Human Resource Development

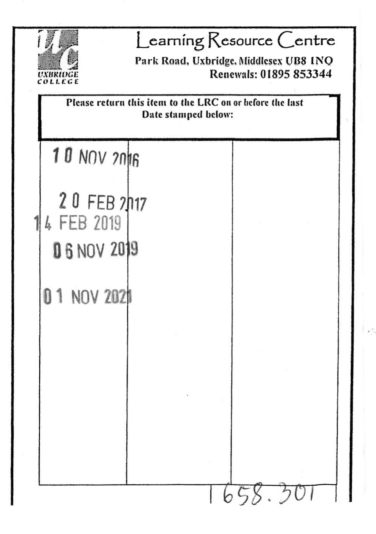

Human Resource Development

DAVID MANKIN

OXFORD
UNIVERSITY PRESS

OXFORD
UNIVERSITY PRESS

Great Clarendon Street, Oxford ox2 6DP

Oxford University Press is a department of the University of Oxford.
It furthers the University's objective of excellence in research, scholarship,
and education by publishing worldwide in

Oxford New York

Auckland Cape Town Dar es Salaam Hong Kong Karachi
Kuala Lumpur Madrid Melbourne Mexico City Nairobi
New Delhi Shanghai Taipei Toronto

With offices in

Argentina Austria Brazil Chile Czech Republic France Greece
Guatemala Hungary Italy Japan Poland Portugal Singapore
South Korea Switzerland Thailand Turkey Ukraine Vietnam

Oxford is a registered trade mark of Oxford University Press
in the UK and in certain other countries

British Library Cataloguing in Publication Data
Data available

Library of Congress Cataloging in Publication Data
Data available

Typeset in 8.8/13pt Stone Serif by Graphicraft Limited, Hong Kong
Printed and bound in Great Britain by
Ashford Colour Press Ltd, Gosport, Hants

ISBN 978–0–19–928328–6

5 7 9 10 8 6

PREFACE

Today we talk about human resource development when previously we talked about training. Both concepts have learning at their core but human resource development embraces a much broader array of learning theories than training. When I first graduated in 1977 most large organizations relied upon a centralized training department to cater for their training needs. Often in larger organizations these departments would comprise a training centre, ranging from a small suite of rooms at a company location to a purpose-built residential training complex, sometimes set in attractive grounds, and staffed by a team of trainers and administrators, who would report through to a training manager who would in turn report to a senior manager or director. These departments tended to produce an annual brochure listing the organization's training provision so that line managers could nominate individuals for specific courses. Often success was measured in terms of the ability of staff in the training department to fill these courses. It was not always clear the extent to which such departments were either supporting the achievement of business objectives or adding any value to the organization. Often the evaluation of the effectiveness of training was non-existent or grossly inadequate (e.g. restricted to end-of-course reaction questionnaires).

In developed countries across North America, Europe, Australasia, and parts of Asia this traditional approach to training still exists but it does so alongside a wider range of strategies that constitute what is now referred to as human resource development. The focus has shifted from training to strategies involving, amongst others: organization development, organizational learning, lifelong learning, situated learning, informal learning, and workplace learning. The aim of this book is to explain the transition from training to human resource development and the implications of this for organizations operating around the world in a range of sectors. As shall be seen many organizations still rely on centralized training departments albeit under a variety of guises such as corporate universities and learning resource centres. To date much of the debate about the theory and practice of human resource development has been dominated by Western perspectives on the concept. It is almost certain that as the twenty-first century progresses more indigenous perspectives will emerge in developing economies such as China and India.

Throughout the book you will encounter a wide range of terms and abbreviations, including the jargon that is a perennial characteristic of any profession. In particular, the term *intervention* is used to describe any formal activity such as a training course or workshop, a planned coaching session, an organization development project, or a career counselling session. Where an intervention forms part of a wider initiative the term *programme* is used. For instance, a training intervention designed to teach presentation skills may be one element in a management development programme that comprises a series of interventions focusing on different management competencies. As you will discover line managers and employees have an important role to play in the practice of human resource development. The concept of *practice* covers all aspects of human resource development, including activities that support the design, implementation, and review of interventions, such as: administrative responsibilities, data analysis, briefings, meetings, and informal discussions. New concepts are always defined and a glossary of terms has been included for quick and easy reference.

Structure of the book

The book comprises three parts which cover different aspects of human resource development (HRD). *Part One* (chapters 1 to 3) discusses the conceptual foundations of human resource development so that you can better understand the relationship between theory and practice. This discussion includes an analysis of the changing external context so that you gain an insight into the implications of globalization for the practice of human resource development. *Part Two* (chapters 4 to 9) focuses on formal interventions including analysis of needs, the design process, different approaches to delivery or implementation, and the options for measuring the effectiveness of interventions. In many respects this is the nuts and bolts or 'basic toolkit' of practitioners, although the types of intervention discussed extend beyond traditional training interventions. *Part Three* (chapters 10 to 15) is intended to illustrate the changing nature and scope of human resource development practice by focusing on the role of human resource development in relation to knowledge management, informal workplace learning, corporate social responsibility, and small and medium sized enterprises. These are neglected themes in the mainstream literature on human resource development.

Chapter 1 focuses on the external context of organizations and the implications of globalization for the practice of human resource development. Key themes are the effects of economic globalization, trends in communications and information technologies, and changes to organizational structures. The concept of national human resource development is introduced and contrasted with the more traditional concept of national vocational education and training.

Chapter 2 explains in detail how the concept of human resource development has evolved from its roots in training. The 'learning continuum' is introduced to illustrate this story and provide an underpinning conceptual framework to help readers appreciate the full scope of the theory and practice of human resource development.

Chapter 3 is devoted to the strategic implications of human resource development and introduces the concept of vertical alignment to explain the relationship between human resource development and organizational (or business) strategy; and horizontal alignment to explain the relationship between human resource development and human resource management respectively. A typology for HRD strategic choices is presented which informs discussion in subsequent chapters.

Chapter 4 provides a detailed discussion on learning theories associated with the two principal perspectives on learning: the psychological and the sociological. This underpins much of the discussion in subsequent chapters. The concept of reflective practice (or critical reflection) is also introduced.

Chapter 5 introduces the concept of the human resource development cycle. This is a four stage model used by practitioners to identify HRD needs and then design, deliver, or implement, and evaluate an intervention. The chapter explains how this cycle differs from the traditional systematic training cycle.

Chapter 6 focuses on stage one in the human resource development cycle: identifying HRD needs. Often these are learning and development needs identified by the employee or line manager (e.g. at the annual performance appraisal). On other occasions the technical expertise of the HRD practitioner is required and the chapter provides several examples of the techniques and methods used in these situations. The outcomes from this stage may be anything from a formal training course to an organization development project.

Chapter 7 focuses on stage two in the human resource development cycle: designing the HRD intervention. This stage draws heavily on the expertise of the HRD practitioner although the line manager and/or employee can also be involved. This chapter introduces readers to a range of design options including e-learning and blended learning (both of these have emerged over the last decade).

Chapter 8 focuses on stage three in the human resource development cycle: implementation or delivery (depending on the type of intervention). The chapter explains the full range of options and the implications this has for HRD practitioners, line managers, and employees.

Chapter 9 focuses on stage four in the human resource development cycle: evaluation. Arguably this is the most critical stage in the cycle but it is also the most neglected by practitioners and organizations despite the huge investments in HRD, particularly training budgets. This situation is changing slowly as more use is made of quantitative performance measures.

Chapter 10 explores the implications of knowledge management for HRD practitioners. Until recently this has been another neglected area in the literature on human resource development. The chapter argues that HRD practitioners can play an important role in facilitating knowledge formation processes within and between organizations (e.g. knowledge creation, knowledge sharing, and knowledge transfer).

Chapter 11 discusses informal workplace learning and the role of the HRD practitioner and line manager in facilitating this process. Informal learning occurs in all organizations on an ongoing basis and often individuals are unaware that learning has taken place.

Chapter 12 looks at the role of human resource development in small and medium sized enterprises. The vast majority of these organizations lack a dedicated HRD practitioner with responsibility for employee learning and organization development resting with the owner-manager. As the chapter explains many owner-managers lack the expertise to carry out the role.

Chapter 13 analyses the different ways in which larger organizations can organize the HRD function. A range of options are discussed along with some of the principal implications of each option for the practice of human resource development.

Chapter 14 discusses the implications of business ethics and corporate social responsibility for the practice of human resource development in a range of organizational settings.

This is another neglected area in the literature on human resource development despite the importance and topicality of ethical and socially responsible management.

Chapter 15 looks at the importance of continuing professional development for HRD practitioners, line managers, and employees. Specific HRD competencies are identified from the content of preceding chapters and summarized for each of the three stakeholders. The remainder of the chapter provides a closing summary of the principal challenges facing the HRD practitioner by returning to the themes identified in chapter 1 and attempting to predict how these trends may continue or change in the future.

ACKNOWLEDGEMENTS

A great many people have helped me directly and indirectly in the writing of this textbook. In terms of those who have helped me directly, I would like to thank the following for reducing the burden of this task by writing or co-writing some of the chapters: David Simmonds, for writing chapter 9, John Roscoe, for co-writing chapter 7, and Rod Stone for co-writing chapter 12. I would particularly like to thank Sarah John, Director, Acorn Group, Tom Holden, Managing Director of TCW Consulting, and Ian Yates, Learning and Development Manager not only for providing case material but also giving up their time to meet with me and discuss the project. In addition I would also like to thank Fiona Argent, Training and Development Consultant, Acorn Group, Michelle Armitage, HR Director, and Jane Chilman, Director of People First Associates, for providing additional case material.

I would like to thank the team at OUP and in particular my editor Angela Adams for her unerring support and guidance and providing me with some invaluable feedback. Finally, thanks to all the reviewers who also provided very detailed feedback on each of the chapters.

Those who have helped me indirectly are too numerous to mention and have already received my thanks in person. However, I would like to acknowledge Gareth Jones (UWIC) for allowing me the flexibility to write the book, Alyson Stonier (UWIC) who relieved me of some administrative burdens in the final weeks so that I could complete the editing process as well as former teaching colleagues Richard Beresford, Joy Butcher, Savita Kumra, and Carol Mason for all the informal discussions we had at Oxford Brookes University. Finally I would like to thank my wife Kay for her unending support and patience.

I am grateful to *People Management* and the following authors for permission to reproduce copyright material from the magazine: Lara Ashworth (It's time HR professionals got their teeth into bite-sized training programmes. *People Management*, 5 May 2005, p. 42—used in chapter 7); Liz Hall, currently editor of *Coaching at Work* (Costume change. *People Management*, 5 April 2007: 42–3—used in chapter 8); Bill Lucas (Method to the madness. *People Management*, 23 October 2003: 61—used in chapter 7); Steve Smethurst (Course of treatment. *People Management*, 9 March 2005: 34–6—used in chapter 7); Claire Warren (Stars of India. *People Management*, 22 February 2007: 26–30—used in chapter 6).

BRIEF CONTENTS

PART 1 The Fundamentals of Human Resource Development

PART 2 The Operational Role of Human Resource Development

PART 3 The Key Themes in Human Resource Development

DETAILED CONTENTS

PART 1   The Fundamentals of Human Resource Development

LIST OF FIGURES

LIST OF TABLES

GUIDE TO *INSIGHTS INTO PRACTICE* BOXES

HOW TO USE THIS BOOK

My original aim was to write a textbook that would demystify the concept of human resource development and explain different aspects of the concept in an accessible and student-friendly manner. I hope that I have achieved this aim. Various pedagogical features have been used to make the content more interesting, and to encourage readers to find out more about specific topics.

David Mankin

Key concept   Reflective practice

Reflective practice involves thinking critically about specific incidents and examining what happened, how it happened and why it happened. The outcome of this process is often some form of learning that involves an adjustment to how we think and act in the world.

Key concept boxes provide succinct explanations of concepts important to developing an understanding of human resource development.

INSIGHTS INTO PRACTICE

Working life in Asian firms

Despite the convergence of business practices that is claimed to be a feature of economic globalization there are still huge variations between countries. The bulk of Asian firms are small town and village enterprises which are underpinned by family and community ties. This results in organizational cultures characterized by cohesion and uniformity and where employees are prepared to work hard for long hours. The principal business drivers for all sizes of firm are productivity, cost reduction, and profit. HR practice is still predominantly administrative in larger firms. It is not viewed as a strategic function and most directors are not interested in soft measures. The principal purpose of induction is to instil loyalty and many employers are reluctant to provide additional training. Employees who wish to expand their knowledge and skills so that they can get a better job have to do so in their own time through private study (relying on support from family and friends). Those with foreign qualifications have better career prospects because they are viewed as talented employees.

Source
Harry, W. 2007. East is East. *People Management*, 29 November: 36–8.

Insights into practice/Personal reflection boxes contain examples of business practice or HRD practice relevant to a chapter's content. Some of these are taken from primary sources, such as HRD practitioners I have interviewed for the book. Others are personal reflections on my own experience as a manager and HRD practitioner before I embarked on an academic career. The remaining examples are drawn from secondary sources such as academic journal articles and other textbooks.

MEDIA WATCH BOX

Change management in the non-profit sector

This case illustrates the role training and development can play in the support of change management. Taken as a whole, the HR function is undertaking a major organization development project that relies on the close alignment of HRD and HRM elements (see also chapter 3 on horizontal alignment).

The Children's Trust is a UK based charity which helps to support children who are severely disabled and suffering from brain damage. As part of a change management strategy to move away from an avoidance culture the charity implemented a

Media watch boxes contain topical summaries of articles published in the news media (e.g. newspapers and magazines) or on the Internet. These are intended to help you place the chapter's topic in a wider context.

TIPS AND HINTS

In many contexts using problem-solving processes and techniques is a very useful way of building credibility for the role of the HRD practitioner as the focus is on finding practical solutions to practical problems.

Tips and hints boxes offer practical advice about the application of theory to practice.

Activity boxes are intended to encourage readers to deepen their understanding of a particular topic. Tutors may wish to use some of these activities in the classroom.

> **ACTIVITY 10.1**
>
> Returning to Polanyi's example of learning how to ride a bicycle write down a set of instructions explaining how to ride a bicycle and share this with a relative, friend or colleague. What is their reaction? Would it be better to do this exercise using an actual bicycle? How easy is it to explain how to balance, how to judge distances etc?

Review questions at the end of each chapter provide another opportunity to check understanding.

> **Review questions**
>
> 1 What are the principal knowledge and skills required by an HRD practitioner to be an effective trainer?
> 2 How has e-learning impacted on the delivery role of the HRD practitioner?
> 3 In what ways do the skills required to be an effective OD project manager differ from those needed to be an effective facilitator?
> 4 In what ways are the requirements of coaching different to mentoring?

Case studies at the end of chapters include questions to answer. There is a case study at the end of every chapter and these have been kept relatively short so that they can be used for group work in the classroom.

> **Case study**
>
> **Acorn and a client centred approach to training**
>
> Established in 1992, Acorn is an award-winning business that is now Wales' leading recruitment and training organization, with an annual turnover of just under £100m. With offices across South Wales, the West Country, North Wales, Scotland and the North West of England the company places 5,500 people into 750 different client companies each week and makes some 1,500 permanent placements each year. It is a previous winner of both best regional recruitment firm and best national firm at the Professional Recruiter Awards. Acorn's

Glossary of terms provides easy accessibility to definitions of all the principal concepts contained in the book.

> Action learning Action learning involves a group of learners working together in an action learning set to solve real problems in the workplace. A series of meetings are held during which set members question and challenge the causes of the problem and potential solutions.
> Added value Added value is about identifying what really matters to key stakeholders and delivering the services and products that achieve this. In many respects it builds on the total quality management ethos of delivering products and services that create 'customer
>
> Codification Codification is based on the assumption that it is possible to encode knowledge as text, figures, or digital data. Many observers argue it is information rather than knowledge that is being encoded in this way. See also knowledge management.
> Cognition Cognition involves the development of representations or mental models of the world around us within an individual's mind (Bowden and Marton, 2004). See also situated cognition.
> Communities of practice 'Communities of

HOW TO USE THE ONLINE RESOURCE CENTRE

To support this text, there is a wide range of web-based content for tutors and students. Students can go to the online resource centre to find web links, media-watch updates, and a training plan exercise. Tutors will be able to access a suite of customizable PowerPoint slides which can be used in lectures and seminars, alongside a bank of additional case studies.

@ www.oxfordtextbooks.co.uk/orc/mankin/

FOR LECTURERS

PowerPoint lecture slides

A suite of chapter-by-chapter PowerPoint slides has been included for use in your lecture presentations. They are fully customizable so you can tailor them to match your own presentation style. All the figures from the book are also provided electronically for inclusion in your slides or handouts.

A bank of additional case studies

In addition to the many case studies included in the text, a further collection of relevant and engaging case studies are available for your use in group tutorial work and assignments.

Suggested answers and discussion points for end-of-chapter case studies

Suggested answers to the end-of-chapter case study questions succinctly highlight the main points students should be covering in their answers.

FOR STUDENTS

Annotated web links to government policy and initiatives

A series of annotated web links to government policy updates and initiatives provide a guide to contemporary and relevant material.

Media-watch updates

Updates from news sources allow you to place the chapter topics into a wider context.

Suggested answers to the end-of-chapter self-assessment questions

Suggested answers to all of the end-of-chapter questions provide the opportunity to discover how well you have understood the key topics.

Web links

Links to websites relevant to each chapter direct students towards valuable sources of information and professional associations.

Training plan exercise

Examples of real-life training plans and evaluations to illustrate the systematic training cycle in operation.

The Fundamentals of Human Resource Development

Part 1 explains the fundamentals of human resource development. The topics covered act as a foundation for parts 2 and 3. These fundamentals encompass a wide range of issues including an analysis of the relationship between the theory and practice of the concept.

The Context of Human Resource Development

- The emergence of national human resource development (NHRD)
- Global approaches to NHRD
- The implications of NHRD for HRD practitioners

Key concepts:

Globalization

Supply chain

Human resource development (HRD)

Human capital

Social capital

National human resource development (NHRD)

National vocational education and training (NVET)

1.1 Introduction

A variety of terms have been used by academics and practitioners to describe the topic covered in this book: training, training and development, employee development, learning and development, and human resource development (HRD). Do these different terms mean different things? Or, can they be used inter-changeably? Who is responsible for HRD in organizations: HRD practitioners or line managers or both? What are the responsibilities of the learner? What is the relationship between HRD and human resource management (HRM)? Why do academics rather than practitioners prefer the term Human Resource Development (HRD)? The aim of this book is to provide answers to these questions. This is not an easy task as there are multiple perspectives on the meaning and purpose of HRD which can confuse anyone who is unfamiliar with the topic. Much of the academic literature published over the last decade has been characterized by an ongoing and robust debate on these different perspectives. This has been important for three reasons: it has strengthened the breadth and depth of HRD theory; it has generated empirical studies on different aspects of HRD practice; and, it has helped to establish the academic credibility of the subject. But there is still a sense that the academic and practitioner communities are not as closely inter-twined as they should or could be; although tensions between theory and practice are not confined to the field of HRD but appear to be endemic in the management and organizational sciences generally (Kuchinke, 2004).

It is not the purpose of this chapter to critique the relationship between the academic and practitioner communities and the implications that this has for the theory and practice of HRD. This is covered in the next chapter where you will gain an insight into the often ambiguous and contested nature of the concept. Chapter 2 will focus in particular on an analysis of the two principal perspectives on HRD: the *performance* and *humanist* perspectives. These perspectives have fuelled some of the most controversial debates about the meaning and purpose of HRD. To date these debates have been dominated by Anglo-American perspectives but this is now changing as more indigenous perspectives on HRD emerge across Europe, the Middle East, and Asia. This reflects the way in which the theory and practice of HRD are evolving within the context of a dramatically changing world.

Globalization has witnessed the deregulation of markets, the relocation and outsourcing of production and service facilities, particularly to China and India respectively, and the inter-connectedness of markets, principally as a result of increasingly sophisticated information and communications technologies, symbolized by the Internet. This has resulted in changes to how many organizations are structured, how they are managed, how they conduct their operations, and how they plan for the future. Globalization is not a new phenomenon but what differentiates this current phase from previous ones is the sheer scale. The number of countries affected, the volume of trade, and the rate of growth are far greater than in any previous phase (Stark, 2005). Inevitably globalization is having a huge impact on the role, nature, and purpose of HRD in organizations of all sizes and sectors across the world. However, much of the literature on HRD has been written from the perspective of large private sector organizations (i.e. national and multinational corporations). Examples taken from the public and non-profit sectors tend to be used less frequently by authors. This is also the case with small and medium sized enterprises (SMEs). Yet, public sector organizations are significant employers in most developed countries and non-profit organizations play a crucial role in addressing a wide range of humanitarian issues around the globe and make a significant contribution through a wide range of training initiatives. While smaller businesses are now able to compete globally and, in many countries such as Australia and Finland, are critical to the national economy. Consequently, throughout the book I shall endeavour to highlight the challenges that different sectors and types of organization pose for the theory and practice of HRD. Similarly, when referring to the practice of HRD it is important to understand that this involves several stakeholders, in particular the HRD practitioner, the line manager, and the learner at an operational level, and the HRD practitioner and senior manager at a strategic level. The contribution made by each of these stakeholders varies considerably depending on the context. This will be illustrated throughout the book using case examples drawn from a wide range of contexts.

Key concept   Human resource development

Human resource development (HRD) encompasses a range of organizational practices that focus on learning: training, learning, and development; workplace learning; career development and lifelong learning; organization development; organizational knowledge and learning (see chapter 2 for a detailed explanation).

1.2 **Globalization**

What is globalization?

It is easy to understand why people often use the expression 'the world is getting smaller'. Cheap flights have opened up new holiday destinations; news coverage from around the world now unfolds in real time on a 24/7 basis; more people are migrating to other countries than ever before; the Internet is enabling instant access to just about any aspect of social, cultural, scientific, and economic life in other parts of the world; and, the mobile phone has revolutionized communications. Some observers believe we are in the process of creating a form of cultural homogeneity as once disparate communities are connected together in a new, global society (Water, 1995; Kingsnorth, 2008); a trend Gray (2000) refers to as *de-localization*. An example of this is the decline in the number of languages in the world, currently around 6,900, but predicted to fall by anywhere between 50 and 90 per cent over the next hundred years (MacGillivray, 2006).

From an economic perspective globalization is about the primacy of an integrated global market which transcends national markets and frontiers (Wolf, 2005): each day more than US$1.5 trillion flows across international borders (Cunningham, 2004). The

> **Key concept** Globalization
>
> Globalization is about the creation of a borderless global economy that allows unhindered movement of finance, products, services, information, and people.

underpinning principle is that global markets create competition which ensures better products and services at better prices (Marquardt, 2005). However, for this to work there needs to be deregulation of markets: organizations need to be able to compete freely against each other and without the hindrance of any trade restrictions (for instance, national trade barriers and tariffs). Unfortunately, the lowering of trade barriers is not without its problems as was illustrated by the trade dispute in Europe during 2005: the ending of ten-year quotas on the import of cheaply produced clothes and shoes from China triggered a temporary embargo which resulted in stockpiles of goods in ships and warehouses at UK and European ports. Retail outlets warned that failure to release these goods would result in higher shop prices and, consequently, it was the consumer who would be penalized.

Until very recently globalization has always been associated with the transnational or multinational corporation which is characterized by the geographical dispersion of business operations (Shoobridge, 2006). Leading Western brands have become global brands, for instance: the Apple iPod, Google, Microsoft, HP, GAP, Nike, and Coca Cola. When considering these multinational corporations you have to think in terms of billions of dollars or pounds, for instance: Hewlett-Packard's annual revenue of US$73 billion is more than double the GPD of Kuwait (*The Times*, 12 February 2005: 66); Wal-Mart's annual turnover exceeds the GDP of all but 22 countries (Rothkopf, 2008); and Google has a market value of US$120 billion (*The Independent*, 12 May 2006: 47). The downside is that the market power of dominant companies such as Microsoft can result in a virtual global monopoly that makes the emergence of new, innovative competitors almost impossible (Stiglitz, 2007).

MEDIA WATCH BOX

Global brands

Recent research has revealed that for consumers in Europe the most trusted global brands are those of non-government/non-profit organizations such as Greenpeace, WWF, and Amnesty International. The values of these organizations have a universal appeal to consumers.

Source
Independent on Sunday (Business section), 14 August 2005: 4.

At the same time the efficacy of the traditional organization structure, based on the division of labour, hierarchy, mass production, and large size has lost ground to alternative structural principles (Alvesson, 2004) which can offer organizations greater levels of flexibility and adaptability. Since the turn of the century there has also been signs of a transfer of power from the multinational corporation to the individual (Friedman, 2006). As a result of convergent advances in information and communications technology (both hardware and software) it is now possible for individuals to collaborate and compete globally. Size is no longer a key determinant of whether an organization can be described as global. An anecdotal example of this is when I was chatting to another delegate at a business conference who described the company she owned as being 'global'. I asked her what this meant and she replied: 'I run a business which specializes in importing and exporting high quality wines around the world. I have two people working for me and we do everything over the Net.' The transfer of knowledge, which is particularly critical for multinational companies (Liu et al., 2006), has been aided considerably by these technological developments. Indeed technology has made possible collaboration among large numbers of workers thus enabling some companies, such as General Electric, to become a *talent-intensive* mega-institution (Bryan and Joyce, 2007).

To date the concept of globalization has proven highly contentious, having both its supporters and its detractors. Multinationals are often portrayed as villains (Stiglitz, 2007) and Klien (2008) argues that even natural disasters are being viewed as market opportunities, a trend she describes as 'disaster capitalism'. One of the key problems is the perceived primacy of the American approach to business although Kay (2004) notes that Europeans have always demonstrated some scepticism about its suitability as a universal

---

(•) INSIGHTS INTO PRACTICE

Working life in Asian firms

Despite the convergence of business practices that is claimed to be a feature of economic globalization there are still huge variations between countries. The bulk of Asian firms are small town and village enterprises which are underpinned by family and community ties. This results in organizational cultures characterized by cohesion and uniformity and where employees are prepared to work hard for long hours. The principal business drivers for all sizes of firm are productivity, cost reduction, and profit. HR practice is still predominantly administrative in larger firms. It is not viewed as a strategic function and most directors are not interested in soft measures. The principal purpose of induction is to instil loyalty and many employers are reluctant to provide additional training. Employees who wish to expand their knowledge and skills so that they can get a better job have to do so in their own time through private study (relying on support from family and friends). Those with foreign qualifications have better career prospects because they are viewed as talented employees.

Source
Harry, W. 2007. East is East. *People Management*, 29 November: 36–8.

model. The different perspectives have been summarized as 'pro-globalization' and 'anti-globalization' in table 1.1.

As can be seen from table 1.2 the principal drivers of globalization are: advancements in technology and communications, global competition, and changing organizational structures. These have impacted on businesses in a variety of ways (described in the table

Pro-globalization	Anti-globalization
Provides an integrated global market through the removal of barriers to free trade.	A flawed economic concept that has failed to deliver on its early promise. It is characterized by a process of homogenization that poses a threat to individual nation states (e.g. the erosion of national cultures and the distinctiveness of the local communities that make up nation states).
Promotes the mobility of financial capital across the globe.	The movement of financial capital from the rich developed nations to the poorer developing nations has been relatively modest. There is an increasingly polarized global distribution of income and wealth between the nations of the North and South. Wealth remains in the North.
Foreign direct investment (FDI) by multinational corporations stimulates the transfer of technology and management practices to less developed countries.	FDI by multinational corporations is actually restricted to a few countries.
Economic convergence over time resulting in an equalization of wages across the globe.	There is a lack of any economic convergence: income inequality between the developed and less developed nations is actually increasing. Wages may have increased in developing economies but are not keeping pace with wages in developed countries. Also there are downsides: lack of job security, long hours, and poor working conditions. The migration of low-skilled work to Asia and the Far East also means supporting low-skilled indigenous workers in Western countries is becoming unsustainable.
Global markets create competition which ensures better products and services at better prices.	Global markets are producing cheaper products but manufacturing processes are posing a threat to the world environment: they are characterized by a competitive exploitation of natural resources and a lack of adequate conservation strategies. They are unlikely to deliver the sustainable technologies needed to tackle environmental problems.
Globalization is best driven by a Westernized form of free-market capitalism.	Globalization should not mean the Americanization of other economies and cultures.
Globalization can be a force for good: economic integration is a prerequisite for tackling global issues such as poverty.	An economic focus is too narrow: globalization should be seen primarily as a social process. The short term financial interests of developed countries do not always coincide with the needs and well-being of citizens in developing nations.

Table 1.1 Different perspectives on globalization

Sources: Gray, 2000; Turner, 2001; Stiglitz, 2002; Kay, 2004; Boon et al., 2005; Dymski, 2005; Jenkins, 2005; Marquardt, 2005; Saul, 2005; Wolf, 2005; Baddeley, 2006; Friedman, 2006; MacGillivray, 2006; Gualerzi, 2007; James, 2007; Mishkin, 2007; Stiglitz, 2007; Kingsnorth, 2008; Klein, 2008; Sachs, 2008.

Drivers of globalization	Organizational requirements
Technology and communications • Digital technology (speed, efficiency) • Portability (laptops, palmtops, mobile phones) • Workflow/collaboration software (24/7 working, higher productivity) • Connectivity (Internet, intranets) • Customization (products, services) **Global competition** • Integrated global market • Free market capitalism (US Model) • Global brands • Deregulation • Offshoring (labour intensive and low automation) • Outsourcing (low value-added activities) • Disintegration of supply chains and fragmentation of production processes (having different parts of the process carried out in different countries to minimize costs) **Organizational structures** • Mergers, acquisitions, and alliances • Restructuring • Migration of work (manufacturing, services and specialist/knowledge functions) • Workforce demographics (diversity: gender, ethnicity, age) • Health (longer life spans in developed countries)	• Global leadership (understanding global markets; matching management practices to the needs of a global business) • Adaptable and flexible organizational structures (e.g. flexible firm; integrating offshore and outsourced elements of the firm; matching structure to innovation requirements) • Managing supplier chains (implications of outsourcing and offshoring; preparing managers for international assignments) • Managing a diverse workforce (external and internal labour markets) • Updating core competencies and skills • Innovation (better products and services but at a lower cost; shorter product life cycles) • Knowledge management systems for knowledge creation, sharing, and transfer • Retention of intellectual capital • Cost reduction (e.g. labour) • Increased productivity (quality of service) • Market expansion

Table 1.2 The impact of economic globalization on organizations

Sources: Dowling and Welch, 2004; Kay, 2004; Price, 2004; Dymski, 2005; Friedman, 2005; Ulrich and Brockbank, 2005; Amighini and Rabellotti, 2006; Bardham, 2006; Gough et al., 2006; Jenkins, 2006; Johnson, 2006; Bryan and Joyce, 2007; Boxall and Purcell, 2008; Fung et al., 2008

as 'organizational requirements'). Historically technology has always had a significant impact on society, from the invention of the printing press through to the invention of the telegraph. Today some of the major trends in technology are: the speed at which technological changes are occurring, the gains in efficiency as processing speeds increase, the increasing degree and complexity of connectivity, and the greater ease with which organizations can produce customized products and services (Ulrich and Brockbank, 2005). Improvements in technology and communications have helped to make the world become 'flatter' as people make connections across organizational and national boundaries and collaborate and compete in real time on a 24/7 basis (Friedman, 2006; Fung et al., 2008). Not surprisingly the Internet is closely associated with globalization. Today businesses, whatever their size, can use the Internet to promote their products and/or services (see *Media-watch* box). This type of e-commerce has been fundamental in helping SMEs to carve out niche markets on a world stage. For instance, Finland has been particularly adept at exploiting the Internet for e-commerce having one of the highest Internet connection rates globally (Ohmae, 2005). Technology is also helping emerging economies to develop much faster than their Western counterparts were able to in the past (Turner, 2001). Although organizations feel compelled to use new technology it is not a panacea as a series of failed and over-budget projects in the UK public sector has illustrated (for instance, the NHS National Programme for IT with a budget of £6 billion has been projected to cost anywhere up to £30 billion). There is also a *dark-side* to technology with increased surveillance of employees through CCTV in some countries and the use of electronic tagging in some distribution centres to monitor the employee's completion of tasks.

MEDIA WATCH BOX

E-commerce

The Sixtus monastery in Flanders has been receiving 2,000 hits a day on its website after beer made by its Trappist monks won a prestigious quality award. As a result supplies of the beer quickly became exhausted.

Source
Independent, 10 August 2005: 19.

Global competition is increasing as more and more businesses enter the global marketplace, particularly from China and India. These two countries are not only experiencing rapid economic growth but are developing their own indigenous forms of capitalism rather than replicating the prevailing Westernized model of capitalism, which is based on liberal democratic principles (Ferguson, 2006). Both countries are creating jobs but are focusing on different sectors. So far China has been concentrating on manufacturing, construction, and transport and has adopted a classic Asian strategy of exporting low-priced manufactured goods to the West (Das, 2006). Her competitive advantage comes from a combination of cheap labour and modern production facilities (Kynge, 2006). Meanwhile India has been concentrating on services and software design and has relied on domestic rather than export markets (Das, 2006). As a result the software development sector in India has grown significantly and is diversifying from offering basic services to developing high level software development. Leading companies, such as Motorola, Hewlett-Packard, and Cisco Systems, now rely increasingly on Indian software development teams for next generation products with Bangalore becoming India's own 'silicon valley' (*The Independent on Sunday*, 21 August 2005, page 8, Business section). However, there are also examples of significant manufacturing success: India is now the world's third largest maker of small cars. The growth of the Indian automotive industry has been underpinned by low wage costs and the adoption of Japanese manufacturing techniques. Over 100 indigenous companies are now valued at over a billion US dollars, including Bharat Forge, Jet Airways, Wipro Technologies and Tata Motors (Das, 2006). Unfortunately, there is a downside to this growth, particularly in China: the consequent damage to the environment (see chapter 14).

MEDIA WATCH BOX

Developments in China and India

The first three examples illustrate the pace at which the Chinese and Indian economies are developing. The fourth and fifth examples give an insight into the downside of rapid economic growth.

By April 2006 China had overtaken Britain as the fourth ranked economy in the world.[1]

By early 2006 China had overtaken Japan as the world's largest holder of foreign reserves, some £490 billion.[2]

India is investing £35 billion to upgrade its road network.[3]

China's famous Yellow River is disappearing and what water remains is heavily polluted. Riverside cities such as Lanzhou and Shizuishan are now among the most polluted in the world. This situation is contributing to a growing water crisis as the country drains its rivers dry.[4]

India has experienced riots as people in the northern parts of the country reacted violently to widespread power cuts that left homes without electricity or water. The economic boom may be creating a wealthy consumer class but the country is struggling to improve the basic infrastructure demanded by the rest of the country's population. The government has pledged to provide power for everyone by 2012 but this highly ambitious target is unlikely to be achieved.[5]

Sources
[1] *The Times*, 17 April 2006: 32.
[2] *Sunday Times*, Business section, 9 April 2006: 14.
[3] *Guardian*, 2 May 2006: 25.
[4] *National Geographic*, May 2008: 146–69.
[5] *The Times*, 3 May 2008: 41.

Organizations have had to make structural changes in order to keep pace with global trends. The increase in mergers, acquisitions and alliances reflects the extent to which multinational corporations are using size and brand name to exploit global markets. At the same time many organizations have had to relocate or outsource elements of the supply chain in order to take advantage of lower labour costs in other countries.

Key concepts   The supply chain

The supply chain is the network of organizations that are involved in the processes that create value for customers in the form of products and/or services.

A wide range of products previously manufactured in the US and Europe are now made in Asia and China from toys to footwear and clothes. More recently, there has been an increase in the outsourcing and offshoring of more complex, non-routinized functions such as research and development (Bardham, 2006): some 125 of America's leading companies now have research and development facilities in India (Das, 2006). In the US the jeans manufacturer Levi Strauss has outsourced much of its design activity (Johnson, 2006). Consequently, a wide range of products and services are now handled by customer service staff in the Asian sub-continent, from the preparation of tax returns by Indian accountants to the initial analysis of medical scans for American hospitals by Indian doctors (Friedman, 2006). The good level of English language skills of many graduates gives India an advantage over many other countries such as China. This advantage can be seen in sectors, such as financial services, where the outsourcing or off-shoring of call centres to India has enabled many organizations to drive down wage bills while at the same time employing well educated employees. India is a popular choice for UK companies (*People Management*, 1st June 2006, page 13). Companies that have set up offshore call centres include: Prudential, HSBC, Lloyds TSB, Barclays, and Royal and Sun Alliance; while those that use Indian-owned services include BT, British Airways, and the NHS.

! TIPS AND HINTS

When analysing the impact of globalization on an organization try to think about the social and environmental implications as well as the economic. If you want to know more about these then read chapter 14.

MEDIA WATCH BOX

Developments in the Middle East

China and India are not the only countries currently experiencing huge investment levels. Massive investment is a characteristic of several Middle East countries although this is a result of revenues from oil and reflects a need to invest and diversify as a long term strategy for when oil reserves are exhausted. For instance, Saudi Arabia, which has the largest economy in the Middle East, has embarked on a £350 billion investment programme in order to diversify its economy away from a dependence on oil. Meanwhile Dubai, which has a population of one million, is spending £140 billion to transform itself into a 'capitalist powerhouse' that will increase the number of visiting tourists from 6 million to 10 million by 2010.

Sources
The Times, 14 January 2006: 64; *The Sunday Times*, Business Section, 21 May 2006: 3.

The large populations of China and India are enabling these two countries to achieve a global domination that eluded countries like Japan and South Korea. A potential brake on growth may occur because of rapidly rising wages and a requirement to address environmental issues but it is likely that by the middle of this century China and India will be the world's two dominant economies, closely followed by Russia, with its vast stock of natural resources, particularly oil and gas.

ACTIVITY 1.1

Find two publications (e.g. articles, books, or book chapters) that adopt different perspectives on globalization. Summarize the arguments in each and then share your analysis with a colleague or fellow student who has carried out the same activity. What are the similarities and differences between your summaries?

1.3 The implications of globalization for HRD

For those working in an international context globalization presents HRD practitioners with the opportunity to deliver a wide range of HRD interventions that add value to an organization. In order to achieve this they need to work in partnership with key stakeholders at both a strategic and operational level. Managing these stakeholder relationships is a challenging and complex task and is influenced by how the HRD function is structured (see chapter 13). To be successful HRD practitioners must understand global trends and the issues that matter most to their stakeholders (Ulrich and Brockbank, 2005). This knowledge needs to be integrated with an understanding of the global economy and different national HRD policies and practices (Swanson and Holton, 2001); and an understanding of cultural differences and how these can impact on formal and informal workplace learning (Marquardt et al., 2004). In addition HRD practitioners must know how to design, deliver and evaluate strategic global training in a multinational environment (Petranek, 2004). This enables the HRD function to design interventions that are linked to the achievement of organizational goals. For business corporations most of these goals will be financially oriented.

Marquardt (2002, 2005) argues that HRD should adopt a leadership role to ensure globalization brings benefits to humanity. In a similar vein Bierema and D'Abundo (2003) argue for 'socially conscious' HRD which involves promoting ethical and socially responsible management and leadership. These ideas reflect two things: first, the growing influence on organizations of business ethics and corporate social responsibility (CSR), which are the focus of chapter 14; second, the influence of a humanist perspective on learning and HRD, which is discussed in the next chapter. The problem for many HRD practitioners is that a leadership role remains an aspiration rather than a reality.

A further problem is that there has been limited and inconsistent evidence that HRD interventions do add value by impacting positively on employee and organizational performance. For instance, there are doubts about the effectiveness of management

> **⚠ TIPS AND HINTS**
>
> There are some significant differences between US and UK perspectives on HRD that can have implications for how you interpret the role of HRD in an organization. When analysing an organization (e.g. in a case study) make sure that you differentiate between perspectives rather than simply treat HRD as a universally agreed concept. If you want to know more about this then read chapter 2.

training in leadership skills (Parry and Sinha, 2005). This needs to be placed in the context of an annual global expenditure on management education generally of $2.2 trillion (Monaghan and Cervero, 2006). A major research study for the Chartered Institute of Personnel and Development (CIPD) by Purcell et al. (2003) revealed that it is possible only to discern some positive associations between specific HR practices and performance. However, these do include training, career development, communications, and job design; all of which can fall within the remit of the HRD practitioner working in conjunction with line managers and other stakeholders. Added value can be measured in other ways; for instance, effective HRD interventions can contribute to building an organization's reputation (Clardy, 2005). This brings benefits to an organization in any sector. Despite the lack of any definitive and conclusive evidence HRD functions have become much more business-focused over the years often operating as profit-centres rather than cost-centres. At the same time the number of training consultancies, from independents to international enterprises, have grown. These issues are developed further in chapters 9, 12, and 13.

The nature and purpose of HRD at an organizational level differs across countries and regions and between different types of organization. There are examples of sophisticated indigenous approaches to HRD in the developing economies of India and China, although training costs are minimized in the Chinese manufacturing sector (see *Insights into practice* box). Foreign direct investment (FDI) companies invest in HRD more than indigenous companies and this is helping in the transfer of HRD practices between developing and developing economies. This trend is not restricted to Western multinationals. For instance, the Korean car manufacturer Hyundai has applied some of its own HRM policies in India, particularly training programmes which have been designed to reinforce employee loyalty to the company (Lansbury et al., 2006).

Perhaps the greatest challenge facing HRD practitioners working in an international capacity is how to operate effectively at both a global and a local level (Hall, 2005); to have the ability to *think globally* but *act locally* (Hatcher, 2006). This is important because it has been increasingly recognized that country and local context influence the HR practices of multinationals (Cooke, 2004). A topical example of this is the need for HRD practitioners in multinationals to have 'a comprehensive understanding of the cultural context in China' if Westernized HRD practices are to be adapted effectively to the Chinese environment (Wang et al., 2005: 323). Although many smaller organizations now operating in the global market place tend not to employ specialist HRM or HRD practitioners there is still a need for managers to think in this way. Table 1.3 sets out the key organizational requirements that HRD interventions need to address. The HRD

(•) INSIGHTS INTO PRACTICE

Training in China

These examples illustrate the extent to which formal training interventions are a feature of both the private and state sectors that co-exist in China. The country still has some way to go in terms of the full range of HRD interventions found in most developed countries. China is a country that expatriate managers find particularly challenging to adjust to (Selmer, 2006) and the country's preference for indigenous approaches to HRD has led to some Western managers becoming frustrated when collaborating with their Chinese counterparts (Wang et al., 2005). The third example reveals how Western approaches to learning and development are starting to impact on indigenous approaches to training.

A study of a toy manufacturing company in China revealed that new recruits undertook a 3-month training process but were paid less than half the wage of a fully trained employee.[1]

The selection of public servants in China involves candidates undergoing pre-job training. Two approaches are used: (a) a period of internship, under the guidance of an experienced official, and (b) intensive training, involving attendance on a formal training course of at least ten days' duration. Public servants about to be promoted to senior positions receive short term position-targeted training, which is customized, practical and case-based, so that it reflects the demands of the position. Other types of training available to public servants are: expertise training, usually off-the-job intensive training, and knowledge-renewing training, which can be delivered in a variety of ways.[2]

Infinite Shanghai Communication Terminals, a joint venture between a US and Chinese company, has introduced a new training initiative which involves a series of one day workshops on a range of topics (e.g. communication skills, presentation skills). The workshops are delivered in Mandarin Chinese by a Chinese consultancy firm using university premises. The firm's HR manager would like to see a move towards more participatory learning methods by setting up short workshops, to be held on the firm's own premises, which enable participants from the one day workshops to share experiences and knowledge with each other.[3]

Sources

[1] Cooke, F. L. 2004. Foreign firms in China: modelling HRM in a toy manufacturing corporation. *Human Resource Management Journal*, 14 (3): 31–52.

[2] Shan, A. 2004. Present situation, problems, and prospects of China's public servant training. *International Journal of Public Administration*, 27 (3 and 4): 219–38.

[3] Sloman, M. 2007. Chinese puzzle. *People Management*, 11 January: 40–3.

interventions are categorized as 'formal interventions' and 'informal activities' with both requiring collaboration between HRD practitioners and senior/line managers to differing degrees depending on the organizational context. Although these requirements are biased to multinationals, many affect other types of organization to a lesser or greater extent. For instance, non-profit organizations operating in several countries or regions and

Organizational requirements	HRD interventions and practices
The development of global leaders Developing leaders who can think and act from a global perspective is a critical success factor for organizations operating in global markets. There is a view that organizations need to create a unique leadership brand	**Formal** • Management development programmes that focus on the development of leadership skills. This includes in-house and external programmes (T&D) • Educating managers to behave in ethically and socially responsible ways. This can be achieved through workshops, courses, conferences and seminars, mentoring programmes, and executive coaching (T&D) • Identifying and developing less senior managers who demonstrate potential senior managerial talent. This can be linked to organizational systems for career development and succession planning (CD) **Informal** • Promoting ethical management and leadership as part of daily activities (HRD practitioners and senior managers as role models) • Informal mentoring and coaching (can include upward coaching)
Adaptable and flexible organizational structures There are an increasing number of mergers, acquisitions, alliances, and joint ventures, often involving cross-national and cultural boundaries. Management need to help ease any transition and counter engrained attitudes that may hinder the process of change. Organizations of all sizes seek some degree of flexibility.	**Formal** • Creating and sustaining new forms of organizational structures with cultures based on cooperation and collaboration (OD) • Management training in change management processes (T&D) • Keeping departments and employees affected by an impending merger or acquisition informed about the change using multiple communication channels (OD) • Educating management about potential reorganization options and the implications for the organization and its workforce of those options (T&D) **Informal** • Keeping departments and employees affected by an impending merger or acquisition informed about the change using informal communication channels
Managing supplier chains The offshoring and outsourcing of parts of the supplier chain (e.g. production) has resulted in the dispersion of core assets and the creation of competence clusters around the globe. The number of global organizations has continued to rise and the	**Formal** • Creating and sustaining new forms of organizational structures (OD) • Building global teams that can handle problems of diversity and distance (OD, T&D) • Training local customer service/call centre staff in British or American language and voice skills (as well as product and customer skills training). This is important as it helps create empathy with the customer (T&D)

Table 1.3 The implications of globalization for HRD interventions and practices

(*Key*: T&D = training and development; CD = career development; OD = organizational development)

Sources: Kim, 1999; Bierema et al, 2002; Jeris et al, 2002 ; Marquardt, 2002; Noe, 2002; Beaumont and Hunter, 2002; Bierema and D'Abundo, 2003; Hytönen, 2003; Iles and Yolles, 2003; Marquardt and Berger, 2003; Rocco et al, 2003; Marquardt et al, 2004; Rees, 2004; Wentling, 2004; Downey et al, 2005; Lien, 2005; Littrell and Salas, 2005; Short and Callahan, 2005; Ulrich and Brockbank, 2005; Wang et al, 2005; Yorks, 2005; Zhao, 2005; Bardham, 2006; Greer et al, 2006; Littrell et al, 2006; Selmer, 2006; Shoobridge, 2006; Awbrey, 2007; Ulrich, 2007.

Organizational requirements	HRD interventions and practices
number of employees, primarily managers, relocating abroad continues to increase. However, there is a lack of consistency in preparing managers for international assignments. For instance, many US companies are sending employees abroad without any preparation	• Training local, indigenous managers in modern management techniques and behaviours (T&D) • Cross-cultural training for managers: educating them in 'cultural fluency' (i.e. the ability to work effectively within and between multicultural environments) (T&D) • Increasing the cultural competence of employees generally (OD, T&D) • Preparing employees and managers for expatriation (T&D, CD) **Informal** • Facilitating the activities of global teams • Preparing employees and managers for expatriation
Managing a diverse workforce Internal and external labour markets are becoming increasingly diverse. For instance: the skills needs of immigrant workers; the rising number of female workers; employees working beyond the traditional retirement age. It is likely that those organizations with cultures that support diversity will be better positioned to retain the best talent needed to remain competitive. There is also a need to improve basic literacy and numeracy skills among low-skilled and low-paid employees	**Formal** • Diversity education and training programmes. These communicate the importance of diversity and help to remove barriers, such as employees not understanding the value of diversity (T&D) • Developing cross-cultural team working and communication skills. Cross-cultural training, traditionally restricted to preparing employees for expatriate assignments, can be used to help domestic employees interact with colleagues from diverse cultural backgrounds (T&D, OD) • Training immigrants in technical and customer service skills (T&D) • Reskilling and retraining of older employees beyond the traditional retirement age (T&D) • Providing employees with opportunities to improve their basic literacy and numeracy skills to give them the potential to break out of the low-wage cycle (CD, T&D) **Informal** • Promoting cultural sensitivity • Helping employees to understand how they can learn from team experiences
Updating core competencies and skills The core competencies and skills needed by employees are changing rapidly as new forms of technology are introduced, new products and services are developed, new markets are opened up, and suppliers are sourced from around the globe	**Formal** • Systems for the identification and monitoring of core competencies and skills (OD) • Training and development programmes to enable employees to upgrade or learn new competencies and skills (T&D) • The promotion of lifelong learning (CD) • Developing alliances with regional and national institutions (e.g. Learning Skills Councils in Britain; labour–market partnerships in the US) (OD) **Informal** • The promotion of lifelong learning and facilitation of informal workplace learning

Table 1.3 *(cont'd)*

Organizational requirements	HRD interventions and practices
Innovation The need for innovative products and services. The life cycles of many products and services are becoming shorter and shorter, which places increasing demands on the ability of organizations to be innovative	**Formal** • Developing a global culture of continuous learning which instils employees with a spirit of innovation (OD) • Helping employees to unlearn old behaviours and skills and to learn new ones (T&D, OD) • Creating new ways to work (OD) **Informal** • Promoting the role of informal groups and social networks as sources of innovation and problem-solving • Facilitating the activities of informal groups and social networks • Helping employees to unlearn old behaviours and skills and to learn new ones
Knowledge management systems Knowledge management (KM) systems are needed to ensure the effective creation and sharing of knowledge within an organization and transfer around the globe. The latter, in particular requires sophisticated technology.	**Formal** • Developing employee competencies in knowledge creation, sharing, and transfer (T&D) • Creating a learning infrastructure that maximizes opportunities for organizational learning and knowledge sharing between organizations (OD) • Improving employee familiarity with technology-based KM systems through the utilization of new technologies to deliver e-learning programmes around the globe (T&D, OD) **Informal** • Facilitating knowledge management processes involving both electronic and face-to-face interactions • Identifying and improving opportunities for knowledge creation, sharing, and transfer

Table 1.3 *(cont'd)*

competing for funding need senior managers to have effective global leadership skills; and, all organizations operating in global markets, from small business to multinationals, need to understand about change management. Formal interventions and activities have been categorized as training and development, career development or organizational development (see key in table). Arguably, all informal activities are forms of organizational development which depend on a mix of facilitation and coaching skills by HRD practitioners and line managers.

ACTIVITY 1.2

Find organizational examples of HRD interventions that address any three of the above organizational requirements. As above, you should use the Internet, textbooks, articles or any other form of learning resource for this activity.

In tackling these issues HRD practitioners face ethical challenges. As chapter 14 will highlight, there have been numerous examples of decisions made by senior managers in global organizations that have resulted in unethical outcomes (from corruption to the dumping of waste; from deception to the exploitation of child labour). Corporate social responsibility (CSR) has emerged as an important aspect of an organization's strategy, reflecting the heightened awareness in society of concerns for the environment and for ethical practices (for instance, promoting fair trade products). We live in an age when for some the modern corporation is portrayed as a demonized entity possessing psychopathic (Bakan, 2004) as well as undemocratic and dysfunctional characteristics (Hatcher, 2004). Globalization may be driven by a basic human desire for a better life (Friedman, 2000) but it creates tensions and contradictions for the HRD practitioner that I refer to as the *dark-side* of organizations. The ethical issues associated with poor working conditions and pay are not simply a characteristic of third world or developing cultures but exist already in developed societies. There are fears that society will become increasingly characterized by social exclusion (Nijhof, 2005) or economic segregation (Scully-Russ, 2005).

1.4 National HRD and vocational education and training (VET)

Traditionally HRD texts have referred to national vocational education and training (NVET) rather than national HRD and this is still the case in much of the current literature. NVET is focused on developing a country's human capital and represents a strategic response to the long term skills needs of its indigenous private, public, and non-profit sectors. National priorities place considerable emphasis upon transferable skills (Rigby, 2004). Getting this right is critical to the competitiveness of a nation's economy (Van den Berg et al., 2006) and is becoming more difficult in an era of increasing global competition where new economies are emerging and developing rapidly (e.g. China and India). For instance, many developed countries are still struggling with skills shortages (see *Media-watch* box) and across Europe apprenticeship schemes are in crisis (Clarke and Winch, 2007). The adoption of long term policies may become difficult to sustain as they come under pressure from short term challenges (e.g. changes in government; economic recession; mass migration; changes in technology).

The shift from an industrial to a post-industrial knowledge economy in developed nations has created a rising demand for workers with higher level skills. For instance, the US has seen an increase in the demand for certified skills training based on national standards in response to increased employer demands for more highly skilled employees (Carter, 2005). Much of the demand for higher skills has been addressed at an organizational level through a combination of strategies encompassing retraining, recruiting from abroad, offshoring, and out-sourcing. These strategies can be implemented relatively quickly while changes to a country's education and vocational training systems can take years to come to fruition and even then there is no guarantee of success. Arguably, national VET initiatives are always playing 'catch-up'.

MEDIA WATCH BOX

Skills shortages in the UK

People Management is the bi-weekly magazine published by the Chartered Institute of Personnel and Development. These items illustrate some of the problems facing UK organizations.

Basic literacy and numeracy continue to be a problem with 3.5 million workers in the UK lacking these skills.[1]

Despite an estimated employer investment of £23.7 billion in education and training in the UK, 20 per cent of companies still have skills gaps costing some £10 billion in lost revenue.[2]

The *Leitch Review of Skills* published in the UK in December 2006 highlighted that the UK would continue to have problems with workforce skills and productivity.[3]

Sources
[1] *People Management*, 29 July 2004: 14.
[2] *People Management*, 29 December 2005: 9.
[3] *People Management*, 9 August 2007: 28–31.

! TIPS AND HINTS

One of the first things a HRD practitioner should do upon appointment is to investigate the NVET initiatives available in his/her country of operation. Often funding and other incentives are available which many organizations, particularly smaller firms, are unaware of.

Over the last twenty years many European countries have expanded their training infrastructures (Ramirez, 2004) and introduced reforms to vocational education and training in order to make the education sector more responsive to the needs of employees (Smith, 2006). These reforms have been influenced by European Union (EU) policy which is characterized by an emphasis on competence-based approaches to vocational training, although there are variations between countries. In France vocational and technology-based baccalaureates have experienced sustained growth since the 1980s and vocational-based courses offered by universities have been increasing (Géhin, 2007). The UK's national VET strategy has also focused on vocational qualifications (e.g. national vocational qualifications or NVQs) although these have met with limited success. Presently, the UK government is encouraging universities to be more business-facing although this has met with mixed reactions from various stakeholders. The aim of the EU is to address variations between countries so that the concept of transferable vocational qualifications can be realized (this is consistent with a move to a single labour market in Europe). This approach does create problems for individual nations. For instance,

Germany's traditional craft-based approach to vocational education and training, which underpinned the success of its manufacturing sector and was universally admired (Kay, 2004), is now under threat from a combination of the shift to a service-based knowledge economy and the EU's desire to harmonize VET across Europe (Greinert, 2007). Indeed, apprenticeship schemes in many countries are in crisis as VET has become increasingly the preserve of schools and colleges (Clarke and Winch, 2007). Additionally, the recent growth of interest in on-the-job informal learning (see chapter 11) is now challenging the efficacy of competence-based qualifications (Hager, 2007).

Although NVET encompasses the concept of lifelong learning, which has received much attention as part of government policy-making, in many European countries this has been from a rather narrow economic perspective: completing new education courses and acquiring new skills in order to keep pace with the changing job market (Pring, 2007). This is consistent with a performance perspective on learning and HRD while a humanist perspective focuses on how learning can support personal growth and enrich individuals' lives (see chapter 2).

Key concept   National HRD

National HRD is intended to provide a coherent set of policies for the social and economic development of a country. It encompasses a wide range of concerns including: public health, environmental protection, diversity, education, and vocational training. The way in which national HRD is handled varies from country to country.

The concept of national human resource development (NHRD) has emerged in response to global trends that have political, social, and environmental as well as economic implications. It encompasses a broader range of issues than NVET, such as health, safety, community, and culture (McLean, 2004) and considers the implications of developing a country's human *and* social capital (Paprock, 2006). As globalization makes the disparities in education and skill levels between different countries and regions of the world much more visible (Metcalfe and Rees, 2005) there is an opportunity for HRD practitioners to lobby for a wider political, economic and social influence. Chapter fourteen discusses the implications for HRD practitioners of ethical and socially responsible management. Although the nature and purpose of HRD at national level differs from one country to another it is possible to discern five emerging models of NHRD: centralized, transitional, government-initiated, decentralized/free market, and small nation (Cho and McLean, 2004). These are defined in table 1.4 along with illustrative examples drawn from a range of literature.

Outside the US and Europe countries which are moving intentionally toward a NHRD policy include South Korea, New Zealand, India, South Africa, and Kenya (McLean, 2004). In China a NHRD policy has emerged in recent years as an important component of the country's social and economic development (Yang et al., 2004). In several other countries

Type of NHRD	Illustrative examples
Centralized Central government is responsible for the provision of education and training (a top–down approach)	**China** In China today a growing private sector exists alongside traditional state-owned enterprises as the country shifts from a centrally planned to a market-driven economy. This has fuelled demand for skills training. However, this transition is being controlled by the state whose interpretation of NHRD is heavily influenced by a socialist concept of human resources. Until recently the principal focus of the Chinese government has been on general education rather than vocational education and training. Since 1980 there has been growing interest in vocational education at school level, but beyond this the country's training and development infrastructure is still relatively weak and disorganized—although the situation is changing as the economy continues to develop. Traditionally training has been viewed as inferior to education and treated as a low priority by central government. Consequently training carried out within private sector enterprises, and which is in principle heavily regulated by legislation, is rarely monitored. The country has been criticized for the low quality of its labour market with only one third of employees in state-owned enterprises having undertaken some form of vocational education or training. Private enterprises invest much more heavily in training programmes. VET is offered by vocational schools and technical colleges. The latter are controlled by local or regional authorities and tend to focus on qualifications in nursing, nursery teaching, and banking. Vocational schools are accountable to the Ministry of Labour and focus on technical skills training for state-owned enterprises. Larger, more economically developed cities have better VET provision than smaller, less developed cities. However, the historic underinvestment in VET has impacted negatively on the country's economic development. Many technical posts remain unfilled and there is a shortage of qualified managers (consequently management training is an important area for private sector enterprises) **France** This is a country that relies heavily on the state for solutions to its VET problems. Historically, there has been a clear distinction made between initial training, including formal academic qualifications, and continuing education and training. Legislation is used to enforce national policy (e.g. accreditation of prior experiential learning is legally binding on all private sector organizations). All workers have an individual right to training and are expected to negotiate their own training and development needs with their employer. This includes attending courses that lead to a formal qualification, with employers paying fees and related expenses as well as altering job descriptions or offering promotion opportunities upon successful completion of the course

Table 1.4 National HRD in a selection of countries

Sources: Smith, 1999; Pickersgill, 2001; Xie and Wu, 2001; Venter, 2003; Bartlett and Rodgers, 2004; Cho and McLean, 2004; Kay, 2004; Lee, 2004; Lynham and Cunningham, 2004; Marquardt et al., 2004; Osman-Gani, 2004; Rao, 2004; Yang et al., 2004; Bhatnagar, 2005; Carter, 2005; Cooke, 2005; Jeris et al., 2005; Ohmae, 2005; Xiao and Lo, 2005; Lynham and Cunningham, 2006; Van Horn, 2006; Wynne, 2006; Xiao, 2006; Halliday, 2007; Keep, 2007; Lewis, 2007; Méhaut, 2007; Winch, 2007.

Type of NHRD	Illustrative examples
Transitional Reflects a situation in which the responsibility for NHRD is in transition from a centralized to a decentralized model	**India** NHRD policy can be traced back to 1985 when a comprehensive review of education policy was initiated which subsequently led to a significant increase in the number of schools, teachers, and pupil enrolments; although many in the country remain desperately poor and in need of education. With the opening up of the economy to foreign multinationals since 1991 the rapidly developing private sector has realized that competitive advantage comes from an investment in human resources. In contrast central government have been slow to understand the implications of a global economy. Rather it is the cities and region-states that have become integrated in the global economy and it is only recently that the government has started involving the private sector in the development of NHRD. A key strength of the country is its higher education system which has been particularly successful in producing graduates in science and technology subject areas **Singapore** The country's education system is geared towards meeting the country's human capital needs (e.g. it is this which determines the courses offered by universities) and in this way is an integral part of NHRD policy. Political leaders are deeply committed to developing a better life for the country's citizens. Historically the Ministry of Manpower, which is responsible for the Workforce Development Agency, has been principally responsible for national policy. However, the government now relies on a tripartite approach involving cooperation between the government, employers, and trade unions. For instance, unions provide education and training to enable members to upgrade their skills; and, distance learning programmes are available in the private sector. The benefits of investment in education and training and infrastructure are now showing through in the shape of a thriving private sector. This sector is also supported by the Singapore Institute of Management which provides training each year for over 11,000 managers
Government-initiated NHRD initiatives are initiated by government	**UK** The focus of recent governments has been on updating skills and developing the concept of lifelong learning which is broadly in line with EU policy. Historically, the UK has been characterized by a market-driven voluntary approach to vocational training, in which the primary responsibility for addressing skills shortages has been placed on employers supported by a range of government-led initiatives. These include: national vocational qualifications (NVQs) and apprenticeships (formerly referred to as 'modern apprenticeships'); although the reality is that vocational education has often been perceived as inferior to traditional educational qualifications. In 2001 the New Labour government set up the Learning and Skills Council (LSC) to oversee education and training for students over the age of 16 (this did not include university education). The LSC comprises representatives from employers, learning providers, and community groups. Since its establishment it has invested heavily in further education programmes as well as in initiatives such as apprenticeships (in 2004–5 its total spend was £9.2 billion). As with previous initiatives this approach has been criticized. One particular trend that can be discerned is that since the

Table 1.4 *(cont'd)*

Type of NHRD	Illustrative examples
	1980s central government and its agencies have been increasingly taking control of VET and relegating other stakeholders, such as employers and trade unions, to a more subordinate role. This incremental process of centralization is out of step with trends in other European countries, such as Italy, Holland, Sweden, and Finland which have focused on devolving responsibility to local social partnerships

Australia
The VET strategy adopted by the Australian government in the late 1980s was an attempt to replicate the UK market-driven approach. In 1988 a new central government department with responsibility for VET was created. This replaced previously fragmented state-based systems. Since then the government has promoted: competency-based training; the development of nationally recognized qualifications; the amalgamation of entry-level traineeships and apprenticeships as 'New Apprenticeships' in order to provide a unified entry-level training system; and, the development of a national training market in which private training providers could compete against established systems of state provision. The push for nationally recognized qualifications mirrors the UK's strategy for NVQs (see above) as well as the EU aim for transferable vocational qualifications among all member states. Unlike the situation in many European countries the demand for apprenticeships has remained buoyant. However, much of the training based on competency standards has been criticized for being too short term, fragmented and enterprise specific |
| **Decentralized/ free-market** Vocational education and training are the responsibility of the private sector with indirect support from government | **US**
The federal government plays a limited role in VET with principal responsibility resting with individual states and below, although the 1990s did see increased promotion by central government of certified skills training in order to address skills shortages (e.g. electricians). Vocational education in high schools has been viewed traditionally as an option for underachieving students to help them prepare for employment. However, new models are now emerging which are not based solely on the needs of employers but offer a more rounded education experience. However, many employers are complaining that schools are not teaching basic skills effectively and that more needs to be done to address the needs of lower-paid and lower-skilled workers. In terms of higher education the US is seen as leading the world with the top universities being private institutions. As with VET the federal government does not provide any central direction that is commonly found in Europe but does inject substantial research funding into the sector |
| **Small-nation** Small nations need to cooperate and share resources through regional initiatives | **Pacific Islands**
These provide a unique regional response to NHRD. The goal of regional inter-governmental organizations is to promote the sustainable development of the region to ensure that quality of life is maintained. This is reflected in the mission of the Pacific Institute of Management and Development, which provides management education to managers in the private and public sectors. This is achieved through a combination of education qualifications (e.g. MBA), short courses, seminars, and conferences aimed at senior managers, and applied research and consultancy. |

Table 1.4 *(cont'd)*

INSIGHTS INTO PRACTICE

HRD in the United States and Australia

These two examples contrast HRD practices in two developed countries: the US and Australia. The US has a strong tradition of adopting a structured and systematic approach to formal training interventions (see chapters two and five) yet ensuring the knowledge, skills and attitudes learnt on these interventions is transferred to the workplace remains a major problem.

Manufacturing companies in the US are pushing decision-making and problem solving down to frontline production employees. A variety of formal training interventions are being used to do this, including: classroom-based instruction, on-the-job training, and training workshops. However, research indicates that transfer of learning back to the job is poor.[1]

Survey data from the 1990s indicates that expenditure on training by Australian corporations is increasing and yet the organization of training in Australia tends to be ad hoc and unsystematic (for instance, formal methods for the identification of training needs are rarely used). The majority of enterprises do not employ qualified trainers or produce written training plans.[2]

Sources
[1] Brockman, J. L. and Dirkx, J. M. 2006. Learning to become a machine operator: the dialogical relationship between context, self, and content. *Human Resource Development Quarterly*, 17 (2): 199–221.
[2] Smith, A. 1999. International briefing 4: training and development in Australia. *International Journal of Training and Development*, 3 (4): 301–13.

there are the first signs of emergent approaches to NHRD. For instance, Sri Lanka has launched skills development projects based on competency-based training in order to build a much closer partnership between the private sector and vocational training (Jeris et al., 2005). However, there are still significant gaps in the literature. For instance, little attention has been given to Middle East countries although several countries, Bahrain, Kuwait, Jordan, Oman, and the United Emirates have NHRD programmes (Metcalfe and Rees, 2005). In Saudi Arabia the government is attempting to tackle unemployment levels through a policy of replacing foreign workers with Saudis and forcing the public sector to recruit Saudis for jobs that do not exist rather than by strengthening the country's approach to education and vocational training (Al-Dosary and Rahman, 2005). In North Africa, Morocco has started by focusing on primary education and improving enrolment at this level (Cox et al., 2005).

ACTIVITY 1.3

Identify one national training initiative from your own country and investigate how successful it has been.

1.5 **The implications of national HRD for HRD practitioners**

HRD practitioners require a good understanding of the full range of national HRD initiatives for the country they are working in. This becomes more complex when they are working in an international context and need to be familiar with any number of national HRD policies. In turn these policies will influence HRD strategy and practice in a variety of ways as can be illustrated by returning to the five models proposed by Cho and McLean (2004):

- In the centralized model HRD practitioners in indigenous and FDI enterprises will have to manage the implications of any restrictions created by the tight political control exercised by central government.

- In the transitional model HRD practitioners have the opportunity to make an important contribution to the development of national HRD because this model reflects a tripartite approach that draws upon the government, unions, and employers.

- The government-initiated model is dependent on the quality and appropriateness of government initiatives in meeting the needs of organizations. For instance, in the UK successful participation in the Investors in People scheme, which recognizes excellence in an organization's investment in human capital, can strengthen the role, status, and contribution of HRD.

- The decentralized/free-market model offers HRD practitioners the opportunity to be part of the primary force that is driving national education and training policy.

With regard to the small-nation model Cho and McLean (ibid) make the point that it is difficult for countries to make this work. It is likely that the majority of organizations within such countries lack the necessary HRD expertise.

Engaging with national HRD enables the HRD practitioner to adopt a broader and more strategic perspective on the role of HRD. For instance, lifelong learning can be integrated into an organization's HRD strategy (see chapter 3); basic skills, such as numeracy and literacy, can be improved through learning and development interventions (see chapter 5); and, viable apprenticeship schemes and vocational qualifications can be used to address specific performance-related problems (see http://www.oxfordtextbooks.co.uk/orc/mankin for more details). From a wider political and societal perspective Marquardt et al. (2004) argue that HRD practitioners can assist national governments in ensuring globalization provides long term benefits for society. Whilst this role is likely to be restricted to a small minority of practitioners it does merit serious consideration in an era where ethically and socially responsible management is receiving increasing media attention (see chapter 14). Stewart and Tansley (2002) also argue that HRD practitioners can work together with employers and government to support new approaches to learning. The need for this approach is echoed in pleas for solutions to global problems that are based on nations collaborating and tapping into the expertise and creativity of the non-government sector (Sachs, 2008). This should include building on the HRD expertise of global non-profit organizations (see *Insights into practice* box).

(•) INSIGHTS INTO PRACTICE

Training provided by non-profit organizations

The majority of training provided by non-profit organizations is externally rather than internally focused as illustrated by these examples. HRD interventions are, in effect, an integral aspect of the 'brand' identity of these organizations (see also *Media Watch Box* above):

The provision of training has been a key feature of many Oxfam projects. For instance, a joint project between Oxfam Australia and the Chicomo Rural Development Project in Mozambique on sustainable water supplies in remote rural communities involved training local communities in how to maintain and repair water pumps: 'Maintaining a functional hand pump and creating a sense of ownership of the water source are essential and require more than a single training session and a formal handover of the hand pump and borehole to the local community' (Mann, 2003: 66).[1]

The International Federation of Red Cross and Red Crescent Societies have provided: training for emergency response teams in Panama and Argentina; training for the prevention of SARS in East Asian countries; and, training in water sanitation and other relief techniques for members of regional disaster response teams in West Africa.[2]

Sources
[1] Mann, E. 2003. Sustainable water supply for a remote rural community in Mozambique. *Greener Management International*, 42, Summer: 59–66.
[2] Marquardt, M., Berger, N. and Loan, P. 2004. *HRD in the Age of Globalisation*. New York: Basic Books.

! TIPS AND HINTS

A secondment to a non-profit organization or a period of voluntary work is an excellent way of developing your HRD skills and broadening your knowledge base.

Summary

This chapter defined and explained the concept of globalization by drawing upon two contrasting perspectives. The dominance of the economic perspective was highlighted and discussed. The principal drivers of globalization were identified as advancements in technology and communications, global competition, and changing organizational structures. The implications of these for organizations were highlighted and summarized in table 1.2 (the impact of economic globalization on organizations). Particular attention was given to the emerging economies of China and India and the potential for a shift in economic power from the developed nations of the West to these developing nations in Asia and the Far East. The organizational requirements that emerged from this discussion were used as the starting point for an analysis of the implications of globalization for the practice of HRD. These were summarized in table 1.3 (the implications of globalization for HRD interventions and practices).

It was argued that particularly for those working in an international context globalization presents HRD practitioners with the opportunity to deliver a wide range of HRD interventions that add value to an organization. But to achieve this they need to work in partnership with key stakeholders at both a strategic and operational level. This theme is developed further in the next chapter and is one of the key themes in this book. The discussion on national HRD explained how the previous focus on education and vocational training is being replaced by a much broader perspective that incorporates a range of social and environmental issues. Consequently, the twenty-first century poses a great many challenges for practitioners and managers in the implementation of HRD practices. In moving forward both line managers and HRD practitioners will need to develop and/or improve new competencies; and, in some cases, they will also need to engage with the wider community and contribute to the agenda for national HRD.

Review questions

1   How can the concept of human resource development be defined?

2   What are the principal perspectives on globalization?

3   Summarize how globalization is impacting on organizations generally. What are the principal implications for human resource development practices?

4   Is it really possible for business corporations to operate ethically in a global economy when their primary goal is to maximize profits? Can you identify any examples of good and bad practices?

5   Why is the concept of national HRD important for the future development of countries?

Suggestions for further reading

1   Bierema, L. L. and D'Abundo, M. 2003. Socially conscious HRD. In A. Maycunich Gilley, J. L. Callahan and L. L. Bierema (eds.) *Critical Issues in HRD: A New Agenda for the Twenty-first Century*. Cambridge, MA: Perseus Publishing.

    This book chapter explains the concept of 'socially conscious' HRD.

2   Dirani, K. 2006. Exploring socio-cultural factors that influence HRD practices in Lebanon. *Human Resource Development International*, 9 (1): 85–98.

    This is an interesting article because it explores the nature of HRD in an Arab country. The Arab countries remain a much neglected topic in the literature on HRD.

3   McLean, G. N. 2004. National human resource development: what in the world is it?, *Advances in Developing Human Resources*, 6 (3): 269–75.

    A very short article that summarizes the concept of national HRD.

4   Marquardt, M., Berger, N. and Loan, P. 2004. *HRD in the Age of Globalisation*. New York: Basic Books.

There is an abundance of useful material in this book especially on specific countries and regions.

5   Stiglitz, J. 2007. *Making Globalisation Work*. London: Penguin Books.

There are many texts on the subject of globalization but this one offers a particularly searing critique.

Case study

National HRD in Finland, Russia, and South Africa

Finland

HRD practice in Finland is diverse as it is primarily the responsibility of the employer with some steering from government through legislation and government-led initiatives such as the Finnish Workplace Development Programme. The labour market in Finland is characterized by high levels of education. Since the mid-1990s adult education and training has become an increasingly important feature of national policy and is available in over 1,000 institutions although the majority of adult learning takes place within organizations in the form of training provision or workplace learning. For young people who decide upon a vocational route after comprehensive school there are a wide range of training options to choose from: there are 75 initial vocational qualifications. This type of training is offered by education institutions and as apprenticeship schemes. Training is a mix of theoretical studies and practical sessions plus on-the-job training in actual workplaces. Higher education is studied at universities or polytechnics with the latter having a vocational orientation. Finland has been able to realize the benefits of a knowledge-based economy achieving excellent levels of productivity, innovation, and competitiveness. National VET has been heavily influenced by the EU commitment to the development of a learning society and competence-based training, particularly in the public sector. SMEs in Finland demonstrate high levels of innovation which reflect the country's prioritization of investing in research and development. This has also been reflected in the past in HRD practice in Finnish organizations which has been regarded as being quite innovative; drawing upon a wide range of HRD interventions including the implementation of new types of training course, the facilitation of workplace learning and the utilization of organizational intranets.

Russia

Today Russia is no longer characterized by Soviet-era practices or a labour market that is under the direct control of central government. Instead, Russian enterprises are being forced to improve their ability to recruit and retain human capital. Since the early 1990s there has been a significant reduction in state-sponsored vocational training and a consequent increase in opportunities for private training and education companies, along with the setting up of their own training and development facilities by subsidiaries of foreign companies. The once world class higher education sector is now run down but still produces every year over 200,000 science and technology graduates (there are some 3,500 universities and research institutes in the country). However, access to a good education can often depend on parental connections and corruption is rife.

South Africa

The situation in South Africa has been deeply influenced by recent political, social, and economic developments and the legacy of apartheid. A significant proportion of the population is unemployed and has low skill levels. The country is also experiencing skills shortages at the high and intermediate levels. National government is committed to developing the country's human capital and has used legislation to promote vocational education and training. In 1995 the South African Qualifications Act was introduced with the aim of promoting national standards for training through transferable qualifications and the accreditation of prior learning. In 1998 the Skills Development Act was an attempt to make employers treat training more seriously and included the introduction of a training levy and a requirement that firms produce and submit an organizational skills development plan. Since the ending of apartheid the government has introduced measures to address racial imbalances in education, high levels of unemployment, and skills shortages in science and technology.

Sources

[1] Hytönen, T. 2003. International briefing 14: training and development in Finland. *International Journal of Training and Development*, 7 (2): 124–37.

[2] Bonnin, D., Lane, T., Ruggunan, S. and Wood, S. 2004. Training and development in the maritime industry: the case of South Africa. *Human Resource Development International*, 7 (1): 7–22.

[3] Lynham, S. A. and Cunningham, P. W. 2004. Human resource development: the South Africa case. *Advances in Developing Human Resources*, 6 (3): 315–25.

[4] Ardichvili, A. and Dirani, K. 2005. Human capital practices of Russian enterprises. *Human Resource Development International*, 8 (4): 403–18.

[5] Kraak, A. 2005. Human resources development and the skills crisis in South Africa: the need for a multipronged strategy. *Journal of Education and Work*, 18 (1): 57–83.

[6] Ohmae, K. 2005. *The Next Global Stage: Challenges and Opportunities in Our Borderless World.* Upper Saddle River, NJ: Wharton School Publishing.

[7] Walburn, D. 2005. The Lisbon Agenda: regional performance in a two speed Europe: the important contribution of local programmes of SME support. *Local Economy*, 20 (3): 305–8.

[8] Lynham, S. A. and Cunningham, P. W. 2006. National human resource development in tansitioning societies in the developing world: concept and challenges. *Advances in Developing Human Resources*, 8 (1): 116–35.

[9] Lucas, E. 2008. *The New Cold War: How the Kremlin Menaces Both Russia and the West.* London: Bloomsbury.

[10] Education and training in Finland http://virtualfinland.fi (accessed 29 May 2008).

Case questions

1. Using the five models proposed by Cho and McLean (2004) how would you categorize each country's approach to national HRD?

2. To what extent should employers be taking responsibility for basic skills training in areas such as numeracy and literacy?

Online resource centre

Visit the supporting online resource centre for additional material that will help you with your research, essays, assignments, and revision.

 www.oxfordtextbooks.co.uk/orc/mankin/

2

Global Perspectives on Human Resource Development

Learning objectives

By the end of this chapter you should be able to:

* Appreciate how the theory and practice of human resource development has evolved over the last 30 years

* Discriminate between different perspectives on HRD

* Define and explain the concept of HRD

* Understand the centrality of performance and learning theory to perspectives on HRD

* Explain perspectives on HRD emerging in the developing economies

In order to achieve these objectives it is important that you not only read the chapter carefully but also complete the activities and review questions, but also undertake some of the suggested further reading.

Indicative content

■ Definitions and explanations of training, learning, and development

■ The performance perspective on HRD

■ The humanist perspective on HRD

■ Reconciling the performance and humanist perspectives

■ The evolution of the theory and practice of HRD

■ The role of individual and organizational learning

■ The emergence of informal learning

- The relationship between psychological and sociological perspectives on learning

- The concept of business partnership between HRD practitioner and managers

- The importance of intellectual capital (combining human and social capital)

- The structure and design of the HRD function

- HRD in the developing economies

Key concepts:

Human resource development (HRD)	Lifelong learning
Organization development	Vertical strategic alignment
Career development	Horizontal strategic alignment
Training, learning, and development	
Organizational learning and the learning organization	

2.1 Introduction

From an academic perspective human resource development (HRD) has been perceived as an ambiguous and problematic concept (Mankin, 2001). Despite the efforts of a great many academics, along with several practitioners who have written for academic publications, the concept continues to defy a universal definition. The theoretical foundations of HRD have been discussed at length since the late 1980s (Torraco, 2004) and although there has been much debate about the meaning and purpose of HRD in academic literature most practitioners and managers remain unaware of these arguments. Indeed, while academics discuss HRD most practitioners and managers simply talk about training, learning, and development. From their perspective there is nothing unusual or ambiguous about the meaning and purpose of training, learning, and development nor are they concerned that the constituent elements of HRD are rarely brought together in a single function. Rather it is HRD academics who have been preoccupied with these issues as they strive for academic credibility in the form of a discipline identity (Mankin, 2003). This has generated many attempts to define boundaries for the theory and practice of HRD. That this has proven to be challenging and problematic suggests that the ambiguous nature of HRD should be regarded as its defining feature:

> If HRD has a role to play in helping organizations develop in an era of rapid change, then there is a need for HRD professionals (from practitioners to academics) to accept that HRD itself is a continuously evolving, adaptive concept . . . Perhaps less time should be devoted to debating the merits of different definitions and more to better understanding how HRD, as a fluid, amorphous concept, can contribute to organizational change. (Mankin, 2001: 67)

The latter sentiment is a consequence of my former career, specifically the time I spent working in the manufacturing sector as a HRD practitioner and before that as a total quality manager. It is that latent urge to identify practical solutions to practical problems. It is about being pragmatic and adopting whatever methods, techniques, or processes work in a given context at a particular moment in time. As Lynham and Cunningham (2006) note about HRD there is no need to be pre-occupied with 'one-size-fits-no-one' models. Rather, as they go on to suggest, the focus should be on recognizing the situated nature of HRD. This has implications also for the strategic dimension of HRD which is discussed in the next chapter.

The current situation continues to be characterized by a widening gap between the theory and practice of HRD (Torraco and Yorks, 2007):

> Although we have conducted interesting and lively debates on the nature of HRD and its place in the modern organisation, this has been a debate conducted by insiders largely for the benefit of the HRD academic community. Meanwhile, the world of policy making and practice has moved on, and we have failed to have an impact on either. (Smith, 2006)

To date there have been relatively few empirical studies on the relationship between the theory and practice of HRD (Short, 2006). A classic academic stance is illustrated by

McGuire et al. (2006) who argue that 'there is significant value in HRD practitioners understanding how these various perspectives may critically inform their day-to-day activities' (McGuire et al., 2007). The efficacy of this remains questionable until there is more two-way dialogue between academics and practitioners and, importantly, organizational managers who play an increasingly crucial role in the practice of HRD. While there has been a considerable amount of theory-building there has been less investigation into organizational practices. There is still limited empirical evidence of the existence of HRD strategies, processes, and practices within many organizations (Beattie, 2006). As Short (2006) notes academics need to: maintain an ongoing involvement in business (or other sectors), adopt different ways of doing research, carry out more research in authentic contexts, and improve the dissemination of research findings. Fora that can facilitate this process already exist. For instance, the University Forum for HRD (UFHRD) and Chartered Institute of Personnel and Development (CIPD) in the UK; and the Academy of HRD (AHRD) and the American Society for Training and Development (ASTD) in the US.

This chapter will endeavour to explain how the concept of HRD has evolved and the implications this has for HRD practitioners and organizational managers. Speculations about the future of HRD will be confined to the final chapter (15). The first section defines the concepts of training, learning and development. The second explores some of the concepts and theories that have informed definitions of HRD. This is followed by an explanation of the 'learning continuum', a framework designed to illustrate changes in the theory *and* practice of HRD. Key trends are identified and explained in more detail in subsequent sections. As part of this process a model for HRD is developed. Given the comments above this may appear somewhat contradictory. I justify this approach on the basis of pedagogy: the model is intended to be an aid to learning. Those of you who compare this new model with that proposed at the turn of the century (see Mankin, 2001) will see some significant differences that reflect changes in the theory and practice of HRD since then. My concluding remarks at the end of that article are still pertinent: 'The irony of this article is that by the time it is published the model will already have changed' (ibid.: 81). The chapter concludes with a brief discussion on HRD practices emerging in developing economies.

2.2 Defining learning, training, and development

Learning

Before embarking on the story of how HRD has evolved it is important to define and explain the concepts of learning, training, and development. Learning is about the acquisition of new knowledge and how this changes the individual in some way (e.g. in terms of how they think about something, or how they carry out a task, or how they behave). As chapter 4 reveals there is no universal definition of learning although different theories are based on two broad perspectives: psychological (i.e. all learning takes place inside a person's mind) and sociological (i.e. learning is influenced by the social context).

Increasingly, HRD practitioners have been endeavouring to create organizational contexts that foster learning with terms such as 'learning environment' (Noe, 2002) and 'learning climate' (Gilley et al., 2002) being used to describe such a context. Critical to this process is the need for employees to understand how they learn and how they can learn more effectively. As chapter 11 explains much of the learning in organizations is informal. Often this informal learning happens accidentally or incidentally in the workplace and people are not necessarily aware that learning has occurred.

Training

Training involves planned instruction in a particular skill or practice and is intended to result in changed behaviour in the workplace leading to improved performance. During the training the trainee acquires new knowledge in the form of explicit knowledge or 'know-what' (e.g. understanding and being able to explain the principles of health and safety when using equipment) and tacit knowledge or 'know-how' (e.g. developing the practical skills to use equipment in a safe manner). For a more detailed explanation of explicit and tacit knowledge refer to chapter 10. Some popular training techniques are demonstration, guided practice, and coaching. Training interventions are determined by the needs of the organization and are usually designed to bring about an immediate improvement in job performance. As Noe (2002: 4) observes: 'the goal of training is for employees to master the knowledge, skill, and behaviours emphasized in training pro-grams and to apply them to their day-to-day activities'. However, as shall be discussed later in the book, the transfer of learning from the 'classroom' to the workplace is notori-ously fraught with difficulties.

Development

Development is much broader than training and usually has a longer term focus. It is concerned with the enhancement of an individual's personal portfolio of knowledge, skills, and abilities (i.e. competencies). Development activities can be determined by both the needs of the organization and the needs of individual (e.g. attending a series of man-agement development workshops in preparation for future promotion may be part of an organization's strategy for succession planning and therefore can be beneficial to both parties). For many professional practitioners, such as members of the Chartered Institute of Personnel and Development (CIPD), development activities are an integral aspect of an individual's continuing professional development (CPD), which is discussed in more detail in chapter 15. Development also embraces education. Education can range from courses in basic literacy and numeracy through to post-graduate qualifications such as an MBA. National HRD policies have a very strong focus on education as the funding of primary, secondary, tertiary, and higher education is normally the responsibility of central government. Increasingly education is also seen as embracing lifelong learning which has become part of the political landscape in the European Union over the last 20 years. Training focuses on work, education focuses on the whole person; development is often a mix of the two of these.

> **Key concept**   Lifelong learning
>
> Lifelong learning is the ongoing acquisition of knowledge and skills by study and experience throughout the duration of an individual's career.

2.3 The foundations of HRD

The performance perspective

US perspectives on HRD have dominated academic literature since 1970. This was the year that one of the earliest definitions of HRD can be traced back to (Walton, 1999; Swanson and Holton, 2001). Since then academics have had 'gut feelings about what is central to HRD and what might be viewed as tangential' (Roth, 2004: 15) but have been unable to reach a clear consensus on the meaning and purpose of the concept. US definitions emphasize the importance of performance, as illustrated by Gilley et al. (2002) who define development as 'the advancement of knowledge, skills, and competencies for the purpose of improving performance within an organisation' (p. 5). This emphasis on performance pervades US definitions of HRD and reflects a preoccupation with the needs of the organization. It is underpinned by an economic perspective (Wang and McLean, 2007) that focuses on the role of human capital. An appreciation of the value of human capital within an organization is well established (Geroy and Venneberg, 2003) although it is a theory that ignores the social processes that underpin human activity in the workplace (the implications of this are discussed in section 2.9 below and in chapter 10).

> **Key concept**   Human capital theory
>
> Becker (1964, 1975) popularized Schultz's (1961) human capital theory that organizations derive economic value from employees' skills, competence, knowledge, and experience. Schultz (ibid.) argued that human capital can be developed through education and training.

The theory and practice of HRD in the US have been informed by economics, systems thinking, and psychology (Swanson and Holton, 2001) as well as the systematic approach to training used by the Training Within Industry Service of the US government during the period 1940 to 1945 (Smith and Sadler-Smith, 2006). The development of this systematic approach is discussed in chapter 5. A seminal definition of HRD is provided by McLagan (1989) who suggested that HRD comprises three domains: organization development, training and development, and career development. This was more specific than Nadler's (1970) reference to 'organised activities' (p. 3, cited in Swanson and Holton, 2001). Subsequent definitions have either referred to similar domains (e.g. training, education, and development; training, career development, and organization development) or have emphasized the role of learning (e.g. organized learning activities; organized learning experiences; learning-based interventions). However, the focus on performance has remained the primary outcome in these definitions.

Key concept   Career development

Career development is a planned and structured response to the career aspirations of key employees.

An often quoted definition of HRD is offered by Swanson and Holton (2001) who describe the concept as:

> a process of developing and unleashing human expertise through organisation development (OD) and personnel training and development (T and D) for the purpose of improving performance. (p. 90)

There is something rather powerful and dramatic about the phrase 'unleashing human expertise' that is absent from the rather more staid language found in British and European definitions. However, what is more important than the cultural influence on language is the fact that this definition remains locked in a relatively narrow economic-rationalist view of organizations. It does not differentiate between formal and informal activities and processes (see section 2.6 and chapters 10 and 11); it does not acknowledge sociological as well as psychological perspectives on learning (see section 2.7 and chapters 10 and 11); and, it does not address the implications of managing social as well as human capital (see section 2.9 below and chapter 10). This narrow perspective is also evident in the literature of other leading American theorists (Kuchinke, 2003).

Key concept   Organization development

Organization development is a systematic and methodical approach to the management of change that is aimed at improving organizational performance and competitiveness.

The humanist perspective

In contrast, many of the British and European definitions are based on humanist thinking which has its roots in humanist-psychology (McGuire et al., 2005). From this perspective HRD is about enhancing personal growth and developing human potential (Yang, 2004). Learning remains within the control of the individual and is the primary outcome of HRD; improvements in performance follow-on as a consequence of this learning. Arguably it is a more holistic perspective although it does underestimate the extent to which short term pragmatism is embedded in business corporations (Beattie, 2006).

MEDIA WATCH BOX

Organization development

Apparently many HR practitioners in the UK have had their job titles changed to include the phrase organization development. However, a US organization development consultant is sceptical about the ability of many HR practitioners to get to grips with the breadth and range of the concept, pointing out that the US has education programmes in the subject because it is regarded as an important academic discipline.

Source
People Management, 12 October 2006: 40–1.

MEDIA WATCH BOX

The demise of organization development

According to Andrew Mayo, a leading HRD consultant, the growth of interest in competency frameworks, which focus on the individual, has resulted in the demise of organization development skills. He feels that too much attention is being given to training interventions designed to develop the individual.

Source
People Management, 24 November: 16–17.

Enriching the lives of employees may bring long term gains but the vast majority of organizations are small and medium sized enterprises which are focused on the short term and are concerned about basic skills. They often see training and development as a cost rather than an investment (see chapter 12).

Reconciling the performance and humanist perspectives

Are performance and learning incompatible? This question goes to the very heart of the debate about the meaning and purpose of HRD. Swanson and Holton (2001) describe learning and performance as 'partners in a formula for success' (p. 4) arguing that 'learning and growth for the sole benefit of the individual and which will never benefit the organization is not acceptable for *organized-sponsored HRD*' (p. 145; emphasis in the original). Therefore from a humanist perspective learning remains subsidiary to performance. For this reason a great many academics, particularly in Europe, remain unpersuaded. However, the performance perspective has now achieved a degree of ascendancy (Smith, 2006) and the humanist position is being challenged: McGuire et al. (2005) argue that humanist rhetoric is no longer matched by organizational actions which are driven much more by economic imperatives. Whilst it may be virtuous to advocate the humanist perspective this is unlikely to go down well with senior managers in many private or public sector organizations. Their priority will be on organizational performance. Even organizations in the voluntary sector may struggle to reconcile an altruistic commitment to their employees with the financial pressures that they have to operate under. The reality in many organizations is that 'HRD programs are funded with the expectation that they will benefit the larger system (e.g. the organization or nation). Financial and non-financial outcomes can result, but financial outcomes are usually the top priority' (Sleezer et al., 2004: 28). Indeed, improving performance 'was the early rationale for training and development' (Yorks, 2005: 15). The dominance of economic globalization impacts on the viability of the humanist perspective. It is unlikely that there will be a convergence of the two perspectives but an increase in empirical studies, as suggested above, may prompt a 'meeting of minds'.

In order to justify the resources invested in HRD activities it is increasingly important to identify the benefits that accrue to the organization particularly in terms of improved performance. Recent studies are beginning to confirm that better organizational performance *is* linked to an investment in learning and development (Clarke, 2004). This does not mean the HRD profession should become complacent. Rather, it emphasizes the importance of making a business case for HRD activities. The rationale underpinning the evaluation of HRD activities is driven by the need to prove, in the language of economics and finance, that HRD can add value to an organization through the improved performance of employees. Unfortunately, HRD functions have often struggled to translate business objectives into appropriate HRD objectives with measurable outcomes. It is not always easy to measure the benefits of HRD activities and this raises some practical

---

INSIGHTS INTO PRACTICE

A personal reflection

Ironically, HRD practitioners are often more attuned to the needs of employees across all parts of the organization. One of the criticisms I have heard often over the years is that employees may leave an organization after a significant investment in their personal development has been made. This is short-sighted. Given the significant changes that have taken place over the last generation and the nature of the employer–employee psychological contract such movements are inevitable. This may make the management of an organization's intellectual capital more challenging but this should not be allowed to detract from maximizing employees' contributions to an organization's performance while they are employed by that organization.

Source
The author

difficulties for HRD practitioners who are often struggling to gain greater credibility inside their organization. The political reality in many organizations is that HRD practitioners are perceived as being less relevant to the needs of the business than their colleagues in other functions (such as marketing, sales, production, research and development, etc.).

It was not until the mid-1990s that academics in the UK started to use the term HRD in preference to its antecedents, such as training and development, employee development, or learning and development. At this time British definitions of HRD tended to emphasize the role of formally-planned activities and processes:

> Human resource development encompasses activities and processes which are *intended* to have impact on organisational and individual learning. The term assumes that . . . both organisations and individuals are capable of influence and direction through deliberate and planned interventions. Thus, HRD is constituted by planned interventions in organisational and individual learning processes. (Stewart and McGoldrick, 1996: 1)

Subsequently, new definitions have emerged that incorporate current trends. For instance, Harrison and Kessels (2004: 89) define HRD as an organizational process that:

> comprises the skilful planning and facilitation of a variety of formal and informal learning and knowledge processes and experiences, primarily but not exclusively in the workplace, in order that organisational progress and individual potential can be enhanced through the competence, adaptability, commitment and knowledge-creating activity of all who work for the organisation.

There are few organizations in the UK which have departments labelled as 'Human Resource Development'; and this is also true of the US (Yorks, 2005). Often the role is subsumed within the HR or HRM function. This does not mean, however, that HRD should be viewed only as an abstract concept. The elements that constitute HRD make an important contribution to organizational performance regardless of how the function is structured. Interestingly, it has been argued that the status of HRD practitioners is rising (Gold et al., 2003), a point of view that is touched on again in chapters 13 and 15.

ACTIVITY 2.1

Carry out a search of job adverts for HRD-type positions. How many different job and function titles can you identify? How commonly used is the term HRD to describe jobs or functions? Are there any similarities or differences between sectors or type of organization?

Although there is no universal definition of HRD is there anything which is common to the multitude of theoretical definitions? From analysing previous debates on the meaning of HRD it is possible to identify several salient features of the concept:

1. The theory of HRD has its roots in a diverse range of concepts and disciplines.
2. The practice of HRD has its roots in training and human capital theory.

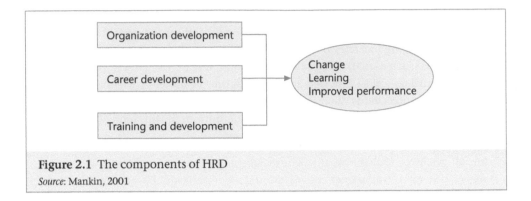

Figure 2.1 The components of HRD
Source: Mankin, 2001

3. The theory and practice of HRD encompass strategic and operational processes and practices.
4. The theory and practice of HRD focus on individual and collective learning, career development, and organization development.

Each of these points is developed further as part of the analysis and discussion in this chapter. The initial components of the HRD model are shown in figure 2.1 which replicates the model in Mankin (2001).

2.4 The evolution of the theory and practice of HRD

One way of illustrating the evolution of the theory and practice of HRD is through the *learning continuum* (see figure 2.2). This shows the principal changes that have taken place and how the concept of HRD has evolved from an operational focus on training designed to develop employees' skills to a broader strategic focus on interventions designed to develop an organization's intellectual capital (i.e. the individual and collective knowledge found within an organization). This emphasis on intellectual capital reflects the shift from an industrial to a post-industrial or knowledge society. Knowledge that has accrued over time and is unique to an organization (i.e. difficult for competitors to replicate) has become a valuable source of competitive advantage. This knowledge can manifest in variety of ways, for instance as the expertise underpinning innovative products and/or services. Bryan and Joyce (2007) refer to this as the 'mind power' of an organization. Competitive advantage is normally associated with business corporations and can be measured in terms of enhanced market share, higher levels of profitability and returns on investment, and increased market capitalization. Other sectors, such as the public and non-profit, are likely to focus on maximizing organizational performance through the efficient and effective utilization of their people.

The learning continuum fulfils four functions:

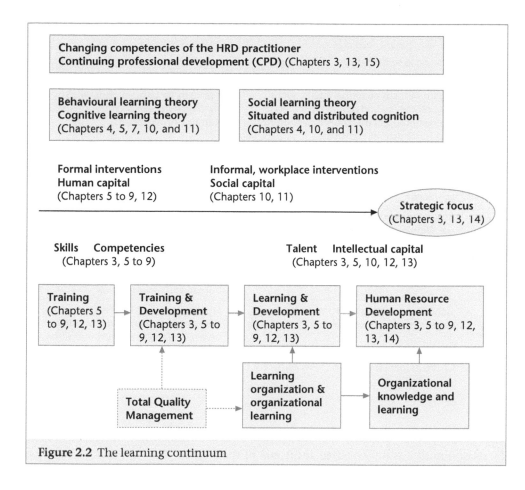

Figure 2.2 The learning continuum

1. It tells the story of HRD albeit from a predominantly Anglo-American perspective.

2. It conveys a sense of the range of HRD strategies available to organizations. For instance, informal workplace interventions can be combined in different ways with formal training interventions (see chapters 5 and 11).

3. It enables comparisons to be made between organizational practices. For instance, small and medium sized enterprises are less likely than large businesses to invest in formal training interventions (Webster et al., 2005) (see chapter 12).

4. It enables comparisons to be made between countries (and regions). Indigenous organizations in developing countries are still playing catch-up. For instance, in a study of Russian enterprises Ardichvili and Dirani (2005) discovered that HRD interventions tend to focus on short term job-related training needs rather than long term employee development (although the same study revealed the reverse was true for management positions).

The principal changes in the evolution of the theory and practice of HRD are set out in table 2.1 and explained in more detail below. These changes have impacted on the competencies needed to be an effective HRD practitioner.

	From	To
1.	Training as something you do to people	Learning as something people take responsibility for
2.	A primary focus on formal interventions (e.g. off-the-job and on-the-job training interventions, such as courses, workshops, and apprenticeship schemes)	A primary focus on informal workplace learning (e.g. learning from colleagues, learning from mistakes)
3.	The trainer as an instructional expert working at an operational level and providing line managers with training solutions	The HRD practitioner as a facilitator of learning working at both a strategic and operational level in partnership with senior managers and line managers
4.	Psychological perspectives on learning (i.e. learning theories associated with individual cognition)	Sociological perspectives on learning (i.e. learning theories associated with situated and distributed cognition)
5.	An emphasis on developing employees' skills (i.e. human capital)	An emphasis on developing an organization's intellectual capital (i.e. human and social capital)
6.	Centralized training departments and large teams of internal trainers	Smaller centralized, decentralized and outsourced teams delivering training on a more flexible and just-in-time basis

Table 2.1 Principal changes in the evolution of the theory and practice of HRD

In order to better illustrate the evolution of HRD a model will be developed section by section until it is fully realized at the end of the chapter. This will then provide the overarching framework for subsequent chapters which explore specific aspects of HRD.

2.5 The shift from training to learning

In terms of the employee the shift from training to learning manifests in several ways:

1. **There is an expectation that employees will take more responsibility for their own learning,** for instance: sharing the cost of education programmes with the employer; identifying their own learning needs on an ongoing basis; learning from work-related situations; learning from colleagues. Rather than relying predominantly on formal training interventions provided by the organization, such as classroom-based workshops, employees are now engaging with different forms of self-managed and self-directed learning. The former is usually associated with formal interventions, such as e-learning programmes, while the latter involves the integration of learning with work (see the discussion on informal workplace learning below). As a consequence the focus has shifted from training and development to training, learning, and development. As chapter 5 will explain there is still an important role for traditional training interventions but these are no longer the predominant form of HRD provision.

2. **Employees need to demonstrate a commitment to *lifelong learning* in order to remain employable**. As individuals increasingly build portfolio careers they will move from one organization to another; for instance, an average American will hold ten or more different jobs in their career (Luthans et al., 2006). Career development (CD) is a 'process of professional growth brought about by work-related learning' (Van der Sluis and Poell, 2003: 162). It is concerned with an individual's future development and career progression. Definitions vary in focus from the individual to the organization (McDonald and Hite, 2005). In the past, the term career management has often been used to reflect an organization's perspective and responsibilities as the career development needs and expectations of an individual do not always converge with the needs and expectations of the organization. An organization may have systems in place to manage careers, as part of an organization's succession planning and management development strategies, but limits may be placed on direct and indirect support of career development activities that are seen to benefit the individual more than the organization. A key determinant here is how long the employment relationship is expected to last linked to the likely level of return on the investment made. This approach does require individuals to develop *career consciousness* which is still lacking in many employees (van den Berg et al., 2006).

3. **Employees are being encouraged to understand how they learn and how they can learn differently.** This requires them to reflect on their learning (i.e. *reflective practice*) which can be difficult to grasp. They need something to act as a trigger to make them conscious that learning has taken place. Donald Schön (1983) refers to these triggers as 'surprises'. For instance, you might find yourself giving feedback to a colleague and are surprised at their reaction. Perhaps they disagree strongly, use colourful language; perhaps they are unhappy because you have not given specific examples to support your feedback; or perhaps you have used inappropriate language. Subsequently, however, you may reflect on the incident and decide whether to adjust your approach the next time a similar situation arises. This process of reflection has been triggered by the

---

(•) INSIGHTS INTO PRACTICE

Career development

A study carried out by Chen et al. (2004) concluded that the levels of job satisfaction, professional development, and productivity among research and development personnel increase with their increasing satisfaction with career development programmes. Not surprisingly, many organizations have been introducing career planning workshops to help managers learn how to plan their own careers with confidence and some sense of independence or are using competency frameworks to make the process of spotting and developing talent less subjective.

Source
Chen, T-Y., Chang, P-L. and Yeh, C-W. (2004) An investigation of career development programs, job satisfaction, professional development and productivity: the case of Taiwan.

MEDIA WATCH BOX

HRD in non-profit organizations

Aid agencies recognize the importance of having properly trained staff who can cope with the latest emergencies. Care International, a non-government organization, is restructuring its emergency response capacity into three levels: local, regional, and global. Each level has specified skills that reflect core competencies which have been designed to ensure appropriately qualified personnel are on standby for any emergency response. The organization also provides career development opportunities. World Vision has introduced a rapid induction pack that can be tailored to local contexts so that members of emergency teams at the local level can be made quickly familiar with the organization (many of these people are on short term contracts). Meanwhile Save the Children has implemented facilitation training so that trained facilitators can help emergency response teams.

Source
People Management, 29 May 2008: 18–21.

incident acting as a surprise (i.e. not conforming to your expectations). Over the years I have asked the same question to numerous groups of students: can you identify anything unusual that has happened to you at work recently? Invariably the answer is a mix of 'no' and shakes of the head. Then I ask the next question: can you tell me about the last time you learnt something? Invariably the responses are about training courses, workshops, or seminars. The problem is that so much of what we do at work has become routinized and no longer surprises us.

All three of these are inter-related and result in some form of change at the level of the individual (see section 2.2 above and chapter 4). This shift has altered the balance of the relationship between the three primary stakeholders traditionally involved in training: the HRD practitioner, the learner, and the learner's line manager (which is discussed below).

TIPS AND HINTS

It can be helpful to view lifelong learning from the perspective of marketability rather than employability as this reminds people that they are participating in a highly competitive labour market.

From an organizational perspective the shift from training to learning has generated a wide range of literature on the concept of organizational learning. It is argued that all organizations learn (Argyris and Schön, 1996) or learn to some extent (Garvey and Williamson, 2002). Distinctions have been drawn between learning *by* an organization

INSIGHTS INTO PRACTICE

Petronus

Petronus (Petroleum Nasional Berhad) is the national petroleum company of Malaysia. It is a multinational corporation with interests in over thirty countries. The company's education division has shifted its focus from 'trainer-dependent' to 'learner-centred' approaches (i.e. from training to educating). The education division is promoting lifelong learning as part of their overall strategy and this is reflected in several initiatives, including: educating younger employees for long term roles; re-skilling employees; developing self-awareness and the ability to work independently (thus avoiding the need for micro-management); and, preparing staff for retirement by educating them in how they can continue to make an economic contribution even after they have retired.

Source
Johari, P. J. (2005) Learning strategies for global competitiveness—the Petronus experience. In A. G. PG HJ Metusin and O. K. Beng (eds.) *HRD for Developing States and Companies: Proceedings of the 2005 Brunei Darussalam AEMC Convention.* Singapore: ISEAS Publication.

and learning *within* an organization (Huysman and de Wit, 2003). The latter perspective emphasizes *organizational learning* processes which explain how individuals and groups learn (e.g. the individual acting as an agent of the organization; group members learning from each other) and how that learning can become institutionalized; while the former perspective emphasizes the concept of the *learning organization*. This has always been an aspirational concept that does not reflect the realities of HRD practice, which tend to be very different (Nijhof, 2004). As training and development has been viewed historically as the core activity of HRD the concept of organizational learning has never been fully embraced (Callahan, 2003).

Organizational learning is not only closely linked with individual and group learning but also with organization development. Indeed, it is this organizational perspective that is critical to HRD being treated as a strategic partner (Callahan, 2003). The boundaries between organization development and organizational learning have become blurred (Yorks, 2005) as HRD practitioners undertake large-scale organizational learning and change initiatives (Marquardt and Berger, 2003). Organization development is concerned with planned change programmes that are designed to improve organizational performance and competitiveness. Initiatives usually involve a total organization system, treat the organization from a systems perspective, and have long term goals (Gilley et al., 2002). Examples include changing an organization's culture, implementing a new organizational structure, and introducing new organization-wide ICT systems. Organization development is relevant to HRD practice because change programmes normally involve the development of people as well as systems and structures. Noe (2002) argues that organization development is important because it 'helps to create a learning environment' (p. 443). A learning environment embraces individual, group, and organizational learning processes.

The relationship between organizational learning and organization development has been further cemented by the emergence and evolution of knowledge management systems and processes. Knowledge formation processes such as knowledge acquisition, knowledge creation, knowledge sharing and knowledge transfer are inextricably linked with learning and draw upon both psychological and sociological theories of learning (see section 2.7 below and chapter 4). The academic focus is now on organizational knowledge and learning as a field of study and this is reflected in the model for HRD. It is somewhat ironic that although the theory and practice of human resource development has evolved in parallel to that of knowledge management it is the latter that has captured the imaginations of organizations reflecting how contemporary society has become increasingly dependent on knowledge (Delanty, 2001). Knowledge management seems to have a seductive quality (Alvesson, 2004) that HRD appears to lack and unlike the term HRD has gained widespread usage in organizations. The strategic implications of knowledge management are discussed in the next chapter while chapter 10 explores the relationship between HRD and knowledge management in some detail.

HRD practitioners can make an important contribution to the overall design, delivery, and evaluation of a change initiative in a leadership, coordination, or facilitation capacity. They have considerable experience in diagnosing individual, group, and organizational training and development needs. This is a transferable skill that, along with expertise in design and evaluation processes, can make a significant contribution to the effectiveness

MEDIA WATCH BOX

Change management in the non-profit sector

This case illustrates the role training and development can play in the support of change management. Taken as a whole, the HR function is undertaking a major organization development project that relies on the close alignment of HRD and HRM elements (see also chapter 3 on horizontal alignment).

The Children's Trust is a UK based charity which helps to support children who are severely disabled and suffering from brain damage. As part of a change management strategy to move away from an avoidance culture the charity implemented a range of HR initiatives. These included a senior manager development programme aimed at identifying managers' training needs and improving their confidence and their skills in areas such as communications and objective setting. The initiative involved the use of psychometric instruments and 360 degree appraisal. This helped to make managers feel more positive. The change management strategy also involved more competence-based training for other staff (e.g. nurses and carers) and the implementation of a new performance appraisal system, a review of pay scales for carers, and new job descriptions.

Source
People Management, 15 November 2007: 42–4.

INSIGHTS INTO PRACTICE

A personal reflection

When I was a training and development manager I was invited to a meeting at head office to discuss the implementation of a new computer system for the sales division which was based on the latest lap-top technology. It was an innovative project and I was impressed by the level of investment. Imagine my surprise though when I was advised that the project would go live 'in one month's time' and that I had until the following week to design the training programme! However, it was the deadly silence that greeted my next question that illustrates how someone with a training and development background can contribute to major change programmes. My question was a simple one, 'how are you going to evaluate the project?' It was apparent that no one had thought about this until I had asked the question. It was tacitly accepted that the project would be successful and guarantee a return on the company's investment.

Source
The author.

of OD initiatives. Also, an HRD practitioner is usually someone who is adept at steering him/herself through the morass of organizational politics encountered in organizations. Politics are a reality of organizational life and HRD practitioners should not be frightened about having to 'play the political game' in order to get results; although it is important not to compromise ethical standards and thus be drawn into the 'dark side'. This does not mean that a HRD function owns OD. Several of the projects I was involved with as a total quality manager were change projects that required me to operate in what could be described as either an OD or HRD capacity.

From the above it can be seen that learning and change are common across the three domains of HRD practice that have been identified (see figure 2.3).

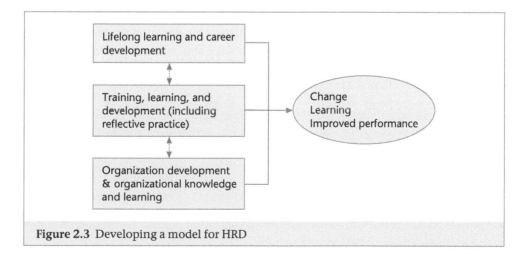

Figure 2.3 Developing a model for HRD

2.6 **The shift from formal interventions to informal workplace learning**

Swanson and Holton (2001), drawing upon the work of Weinberger (1998), identify 18 definitions of HRD between 1970 and 1995 many of which refer to organized, systematic or planned activities and processes. Yet it is now recognized that the majority of adult learning occurs informally in the workplace regardless of the activities of HRD practitioners and managers (Hytönen, 2003). The first time any differentiation was made between formal and informal learning in a definition of HRD was in 1986 by Nadler and Wiggs (cited in Swanson and Holton, 2001) who differentiate between classroom-based learning and experiential on-the-job learning. Employees learn through their jobs in a variety of ways: learning from colleagues; learning from doing (e.g. chairing a meeting, leading a project team, attending an interview); and, learning from mistakes. An advantage which informal learning in the workplace shares with on-the-job training is that learning is not de-contextualized. This has always been a problem with classroom-based interventions which rely on the transfer of learning from the classroom to the workplace through methods such as action plans and post-course/workshop reviews. Although it is recognized that the transfer of learning from the classroom to the workplace is critical to the success of any training intervention many organizations have been slow to establish systems to measure this effectively. Research studies have tended to support anecdotal evidence that transfer of learning is a very hit and miss affair (see chapter 9 for a more detailed discussion). However, informal workplace learning is not without problems: it is not necessarily always effective and can be difficult to measure (Stern and Sommerlad, 1999); and, opportunities for low-grade staff, such as manual and clerical workers, tend to be limited (Nieuwenhuis and van Woerkom, 2007). These points are developed further in chapter 11 which includes an analysis of the respective roles of the HRD practitioner, line manager and learner.

Figure 2.4 illustrates the implications of this shift on the respective roles of the HRD practitioner and line manager. The principal changes are:

- Less emphasis on content-driven formal interventions designed to develop specific job-related skills (e.g. workshops, guided practice) and more on informal learning opportunities that help employees develop competencies critical to organizational performance (see chapter 11).

- Less emphasis on validation (e.g. did participants enjoy the training workshop?) and more on evaluation (e.g. has there been a change in performance that brings benefits to the organization as well as the learner?).

- Less emphasis on instructional design and delivery by the HRD practitioner and more on the facilitation of learning (e.g. helping individuals to learn in the workplace).

- More involvement by the line manager in the evaluation process (see chapters 5 and 9) and in the facilitation of workplace learning.

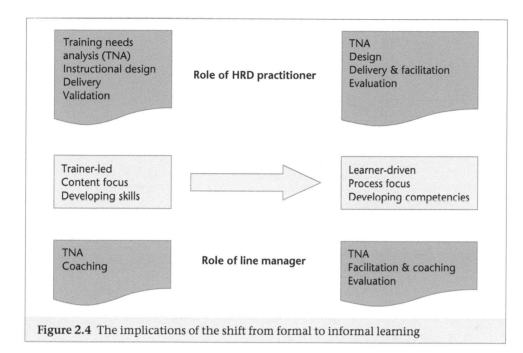

Figure 2.4 The implications of the shift from formal to informal learning

---

! TIPS AND HINTS

Line managers need to make a conscious effort to understand the role of informal learning within their area of responsibility and the impact it is having on team performance. This requires managers to be actively engaged with team members through regular chats and discussions (i.e. the concept of managing by wandering about).

From the above it can be seen that the HRD model being developed in this chapter needs to reflect the role of informal learning, competencies, and evaluation. Informal learning can impact on all three domains of HRD but is not under the direct control or management of the HRD practitioner or line manager. Both can have an indirect impact through a facilitation role or the provision of formal interventions that can aid the cultivation of a learning environment conducive to informal learning. Consequently, it is shown as a type of 'shadow' activity against each of the domains. This helps to capture more of the complex nature of organizations as 'shadow' activities are entwined with formal structures and processes in symbiotic relationship that can be difficult to unravel on a day-to-day basis (Mankin, 2007). This partly addresses the criticism that 'much HRD theory and research treat organization systems as complicated linear systems directed toward producing predictable outcomes' (Yorks and Nicolaides, 2006). Improving competencies is one of the primary aims of HRD activity and therefore can be treated as an output. The primary focus of evaluation is the measurement of improved performance (and the benefits this brings to the organization), so this highlights the importance of improved performance as an output of HRD (see figure 2.5).

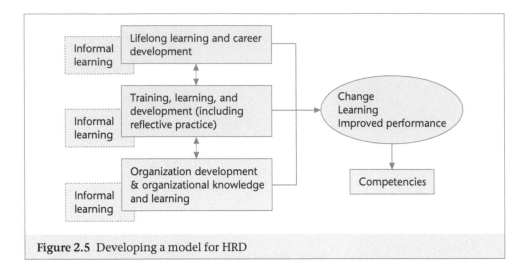

Figure 2.5 Developing a model for HRD

2.7 The shift from psychological to sociological perspectives on learning

Formal training interventions are usually designed using rational models for instructional design which are based on psychological perspectives on learning such as behavioural and cognitive learning theories (i.e. learning takes place within an individual's mind and the individual's understanding and behaviour can be modified through learning). This is why many training techniques and methods focus on the individual acquisition of knowledge, often in a passive manner, for instance: reading hand-outs, case studies and slides; making personal notes; listening to presentations by the trainer; thinking about and reflecting on content; preparing individual action plans. The inclusion of group activities, such as team exercises and group discussions, are a concession to social learning (i.e. learning-from-others) but the emphasis remains the acquisition of knowledge by individual participants. However, learning is a multifaceted concept and sociological perspectives on learning have become more prominent in the theory and practice of HRD. Sociological theories of learning focus on the inherently social nature of learning; for instance, learning emerges from social interactions (Easterby-Smith and Araujo, 1999). One particular sociological perspective that has provoked much interest is *situated learning* (Lave and Wenger, 1991) which focuses on learning from colleagues in a work context. This has contributed to the growing interest in informal and collaborative workplace learning and the role of HRD practitioners and line managers in supporting learning that is integrated with work (see chapters 10 and 11). Chapter four contains a detailed explanation of different learning theories. Figure 2.6 illustrates the principal characteristics of this shift.

The implications of this shift can be added to the HRD model (see figure 2.7). However, do note that the key for underpinning learning theories are based on generalizations about the practices within each of the three domains.

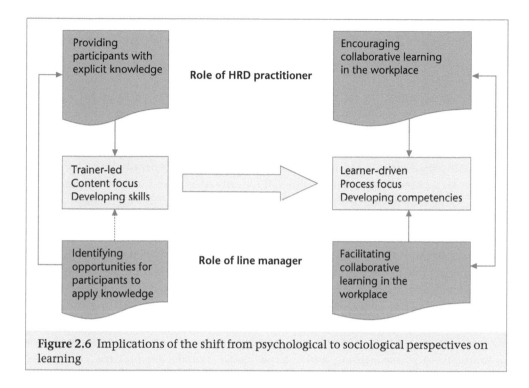

Figure 2.6 Implications of the shift from psychological to sociological perspectives on learning

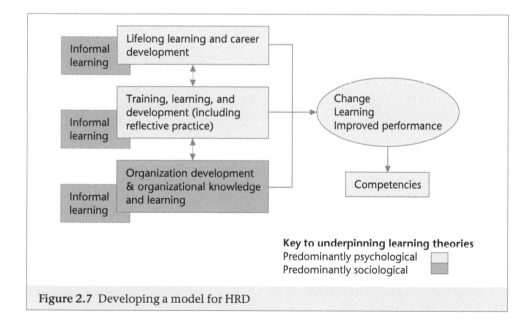

Figure 2.7 Developing a model for HRD

2.8 The shift from the trainer as an instructional expert to a business partner

As figure 2.2 illustrates the traditional role of the HRD practitioner was that of a trainer; someone who was seen as an instructional expert; someone knowledgeable in course design and delivery (see chapters 5, 13, and 15). Line managers tended to nominate employees for courses and workshops that were designed and delivered by members of the training department. The role of the line manager was generally restricted to the identification of training needs (e.g. through the annual appraisal interview) and, where willing, in the briefing and debriefing of participants. Today the HRD practitioner seeks to adopt a business partner approach to working with management. This involves a variety of roles, including: change agent, business expert, knowledge manager, and internal consultant (Ulrich and Brockbank, 2005). This reflects the extent to which line managers play a more critical role in the facilitation of learning in the workplace than the HRD function (Beattie, 2006). Increasingly, the HRD practitioner and line manager are collaborating on all aspects of an HRD intervention: the identification of learning needs and the design, delivery, and evaluation of the intervention (see chapters 5 to 9). Line managers can support HRD in a variety of ways including acting as a coach or mentor, as a facilitator of informal workplace learning, and as a role model for reflective practice. These issues are discussed in more detail in chapters 5 to 9, 11 and 15. The implications of business partnership are discussed in chapter 3. Figure 2.8 illustrates the implications of this shift to business partner.

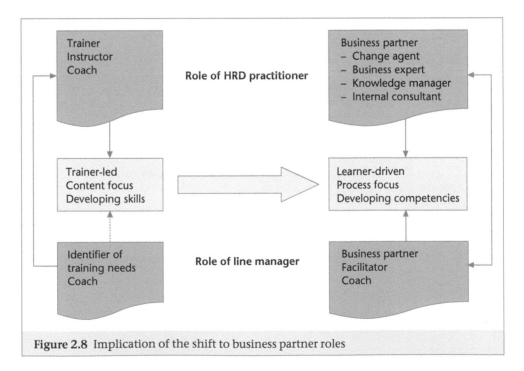

Figure 2.8 Implication of the shift to business partner roles

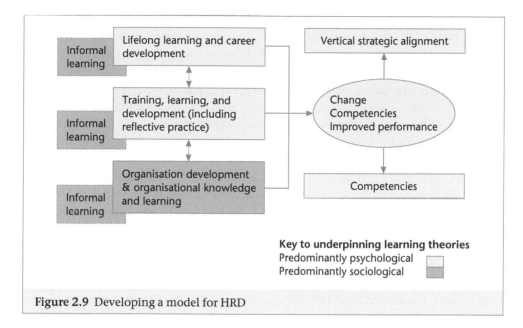

Figure 2.9 Developing a model for HRD

The implications of the above have been added to the HRD model in figure 2.9. The principal implication is the strategic nature of the business partner role. This is shown as vertical strategic alignment in the model. The outputs from the three domains of HRD practice need to support the organization's strategy. How this can be best achieved is discussed in the next chapter.

Key concept   Vertical strategic alignment

The process by which HRD strategy, policies, and plans are aligned with an organization's strategic goals and objectives.

! TIPS AND HINTS

Although the business partner role provides a framework for the HRD practitioner the reality of trying to establish a strategic role comes down to gut instinct, working hard, getting involved whenever possible and hoping for a fair degree of luck. There is no route-map to success.

2.9 The shift from the development of human capital to the development of intellectual capital

Approaches to training have been underpinned by human capital theory which provides an economic rationale for the education and training of employees. Human capital manifests as the experience that an individual brings to an organization in the form of the knowledge, skills, abilities, and values that he/she has accumulated over time (Bertels and Savage, 1998; Scarborough and Carter, 2000). Consequently, the employees of an organization are viewed as an asset or a resource that can be improved through investment in the same way as other assets or resources such as buildings and equipment. Traditionally the principal focus was on on-the-job training (Wang and Holton, 2005) although this has since broadened to encompass a wide range of formal interventions. More recently, the emphasis has shifted to intellectual capital which embraces social capital as well as human capital; and it is important that organizations develop both forms of capital (Harrison and Kessels (2004)). Social capital is knowledge that is socially embedded in social networks and informal groups (Lam, 2000). It can be described as the potential knowledge that can be created when individuals collaborate with colleagues in these networks and groups. Consequently, intellectual capital brings together the individual and collective dimensions of knowledge.

Research reports published in the UK by the Chartered Institute of Personnel and Development (CIPD) have acknowledged the role that social capital plays in promoting learning and the sharing of knowledge in organizations (Stewart and Tansley, 2002; Swart et al., 2003). Kessels and Poell (2004) suggest that HRD practitioners can help develop social capital within an organization by: bringing people together (who have different backgrounds and perspectives); building informal work groups known as communities of practice (where people share a common interest); helping employees to gain access to social networks; sustaining social networks; making gains in social capital explicit; and developing a language for people to recognize gains in social capital. Increasingly,

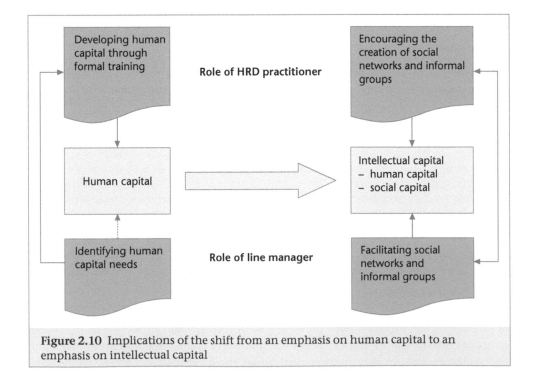

Figure 2.10 Implications of the shift from an emphasis on human capital to an emphasis on intellectual capital

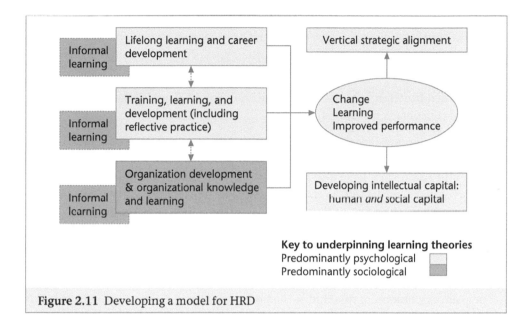

Figure 2.11 Developing a model for HRD

informal groups and networks are being recognized as an important source of support for problem solving, innovation, and adaptation although presently managers seem to do relatively little to assess and support such networks (Cross et al., 2002). You will find a more detailed discussion on these issues in chapters 10 and 11. Figure 2.10 illustrates the principal implications of this shift.

The implications of this shift for the HRD model are shown in figure 2.11. The development of intellectual capital is the ultimate goal of HRD practices and if successful this should result in competitive advantage for private sector enterprises and performance advantage for organizations in the public and non-profit sectors. The combination of human and social capital also helps to capture the complex nature of organizations because of the relationship between social capital and informal learning processes.

2.10 The shift from centralized training departments and large teams of internal trainers to more varied and flexible approaches

Today there are many different ways of structuring the HRD function in larger organizations. Options include:

- **Centralization** (e.g. the traditional training centre model). Training centres remain popular and have gone through various reincarnations such as corporate universities which have not proven as popular as was originally predicted (see chapter 13). The Indian company Tata Group, which includes Tata Steel and Tata Motors, has a highly successful training centre (see chapters 13 and 14).

- **Decentralization** (e.g. line managers have a devolved responsibility for training and work in collaboration with a very small team of HRD practitioners who operate on an internal consultancy basis and coordinate other types of HRD interventions across divisions and departments).

- **Outsourced function** (e.g. line managers with devolved responsibilities working with external consultants as required).

Walton (1999) proposes a virtual HRD function which uses the latest technologies to link together autonomous business units in a virtual network. Improvements in communications and technology have also facilitated the emergence of more flexible learning systems. For instance, the shift from static learning resource centres to flexible e-learning programmes that can be delivered via intranets and the Internet on a 24/7 basis anywhere in the world. By the turn of the century HRD practitioners were combining e-learning and face-to-face methods in a wide variety of ways giving rise to the concept of *blended learning* (see *Insights into practice* box). Chapters 12 and 13 focus on how the HRD function is managed in different types of organization.

The main implication of this shift is the horizontal strategic alignment between HRD and HRM whether they are part of the same function or independent of each other. The HRD model has been updated in figure 2.12 to reflect this. This theme is developed further in the next chapter.

The model highlights priorities for the organization which are consistent with previous findings. For instance, Beattie (2006) identifies a number of themes that have emerged from the literature on the role and practice of HRD including: developing policies which

INSIGHTS INTO PRACTICE

Developing managers in IKEA

This is an example of how companies are adopting a blended learning approach to the training and development of managers. Blended learning is a combination of face-to-face training interventions and e-learning.

The initial training of new managers involves them in: gaining practical work experience in all areas of a store; understanding how business operations are inter-connected; and completing an e-learning programme ('Managing at IKEA'). The e-learning programme includes trainer-led, online tutorials and tasks that are designed to encourage interaction with colleagues. Following induction managers are required to attend a bi-annual three-day leadership course. Other courses are available which expose them to both self-managed and structured learning. These programmes can involve the utilization of a range of techniques such as 360 degree feedback, goal setting, and business planning.

Source
Weinstein, M. (2006) Teaching the TOP. *Training*, 43 (2): 30–3.

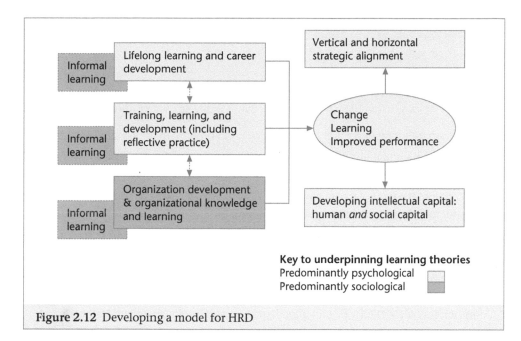

Figure 2.12 Developing a model for HRD

ACTIVITY 2.2

Find one illustrative example of each of the following:

1. An e-learning or blended learning initiative

2. An organization that uses a centralized training centre

3. An adult education or vocational training initiative

You should use the Internet, textbooks, articles, or any other form of learning resource for this activity.

Key concept   Horizontal strategic alignment

The process by which HRD strategy, policies, plans, and practices are aligned with an organization's HRM strategy, policies, plans, and practices.

---

integrate business and HRD strategies (see chapter 3); creating a learning environment (see chapters 3 and 11); designing HRD interventions that add value (see chapters 5, 7, and 11); having a systematic learning system in place (see chapter 5); adopting a partner-ship approach with line managers (see chapters 3 and 13); helping employees learn how to learn and encouraging reflective practice (see chapters 4 and 11); and, assessing HRD interventions for the value they add (see chapters 5 and 9).

 **INSIGHTS INTO PRACTICE**

Bank of Tokyo-Mitsubishi

When the Bank of Tokyo-Mitsubishi reorganized its US operations and reviewed its business strategy it identified four key objectives for developing its human capital:

1. To prepare succession plans for all employees in order to maintain stability.
2. To implement training that focuses on a key competency for the bank: credit risk management.
3. To ensure the workplace is characterized by teamwork, safety, and fairness (the latter focusing on preventing discrimination);
4. To change the reward strategy to a mix of Japanese and US systems (i.e. seniority-based and performance-based).

This case illustrates the role of horizontal alignment with HRD activities being inter-woven with HRM activities. It also highlights a mix of HRD activities that reflect the components of the HRD model in this chapter: career development and lifelong learning in the first objective; training, learning and development in the second (and also implicit in the third); and, organization development/organizational knowledge and learning implicit in the third.

Source
Kaplan, R. S. and Norton, D. P. 2004. *Strategy Maps: Converting Intangible Assets into Tangible Outcomes.* Boston, MA: Harvard Business School Press, pp. 18–24.

2.11 **The current debate**

What do these shifts tell us about HRD in today's organizations? The first is that learning is central to HRD. Some theorists prefer to use the term adult learning when discussing HRD as it is argued that this term not only distinguishes between psychological perspectives that are relevant to adults rather than children but it also encompasses both psychological and sociological perspectives on learning (Yang, 2004). The second is that performance is also critical to HRD. The emphasis on evaluation, competencies, intellectual capital, and business partnership reflects the extent to which HRD practices are expected to contribute to organizational performance and provide added value. As was explained at the start of the chapter much of the debate on the meaning and purpose of HRD has focused on whether or not learning and performance are mutually exclusive.

Gilley and Maycunich (2002), and Maycunich et al. (2003) differentiate between what they term 'activity-based HRD' and 'results-driven HRD'. Activity-based HRD is where HRD practice focuses on a systematic approach to training (i.e. identifying training needs, designing a training intervention, delivering and evaluating an intervention).

This equates to the training end of the learning continuum and a focus on improving individual performance through the acquisition of new knowledge and skills. Results-driven HRD requires HRD practitioners to work collaboratively with management at all levels of the organization in order to improve organizational performance through the development of intellectual capital. The extent to which this is an evolving perspective is illustrated by Gilley et al.'s (2002) modification of an earlier definition of HRD by Gilley and Maycunich (2000) which is cited and amended with the insertion of 'formal and informal' in square brackets:

> we can define HRD as 'the process of facilitating organisational learning, perform-ance, and change through organised [formal and informal] interventions, ini-tiatives and management actions for the purpose of enhancing an organisation's performance capacity, capability, competitive readiness, and renewal'. (Gilley and Maycunich, 2000a, 6) (cited and amended by Gilley et al., 2002: 6–7)

Lee (2007) argues for the adoption of a holistic perspective on HRD that encompasses the global and local challenges now facing HRD practitioners in an increasingly complex world. Her proposals address global trends such as migration, climate change, and the changing world of work. This views organizations and the context they operate in as a complex system. Complex systems 'are characteristically dynamic and usually annoy-ingly unpredictable' (Yorks and Nicolaides, 2006: 145). They also cannot be reduced to their constituent parts, as the model for HRD in this chapter has attempted to do. However, as with most models the purpose is to aid understanding by providing a lens through which organizations can be analysed. The downside to this is that there can be 'a consequent loss of richness of the picture that confronts the practitioner' (Sadler-Smith and Smith, 2006).

In many respects the HRD model developed in this chapter builds on the three domains traditionally associated with HRD: organization development, training and development, and career development (McLagan, 1989). By linking these to evolving perspectives on learning it has been possible to produce a model that reflects much of the current think-ing on HRD. But it is by no means a complete or perfect model. For instance:

- Although career development is often regarded as being central to HRD there is a paucity of literature on the topic suggesting it is in fact a relatively minor aspect of HRD (Egan et al., 2006). Should the lack of theoretical discussion and empirical studies alter the perspective developed in this chapter? Probably not. Rather the importance of career development has been overlooked (Swanson and Holton, 2001). Chapter 1 dis-cussed various trends linked to globalization including the changing nature of work, the shift towards more flexibility, and the migration patterns affecting labour markets. Career development remains an important concern for many individuals particularly in an era characterized by lifelong learning and knowledge work.

- A clear definition of organizational learning has remained elusive (Lopez et al., 2005). Psychological perspectives on learning tend to use agency theory to describe and explain organizational learning (i.e. individuals learning on behalf of the organization with knowledge held by the individual). In contrast sociological perspectives focus on the social context within which learning occurs (i.e. individuals learning through social interaction with knowledge being socially embedded). Regardless of perspective learning needs to become institutionalized for it to be described as organizational learning. Institutionalization can take several forms: new routines or ways of doing things either formally or informally that have consolidated over time (for instance, colleagues with similar roles, but working in different areas, having regular informal meetings to discuss common problems and thus speed up the decision-making process at formal meetings); systemic changes (for instance, how information about the external environment is collected, analysed, and disseminated; how knowledge generally is acquired, distributed, and stored); and, the embedding of techniques and methods that lead to improved performance (for instance, continuous improvement techniques used by production operatives).

A tension can arise when you try to analyse HRD from both an individual and an organizational perspective. HRD is rather like the ancient Roman god Janus: it is a concept that can look both ways at the same time even though individual and organizational goals are not always compatible or convergent. This dilemma is aptly captured by Garavan et al. (2004):

Individual-level analysis tends to characterise HRD as voluntary, both formal and informal, focusing on the future, largely incremental, predominantly introspective, emphasising the development of generic competencies, and enhancing labour

INSIGHTS INTO PRACTICE

A personal reflection

I recall the implementation of a new performance appraisal system that utilized a numeric scale for rating individual performance. Prior to this the appraisal system had been based on a qualitative assessment only and this had been very popular amongst line managers and employees generally. People were suspicious that the numeric rating system was the prelude to the introduction of a new performance related pay-scheme in place of the annual cost-of-living pay rise. At the workshops for training on the new system I was challenged on this point by many of the participants and had to deny vigorously that the company had any intention of changing its policy. Most people accepted my word on this. Yet I was aware of a very strong possibility that such a change was being seriously considered by senior management. They believed that if implemented employee performance would be better focused on achieving organizational goals. I had my own views on this matter and had expressed them to senior managers, but in terms of rolling out the training initiative I had no option but to adhere to the 'company line'.

Source
The author.

mobility, and it assumes that the individual is the decision maker. Organisation-level analysis emphasises a contrasting set of characteristics. HRD provision is more likely to be involuntary, organisationally sponsored, focusing on formal activities, dealing with predominantly current issues . . . and emphasising inter-active learning processes rather than introspection. (p. 427)

Is this actually something that need concern HRD practitioners and other stakeholders such as line managers and employees? In one sense it is because HRD practice could be criticized for being contradictory. Sometimes a HRD practitioner may struggle to convince sceptical employees why a particular training intervention has been launched. In another sense this dichotomy simply reflects the ambiguities and realities of organizational life and HRD practitioners just have to learn how to manage such situations (see *A personal reflection* box).

Looking to the future there certainly appears to be a need to develop:

- More comparative studies in order to better understand the relationship between Western and indigenous approaches (Dirani, 2006)

- New theories that are grounded in cultural contexts other than the US (Woodall, 2005)

- New perspectives on adult learning in the workplace which reflect the rich diversity of worldviews on the subject (McLean, 2006)

2.12 Emerging perspectives on HRD

While the theory of HRD is well established in US and Europe (Wang and McLean, 2007), '[i]n much of the rest of the world labour remains a commodity to be hired and fired . . . and HRD in such markets is largely driven by narrow instrumental concerns' (O'Donnell et al., 2006: 13).

HRD in developing economies: China

China is still in the process of transition from a rural, agricultural-based economy reliant on central planning to an urban, industrialized free market economy that lacks any tradi-tion of HRD (Yang et al., 2004). The rapid rate of change and economic growth associated with this transitional phase requires HRD practitioners to work within a business environ-ment that is characterized by high levels of ambiguity and uncertainty (Wang and Wang, 2006). The concept of human resources, including HRD, is relatively new with managers and practitioners in indigenous firms very much locked into a game of 'catch up'. Since 1978:

many Western concepts of management, such as HRD and human resource man-agement (HRM), have been brought in, and they coexist with some old terms. In fact, although the majority of newly created organisations, such as privately owned enterprises, joint ventures, and foreign investment firms, tend to use the new term *human resources* (HR), most government agencies, the ruling communist party and its local organisations, and state-owned-enterprises (SOEs) continue to use older terms (e.g. *personnel*). (Yang et al., 2004: 298)

An emphasis on pre-employment training (Cooke, 2005) suggests there is still some way to go before new perspectives on the theory and practice of HRD emerge and challenge established perspectives. At this time it is possible to discern that the Chinese approach to training is characterized by strong social and moral responsibilities (Yang and Zhang, 2003) reflecting Confucian traditions (Yang et al., 2004). Wang et al. (2005) argue that Western HRD practices should not be adopted uncritically by indigenous organizations but adapted to reflect China's different cultural values. In terms of future developments it is predicted that continued economic growth will be underpinned by an increase in smaller firms that draw heavily on the capabilities of Chinese who have been trained abroad but now want to make their career in China (Fuller and Thun, 2006). At the same time it is likely that new Chinese brands will emerge. Given the relative lack of interest in HRD strategy in SMEs in the Anglo-American literature, this predicted growth in smaller businesses may result in the emergence of new perspectives on HRD theory and practice.

HRD in developing economies: India

In relation to India, the first dedicated HRD department was created in an engineering company in 1975 and by the mid-1980s HRD had become an accepted role within many organizations (Rao, 2004). While public education remains the government's most damaging failure private schools and institutes have been meeting the educational and training needs of the private sector (Das, 2006). Pattanayak (2003) has identified performance improvements within an Indian organization following the implementation of a range of HRD strategies over a two-year period. These improvements included increased production and reduced down-times. He concluded that this illustrated the importance of the human dimension of performance and the alignment of HRD activities with business strategy. However, as he commented more generally about organizations in India:

> in most Indian family-owned businesses, alignment of HRD tends to be hindered by the ritualistic nature of confining strategy decisions to the top decision-makers. This limits the synchronisation between the competencies required to deliver future business activities and the competencies available in the organisation. In order to bridge this gap, larger organisations have tended to develop existing employees, whereas smaller organisations have tended to hire developed people. (pp. 405–6)

HRD in other countries

There have been far too few studies of HRD in other countries; for instance, Greece, Kenya, Singapore, Thailand, and Vietnam. However, these perspectives are at an emergent stage and it is likely to be some time before they can influence or challenge Anglo-American perspectives. But already there are doubts about the universality of

Anglo-American perspectives. For instance, Petridou and Glaveli (2003) question whether the Anglo-American approach to HRD is actually transferable to countries such as Greece. Much of the discourse on HRD in other countries is influenced by what happens in multi-nationals which do not reflect emergent indigenous theory and practice. Globalization appears to be creating a universal approach to HRD (Metcalfe and Rees, 2005) but this may turn out to be illusory as the economic balance of power gradually shifts to an Eastern rather than Western orientation.

ACTIVITY 2.3

Find an academic journal article that discusses human resource development in a different country to your own. To what extent does this correspond with your understanding and/or experience of human resource development in your own country?

Summary

In this chapter we have looked at some different perspectives on the meaning of HRD and contrasted American and British definitions. This has been placed in the context of a brief history of the concept from 1970 to the present which also included definitions of training, development, and learning. The chapter has explained how the concept of HRD has evolved over the years to embrace organizational learning, individual learning, and lifelong learning. It has highlighted the principal perspectives on HRD, the performance and humanist perspectives, and explained some of the tensions between these. Using these perspectives as analytical lenses helps us to understand why the practice of HRD varies so much from organization to organization. Humanist thinking involves long term investment in training, learning, and development as the primary focus is on developing the individual with performance improvement as a consequence of this. Performance thinking is often driven by short term needs and is primarily focused on the organization with investments in training, learning, and development being made to secure performance gains for the organization with benefits to the individual being consequential. There is still a lack of consensus on whether HRD practices should focus on organizational performance needs or individual development needs although the humanist perspective is being challenged. This theme is developed further in the next chapter which explores HRD strategy, policies, and plans. As other countries start to adopt HRD strategies and practices it is likely that the prevailing Anglo-American perspectives will be challenged making it very likely that a universal definition of HRD is unattainable.

Review questions

1   What are generally regarded as the principal components of HRD? Can you identify specific case study examples that illustrate how well organizations are handling each of these components?

2   Without referring back to the chapter contents write an explanation of how development is different to training.

3   Carry out a literature search and identify two further definitions of human resource development that are not used in this chapter. In what ways are they similar or different to the examples used in this book?

4   The learning organization is regarded by many theorists and practitioners as an unattainable ideal. Produce an argument of no more than 500 words that supports or refutes this statement. Draw upon sources as appropriate to support your argument.

5   What do you see as the principal advantages and disadvantages for the employer and the employee of career development interventions such as career planning workshops and career counselling sessions?

Suggestions for further reading

1   Swanson, R. A. and Holton, E. F. 2001. *Foundations of Human Resource Development*. San Francisco, CA: Berrett-Koehler.

Refer to this book to learn more about the history of HRD.

2   Kuchinke, K. P. 2004. Theorising and practicing HRD: extending the dialogue over the roles of scholarship and practice in the field. *Human Resource Development International*, 7 (4): 535–9.

An interesting article that makes a good contribution to the current debate about the relationship between theory and practice.

3   Egan, T. M., Upton, M. G. and Lynham, S. A. 2006. Career development: load-bearing wall or window dressing? Exploring definitions, theories, and prospects for HRD-related theory building. *Human Resource Development Review*, 5 (4): 442–77.

This article discusses an important but much neglected topic in HRD literature: career development.

4   McGuire, D., Garavan, T. N., O'Donnell, D. and Watson, S. 2007. Metaperspectives and HRD: lessons for research and practice. *Advances in Developing Human Resources*, 9 (1): 120–39.

This article contains an interesting discussion about different perspectives on HRD and the implications for both theory and practice. The key findings are summarized in a series of tables and provide some interesting insights.

5   Wang, X. and McLean, G. N. 2007. The dilemma of defining international human resource development. *Human Resource Development Review*, 6 (1): 96–108.

This article contains a brief synopsis of the evolution of HRD and discusses the difficulties of developing an international definition of HRD.

Case study

Applying the 'learning continuum' to Wipro

Wipro is one of India's leading technical services companies, ranked third behind Tata Consultancy Services (1st) and Infosys Technologies (2nd). The company's revenues have increased from US$400 million in 1999 to US$2.4 billion in 2006. Wipro's values are captured in the 'Wipro Promise' which focuses on respecting people, integrity, innovation, and value for money. The company has identified 24 competencies including: initiative, problem-solving, innovation, inter-personal sensitivity, teamwork, flexibility, decisiveness, and global thinking. The company is committed to training, which starts with induction when new recruits undergo training on the company's values. This commitment was demonstrated by the fact that when there was a downturn in business in 2001 and 2002 the company actually increased the training budget rather than cutting it as you would normally expect an organization to do.

The training resources are such that up to 5,000 employees a day can be trained at its training facilities in Bangalore where 120 full time specialists are available to deliver the programmes. E-learning programmes are also available. The induction of new recruits starts every two weeks for groups of 300–400 and is followed by eight to ten weeks of classroom training on various technical subjects as well as sessions to familiarize participants with various business functions. Subsequently, on-the-job training is available. The company offers two career paths: management and technical. A range of courses are available which help them to improve their performance and 'enrich their professional lives' (p. 95). All employees must complete ten days of training each year and are encouraged to average 12. A computer program is provided to help employees plan their career paths. Much of the technical training involves certification and the company provide a team of online mentors to help answer queries and concerns. As managers progress they are required to increase their knowledge of business and general management. Week-long training modules are available to support this process. Self-improvement programmes are also available to all employees and cover such things as cross-cultural and languages training. Some sessions cover personal issues such as mental health and the work–life balance.

Wipro's strategic goals are categorized under the following headings: quality, financial, people, innovation, business development. Each business unit can choose their own sixth category. Goals are cascaded downwards and monthly progress reports are produced in each business unit. The company uses 360 degree feedback for the performance reviews of managers who then receive help from the HR function in compiling action plans which they communicate to their team. All employees undergo a performance appraisal which is linked to the 24 competencies and the system has been descried as fair and useful by employees. As part of the strategic planning process employees are invited to make performance improvement suggestions. Wipro works to a one- and three-year planning cycle (by comparison Infosys Technologies works to a five-year cycle). The company has engaged in visioning exercises and managers have been encouraged to hold regular off-site meetings to think up ideas.

Source
Hamm, S. 2007. *Bangalore Tiger: How Indian Tech Upstart Wipro Is Rewriting the Rules of Global Competition.* New York: McGraw-Hill.

Case questions

1. Where would you position Wipro on the 'learning continuum'? What are the reasons for your decision?

2. What else would you need to know in order to make a more informed decision?

Online resource centre

Visit the supporting online resource centre for additional material that will help you with your research, essays, assignments, and revision.

 www.oxfordtextbooks.co.uk/orc/mankin/

Developing an HRD Strategy

Key concepts

Strategic HRD

Business strategy

Organizational structure

Human resource management

Organizational culture

Vertical and horizontal strategic alignment

Resource-based view (RBV)

HRD strategy

HRD policy

3.1 **Introduction**

Organizational strategy is often referred to as corporate or business strategy and for the purposes of this chapter the term business strategy will be used (apologies to anyone working in the public or non-profit sectors). In many large organizations the HRD function operates in a reactionary role and has limited or no involvement in strategic management, particularly the planning phase. In most SMEs there is no HRD function or, at best a single person in an HRD role. Often HRD is the responsibility of a general manager or the owner-manager in smaller firms. In these situations there is limited evidence of strategic management processes (see chapter 12 for a discussion on this issue). Consequently much of the content of this chapter is aimed at larger organizations (defined in Europe as having 250 or more employees) although many of the principles can still be applied in SMEs.

Vision and mission statements have become a popular way of summarizing and communicating an organization's strategic goals although they have been criticized as time-wasting distractions. Although a difficult concept to pin down at times vision can be defined as an image of what the organization will look like in the future. It is, in effect, a visualization of the future and therefore is aspirational. The mission can be described as an articulation of how the vision will be achieved setting out the principal goals and summarizing key organizational values (e.g. 'We always put our customers first'; 'Our employees are our most important asset'; 'Quality matters'). Subsequently, as part of the strategic planning process, objectives are identified which will enable the organization to achieve its mission. These objectives represent the core of the business strategy. The business strategy is a plan that integrates an organization's vision, mission, goals and objectives and determines how resources will be used. This, in turn, influences the HRD strategy and then HRD policies, plans, and practices; for instance, a business that is expanding through mergers and acquisitions is likely to focus on culture change and team-building training as part of its HRD strategy. This is a top–down linear process that is an over-simplification of what actually happens and how it happens (see figure 3.1).

This chapter will argue that ongoing strategic level collaboration between the HRD function and key stakeholders (e.g. senior managers and line managers) is needed to maximize the effectiveness of the HRD strategy. This requires the HRD function to operate as a business partner, a role which has several dimensions: business expert, change agent, knowledge manager, and consultant (Ulrich and Brockbank, 2005). These dimensions reflect the changing nature of work and organizations discussed in chapter 1 and the trends captured in the 'learning continuum' in chapter 2. Operating as a strategic partner is about *shaping* rather than supporting business strategy (Torraco and Swanson, 2001). To do this successfully HRD practitioners need to develop a range of inter-related skills and an ability to *think strategically* (Gilley et al., 2002). This, in turn, needs to be underpinned by business or commercial acumen which includes business understanding and cross-functional experience (Griffiths, 2004). This is a challenging agenda for HRD practitioners who must overcome stereotypical perceptions of their historical role. In the past training was regarded as a peripheral activity (Sloman, 2007). The trends (i.e. 'shifts')

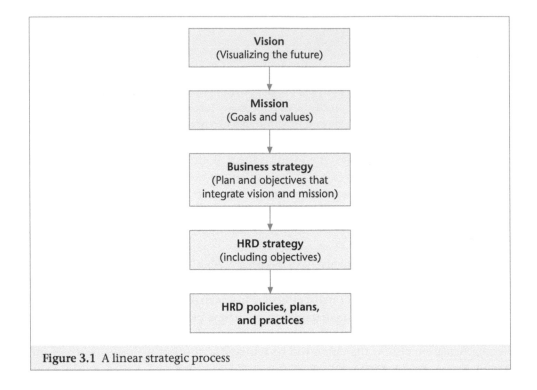

Figure 3.1 A linear strategic process

identified in the previous chapter illustrate how the practice of HRD has become more strategic. Employees provide an organization with intangible assets that are critical to achieving and sustaining competitive advantage (Ghosal and Moran, 2005). The aim of HRD is to create and sustain a learning infrastructure within which organizational knowledge and learning processes can be used to leverage these assets in support of an organization's strategic objectives.

Many of the ideas about the strategic role of HRD, such as vertical alignment and the collaborative role of managers can be traced back to a seminal article by Garavan (1991). More recently he has proposed a model for strategic HRD (Garavan, 2007) which has been cited in this chapter. The first section discusses the internal factors that influence strategic HRD: strategy and structure; organizational culture; and, human resource management (HRM). The second section builds a model for strategic HRD that better reflects the complexities of organizational processes than the linear process shown in figure 3.1. The third and final section discusses some of the implications for practice of a strategic approach to HRD.

> **ACTIVITY 3.1**
>
> Carry out an Internet search and identify two examples of an organizational vision and/or mission statements. How similar or different are they? What is your reaction to the language that is used? Can you identify any potential HRD implications?

3.2 Factors influencing strategic human resource development

Chapter 1 discussed the implications of globalization for the practice of HRD. This focused on external factors and how these influence HRD interventions (for instance, training programmes on diversity in response to changes in external and internal labour markets). The principal internal factors that influence HRD are set out in figure 3.2. These reflect the argument that strategy, structure, and culture need to be aligned (Morgan et al., 2007).

Strategy and structure

As stated above strategy is often described as a process involving a series of steps or phases involving: analysis and planning; implementation; review. This approach is useful as a pedagogical aid but does not always convey the complexities of the processes involved or their iterative nature. It can be traced back to the 1960s and the emergence of rational models for strategic management which fuelled the creation of central planning departments in large organizations. More sophisticated models have been developed since then; for instance, see the work of Michael Porter and how this has influenced strategic thinking: the 'five industry forces' (1980), the 'generic strategy choice' (1980), and the 'value chain' (1985). The underlying assumption is that the external environment can be analysed objectively thus enabling an organization to design strategies that fit that external

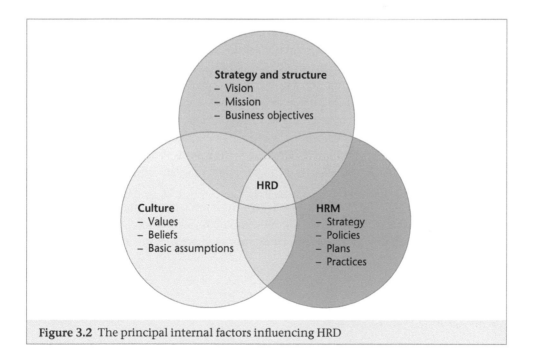

Figure 3.2 The principal internal factors influencing HRD

environment (Morgan et al., 2007). Internal resources and capabilities are structured to respond to the market demands identified in the analysis. However, Mintzberg (1994) makes the point that successful strategies tend to emerge and few planned strategies are ever realized. This reflects how difficult it is to make predictions about the future (Bryan and Joyce, 2007). Consequently, strategic HRD 'must be sensitive to both emergent and planned strategies' (Garavan, 2007: 12); hence the emphasis below on continuous scanning of the external and internal environments.

MEDIA WATCH BOX

Business strategies

These scenarios give an outline of each company's business strategy and are linked to activity 3.1.

In 2007 Guy Hands' investment firm paid £3.2 billion for EMI, the UK record company with acts including Coldplay, Radiohead, and Robbie Williams. Mr Hands has an abrasive management style that has upset artistes as well as employees. His previous experience has been the acquisition and disposal of companies in property and waste disposal industries. Although many of his deals have been highly profitable the purchase price of £1.9 billion for the Le Meridien hotel chain in 2001 had to be written off in 2003.[1]

When Premier Foods acquired RHM for £1.2 billion and the company doubled in size it was continuing what had been a highly successful acquisitions strategy since the 1990s. Premier Food's share price rose as factories were merged and depots were closed affecting some 1,000 jobs. However, Hovis started to lose market share to the privately owned Warburtons (whose market share has risen from 15 per cent to nearly 23 per cent), wheat prices rose, and the company's share price fell from a high of 330pence to 92pence valuing the company at £777 million (against a high of £2.8 billion). The company is making profits but with debts of £2 billion is facing cash flow problems. To save money the company has to cut the dividend payable to shareholders.[2]

When Nick Salmon took over as chief executive of Cookson in 2004, a long established group of companies, he implemented a new business strategy that involved the disposal of non-core businesses. The new focus was on the production and supply of industrial ceramics to the steel and solar panel markets. Both of these markets are growing globally (solar panels at 30 per cent per annum). As a result of this new strategy Cookson is now the market leader for the supply of ceramics with a market share of 80 per cent and profits of £170 million in 2007. The company has prepared for any economic downturn by implementing cost reductions and productivity improvements.[3]

Sources
[1] *Daily Mail*, 15 January 2008: 76.
[2] *The Sunday Times* (Business Focus section), 2 March 2008: 3.5.
[3] *The Mail on Sunday*, 16 March 2008: 74.

> **Key concept** Strategic HRD
>
> Strategic HRD is when HRD strategy, policies, plans and practices are vertically and horizontally aligned and learning is embedded in the organization's strategic processes.

ACTIVITY 3.2

1. How might HRD respond to the business strategies in each of these companies?
2. What might be the implications for the role of HRD in each of these companies?

This rational approach to strategic management assumes that HRD strategy is directly influenced by business strategy in the following way. The business strategy flows from an analysis of external factors (e.g. market conditions, economic projections). Subsequently, the business strategy is analysed and HRD implications identified so that these can then be converted into HRD objectives and an HRD strategy for the organization. The HRD strategy should communicate clearly how HRD objectives support each strategic objective. For instance, a strategic objective might be to launch a new product or service in order to increase the organization's overall market share by 5 per cent over two years. This might then involve an HRD objective which focuses on providing sales and customer service personnel with new product/service knowledge. This can be achieved through a mix of HRD interventions such as: training courses, e-learning, or coaching. The chosen option(s) are then included in the overall HRD plan or set of plans depending on the size and structure of the organization (see chapter 13). The HRD plan should convey the implementation implications of all identified HRD objectives; for instance: what type of HRD intervention is needed, how it will be delivered (e.g. in-house, external, electronically such as a virtual project team or e-learning), who will be involved (i.e. target audience), what the cost implications are and so on. As the bulk of HRD practice is focused on training, learning, and development it is more likely the plan will be published as the organization's 'training plan'. It may also be necessary to amend HRD policies, such as the training and development policy. This approach represents a form of top–down vertical strategic alignment (variants of this term include: vertical integration and external fit). This concept was introduced in section 2.8 of chapter 2 and defined as the process by which the HRD strategy, policies, and plans are aligned with an organization's strategic goals and objectives.

> **Key concepts** The resource-based view (RBV)
>
> The resource-based view is based on the assumption that organizations can develop human and technical resources that help the organization secure competitive advantage but are difficult for competitors to imitate.

A strategic perspective that has become popular in the literature on both HRM and HRD is the resource-based view (RBV) (Wernerfelt, 1984). The RBV focuses on the role of internal resources and organizational capabilities with the latter defined as:

> the capacity of an organisation to use resources, get things done, and behave in ways that accomplish goals. They characterise how people think and behave in the context of the organization . . . Capabilities define what the organisation does well. (Ulrich and Brockbank, 2005: 49)

These are intangible assets and represent something an organization does well relative to competitors and from a RBV perspective it forms the basis of the organization's strategic direction (Özçelik and Ferman, 2006). Organizational capabilities can also be described as an organization's core competence. This was a popular term in the management strategy literature of the 1990s (Le Deist and Winterton, 2005) and was defined as 'a bundle of skills and technologies that enable a company to provide a particular benefit to customers' (Hamel and Prahalad, 1994: 219). The HRD literature has tended to associate core competence or capabilities with the concept of human capital. For instance:

> Human capital that possesses organisation-specific knowledge is an invaluable asset that has the potential to produce a competitive advantage and sustain it. Hence, firms should be very selective with the employees they decide to train and develop. (Carmeli and Weisberg, 2006: 202)

With the growth of interest in knowledge management attention has shifted to intellectual capital which embraces both human and social capital (see chapter 2). This is not a large firm only response to business strategy. Studies show that intangible factors, such as organizational change, innovation, and human resource management contribute to the competitiveness of SMEs (Aragón-Sánchez and Sánchez-Márin, 2005).

! TIPS AND HINTS

It is important to place the RBV within the context of the external environment as there is a danger of adopting an either–or stance on strategy. Porter (1991) points out that resources help to create value in markets and are not an end in themselves.

Kaplan and Norton (2004) identify four ways in which intangible assets differ from tangible assets:

1. Intangible assets impact *indirectly* on value creation. This has implications for the evaluation of HRD interventions and activities (see chapters 9 and 13).

2. The value of intangible assets is *context-specific*. This is why organizations are keen to retain talented employees who have accrued expertise critical to organization performance and competitiveness over a number of years.

3. Intangible assets provide *potential value*. For instance, knowledge that is socially embedded (see chapters 2 and 10) is latent until it is leveraged in some way (e.g. as part of the research and development processes in the organization).

The power of ideas

Cemex, a Mexican producer of cement, holds nine 'innovation days' a year to capture the ideas of its employees. These events can generate hundreds of ideas and the best get implemented (e.g. ten were implemented from 250 proposed by employees at one event). Companies should not expand research and development departments until they have fully exploited the creativity embedded in their workforce. This concept can be extended to include outsourced elements of the supply chain.[1]

This case illustrates the continued influence of total quality management on current thinking. This approach to innovation requires an appropriate learning environment, one that is characterized by devolved and/or empowered informal learning (see step 3 in section 3.3 below) as employees need to feel able to question and challenge an organization's strategy and business model.

Source
[1] Hamel, G. and Getz, G. 2004. Freeing radicals. *People Management*, 30 September: 34–6.

4. Intangible assets need to be horizontally and vertically *aligned*. They need to be combined with organizational systems and processes that are focused on strategic objectives in order to generate value.

This focus on intangible assets offers an opportunity for HRD to play a more pivotal role in strategy-making although this has not materialized in practice. A study by Jeris et al. (2002) reveals a lack of involvement by senior HRD practitioners in the strategic planning stage of mergers and acquisitions although HRD expertise was seen as essential during the implementation stage. As Garvan (2007) observes 'in planned approaches it is unlikely that SHRD will have any major role to play at the strategy formulation phase. It will make its most effective contribution at the strategy implementation phase' (p. 12). This suggests a tactical rather than strategic role for HRD (Jeris et al., 2002) which can result in problems if the transition from planning to implementation is not seamless (see *Media Watch Box*).

Because it can take time to develop unique resources tensions can arise between the cost of investment (including HRD inputs) and the timescale needed to achieve a return on investment (ROI). Western businesses in particular have been criticized for focusing on short term financial returns (see *Insights into practice* box). The replication of best practice is often seen as providing a quicker route than the RBV but:

The notion of best practices' implies that organisations can pick and choose predefined tools and blueprints in performing HRD activities within the firm, and that firms can reap the advantages of closely imitating others. (Lervik et al., 2005: 346)

British Airways and terminal five (T5)

British Airways (BA) has a troubled history including multimillion pound fines on both sides of the Atlantic for price fixing on passenger flights (e.g. £122 million by UK Office of Fair Trading; £148 million by the US Department of Justice). In March 2008 the new terminal 5 (T5), built at a cost of £4.3 billion, was launched but within days the new state-of-the-art baggage handling system had collapsed and 23,000 bags had been lost. Because of the chaos this caused hundreds of flights to end up being cancelled at a cost of £16 million. The reputation of BA was badly damaged by this incident. Reports indicated a range of inter-related problems had impacted on the new system, including: a lack of staff car parking spaces; only one security checkpoint was operating; some staff were unable to log onto the system; problems with the hand-held devices which passed instructions onto baggage handlers; poor communications on the ground; and, conveyer belts that became seized up. Unions and BA staff claimed they had not been properly trained to operate the new baggage system although this was refuted by the company. Inadequate training was attributed to many of the problems referred to above. A representative of the Public and Commercial Services Union (PCS) claimed that the company had ignored requests for meetings before the launch to discuss and better understand work practices and contingency arrangements. It was claimed by two unions that senior managers in BA had been warned that the launch plans would result in chaos because some 2,000 staff had not been properly trained. BA has sought to place some of the blame on the British Airways Authority (BAA). Despite the baggage problems the company announced it would transfer the lucrative Heathrow to New York services from terminal 4 to T5 in June 2008. In May 2008 BA announced record pre-tax profits of £883 million. The chief executive of BA, Mr Willie Walsh, decided to waive his £700,000 bonus. The company currently has a cash balance of £1.8 billion.

Sources
[1] *Daily Mail*, 15 February 2008: 82.
[2] *Guardian*, 29 March 2008: 4–5.
[3] *The Times*, 29 March 2008: 36.
[4] *Daily Mail*, 15 April 2008: 66.
[5] http://www.cipd.co.uk/news/_articles (accessed 18 April 2008).
[6] *Guardian*, 10 May 2008: 38.
[7] *Guardian*, 17 May 2008: 38.

This case illustrates an apparent misalignment between business strategy and HRD in terms of training to support the new baggage system. Baggage loss has always been a major problem for all airlines and previously BA has sought to reduce the amount of time to recover a lost bag (Morgan et al., 2007).

Rather strategically-aligned HRD is organization-specific and 'the capabilities that under-pin it are likely to be distributed amongst the members of the organization' (Smith and Sadler-Smith, 2006: 199). Bryan and Joyce (2007) suggest there are three inter-linked capabilities that need to be created and developed by organizations: formal networks, talent marketplaces, and knowledge marketplaces. However, these capabilities are also reliant on the informal structures and processes that characterize social capital (i.e. informal groups or communities and informal networks).

INSIGHTS INTO PRACTICE

A personal reflection

Many years ago when I was a newly appointed training and development manager in a national manufacturing company I devoted a great deal of time and care to produc-ing a three year training and development strategy that was linked to the achieve-ment of business objectives, as set out in the company's mission statement and other documents. The strategy was rejected by the managing director on the basis that it covered a period longer than a year! At the time the company was operating within a relatively stable environment.

Source
The author.

Strategy and structure are linked together because an organization's structure is critical to the achievement of business strategy (Bryan and Joyce, 2007). The importance of the relationship between strategy and structure can be traced back to Chandler (1962). An organization's structure should be designed to support business strategy (not the other way round). For instance, strategies that focus on close collaboration with customers and suppliers require a strong matrix structure that 'promotes agility and responsiveness' (Morgan et al., 2007: 116). As chapter 1 explained organizations have become more varied in design as a result of globalization and improvements in information and communica-tions technology. Many organizations are now characterized by flexibility, outsourcing of the supply chain, and virtual working. This acknowledges that in the twenty-first century organizations can no longer create value using the outmoded vertical, top-down hierarch-ical structures that characterized organizations in the previous century including those that have been 'retrofitted with ad hoc and matrix overlays' (Bryan and Joyce, 2007: 28). The concept of structure now needs to be reconceptualized. Traditional definitions of structure involving the:

number of layers, processes, the role people play . . . do not represent the identity of the organisation, the capabilities it can exercise. It is more productive to rewire line managers' concepts of organisation away from structural solutions (downsizing, removing layers, reengineering) to capability-based solutions (talent management, collaboration, learning, speed of change, and so forth). (Ulrich and Brockbank, 2005: 71)

This notion of 'rewiring' explains why culture is an important influencing factor.

! TIPS AND HINTS

An organization's policy on management development and education should be reviewed carefully in the light of any strategic objectives that require potential changes in culture.

Culture

Definitions of organizational culture vary. It can be summarized as the 'collective mindset of the company . . . that is, shared ways of thinking' (Ulrich and Brockbank, 2005: 150) or as 'a commonly held set of beliefs, values and behaviours' (Smith and Sadler-Smith, 2006: 79). Business and HRD strategies need to accommodate these values, beliefs, and behaviours and make them tangible to employees (although some strategies may involve changing the culture in some way). The values and beliefs of an organization have a direct impact on organizational knowledge and learning processes and influence the type of change programmes HRD practitioners may become involved in. One of the dilemmas confronting some HRD practitioners is that the actions and behaviour of managers may contradict the espoused values and beliefs thus damaging the credibility of both the business and HRD strategies. This is often the reason why vision and mission statements are criticized as time-wasting distractions; and dismissed by many employees as mere rhetoric.

Schein's (1992) definition of organizational culture highlights the role of basic assumptions and how these underpin values and beliefs:

A pattern of shared basic assumptions that the group learned as it solved its problems of external adaptation and internal integration that has worked well enough to be considered valid and, therefore, to be taught to new members as the correct way to perceive, think, and feel in relation to those problems. (Schein, 1992: 12)

Not only does this definition demonstrate the inter-relationship between culture and learning it also highlights that regardless of the espoused values and beliefs it is the basic assumptions underlying culture that drive behaviour in the workplace. These basic assumptions usually exist at a subconscious level manifesting in a 'taken for granted' fashion. This is why learning, which aims to change understanding and behaviour, can be pivotal to the fostering of cultural change (Hite, 2004). Changing organizational culture is one of the biggest challenges confronting HRD practitioners. It is much more difficult to change culture than to change strategy or structure (Morgan et al., 2007):

So it is crucial to consider both the existing and desired culture when defining strategy and structure. The most astute corporate leaders know they must either *choose a strategy in line with the existing culture or be prepared to make significant investments to modify or create new cultures.* (p. 93)

While individuals may learn, the organization as a whole will only change if that learning is shared and acted upon collectively (Sambrook and Stewart, 1999). This is why Tata Steel's investment in recruitment, training, and retention has to be combined with a change in culture as part of its strategy to become a global leader in its sector (Seshadri and Tripathy, 2006). The stronger an organizational culture is the more likely that culture will shape the organization's strategy (Özçelik and Ferman, 2006).

! TIPS AND HINTS

It is well worth taking the time to read about Edgar Schein's ideas as he offers some practical advice on how to analyse and change organizational culture.

● ▶ INSIGHTS INTO PRACTICE

A personal reflection

HRD practitioners need to be able to translate HRD jargon, concepts, and philosophies into the everyday language of their organization. I once met an HR Manager who was a great fan of the work of Peter Senge, an American writer on the learning organization and organizational learning. He explained that he had become frustrated with senior management colleagues who did not share his passion for the learning organization concept. When I asked him how he presented the ideas of Senge to managers and employees he produced a slide show on his laptop that was a summary of Senge's book (*The Fifth Discipline*). It used Senge's terms and language and he had made no attempt to explain these in the everyday language of his own company. Even when I pointed this out to him, he still struggled to understand why so many colleagues were as frustrated with him as he was with them!

Source
The author.

In an organization with a highly developed sense of learning it is anticipated that the mission statement, in particular, will reflect the organization's learning philosophy. For instance, successful managers will be those who are able to forge the values and beliefs of the organization through the facilitation of learning activities in the workplace (see also chapter 11). Within such a learning-oriented culture the role of managers in supporting learning will eventually become indistinguishable from other managerial responsibilities. At a senior level this will be reflected in senior managers viewing the strategic planning process as a learning process in itself and not purely as a means to an end (Walton, 1999). At one level an organization can claim to have an HRD strategy if it is harnessing HRD interventions to support business goals; but to be truly strategic, learning processes need to be embedded in all organizational activities—including strategic planning as well as strategic implementation and review.

Achieving such a culture is highly problematic in an era when many of the control principles of scientific management still prevail in a wide range of organizational settings. Hamel and Prahalad (1996) refer to 'managerial frames' which are 'the corporate equivalent of genetic coding, [and] limit management's perception to a particular slice of reality. Managers live inside their frames and, to a very great extent, don't know what lies outside' (p. 54). Altering these frames is difficult as this involves challenging some of the basic assumptions driving management behaviour. This equates to the notion of 'rewiring' referred to above. Consequently, incremental change is likely to be the most successful approach (Dirkx et al., 2004). This 'rewiring' of senior managers in particular is critical to strategic HRD. Without it senior managers may continue to focus on the tactical role of training and development.

> ### (•) INSIGHTS INTO PRACTICE
>
> ## Motorola
>
> As a result of rapidly changing technologies and increased competition in Europe and Asia during the 1990s the HR function ('HR leadership team') in Motorola developed a new HR strategy with goals that included: linking HR practices to the requirements of key stakeholders (i.e. customers and shareholders); developing the culture so that it was consistent with the company's brand identity; and, gaining the commitment of all employees. HR put culture at the heart of the strategy. They identified that the company culture needed to change if the company was going to respond effectively to increasingly competitive global markets.
>
> **Source**
> Ulrich, D. and Brockbank, W. 2005. *The HR Value Proposition*. Boston, MA: Harvard Business School Press.

Human resource management (HRM)

HRD and HRM need to be understood as integrated concepts although each has its own distinctive characteristics and role. McLagan (1989) suggests that the focus of HRD should be on *improving* while that of HRM should be on *creating* and *maintaining*. This relationship does not necessarily have to be reflected in organizational structures: the HRD function may be part of a larger HRM department but it may also be a free-standing. What is important is that HRD and HRM strategies, policies, plans, and practices are horizontally aligned and not in conflict. The focus on improving reflects the centrality of learning to HRD (for instance, see the discussion in chapter 4 on double-loop learning and the role of questioning and challenging in the learning process). Maintaining an effective working relationship with the HRM function is an important aspect of the HRD practitioner's role.

In horizontal alignment (also termed horizontal integration or internal fit) the HRD function ensures that the HRD strategy, policies, plans, and practices are consistent with the HRM strategy, policies, plans, and practices. For instance, ensuring the set of competencies underpinning a management development programme is the same as that used for recruitment and selection. Smith (2006) refers to studies in the US on high-performance work systems which show that skills and training make a more significant contribution to organizational performance when combined with complementary HRM practices. Horizontal alignment is illustrated in figure 3.3.

However, horizontal alignment goes beyond ensuring consistency between HRD and HRM. There is a need for a wider horizontal integration of organizational processes and activities (Ghosal and Gratton, 2005: 316–24):

• **Operational integration:** creating a standardized technological infrastructure. This is made possible through the advances in information and communications technologies discussed in chapter 1.

• **Intellectual integration:** creating a shared knowledge base. This equates to a technology-based knowledge management system and reflects the growth of interest in knowledge work and intellectual capital (see chapter 10).

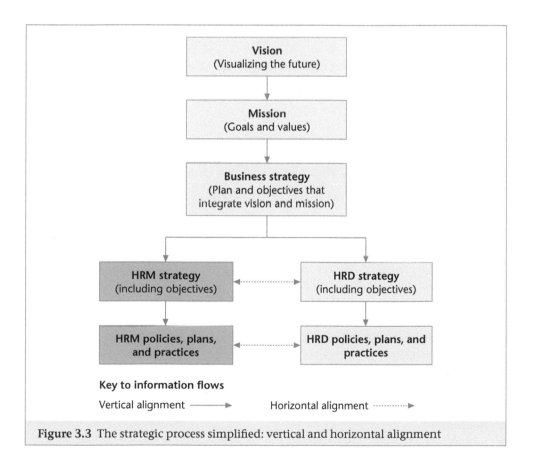

Figure 3.3 The strategic process simplified: vertical and horizontal alignment

INSIGHTS INTO PRACTICE

All change at RUSAL

RUSAL is Russia's largest producer of aluminium and the third largest in the world. The company was created in 2000 as a result of various mergers and now employs over 50,000 people across 12 countries. RUSAL has focused on performance management and this has been credited with a doubling of productivity. During the Soviet Union era the original Siberian companies that now comprise RUSAL were characterized by low employee morale, poor levels of health and safety, and corruption. As part of the change process new training initiatives have been implemented including: induction programmes, personal development plans, sponsorship for education courses, management training, and e-learning. The company has also introduced new communications systems, a code of conduct based on a new set of core values, and a corporate social responsibility programme.

This case illustrates how training and development interventions play an important role in the implementation of change initiatives (in this case focused on culture change through the introduction of modern management practices). These initiatives are both horizontally aligned (with the performance management system) and vertically aligned (supporting the strategic change in culture).

Source
Fuller, G. 2005. Come the revolution. *People Management*, 1 September: 38–40.

INSIGHTS INTO PRACTICE

Vertical and horizontal alignment of HR in the Tata Group

The India-based Tata Group comprises over 80 companies (see also main case in chapter 14). Each company has its own business strategy and HR function. However, there is also a small corporate HR function which sets overall direction for the other HR functions but does not dictate the business strategies in their companies. The corporate HR function sets overall direction 'by crafting a general HR framework and setting minimum standards, spearheading specific HR interventions in Tata companies, and linking their needs with the overall corporate vision' (page 181). It also provides the other HR functions with the process tools to 'design and implement high value-added and business-focused HR agendas' (p. 181).

Source
Ulrich, D. and Brockbank, W. 2005. *The HR Value Proposition*. Boston, MA: Harvard Business School Press.

DEVELOPING AN HRD STRATEGY

- **Social integration:** creating bonds between employees that stimulate knowledge sharing. This equates to a knowledge management strategy based on face-to-face social interactions and also reflects the growth of interest in knowledge work and intellectual capital (see chapter 10). Bryan and Joyce (2007) argue that organizations need to increase the number of productive interactions between employees while decreasing unproductive ones.

- **Emotional integration:** creating a common purpose and shared identity. This emphasises the role of culture and corporate leadership. The culture needs to be monitored by the HR function to ensure that it supports the organization's strategic direction (Özçelik and Ferman, 2006).

3.3 Developing an HRD strategy

In order to explain some of the fundamental principles underpinning strategic management a step-by-step approach is adopted. In reality this is an ongoing process in which information is flowing continuously across as well as between steps; and, where any published documentation that tries to capture the outputs of this process (e.g. a written business strategy) actually represents a 'snapshot' in time. The 'simplified strategic process' shown in figure 3.3 will be built upon and developed further.

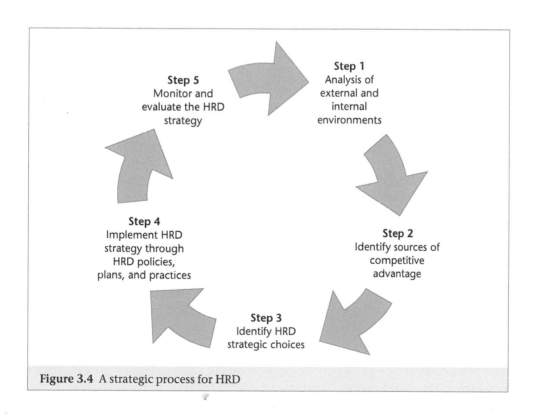

Figure 3.4 A strategic process for HRD

Step 1 Analysis of external and internal environments

Data from external and internal environments can be analysed to provide information which then informs decisions about business strategy, and in turn, HRD strategy and HRM strategy. Analysis of the external environment includes market trends, economic forecasts, technological changes, labour market, and demographic trends and government initiatives. This analysis is not the preserve of a single function although marketing usually plays an important role in developing a strategic view of the organization (Brassington and Pettitt, 2003). HRD and HRM practitioners may be particularly involved in the analysis of external labour markets and government initiatives. The internal analysis focuses on business processes, the internal labour market, and organizational culture; as well as assessing the implications of organizational structure (e.g. flexibility; outsourcing and off-shoring) and the changing expectations of employees (e.g. work–life balance; employability). The HRD practitioner needs to scan the external and internal environments on a regular basis in order to be in a position to react to changes in trends (e.g. increasing scarcity of qualified engineers in external labour markets; changes in performance levels in departments). This process is more complex in a global organization where there is a mix of global and local trends (see chapter 1).

! TIPS AND HINTS

Do not fall into the trap of confusing an organization-wide training analysis with a strategic level analysis of the internal environment. The former has a much more narrow focus than the latter.

A particular problem with analysing information for strategic decision-making is 'bounded rationality' (Simon, 1985). It is not possible to know everything about the external environment although it is assumed that people will always choose the best course of action and will make rational decisions based on that information. Any search for information is inevitably incomplete thus resulting in satisfactory rather than optimal decisions (Simon, 1985). The implications of this for HRD practice are summarized by Herling (2003):

> If HRD is to be strategic within the organisation then, when involved in organisational decision making or the initiation of complex organisational change, HRD professionals must be willing to continually raise the issue of bounded rationality and its impact on the choices being made. We must be willing to ask all the questions and question all the answers, we must insist that we have explored all the possibilities and not opted for a satisfactory solution over the best solution. (p. 405)

This helps to explain why planned strategies often fail and successful strategies emerge (see above). The strategic process diagram in figure 3.5 has been amended to reflect step 1.

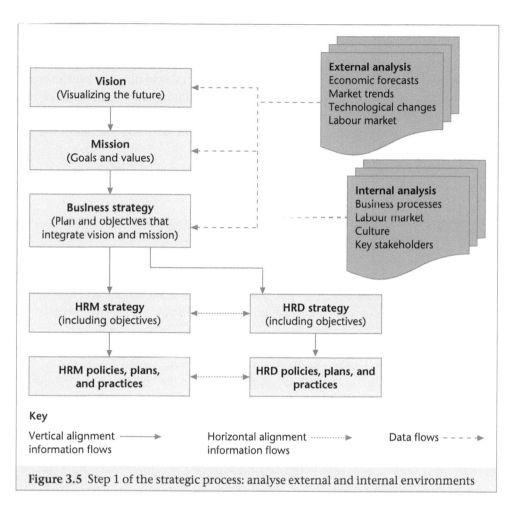

Figure 3.5 Step 1 of the strategic process: analyse external and internal environments

Step 2 Identify sources of competitive advantage

Analysis of the external and internal environments is used to corroborate existing sources of competitive advantage and to identify potential new ones. Ulrich and Brockbank (2005) provide several examples of these, including: innovating new products and services (e.g. Intel); quality (e.g. Toyota); branding (e.g. Coca Cola); on-time delivery (e.g. FedEx); and, customer service (e.g. Virgin Atlantic Airways). These sources of competitive advantage (or in the case of public and non-profit sectors performance advantage through the delivery of best value) reflect the core capabilities of an organization. These core capabilities are underpinned by the intellectual capital of the organization in the form of employee competencies. For instance, innovating new products and services is likely to be underpinned by competencies such as creativity, problem solving, change orientation, and knowledge sharing. The HRD strategy focuses on how these competencies and potential new ones can be developed in order to achieve the organization's strategic objectives.

For example, an organization which has a business strategy focused on increasing market share through excellence in customer service may need to improve the training of its sales force in customer care competencies such as verbal communications, demonstrating empathy, and problem solving. Some organizations may need to undergo a major transformation in order to remain competitive and maintaining the momentum of this process requires changing how managers think and act (Ghosal and Bartlett, 2005). This links to the discussion above on culture and managerial 'frames' and the role of HRD in developing culture.

The strategic process diagram in figure 3.6 has been amended to reflect step 2.

● INSIGHTS INTO PRACTICE

Nokia

This case illustrates the important role that organizational knowledge and learning processes play in the development of core capabilities (in this case the core capability is strategic agility).

Nokia, which has over 100,000 employees in over 100 countries, achieved an annual profit of £6.3 billion in 2007. Its culture is characterized by change and renewal. The latest trend the company is focusing on is the convergence of mobile phones and devices with Internet services. New competitors are emerging including Apple, Google, and Microsoft. Nokia has a value-culture (expressed as four values: engaging you; achieving together; passion for innovation; and, very human). The company encourages employees to switch roles and functions during their career with the company. Not surprisingly, Nokia is regarded as a strategically agile company. Strategic agility is characterized by strategic sensitivity (i.e. an early awareness of changing trends), leadership unity (i.e. senior managers are able to make bold and important decisions quickly), and resource fluidity (i.e. the ability to reconfigure and redeploy firm resources). Nokia has used learning systems and processes to support its ability to be strategically agile. For instance, creating new ventures to stimulate experiential learning about new opportunities (these new ventures were allowed to operate independently of the core business so that learning was maximized), and learning the lessons from early commercially unsuccessful 3rd Generation (3G) products. The company has created a 'core framework' for countering what it sees as the natural decay of strategic agility which embraces the role of learning (e.g. encouraging the generation of new ideas; reframing new opportunities; and, learning from the innovative experiences gained from working with new products and/or services). These learning processes are consistent with the company's culture and values.

Sources
[1] Doz, Y. and Kosonen, M. 2008. The dynamics of strategic agility: Nokia's rollercoaster experience. *California Management Review*, 50 (3): 95–118.
[2] *People Management*, 17 April 2008: 34–7.

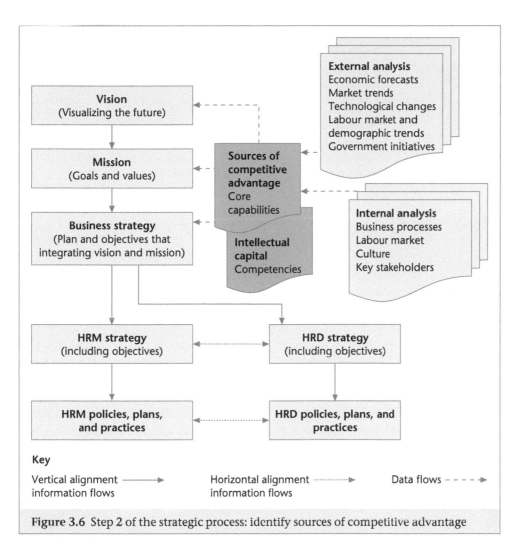

Figure 3.6 Step 2 of the strategic process: identify sources of competitive advantage

Step 3 Identify HRD strategic choices

Broadly speaking there are four principal HRD strategic choices for developing an organization's intellectual capital and these are summarized in figure 3.7 below. These are not intended to be either–or choices; rather it is anticipated that an organization will use some combination of these depending on a variety of organizational factors such as size and structure, culture, and availability of resources. It is implicit in these choices that HRD practitioners ensure all HRD interventions and activities are aligned with the organization's strategic direction (Ulrich, 2007). Where the emphasis is on indirect interventions the role of HRD practitioners is secondary to that of managers and employees. This reflects the need for a holistic approach to strategic HRD which is based on a shared responsibility for the successful implementation of strategic HRD.

Indirect interventions	**Devolved informal learning** Developing awareness of learning opportunities	**Empowered informal learning** Creating a learning environment (i.e. a context conducive to social capital)
Direct interventions	**Learning as socialization** Delivering formal training, learning and development interventions	**Engineering** Creating and controlling communities-of-practice and social networks
	Human capital	Social capital

Figure 3.7 HRD strategy choices

Learning as socialization reflects traditional approaches to the development of human capital that are associated with the left-hand end of the learning continuum shown in chapter 2 and the systematic approach to training discussed in chapter 5. The focus is on formal, structured interventions such as training courses, coaching sessions, and education programmes where primary responsibility is with the HRD practitioner as a 'training expert'. The aim of these interventions is to ensure employees conform to the values and beliefs of the organization (see *Insights into practice* box on Singapore Airlines later in the chapter) and have the ability to meet performance targets and standards. For instance, a business strategy that is cost-oriented will focus on skills training in order to maximize productivity and efficiency (Garavan, 2007). This type of socialization is not targeted at organizational renewal but has 'been designed to perpetuate a stable and unmoving organization [which] could hinder an organization's ability to be agile and change' (Danielson, 2004: 355).

MEDIA WATCH BOX

Training as control

According to a group of leading consultants and academics too many organizations are using training to control employees which is resulting in failed training and development initiatives. The group argue that managers need to accept that most learning is actually informal and beyond managers' control.

Source
People Management, 24 November: 16–17.

Devolved informal learning is where day-to-day operational responsibility for learning is devolved to line managers and employees. Their ability to understand about learning and development (e.g. how individuals learn; how individuals can learn differently; how individuals can use reflection to improve their personal learning etc.) is supported by a mix of formal interventions designed and delivered by HRD practitioners (e.g. training workshops on learning styles and reflective practice; e-learning courses that encourage self-managed learning; coaching sessions to help line managers develop facilitation skills etc). This strategy is usually associated with an emphasis on lifelong learning and career development. The HRD practitioner can also be involved in the development of organizational knowledge and learning processes that rely on formal teams, knowledge sharing activities, and problem solving projects.

Engineering of learning is where HRD interventions are focused on organization development interventions that are intended to develop social capital. This strategic approach to HRD reflects a managerial control mode (Alvesson and Kärreman, 2001) where managers interpret learning 'as a vehicle for manipulating employees and persuading them to adopt organizational aims' (Slotte et al., 2004: 482). Whilst it is possible to exercise a high level of control over direct interventions designed to develop human capital the situation is very different with social capital which has been shown to be most successful when allowed to emerge within the workplace. Social capital is about the development of communities (physical, virtual, co-located, or dispersed). As Alvesson and Kärreman, (2001) observe:

> Community is difficult to accomplish or control for management. It is basically an organic, social quality, associated with background, long term commitments, downplayed hierarchy and considerable space also for non-instrumental virtues in a social context. The corporate form is typically not a setting that encourages community formation, but tends to work against it, at least on the level of the whole organisation. (p. 1006)

For this reason empowered informal learning is the preferred choice for developing social capital (although there is no guarantee that social capital will always work in the organization's favour). Primary responsibility for HRD in this quadrant is held by the line manager in partnership with employees. The HRD practitioner can provide support and guidance but is more concerned with developing the learning infrastructure required for successful devolved informal learning. This infrastructure includes further processes for organizational knowledge and learning such as the design of work areas and the provision of shared spaces (e.g. communal areas). However, for indirect interventions to be successful high levels of trust need to be in place. Developing trust should be an integral aspect of the development of any learning environment. A lack of trust will impact on the development of a strategic partnership between HRD practitioners and managers.

Devolved informal learning and empowered informal learning are both underpinned by workplace learning (see chapter 11). This type of learning is important in all types and size of organization as it acts as a prerequisite for organizational change. However, the need for a mix of choices is justified by Skule (2004) who states that 'Along with education and formal training, informal learning is the key to corporate competitiveness as well as to employment and employability' (p. 8). It is also suggested that these two strategic choices provide the humanist perspective on HRD (see chapter 2) an opportunity to co-exist with the performance perspective.

MEDIA WATCH BOX

The power of empowerment

Analysis of surveys conducted in UK manufacturing companies reveals an important link between empowerment and learning that helps employees cope better with their jobs and stimulate knowledge sharing with colleagues.

Source
People Management, 22 February 2007: 40–2.

There is a fifth strategic choice which is to do nothing; and many organizations, particularly small and medium sized enterprises adopt this strategy (see chapter 12). Marsick and Watkins (1990) note that informal learning can take place despite an environment not highly conducive to learning. Similarly, social capital will always exist alongside the formal structure of an organization—often employees, individually or in groups, get on and achieve things in spite of the organization rather than because of it.

The strategic process diagram in figure 3.8 has been amended to reflect step 3.

! TIPS AND HINTS

Distinguishing and deciding between these strategic choices requires a great deal of accumulated experience, ideally including line manager experience at some point.

Step 4 Implement HRD strategy through HRD policies, plans, and practices

Implementation of HRD strategy is achieved through the implementation of HRD policies, plans, and practices. The mix of HRD strategic choices chosen at step 3 will influence how this happens. The formulation and publication of an HRD policy statement is an important aspect of the HRD strategy process because a policy is a practical expression of an organization's commitment to HRD. Policies exist to enable others to make decisions (Mayo, 1998). Consequently, the HRD policy should explain the purpose of HRD (i.e. how HRD processes support the achievement of the organization's vision, mission, and strategy); clarify who is responsible for different aspects of HRD practice (this is particularly important for the line manager and learner); explain of how resources will be allocated (e.g. are professional development programmes sponsored by the organization); and, specify success criteria. Although the format of an HRD policy will vary from organization to organization it should include these essentials. Sometimes it can be

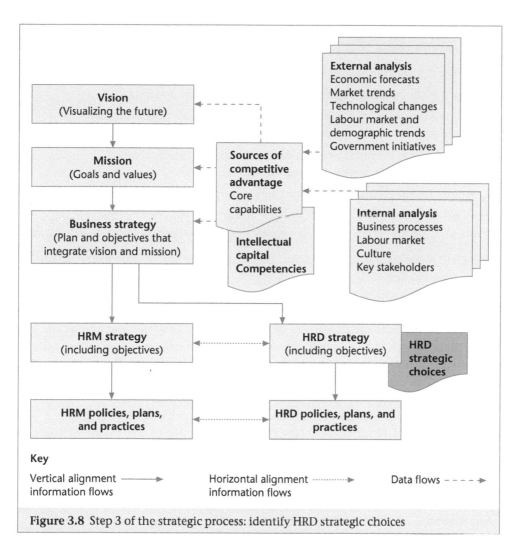

Figure 3.8 Step 3 of the strategic process: identify HRD strategic choices

useful to ensure that the organization's overall HRD strategy is captured in writing to ensure that all employees fully understand the contribution the HRD function makes to the organization (though this needs to be updated regularly).

Key concept   HRD policy

The HRD policy should communicate an organization's HRD philosophy to all employees so that informed decisions can be made about HRD activities.

HRD plans are normally produced for the organization as a whole, business units, divisions, departments, and individual employees. There are no hard and fast rules for the format of HRD plans. It does not matter as long as the approach adopted preserves the important principles of:

- Accuracy (i.e. the plan reflects the needs of the business)
- Clarity (i.e. the plan uses language that all employees can understand)
- Timeliness (i.e. the plan is published in advance to give all stakeholders an opportunity to reflect on the proposals)
- Informative (e.g. the plan specifies who is to be trained; when; why; solution/intervention selected; duration; cost)
- Ongoing (i.e. the plan is used as a working document and updated as required; it is not simply an annual publication which gets filed and forgotten about)
- Names (i.e. people feel happier about contacting a named person rather than a job title)

The ACTION acronym can be used as a checklist to ensure any HRD plan contains all relevant information.

HRD practices include a range of interventions and activities. Interventions can be training courses, coaching sessions, career counselling sessions, and change projects; while activities include offering advice on training needs, analysing questionnaires, and giving presentations to management teams. The HRD strategy will specify the strategic choice (e.g. learning as socialization) but it is the plan that sets out the specifics of that choice. These can take the form of HRD interventions and/or activities and examples of these and how they support specific capabilities are shown in table 3.1.

The strategic process diagram in figure 3.9 has been amended to reflect step 4.

Source of competitive advantage	Innovation	Customer service
Capabilities	Creativity and problem solving	Empathy and interpersonal skills
Requirement	R&D personnel to be knowledgeable in the latest thinking in their specialist areas	Sales and customer service personnel to demonstrate high levels of product and technical knowledge and high standards of customer care
Training, learning and development	Attending courses, conferences, seminars, inter-company visits; self-managed learning	Attending courses on product and technical knowledge, and customer care; being coached by experienced colleagues
Career development and lifelong learning	Presenting papers at conferences; developing social networks	Participating in development centres
Organization development/ organizational knowledge and learning	Nurturing informal learning in the workplace; facilitation of knowledge creation and sharing processes	Empowered learning and self-managed teamwork

Table 3.1 Examples of how HRD can support organizational capabilities

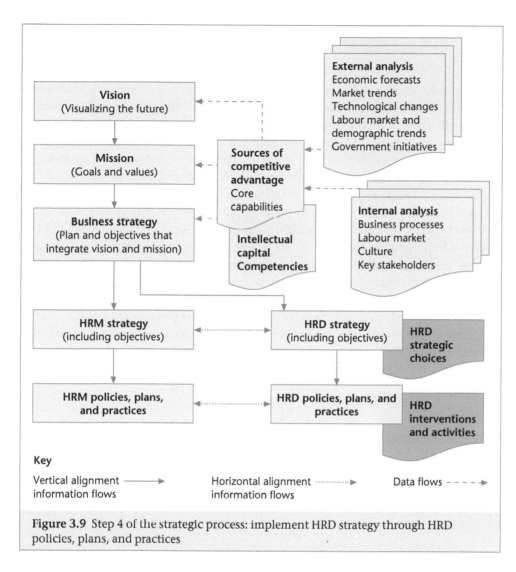

Figure 3.9 Step 4 of the strategic process: implement HRD strategy through HRD policies, plans, and practices

Step 5 Monitor and evaluate the implementation of HRD strategy

This is an often neglected aspect of HRD practice in organizations. Chapter 9 highlights some of the issues around the evaluation of discrete HRD interventions while chapter 13 discusses the importance of evaluating the effectiveness of the HRD function. The evaluation of the HRD strategy forms part of the latter. Often there are constraints which impact on the implementation of HRD interventions and activities such as limited resources (e.g. a capped training budget; little internal expertise) or restricted access to certain aspects of the business strategy (see *Insights into practice* box). These constraints often create situations in which HRD is not strategically aligned:

Few organisations attempt to show a positive link between training and positive change . . . highly qualified practitioners, ready to assess needs and evaluate

> results, may be stymied by management's unwillingness to spend time and money
> on proper design. Practitioners face enormous pressure from organisation leaders
> to embrace the latest training fad or quick fix. (Bunch, 2007: 145)

Proposed interventions and activities should be prioritized using criteria such as relevance to strategic objectives or a mandatory legal requirement. Financial techniques such as cost-benefit analysis and return on investment can be used (see chapters 9 and 13). Sometimes it is necessary to demonstrate the potential cost implications of not doing anything. In a nutshell, evaluation is about demonstrating a business case for HRD. An important aspect of this stage is demonstrating how the development of intellectual capital is integrated with the other forms of capital. For instance: information capital, held by the technological infrastructure, and organization capital, such as culture, leadership, and teamwork (Kaplan and Norton, 2004). The balanced scorecard was devised to highlight the importance of investing in the future; by investing in areas such as people, systems, and procedures and not purely equipment and R&D (Kaplan and Norton, 1996). It can be used to measure the effectiveness of component elements of business strategy (i.e. financial measures, customer measures, internal business process measures, and learning and growth measures). It is particularly interesting because of the role of non-financial data as a key measurement of performance necessitating a need to identify what could be termed non-traditional strategic performance measures:

> The balanced scorecard is premised on the notion that measurement motivates
> and aims to move away from the problems that a short term reliance on financial
> measures alone creates. (Houldsworth, 2004: 89)

For instance, Tata Steel relies heavily on this approach (Seshadri and Tripathy, 2006).

(•) INSIGHTS INTO PRACTICE

A personal reflection

Several years ago I was working with an external consultant who needed to be briefed in detail on the company's strategy. The consultant was seated in a room with a senior manager present and told he could read the 'business plan' there but was not allowed to remove it, make copies, or take any notes. At the end he had to sign a disclaimer stating that he would not divulge the contents to any other person (including employees). The real problems started when he had to facilitate sessions with employees and it became apparent that the employees had no real sense of what the company was trying to achieve. This type of situation can be a real dilemma for HRD practitioners. Usually their work is linked to improving employee performance, be it in terms of better customer service, reduced wastage, and higher quality, or fewer accidents. But this can be difficult to achieve if employees have no real sense of how their individual performance contributes to the organization's plans.

Source
The author.

The strategic process diagram in figure 3.10 has been amended to reflect step 5. As evaluation acts as a feedback loop various flows in the strategic process have been made two-way to highlight this fact and to convey the iterative nature of strategic processes found in organizations.

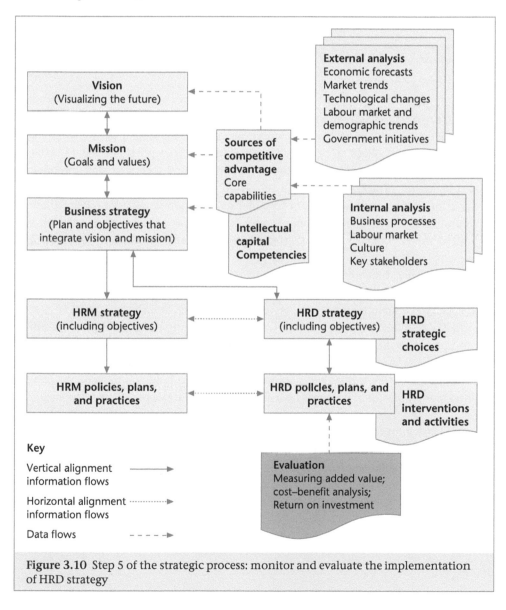

Figure 3.10 Step 5 of the strategic process: monitor and evaluate the implementation of HRD strategy

3.4 Implications for practice of a strategic approach to human resource development

Effective communication and information systems need to be in place to ensure vertical and horizontal alignment are effective. Formal communications are critical to the dissemination of organizational values in larger organizations (see *Insights into practice* box). It is difficult for such systems to replicate the immediacy and informality that characterize smaller organizations.

Information flows are critical to the formulation and implementation of HRD strategy. A good starting point is for the HRD practitioner to ask him/herself a basic question: *if the HRD function were my own business what information would I require, in what format and how*

(••) INSIGHTS INTO PRACTICE

Singapore Airlines

Singapore Airlines has a reputation for being a world class airline company that has been in existence since 1972 and employs nearly 14,000 people. It is renowned for the quality of its in-flight service which can be linked to its corporate values of pursuit of excellence, and customer first. Other values are safety, concern for staff, integrity, and teamwork. The company has a HR division that includes a people networks department that is responsible for communicating Singapore Airline's mission, core values, and strategic goals to all employees. Communication channels used include: printed media, online systems (e.g. bulletin boards and email), and face-to-face meetings and road-shows; as well as corporate events. There is also an organizational climate survey. Different publications and road-shows are used to target specific occupational groups within the company. Training and development interventions are used to communicate the company's mission, values, and strategic goals (e.g. at induction, on training programmes). Cabin crew undergo a four month immersion programme so that their behaviour is consistent with the brand image projected to customers (even down to details such as how they should greet customers and maintaining eye contact at boarding). Subsequent, ongoing training interventions continue to reinforce the alignment of personal and corporate values. In order to ensure employees behave in line with corporate values there is an evaluation system in place.

This case illustrates the interweaving of ongoing communications with ongoing training as a way of achieving vertical strategic alignment. It reinforces the role of organizational culture and demonstrates how formal training, learning and development interventions can help to change behaviours. See chapter 4 for a discussion on different learning theories, including behavioural learning.

Source
Chong, M. 2007. The role of internal communication and training in infusing corporate values and delivering brand promise: Singapore Airlines' experience. *Corporate Reputation Review*, 10 (3): 201–12.

easy would it be to obtain? At one level the HRD practitioner needs information in order to conduct good housekeeping. At another level it is needed to justify the function's existence: are the strategic HRD objectives being achieved? Is the HRD function adding value to the organization? As HRD practitioners tend to be non-IT specialists it is important that they acquire knowledge and skills which enable them to appreciate and maximize the potential benefits of the information and communications technology at their disposal. Blockages in these systems will compound the problem of bounded rationality and impact on the quality of decision-making at all levels. This can result in the creation of 'silos' of activity that may be individually characterized by high levels of knowledge sharing but which act as barriers to the transfer of knowledge across the organization. In this situation highly sophisticated processes for organizational knowledge and learning are needed which the HRD practitioner may not have the authority or expertise to create.

However, information systems are useless unless there is effective analysis of the information by the HRD practitioner. As Grieves (2003) observes, it is interpretation that matters:

> Skilful organisational analysis has little to do with the accumulation of facts and should be more concerned with the relationships between them, that is, with interpretation and insight. (p. 24)

Traditionally, the principal focus of organizational analysis has been on the identification of training needs (see chapters 5 and 6). This involves the identification of knowledge, skills, and attitudes that are currently deficient in the organization rather than gaps in business results that impact on performance (Gilley and Maycunich Gilley, 2003). The HRD practitioner now needs to adopt a much broader perspective and identify the underlying causes of these gaps:

> By constantly exploring and asking questions, HRD professionals are not focusing on the status quo but are continuously looking for new and improved ways of enhancing the organisation's effectiveness. (Gilley et al., 2002: 254)

Along with skills such as the ability to influence others, the ability to negotiate effectively, and the ability to communicate ideas with fluency, HRD practitioners are potentially well equipped to initiate a process for the development of an HRD strategy. But these skills need to be combined with business or commercial acumen and, arguably most importantly, political acumen.

Mintzberg (1994) observes that 'strategists' are people who immerse themselves in the daily detail while still being able to abstract the strategic messages from it. This is akin to the often used 'helicopter' perspective, the ability to rise above the morass of day-to-day activity and to take a broader perspective. This has implications for the HRD practitioner who has to be able to understand and contribute to the strategic management process of the organization. Depending on the perceived role and status of this position the level of involvement may be to a lesser or greater extent. A range of options are shown in table 3.2.

These options are intended to be illustrative only and you can encounter a mix of two or more within an organization. The challenge for the HRD practitioner is to develop the

Role	Description
Guerrilla fighter	They have to identify tactical opportunities to impact upon strategic management. This may be through the exploitation of close working relationships with particular directors or senior managers; or by maximizing the opportunities presented by particular projects
Politician	Their status is such that they can operate at senior management and director level with ease and assurance; although they may not necessarily hold a directorship. They have highly effective political and influencing skills. Although not necessarily in attendance at strategic management meetings, their closeness to all the directors enables them to have an indirect input to strategy formulation
Idealist	Tends to have very little input to the strategic management process. They are viewed by directors and senior managers as *having their heads in the clouds*. They lack the pragmatism of the guerrilla fighter and believe that training and development is an investment that should be resourced as a right; and consequently argue they should be involved in strategic management discussions (even if they lack an appreciation of commercial and strategic issues)
Administrator	Accept their role and status in the organization and do not question their lack of involvement in the strategic management process. They are happy to do as instructed, not to question decisions or assumptions, and believe the focus of their role is to provide an efficient training and development service
Change facilitator	Recognizes that one of the best ways to get HRD much more closely aligned with business strategy is through cultural change programmes. These cannot be achieved without the support of the HRD function

Table 3.2 Strategic options for the HRD practitioner

competencies and credibility to be able to contribute to the strategic management process effectively. Not all HRD practitioners are able to convert such theory into practice. This is because different organizations have different perspectives on the role and purpose of HRD and this subject is explored in more detail in chapter 13. For instance, there are many different examples of strategic HRD as well as non-strategic HRD, and sporadic-strategic HRD. As explained above strategic HRD is where the HRD practitioner is seen as a business partner in helping to bring about fundamental changes to the organization. Non-strategic HRD is where the focus is on rectifying skills deficiencies. This was characteristic of the period leading up to the 1990s. The HRD practitioner had very little, if any, input into the strategic planning process. Sporadic-strategic HRD is where the HRD practitioner is involved in some key change programmes only; and their involvement is carefully controlled by directors on a highly selective basis (to quote a Sales and Marketing director from a few years ago: *training is something you take out of the drawer every now and again and then kick back in when you don't want it for a while*).

There are a range of barriers to the existence of strategic HRD which include:

• The lack of incentives for organizations to invest in HRD activities, such as training and development interventions. This is despite a series of different government initiatives over the years which have attempted to encourage more investment through the provision of grants (e.g. National Vocational Qualifications) or through the achievement of publicly recognized standards of quality (e.g. Investors in People)

- The lack of incentives for individuals to invest in their own development—the concept of lifelong learning is still very much in its infancy

- The lack of a well formulated business strategy or effective strategic planning process; the continued dominance of short term financial pressures; the continuance of the perspective that HRD does not have a strategic-level role

- The inability of HRD practitioners to promote the need for an HRD strategy. This may be due to a variety of factors (e.g. lack of determination and perseverance; lack of strategic understanding; lack of business and commercial acumen; the prevailing organizational culture)

Summary

HRD has an important role to play in helping organizations develop in an era of rapid and continuous change. Although rational step-by-step processes are fallible in organizational contexts they do provide useful pedagogical aids. The models developed in this chapter can also assist HRD practitioners in the development of an HRD strategy but ultimately practitioners will have to rely on their skills and intuition to handle many of the problems they are confronted with. An important aspect of the strategic process is the business partner concept whereby the development of a strategic approach to HRD is dependent on collaborative working between the HRD practitioner and key stakeholders, particularly senior and line managers. This relationship underpins the practice of HRD on a day-by-day basis. As chapter 2 explained the HRD practitioner operates differently to the traditional trainer role.

The chapter has highlighted the importance of vertical and horizontal alignment. HRD strategy, policies, plans, and practices need to be aligned with the organization's vision, mission, and strategic objectives as set out in the business strategy. Effective communications and information systems need to be in place to support these processes. At the same time HRD and HRM need to be aligned whether or not they are part of the same function. This horizontal alignment also needs to extend beyond these two areas and encompass other operational and functional activities. Whatever approach is adopted for the strategic planning and implementation consideration must be given to the review and evaluation stage. This is an important theme that is returned to in chapter 13 which discusses the management of the HRD function.

Review questions

1 Explain the difference between vertical and horizontal alignment.

2 Summarize the key challenges facing the HRD practitioner in developing a strategic approach to HRD.

3 What is the relationship between an organization's mission statement and business strategy?

4   What does RBV stand for and how is it relevant to human resource development?

5   What are the implications of the business partner role?

Suggestions for further reading

1   Walton, J. 1999. *Strategic Human Resource Development*. Harlow: Prentice Hall.

Although now dated this important text still contains some relevant material and is worth regarding as supplementary reading.

2   Pattanayak, B. 2003. Gaining competitive advantage and business success through strategic HRD: an Indian experience. *Human Resource Development International*, 6 (3): 405–11.

An interesting article that is well worth reading because of its focus on India rather than Anglo-American contexts.

3   Özçelik, G. and Ferman, M. 2006. Competency approach to human resource management: outcomes and contributions in a Turkish cultural context. *Human Resource Development Review*, 5 (1): 72–91.

An interesting article that encompasses much of the debate on the role of competency movement.

4   Garavan, T. N. 2007. A strategic perspective on human resource development. *Advances in Developing Human Resources*, 9 (1): 11–30.

A good article if you want an alternative model to the one proposed in this chapter.

5   Ulrich, D. and Brockbank, W. 2005. *The HR Value Proposition*. Boston, MA: Harvard Business School Press. Well worth reading although it focuses on HR generally rather than HRD.

There have been several articles in the CIPD's People Management magazine about the concepts discussed in this book.

Case study

Toyota

Toyota, valued at US$188 billion or £98 billion, is the world's second biggest car maker, just behind General Motors of the US, but is expected to claim the top spot in 2009. The potential key competitors of the future are likely to be from South Korea, China, and India where companies such as Hyundai, Kia, and Tata are making cheap cars of a good quality. Toyota has been able to combine product quality and reliability with low pricing, fuel efficiency, and good design. It has been successful at aligning its operational activities with strategic goals. The company is driven by what it terms the 'Toyota Way' rather than by cost reduction (which characterizes many Asian and Far East manufacturing companies). The 'Toyota Way' has been evolving since the company was originally founded in 1926. It is all about the culture of the company and emphasizes mutual trust and respect for everyone involved in and with the business.

Toyota is regarded as one of the most efficient companies in the world because of the Toyota Production System (TPS) based on lean production and *kaizen* (continuous improvement) principles. These are at the heart of its approach to business strategy. The approach adopted by Toyota has resulted in the institutionalization of lean manufacturing skills and *kaizen*. Over 20 million suggestions in 40 years have been generated by the company's suggestion system which is only one aspect of its approach to continuous improvement. The company places great emphasis on teamwork that reflects a culture characterized by collaboration, cooperation, and trust. The company believes that teams are better at solving problems, and that people learn from each other.

In terms of its approach to HRD the principal emphasis is on training. The HR function itself is viewed as playing a key leadership approach in the company's improvement processes and has a coordination role when it comes to training. The training and development team is part of a broader 'Human System' which focuses on development, recruitment, and retention. The aim of the 'Human System' model is to make everyone a member of the Toyota culture. In the US a corporate university[1] (University of Toyota) has been created to provide training and consultancy on Toyota's business practices, particularly lean manufacturing. The principal strength of the company has always been its approach to on-the-job training although this has become increasingly supplemented with classroom training (although the latter was not greatly appreciated in the past). The company prefers the term on-the-job development because it is felt to be broader than training. This approach includes methods such as job rotation which reflects this broader development. Team leaders are trained as facilitators and instructors and do most of this classroom training. It is a requirement that anyone in this role has production experience. The increase in classroom training reflects the influence of globalization on the company. Employees are able to identify personal training opportunities which are referred to as 'self-initiated development'. The training of general managers involves learning about business planning and policy, Toyota Business Practices, and several other related issues. Most of this is handled by the Toyota Institute in Japan although job rotation is also a characteristic of this level.

Toyota has always stressed the importance of recruiting people who not only have the capacity to learn but also possess the motivation and desire to do so. The company is always trying to find ways to improve the training methods it uses because people are trained without slowing down the line. This is a challenging situation for anyone new to the job. This is because the TPS is so interconnected that to slow down one part affects the whole system. Standardized instruction methods are used across the company. Recently, the company has been trying to drive down costs and there are concerns that this is harming its long standing reputation for quality. In the past it has found ways of realigning its strategy and operations to cope with issues such as environmental concerns without resorting to a cost reduction strategy. It will be interesting to see how the next few years turn out.

Sources

[1] *The Times*, 7 August 2006: 35.

[2] Ulrich, D. and Brockbank, W. 2005 *The HR Value Proposition*. Boston, MA: Harvard Business School Press.

[3] Bryan, L. L. and Joyce, C. I. 2007. *Mobilising Minds: Creating Wealth from Talent in the 21st-Century Organisation*. New York: McGraw-Hill.

[4] Liker, J. K. and Meier, D. P. 2007. *Toyota Talent: Developing Your People the Toyota Way*. New York: McGraw-Hill.

[5] Morgan, M., Levitt, R. E. and Malek, W. 2007. *Executing Your Strategy: How to Break it Down and Get it Done*. Boston, MA: Harvard Business School Press.

[6] *The Times*, 1 March 2008: 73.

[7] Liker, J. K. and Hoseus, M. 2008. *Toyota Culture: The Heart and Soul of the Toyota Way*. New York: McGraw-Hill (written in collaboration with the Center for Quality People and Organisations).

Notes
1 See chapter 13.

Case questions

1. How would you describe Toyota's approach to HRD?

2. To what extent do HRD activities appear to be vertically and horizontally aligned?

3. What are the advantages and disadvantages of Toyota's approach to HRD?

Online resource centre

Visit the supporting online resource centre for additional material that will help you with your research, essays, assignments, and revision.

 www.oxfordtextbooks.co.uk/orc/mankin/

The Operational Role of Human Resource Development

Part 2 explains the operational role of human resource development. This role encompasses a wide range of activities that range from analysing the training needs of employees to evaluating the effectiveness of HRD interventions such as training courses, organization development projects, and career development sessions. In many respects these are the 'nuts and bolts' of human resource development.

The Role and Theory of Learning

Learning objectives

By the end of this chapter you should be able to:

* Appreciate the reasons why it is difficult to arrive at a universal definition of learning

* Explain the importance of adult learning theory for HRD practice

* Understand and explain the differences between psychological and sociological perspectives on learning

* Appreciate the role of several different approaches to learning: problem-solving, reflective practice, and self-directed learning and e-learning

* Understand the role of motivation to learn in adult learning

* Identify potential barriers to learning

Indicative content

■ Psychological theories of learning: behavioural, cognitive, and experiential

■ Learning styles and how they can help the HRD practitioner

■ The role of emotional intelligence in learning

■ Sociological perspectives on learning: social and situated learning

■ Single-loop and double-loop learning, deteuro learning, and action learning

■ The principles, role, and importance of reflective practice

■ Self-directed learning, e-learning, and blended learning

■ The role of motivation in adult learning

■ The role of the psychological contract

■ Potential barriers to learning

Key concepts

Psychological theories of learning: behavioural; cognitive; experiential

Sociological theories of learning: social learning; situated learning

Learning styles

Reflective practice

Self-directed learning

E-learning

Blended learning

Motivation to learn

Barriers to learning

4.1 **Introduction**

The previous chapters have explained the pivotal role of learning to the formulation, implementation, and review of HRD strategy and practice. Consequently, HRD strategies and processes now embrace a wide range of learning theories. The recognition of informal learning, incidental learning, and situated learning (the latter as a variant of social learning) has elevated the importance of the workplace as a context for learning. A study by Slotte et al. (2004) revealed that HRD practitioners attach great value to informal learning in the workplace (as part of an integrated strategy with formal interventions). For an increasing number of organizations learning in everyday work situations now takes primacy over learning in the classroom; although there is still a need for more empirical studies to support this claim (Poell and Van der Krogt, 2003):

> It could be argued that the most frequent and most important forms of learning are by-products of other activities without particular arrangements being made to facilitate learning . . . Even developing professional competence can be seen more or less as a by-product of becoming a member of a professional group. (Bowden and Marton, 2004: 57)

What is open to debate is whether workplace learning should be subject to direct and systematic HRD interventions that characterize traditional approaches to training and development. Or should the role of the HRD practitioner be to devise strategies that focus on developing an appropriate context through indirect interventions? This can be at the micro and macro levels of an organization and is often referred to as cultivating the learning climate of an organization (see strategic choices in chapter 3). In order to create an appropriate learning climate, HRD practitioners need to understand the strengths and limitations of a range of learning theories as well as the role of motivation in adult learning. Adult learning should be referred to as *andragogy* as opposed to *pedagogy* which refers to child learning. Yet it is the latter term that tends to be used to describe the study of learning processes at university level although undergraduates are clearly of an adult age.

Broadly speaking, learning theories can be categorized as either psychological or sociological. This means learning can be examined in terms of the *individual*, the *group* and the *organization* (the latter as a 'collection' or 'grouping together' of groups). Theories to explain individual learning have been produced primarily from a psychological perspective; these theories focus on human cognition and the development of representations or mental models of the world around us within an individual's mind (Bowden and Marton, 2004). This perspective underpins traditional approaches to education where knowledge is stored in books, articles, web-pages, lecture slides, and tutor hand-outs and is acquired by the student through reading, listening, and writing. To understand learning within group contexts it is necessary to understand sociological theories of learning. These argue that cognition is also situated in the workplace, distributed across group members and learning occurs as a result of the social interaction between group members. Knowledge that is socially constructed as a result of these interactions differs from the knowledge acquired by students as a result of reading, listening, and writing. As students you gain an insight into this type of learning when you become involved in group-based activities or when you chat with each other socially. Some of the key theorists are shown in figure 4.1. Psychological and sociological perspectives are shown as overlapping because this is not about an 'either–or' choice. The two perspectives are inter-related and mutually dependent on each other. Not surprisingly, there is no universal definition of learning although Jarvis (2006) has attempted to produce an overarching definition which combines a range of theories:

> The combination of processes whereby the whole person—body (genetic, physical and biological) and mind (knowledge, skills, attitudes, values, emotions, beliefs and senses) experiences a social situation, the perceived content of which is then transformed cognitively, emotively or practically (or through any combination) and integrated into the person's individual biography resulting in a changed (or more experienced) person. (p. 13)

This definition shows how difficult it is to produce a simple definition of the concept.

Employees are adults and yet the contribution of adult learning theory to HRD theory and practice has never been fully explored as it has been assumed that learning processes are the same for both children and adults (Yang, 2004). Holton et al. (2001) have made a similar point by suggesting that not enough attention has been given to adult learning in the literature on performance improvement and that HRD practitioners need to develop expertise in this area. This is not a straightforward task as there is no definitive theory of adult learning, rather:

> adult learning theory refers to a collection of several concepts and theories that explain how adults learn, and adult learning is reviewed as a process that adults engage in that results in a relatively long-term change in the domains of attitude, knowledge, and behaviour. (Yang, 2004: 130)

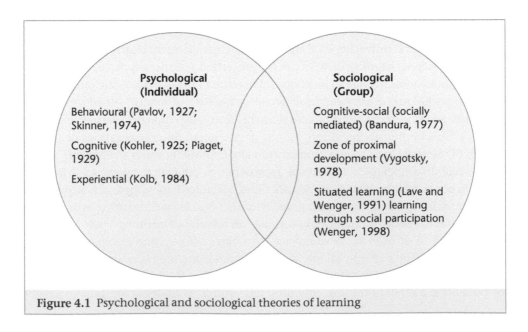

Figure 4.1 Psychological and sociological theories of learning

This involves the utilization of different learning theories, individually or in combination, depending on the nature and context of the HRD intervention. The challenge for HRD practitioners is to focus on those learning theories that are most relevant to a particular type of intervention and to build this into the design process (see chapter 7). Some examples are given in table 4.1 below. In contrast informal learning is usually unplanned, unstructured, and experiential in nature and the 'quality' of learning that takes place is often dependent on the 'learning competence' of the individual(s) involved. A distinction should also be made between conscious, subconscious, and unconscious learning as some learning will always remain inaccessible (Lee, 1996). These points are developed further below.

> **! TIPS AND HINTS**
>
> HRD practitioners need to work closely with line managers to help them understand the characteristics of informal learning and to develop their facilitation skills. The line manager is best placed to facilitate and nurture informal learning and assess its impact on employee performance.

> **INSIGHTS INTO PRACTICE**
>
> **Adult learning**
>
> Research shows that trade union organized adult learning interventions in the UK are having a positive effect on employee morale and helping to improve employee retention.
>
> **Source**
> Mahoney, C. 2007. A collective bargain. *People Management*, 6 September: 36–7.

Type of intervention	Learning theory involved
Basic skills training	Behavioural (see chapters 7 and 8)
Knowledge acquisition	Cognitive (see chapter 10)
Competence development	Experiential (see chapters 5 and 7) Situated (see chapters 10 and 11)
Problem-solving	Single- and double-loop (see this chapter) Action learning (see chapter 8)
Reflective practice	Learning styles (see chapter 7) Reflection-in-action/on-action (see chapter 15) Deutero (see chapter 15)
Workplace learning	Self-managed or self-directed learning (see chapters 7 and 8) Blended/e-learning (see chapters 7 and 8) Informal learning (see chapters 2 and 11)

Table 4.1 Learning theories and illustrative examples of interventions

MEDIA WATCH BOX

To train or not to train gardeners

The British television personality and gardener Rachel De Thame has upset providers of education and formal training in gardening by declaring that formal learning is not the most important thing a good gardener needs. Rather it is having a 'good eye'. She does not have any formal qualifications in gardening.

Source
Daily Express, 13 May 2008: 19.

4.2 Psychological learning theories

Traditional perspectives on learning within a training context have focused on psychological theories of learning; in particular, behavioural and cognitive theories. Consequently, traditional approaches to training and development have relied heavily on the notion of transfer of learning (sometimes referred to as transfer of training). Holton et al. (2003) define this as the degree to which individuals apply knowledge, skills, behaviours, and attitudes learned in training to their job role. Kim (2004) describes this as a socio-political process because:

> it requires that stakeholders having different interests in specific organisational contexts go through a negotiation process to define objectives or criteria for expected individual and organisational performance and to determine the extent to which training interventions are contributed. (p. 499)

Only about 10 to 15 per cent of employee training results in transfer to the workplace (Cromwell and Kolb, 2004). The implications of ineffective transfer of learning are discussed in detail in chapter 9 on evaluation. We will now look at the different types of learning.

Behavioural theory

Skills training through coaching, guided practice, and instruction are typical examples of the application of this learning theory in an organizational context. Behavioural learning theory focuses on behavioural outcomes as a result of a learning process (i.e. the purpose of learning is to produce specific, prescribed behaviours). From this perspective learning is portrayed as 'a mechanistic and involuntary process over which learners can exert little control' (Starbuck and Hedberg, 2001: 330). An oft quoted definition of this type of learning in textbooks on training and development is that 'learning is a relatively permanent change in behaviour that occurs as a result of practice or experience' (Bass and Vaughn, 1967: 8).

The work of Pavlov (1927) and Skinner (1974) is normally used to illustrate this type of learning. Pavlov's research showed how dogs would salivate when presented with a dish of food. At the same time a bell was rung to indicate to the dogs that the food was available. After a period of time the dogs would salivate when the bell was rung even if no food was made available. The dogs' behaviour had been altered through a form of conditioning; they had learnt to behave differently because of the association of the sound of a bell with food. This is referred to as *classical* or *respondent conditioning* (the dogs initial salivation when presented with the food was an unconditioned response).

Skinner (1974) built on the work of Pavlov by arguing that respondent conditioning does not alter an animal's actual behaviour but simply the timing of its behaviour. He is credited with the concept of *operant conditioning* which is when animal behaviour is shaped by experiences in its environment; in particular, by rewards or punishments (i.e. behaviour can be modified through positive or negative reinforcement, although the former is usually more effective). The reward needs to follow immediately after the desired response. As a result the animal will continue to repeat the desired response while it continues to be rewarded for doing so. I am certain dog owners will recognize the use of 'treats' to encourage obedience in their pet. This is a good example of a reward being linked to a specific behaviour.

MEDIA WATCH BOX

Behavioural learning in China

The Bainen Toy Factory in China has a great many rules which its employees must learn. If any rule is infringed the employee is fined. Rules include no laughing or talking at work, a fine of two hours' wages for each minute the employee turns up late, a fine or dismissal for poor work, and a fine for working too slowly. Employees are paid too little to save any money and if they want to leave the company they must forfeit six weeks' wages which few can afford to do.[1]

This institutionalization of employee behaviour is further reinforced by the requirement that all employees sleep in dormitories on the same site as the production facilities. See also the Singapore Airlines case in chapter 3.

Source
[1] *Daily Mail*, 16 August 2007: 54–5.

Rote learning is typical of this approach. This is often required for basic skills training for jobs that involve frequent, if not continuous, repetition of tasks (which need to be carried out precisely and accurately). An example of this is the standard list of statements and questions that a customer services administrator is required to comply with every time he/she contacts a customer. Another example is an automotive production assembly operative who has responsibility for fixing a component (e.g. the front passenger side door) to a car as it moves along the assembly line. I have used the latter example because I

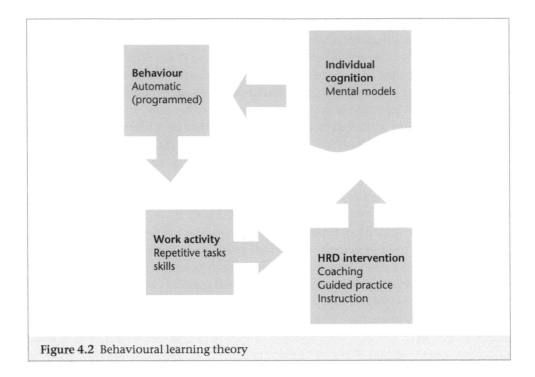

Figure 4.2 Behavioural learning theory

recall my first visit to an automotive factory in 1990. I spent some time watching an operative complete the same task over and over again. The production manager explained that a detailed breakdown of actions, including precisely timed arm and hand movements, underpinned how and what this operative did. Restaurants and coffee shops offer further examples; for instance, the frequency of terms such as 'have a nice meal' followed up by 'is everything okay for you?'; or the way a barista states 'enjoy' as a take-away cup of coffee is thrust into your hand. These automatic phrases have been programmed into staff

MEDIA WATCH BOX

Is age an issue?

Although the brain loses some nerve connections as we grow older it compensates for this by creating new ones. Consequently, people's capacity to process information and learn continues as they age. It is behaviour that is difficult to change.[1]

Sir Alex Ferguson, the highly successful football manager of Manchester United, claims the secret of his success is a willingness to embrace new ideas.[2]

Sources
[1] *People Management*, 17 April 2008: 32–3.
[2] *The Times*, 24 May 2008: 112.

(although there can be a dissonance with body language!). This type of learning is best suited to the workplace rather than the classroom, although it does underpin instructional approaches to training and education.

> **! TIPS AND HINTS**
>
> Understanding behavioural learning theory can help the line manager to better understand the implications of interventions based solely on 'learning through socialization' (see chapter 3).

Cognitive theory

Knowledge acquisition through reading (e.g. books, articles, websites), independently or as part of an education programme, are typical examples of the application of this learning theory in an organizational context. The behavioural theory of learning, with its emphasis on behavioural change, ignores the acquisition of knowledge and the implications this has for how an individual conceptualizes the world around him/herself (Ramsden, 1992). From a cognitive perspective learning can be defined as 'a qualitative change in a person's way of seeing, experiencing, understanding, conceptualising something in the real world' (Marton and Ramsden, 1988: 271). This involves the processing of information inside individual human minds. Consequently, cognitive theory is essentially about how we think (Jarvis, 2006) and how we think is the result of learning which involves the development of representations or mental models of the world with a high degree of general applicability (Patriotta, 2003).

From this perspective knowledge is understood as information that can be acquired and processed by an individual (i.e. knowledge about something, such as 'I know how tall Mount Everest is' or 'I can recite all the songs of Bob Dylan'). This type of learning is something that cannot be easily observed or measured empirically (Jarvis, 2001) although schools, colleges, and universities attempt to do so through assessments such as coursework and examinations. In many respects this is about treating knowledge as an object or commodity, as something external to individuals that can be internalized. In contrast it can be very difficult to teach practical knowledge (often referred to as tacit knowledge, tacit knowing, know-how, or practical skills) in classroom settings, as many readers will surely vouch. If transfer of learning from the classroom to the workplace is to be successful then learners need to be able to tackle practical activities in the workplace as soon as possible. One way in which trainers and teachers attempt to address the lack of practical knowledge in classroom-based learning is through the utilization of practical exercises and activities (although this can be constrained by such factors as budget, venue, and number of trainers). Leading theorists include Kohler (1925) who studied the chimpanzees and argued they could solve problems through insight, and Piaget (1929) who identified that childhood is made up of several stages of intellectual development.

Examples of cognitive learning include staff attending seminars where they remain passive and select what interests them and what seems relevant to their job and/or organization. They may or may not take notes and may or may not read any material after the

> **◉⟩ INSIGHTS INTO PRACTICE**
>
> ## A personal reflection
>
> I once had to design a problem-solving course for a group of engineers. This meant making the course as practical as possible in order to satisfy their learning preferences. My solution? The course focused on the design and construction of racing cars built from Meccano sets. At different stages over two days they had to race their cars against each other and identify improvements to their designs. Whilst it was a highly enjoyable experience for the participants and was subsequently shown to have had an impact on their approach to problem-solving in the workplace, methods such as this remain imperfect simulations only of workplace activity.
>
> **Source**
> The author.

seminar (it is not uncommon for individuals to place the seminar material on a bookcase and never look at it again). Waiters in restaurants may not know how to cook, but having knowledge about the menu is an important aspect of superior customer service (e.g. what produce is in season, what produce has been sourced locally, how long different choices take to cook, what specials are on offer etc). In leading chains of coffee shops baristas attend training courses to learn about the process of coffee making, where the coffee is sourced from (e.g. is it Fairtrade?), and the stages in getting the coffee beans from the farmer to the customer.

> **MEDIA WATCH BOX**
>
> ## Learning the Starbucks' values
>
> Starbucks' business strategy is underpinned by six core values which include to 'provide a great work environment'. The company refers to its employees as 'partners' and provides them with a structured training programme that involves learning about the origins of the company so that partners can live and breathe Starbucks' values. The company has a strong commitment to training. In 2007 the company closed its stores in the US (all 7,100) in order to run a nationwide hands-on training session for all its employees (135,000) aimed at deepening partners' passion for coffee (which in turn should transform the customer experience).
>
> **Sources**
> http://www.starbucks.co.uk (accessed 14 April 2008).
> http://www.guardian.co.uk/business/2008/feb/26/starbucks (accessed 14 April 2008).
> http://news.bbc.co.uk/2/hi/americas/7266065.stm (accessed 14 April 2008).

Can animals think?

The behavioural perspective on how animals learn is starting to be challenged. Many researchers are starting to embrace the notion that some animals can think. It has also been shown that the human language is no longer a purely cognitive ability but is equally the product of some form of innate programming.

Source
Gould, J. L. and Gould, C. G. 1998. Reasoning in animals. *Scientific American*, Winter, 9 (4): 52–9.

Experiential learning theory

Experiential learning theory sits in the cognitive camp of theories and helps us understand how an individual learns something. This includes learning both explicit knowledge *and* practical knowledge. Learning is defined in terms of a cyclical and continuous process (Kolb, 1984) whereby individuals learn from experience (often from deliberate experimentation or trial and error; or from making a mistake while doing something else). This perspective can be traced back to the work of Dewey (1916) who argued that everyone is able to learn from experience. He argued that the starting point for learning was a real world problem or situation which acts as a catalyst for inquiry and reflection. This stage is followed by three further stages comprising: reflection, ideas generation, and application and testing (in real situations). Kolb based his experiential learning cycle,

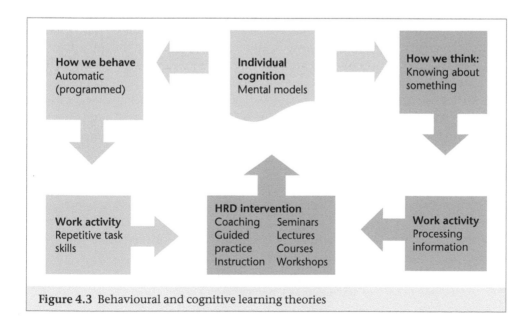

Figure 4.3 Behavioural and cognitive learning theories

which is often referred to as the Kolb cycle, on Dewey's four stages. The four stages in the Kolb cycle are: having a concrete experience which is personal and immediate (this corresponds to Dewey's empirical situation); observation and reflection (reviewing the concrete experience); abstract conceptualization (drawing conclusions and generalizing about concepts and theories); and active experimentation (testing new concepts or concepts in new situations). The humanistic perspective discussed in chapters 2 and 3 is largely dependent on this form of learning (Fenwick, 2006).

The experiential learning cycle is probably the most popular learning theory in use today by HRD practitioners. Because it describes how people learn, independently of any particular situational constraints, such as formal or informal settings (Yorks, 2005) it can be applied to a range of activities and interventions or organizational settings. It can be used by the HRD practitioner to underpin the design of formal interventions or by an individual to guide their informal learning in the workplace. The latter requires individuals

---

MEDIA WATCH BOX

Learning from experience and career progression

Much of the learning that takes place in the workplace tends to be context specific although some aspects of this learning can be transferred to other contexts, such as a different organization. Unlike education which is made explicit in CVs most applicants only infer learning from experience in an 'experience' section. Consequently, there is an argument for recognizing this learning through accreditation by universities. This is a potentially lucrative market for universities.[1]

The questions that need to be asked are these: Should such learning be formally captured in this way? Can any formal accreditation process truly capture all aspects of this type of learning? Much informal learning involves tacit knowledge (i.e. practical knowledge) which is notoriously difficult to articulate and share with others (see chapter 10) suggesting any accreditation process would reflect a superficial understanding only or require incredibly complex and time-consuming processes. This argument can be countered partly by referring to vocational qualifications in countries such as Finland and the UK, which are competence-based and therefore designed to measure certain aspects of practical knowledge. The next example illustrates that individuals do not need to have their experience measured through accreditation; what really matters is the added-value that the experience itself provides.

Many women who take a career break to raise children often feel apprehensive about returning to work after a gap of several years. This is where using a work experience route can help them experiment with different jobs and contexts.[2]

Sources
[1] *The Times Higher Education Supplement: Work-Based Learning*, 11 May 2007: 6–7.
[2] *The Guardian* (Saturday *Work* supplement), 11 August 2007: 1.

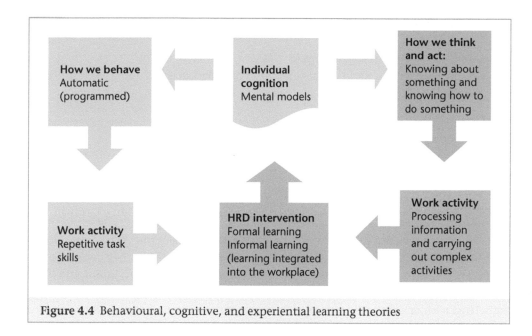

Figure 4.4 Behavioural, cognitive, and experiential learning theories

to understand learning theory and this is discussed in more detail below in the section on reflective practice. Chapter 7 discusses in detail how HRD practitioners utilize the Kolb cycle when designing formal interventions.

 **TIPS AND HINTS**

Line managers can ask employees to complete a learning styles questionnaire as part of the appraisal process so that the implications can be discussed as part of an individual's personal development plan.

However, individuals tend to have experiences that are grounded in social interactions and in this sense experiential learning can be described as a bridge between purely psychological and purely sociological perspectives on learning. The reflective observation, abstract conceptualization and active experimentation stages normally take place within the individual's head, while the concrete experience stage often is reliant on social interaction. Whenever I have asked students to apply Kolb's cycle to a real-life situation that they have experienced recently, they invariably cite examples of the concrete experience involving at least one other person (with the fourth stage often focusing on doing something differently or behaving differently within a social context). You can have a go at doing this yourself by completing activity 4.1 (even better, share and discuss your results with other students). For learning to take place all four stages must be completed.

Although Kolb identified four learning styles associated with the experiential cycle, it is the Honey and Mumford (1992) learning styles typology that has been popularized and favoured by HRD practitioners. Learning styles, sometimes referred to as learning

ACTIVITY 4.1

Using the experiential learning cycle
As an individual think about a recent situation or experience and apply the learning cycle to it:

The concrete experience was . . .
My reflections on the experience are . . .
The conclusions I drew are . . .
Next time I plan to . . .

preferences, explain how information is organized and processed (i.e. how we prefer to *think* about something). Unlike Kolb, who focused on learning behaviour, Honey and Mumford decided to focus on general management behaviour as they believed managers rarely think about learning behaviour (Yorks, 2005). Honey and Mumford (1992) also identified four learning styles: activist; reflector; theorist; pragmatist. Each one is associated with one of the four stages in the experiential learning cycle as follows: activist (having a concrete experience); reflector (observation and reflection); theorist (abstract conceptualization); and, pragmatist (active experimentation). Each of these four learning styles is explained in more detail in table 4.2.

Activists	Enjoy the immediacy of new and different experiences. They like to have a go at doing things often 'diving in at the deep end' and not thinking through the implications of their actions. They can get bored very quickly and start to look for new experiences. They tend to dislike classroom-based learning methods where they are passive (e.g. seminar, lecture, information-giving sessions)
Reflectors	Prefer to think through the potential implications of any activity before doing it. They tend to be cautious and thoughtful, and quieter in group discussions. They like to listen to and observe other people before putting forward their own point of view. They dislike learning methods that 'force' them into the limelight, such as role-play
Theorists	Like to think things through in a logical, methodical, and systematic manner. They like to assimilate all the facts before acting or making what they would describe as a 'rational' decision. They have a strong preference for reading and thinking, and like to take their time to think things through before joining a discussion. They may not like the immediacy of problem-solving and decision-making that characterizes many training interventions
Pragmatists	They are keen to try out new ideas, theories, and techniques to see if they actually work in practice. Consequently, they enjoy experimenting with different ways of doing something. But they can be impatient with discussions that are wide-ranging and open-ended. They are very practical individuals who enjoy solving problems and making practical decisions. They can be dismissive of training interventions that appear to offer no apparent benefit (i.e. the 'Why am I here?' syndrome)

Table 4.2 Learning styles
Source: Table has been created from the description of learning styles by Honey and Mumford (1992)

Learning styles are not theories of learning. Instead, they acknowledge how individuals can vary in their response to learning situations, methods, and techniques. This information can be used in a variety of ways:

- By HRD practitioners to inform the design process (see chapter 7)

- By the learner to identify appropriate learning methods to develop his/her approach to CPD; to identify weaker preferences that might need to be improved in order to develop the learner's overall approach to learning and CPD (i.e. become a more proficient learner) (see chapter 15)

- By the line manager to inform decisions about how best subordinates can achieve their personal development plans; for instance, during appraisal discussions (see chapter 6)

However, it is important to recognize that the Kolb and Honey and Mumford learning styles questionnaires are self-rating instruments and, therefore, subject to bias or misinterpretation that may render some results questionable. Although Honey and Mumford have published norm table data this is still based on relative strengths within the learner and not in relation to others. That said, such data is still of interest as it suggests that differences do exist across different professions. For instance, Burns (2001: 32) notes that 'entrepreneurs tend to learn by doing. They act first and then learn from the outcomes of the action' and that this is an integral aspect of an incremental decision-making process favoured by many entrepreneurs.

Yorks (2005) makes an important observation about these learning theories when he argues that emotions are an integral aspect of learning but are often neglected in the literature. This can be seen, for instance in the abstract conceptualization stage of the Kolb cycle which involves the use of logic and ideas to understand problems or situations rather than feelings. This is very much a rationalist perspective. The role of emotions is usually referred to as the *affective* dimension to learning. Emotions comprise a combination of the physical and the cognitive, both of which affect individual behaviour and learning (Jarvis, 2006). Over the last decade or so there has been increased interest in the concept of emotional intelligence, a person-centred approach to learning which emphasizes emotions. Yet there have been very few empirical studies of development programmes that focus on emotional intelligence (Clarke, 2006).

Key concept   Emotional intelligence

Emotional intelligence is about dealing with emotions effectively and can be viewed as an ability or competency (McEnrue and Groves, 2006).

Relatively straightforward examples of emotions that are associated with learning are a sense of achievement and a sense of failure. Yorks (2005) cites Short and Yorks (2002) to explain how HRD practitioners can take emotions into account, including: recognizing the different emotional needs of individuals and creating an environment conducive to the discussion of emotions and feelings. I know from my own experiences that in Britain many individuals are reticent to discuss their feelings and emotions. However, people will open up if they trust you. This was certainly the case when I facilitated open and frank discussions amongst management teams as part of a long term development strategy; or when I carried out career counselling sessions. This takes time, effort, and consistency of approach to achieve.

MEDIA WATCH BOX

Too much emotion?

A 'therapy culture' is pervading the UK education system with children and young people becoming anxious about under-achieving at school and university. This culture is characterized by a preoccupation by government ministers and some educators with asking pupils to share their feelings and emotions as part of the education process. This criticism follows on from the implementation of lessons on the social and emotional aspects of learning in schools.

Source
Daily Mail, 12 June 2008: 3.

ACTIVITY 4.2

Search for an academic journal article on emotional intelligence. Read it and then summarize the article in less than 250 words.

4.3 Sociological learning theories

From a sociological perspective learning is deeply influenced by the social context within which it occurs (Reynolds et al., 2002). 'Conventional psychology views learning as an individual process and normally excludes social and political factors of learning' (Yang, 2004: 130). This is often cited as a criticism of university education as learning is usually separate from the work or social context (Lave and Wenger, 1991; Bowden and Marton, 2004). This can be offset partly by encouraging students in an educational context to develop a deep, rather than surface approach to learning. A deep approach to learning involves really trying to get to grips with understanding a problem or subject. For instance, students studying an organizational behaviour (OB) module look for links and relationships between different topics and try to develop a holistic understanding of how and why people behave as they do in organizations. When answering an examination question on organizational culture as well as discussing the principal theories and models and applying them to organizational contexts, they will also demonstrate an understanding of how culture is linked, for example, to leadership and motivation theories. In contrast, surface learning involves a cursory and rudimentary understanding of discrete topics. In an examination answer theories and concepts will be presented in a highly descriptive manner, few if any links will be made to organization contexts, and no attempt will be made to explain any relationships with other topics. It is associated with rote learning (Bowden and Marton, 2004).

Situated learning

Situated learning is a variation on social learning or as it is often termed, social cognitive theory and is about developing individual competence (i.e. the ability to do a particular job to a high standard). Discussions with colleagues, mentors, and specialist experts, usually within the same community or social network, is a typical example of this type of learning in a work context. Initially social learning theory focused on learning from others in a passive way through observation and imitation (Bandura, 1977); and was essentially, a refinement of the behaviourist perspective on learning. In recognizing the importance of observation the theory acknowledged the importance of cognitive processes as part of individual learning. However, it was noted that inquiry is restricted to what is directly observable (i.e. what people do and how they behave) (Bowden and Marton, 2004). As a result of this people might learn inefficient ways of working, develop inappropriate behaviours, or simply lack the ability to decipher some of the tacit skills used by experienced workers (Marchington and Wilkinson, 1996).

> **! TIPS AND HINTS**
>
> Bandura's (1977) theory of social cognitive learning illustrates why it is important for line managers to act as role models: employees observe the behaviour of managers and respond accordingly.

Subsequently, social learning theory has evolved with the situated learning perspective (Lave and Wenger, 1991) focusing on the organization as a social and cultural context within which learning takes place. Learning is *situated* in a real-life or work-setting and is a social activity which 'allows people to hold learning conversations, where they solve problems, tell *stories* and share insights, from hunches and feelings to analysis and well-researched ideas' (Sallis and Jones, 2002: 96). The focus is on shared practice, such as collaborating in the same specialist area, as university academics tend to do, or sharing a common interest. In this sense, learning is a by-product of the learners' participation in social practices which do not necessarily have learning as their primary aim (Bowden and Marton, 2004) but is also 'an integral and inseparable aspect of social practice' (Lave and Wenger, 1991: 31). Within this shared context the focus is on the progression from novice/apprentice- to expert-status. Lave and Wenger (1991) describe this process as *legitimate peripheral participation* (LPP). Lave and Wenger (1991) are highly critical of formal, traditional approaches to learning which focus on the acquisition of explicit knowledge; for them, learning does not simply take place in the mind but 'concerns the whole person acting in the world' (p. 49). This perspective has also been termed *learning through social participation* by Wenger (1998).

This strand of learning draws upon the work of educational psychologists such as Vygotsky who worked in the Soviet Union. Vygotsky (1978) was interested in the relationship of individual human beings with both their physical and social environments. He felt that the development process was 'deeply rooted in the links between individual

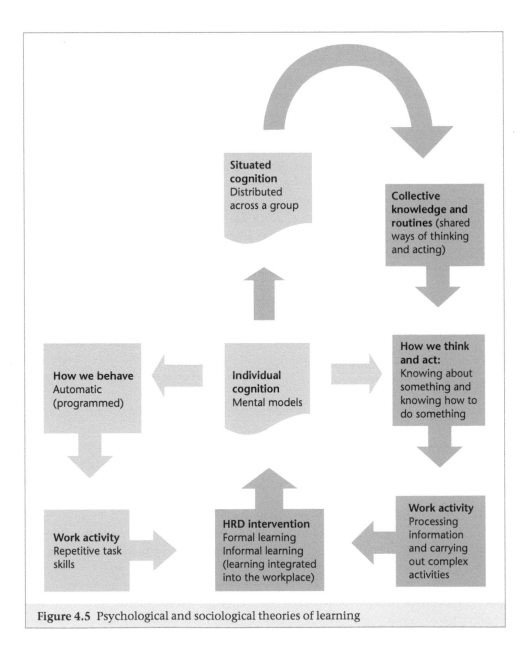

Figure 4.5 Psychological and sociological theories of learning

and social history' (p. 30) and that learning was a profoundly social process. He proposed the concept of the *zone of proximal development* to explain the influence of the social context on an individual's learning and development. This is usually described as constructivist theory, and although there are several different constructivist positions it is not intended to go into each of these at this stage. The constructivist approach emphasizes how the individual constructs meaning from his/her participation in social activities (Gergen, 1995). From this constructivist perspective the reality of the world is always changing and knowledge is transitory (Wallerstein, 2004) and the subject of continuous, ongoing debates and exchanges (Seiler, 2004). Unlike cognitive theory, constructivist theory argues all knowledge is personal and learning is an individual's construction of meaning out of experience (Reynolds et al., 2002: 22–4).

Although Vygotsky focused on children his constructivist ideas have influenced the development of Lave and Wenger's theory of situated learning. It can be seen also that psychological perspectives have informed the work of Lave and Wenger. For instance, Dewey (1916) referred to above, believed that learning takes place all the time when individuals interact, reflect, and think (Elkjaer, 2000). Traditionally HRD practitioners have focused on learning within a formally constituted team or group (e.g. work unit; project team; task group; quality control circle; etc). Formal work-groups and teams are an important source of learning (Rainbird et al., 2004) but much of the current interest in situated learning is focused on informal groups, such as communities of practice and social networks (see chapters 10 and 11 for a more detailed discussion). Practices used to encourage formal team learning are not necessarily transferable to an informal context. There is currently a wide ranging debate on this issue.

The arguments about whether or not learning is essentially individual or social remain largely rhetorical (Griffin, 2001) despite the proliferation of theories about learning being attributed to communities, organizations, and society itself (Griffin and Brownhill, 2001). It is difficult to identify precise boundaries between individual and social learning. Indeed, a study by Mankin (2007) has found that psychological and sociological perspectives on learning are inextricably linked in a form of symbiotic relationship (see figure 4.5 and chapter 11).

4.4 **Learning approaches to problem-solving**

Learning approaches that focus on problem-solving span individual, group, and organizational learning. Argyris (1995) focuses on the individual as an agent of the organization in his discussion of *action science* which distinguishes between Models 1 and 2 of theory-in-use. Single and double loop learning reflect the type of learning that is associated with Models 1 and 2 respectively. Single-loop learning occurs when an individual realizes a mistake has been made and subsequently corrects that mistake and/or identifies a way of preventing it from happening again (i.e. an incremental improvement). For example, some data is entered onto a computer system so that a report can be produced; and when the report is checked a mistake, such as incorrect figures, is spotted. The computer system is amended and a new, correct version of the report is produced along with a way of preventing such a transcription error from reoccurring. Such learning is taking place daily in organizations. However, when using double-loop learning individuals are encouraged to ask 'what if' questions. In the previous example individuals might question why the report is produced in that way or why there is a need for the report in the first place. Such questioning may run counter to the organizational culture and, consequently, double-loop learning may not be encouraged in an organization where conformance and compliance prevail.

TIPS AND HINTS

In many contexts using problem-solving processes and techniques is a very useful way of building credibility for the role of the HRD practitioner as the focus is on finding practical solutions to practical problems.

The term theory-in-use is used to describe actual practice. Argyris and Schön (1974) identified that there can be a significant difference between the theories espoused by practitioners and the theories that they actually practise. I have come across many examples of this in the past and concluded some years ago that this contradiction often reflects a practitioner's unwillingness or inability to reflect critically on their own practice. Single-loop learning reinforces the theory-in-use espoused by an organization. Double-loop learning questions and challenges the existing theory-in-use when practice is seen to be different to what the organization espouses.

Another leading approach to problem-solving is action learning which was developed by Revans (1983, 1991). It is a form of learning-by-doing that involves a group approach to solving problems encountered in the workplace. A small team or 'set' is established and members share ideas and experiences in order to identify a solution. The group does not disband until the problem has been resolved. Revans developed the formula $L = P + Q$ to explain action learning: learning (L) comprises programmed knowledge (P) in combination with insightful questioning (Q). A structured and disciplined approach is required. Action learning implies both individual and organizational development because any action on the problem changes both the problem and the person who is acting upon it (Pedlar, 1991). Several assumptions underpin action learning:

- Learning occurs from action in real situations
- Learning and understanding come from reflection
- Learning has a social dimension
- The actual work context is the best place to test ideas

Additionally, line management must be involved and committed to the project. During my time as a total quality manager in the early 1990s improvement project teams used action learning, in combination with a systematic approach to problem-solving, to address quality problems; often producing significant results.

4.5 Learning approaches to reflective practice

Reflective practice can take place in isolation and within a social context. Indeed, reflection within a social context is often more effective (van Woerkom, 2004). Social interaction, in the form of collaborative discussions for instance, acts as a catalyst for reflection by and between individuals. Schön (1991) developed the idea of reflective practice because traditional approaches to educating professionals focused on explicit knowledge (which he referred to as propositional knowledge) which does not take into account the realities of professional practice; which, as explained above, involves the development of professional competence through the acquisition of practical knowledge (i.e. tacit knowledge or know-how).

Key concept   Reflective practice

Reflective practice involves thinking critically about specific incidents and examining what happened, how it happened and why it happened. The outcome of this process is often some form of learning that involves an adjustment to how we think and act in the world.

Tacit knowledge is difficult to articulate: 'often we cannot say what it is that we know' (Schön, 1991: 49) (for instance, to use a simple analogy, try to write down some instructions that will explain to someone else how to ride a bike). In arriving at an explanation of reflective practice he differentiates between *reflection-on-action* and *reflection-in-action*. Professional practitioners reflect on the knowledge they have; but they 'often think about what they are doing, sometimes even while doing it' (ibid.: 50), particularly when that

MEDIA WATCH BOX

Changing manager mindsets in the UK

According to Henley Management College there are too many managers in the UK who are entrenched in old mindsets and failing to adapt to changing work practices such as flexible working. Less than 20 per cent of managers have had any training in how to adjust their management style from one based on all staff being physically located together to one based on flexible work arrangements. The key issue revolves around managers trusting their employees.[1]

A short supporting article compares some managers to the character of David Brent from the Ricky Gervais comedy *The Office*.

Source
[1] *The Times*, 28 May 2005: 59.

reflection is triggered by 'surprise' (i.e. something unexpected happens). Schön's concept of reflective practice is discussed in more detail in chapter 15 along with other perspectives on the topic.

Reflective practice involves the questioning and challenging of prevailing beliefs and assumptions and is intimately linked to the concepts of double-loop learning and deutero learning. Deutero learning is learning to understand how you learn. Learning how to learn provides the foundation for all other skills (Carnevale et al., 1990) and is a critical component of continuing professional development (see chapter 15). There is still a need to carry out more research into the operationalization of reflective practice. Many students on professional development programmes (as well as degree and post-grad courses) struggle to get to grips with the concept. This approach also underpins national policy in countries like Finland where there is a government commitment to improving the learning to learn skills of the poorly educated (Finland's Ministry of Education, 2008).

INSIGHTS INTO PRACTICE

Managers and reflective practice

The workplace is providing managers with plenty of opportunities to learn but many lack an awareness or understanding of how they can learn from these experiences. This requires managers to focus on learning how to learn, a process that can be helped through the analysis of learning styles. Over the years different approaches to management development have come and gone. A recurring theme of these has been a lack of appreciation of underpinning learning theory.

Source
Mumford, A. 2004. Going the extra mile. *People Management*, 25 November 2004: 40–1.

4.6 Learning approaches to self-directed learning and e-learning

Self-directed learning (SDL) reflects the extent to which individuals are believed to be taking more responsibility for their own learning (see the 'learning continuum' discussion in chapter 2). Often this is being driven by an individual's career aspirations; in other cases it is being driven by the organization (e.g. as a consequence of an organizational commitment to lifelong learning which flows from the organization's values). The traditional view of this approach, often encapsulated in the past in the concept of distance learning, is of an individual learning in isolation. This is both inaccurate and overly simplistic. Whilst the individual takes responsibility for identifying their learning needs and managing the learning process (including: identifying and evaluating the learning approach), as with reflective practice this form of learning can also take place within a social context in which individuals share their knowledge with others. Both the individual learner and the organization benefit from this type of learning. As Smith (2002: 111) comments:

> there is considerable commercial value in encouraging employees to become effective self-directed learners such that they can develop and pursue their learning goals and outcomes that contribute to competitiveness without the need for all learning to occur when there is direct training by an instructor.

Increasingly technology is playing an important role in this approach to learning. I suspect every reader has heard of the term e-learning. E-learning emphasizes cognitive learning; and to date has not produced any new theory of learning (Reynolds et al., 2002). Although technology may provide an efficient system for the transmission of explicit knowledge, it cannot replace the benefits of social interaction (see *Media watch* box). However, there is plenty of evidence to support the existence of on-line communities which function in a similar, but ultimately less effective way, than communities whose members are physically located together. Face-to-face contact engenders a greater degree of trust between community members; and this has been shown to be the case with academic communities in the business schools of UK new universities (Mankin, 2007).

(•) INSIGHTS INTO PRACTICE

The power of telling stories

People can learn from each other through sharing stories. A one-day workshop on storytelling organized by Openreach (part of UK company BT) was designed to help learners (in this case managers) improve skills in communications and persuasion. As part of the workshop learners were asked to create a story together. A spokesperson for the company argues that this type of intervention is ideally suited to firms operating in people-intensive markets.

Source
Syedin, H. 2007. Tell-tale influence. *People Management*, 15 November: 30–5.

To date four types of e-learning appear to have emerged: web-based training which tends not to involve any support from HRD practitioners (i.e. treated very much like a distance learning approach); supported on-line learning which involves on-line trainer support; e-learning community which involves on-line knowledge sharing amongst a group of learners (and can be supported by an online facilitator); and, informal e-learning whereby learning occurs as a result of on-line communications with others who can be internal or external to the organization (Sloman and Reynolds, 2003).

In recent years there has been a move away from pure e-learning to blended learning in which a range of learning methods, underpinned by a range of learning theories, are combined or blended together. Blended learning has emerged as a result of e-learning not being the panacea many practitioners and theorists first thought it would be. Blended learning incorporates e-learning as part of a planned blend or mix of other learning

> **Key concept**   E-learning
>
> E-learning is a learning and development delivery system that relies on technology and normally requires the learner to engage in self-directed study. It is not a learning theory.

strategies. It tends to be more effective (for the learner) and often more efficient (for the organization). In terms of learning theory, blended learning:

> Provides traditional social interaction forums, and uses technology to create links to repositories of information that can be used to share knowledge and to learn. (Macpherson et al., 2004: 300)

INSIGHTS INTO PRACTICE

A personal reflection

In the mid-1990s I experimented with the integration of computer-based training in workshop-based soft skills training (e.g. training on Powerpoint as part of a presentation skills workshop; CBT video-based business games as part of a management development workshop). In approaching the design of these interventions, along with a skilled IT training consultant, I adopted the same approach as normal (i.e. the utilization of cognitive, experiential, and social learning theories). This illustrates how design strategies for blended learning are underpinned by existing learning theory and how technological approaches to learning can complement face-to-face social interaction on more traditional training interventions. Of course, the technology has become a lot more sophisticated since then.

Source
The author.

MEDIA WATCH BOX

Blended learning

Regardless of advances in technology underlying learning methodologies will remain the same. The importance of social capital (see chapter 2) means that learning through face-to-face social interaction will remain a critical component of an organization's approach to learning and development.

Source
People Management, 12 June 2008: 21.

4.7 **The role of motivation in adult learning**

The motivation to learn has been studied in relation to formal learning interventions (i.e. training). Noe (1986) defines the motivation to learn as a trainee's desire to learn the content of training and development activities. Analysis of the motivation to learn at the individual level tends to assume strong intrinsic motivation (Garavan et al., 2004) such as self-esteem, recognition, a better quality of life, and self-confidence, as well as self-actualization (Knowles (1970, 1984) cited in Waddill and Marquardt, 2003: 408). Unfortunately this topic is still relatively under-researched. However, the motivation to learn is felt to be an important pre-condition of learning (Naquin and Holton, 2003) and for the transfer of learning from the classroom to the workplace (Mathieu and Martineau, 1997). The results of a survey study by Naquin and Holton (2003) led them to conclude that motivation:

> cannot be thought of as just motivation to learn or train. Because both learning and performance outcomes are desired from learning events, the motivation construct must encompass both motivation to learn and motivation to perform using that learning . . . and that such a re-conceptualisation might lead to new practices aimed at enhancing motivation to improve work through learning. For instance, pre-training interventions designed to address *both* the learners' motivation to train and motivation to transfer can serve to enhance the training effectiveness. (p. 368; emphasis in original)

❗ TIPS AND HINTS

Both the HRD practitioner and line manager need to devote effort and time to understanding how individual learners are motivated. This may be more time consuming than making generic assumptions about their motivation but ultimately time invested at an early stage in the design process can have a potentially significant impact on the learning outcomes and effectiveness of any intervention.

Key reasons why and how learners are motivated to learn include:

- Learners decide the need for training (as opposed to being imposed. When a training and development practitioner the author often encountered individuals on training workshops who, when asked about their personal objectives, would comment: 'I don't know why I'm here', 'I got a memo from my manager telling me I had to attend').

- Previous experiences on training courses (which can be negative, de-motivating, or positive, motivating).

- Supportive work context that will encourage transfer of learning and further experimentation/learning (post-training reviews by the line manager can help here but if the training content is not relevant or the learner is under too much pressure from work routines, then it is likely that any potential benefits will be dissipated and the learner will be less motivated to attend future training workshops). A supportive workplace encompasses peers and line managers. A research study by Cromwell and Kolb (2004) shows that the support of peers is influential in the transfer of learning process while various studies have highlighted the important role of line managers in the transfer process. Gilley et al. (2002) argue that learning fails to be transferred because no one takes responsibility for owning the process.

The performance of the most able employees can be impacted by a low motivation to learn. In some organizations there will be individuals who have poor numeracy and literacy skills. There is a body of research that suggests that workplace literacy skills are a key factor in the trainability of individuals (Bates and Holton, 2004). I can recall several instances when I encountered resistance to training because of this issue (in one particular case the individual was terrified of being asked to write something on a flipchart by his fellow trainees who were oblivious to his problem. He spent the entire two day workshop developing strategies to avoid such a situation and, consequently for him little learning took place and the experience simply reinforced his belief that he should avoid training courses).

However, there is a need for much more research into the motivation to learn in informal contexts. Factors which appear to influence employee's motivation include:

- The existence of a supportive learning climate (macro-learning climate)
- Support from immediate team/community/network colleagues (micro-learning climate)
- Job satisfaction (linked to a sense of belonging)
- The relevance of the learning to present and future roles (learning embedded in and focusing on professional practice is important here)

A study by Egan et al. (2004) suggests that job satisfaction is associated with the organizational learning culture of an organization (i.e. the macro-learning climate referred to above); and this illustrates the inter-related nature of the above factors. The transfer of learning is often impeded by the lack of line management support back in the workplace. Also important is the active support from senior management (McCracken, 2004). Implicit in the above is the notion of the psychological contract. A research study carried out by Bartlett and Kang (2004) indicates that attitudes towards training may be influenced by the level of psychological tie or attachment that an individual feels towards his/her employing organization. This reflects the importance of the psychological contract between the individual and the organization. Consequently, the line manager can help strengthen employees' commitment to the organization by being supportive of training activities.

Key concept   Psychological contract

The psychological contract is the set of unwritten reciprocal expectations between an organization and an individual employee (Schein, 1978). It reflects the existence of an emotional as well as economic attachment to the organization which is highly subjective and subject to change (Boxall and Purcell, 2008).

4.8 Potential barriers to learning

The potential barriers to learning are many and varied. However, it is possible to identify those which are commonly encountered. These include: lack of time and/or financial support; fear of failure, lack of facilities and/or equipment; an unsupportive organizational culture; limitations of individual ability; and, strongly entrenched learning preferences. A survey of 973 delegates at the CIPD HRD conference in 2004 revealed that 48 per cent blamed time pressures and 31 per cent lack of support from line managers. The HRD practitioner can help individuals to reflect upon any potential barriers and identify strategies for overcoming or, perhaps more realistically, minimizing them.

Knasel et al. (2000) have categorized barriers to learning in the following way:

- **Personal:** many individuals have memories of bad experiences from earlier in their lives, especially about school. Consequently, confidence and self-esteem can be affected adversely. Anxiety and negative attitudes may need to be overcome. Additionally, the motivation to learn, to sustain a commitment to continuous learning, may be lacking; as well as specific learning skills.

- **Practical:** this category covers a wide range of factors, including lack of financial support, lack of time, lack of facilities and equipment, etc.

- **Organizational:** many organizations do not make learning a priority and the culture that evolves is not conducive to supporting continuous development. Additionally, the way in which work is carried out and the structure of the company may inhibit learning—a rigid, hierarchical bureaucracy is not the best place to learn from others in the workplace!

- **Social:** depending on the extent to which an organization is dependent on the local labour market rather than the external labour market generally, problems of literacy and the motivation to learn may be more or less prevalent.

There are a variety of strategies for overcoming these different barriers.

ACTIVITY 4.3

Identify *three* barriers to your own learning that you have experienced. What strategies did you use to overcome these? Do you foresee any potential barriers or obstacles to your current personal development plan? What strategies do you intend using to overcome these?

As well as the above categorization of barriers you may have identified some from the following list compiled by Mumford (1988):

- Perceptual—not seeing that there is a problem
- Cultural—the way things are done around here

- Emotional—fear or insecurity
- Motivational—unwillingness to take risks
- Cognitive—previous learning experience
- Intellectual—limited learning style; poor learning skills
- Expressive—poor communication skills
- Situational—lack of opportunities
- Physical—place, time
- Specific environment—boss/colleagues are unsupportive

The above lists acknowledge the affective dimension to learning that was discussed briefly earlier. Boud et al. (1985) make the important point that negative feelings can be a major barrier to learning because 'they can distort perceptions, lead to false interpretations of events, and can undermine the will to persist' (p. 11). Line managers and HRD practitioners need to be conversant with these barriers. The line manager in particular needs to be aware of how to minimize them so that the benefits of both formal learning and development interventions and informal learning activities are maximized (see chapters 5 and 11 respectively).

Summary

In this chapter you have been introduced to some of the principal theories of learning. These can be categorized as psychological or sociological perspectives on learning with training and development being associated traditionally with the former. The psychological perspective includes behavioural, cognitive, and experiential theories. These regard cognition as something which happens inside individual minds resulting in an emphasis on the transfer of learning from the classroom to the workplace. Behavioural theory underpins coaching, guided practice, and instruction in basic skills and is associated with socialization processes. Cognitive theory involves the processing of information which can lead to a qualitative change in how an individual sees the world (new mental models are created). Experiential leaning is about learning from experience and has been a popular theory with HRD practitioners when designing courses, workshops, and seminars. It also helps us to analyse the learning styles or preferences of individuals.

More recently, there has been increased recognition of sociological theories such as social learning and situated learning. These have made an important contribution to adult learning theory although this relationship has never been fully explored. Situated learning has particular implications for learning that is integrated with work (see chapter 11). Important approaches to learning that are underpinned by psychological and sociological perspectives are problem-solving, reflective practice, and self-directed learning (incorporating e-learning). The role of motivation in adult learning is still an under-researched topic despite having a major influence on how adults engage with learning activities. Other potential barriers to learning were highlighted and discussed. These theories and approaches to learning underpin much of the content in subsequent chapters on topics such as designing formal interventions, integrating learning into the workplace, and continuing professional development.

Review questions

1   Returning to the definition of learning by Jarvis (2006) above, at the start of the chapter, explain which learning theories can be related to specific elements or parts of this definition.

2   List what you feel are the principal strengths and weaknesses of each of the learning theories covered in this chapter.

3   Think of a problem or situation that you are trying to resolve. This can be anything, for instance: a difference of opinion with a student or colleague, a challenging project you are involved in, or an unrealistic deadline for a piece of work. Select a learning theory and apply it to this problem or situation. Does this offer any new insights?

4   Carry out a search to see if you can find any case study examples of organizations using a particular learning theory or theories to underpin their learning and development strategy or policy.

5   What do you see as some of the potential difficulties facing line managers in encouraging employees to engage in reflective practice?

Suggestions for further reading

1   Kolb, D. A. 1984. *Experiential Learning: Experience as the Source of Learning and Development*. Englewood Cliffs, NJ: Prentice-Hall.

A seminal text well worth refering to in order to improve your understanding of experiential learning.

2   Holton, E. F., Swanson, R. A. and Naquin, S. S. 2001. Andragogy in practice: clarifying the andragogical model of adult learning. *Performance Improvement Quarterly*, 14 (1): 118–43.

This article provides a useful overview on adult learning.

3   McCracken, M. 2004. Understanding managerial propensity to participate in learning activities: the case of the Scottish life assurance company. *Human Resource Development International*, 7 (4): 501–17.

This article places various aspects of learning within a case study context.

4   Clarke, N. 2006. Emotional intelligence training: a case of caveat emptor. *Human Resource Development Review*, 5 (4): 422–41.

Read this article if you want to find out more about emotional intelligence.

5   Jarvis, P. (2006) *Towards a Comprehensive Theory of Human Learning*. Abingdon: Routledge.

An excellent and detailed discussion of learning theories.

Case study

Learning alone or learning together?

The following statements have been taken from a research study carried out by the author over a three year period. Participants work in various business schools in the UK. Their names and universities have been made anonymous for reasons of confidentiality.

Kirk: My subject group has been a place where we've shared experiences, that is practical experiences; and, in a sense it's just been a home for subject developments.

Jilly: You can come out of your office door and have a conversation with somebody on the stairs which is incredibly useful and I don't see that happening in the rest of the business school that much. We all have coffee together in the morning, whoever's there, and we talk about what we're going to be doing that day and it will spark off something, 'oh, have you seen this or whatever?'. So I find that very useful although there are advantages and disadvantages.

Kirk: You've got to kick people from time to time. Kick yourself as well, saying, come on, you need to look at this.

Meryl: Most of our time is taken up with conversations about process at the expense of more meaningful conversations. We know what's wrong with courses but we can't change them. We know what's wrong and how we could run it but we can't do that. More and more of the freedom and flexibility are going as more and more processes and protocols are put in.

Sophie: Committees are very useful and often they are the only way that you get to know what is happening in the university. You know, the decisions that are made further up. If I wasn't on that committee I would have no other way of finding out that information because it isn't communicated and we don't have regular team meetings. So these meetings, though they can be long and laborious, they are actually worth going to because they are the only way of getting information and you need to have the information.

Zoe: Often you have a problem with teaching and learning. You'll often find that other people have had similar problems and propose, help you with solutions and things. I drop in on Jilly or so and so, and say, I'm trying to do this. Or you stand upstairs and you, you're drinking coffee and say, I've got this real problem, and then four or five people come out of their rooms bearing you bits of paper.

Craig: We are very good friends, we socialise outside and inside the university. We have worked together now for eight years. I can honestly say working here, really, that there is very rarely a day goes by that one of my colleagues doesn't make me feel good about myself in some way. And of course I have got some very close colleagues and friends in that particular group.

Phil: From a personal perspective, being involved in a lot of committees I find very interesting just because you get to know an awful lot more that is going on about the university, and with it being a large organisation it can be difficult at times.

Zoe: Well, it's a lot of learning by doing here . . . because you're sort of thrown in, you know.

Joanne: I do reflect upon things. I think that's the only way you can survive. I do, quite often, again on the bike. I find that a useful, literally, mechanism for resolving the hiccups or the difficulties that may have occurred during the day and perhaps on the way, devising strategies for dealing with them.

Case questions

1. Which learning theories appear to be evident in each of the above statements? In some cases there may be more than one theory involved.

2. Can you identify any barriers to learning in any of the statements?

Online resource centre

Visit the supporting online resource centre for additional material that will help you with your research, essays, assignments, and revision.

 www.oxfordtextbooks.co.uk/orc/mankin/

5

A Systematic Approach to HRD

Learning objectives

By the end of this chapter you should be able to:

* Appreciate the reasons why it is important to adopt a systematic approach to the design of formal HRD interventions

* Understand and explain the differences between the systematic training cycle (STC), and the human resource development (HRD) cycle

* Explain the skills needed by a HRD practitioner to implement the HRD cycle effectively

* Explain the respective roles of the HRD practitioner, the learner, and the learner's line manager in the HRD cycle

Indicative content

■ The role and purpose of the systematic training cycle (STC)

■ An overview of each of the four stages in the STC: identifying training needs, designing training interventions, delivering training interventions, and evaluating training interventions

■ The respective roles of the trainer and line manager in the STC

■ The role and purpose of the HRD cycle

■ An overview of each of the four stages in the HRD cycle: identifying HRD needs, designing HRD interventions, delivering HRD interventions, and evaluating HRD interventions

■ The respective role of the HRD practitioner, line manager, and learner in the HRD cycle

■ The role of continuous improvement and problem-solving techniques

- The role of the line manager as a coach and mentor

- The importance of management development

Key concepts

The systematic training cycle (STC)

The human resource development (HRD) cycle

Identifying training needs (ITN)/
Training needs analysis (TNA)

Entry behaviour

Design

Training strategy

Delivery

Evaluation

5.1 Introduction

Much of HRD practice still involves the design and delivery of formal interventions although the focus appears to be shifting from off-the-job to on-the-job interventions. As shall be discussed in chapter 11 this trend has been paralleled by a growing appreciation of the importance of informal learning. This is when learning occurs unexpectedly in the workplace: characteristics of informal learning include 'unintended, opportunistic and unstructured learning and the absence of a [trainer]' (Eraut, 2004: 250). Although the level of classroom-based training is declining (Dilworth, 2003) it is still unclear whether informal learning opportunities have really overtaken traditional approaches to training and development. The CIPD's 'Learning and Development Survey 2006' indicated that the formal training course is no longer seen as the most effective way to achieve learning outcomes (J. Jarvis, 2006). Yet a year later when the 2007 survey results were published it was noted that traditional training methods were still very popular (Wain, 2007). A study by Slotte et al. (2004) reveals that formal interventions are still viewed as essential for the provision of the skills and knowledge needed by employees to achieve an organization's goals and objectives.

Sloman (2005) argues that formal interventions still offer important advantages, including: learners can share experiences with other learners on a course; learners can practise skills in a safe environment; a trainer can give immediate feedback; and, compulsory courses signal to learners what is important to the organization. Induction continues to be a good example of a formal intervention and research shows that tailor-made or bespoke induction programmes increase staff retention (CIPD, 2006). As Eraut (1994) cautions, it is 'dangerous to underestimate the contribution which a well-designed course . . . can make' (page 82). What is important here is the emphasis on a *well-designed* course, which is the subject of chapter 7. The knowledge and skills required to design formal interventions *remains* an important aspect of the HRD practitioner's toolkit. The HRD practitioner may no longer be involved in designing as many classroom-based interventions but he/she still needs the knowledge and skills to identify, design, implement, and review a wide range of formal, planned workplace-based interventions, including: secondments, special projects, coaching and mentoring schemes. These types of interventions can also have implications for career development and lifelong learning, as well as organization development and organizational knowledge and learning. This illustrates the extent to which the boundaries between the components of HRD are becoming blurred in terms of day-to-day practice.

The purpose of this chapter is to provide an overview of how formal interventions are designed, implemented, and evaluated by HRD practitioners and line managers following the identification, of a legitimate need for the intervention in the first place. The chapter will take as its starting point an explanation of how this has been handled in the past, before the emergence of HRD and when the emphasis was on training and development. This discussion focuses on a specific framework referred to as the systematic training cycle (STC). In the remainder of the chapter the STC will be developed to take into account the other components of HRD and the range of HRD strategic choices set out in chapter 3.

MEDIA WATCH BOX

Secondments as a formal intervention

Civil servants working in the Scottish Executive have been able to take advantage of secondments since 1999. Referred to as 'interchanges', the number of employees taking advantage of this approach has been gradually increasing. However, the potential benefits of this type of intervention can be difficult to measure as any new skills may not be immediately obvious when the employee returns to his/her original role.

This example illustrates one of the potential dilemmas facing the HRD practitioner: persuading managers of the benefits of an intervention where the learning gained may take a long time to emerge. Many managers in the private sector may not be as patient as their counterparts in a public sector organization like the Scottish Executive.

Source
People Management, 8 March 2007: 16.

This chapter provides an overview for chapters 6 to 9 which each explore in more detail a specific aspect of this framework: needs identification (chapter 6), design (chapter 7), delivery (chapter 8), and evaluation (chapter 9).

5.2 Formal training and development interventions

The systematic training cycle (STC) is a generic framework that has been used for many years to guide the design of formal training and development interventions. The STC comprises four stages: the identification of training and development needs followed by the design, delivery, and evaluation of the training and development intervention (see figure 5.1). This approach has been associated with supply-driven interventions that reflect what Yorks (2005: 39) terms a 'cafeteria-style delivery of programs'. In the US its origins can be traced back to the post-World War II ADDIE training model—analysis, design, development, implementation, and evaluation (Allen, 2006); whilst in the UK the STC emerged in the 1960s (Bratton and Gold, 2007).

> **Key concept**   The systematic training cycle
>
> The systematic training cycle is one of several different terms used to describe a methodical step-by-step approach to the key stages in developing a training intervention: identification of needs, design, delivery, and evaluation.

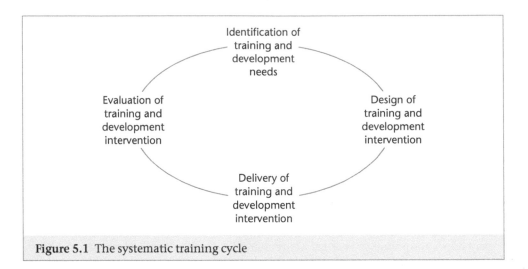

Figure 5.1 The systematic training cycle

❗ TIPS AND HINTS

Although authors have modified the framework to reflect new insights or individual preferences the underlying framework has proven a robust and reliable tool. The HRD practitioner needs to demonstrate the potential benefits of this approach when working with line managers.

Each of the four stages will now be explained in more detail.

Stage 1: Identification of training and development needs

As Sloman (1994) identified there are broadly two types of training and development need: supply-led and demand-driven. A supply-led training and development need is one that has to be addressed in order for an organization to be capable of achieving its strategic goals. For instance the introduction of a new computerized sales order processing system to support the expansion of business in new markets will require staff to be trained in its use. In order to prepare the organization for successful implementation of the system the HRD practitioner needs to be aware of the organization's business strategy and how this new system is linked to specific business objectives. Another example could be technical skills training and/or health and safety training as a result of an organization's decision to introduce new production equipment in order to manufacture a new product range. A demand-driven training and development need is one that has arisen as a result of an individual employee or line manager identifying a performance gap or development need, for instance during an appraisal or performance review discussion. This is why the line manager has to adopt a 'hands on' approach to training and development: often the way in which a performance appraisal is handled by the line manager has an important bearing on how training and development is perceived by employees.

Formal interventions

Formal training interventions are used around the world and still form the bedrock of HRD strategies in a wide range of contexts. The first two illustrate the internal and external focus of training in a leading charity, Oxfam. The third illustrates the role of formally structured interventions to support career development strategies for potential leaders of the future. The fourth example focuses on a different approach to leadership development.

Oxfam has 5,000 people on its payroll who are spread across 70 countries. The charity also has 700 shops in the UK. Formal training initiatives include coaching and mentoring for managers, and 'pick up and go' training packs for managers which can be used anywhere in the world.[1]

Oxfam has a training programme in place in Bolivia which focuses on training those who live in highland communities in herd management (including how to improve the quality of the meat and wool produced).[2]

Ernst & Young, the international accountancy firm, have introduced development centres to help the company identify future leaders. They have been designed in conjunction with Pearn Kandola (PK), the occupational psychologist firm.[3]

BP introduced a new structured leadership development programme to replace its previously ad hoc approach to this issue. The programme took 18 months to design and develop and was focused on the development of 'first level leaders'. The programme comprises a mix of methods including face-to-face sessions and web-based content (although the latter is seen as supplementary to the former). Sessions last between two and four days and use methods such as role play. Outside of these sessions there is peer coaching of learners.[4]

Sources
[1] Carrington, L. 2005. The third way. *People Management*, 19 May 2005: 24–8.
[2] http://www.oxfam.org (accessed 29 May 2008).
[3] Trapp, R. 2005. The mirror has two faces. *People Management*, 19 May 2005: 40–2.
[4] Priestland, A. and Hanig, R. 2006. Fuelling the fire. *People Management*, 23 February: 40–2.

In order for this stage to be successful the HRD practitioner has to understand the methods for carrying out an organization-wide training needs analysis (TNA); such as data collection and interpretation of organizational strategy, objectives, and policies. Conducting an organization-level TNA enables the HRD practitioner to ask some important questions, such as: *how well matched is our workforce to the needs of the business? What levels of expertise do we have now; and what will we require in the future in order to achieve our business objectives?* The HRD practitioner also needs to understand how to collect and interpret data at the individual and department or operational level (e.g. appraisals; job analysis; questionnaires; interviews). Analysis at the department or operational level usually involves some form of job and/or task analysis. Job analysis is a systematic method or process for obtaining detailed information about a job (Gibb, 2002). Task analysis focuses on specific tasks within the job. Analysis at the individual level (sometimes referred to as person analysis) involves a diagnosis of individual performance with the performance review or appraisal often being an important source of information (Wexley and Latham, 2002). The line manager is involved in this process either directly or indirectly depending on his/her knowledge of needs assessment techniques. The different levels of analysis are often carried out at the same time 'because it is often difficult to determine whether performance deficiencies are a training problem without understanding the tasks and the work environment' (Noe, 2002: 74). Consequently, analysis is at the heart of the first stage of the STC. Undoubtedly, the time spent in identifying training and development needs is time well invested as it should result in training being directed to the areas where it is really needed.

Stage 2: Design of training and development intervention

Having identified that a training and development intervention is the appropriate solution it is important to move onto the design phase. Some of the key issues to agree right at the start are:

- **The learning objectives:** What is the intervention being designed to achieve? For instance, if the training and development need(s) identified in stage 1 are skills-related there is little point in designing a course or workshop that focuses on the acquisition of explicit knowledge about the topic (i.e. know-what) unless this is coupled with opportunities to practise and develop the skill(s) (i.e. practical knowledge). Learning objectives should relate to performance objectives wherever possible so that the impact of the training on job performance can be evaluated post-training. The line manager can refer the designer to key targets and metrics in his/her area of responsibility.

- **The budget:** who is funding the intervention and is there a budgetary limit? What are the indirect as well as direct costs of the intervention? Direct costs usually comprise the course fee which should cover the cost of the trainer(s), room, and equipment hire, and the costs incurred in the design of the intervention. Indirect costs include time lost on the job due to attendance at the training event as well as the cost of temporary cover in some situations, travel costs, and often overnight accommodation as well as incidental expenses. Agreement needs to be reached about who is funding what element. Often direct costs are covered by the training budget and indirect costs by the line manager's budget. In the UK nearly 80 per cent of organizations have a training budget with the average spend per employee being highest in the voluntary (non-profit) sector (CIPD, 2008).

- **Entry behaviour of learners:** what are the learning styles or preferences of the learners? What motivates them to learn? What are their present skills profiles? There is nothing worse than organizing a training intervention around a specific group of individuals to discover on the day that a line manager has sent someone else who may or may not match the person's needs that he/she is replacing (usually they don't match!). I have delivered workshops where one or more participants have admitted 'I don't know why

A personal reflection

I devoted a great deal of time to the implementation of a company-wide programme for IT skills training which included a mix of customised courses, standard courses, and surgery sessions (where an IT trainer would visit a site and help staff on a one-to-one basis). As part of the monitoring and review process I was attending the morning session of a customized workshop for experienced users of a specific spreadsheet (Microsoft Excel). The participants had been identified through an analysis of their responses to a detailed questionnaire sent in advance. This was to ensure that the training matched the needs of participants. After half an hour it became apparent that one of the participants was failing to keep up with the others. When questioned he explained that he had never used Microsoft Excel before. 'So why did you say you had on the questionnaire?' I asked. 'Because I didn't think it mattered. I mean in my last job, four, five years ago I used a different spreadsheet so I thought it didn't matter.' I groaned inwardly particularly when it then emerged he hadn't even used many of the functions available but had ticked all the boxes because he had 'looked at them once or twice before'.

Source
The author.

I'm here', 'I've done something like this before', or 'This wasn't identified at my appraisal as an issue'. Sometimes it is the actual learner who is at fault (see *personal reflection* box). Again, this highlights why the line manager and trainer need to work collaboratively.

- **Training strategy:** this means the specific approach being adopted by the trainer (e.g. in-house workshop; on-the-job training; self-managed learning etc). Many programmes involve a combination of training strategies. For instance, a leadership skills programme can involve: workshops, coaching sessions on-the-job, secondments and/or special projects, and being mentored by an experienced manager.

- **Time constraints:** often the HRD practitioner has to reach a compromise over the timing and/or duration of the training intervention. E-learning and blended learning interventions are being increasingly promoted as more flexible delivery systems than traditional interventions. However, the significant rise in this delivery approach has failed to materialize (CIPD, 2008). Over the last thirty years there has been a significant shift in the design of formal programmes from long to short durations. For instance, when I first worked in the private sector in the late 1970s the company offered week-long management development courses. By the time I took up an HR appointment in 1993 in the same company most formal interventions were one or two days' long. By 1998 the company was providing health and safety training in ten to fifteen minute 'chunks'. This transition to 'bite-sized chunks' reflects a wider social change that can be seen in the use of media-based technologies generally, particularly amongst the younger generation (see *Media watch* box).

- **Accountability:** The HRD practitioner, the learner, and the learner's line manager need to be accountable for their respective contribution to the intervention (Gilley et al., 2002). In the past it was all too easy to blame the trainer for any problems. Today line managers can offer ideas and feedback to the HRD practitioner about the design process. Whilst line mangers may not necessarily be asked to deliver training courses they are expected to act as a coach or mentor that requires certain skills (see chapter 8). Over 70 per cent of UK organizations now undertake coaching activities with the bulk of responsibility being with line managers or their direct reports (CIPD, 2008). Increasingly, line managers are being asked to act as a facilitator in the development of informal learning opportunities (i.e. devolved informal learning and empowered informal learning—see chapter 3). They also *should* play a role in evaluation (Blanchard and Thacker, 2004)

！ TIPS AND HINTS

Evaluation needs to be agreed at an early stage and should flow from the performance *and* learning objectives. Too often training and development interventions are implemented without considering how the programme will be evaluated or evaluation is discussed but is then not followed through at the post-training stage (this can be for a variety of reasons as discussed in chapter 9).

MEDIA WATCH BOX

Bite-sized training

The Financial Services Authority (FSA) in the UK is planning to offer short seminars on personal finance topics including budgeting, borrowing, and saving. These seminars will be offered to employees of organizations around the country and delivered by trained personnel during lunch breaks.

Source
Guardian, 28 March 2006: 23.

When these issues have been addressed the detailed design can start; and appropriate methods and media can be selected. Ideally this phase should involve the trainer who will be delivering the intervention; although this may not always be possible. In the US the design stage is often the responsibility of an *instructional designer* who is seldom involved in the delivery of the intervention (Gilley et al., 2002). The HRD practitioner also has to decide whether it is appropriate to involve an external agency (e.g. training consultant; training provider) rather than utilize an internal resource. It will be necessary also to consider a range of other design issues including the actual venue or learning environment:

location; availability; accessibility; comfort; heating and ventilation; lighting; room capacities; shape of rooms; power sockets; light switches; acoustics; equipment; wall space and fixings; residential facilities; parking; reception; refreshments; toilets; leisure facilities; emergency procedures; and so on.

Stage 3: Delivery of training and development intervention

The HRD practitioner must ensure that all trainers or consultants deliver to an appropriate standard. This stage is described by Swanson and Holton (2001: 219) as a 'pressure point' because the trainer wants to succeed and participants have high expectations. Relatively simple matters such as the layout of the room or the readability of training materials can have a massive impact on the participant's assessment of the intervention. There is nothing worse than as a participant:

- Sitting in a training venue and watching a poor quality video that has faults with sound and picture
- Listening to a trainer who thinks he/she is being funny or who trivializes important points with too much forced humour
- Being forced to accept one point of view only—the trainer's
- Having nothing to do except listen to the trainer because there are none or very few interactive exercises to engage participants
- Being patronized

As Ian Yates, a learning and development manager, recently said to me: 'People must come to the training without any sense of trepidation. They mustn't be scared by it. The course should be fun as well as educational and the trainer must display pace, energy and enthusiasm. Also we always try to build our sessions around the learning preferences of all the participants so that everyone has an opportunity to shine'.

Stage 4: Evaluation of training and development intervention

Evaluation needs to be viewed in two ways. First, at the level of the training activity itself (which I refer to as Type 1 Evaluation); second, at the level of the HRD function (which I refer to as Type 2 Evaluation). Techniques used at the first level will complement the second level although the evaluation of the effectiveness of the HRD function itself will not be achieved solely through the use of standard type 1 evaluation models or frameworks (and this point is discussed in detail in chapter 13). In terms of some of the most commonly used evaluation frameworks for type 1 evaluation the most well known is probably Kirkpatrick's (which was originally developed in 1959 by the American Donald Kirkpatrick). It comprises four levels of evaluation:

1. **Reaction:** this is the most commonly used level of evaluation and is about measuring learner satisfaction with the training intervention, normally at the end of the intervention through the use of a questionnaire.

2. **Learning:** this is about assessing the learner's achievement of specific learning objectives.

3. **Behaviour or performance:** this is about measuring improvements to the learner's on-the-job performance.

4. **Results:** involves assessing the impact of the intervention on organizational performance and is the most difficult level to measure.

These levels are discussed in detail in chapter 9. Interestingly, this framework suggests that evaluation starts at the end of the learning event and does not make explicit the need to build evaluation into the planning and design phases. As evaluation data is obtained for each level it becomes increasingly difficult to secure appropriate data for the next level as it is difficult to prove a direct link, say, between a training event and improved business results (e.g. profits; return on capital employed; etc.). A 1990 report by Carnevale and Schulz for the American Society for Training and Development identified the following characteristics of a rigorous evaluation system and these remain pertinent today:

• Data is collected from many, if not all, participants

• Data is collected more than once; perhaps several times

• More evaluation at the organizational level is carried out

• Quantitative data collection methods are used

• It is more expensive to do

• It is more time-consuming

• Formal reports are produced

• Decisions about programmes are made (e.g. continuation; cutback)

• Evaluation is always carried out when training's success is critical for safety or strategic business purposes

This list can seem daunting to many HRD practitioners who are often under pressure to focus predominantly on delivery. They also need the direct help of the line manager who monitors performance and who can also hold pre- and post-briefings with learners. This latter process sends a signal to employees about the importance of training and development. The implementation of a rigorous evaluation system can be seen as problematic for a variety of reasons:

• It is felt to be too time-consuming

• Line managers are not always interested in the information

• Line managers are not always cooperative in collecting, analysing, and interpreting the data

• It is difficult to identify a practical evaluation system

• Some of the data collection methods, such as interviews, pre-briefings, and post-debriefing sessions, require skill and patience

• There is too big a gap between the rhetoric and reality

- Lack of pressure from the top
- Some training interventions are just too complex or long term to collect meaningful data to satisfy the short-term perspective of senior managers

Clearly, there is a need for HRD practitioners to carry out evaluation if they are to raise their profile and credibility in the eyes of internal stakeholders. However, they also need to consider very carefully the implications of the shift from formal to informal learning. How do you evaluate learning which takes place 'outside' of formal events? What is the role of the employee and line manager in such situations?

INSIGHTS INTO PRACTICE

Systematic training in Malaysian SMEs

A study of TQM best practice in three Malaysian SMEs reveals the importance of 'targeted training in quality techniques and awareness' (p. 501). Examples of a systematic approach from these cases include: a skills-mapping exercise to identify employees' training needs; the design and implementation of a management development programme focused on developing management capability in TQM concepts and practices; and, the measurement of benefits of the whole TQM strategy (including training) which were in one case 'reduced costs, increased line efficiency and improved employee morale' (p. 498).[1]

This is very much a performance orientation to training which involves the adoption of 'a total system (systemic) approach to organizational performance' (Gilley et al., 2002: 179). The role of HRD is that of a *performance engineer* which focuses on helping organizations to achieve strategic goals and objectives through improving organizational performance (Gilley and Maycunich Gilley, 2002).

Source
[1] Ab Rahman, M. N. and Tannock, J. D. T. 2005. TQM best practices: experiences of Malaysian SMEs. *Total Quality Management*, 16 (4): 491–503.

ACTIVITY 5.1

Assume you are a HRD manager and draft an email of up to 250 words that you could send to line managers to explain the importance of one of the four stages in the STC.

Criticisms of the systematic approach

In the past the STC has been criticized for being too mechanistic and over-reliant on the role of the professional trainer. Often it is not used because it is felt to be too time-consuming and rigid. Yet, in my experience it is not the STC framework itself that has

(•) **INSIGHTS INTO PRACTICE**

Systematic training in India

This case involved a questionnaire-based survey of training practices in 252 organizations spanning SMEs to multinational corporations and both the private and public sectors. The results reveal that there are more organizations evaluating training than carrying out training needs analysis. 100 per cent of multinationals, 86 per cent of private firms, and 81 per cent of public sector organizations conduct some form of monitoring of training effectiveness; although the figures for reporting this information to relevant managers falls to 56 and 63 per cent respectively for the private and public sectors. This reflects the fact that these sectors focus on validating the learner perception of the training event itself rather than evaluating the impact on performance (as carried out by the multinationals). Although all the multinationals surveyed conduct TNAs *and* carry out some form of evaluation this figure is only 67 per cent for private firms and 44 per cent of public sector organizations. Indeed, the study shows that there is also a lack of a systematic approach to TNA in the private and public sectors. In terms of training design and implementation, this is carried out by all the multinationals, 94 per cent of private firms and 87 per cent of public sector organizations. The study also reveals a lack of training and development policies in the private and public sectors.[1]

It seems odd that more organizations focus on evaluation than on the TNA stage given the importance of the linkage between performance and learning objectives. This should drive the design process. The data suggest that much of the training provision in these organizations is supply-led.

Source
[1] Yadapadithaya, P. S. 2001. Evaluating corporate training and development: an Indian experience. *International Journal of Training and Development*, 5 (4): 261–74.

been the cause of problems, such as poor evaluation, but rather the way in which it has been used or rather *mis*used. Rigid adherence to any framework at the expense of commonsense and intuition can create problems. But this does not mean the framework should be rejected. There is still much good practice that is implicit in the STC as shall be covered in the next four chapters. Indeed, using the STC can minimize the faddish nature of many programmes (Wexley and Latham, 2002). As McClernon (2006) observes:

> Probably the biggest rival to systematic training is simply non-systematic training such as training events produced without applying the discipline associated with a training-for-performance approach. Often these quasi-training events are developed by well intentioned individuals unskilled in systematic performance improvement approaches. Little if any emphasis is focused on the analysis and evaluation phases . . . and the impact is generally negligible and even negative.
> (p. 443)

However, rigid adherence to the STC can be counter-intuitive and it is important to recognize the validity of different perspectives. Ideally, an experienced HRD practitioner will judge when it is prudent to adopt a systematic approach and when not to.

(•) INSIGHTS INTO PRACTICE

Why the systematic approach still matters

In the US the Internal Revenue Service (IRS) implemented training for thousands of its employees to improve the accuracy of information provided to taxpayers (the training had been triggered by taxpayers complaining about the lack of accuracy). The IRS were subsequently criticized in a report for not setting any training goals, not being able to provide any data on the cost of the programme, and for relying on inadequate evaluation methods.[1]

Although triggered by a legitimate (supply-led) performance problem, this example illustrates how the failure to adhere effectively to a systematic approach can impact on the overall quality and effectiveness of a training programme or intervention.

Source
[1] Bunch, K. J. 2007. Training failure as a consequence of organisational culture. *Human Resource Development Review*, 6 (2): 142–63.

ACTIVITY 5.2

Search the Internet for three examples of different formal interventions that appear to be based on a systematic approach. Examples of formal interventions include: training courses and workshops; mentoring programmes; coaching programmes; secondments. You may find it useful to refer to the CIPD's *People Management* magazine and HRD journal articles.

5.3 The HRD cycle

Traditionally the STC is seen as separating the role of the professional trainer from that of the line manager. This is not the case if a partnership approach is adopted in which the principal stakeholders are: the HRD practitioner, the learner, and the learner's line manager. This is shown diagrammatically in figure 5.2. In terms of the work of non-profit organizations, such as Oxfam, members of poor communities are often stakeholders in the HRD process. For most formal interventions the line manager has an important role in all four stages and, in particular in the first and fourth. The HRD practitioner can assist line managers in identifying the learning and development needs of their subordinates. These needs will differ greatly depending on the job a person is doing and the level of skill they possess. Even in a team where everyone does the same job the learning and

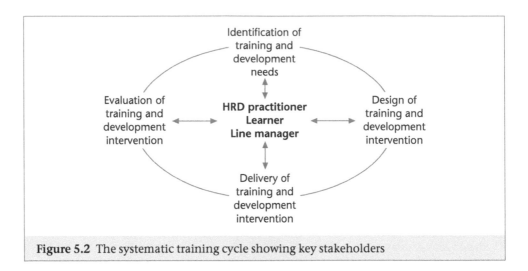

Figure 5.2 The systematic training cycle showing key stakeholders

development needs may vary significantly—some team members may already carry out tasks competently; others may have little experience and be less competent; others may be interested in developing themselves for future roles. Yet, the CIPD's 2007 *Learning and Development* survey revealed that only 40 per cent of organizations trained all or the majority of their line managers in how to support learning and development (Winkler, 2007).

Key concept   The HRD cycle

The HRD cycle builds on the systematic training cycle (STC) by providing a methodical step-by-step approach to the key stages in developing HRD interventions that span learning and development, career development and lifelong learning, and organization development and organizational knowledge and learning. Like the STC it comprises four stages: identifying HRD needs, design, delivery, and evaluation of HRD interventions.

This framework can be developed further to incorporate the shift in emphasis from training to learning. This places much more emphasis on the role of the learner who, as part of the partnership approach, should be taking responsibility for their own learning. Learning ceases to be something that is 'done' to employees as was implicit in the STC where the emphasis was on training. The STC has been updated in figure 5.3 to reflect this shift in emphasis.

As it stands this still reflects a potential piecemeal design process with the cycle focusing primarily on individual learning and development interventions. The HRD cycle builds on the STC by incorporating a holistic approach which embraces humanist and performance thinking. As before the cycle involves four stages.

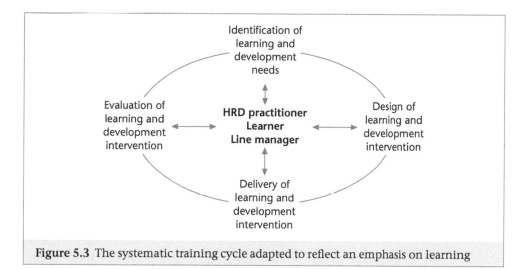

Figure 5.3 The systematic training cycle adapted to reflect an emphasis on learning

Stage 1 'is seen as the foundation to strong human resource development (HRD) practice' (Roberts, 2006: 476). It operates at three levels: strategic, operational, and individual. The strategic level requires HRD practitioners to produce an organizational analysis of HRD needs which is based on an assessment of: the organizational strategy, performance problems and gaps, and the implications of HR plans; as well as the career aspirations of employees. This last point comes with a caveat: put simply, not all organizations will be able to accommodate these career aspirations. This may be due to a shortage of funds or a lack of interest. Indeed, career development is often regarded as the 'bridesmaid' of the HRD function despite the increased interest in the work-life balance in recent years.

TIPS AND HINTS

As was discussed in chapter 3 the organizational analysis of HRD needs is only one aspect of the strategic analysis of the internal environment.

The organizational analysis incorporates the requirements identified at the operational and individual levels. This approach requires HRD practitioners to think strategically as was discussed in chapter 2. Gilley et al. (2002) are correct in asserting that this stage 'is as much a state of mind as it is a series of techniques and processes' (p. 254). The strategic analysis involves an assessment of whether the HRD intervention needs to be an OD project, learning and development programme, or a career development activity (or combination of all three). At this level the HRD practitioner adopts a business partner role in order to work collaboratively with senior managers. In terms of OD projects which can be pro-active as well as reactive, the HRD practitioner operates as a change agent (Grieves, 2003). As McLean et al. (2005) argue:

Organisation development (OD) is playing an increasingly key role in helping organisations to change themselves and improve organisational effectiveness and employee well-being in order to survive and thrive. (p. 157)

In 2002, when Network Rail took over from Railtrack in the UK, the company was characterized by very low employee morale; and so it was decided that a huge investment in training and development was the best way to bring about culture change: the company invested in a leadership development centre and five new training centres, an updated graduate programme, and a foundation degree in railway engineering (Smedley, 2007). This example also illustrates an important observation by Swanson and Holton (2001) that every training and development intervention has an OD component and vice versa. It also highlights the role of training centres as a key part of organization's HRD strategies (see *Media watch* box).

MEDIA WATCH BOX

Global training in Nissan

Nissan have announced the opening of a new global training centre at its UK Sunderland plant that will provide 15 week training programmes as part of an initiative to standardize training and education and share good practice between sites.

Source
Personnel Today, 19 June 2007: 6.

The operational level requires HRD practitioners to collate information on performance gaps. Depending on the size of the organization this exercise focuses on departments, divisions, or business units. At this level the HRD practitioner and line manager have to work collaboratively with the latter taking advantage of the HRD practitioner's technical knowledge on how to conduct needs analyses. The differentiation between strategic and operational levels reflects the distinction made between strategy and operational effectiveness:

> Strategy involves creating a unique, sustainable position of providing value by performing activities in a distinctive pattern that cannot be easily duplicated or imitated by competitors without compromising their existing strategic position. Operational effectiveness involves performing activities better, that is, faster and/or with better quality and cost effectiveness than competitors; increasing operational effectiveness involves process improvement. (Yorks, 2005: 38)

This quote not only illustrates the American emphasis on performance improvement but also the role of continuous improvement as part of the HRD practitioner's toolkit.

To reflect this improvement facet of HRD, the HRD cycle incorporates the PDCA cycle that was originally developed in the 1920s but came to prominence as a critical component in Japan's *kaizen* or continuous improvement philosophy. This is shown diagrammatically in figure 5.4. 'Act' involves identifying the symptoms and underlying causes of any problems. 'Plan' is the design phase of the problem solving intervention. 'Do' is the implementation phase; and 'Check' equates to the evaluation phase. The 'act'

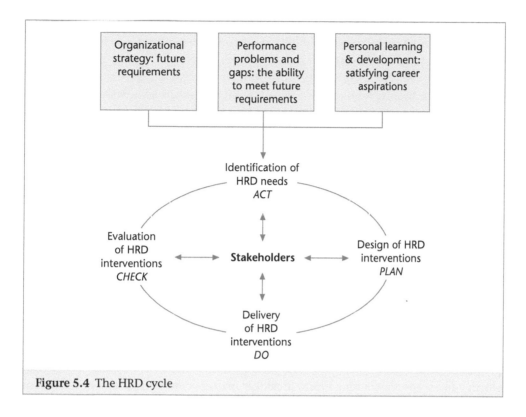

Figure 5.4 The HRD cycle

! **TIPS AND HINTS**

My experience as a total quality manager was invaluable when I became a HRD practitioner. Understanding how to analyse and improve processes even though I had no direct experience of working with those processes enhanced my ability to carry out effective analyses of HRD needs and to facilitate HRD interventions that involved organization development, learning and development, and career development.

(or 'action') stage of the PDCA cycle is associated with stage 1 of the HRD cycle to reflect the extent to which the evaluation of HRD interventions (stage 3) informs the analysis stage and thus ensures the cycle is a continuous process or open loop (rather than a closed loop as the original STC is often viewed).

The individual level tends to focus on the development of specific knowledge, skills, or competencies. It is heavily reliant on the line manager and, in particular, on his/her ability to achieve constructive outcomes from the performance review or appraisal process. This information can then be passed on to the HRD practitioner who may or may not feel the need to carry out a supplementary investigation (e.g. observation, questionnaire, or interview). In order to maximise the transfer of learning from the formal intervention to everyday activity in the workplace requires the identification of transfer needs:

in training needs assessment, distinguishing transfer from learning needs is an important task for HRD professionals since not all learning needs can be converted to transfer needs . . . Assessing trainees' and organisations' transfer needs is different from assessing learning needs; the former requires a precise transfer needs assessment reflecting human and organisational barriers and constraints that may impede training transfer. (Lim and Morris, 2006: 106)

This requires HRD practitioners to be knowledgeable in continuous improvement and problem solving techniques. In many respects the role of the HRD practitioner can be described as that of a problem solver with problems occurring at the strategic, operational, and individual levels. There are two dimensions to this: just as management practice is defined as a science and an art, HRD practice involves a scientific or rational dimension, in the form of the HRD cycle, and an artistry dimension in the form of an HRD practitioner's experience and expertise (e.g. a form of 'craft knowledge') which can be heavily reliant on intuition. Although intuition is highly subjective it is rooted in individual experience (Hislop, 2005). In SMEs the boundaries between these three levels may blur or merge. For very small businesses in particular the distinction between these levels may be totally artificial.

Stage 2 requires the ability to design a range of interventions, including: OD projects to bring about organizational change; organization- or unit-wide learning and development programmes such as mentoring and/or coaching for line managers; workshops or courses which address specific training needs, including management skills; career development seminars and counselling sessions. Each of these interventions is underpinned by the same design principles although the activities themselves can be vastly different. For instance, mentoring programmes may focus initially on 'learning as socialization' but have as a long-term goal the achievement of 'devolved informal learning' as line managers develop expertise in mentoring and no longer require formal training or facilitation. In contrast a standard induction course tends to be concerned solely with 'learning as socialization'. Induction reflects a socialization 'process by which new employees are transformed into effective members of the company' (Noe, 2002: 397) while the mentoring example reflects the fact that socialization is in fact an *ongoing* and *continual* process. The problem with socialization is that it:

is not intended to facilitate renewal; rather, its purposes, desired outcomes, and characteristics have been designed to perpetuate a stable and unmoving organisation. This could hinder an organisation's ability to be agile and change. (Danielson, 2004: 355)

As with the STC, the design stage of the HRD cycle can be broken down into a number of elements as shown in table 5.1.

In applying the PDCA cycle an important task is the identification of the causes of any problem. Just as the PDCA cycle was used to identify root causes and improvement solutions as part of an organization's continuous improvement strategy, so the same is true for the HRD cycle. The PDCA cycle and associated techniques, such as cause and effect analysis and process mapping, are important aspects of the HRD practitioner's toolkit.

Stage 2	OD	Learning and development	Career development
Objectives	Performance objectives	Performance and learning objectives	Development objectives
Budget	High direct costs High indirect costs	Low to medium direct and indirect costs	Medium to high direct costs Low to medium indirect costs
Entry behaviour	Assessment of expertise of project team members; assessment of organizational readiness for the change	Assessment of the knowledge and skills of learners; and their learning preferences	Assessment of career potential within and without the organization; and of the individual's career interests
Implementation methodology	Project team(s) in combination with other methods (e.g. workshops, team briefings, focus groups, etc.)	Appropriate training strategy	Combination of one-to-one counselling session(s), psychometrics and workshops, seminars or on-the-job development activity
Evaluation	Measurement of performance indicators at all three levels; and of qualitative feedback from employees	Measurement of learning and performance (this may be at all three levels)	Performance review or appraisal metrics; staff retention and/or attrition rates
Time constraints	Likely to be medium to long term	Likely to be short to medium term	Likely to be medium to long term
Accountability	All stakeholders	HRD practitioner, learner, and learner's line manager	HRD practitioner and the individual (also the line manager depending on the nature of the intervention)

Table 5.1 The design stage of the HRD cycle

Stage 3 can often make or break an intervention. There are several basic requirements that need to be covered. A problem with any one or more of these requirements can result in dissatisfied learners or ineffective outcomes. Basic requirements include:

- For OD projects a good understanding of the levels of expertise available within the project team (and, conversely, an awareness of any gaps that need to be addressed) is essential. In terms of learning and development interventions a good match between entry behaviour and the learning methods adopted by the HRD practitioner. The HRD practitioner needs to be adaptable and not tied to a particular approach to delivery (see *Insights into practice* box) while the line manager needs good skills in change management and, as stated above, facilitation.

- Good delivery skills. In terms of learning and development interventions there is nothing worse than a boring and/or unskilled trainer. An effective trainer encourages

> **(•) INSIGHTS INTO PRACTICE**
>
> ## Using targeted training to solve recruitment problems
>
> The UK charity Broadway, which offers support to homeless people, was struggling to recruit good staff and so decided to design a programme that would enable them to 'grow their own'. The new programme is a year-long trainee scheme that comprises a mix of interventions, including: placements at different Broadway hostels and centres; seminars; course-work; and, off-the-job training sessions. Broadway also runs action learning sets (see chapter 8) and every employee has a personal development plan. The programme has had a measurable impact on the charity's performance.
>
> **Source**
> Johnson, R. 2007. On Broadway. *People Management*, 19 April 2007.

active listening through the deployment of appropriate skills: using appropriate language, avoiding or explaining acronyms, varying the tone of his/her delivery, maintaining a consistent level of eye contact with learners, and so on. In terms of career development the HRD practitioner needs to be able to establish a good level of rapport with the individual and create a climate of trust. This is why many managers are not suited to the delivery of a wide range of HRD interventions.

- Good project management skills so that OD projects can be designed, implemented, and evaluated effectively. This is true for both the HRD practitioner and the line manager. Good project management skills are important also for other types of HRD intervention.

- A physical environment conducive to learning. Ensuring adequate ventilation and/or appropriate heating may seem fairly prosaic but can make or break an event. This is equally applicable to OD projects and career development sessions.

> **! TIPS AND HINTS**
>
> The HRD practitioner sometimes needs to block or adjust the involvement of a manager in the delivery of a training event if it has become a 'vanity project' for the manager. Some assume that delivery is easy—it isn't.

Stage 4 evaluation is important for all types of HRD intervention. The evaluation methodology needs to be agreed at an early stage in the design process and should be linked to the performance and/or learning/development objectives. The transfer of learning from the 'classroom' to the workplace is seen as the ultimate goal of training (Lim and Morris, 2006). Yet one of the principal criticisms of formal learning and development interventions has been the poor levels of learning transfer achieved:

A personal perspective

When I was a line manager I had arranged for one of the company's IT trainers to conduct a series of one-to-one coaching sessions with several customer services assistants. Towards lunchtime I was standing with the customer services manager discussing an issue when I was both startled and surprised by a loud bang caused by the IT trainer slamming his fist on one of the assistant's desks. He exclaimed, 'Why don't you understand what I'm telling you?' and stormed out of the office. I followed him and asked what the problem was, to which he replied, 'She's not bright enough. She just doesn't understand what I'm telling her. She's useless.' My response was simple and straightforward, 'Perhaps it's more to do with your coaching style.' He glared at me and without saying a word in reply strode towards the car park. I didn't invite him back. Some years later when I became a HRD practitioner I used this incident to remind me of the importance of understanding entry behaviour and not forcing learners to learn in one particular way. In terms of career development an ability to obtain in-depth knowledge of the aspirations, concerns, strengths, and weaknesses of the individual is essential. I have to admit though that the career development initiatives I was involved with were extremely time-consuming and did not necessarily benefit the organization (and this can be a major factor in the decision-making process for the allocation of funds).

Source
The author.

Before learning can be translated into value for the organisation, it must be applied to the job. Unfortunately, many employees are left on their own immediately after participating in an intervention. Management's failure to assist in integrating change, skills, or knowledge on the job causes confusion and frustration on both sides. Consequently, much of the change is lost. (Gilley et al., 2002: 351)

There are other factors affecting transfer of learning, and these are discussed in chapter 9, however the above quote is illustrative of the most commonly encountered problem.

Evaluation is a highly problematic process as revealed by the findings of the CIPD's *Learning and Development Survey 2006*. This survey revealed that while only 36 per cent of organizations evaluate the impact on financial performance some 80 per cent of respondents felt that their activities have delivered greater value to the organization than they are able to prove. The survey highlights barriers to effective evaluation, such as lack of resources or time, but also makes the valid observation that much more needs to be done to demonstrate the link between formal interventions and the bottom line. Chapter 9 focuses on some of the financial measures long adopted in US organizations that could be utilized more widely. Chapter 13 continues the discussion but in relation to the HRD function as a whole (returning, for instance, to the role of the balanced scorecard which was introduced in chapter 2).

5.4 **A robust approach?**

The principles underpinning the HRD cycle are alive and well as can be seen from the pages of the CIPD's *People Management* magazine which regularly highlights formal interventions that are clearly predicated on the original STC. Examples include: the design of e-learning programmes; leadership programmes; NVQ programmes; and offshore call centre training. Training is still one of the most widely used strategies for managing diversity in organizations (Wentling, 2004). The focus of the HRD practitioner is much more on finding ways to support the line manager; for instance, in the design and implementation of HRD interventions that focus on skills in coaching, mentoring, and facilitation. In this way the work of the HRD practitioner also has an indirect impact on employees. Ellinger (2005) argues that HRD practitioners can:

> educate managers and leaders about the conditions that trigger informal learning as well as the process of informal learning so that creation of learning opportunities can be enhanced for employees and the process of informal learning can be supported . . . [and] can assist with development of coaching and mentoring skills that enable managers and leaders to play more pivotal roles in this process. Becoming more skilful in providing feedback and helping employees assess, evaluate, and reflect on the outcomes of their informal learning activities are also critical competencies required of managers and leaders. (p. 412)

Line managers in the role of coaches and mentors can create settings which stimulate reflective practice (London, 2003). The development relationship created between the mentor and learner or coach and learner also reflects the role of social learning theory in certain types of formal HRD intervention (see chapter 4).

The role of coaching

> **Key concept**   Coaching
>
> A coach is a peer or manager who works with an employee to motivate her, help her develop skills, and provide reinforcement and feedback (Noe, 2002: 452).

According to the CIPD's 2007 and 2008 'Learning and Development' surveys the majority of UK organizations are now using coaching (Knights and Poppleton, 2007). Coaching interventions require formal support in the form of training of coaches, and support from line managers. Knights and Poppleton (2007) have identified from case study research that there is a continuum of coaching that ranges from a 'hands off' approach to a highly formalized one. Coaching can be used as both an OD and learning and development intervention. It can be used to change the relationship between manager and employee with the evolution of more self-managed teams (McLean et al., 2005). Ultimately, coaching is a flexible and adaptable method of training that is well suited to

> **INSIGHTS INTO PRACTICE**

The role of the line manager

The role that line managers play is illustrated by the following findings from a research study based on six organizational case studies.

The study identified five inter-related factors:

1. Line managers placing more emphasis on the development of employees who are critical to the success of the business, such as knowledge workers (see chapter 10).
2. Having a shared language for learning and development.
3. Having a culture that is supportive of learning and development.
4. Having an effective performance management system that helps managers to support learning and development.
5. Line managers having the skills to support learning and development.

The case study organizations feel that management development programmes need to be supported by other HR practices such as 360 degree appraisal and structured coaching programmes.

Source
Hutchinson, S., Purcell, J. and Winkler, V. 2007. Golden gate. *People Management*, 19 April: 38–40.

the changing demands of organizations and therefore it is not surprising that it is a popular intervention. In recent years, the coaching of senior managers, referred to as executive coaching, has grown in popularity although it remains an ill-defined concept:

> Although executive coaching has been proposed as an intervention to help executives improve their performance and ultimately the performance of the overall organization, whether or not it does what it proposes remains unknown due to the lack of empirical evidence for what happens, why it happens, and what makes it effective or ineffective. (Joo, 2005: 463)

Not only is executive coaching dependent on some form of formal training programme facilitated by an external professional coach but the above quote illustrates the need for a systematic and structured approach to the design process in order that relevant evaluation methods can be implemented.

Key concept   Mentoring

Mentoring involves a more experienced and usually more senior person helping a less experienced employee through discussion and guidance. It is a developmental relationship which is focused on supporting the employee's ability to achieve his/her career ambitions.

Mentoring is well suited to helping individuals with their career development (McDowall-Long, 2004). Formal mentoring programmes are particularly prevalent in business and industry (Hegstad and Wentling, 2005). Mentoring programmes not only enhance career development strategies but also impact on organization development:

> Three major kinds of possible organisational outcomes of mentoring that have been suggested include developing human resources (e.g. improved motivation, job performance, retention and succession planning), managing organisational culture (e.g. strengthening or changing culture), and improving organisational communication. (Hezlett and Gibson, 2005: 455)

Formal mentoring programmes have become increasingly popular as they are believed to offer benefits to both the organization and employee (Allen and O'Brien, 2006) and help to instil loyalty and commitment to the organization (Gilley et al., 2002). Hegstad and Wentling (2004) identified that a systematic design process underpins the development of 'exemplary' mentoring programmes in business organizations:

> A thorough needs analysis . . . should be conducted to determine current organisational needs and to brainstorm possible remedies. If a structured mentoring process is determined to be the most effective way to address an organisational need, then a structured design process should be utilised. A thorough needs analysis will improve the design of the program as well as allow for more accurate evaluation. (pp. 441–2).

This illustrates the continued need for an underpinning systematic approach to the design of HRD interventions.

Developing managers

Organizations have tended to tackle the development of managers through formal management development programmes and education courses. These are theoretically underpinned by a systematic approach but often the learning objectives are generic reflecting the supply-led nature of much of this provision; and, evaluation is rarely carried out (Mabey, 2004). Often management development programmes suffer from a lack of vertical alignment with the business strategy (Espedal, 2004). Increasingly, training is focusing on management *and* leadership (Collins and Holton, 2004). Gilley et al. (2002) argue that management and leadership development is important for four reasons:

1. Organizational performance is dependent on the quality of managers and their respective practices.
2. Managers act as the lifeblood of an organization: 'they are the interpreters of the organization's vision and the executors of its strategy' (p. 127).
3. Managers act as the gatekeepers of quality and performance improvement including the facilitation of employees' learning and development.
4. managers 'are the primary conduit used to improve employee motivation and satisfaction' (p. 127).

Over the last fifteen years or so there has been an increase in public policies aimed at improving the calibre of European managers (Gray, 2004); although actual practices vary considerably across European countries (Brewster, 2004).

To date, the preferred methods for management development in European countries have been internal skills programmes and external courses, with mentoring and coaching the next most popular (Mabey, 2004). More recently in the UK, higher education institutions have been catering for a growth in demand from private sector organizations for leadership development programmes (see *Media watch* box). In the US there has been a continuous growth in the provision of management and leadership development interventions since the 1940s although the quality and integrity of much of this provision by university business schools and training consultancies is now being challenged and criticized (Swanson and Holton, 2001).

MEDIA WATCH BOX

The role of higher education in management development

Surprisingly it is university business schools in particular that are dominating the management development market and not training consultancies.

Source
Times Higher Education Supplement, 16 November 2007: 14.

Courses provided by universities adhere to many of the underlying principles found in formally-designed training and development interventions. However, uncertainty exists over the most effective method for training managers and whether or not there exists a set of universal best practices that transcends national boundaries (Ramirez, 2004). Megginson (1996) defines two types of learning behaviour in managers: planned learning (i.e. a deliberate and thought-out approach to a work situation as a potential learning opportunity) and emergent learning (i.e. an unplanned exploration of a work experience as a learning opportunity). The latter equates to informal learning and it is now recognized generally that informal learning does have an important role to play in management learning and development. Indeed it has been argued for some time that much managerial learning takes place informally on the job as a result of job-related development opportunities (Lowy et al., 1986).

A key challenge for HRD practitioners and line managers is to address barriers to managerial learning. These include:

- Perceptual (not seeing there is a problem), Intellectual (inadequacy of previous learning) and Environmental (the influence of the learning climate on individual behaviour) (Temporal and Boydell, 1981 cited in McCracken, 2004)
- Lack of opportunity to learn (Mumford, 1988)

> **MEDIA WATCH BOX**
>
> ## It's never too late to learn
>
> In SMEs it is often the owner-manager or entrepreneur who is the focus of management development (see chapter 12). Often they are too busy to attend a training course. However, doing so can have a major impact on firm performance.
>
> Hotel Chocolat is an Internet-based firm that was re-branded from its original name (Choc Express) following a co-founder's enrolment on a business and management course targeted at owner-managers. The course was offered by Cranfield School of Management and included a range of topics (e.g. business strategy, finance, and marketing) delivered through workshops. Angus Thirwell, co-founder of Choc Express found himself very quickly applying his learning and improving firm performance. So much so that he recouped the £10,000 cost of the course.
>
> **Source**
> *The Sunday Times* (Small Business), 13 January 2008: 3.10.

- Fear of change (Sambrook and Stewart, 2000)
- Costs and absence cover (Mabey and Thomson, 2000)

This is a complex issue that is difficult to unravel; the reality is likely to be an intertwining of several barriers rather than any single barrier acting as a root cause in any organizational context.

The challenges ahead

The major difficulty facing HRD practitioners is that 'in many cases, HRD has been relegated to a reactive role, solving problems piecemeal as they occur rather than proactively undertaking large-scale organizational learning and change initiatives' (Marquardt and Berger, 2003: 287). Adoption of the HRD cycle will not resolve all aspects of HRD practice in organizations. Just as the STC oversimplified the complex realities of organizational settings (Smith and Sadler-Smith, 2006) so over-reliance on the HRD cycle may inhibit the development of intuitive approaches to HRD. A great many of the problems encountered by HRD practitioners cannot be resolved through scientific or rational approaches. This is a lesson I learnt very quickly when a TQM manager. The adoption of a systematic approach to problem solving and continuous improvement offers many potential benefits but there are times when you need to place your trust in instinct and intuition. Sometimes you need to challenge the rational approach by asking the question, 'does this feel right?' and if the answer is 'no' then time should be made to reflect carefully on the reasons for this and the implications for any proposed HRD activity. The HRD practitioner needs to embrace change and ambiguity (Mankin, 2001) in order to better understand organizational realities. Doing so requires an intuitive understanding of the complexities of an organizational context that needs to be considered in tandem with the application of the HRD cycle. This perspective is developed further in chapters 10, 11, 13, and 15.

Summary

The chapter started by introducing you to the systematic training cycle (STC), a methodical approach to the design and implementation of formal training and development interventions that has been popular for some fifty years. Although traditional classroom-based training and development interventions are in decline there is still an important role for the STC given that many workplace learning opportunities are planned. The STC has been updated as the HRD cycle to reflect the trends discussed in chapter 2, and in particular the shift in emphasis from training to learning. However, it is the HRD cycle that incorporates the principal components of HRD practice (as outlined in chapter 3). The HRD cycle embraces a problem-solving methodology that was popular with TQM practitioners: the PDCA cycle. This emphasis on continuous improvement is at both the micro and macro levels. At the micro level problem-solving skills will become increasingly important as HRD practitioners are challenged 'to find new ways to implement learning technologies that are efficient and effective and that deliver immediate, strategic, and influential results' (Ruona et al., 2003: 279). At the macro level HRD practitioners can adopt a change agent role that enables them to facilitate systemic changes across an organization.

Review questions

1   List and briefly explain the four stages of the systematic training cycle (STC).

2   What are the potential advantages and disadvantages of the STC?

3   In what ways does the HRD cycle differ from the original STC?

4   Why is it important to consider evaluation at the design stage?

5   What knowledge and skills are required by the HRD practitioner and line manager to implement effectively the four stages of the HRD cycle?

Suggestions for further reading

1   Mabey, C. 2004. Developing managers in Europe: policies, practices, and impact. *Advances in Developing Human Resources*, 6 (4): 404–27.

    This article provides a useful overview of management development in Europe.

2   Hezlett, S. A. and Gibson, S. K. 2005. Mentoring and human resource development: where we are and where we need to go. *Advances in Developing Human Resources*, 7 (4): 446–69.

    Read this article to find out more about mentoring.

3   Joo, B-K. 2005. Executive coaching: a conceptual framework from an integrative review of practice and research. *Human Resource Development Review*, 4 (4): 462–88.

    This article provides a useful discussion on executive coaching.

4   **Allen, W. C. 2006. Overview and evolution of the ADDIE training system.** *Advances in Developing Human Resources*, 8 (4): 430–41.

An interesting review of the evolution of the systematic approach to training and development.

5   **Cowell, C., Hopkins, P. C., McWhorter, R. and Jorden, D. L. 2006. Alternative training models.** *Advances in Developing Human Resources*, 8 (4): 460–75.

This article discusses a range of systematic training models that are alternatives to the traditional STC.

Case study

Estate Agency Co

Estate Agency Co currently employs nearly 1,000 people many of whom are currently studying for a professional qualification, the Certificate in Practice of Estate Agency qualification (CPEA), which takes two years to complete. The company has adopted a strategy of expansion in order to provide a better property service to all its customers including buyers, sellers, developers, landlords, or tenants. This strategy has involved the acquisition of new businesses underpinned by a commitment to training and development, to continuous improvement in its systems and to constant innovation, through experimentation with new ideas and new technology. The current mission statement of Estate Agency Co is 'to be the estate agent of first choice by building a reputation for delivering the highest possible standards of service, integrity and performance'.

Estate Agency Co has a development team comprising a learning and development (L&D) manager and two trainers. The Learning and Development manager reports to the HR director. Prior to 2007 the primary role of this team was to design *and* deliver a wide range of training courses covering topics such as: induction, legislation, and skills training. In 2007 the company launched a new management development programme that included the devolvement of responsibility for much of the training of front-line staff to area managers and, in turn, to branch managers. Traditionally, area and branch managers have been concerned primarily with financial management. This new training and development responsibility is seen as an important strand to the company's commitment to improving the quality of its managers, to making them 'well rounded managers' according to the Learning and Development manager. The L&D team have reduced their level of training delivery to branch staff accordingly in order to focus more of their time on the analysis of training needs and the design of branch training interventions that can be customized for use by individual area and branch managers.

The L&D manager typically spends two to three hours with an area or branch manager on a one-to-one basis discussing their own training and development needs in the light of their new, devolved responsibility for the training of their staff. The emphasis now is very much on coaching line managers in order to develop the skills needed to deliver training. This involves giving comprehensive feedback to managers on their progress and listening to their concerns about their own development and that of their staff. This has improved the effectiveness of training needs analysis (TNA) considerably. Previously, the TNA of managers 'always happened in a sketchy manner . . . but the L&D team has now got more involved in this stage since much of the delivery has been devolved to line managers' according to the L&D Manager whose team are responsible for designing the training interventions that will be delivered by managers. However, information obtained from the interviews is used to customize the design to meet the different requirements of branches. As the L&D Manager comments: 'We talk about what they need, what the current market situation in their local area is like, what performance gaps exist in the branches. They tell me what they would like to see included in the course so that I can go away and produce new material or adjust what we've already got before passing it back to them. Their biggest concern is that they do not have the time, or the expertise, to do the actual design, to prepare the training material. I can do this much more effectively'. However, the long term aim of the company is that

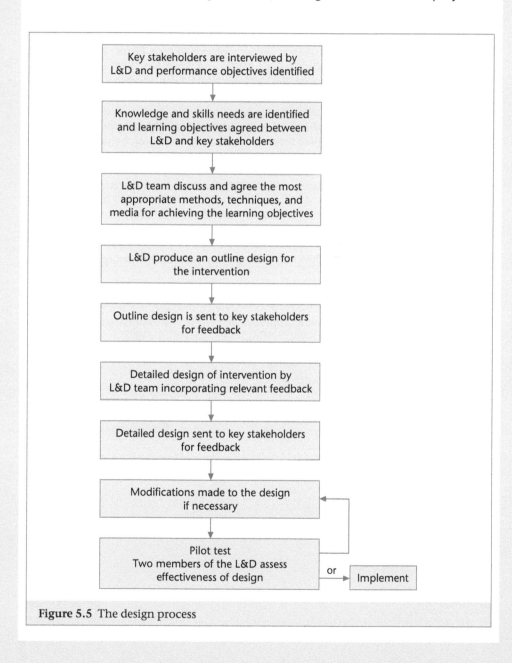

Figure 5.5 The design process

managers will be able to write their own material and design their own courses based on the identification of the training needs of their staff. In terms of the style of the courses these are designed to be as interactive as possible including methods such as role play, quizzes, group discussions, and question and answer sessions. The L&D Manager adds 'We do look at the delegates and consider who they will be sitting next to, whether some personalities will distract others. So we try and cater for a variety of learning styles and therefore suggest to managers that they adjust or drop certain activities accordingly'.

When a manager is delivering his/her first course a member of the L&D sits in so that feedback on the manager's performance can be provided at the end of the course. Typically, the manager will deliver a half-day course in the morning to six participants so that this feedback can take place over lunch. The manager is encouraged to reflect on his/her performance as part of this process (e.g. what he/she felt worked well and what didn't). Where appropriate the manager agrees amendments with the L&D specialist. These amendments range from changes in content to changes in the style of delivery. Then the same course is delivered again in the afternoon to six new participants. A second review and feedback session takes place as before (e.g. how well the amendments worked; how they can be embedded in future courses). An action plan is then produced including a review of the same course at a later date.

In terms of evaluation the L&D manager admits 'It's often the bit that's missed. We're still trying to do more on this. It's partly covered by the feedback from the L&D team member to the manager. We also do look at performance data, such as the number of viewings on a particular property, the number of conversations with customers that are taking place or the number and type of sales and lettings'.

Figure 5.5 above sets out the key stages in the Estate Agency Co approach to the design of training interventions as a result of the new management development programme.

Case study questions

1. To what extent is the Estate Agency Co approach demand-driven or supply-led?

2. How could the company improve its approach to the TNA and design stages illustrated in figure 5.5?

3. What are the benefits of carrying out a pilot test for a L&D intervention?

Online resource centre

Visit the supporting online resource centre for additional material that will help you with your research, essays, assignments, and revision.

@ www.oxfordtextbooks.co.uk/orc/mankin/

6

Identifying HRD Needs

Learning objectives

By the end of this chapter you should be able to:

* Appreciate the reasons why it is important to carry out a comprehensive learning and development needs analysis

* Explain how this stage fits into the HRD cycle

* Describe the three levels at which a needs analysis is normally conducted

* Explain a range of techniques for conducting effective needs analysis at each of the three levels

* Articulate the advantages and disadvantages of the different approaches to needs analysis

Indicative content

■ The purpose of needs analysis and the respective roles of the HRD practitioner, line manager, and employee

■ The reasons why it is important to identify the root causes of performance problems

■ The requirements for an effective organization-level needs analysis

■ Sources of information for organization-level needs analysis

■ The relationship between an organization-wide needs analysis and strategic HRD

■ Performance problems and gaps

■ Techniques for department-level or operational-level needs analysis

■ Job and task analysis using versatility charts, diff-rating scales, task lists, and decision trees

- The relationship between knowledge, skills, and attitudes (KSAs) and competencies

- A problem solving approach to needs analysis

- Techniques for individual-level needs analysis

- The role of performance appraisals in needs analysis

- The general requirements for an effective needs analysis

Key concepts

Learning and development needs analysis/Training needs analysis (TNA)

Attitude surveys

Performance appraisals

Job analysis

Task analysis

Performance gaps

Critical incidents

Problem solving model

Versatility charts

Diff-rating scales

Task lists

Decision trees

Knowledge, skills, and attitudes (KSA)

6.1 **Introduction**

The principal focus of this chapter is the identification of learning and development needs for formal HRD interventions such as training courses, workshops, mentoring programmes, and coaching sessions. It is still an acceptable convention to refer to training needs analysis (TNA) as the first stage in the HRD cycle. TNA embraces a range of analyses that are carried out at the level of the organization, department (operational), and the individual. A training needs analysis is:

> The structured process carried out by a variety of different methods by which information about an organisation's development and training needs is gathered, then reviewed and codified as the basis for [a] development plan. (Mathews, 1997: 10)

The development or training plan sets out identified learning and development needs and the HRD interventions proposed for meeting those needs. Consequently, TNA is an essential starting point for many types of formal learning and development programmes, which as discussed in the previous chapter still account for a great deal of HRD activity in organizations. For instance, mentoring programmes (Hegstad and Wentling, 2004); health and safety training (Senker, 2000); and, coaching interventions (CIPD, 2008). The most significant growth area over the last decade has been in e-learning interventions. These may require HRD practitioners to work with technical specialists in new ways but the overarching process still adheres to the systematic approach discussed in chapter 5 (which also noted that underpinning learning methodologies remain unaltered).

Usually a TNA involves a formal and systematic process but sometimes it can be carried out informally and in a cursory fashion (Blanchard and Thacker, 2004) reflecting the extent to which conducting a TNA is regarded by some as more of an art than a science (Salas and Cannon-Bowers, 2001). This also reflects the extent to which the TNA stage is dependent on collaboration between key stakeholders at each of the three levels. This stage in the HRD cycle is no longer the sole preserve of the 'training expert'. Individuals are taking more responsibility for identifying their own learning and development needs and discussing these with their line manager either at the annual performance review appraisal or on an ongoing basis depending on the organizational context. Line managers have primary responsibility for identifying learning and development needs for their department drawing upon HRD expertise for specialist TNA techniques as and when required. The information from these two levels forms an important part of the organizational analysis reflecting the extent to which much of the HRD practitioner's role at this level is a co-ordination role supplemented by collaborative working with senior managers and, where applicable, with other stakeholders such as suppliers and customers.

The TNA stage can highlight the need for other types of HRD intervention, such as an organization development project, or for the involvement of other departments, such as information technology (IT), marketing, or research and development. Often the role of the HRD practitioner is minimal or redundant in these situations as a different type of expertise is needed to resolve a problem. Consequently, TNA should be seen as a generic term for the investigation of learning and development needs which may or may not result in specific learning and development solutions. The next section discusses the purpose of TNAs in more detail while subsequent sections will explain some of the techniques for conducting a TNA at the three levels of the organization, department (operational), and individual. The final section summarizes the principal requirements for conducting an effective TNA.

6.2 **The purpose of TNAs**

Key concept   Training needs analysis

A training needs analysis (TNA) is a formal and systematic process for analysing the learning and development needs of employees and is usually compiled at three levels: the individual, the department, and the organization.

Analysing learning and development needs enables the HRD practitioner to identify where interventions are needed, who needs to be involved, and what type of intervention is needed. This requires a collaborative approach between the HRD practitioner and key stakeholders. Working in partnership with the line manager is particularly important as they are in the best position to identify the learning needs of employees (Garavan, 2007). The role of the HRD practitioner should be supplementary and supportive: providing specialist advice and techniques when required. The challenge for HRD practitioners is to ensure that line managers have the necessary expertise to carry out their role in this partnership (see *Personal reflection* box). This collaborative approach lies at the heart of the TNA process because:

> Training needs analysis is about gaining agreement on training solutions. It's not about the training department assuming that they know all about the training needs of the employees and the managers. It is paramount that the people are involved in the identification and analysis of needs. (Simmonds, 2003: 42)

Liker and Meier (2007) recommend interviewing employees particularly in smaller firms where it is feasible to talk to every employee directly and identify 'the overall situation and shortcomings of the current system' (p. 59). The simple act of asking employees what works and does not work can be immensely invaluable as Hammersmith Hospitals Trust in the UK discovered when it used a series of workshops to accumulate staff stories about the Trust in order to identify new organizational values that would be grounded in reality (Syedain, 2007).

Often the aim is to identify the underlying, or root *causes* of problems which may manifest as poor performance by an individual or group or as a systemic failure within the organization. Consequently, the first stage in the HRD cycle is regarded as the foundation for effective HRD practice and requires a good knowledge of analytical tools and processes (Roberts, 2006). Once root causes have been identified the line manager and

INSIGHTS INTO PRACTICE

A personal reflection

One of the biggest and recurring difficulties that I encountered as a HRD practitioner was trying to persuade middle-managers, in particular, to adopt a facilitation role. Often this layer of management acted as a barrier to the effective implementation of HRD interventions. Many managers do not understand how their lack of interest in learning and development can act as a barrier to learning. This may appear a somewhat stereotypical portrayal of the middle-manager but the problem has been highlighted in various studies; for instance McCracken (2004) explains that many of the interviewees in his study cited managers paying lip-service to training as a key obstacle to the transfer of learning from the 'classroom' to the workplace. In my experience as a practitioner and academic I have been struck also by how many managers not only have little understanding of learning and development but tend to view it as something to do with individuals only.

Source
The author.

HRD practitioner, in conjunction with the learner(s), can discuss potential solutions. Sometimes these may not require any further input by the HRD practitioner; for instance, where systemic causes are identified that involve other functions such as IT (Information Technology). The involvement of the learner is important because they are actually doing the work; regardless of the type of job involved. Knowledge work, such as research and development, accountancy or human resource management, may be more complex than routine work, such as processing customer orders or transporting materials, but both require the active input of those doing the jobs. This perspective was at the heart of TQM which has informed HRD practice (see chapter 2). One of the principal challenges facing the HRD practitioner is persuading line managers that their role in the practice of HRD is changing (see *Insights into practice* box). This tends to be a large firm perspective with many owner-managers in smaller firms still telling employees what training they need and when they are doing it, or providing little if any training at all (see chapter 12).

In their CIPD research report Stewart and Tansley (2002) argue that the content of formal training interventions will need to be specific to organizational needs and in the case of multinationals adapted to suit local contexts. This strengthens the case for effective TNA in the light of global trends. There may be continued and growing interest in the role of informal learning but there is still a crucial role for formal interventions. Other trends, such as remote working (e.g. from home) and virtual teams are likely to require formal learning and development interventions. The design and implementation of on-line TNA questionnaires is likely to become an increasingly popular method for identifying learning and development needs covering, for instance, health and safety, IT skills, and statistical techniques for problem solving. Many external training consultancies offer

---

INSIGHTS INTO PRACTICE

Barriers to learning

Ian Yates, a Learning and Development comments:

'The two biggest barriers to learning are participants not being prepared by their line manager in terms of a pre-briefing. Not having the opportunity to discuss what they'll be doing, what the learning objectives are and why a debriefing after the training is important. Second, the lack of any debrief or follow-up after the training session. Usually the line manager asks " How did you get on?", the participant says "Great" and the line manager says "Thanks"; and that's all. There is no debrief, no testing of new knowledge and skills, no observation of changed behaviour on the job. Nothing. For us those two things, particularly the latter, are the greatest barriers to effective learning. The learning that takes place in the classroom is lost'.

INSIGHTS INTO PRACTICE

Participating in the TNA stage

Jane Chilman is Director of People First Associates, a training consultancy that specializes in the hospitality and tourism sector. Jane's company offers a range of training interventions covering managing people within the law, discipline and grievance skills, disability awareness, dignity at work, and appraisal skills. In terms of her company's involvement in the TNA stage she comments:

'The only time we tend to get involved with identification of learning and development needs is when we are part of an opening team: we have been involved with the opening of a 5 star 400 bedroom Star London Hotel, 80 bedrooms Boutique Hotel and an Indian Brassiere style restaurant franchise. We normally start with getting the organization to develop their mission statement and company values. Once we understand the business concept we will identify key job roles with the business manager and prepare relevant job descriptions which we will use to identify the skills training required. From this we normally prepare a training plan for each role which forms the basis of the overall Training Plan. In addition we incorporate the necessary statutory training required for each role. The Training Plan is usually in 3 stages, pre-opening, post-opening, and future training requirements. Methods of delivery will depend on the subject matter, style of operation, and budget. Other than on these occasions we tend to be given specific learning requirements which we respond to with an outlined proposal. I consider the lack of involvement in the identification process a weak link, as those carrying out the process do not always identify what their real needs are'.

some form of e-TNA on their websites as a starting point for potential clients; although not all external consultants are given the opportunity to participate in the TNA stage (see *Insights into practice* box). This may be for reasons of cost, (over) confidence in the internal mechanisms for identifying needs, the result of a supply-led approach or an underestimation of the importance of this stage in the cycle.

The traditional focus of the TNA has been on weaknesses or improvement areas. This represents a missed opportunity for identifying what people are very good at and sharing their expertise and achievements across the organization. This type of knowledge sharing has become increasingly important to organizations although the identification of employee strengths 'challenges managers and employees to analyse their behaviours and successes' (Gilley et al., 2002: 37). Often this occurs informally although many organizations have set up knowledge databases to facilitate the sharing of expertise (see chapter 10).

TIPS AND HINTS

The more employees feel they are involved in the analysis of their training needs the more likely any training is going to be seen by them as relevant and meaningful.

6.3 Organization-level TNA

As was explained in chapter 5 an organizational level TNA comprises three elements that reflect supply-led and demand-driven learning and development needs:

- Organizational strategy (referred to generically as business strategy in chapter 3) setting out future requirements for the organization (supply-led)
- Performance problems and gaps that can inhibit the organization's ability to meet its future requirements (both supply-led and demand-driven)
- Personal learning and development that can satisfy career aspirations (demand-driven)

Too often the organizational level of analysis is seen as a 'special' review that only needs to be conducted when triggered by a specific change in the organization's circumstances, such as an organizational restructure or the implementation of a new organization-wide system. Rather, it should be an ongoing, continuous process. This is important also for maintaining the profile of the HRD practitioner. However, a potential danger at this level is information overload. Consequently, an important task for the HRD practitioner is ensuring such information is not only relevant, but also accurate and timely.

Sources of information for an organization-level TNA

The principal sources of information for an organization-level TNA include the organization's (business) strategy and performance indicators. Organizational strategy usually comprises a mix of long term and short term objectives which can cover a range of issues such as:

- Restructuring (including mergers and acquisitions)
- New markets, products, or services
- New technology (e.g. production processes) and computer systems (e.g. customer ordering)
- Changes to legislation (which may be regional, national, or European Union and covers issues from health and safety to discrimination)

The organization's strategy is rarely published as a single, self-contained document. The following observation by Craig (1994) remains as valid today as it did when originally published:

> It is rare for anything more than a passing reference to knowledge and skills to be included in the body of a business plan. Seldom is a clear statement or section included that could be extracted and given to someone with responsibility for learning needs identification. Even where clues are provided it is not commonly within the remit of business plan writing to include such details. (Craig, 1994: 130)

The relationship organization-wide TNA and strategic HRD

The principles of strategic HRD were set out in chapter 3 which also explained that many HRD practitioners are not operating at a strategic level (i.e. their involvement may be partial and sporadic or even non existent). The reality also is that most HRD practitioners are not even given the opportunity to conduct an organization-level analysis (Vaughn, 2005). Many practitioners have a relatively low level of status and find their activities restricted to responding to training demands at the operational and/or individual levels of analysis:

> Training and retraining are responses to particular operational needs and therefore largely reactive and are determined by market demand, rather than being focused on transferable skills. Such training policies may be developed at business unit level without forming part of an organisation-wide training strategy. (Carey, 2000: 33)

HRD practitioners who are involved in organization-wide analysis find themselves needing access to a range of documents and stakeholders in order to be able to deduce the learning and development needs of the organization from a supply-led perspective. Documents include: vision and/or mission statement, marketing strategy, HR plan (traditionally referred to as the manpower plan), corporate policies (e.g. health and safety; environmental); and, performance data. The HR plan is particularly important and illustrates how the boundaries between HRD and HRM practitioners can become blurred:

> Recruiting, developing, and retaining the right employees are crucial for successful strategy execution. The human resources function plays an important role in

developing a sustainable competitive advantage through using people efficiently and effectively as a resource. (Özçelik and Ferman, 2006)

This perspective is typical of a resource based view (RBV) of the organization in which the HRD emphasis is on performance improvement (as was explained in chapter 3). Stakeholders include: board directors, senior managers, heads of department, employees, as well as suppliers and/or customers in many contexts. The HRD practitioner needs to investigate and understand both the internal and external environments. To do this he/she needs to be continuously 'scanning' both of these environments (see *Personal reflection* box and chapter 3 for more on this).

INSIGHTS INTO PRACTICE

A personal reflection

Much of my time as a HRD practitioner was spent visiting sites where I would not only attend formal meetings but also wander around and chat to a wide range of employees. Those working in sales, customer services, and marketing, as well as production and distribution, were good sources of information about the external market; while all were useful in helping me better understand internal dynamics. This may appear to be little more than an anecdotal assessment but such a criticism greatly underestimates the relevance of such an approach to the ongoing analysis of organizational needs. Much of a HRD practitioner's success and credibility is reliant on an intuitive understanding of the sector he/she is working in (as shall be discussed in more detail in chapters 13 and 15). This approach can be formalized through the utilization of benchmarking.

Source
The author.

The scanning of the external environment as part of an organization-wide TNA can involve the use of benchmarking, although this method has its limitations:

It is probably better, though, to see benchmarking as an operational 'trigger' rather than a straight training needs assessment tool. There is no real guarantee that by adapting the best HRD practices in other successful companies, organizational effectiveness or benefits to the bottom line will necessarily result. Training effectiveness is situational and we may not be comparing like with like in all respects. (Reid et al., 2004: 146)

Over the last 10 to 15 years attitude surveys have become a useful source of information, particularly in relation to softer issues such as staff morale, perceptions of managers, understanding of organizational objectives, loyalty to the organization. Attitude surveys provide an insight into an organization's culture. Why is this important?

> **Key concept**   Attitude surveys
>
> Attitude surveys are organization-wide questionnaires that attempt to identify how employees feel about the organization on a range of issues such as leadership and management style, values and culture, reward and recognition, and so on. They are regarded as a useful qualitative measure that can inform decisions about HRD interventions.

First, the environment may affect whether training can produce changes in behaviour that will contribute to organizational effectiveness. Often, if the environment is very poor, employees will resist any kind of training given by the company . . . Second, a careful examination of an organization's culture using a technically sound attitude survey can help pinpoint problem areas within the organization. (Wexley and Latham, 2002: 47)

In many respects the role of the HRD practitioner is similar to that of a detective who is trying to solve a crime: much of the evidence is inferred rather than explicit. Consequently, a combination of good interpersonal skills, intuition, and scientific or rational techniques are needed to be successful.

MEDIA WATCH BOX

The review of training skills development in Tesco plc

Tesco plc currently has 2,318 stores and employs 326,000 people across the world. The Tesco Academy designs and delivers training within the company:

In 2002 a team from Tesco Academy conducted a major review of the company's policy for training skills development. As a result of this review it was decided to implement a new approach to how trainers are developed and have their training skills certified. Tesco was keen for this new approach to embody the latest thinking about adult learning and so The Training Foundation was asked to develop and deliver a tailored trainer development and certification scheme that was compatible with the Trainer Assessment Programme (TAP). Courses were customized to meet the needs of trainers working in the Tesco Academy and across the supermarket chain. Certification is provided jointly by the Training Foundation and Tesco Academy. Over the last three years well over 100 training and line management personnel involved have attended training delivery and training design courses leading to TAP certification.

Source
http://www.trainingreference.co.uk/skills/trainer/tsstudy.htm (accessed 21st November 2007)

Performance problems and gaps

Performance problems and gaps are a feature of organizational life and often reflect the extent to which individuals are deficient in particular skills, knowledge, or attitudes. This is why Chris Argyris argues that single-loop learning (explained in chapter 4) can be found occurring on a daily basis in any organizational setting. Blanchard and Thacker (2004) refer to performance problems as 'triggering events':

> A triggering event occurs when one or more key decision makers communicate that a performance problem exists and it needs to be corrected . . . The performance problem may or may not actually exist, but the key decision maker believes it does. At this point the TNA is initiated. (p. 117)

Most organizations utilize a range of performance indicators, such as: productivity, accidents, absenteeism, waste, customer complaints, down-time (i.e. when a production line is stopped for repairs and/or maintenance). When I visited the Nizsan production facility near Sunderland I was struck by the number of charts, graphs, and tables, based on such indicators that had been placed on public display across the factory. As well as instilling a competitive spirit amongst employees this approach also provided easily accessible and timely data for departments such as training and development.

The traditional assumption that an observable deficiency, such as a task being carried out incorrectly by an employee, simply requires training to solve the problem is flawed (Fenwick, 2006). Often it can be difficult to isolate the underlying causes of a performance problem which can be due to a wide range of factors (see *Insights into practice* box). Many of these underlying causes impact on all three levels of analysis; for instance, poor work climate can be an organization-wide or macro problem as well as a local, or micro one.

INSIGHTS INTO PRACTICE

Possible causes of performance problems

1. The boring and repetitive nature of the work itself
2. Low wages/reward
3. Inefficient work procedures/processes or deficiencies in job design
4. Poor working conditions/work climate
5. Poor motivation
6. Ineffective managers
7. Deficiencies in the way in which performance is managed in the organization
8. Deficiencies in the design of the organization

Sources
Wexley and Latham, 2002; Gilley et al., 2002; McClernon, 2006

HRD practitioners may have to say 'no' sometimes to a request for training in order to help managers tackle the root causes of a problem. What may appear to be a learning and/or development need can sometimes be the symptom of another problem such as an inappropriate procedure, a flawed system or even a poor management decision. HRD practitioners need to be sufficiently assertive to adopt this stance; and also sufficiently creative to offer alternative solutions (see *A personal reflection* box).

(•) INSIGHTS INTO PRACTICE

A personal reflection

I recall a long and difficult discussion with a production manager who was insisting his team leaders needed more training in problem-solving and team-working skills. It became apparent very quickly that the real cause of the problem was the production manager himself. He chaired weekly and ad hoc formal meetings in an autocratic manner always insisting that his 'solution' for any problem was the best. His team leaders genuinely appeared to attempt to implement these 'solutions' even when they knew some were unworkable. Instead of reflecting on his approach the line manager blamed the failed implementation of his 'solutions' on the 'poor' problem-solving and team-working skills of his team leaders. Despite my best efforts I failed to influence his view. The end result? No problem solving and team-working training for the team leaders and very few subsequent discussions between the production manager and myself (I regard this as one of my failures as I should have been able to identify a strategy for persuading the production manager to reflect on his own performance).

Source
The author.

Tackling this type of attitude referred to in the *Personal reflection* box can be particularly difficult when the HRD practitioner has relatively low levels of influence or power. However, the real challenge:

> is not to usurp managers' responsibility for helping their people to meet performance standards. It is to *help* managers identify which problems may have training solutions and to anticipate future learning needs. (Hackett, 2002: 42; emphasis added)

This help can take a variety of forms, including: user-friendly documentation for line managers to use; coaching to help line managers understand the underlying causes of poor performance; advice on potential HRD solutions; ongoing support and encouragement (Hackett, 2002). Coaching, in particular, is seen as being associated with organizational cultures that are characterized by inclusion, involvement, and participation rather than control and compliance (Hamlin et al., 2006).

Sometimes it is not necessary to carry out a TNA (Blanchard and Thacker, 2004). For instance, in 2007 the BBC announced an organization-wide training programme focusing on the corporation's values (see *Media watch* box). This is an example of a supply-led training initiative. However, it is unusual for all departments in an organization to have the same training need and implementing such training can make little sense from a cost-benefit perspective (Wexley and Latham, 2002).

MEDIA WATCH BOX

Helping employees to understand the ethos of the BBC

The Director General of the BBC has ordered the implementation of training in the corporation's ethos for all employees (15,000) and a large number of independent TV producers. This was in response to the revelation that several BBC programme-makers had faked elements of certain shows (e.g. production staff posing as competition winners for premium line phone-in competitions). The training was intended to remind all BBC employees of the corporation's ethos and their responsibility for reporting and broadcasting truthful and accurate information.

Source
http://entertainment.timesonline.co.uk/tol/arts_and_entertainment/tv_and_radio/article2116230.ece (accessed 12 June 2008).

Boydell and Leary (1996) suggest that there are three levels of performance that an organization may aspire to:

1. **Implementing**: which involves bridging the gap between present and desired performance using existing standards to measure against

2. **Improving**: which involves achieving continually rising standards

3. **Innovating**: which involves doing new and better things in order to bring about step change

Consequently, the identification of performance problems or gaps will be driven by the particular level of performance the organization is striving for. What I particularly like about this approach is the recognition of different organizational cultures and the need for HRD interventions that can help improve an organization's performance as opposed to simply maintaining performance. The PDCA model referred to in the previous chapter tends to be used for incremental changes that reflect an 'improving' culture. An 'innovating' culture is often characterized by quantum change which is predicated on a foundation of continuous improvement that is characterized by double-loop learning.

6.4 Department-level or operational-level TNA

The focus at this level is on specific jobs and involves job and task analysis. As was explained in chapter 5 job analysis is a systematic method or process for obtaining detailed information about a job (Gibb, 2002) while task analysis focuses on specific tasks within the job. There are many different approaches to job analysis (Palmer, 1999). A good starting point for this level of analysis is the job description which sets out what the employee does on the job and includes the conditions under which the job is performed (Wexley and Latham, 2002). Job descriptions can be out of date and so the HRD practitioner needs to check the validity of the existing document with the line manager and employee through questionnaires, interviews, and observation.

> **TIPS AND HINTS**
>
> Employees can also be asked to write a synopsis of what they are expected to do in their job or to keep a diary for a period of time that provides a record of what they do and when they do it (Hackett, 2003).

Additional sources of information include:

- Performance standards and/or performance targets
- Management information reports on performance trends, such as: downtime, waste, repairs and maintenance, level of customer complaints (Wexley and Latham, 2002)
- Information from peers, customers, and suppliers; in effect, a form of 360 degree analysis

The next stage is to focus on the specific tasks that comprise the job. Popular techniques for this stage are examples of where the expertise of the HRD practitioner can help the line manager:

- Job or task inventory
- Critical incident technique
- Problem solving model

It is unlikely that many line managers have experience of these. Two other techniques that can be used are time sampling and linear sequencing. Time sampling is where trained observers carry out direct observation of a particular task at random intervals and linear sequencing is where untrained individuals are asked to carry out a task using a step-by-step description of the task (Wexley and Latham, 2002). This is similar to process mapping techniques used in continuous improvement programmes; the flowchart being a popular example. A flowchart for a task is created by the employees who carry out the task, in a session facilitated by a HRD practitioner. This approach highlights potential problem areas such as bottlenecks and corrective loops.

Techniques for job or task analysis

> **Key concept**   Job or task analysis
>
> A job or task analysis involves 'a structured questionnaire that consists of a listing of tasks comprising a particular job' that has been put together by the employees who perform that job (Wexley and Latham, 2002: 58).

By having a list of the tasks required in a job it is possible to develop training interventions that closely resemble the job (Blanchard and Thacker, 2004) and thus improve the likelihood of successful transfer of learning to the workplace (even better if the training can be conducted on-the-job rather than in a classroom or through workplace simulation). Techniques that have been used to assist with the identification of tasks include:

- Versatility charts: a matrix that shows the level of skill for each employee in a work team against a range of tasks (see figure 6.1 for an illustrative example). These charts are used primarily for the day-to-day management of a work team but also provide invaluable information for a TNA. Toyota use a form of versatility chart (see *Insights into practice* box)

- Diff-rating scales: which categorize tasks according to three aspects—their importance, their frequency, and the level of learning associated with them (often referred to as learning difficulty). Within each of these three categories the task can be further ranked. For instance, Importance as: critical, important, not too/minor important, or unimportant; Frequency as: continuously, frequently, occasionally, or rarely; Learning

Task	Bill	Helen	Fiona	Margaret
1	MC		TMC	MC
2	SC	TMC	SC	SC
3		SC		TMC
4	TMC		SC	SC

Key:
C = competent to carry out task
M = main person normally undertaking this task
S = stand-in when main person not available
T = competent to train others in this task

Figure 6.1 Illustrative example of a versatility chart

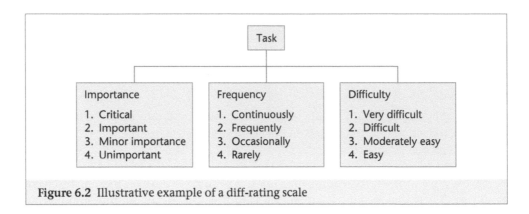

Figure 6.2 Illustrative example of a diff-rating scale

Difficulty as: very difficult, difficult, moderately easy, or easy (see figure 6.2 for an illustrative example)

- Task lists: where individuals list tasks involved in a job and articulate the knowledge and/or skills required for each task along with the proficiency reached (and, where appropriate, any training required) (see figure 6.3 for an illustrative example)

- Decision trees: split tasks into a series of stages on the basis of importance and frequency (see figure 6.4 for an illustrative example).

The identification of knowledge, skills, and attitudes (KSA) and competencies

Traditionally, the information obtained through this level of TNA is used to identify the knowledge, skills, and attitude needed for that job. This is usually referred to as the KSA

⊙› INSIGHTS INTO PRACTICE

The multifunction worker training timetable in Toyota

Toyota has adapted the training plan process to produce Multifunction Worker Training Timetables which show the skill levels of employees in each work area compared against the skill levels actually needed for each job. This approach reflects Toyota's commitment to developing employees who are capable of performing multiple job roles as part of its overall approach to flexibility. Examples can be downloaded from the website: http://www.thetoyotaway.org.

Source
Liker, J. K. and Meier, D. P. 2007. *Toyota Talent: Developing your People the Toyota Way*. New York: McGraw-Hill.

Job title		
Task description	Knowledge/skill required	Proficiency reached
Task 1	Knowledge of health and safety implications	Competent
Task 2	Ability to use manipulation tools	Competent
Task 3	Ability to check for imperfections in product	Not yet competent — further training and guidance needed

Figure 6.3 Illustrative example of a task list

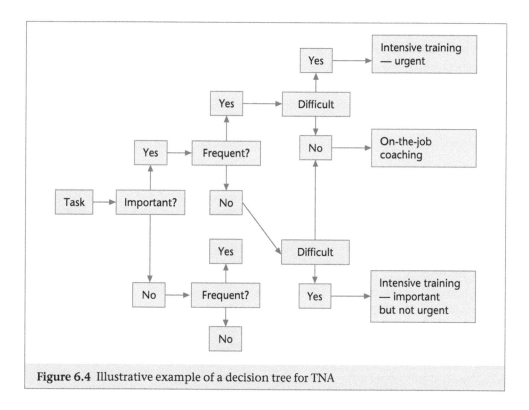

Figure 6.4 Illustrative example of a decision tree for TNA

for a particular job. This information can be used to compile a person specification which sets out clearly the type of person and the types of KSA that they need in order to be able to fulfil the requirements of the job. Knowledge may include such things as: facts (e.g. names, dates, numbers), procedures or sequence of tasks, concepts and principles. Skills may include: thinking and acting in a competent fashion as well as interacting with colleagues. Attitudes manifest as different types of behaviour in the workplace.

Increasingly, organizations are referring to competencies and the design of competency frameworks rather than KSAs; although the extent to which a competency-based approach is applicable will be influenced by national culture as well as organizational culture (Özçelik and Ferman, 2006). The study of competencies can be traced back to the early 1970s and the work of McClelland (1973). Blanchard and Thacker (2004) define a competency as 'a broad grouping of knowledge, skills, and attitudes that enable a person to be successful at a number of similar tasks' (p. 9). Competencies differ from KSAs because, as Dooley et al. (2004) argue, competencies 'establish the *behaviour* requirements needed to be successful in a given profession or task' (Dooley et al., 2004: 317; emphasis added). Blanchard and Thacker (2004) argue that competencies also differ from KSA in several other respects. For instance, they are more general in nature. This means they are not only applicable to a number of jobs or hierarchical levels but they have a longer 'shelf-life' than KSAs which are less adaptive to changing demands on jobs. They also incorporate feelings and emotions and are focused much more on organizational goals. It is the degree of alignment with an organization's strategic goals that determines the long term success of competencies (Özçelik and Ferman, 2006).

This notion of alignment with strategic goals illustrates the extent to which the department/operational level of TNA is inextricably linked to the strategic level. It is important that any analysis at these two levels includes regular reviews of the organization's competency framework to prevent competencies from becoming dated. However, as Simmonds (2003) observes, there are concerns about this competency approach:

> This approach is very limited in both scope and application. There are considerable restraints inherent within competency frameworks. They merely measure what a worker may have been able to do in the past. However, there is no generalisable, transferable, or generic application for the employee's future development. Moreover, there is an all-pervasive sense that there is an in-built competitiveness in such frameworks. There is a desire to perform to the standard that an assessor deems appropriate. One of the major faults of competency frameworks is the concept that a worker is not yet competent. (p. 45)

When I was a HRD practitioner a HRM colleague and I designed the company's first competency framework. This was a time consuming process that took some eighteen months to complete. However, this approach was preferred over the adoption and customization of an off-the-shelf competency framework. Subsequently, the framework was used for recruitment and development purposes and played an important role in the horizontal integration of HRM and HRD processes and practices.

A final observation about the department/operational level of analysis is that employees tend to work in groups, such as sections, teams, and departments. This may be stating the obvious but it can be easily overlooked; for instance, how many recruitment processes incorporate an in-depth consideration of how an applicant may fit into a work group? Self-reporting instruments are particularly popular for the identification of group training needs (Littlepage and Brower, 2004). For instance, some organizations use the Belbin team role inventory to address this issue and this same inventory can also be used as part of a TNA in order to better understand how the existing KSA of team members complement each other and the extent to which gaps may exist which require some form of HRD solution. Group-focused training and development interventions tend to focus on action learning or team problem-solving (Swanson and Holton, 2001) which are discussed in more detail in chapter 7 on delivery.

Key concept   Critical incident technique

Critical incident technique involves identifying those tasks that contribute to effective job performance.

Certain tasks in any job are more *critical* to job performance than others. This technique:

has particular utility when training specialists want to develop a program that concentrates on critical tasks. For example, a restaurant's waiters and waitresses may know how to set up tables and clean them after customers have left. The same waiters and waitresses may have difficulty, however, taking customer orders and relaying these orders accurately to the kitchen. Therefore, the training program should be concerned with these critical tasks. (Wexley and Latham, 2002: 58)

The technique requires detailed information to be collected usually through individual and/or group interviews. The technique focuses on memorable recollections (i.e. critical incidents) rather than on what people think their job should entail (Russ-Eft, 2004). It is well suited to SMEs, particularly in the early stages of organizational growth when training interventions need to unfold rapidly (Reid et al., 2004).

ACTIVITY 6.1

Carry out one of two searches: either on the Internet to find a case study example of the critical incident technique being used as part of a TNA; or in the library to find an article about TNA which mentions the critical incident technique.

Problem solving models have been popular for years. Figure 6.5 sets out a model that I developed and used as a practitioner and which was based on my experiences as a TQM manager. The starting point is to define the nature of the problem using techniques such as flowcharts, control charts, and Pareto analysis. My favourite technique was the flow-chart which is a graphic representation of the sequence of steps that are performed to produce an output. This technique is particularly suited to group discussions where team members can use cards or post-its to write down individual steps and place on a wall or very large wall-chart. The next stage is to identify and prioritize causes using techniques such as observation, discussion and interviews, brainstorming, cause and effect analysis (especially the Ishikawa or 'fishbone' diagram), and ranking techniques. The third stage involves the identification and prioritization of potential solutions by extending the

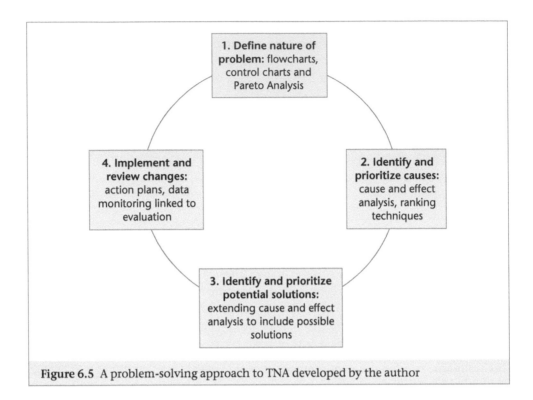

Figure 6.5 A problem-solving approach to TNA developed by the author

techniques used in the second stage. The fourth, and final stage, is the implementation and review of the intervention utilizing action plans, data monitoring, and other forms of evaluation as appropriate to the context of the problem.

> **TIPS AND HINTS**
>
> The problem solving approach to TNA illustrates how this first stage in the HRD cycle can be integrated with an organization's continuous improvement or *kaizen* strategy.

6.5 Individual-level TNA

This level of TNA is often referred to as person analysis because it 'examines those who occupy the jobs to see whether they possess the required KSAs necessary to do the job' (Blanchard and Thacker, 2004: 122). This stage in the HRD cycle needs to be a tailored process if it is going to be successful: a generic 'one-size-fits-all approach' will not work (Bell and Ford, 2007: 59). The respective roles of the line manager and employee are crucial at this level as an important source of information is the performance appraisal or review which can indicate whether a further, more detailed diagnosis of an individuals strengths and weaknesses is needed (Wexley and Latham, 2002). This level does raise some important questions about the validity and accuracy of an organization's performance appraisal or review process. As Buchner (2007) warns:

> Care should be taken to understand the [performance management] system as it is, and how it actually operates, and not simply accept the idealised version typically presented by the organization. (p. 70)

However, an important feature of many performance appraisals is that they provide an opportunity for employees to help identify their own training needs in relation to their present job (Hackett, 2002) as well as development needs in relation to their future career aspirations. Development needs often focus on an individual's potential to progress to other levels and/or roles.

❗ TIPS AND HINTS

It is important to remember though that information obtained from a performance appraisal is dependent on the efficacy of the appraisal process itself.

ACTIVITY 6.2

What skills do you think are required in order to carry out an effective individual-level TNA?

Hackett (2003) argues that there are basically three approaches to performance appraisal:

- **Traits-oriented** which involves an appraisal of personal qualities or attributes such as appearance and punctuality.
- **Results-oriented** which focuses on the measurable outputs or results of an individual (e.g. sales figures; customer complaints; efficiency metrics etc).
- **Competency-based** which focuses on how the individual tackles their job (i.e. emphasizes appropriate behaviours).

Performance appraisals have a dual purpose: they focus on past performance and future needs with the former informing decisions about the latter. However, often appraisals are viewed as simply another method or 'ritual' for controlling performance (Mumford and Gold, 2004) and the development aspects can be lost. This explains why some employees tend to be sceptical about personal development plans. Another problem is that there is a tendency for managers to appraise more leniently for reward-related purposes than for development (Wells et al., 2007).

An aspect of individual TNA which is often overlooked is learner motivation, which as was shown in chapter 4 can be a barrier to learning and thus devalue the potential effect of any learning and development. Consequently:

> In the case of low motivation, interventions that boost motivation to learn could be implemented. Specifically, to increase training motivation, managers could provide training-related information, such as training attributes, training goals, and relevance of training for the respective career. (Rowold, 2007: 27)

In this way the manager can help the potential learner to view the TNA as a credible and meaningful process. A study by Bell and Ford (2007) has shown the credibility of the TNA to be an important driver of learner motivation.

Development centres are becoming increasingly popular as way of identifying learning and development needs. Although development centres are similar in design to assessment centres, which are used for recruitment, they are very different in terms of purpose. Information is reported back to participants in a very different way. Development centres are designed a round a mix of individual and group-based activities and usually incorporate psychometrics: ability or aptitude tests, interest inventories, and personality questionnaires. When I became involved in development centres in the mid-1990s I drew upon Lee and Beard (1994) who described the principal objectives of development centres as:

- Diagnosing development needs through the analysis of individual strengths and weaknesses
- Providing participant feedback
- Identifying and planning the development of individuals, particularly those with higher potential
- Succession planning
- Career planning

Since then development centres have gained in popularity paralleling the increased use of competency frameworks by organizations.

ACTIVITY 6.3

Try to find a case study example of a development centre. What appear to be the advantages and disadvantages of this approach? As well as searching the Internet and journal articles other media publications such as the CIPD's *People Management* magazine can be very useful.

Another popular form of analysis is self-assessment (Hackett, 2002). As with performance appraisals the employee is given responsibility for identifying their own needs (see *Insights into practice* box). However, in some contexts levels of workforce literacy may impact on the viability of this approach (Littlepage and Brower, 2004).

Social learning theory (chapter 4) explains how individuals learn about themselves from others, such as line managers as well as colleagues, customers, suppliers, and so on. Such an approach does have limitations. For instance, it has been shown that supervisors can have very fixed perceptions of subordinates that only change when a remarkable

MEDIA WATCH BOX

Using self-assessment

Jeffrey McIntyre is a vice-president in BNSF railway company which transports freight across the US. When asked about the development of new in-house training and development initiatives for his department, he commented that the company had assembled a team of people who then identified every role and the skills needed for each role which was used as the basis of a self-assessment by employees. Employees rated themselves in terms of skill and level of competence in that skill. This information was then used to produce development plans for each employee. This approach has enabled the company to match appropriately skilled employees with specific projects.

Source
Whitney, K. 2006. On the right track collaboration. *Certification Magazine*, December: 30–2.

situation occurs (Lohman, 2004). You may recall the discussion on reflective learning in chapter 4 and Donald Schön's (1991) reference to 'surprises'. It is possible to develop the self-assessment process further by building in the line manager's perceptions of an employee (see *Personal reflection* box) and further still with the adoption of a 360 degree approach.

INSIGHTS INTO PRACTICE

A personal reflection

As a practitioner I designed a self-assessment process for the company's sales division which was based on a set of KSAs devised through a series of consultations with area and regional sales managers. Area sales managers were asked to rate themselves on a scale of 1 to 6 for each individual KSA. In parallel to this regional sales managers were asked to rate each area sales in a similar way. This data was analysed and presented in graph form which provided a highly visual representation of any perceived differences in perception; thus highlighting KSA gaps that could then be discussed at the performance appraisal. For the vast majority of area sales managers there was a good degree of convergence on perceptions suggesting a high level of honesty. However, there were also a small number of very tricky discussions which usually revolved around an area sales manager over-rating their level of performance across a significant number of KSAs.

Source
The author.

When conducting a TNA at the individual level it is important to take into account relevant work flows or processes (McClernon, 2006):

> In recent years, TandD has learned to think in terms of work processes, not just jobs. The job perspective uses the job as the basis for thinking about and carrying out TandD. When job roles were stable, TandD could be organized around jobs and job hierarchies . . . Given the instability of jobs and the increased focus on how the work gets done, work processes have become increasingly important. (Swanson and Holton, 2001: 250)

The adoption of TQM techniques for TNA provides the HRD practitioner with a much better stocked 'toolbox'. As was explained in chapter 5 the HRD cycle incorporates a systematic approach to continuous improvement referred to as PDCA. Within the 'Do' stage, linked to TNA, techniques such as flowcharts, fish-bone or Ishikawa diagrams, Pareto analysis, and the '5 Whys' are highly effective techniques for identifying learning and development needs through an analysis of work processes.

MEDIA WATCH BOX

TNA at Thames Water

'Thames Water, owned by the German utility group RWE, launched a new UK strategy in October 2004 aimed at making the company the leading water and waste-water company in the UK. Data from staff surveys as part of the strategic review process had revealed that leadership was one of the lowest scoring categories and to address this the company "brought in" business psychologists Kaisen Consulting to carry out a leadership capability exercise or "development needs analysis" (DNA)— a term coined to reflect that, as with genetics, everyone has different development needs. The process for each manager was made up of a day of one-on-one sessions, including interviews, psychometrics and "know how" assessments, followed by a half day for feedback and putting together a detailed development plan . . . Many of the development needs identified through the DNA process have proved to be areas that managers can work on themselves, either with their line manager or their teams. A variety of initiatives have also been introduced, including performance coaching'.

Source
Warren, C. (2005) Still Waters. *People Management*, pp. 34–6.
(Originally published in *People Management*, 29 September 2005, and reproduced with permission)

6.6 **The requirements for an effective TNA**

In order to conduct an effective TNA it is important to:

1. Allow sufficient time and resources to conduct the TNA. TNA is a resource intensive and time consuming process.

2. View TNA as an ongoing, continuous process rather than a once-a-year snapshot. Organizations are constantly changing and the HRD practitioner needs to be aware of these changes (e.g. restructuring, new computer system, new products or services and so on).

3. Consider the relationship between macro- and micro-contexts within the organization. As explained in chapter 5 the different levels of analysis are normally carried out at the same time. This is important because analysis at the individual level, for instance, can be done relatively quickly but tends to be not only a reactive process but fails to take into account the 'bigger' picture provided by an organization-wide analysis.

An important aspect of conducting a TNA at any level is transparency. As a HRD practitioner I heeded the advice of Matthews (1997) which remains valid today:

> An important part of the process is to make sure that staff know why the training needs analysis is being carried out, what their role is and the likely outcomes of their involvement. Team briefing sessions and notices in the staff journal and on the office e-mail will all help to let staff know what is happening and will increase their willingness to participate actively. (p. 7)

Ultimately, the adoption of a TNA reflects a rationalist approach to HRD. It is assumed that a TNA will provide objective data upon which to base the design of an intervention (Cunningham and Dawes, 1997). This reflects a business-driven approach to HRD processes: any investment in HRD interventions is expensive and consequently it is important that such investments be based on a careful analysis of need(s).

Approaching a TNA from a rationalist approach requires the HRD practitioner to undertake a number of stages (see figure 6.6).

Each of the stages in figure 6.6 is explained in more detail:

1. **Decide who else needs to be involved in the TNA.** As well as key stakeholders, such as line managers and learners, he/she may need to involve other HRD practitioners (e.g. colleagues in a central department and/or external consultants). Involving stakeholders at this early stage enhances the likelihood of success when the intervention is implemented. As with so many organizational processes one of the best ways to gain commitment is to involve the people who will be most affected.

2. **Plan the sequence of activities.** This is particularly critical in a large organization where it is likely the three levels of analysis will be carried out simultaneously. Sometimes certain information needs to be treated as confidential or handled in a sensitive manner.

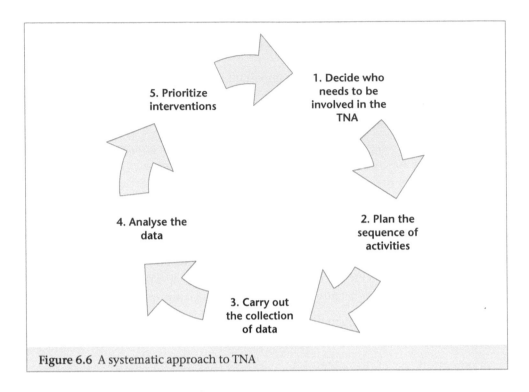

Figure 6.6 A systematic approach to TNA

3. **Carry out the collection of data.** In reality this is likely to be a series of ongoing and overlapping phases with the eventual HRD plan being updated on a continuous basis as a result of data obtained from TNAs and evaluation exercises. You need to ensure that the purpose of this stage is fully understood by stakeholders who may not appreciate the need for a thorough analysis.

4. **Analyse the data.** Interpret the data and identify supply-led and demand-driven HRD needs and categorize potential solutions accordingly: learning and development, organization development (OD), career development (CD), or non-HRD solutions. This may result in further data collection to confirm the findings or help pinpoint solutions.

5. **Prioritize interventions.** In my experience the HRD needs of an organization always outstrip the funds available (in the form of a HRD budget). It is important to decide which issues are of most importance to the organization at the time (while recognizing that this can easily change). The HRD practitioner needs to ask him/herself a range of questions, including: Which interventions will have the most impact on organizational performance? How soon will benefits be realized? What level of resources will be required to support the intervention? Which interventions are the most urgent? What needs to be done before the intervention can be implemented? How will the implementation be evaluated?

The results from the different levels of TNA can be used to compile an organizational HRD plan. This plan should summarize key findings and project the numbers to be trained, the competencies or knowledge, skills, and attitudes (KSA) being developed, the anticipated duration of the training, and anticipated costs (Hackett, 2002). In terms of anticipated duration of the training this should include an estimate of the time needed for successful transfer of learning to the workplace. This can only ever be estimated as individuals will vary in the length of time and the additional support they will need in order to embed new knowledge and/or competencies. Costs should include both direct and indirect costs as explained in chapter 5. An organization training plan which all managers can access also serves another purpose: it can demonstrate the extent to which learning and development is embedded in the organization's culture (Slotte et al., 2004). However, this will involve getting managers to better understand how learning is about more than individualized programmes (Slotte et al., 2004) as highlighted by the discussion of strategic choices for HRD in chapter 3. While many managers understand the importance of the TNA stage their energies are often directed toward the day-to-day control of their department and the achievement of performance targets.

Summary

The first stage in the HRD cycle involves the accurate identification of learning and development needs. This information is normally acquired through training needs analyses (TNAs) conducted simultaneously at three levels: the organization, the department (operational), and the individual. Learning and development needs tend to be a combination of supply-led and demand-driven issues and a variety of techniques can be used to collect relevant data at each of the levels. These techniques comprise the HRD practitioner's 'toolbox'. However, as a wide range of stakeholders are involved in the data collection process this rational approach needs to be combined with the utilization of softer skills, including intuition. Many HRD practitioners are not given the opportunity to carry out a strategic-level analysis and this can lead to an incomplete assessment of the organization's needs. The role is rather like being a detective: much is inferred rather than stated explicitly in an organization's published documents.

Review questions

1   What questions is a HRD practitioner trying to answer by carrying out a TNA at all three levels?

2   What are the principal implications of conducting an effective TNA at all three levels?

3   What are the implications for line managers in each of the five stages of a systematic approach to conducting TNAs?

4   What are the differences between KSAs and competencies?

5   Define and explain a job analysis and a task analysis.

Suggestions for further reading

1   Russ-Eft, D. 2004. Customer service competencies: a global look. *Human Resource Development International*, 7 (2): 211–31.

Read this in conjunction with Özçelik and Ferman (2006) below in order to better understand the role of competencies in HRD.

2   Vaughn, R. H. 2005. *The Professional Trainer*. San Francisco, CA: Berrett-Koehler.

This text offers some insights into the realities of HRD practice, including other stages in the systematic process.

3   McEnrue, M. P. and Groves, K. 2006. Choosing among tests of emotional intelligence: what is the evidence?', *Human Resource Development Quarterly*, 17 (1): 9–42.

This is a useful article for finding out more about emotional intelligence.

4   Özçelik, G. and Ferman, M. 2006. Competency approach to human resource management: outcomes and contributions in a Turkish cultural context. *Human Resource Development Review*, 5 (1): 72–91.

This article includes a good summary of competencies and how they can underpin approaches to formal interventions.

5   Roberts, P. B. 2006. Analysis: the defining phase of systematic training. *Advances in Developing Human Resources*, 8 (4): 476–91.

This is a relatively short but highly informative article on the importance of the first stage in the STC.

Case study

Adopting a systematic approach to training and development

Tom Holden is an independent training and development consultant based in South Wales with over 20 years' experience. During this time he has worked with a range of clients, including the Ministry of Defence (MoD), Home Office, Metropolitan Police Service, IBM/Barclays, Fujitsu, and LloydsTSB. His particular areas of interest and expertise are Training/Learning Needs Analysis, Evaluation and Return on Investment. In tackling training and development projects Tom has devised his own variation on the systematic training cycle which has proven to be highly successful for tackling his clients' problems. This is shown in figure 6.7 (Tom Holden's Vortex© model).

The reason for this methodical approach is explained by Tom: 'How many times has the need for training been recognized, welcomed by all, then criticized harshly after it has been delivered? Too many times? In any economic environment, it makes no sense to throw money at training. Training must be focussed'. Consequently, training needs should be developed from a business case which has resulted from a perceived need to change something: 'A TNA is normally required because there is change taking place within the organization. Mostly, an outside "driver" will have created the need for change, though not all changes will lead to training. Some changes may only lead to an amendment in a manual or the change in a machine setting'. Tom adds, 'It is important for anyone involved with a TNA to be able to question the business need, because it is from the business need that the training need is derived. You should still ask to see the business case in order to understand the driver that created the business need. If there is no written business case there is always a strong risk that you may end up running down the wrong road'.

The next stage is for the training consultant to meet with the client. A face-to-face meeting enables the consultant to: give and receive information; share creative ideas; arrive at joint decisions; and, occasionally to air any differences of opinion about what needs to be done. 'The outcome of this phase can be anything from a simple statement of how you intend to conduct the TNA or a detailed project plan', explains Tom, adding 'If evaluation is required, then the methods for collecting that data must be decided and agreed upon here'. He continues, 'The plan for the TNA must be signed-off by the client before any further work is done'. Tom refers to this as a 'Change Control' point in the process. He explains that 'the most common tool used for the planning of a TNA is an electronic tool such as MS Project. Most clients would expect to see a plan done using such a tool. However, this tool will only take you so far. You will most probably have to support actions listed on the plan with a MS Word document'. Next data are gathered about any training needs: 'This is also an important phase for gathering pre-training evaluation data. Without this data it is impossible to look back and compare on improvements'. The data collation and writing reports phases are about sorting and interpreting the data in order to arrive at potential training solutions. Presenting this report back to the client at a meeting is a critical stage for the consultant.

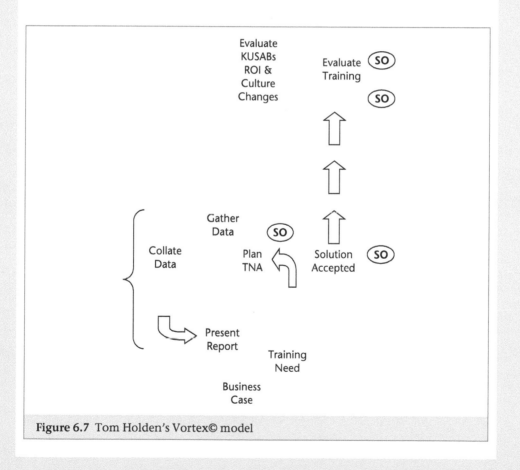

Figure 6.7 Tom Holden's Vortex© model

During these first phases of the project 'it is vital, at every opportunity, to list for the client any risks and assumptions that are related to actions and solutions within the analysis process'.

In terms of the training that is recommended to the client Tom explains: 'The "training solution" you are going to recommend is based upon the data you have gathered in your research. It will be focussed and appropriate. It may be "blended", that is a mixture of learning situations—IT and classroom. It may be just classroom or instructor-led. It may take place on-site at the Client's workplace, or away in a hired classroom. Training can take place anywhere, anytime where planned and controlled learning takes place. What is vital is that the training or learning must meet the need of the organization or individual'. This is critical if the remaining stages, from developing the training through to evaluating training, are to be effective. Tom concludes, 'It is possible for a client to discover that, after evaluation has taken place, there is a need for further training to meet a related business need, exposed by the training. If that is the case, then round you go again!'

Key to figure 6.7:

SO   Sign-off Points for Quality and Change Control and for completion of evaluation. Not all are needed for every training project—just as appropriate.

KUSAB Knowledge, Understanding, Skills, Attitude, and Behaviour.

ROI   Return on investment

Case questions

1. What are the potential benefits of this approach for (a) the client, (b) the training and development consultant, and (c) the learners?

2. What constraints might a client impose on the training and development consultant that could inhibit the effectiveness of the TNA stage?

3. What TNA techniques would you recommend using in each of the following organizational contexts? Assume the employer in each example is interested in improving levels of productivity (therefore start by deciding how productivity might be measured in each context).

   a) The research and development department of an IT software company

   b) Customer service staff in a financial services call centre

   c) Production workers in a factory making concrete roofing products

   d) Lecturers in a university business school

Online resource centre

Visit the supporting online resource centre for additional material that will help you with your research, essays, assignments, and revision.

 www.oxfordtextbooks.co.uk/orc/mankin/

7

Designing Learning and Development Interventions

John Roscoe and David Mankin

Learning objectives

By the end of this chapter you should be able to:

* Explain the relationship between design and other stages in the HRD cycle

* Appreciate the respective roles of the HRD practitioner, line manager and learner in the design process

* List learning and development ('training') strategies and criteria for their selection

* Describe the decisions to be made in designing a learning and development intervention

* Identify and construct a training or learning objective based upon an identified learning need

* Structure a learning and development session to produce a draft design

Indicative content

■ The respective roles of the HRD practitioner, line manager, and learner in the design process

■ The key constraints on the design process

■ The six stages in the design process

■ Agreeing the aim and objectives for interventions and the relationship between performance and 'training' or learning objectives

■ Selecting a 'training' or learning strategy

- Trends in e-learning and blended learning

- Evaluation methods and the different types of assessment

- How to decide the content, methods, sequence, structure, and media for an intervention

- Choosing a venue and the advantages and disadvantages of using internal facilities

- Incorporating relevant learning theory in the design process

Key concepts

HRD designer	Training or learning strategy
Learning objectives	Training methods
Learning outcomes	Evaluation and assessment
Performance statement, conditions statement, and standards statement	Learning theory

7.1 **Introduction**

Design is the second stage in the systematic training cycle and the HRD cycle, and follows on from training needs analysis. Design should not be considered until it has been confirmed that a HRD intervention is appropriate and will be supported by line management, and the organization is prepared to commit resources. As chapter 6 explained HRD needs often relate to a current or future performance problem where developing knowledge and skills is an appropriate response. Other possible causes of performance problems are lack of motivation and support or the environment is wrong for job holders to apply the knowledge and skills they possess. Providing opportunities to learn in such cases will not result in a change of performance because the things preventing performance have not been addressed.

The starting point in the design stage is the identification of learning or training objectives. These are often referred to as the *learning outcomes* of an intervention (i.e. what the intervention is expected to achieve). Consequently, they provide the initial framework for the design stage which

> must be based on a well-thought-out process that will minimise later problems
> and lead to a successful learning experience for all persons concerned. (Vaughn,
> 2005: 19)

It is important also at this initial stage of the design process for HRD practitioners to agree how the intervention will be evaluated.

Different approaches to design for meeting learning outcomes can be equally successful depending upon circumstances or context. For instance, designing a one-to-one coaching session is very different to designing a series of inter-related workshops, although the underpinning principles remain the same. This chapter sets out those underpinning principles. A variety of terms have been used to describe the role of the HRD practitioner in the design phase. For instance, 'instructional developer' (Allen, 2006), 'instructional designer' (Vaughn, 2005; Cowell et al., 2006), 'program developer' (Dobbs, 2006) or 'training designer' (Blanchard and Thacker, 2004). For the purposes of this chapter the term 'HRD designer' will be used. This chapter will focus on the design of formal learning and development interventions, such as training courses and workshops. Other types of HRD interventions, such as OD projects, involve a project management approach and there is a wide range of literature on this topic (although certain implications are covered in chapter 8). There is also a view that increasingly there is a convergence of the 'designer' and 'project manager' roles as a training designer becomes a project manager 'capable of interacting with multiple outsourcing agents or organizations' (Hansen, 2006: 498). This theme will be returned to in chapter 15. Stakeholders such as line managers are not always involved in the design process which still relies predominantly on the expertise of the HRD practitioner. This situation is changing and there is nothing to stop the 'designer' consulting these stakeholders at each stage in the design process. This can assist with stakeholder buy-in of the proposed intervention.

7.2 **Constraints**

There are many decisions that need to be made in designing an intervention. All of them interact so there is no sequence whereby a single decision made is final. Each new consideration can call into question the previous decisions made in the design process. This is often because every design will have some limits imposed by the circumstances or context in which it is being developed. Often these constraints are not made explicit because they are already known and tacitly accepted. For example that the training will be in a classroom in the training centre, it will be delivered by in-house trainers and last no longer than two days. By thinking about the constraints around the design it may be possible to 'think outside the box' and come up with better design solutions or to identify particular barriers to achieving the desired result and what needs to be changed to achieve that result. Typically, the constraints are around four key factors (see figure 7.1).

Each of these constraints will now be considered in more detail:

• **Organization support and culture:** The HRD designer needs to be concerned about identifying the level of support for the intervention. Do the managers recognize the problem and see training as the solution? How supportive are management: will they

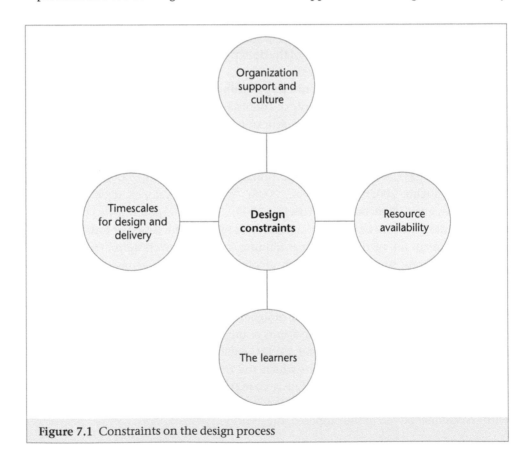

Figure 7.1 Constraints on the design process

be willing to provide resources and release learners? What types of learning activities are seen as legitimate in the organization? The answers to these questions will determine what the final design looks like.

- **The resources available:** The resources that are available in terms of money, training materials, facilities, and trainers needs to be determined. Money is required to develop the design, develop and purchase materials, and then pay for delivery. Who will do the design and delivery is another resource issue. Are there trainers in-house with the capability to design for a particular need? Does the organization have the trainers to deliver the intervention in the locations that will be needed and in the timescale required? When and where existing learning resources can be adapted to meet the need there is an opportunity to reduce development time. Money is also needed for administrative support during the design stage (as well as the other stages).

- **Timescales for design and delivery:** Timings to develop and deliver the learning are dependent on a number of factors. These include the consequences of the problem, might it be threatening to life, costing money, losing customers, or closed down by a regulator? Must the design be a complete solution that gets it right first time or is there an opportunity to pilot and refine the design? The answers to these questions will determine the pressure to start training as soon as possible. Where training is needed immediately it becomes attractive to buy-in an off-the-shelf design.

- **The learners:** Time for training and time to learn must also be considered. How long can the learners be released for training? Will this be sufficient time for them to achieve the objectives? Perhaps the performance at the end of the initial training can be at a lower standard with further practice built in back on the job to achieve the desired performance level. This might be acceptable for an administrative job but not for one where errors could cost lives. How many learners there are needs to be considered: where they are and whether they all have the same level of existing knowledge and skills. Will the same learning intervention be appropriate for all of them? Can they be released for a learning event during work time? How many can be released at once? Can learning be provided for them at the workplace to access between work activities? Do learners have access to computers and the Internet? Will their managers release them for training and support them to apply their learning after the learning event? To produce an effective design to meet the need it is important to have information about the learners. This includes details of the numbers and locations of those having the learning need. This influences selection of the training strategy and the possible locations and timings of learning events. Also learners are not empty vessels and an effective design must build on the existing knowledge and skills of the learners. Information is needed about what the learners already know and can do. The difference between the knowledge and skills needed to achieve the learning objectives and the learners' current level is referred to as the training gap. The learning event needs to focus on bridging that gap. Time and resources should not be wasted on training people in things that they already know and can do. Equally if the training is pitched too high then learners will not benefit from the learning event because they do not have the background to understand. It is also worth considering the learners experience of learning, their learning skills and preferences, and their learning styles.

The way in which these constraints are addressed will vary from intervention to intervention as well as from organization to organization.

Key concept   HRD design

HRD design is the systematic development of a HRD intervention using established methodologies and techniques.

MEDIA WATCH BOX

How valid are instruments for measuring learning styles

A recent study has revealed that very few instruments for measuring learning styles can be trusted in terms of statistically meaningful results. The problem is that some people believe learning styles are stable characteristics of an individual while others argue that they can change. The best instruments can help HRD practitioners but perhaps it is better not to label people in a particular way.

Source
People Management, 29 July 2004: 44.

7.3 **Key stages in the design process**

There are six key stages in the design process (see figure 7.2). Each of these stages requires a range of decisions to be made by the HRD designer, often in conjunction with other stakeholders. Indeed, the involvement of stakeholders is critical to the design stage:

> By connecting with those people who are most likely to be affected by the outcomes, trainers are more likely to be able to achieve their aims. We must, therefore, engage others in a process of questioning dialogue. (Simmonds, 2003: 84)

This is why many HRD designers will produce a 'design brief' which outlines the need, the constraints, and proposed approach. The design brief will help decide whether to undertake the design in-house or outsource it to existing providers or specialists who have the capability to design, develop, and deliver the particular training. The 'design brief' should be agreed with the 'client' and will enable the outsourced provider to develop their design. This provides the line manager with an opportunity to discuss alternative options, potential constraints the HRD practitioner may not be aware of, and any concerns he/she may have about the intervention (for instance, impact on performance,

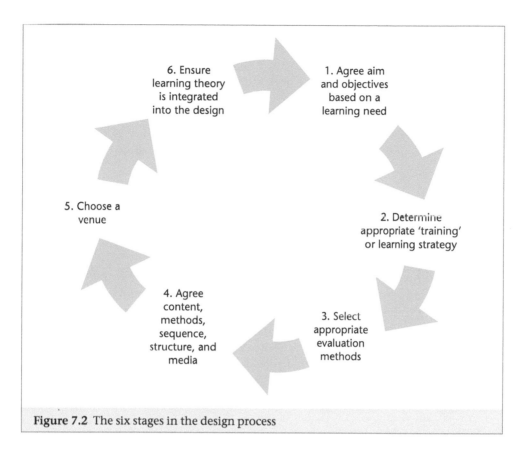

Figure 7.2 The six stages in the design process

A personal reflection

As part of a company-wide change initiative I was approached by the managing director to design a training workshop targeting line managers that could combine change management processes and techniques with a detailed explanation of the rationale for the proposed change. My immediate response was that this could be best achieved with the active involvement of directors in the design and delivery of the workshops. After several discussions with board directors it was agreed that the manufacturing director, sales director, and marketing director would get involved in the project. All three helped to design and deliver the workshop (which ended up as a two-day intervention). This enhanced the credibility of the intervention and enabled learners to ask questions directly to the strategic decision-makers making my role as the lead 'trainer' a great deal easier.

Source
David Mankin.

implications of evaluation methods to be used). The line manager may also want to be involved in the delivery (see *Personal reflection* box).

Learners can also be an integral part of the design process. As was explained in chapter 6 these are the people actually doing the work and therefore are often ideally placed to offer constructive criticisms about the design of the intervention. This will not always be appropriate; for instance, the intervention may be aimed at addressing behavioural problems inherent in the target audience's attitude to performance issues; or time away from the job may be a problem. An example of learner involvement is given in the *A personal reflection* box.

◖•◗ INSIGHTS INTO PRACTICE

A personal reflection

I was asked by one of the company directors to design a development programme for secretaries and personal assistants as part of a career progression and retention strategy. Following a detailed TNA across the company I invited three secretaries to be part of the design team which involved them attending a series of project meetings at which ideas were brainstormed, evaluated, and included or rejected as part of the design. This helped to produce a much more successful intervention and created a strong sense of ownership among the target audience as word spread informally that secretaries were being involved in this way.

Source
David Mankin.

7.4 Aim and objectives

Having started from an identified need the first step is to decide on the learning outcomes required and agree them with the client. The learning outcomes are best captured by developing objectives that specify what the learners will be able to do, under what circumstances and to what standards of performance. The aim of the training should be captured in a single sentence that describes the general intent or purpose. From this can be developed a learning objective that is very explicit about what the learner will be able to do as a result of the training. For instance, the purpose of this textbook is to enable students to develop an understanding of human resource development. To achieve this aim each chapter has been structured around several learning objectives such as: by the end of this chapter you will be able to explain the relationship between design and other stages in the cycle. When designing an intervention, learning objectives can be broken down into enabling objectives which together contribute to achieving the learning objective. These can include underpinning knowledge and component skills learners need to contribute to achieving the learning objective. This can be shown as a hierarchy (see figure 7.3).

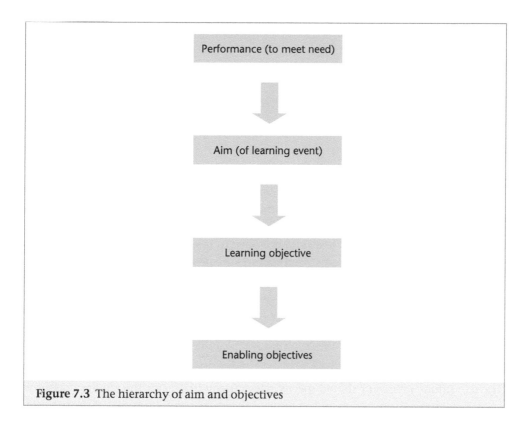

Figure 7.3 The hierarchy of aim and objectives

Key concept   'Training' or learning objective

A 'training' or learning objective is an explicit statement of what a learner is expected to be able to understand and/or do as a result of participating in a HRD intervention.

Why is this part of the design stage so important? The aim and objectives provide the framework around which the design process hinges:

> Effective objectives *help to design the training* precisely to fit the needs of trainees and the organisation. Written objectives indicate that conscious decisions have been made about what skills, knowledge, and abilities to include in the training ... based on the needs analysis process. (Vaughn, 2005: 66; emphasis in the original)

The total number of objectives for a learning event should match the scale of the training. Three or four objectives per day of training is reasonable. Too many objectives can make it difficult for those looking at them to grasp the level of detail implied. A good objective should contain the following components:

- A clear statement of learner performance at the end of training
- The conditions under which the performance will take place
- The standards of performance expected

These three parts of a learning objective are expanded on below.

Performance statement

The performance is determined by the analysis of the training need. It should be an observable behaviour that the learner will be able to demonstrate in order to confirm to themselves and others what they have learned and achieved. It should be complete and self contained in the objective, described by a single active verb. This should result in a performance that will be clear to all and not open to interpretation by different learners and trainers. For the learning objective it captures the performance at the end of training. For instance, in the following learning objective the performance statement is indicated in italics: by the end of this training session *participants will be able to type a letter* at a speed of 120 words per minute using Microsoft Word without making any errors.

Conditions statement

The conditions statement should specify relevant conditions for the required performance. This covers the materials and equipment the learner will use as part of the performance. The location for performance, is it in a workshop or by the side of the road, in the office or on a client's premises? What use of reference materials, online databases, help and advice from colleagues, and other aids to performance will be allowed? The purpose of identifying the conditions is to help the learning to be transferred to the job. For instance, building on the above example: by the end of this training session participants will be able to type a letter *at a speed of 120 words per minute using Microsoft Word* without making any errors.

Standards statement

Standards should specify the level of achievement of the required performance. Standards can be defined in terms of quality, quantity, and completeness of performance. The standards should be specific and unambiguous, as well as realistic and achievable, so that they can be applied objectively (by different persons). The standards help trainers to decide what learning experiences are appropriate and how the performance can be measured. It tells the learners what is expected of them, what they are aiming at through their learning. If the standard required on the job is not going to be achieved during the learning event then this needs to be agreed with the client and how the gap will be closed planned. For instance building further on the above example: by the end of this training session participants will be able to type a letter at a speed of 120 words per minute using Microsoft Word *without making any errors*.

INSIGHTS INTO PRACTICE

The importance of learning objectives

Tim Jones is an experienced HRD practitioner who argues that learning objectives may be hard to articulate but are crucial to the design process for a variety of reasons. He believes learning objectives:

'Define outcomes for both learners and trainers so they are clear about what is expected from the learning. (He has found that learners find it easier to learn when they are clear from the outset what will be expected of them.)

Provide a basis for the evaluation or assessment of results. If standards are not made explicit how can performance at the end of learning be measured?

Help to select the training strategy. Because performance and standards are clear it helps decide what types of training strategy will support the required performance.

Help select training methods. As with selecting the strategy, if the performance requires demonstration of skills then methods that allow development of the skills must be used, if knowledge then methods appropriate for knowledge can be used.

Provide the basis for agreeing outcomes with the client. The objectives make explicit what the learners will be able to do and can confirm to the client that the training need has been correctly identified and the learning to meet that need specified.

Provide the basis for bidding for resources. Depending on the performance required the constraints around the design may prevent achievement of the required performance. If this is the case then agreement with the objectives can be used to support the request for the resources that will be needed to meet the objectives.

Summarize the proposed learning event. The objectives are a summary of what the learning event is all about'.

ACTIVITY 7.1

The following training need has been identified within an organization: to be able to appraise members of staff as part of the performance management system. Draft some potential learning objectives and enabling objectives for this. How could these objectives be checked for appropriateness?

7.5 Selecting a 'learning or training strategy'

Designing training is often thought of in terms of running face-to-face training sessions with a group of learners, such as courses and workshops. In fact there are many different ways to meet learning needs and one way to describe these approaches is to call them *training strategies* or learning strategies. These are shown in table 7.1.

Training strategy	Description
Education	Adopting education as a response to a training need relies on using existing provision in colleges and universities. This is based on generic needs, often to meet professional body requirements. Education can provide learning with subject experts and is usually more appropriate for development needs rather than specific job requirements. For instance, many universities and colleges offer courses that lead to membership of the Chartered Institute of Personnel and Development (CIPD) as well as general management qualifications such as the MBA. Companies such as INA Bearing, a Llanelli based producer of high precision engine components for the automotive industry, has introduced an NVQ level 2 in manufacturing operations for all production operators (Evans, 2004)
E-learning	E-learning has become a very well known option as a training strategy driven by the growth in power and availability of computer hardware and software. IT infrastructure is a major investment for organizations and adopting e-learning can provide an additional return on the investment. E-learning has headline attractions in low costs per trainee, consistency of delivery, and 24/7 accessibility. This method is particularly appealing to organizations operating on a global basis which have to train a geographically dispersed workforce (Downey et al., 2005). E-learning also enables organizations to develop 'bite-sized chunks' and provide learners with information on their progress as has happened in B&Q, the DIY retailer (Sloman, 2004). However, the costs of developing effective tailor-made materials for delivery through e-learning are high and usually more appropriate for large organizations. Generic materials are available for purchase that can fit needs like learning to use software packages. However, there is a potential drawback with this approach as learning and development supported by generic materials may not deliver competitive advantage (Macpherson et al., 2004). One of the principal problems facing HRD practitioners is that there has been very little research into the actual usage and effectiveness of e-learning (Brown, 2005)
Off-the-job external training	This strategy uses commercial providers of training that is run away from the workplace. They might be open courses that have participants from many organizations or a course that is tailor-made for the client organization. The approach can be expensive but has the advantage of not needing to be designed by the organization itself and can be used to address a wide range of specific individual needs
Off-the-job internal training	This strategy is the one often thought about when talking of designing training involving the design of a training session for a group of learners to meet an organization's specific need. It has the advantage of being specific to the organization and being able to use relevant materials. The disadvantages are around the time needed to develop a response and the costs of developing the design, particularly if the numbers to be trained are low
Off-the-job planned development	This is another variation of off-the-job learning and is to use development opportunities such as secondments, visits, and study tours to provide learning to meet the need. These might be provided in associated organizations including suppliers, customers, and even competitors. It could include work with professional bodies and voluntary organizations and charities. Attendance at conferences and seminars may also be included in this strategy as they do not have the specific learning outcomes of a course

Table 7.1 Training strategies

Training strategy	Description
On-the-job training	There are a number of variations on the general approach to learning on-the-job. These range from providing no formal learning and expecting the learner to pick things up as they go along, through coaching by a designated competent person through to planned work experience. Coaching may be provided by colleagues or line manager and sometimes an internal or external tutor may be used. Planned work experience may include delegation, secondments, projects, assignments, job rotation, and deputizing. Someone needs to manage the planned work experience for it to work effectively and tying it in with a mentoring scheme. This can provide support to learners to tie together their learning experiences and put them into context. Although on-the-job training tends to rely on more experienced and skilled employees to train or coach the less experienced (Blanchard and Thacker, 2004)
Self-development	Self-development is a strategy that is perhaps becoming more prevalent. The responsibility lies with the learner to decide what they need to learn to remain competent and employable. The organization may provide some financial support for attending learning events and perhaps mentoring. Where it is the learner's responsibility to identify what learning they wish to undertake using e-learning provision and in-house off-the-job courses then that implies a self-development strategy is being followed

Table 7.1 (*cont'd*)

Key concept   'Training' or learning strategies

A 'training' or learning strategy is a specific approach to the delivery of the HRD intervention that guides the design process.

TIPS AND HINTS

Taking the time to identify the right training strategy enhances considerably the likelihood of a successful intervention.

E-learning and blended learning

It is worth reflecting on e-learning at this point given the rapid growth in this approach to the delivery of learning and development interventions. In the UK e-learning is now being used by nearly 60 per cent of organizations although when these figures are broken down there is a significant contrast between the public sector at 82 per cent and the private sector at 42 per cent (CIPD, 2008). It has been argued that the use of technology changes both the role of the teacher/trainer and the learner by offering a new and alternative mode of delivery for face-to-face teaching which is much more learner focused. There is an overwhelming view that e-learning does require learners to adopt a new approach to learning (CIPD, 2008). But take away the technology and what has changed? Arguably, very little. Technology is simply another form of media that can be used to deliver learning. With today's schoolchildren becoming increasingly IT-literate and sophisticated in their use of technology (through educational and recreational experiences) organizations need to build learning infrastructures and environments that reflect this trend.

INSIGHTS INTO PRACTICE

E-learning in the US and UK health sectors

There is evidence that the use of e-learning in nursing schools is on the increase on both sides of the Atlantic. However, changes need to be made to the learning culture for the benefits of e-learning to be maximized given that nursing education has been based traditionally on high levels of social interaction between learners. Many learners fear e-learning brings a consequent loss of social contact. It seems that learners want more flexibility in how they learn but not at the expense of social interaction.

This case illustrates the role of social learning in developing expertise in a professional practice (see chapter 10).

Source
Farrell, M. 2006. Learning differently: e-learning in nurse education. *Nursing Management*, 13 (6): 14–17.

MEDIA WATCH BOX

E-learning

These two items below provide an interesting contrast in how e-learning is perceived. Interestingly the CIPD's 2008 *Learning and Development Survey* has highlighted that e-learning is perceived as being more effective when combined with traditional face-to-face methods (i.e. blended learning).

Some organizations, including Volvo and the BBC have stopped using the term e-learning. For many people e-learning has a negative image being viewed as dull and boring.[1]

Whitbread, the hospitality sector company, has used an e-learning system, Oracle iLearning, to provide online learning to all of its UK employees. The system allows employees to learn at their own pace and the company has benefited from minimum disruption to daily work activities.[2]

Sources
[1] *People Management*, 2 September 2004: 46.
[2] *Human Capital Management*, a *People Management Briefing*, published 2005: 6.

Increasingly organizations are opting for blended learning strategies that combine e-learning with traditional strategies. The Open University of Shell International Exploration and Production (Shell EP) introduced a blended learning programme that combined e-learning modules with social interaction and collaborative learning and focused on workplace-based activities and/or problems that include supervisor involvement and input by experienced supervisors (Margaryan et al., 2004):

> Technology is an important tool for learning, particularly in terms of facilitating flexibility and reuse of learner submissions. However, technology does not replace the central importance of interpersonal contact: among learners, between the course director and learners, between the learner and his line manager and between the learner and workplace colleagues. Technology is a tool to make this contact richer, more flexible and reusable. (ibid: 272)

The Priory Group, which comprises a workforce of 5000 located in 47 hospitals and schools, has introduced a blended learning approach that:

> Delivers all the online learning materials and acts as a signpost to other training opportunities, venues and dates. All employees have individual programmes created for them and are allocated whatever modules their line managers request for them, plus certain ones that everyone takes. (Smethurst, 2005: 36; originally published in *People Management*, 9 March 2005, and reproduced with permission)

Whilst underpinning principles remain the same there is no doubt that e-learning as a stand-alone option or as part of a blended learning intervention, require the HRD designer to acquire new skills and knowledge as well as working with IT specialists (Waddill, 2006).

The 'training' or learning strategy

Before detailed design can be taken forward the training strategy to be used must be decided. Whilst cost is probably the biggest factor to consider there are other considerations. For instance, if e-learning is proposed then do the learners have access to IT facilities and will accessing them fit in with their job demands? Learners cannot be working in a call-centre responding to calls and studying e-learning at the same time. This illustrates that customer facing jobs may not allow learning through a particular strategy alongside normal work. For other jobs, where the work is controlled by the job holder, it may be quite easy for them to set aside some time for online learning. If the number of learners is very small the best solution may be to identify an external provider and send the learners on an external course. If the number of learners is sufficiently large to justify an in-house group then the choice is whether to design in-house or buy in from outside. The advantages of buying in external courses are: cost effectiveness when few learners are involved, immediacy of availability compared to the time to design and develop a course, not needing expertise on the topic or design skills, and the potential benefits of participants mixing and networking with learners from other organizations. The design of training material into 'bite-sized chunks' is not restricted to e-learning interventions. For instance, Lara Ashworth, head of talent at Metro in 2005, comments that:

INSIGHTS INTO PRACTICE

Implications of using external providers

Lyn Edwards, an independent training consultant and experienced HRD practitioner advises that the first stage in deciding whether an external course is appropriate is to match the identified need(s) with potential external provision. Depending on the nature of the need providers may be general trainers or specialists. They may advertise or be accessed through professional bodies and trade organizations. In selecting external training a number of things need to be considered including details of the course provider as well as of the particular course. Regarding the course provider factors such as how long they have been in business, what range of training do they provide, who are their clients, and what staff do they have are all relevant. The information on a course immediately requires details of the objectives to determine whether it will meet the need. The cost of the training will be next and can be balanced against doing nothing or developing something in-house. Whether the course has been run before may provide useful information together with who attended and what was their feedback. Then issues of when it will run, where, who will attend, how many participants, who are the trainers, what methods are being used will all be part of the basis for an informed decision.

MEDIA WATCH BOX

Training design in BP

As a result of employee attitude surveys revealing that front-line managers were unhappy with the ad hoc training they received, the company decided to set up a design and development team under the leadership of a senior executive to come up with a new training and development programme. This process took 18 months to complete as the project team focused on creating a flexible programme with a global reach. Specific design constraints were: to avoid an over-reliance on e-learning; to cope with the dispersal of managers around the globe; to provide a modular solution. As part of the design process front-line managers were interviewed over the telephone and this enabled the project team to identify some 250 managers who could be involved in the design process. These managers were brought together in sub-groups using one day workshops and gave the project team further insights into learner needs. Following this it was decided to involve HRD practitioners which enabled the project team to take onboard other potential problems, such as compatibility of the new programme with existing provision. The total investment in the design and development phases was US$1.5 million.[1]

This case is interesting because the project is managed by functional executives and HRD practitioners are not brought in until the initial research has been carried out and an outline programme mapped out.

Source
[1] *People Management*, 23 February 2006: 40–2.

More and more, I find that I am procuring bite-sized training for my organisation's bespoke internal programmes. At the moment, for example, all non-management staff are involved in a programme to develop management competencies that takes place for two hours a week over seven weeks. (Ashworth, 2005: 42; originally published in *People Management* 5 May 2005, and reproduced with permission)

Very often when an organization is operating on a global basis it may be necessary to adopt different training strategies in different locations. This may be for cultural as well as logistical reasons. For instance, Hallmark Cards is shifting towards a culture that embraces coaching alongside traditional training programmes, such as management courses, and NVQs for all hourly-paid staff (Simms, 2005).

7.6 **Evaluation methods**

Evaluation is usually considered as the last stage of the systematic approach but often gets neglected. Evaluation includes the assessment of learners during the training intervention itself. Students will be familiar with the concept of assessment from their college or university studies. Assessment may be formative, where the purpose is to provide feedback to the learner so that it can be used to shape future performance. Assessment can also be summative, where the purpose is to check the learning that has been achieved. An example that distinguishes between the two is learning to drive a car. The trainer offers formative feedback during every lesson, it is to help the learner driver improve. The examiner carries out summative assessment to establish whether the learner driver is competent. The examiner offers no feedback during the test and at the end gives a result which is either pass or fail, with reasons for failure.

> **Key concept**   Assessment
>
> Assessment is about measuring learner understanding and/or ability during the delivery phase of the HRD intervention.

Assessment

Assessment measures that can be considered for building into the learning event are generally either to measure reaction of the learners or to establish the learning achieved. Reactions are generally measured through questionnaires and learning through some form of test. The type of test will be determined by the learning to be measured and the purpose of the assessment. Knowledge can be tested by oral questioning, written tests in a variety of forms, and objective tests that can be on paper or on computer. If the purpose is formative assessment then question and answer with immediate feedback may be appropriate. This can be achieved in the classroom with a trainer and online with objective tests. If a formal record of individual learning is required to show an external regulator then a paper or computer based assessment under examination conditions may be required. Depending on the purpose we may test for straight recall of knowledge, have they remembered; comprehension, can they explain it; or application, can the knowledge be applied to a new situation? Testing of skills requires individual performance that is assessed. Depending on the skill it may need to be observed for assessment purposes or the results may be assessed and the skills inferred. The basis for skills assessment is usually some form of product or process checklist that has been developed and is used by a trained assessor. One example of differences between product and process skills is driving. Driving skills are perhaps best assessed by observation (process skills) rather than by whether a driver arrives at a destination safely (product). Assessment to identify the impact of training on job performance is generally not appropriate during the learning event but needs to be considered when designing the training otherwise there will be no resources to carry out the assessment and no benchmark information to show what has changed between the before and after training situations.

Any assessment measures should be considered in terms of whether they are sound and fit for purpose, convenient, and acceptable. Sound in that they measure the required performance and in a consistent, way that provides usable results. So the results should be valid and reliable, knowledge of flying a jumbo jet does not mean that the skills required to fly it are possessed. Someone who gets 100 per cent in a knowledge test about flying may not be able to fly an aeroplane safely and the test is not a valid measure of flying ability. Assessment measures need to be convenient in terms of the resources needed to design, develop, and use the assessment measures in the design. Who has the expertise to design and develop the assessment measures, is there time to develop them, and how much time they will take to use in the training delivery? The assessment of individual performance is particularly demanding if it requires learners to be observed by assessors and given feedback. That generally requires a one to one period for observing skilled performance. The assessors may also need to be trained to use the particular assessment tool developed.

Convenience also relates to the appropriateness to the training strategy selected. E-learning as a strategy lends itself to online assessment of knowledge through objective tests. Objective tests can be presented easily online and the results can be determined immediately. The results can be used to provide the learner with formative feedback. Results can also be used to provide remedial learning if the performance is not at the required level and the results can be recorded to provide a record of the learner's achievement. Objective tests generally measure knowledge and skills are more difficult to assess online, although often not impossible as with flight simulators that test pilots' skills. Thus e-learning has the potential to provide both formative and summative assessments that can be used for a variety of purposes. The demands on the trainer in delivering such a programme are minimized by the technology. All the investment needs to be made in developing the online tests and the feedback mechanisms to the learner and trainer. Whilst e-learning provides that potential the investment in money, time, and design expertise to deliver on the potential does not happen very often. This is understandable for needs that will change quickly when the effort cannot be justified because the life of the finished programme will be short and in fact the e-learning might not be deliverable before the need has moved on.

Finally the assessment methods need to be acceptable to the learner, the trainers, and in the culture of the organization. Will the learner be willing to be assessed in the way proposed? The way the results will be used, who will have access to them, and how they will be stored needs to be considered. Finally whether the assessment approach is acceptable to management. However it is only worth deciding to measure anything if there is a clear purpose and the results will provide useful information that justifies collecting and analysing the information.

> **TIPS AND HINTS**
>
> Never skip this stage. It is no good trying to devise an evaluation approach after the intervention has taken place.

7.7 Content, methods, sequence, structure, and media

Content

Deciding the content of an intervention is relatively straightforward and is determined by the learning objectives. It is the preparation of materials and the identification of appropriate methods and media to deliver these materials that is much more challenging. As Dobbs (2006) observes about the preparation of materials:

> It is essential that quality materials be developed so that learners master the required competencies of their job. Adequate resources are required to develop quality materials in a timely manner . . . To be instructionally sound, materials should support the objectives of the training or program to be implemented, should be learner centred, should build learning on learning, should meet the organisational purpose that was specified in the analysis phase, should ensure that learners acquire the knowledge and expertise specified in the objectives, and should guide them towards mastery of the task. (p. 503)

The mix of materials needs to be considered carefully to ensure the delivery of content will be at the right level and appropriate to the learning objectives (Hackett, 2003). Often this is a trade-off between time spent on developing bespoke material that is highly contextualized as opposed to simply using generic learning materials that are readily available. There is always a tendency to include more content that can be accommodated in the time available. This requires eliminating interesting, but not entirely relevant, content. The agreed learning objective is, again, key to making the decisions. The content should link clearly the objectives to the learning need identified. In the content there needs to be explanation, demonstration, practice, and review. Explanation of the topic involves putting it into context, providing underpinning knowledge about what, how, and why. The content needs to build on the learners' existing knowledge and skills. Not wasting time on things learners can already do yet not assuming they can do things they cannot. Demonstration of the required performance is helpful for learners before they get the chance to practise themselves. Without practice they will not be able to develop skills or apply knowledge to a range of situations. After practice every learner needs feedback on how well they performed to provide reinforcement of performance. 'Feedback guides, motivates, and reinforces effective behaviours or stops ineffective behaviours' (London, 2003: 1). Further practice to use the feedback and embed the knowledge and skills is needed to allow competence to be achieved.

Sequencing the content can be approached from two directions, either the learning outcome to be achieved or the best learning sequence. For some tasks the design should help learners to follow a procedure and the sequence may be followed in the design. For other tasks, where planning is required and the use of concepts and principles will be necessary, the sequence may build the application of the underpinning ideas before putting them all together for the overall performance. The ideal sequence is the one that makes it easiest for the learners to learn as quickly and effectively as possible. The sequence should allow application and practice of knowledge and skills learned so that they are reinforced. The introduction of knowledge should be closely followed with opportunities to use it. After practice specific feedback should follow as soon as practically possible. The academic model of submitting an assessment and then waiting six weeks for the results is not good learning practice. After that delay the learner is unlikely to have much recollection of what they did and why, any feedback is unlikely to be as helpful as being told the next day what was good and less good about their assessment.

Methods

> **Key concept**   Training methods
>
> Training methods are the different ways in which specific elements within an intervention can be delivered to learners.

There are many training methods and some are more appropriate for transferring knowledge and others for skill development. Some have potential for immediate feedback between learner and trainer and others provide little opportunity. One way of looking at training methods is by the role of the learner and trainer. These can help in considering appropriate methods in relation to particular training strategies and learning objectives. As Blanchard and Thacker (2004) warn:

> Whether a method will reach its potential depends on how well the training is designed and implemented. (p. 279)

One of the recurring criticisms of training interventions is the apparently inappropriate choice of methods. 'More often than not, the method used is an arbitrary result of the layout of the room, the trainer's whim or the presence of computer equipment' (Lucas, 2003: 61; originally published in *People Management* 23 October 2003, and reproduced with permission). These quotes also highlight the relationship between design and delivery—that these two stages are inextricably linked, as will be discussed in detail in the next chapter. Table 7.2 shows some typical methods for different types of learning and whether these are suitable for the development of knowledge, skills and/or attitude.

ACTIVITY 7.2

Review the list of methods above and decide to what extent you agree with their rating as appropriate to help learners develop knowledge, skills, or attitudes. Try to identify specific learning objectives that might be achieved through using the particular methods.

The starting point for considering methods is whether they will fit the learning or training strategy. Adopting an e-learning strategy would rule out one-to-one coaching although a lecture using a video sequence could be included. The training methods must support achievement of the objective. The closer the performance in the learning method is to the required job performance the easier transfer of learning should be. If the learning objective requires recall of knowledge then reading or lectures can be suitable. When skilled performance is to be developed then participative methods, like exercises, case studies, coaching and discussion, need to be considered. The selected training methods

---

INSIGHTS INTO PRACTICE

Using different methods

Jane Chilman, director of People First Associates, comments:

'Most of the programmes we deliver are in workshop format. We have found more recently that bite size programmes suit the business area we work in. Normally $1^1/_2$–2 hours interactive workshops using case studies, exercises and role play. This year we are using more actors to role play theatre forums. This is particularly successful when delivering managing disciplines, recruitment interviewing and appraisal training. Participants control the role play, highlighting when inaccuracies occur and directing actors as to what should have happened. Using actors often lightens the mood of what in essence are serious subjects, but really engages the audience in the subject. We accommodate different learning styles by using a variety of activities throughout the programme'.

	Knowledge	Skills	Attitudes
Individual learning			
Assignments		Y	
E-learning: using instruction mode	Y		
Guided reading	Y		
Internet search	Y	Y	Y
Interactive video	Y	Y	Y
Project: individual	Y		
Reading	Y		
Simulation: solo			
Training video			
One-to-one learning			
Coaching	Y	Y	
Counselling	Y	Y	Y
Demonstration	Y	Y	
Exercises: manual skills development		Y	Y
Guided practice	Y		
Mentoring			
Tutorial			
Group learning			
Action Learning Set		Y	Y
Assignment	Y	Y	Y
Brainstorming		Y	
Business game		Y	
Case study: paper-based	Y	Y	Y
Case study: incident	Y	Y	Y
Discovery learning	Y		Y
Discussion: guided and problem-solving	Y	Y	Y
E-learning: using communication features		Y	Y
Field trip	Y	Y	
Group exercise: inter-personal skills	Y	Y	Y
Group project	Y	Y	
In-tray exercise	Y	Y	Y
Learning networks	Y	Y	Y
Lecture	Y	Y	
Lesson	Y	Y	
Micro-teaching			
Open forum			
Role-playing			
Seminar			
Simulation: group			
Training video			
Workshop			

Table 7.2 Examples of training methods

need to be ones that the learners will be comfortable with and can learn from. The method should fit the culture of the organization and not be seen as outlandish or inappropriate. They also need to be able to cope with the numbers of learners. Similarly the methods need to be ones that the trainers will be comfortable and skilled at using and credible in using with the learners.

The methods must fit with the accommodation available such as syndicate rooms and lecture rooms. Some methods will cost much more than others to use: small group work requires much more tutorial support than a large lecture theatre. Some methods require more administrative support as in role-playing where role-players may need to be booked to attend. Also, if say, a case study method is proposed then what case studies are available and what resources will be required to revise existing or create new case studies? The above factors also need to be reconciled to the time available to prepare and deliver the training. Desirable methods may be dropped in favour of those requiring less time. The objectives may need to be revised to reflect these decisions.

Selecting media

Selecting media to support the learning event can be important to save explanation, add interest and support effective learning. Media falls into hardware and software, so a DVD player is the hardware and the DVD disk with a 'video' on it is the software. Training designers may wish to produce their own software that is tailored exactly to the context of the training need. There is a wide range of commercially available material produced with expert input. This includes video, slide presentations, handout materials, case studies and exercises. The attraction of commercial material is that it short circuits the development time and may have higher presentation quality than can be achieved in-house. Media prepared in advance are appropriate for formal input sessions and presenting ideas and situations to learners. These include slides, video, audio and printed materials with case-studies. There are other media that are useful for the trainer to work with learners to capture their ideas and support the learning. These include flipcharts, white boards, and even the chalk board! The trainer can use these to capture and review ideas and learning generated by the learners. This can also extend into using technology for learning where discussion boards, e-mails, telephone conferencing, and video conferencing can be used for supporting learning. E-learning provides a variety of media to support learning delivered through a PC including sound and images and interaction through virtual classrooms, discussion boards, and e-mails.

There is a wide range of media available and the basis of selection is often on availability rather than first principles. Dobbs (2006) warns that the best technology does not always equate to the best media for particular methods. Selection should be based on criteria such as those shown in table 7.3.

Be careful about the seductive nature of some media. For instance, PowerPoint slides have features to support the user in addition to its powerful presentation features. The downside is the many demonstrations of 'death by PowerPoint' as too many slides with too much content are flashed up on a screen with clever transitions and clever background music all of which gets in the way of learning. The range of options today is much greater than it used to be. Software to use in the media selected could be a PowerPoint presentation on a CD, a USB pen-drive, a PC hard drive, or on the Internet projected with a data projector. The slides could even be printed off onto acetates for use with an overhead projector. Software could also be a video on DVD, video tape, or delivered over the Internet or Intranet. Slides can be produced to a good quality in-house and be tailored

Criteria	Explanation
Benefits to learner	• Understanding content more easily (e.g. building models or processes step-by-step with supporting explanations) • Adding interest (e.g. diagrams, images) • Providing an accessible resource (e.g. flipcharts, slides, and hand-outs, hyperlinks) • Giving feedback (e.g. using flipcharts to highlight key points) • Helping transfer of learning (e.g. transportable content that can be referenced easily)
Suitability to support the training method (so that learners get more from the method)	• Ease of use (e.g. flipcharts to capture learning from role plays or group discussions) • Quality of outputs (e.g. PowerPoint slides versus OHP acetates for presentations) • Relevance (e.g. using same equipment as found in the workplace) • Level of complexity (e.g. suitable hardware and software to support business simulations)
Competence of the trainer	• Knowledge of media (e.g. novice or experienced user of media; knowledgeable in which media are better suited to which methods) • Ability to modify content easily (e.g. customization of content and materials to meet the learning needs of different groups) • Resource implications (e.g. buying-in expertise; training the trainer)
Availability	• Hardware is available at the venue and in working condition (e.g. physically check in advance and immediately before the intervention starts; hiring versus purchasing options) • Availability of technical support (e.g. onsite or outsourced) • Availability of alternative equipment (e.g. spare data projector in the event of a breakdown; spare bulbs for an OHP) • Compatibility (e.g. between versions of any software being used)

Table 7.3 Criteria for making media selection decisions

closely to the specific needs of the learning session. Video is easy to record but difficult to achieve a credible quality compared to what can be seen every day on the television. So video is usually best used with commercial products as credibility is lost when things look amateurish. There are many commercial materials available but can be costly. Copyright is also an issue for commercial products and copying is often prohibited. Producing materials in-house requires equipment and takes time as well as requiring skills in design. Underpinning any decisions about the media to include in a training design should be a consideration of whether the aid is worth the cost/effort to support learning.

7.8 Venue selection

Where the training event will be delivered is often a foregone conclusion, as with who will be the trainer. If the strategy selected is e-learning and learners have a PC on their desks the location for the training may be at their desks. If there are dedicated training rooms then they may be expected to be used unless a good case can be made to use other resources that will be chargeable. The venue for training needs to be appropriate for:

- Training objectives: performance, conditions, and standards.
- Assessment measures: individual or group, use and feedback.
- Training methods: group rooms, work rooms, workshop, test place.
- Media: equipment and facilities to use.
- Learners: expectations, status, travelling.
- Trainers: administrative and technical support.
- Image/culture: the organization, training, learning event.
- Budget: costs of use, travel, subsistence.

On the job training provides the real work situation and should thus minimize transfer of learning problems but making time for learning and the cost of errors are difficulties. Off the job training can provide a risk-free, or at least low risk, learning environment which may boost learner motivation and avoid cost of errors. An offsite location can offer a reward element for participants but may also be discriminatory as it may exclude some employees from attending if it requires time away from home.

With all training venues as well as cost and facilities the availability and booking lead time need to be considered. The costs of cancellation are also a factor when using commercial premises. If you are involved in providing a large number of 'classroom-based' events then you will need to balance the cost of using hotels or external residential centres against that of an internal training centre or other internal facilities. There are advantages and disadvantages to the latter which are shown in table 7.4.

Advantages	Disadvantages
You can design purpose-built training facilities that maximize training and learning opportunities (rather than settling for some of the inadequacies of hotel rooms which have not been designed by professional trainers)	You may be pressurized into ensuring it is kept fully utilized. There is nothing wrong in hiring out your own training centre to maximize utilization and generate revenue; however, you must not allow this to distract you from achieving your learning and development objectives
Facilities are directly within your control (and you can make any physical changes you feel to be appropriate)	The organization may not want to increase overheads
Running costs can be cheaper than hiring external facilities (depending on the frequency of usage)	There may be increased travel and subsistence costs in a multisite organization
	It may not be convenient for all employees (e.g. multisite organization)

Table 7.4 Advantages and disadvantages of internal facilities (training centres)

7.9 Incorporating relevant learning theory

One of the considerations when designing an intervention is to ensure that the learners' experience is supportive of their learning. Learning theory helps when making decisions about designing the intervention and how the learners will be involved. When designing learning and development for organizations we are dealing with adults and this has several major implications. First is that they have lots of experience of learning, both formal and informal. Secondly that their existing levels of knowledge and skills need to be taken into consideration so that training effort is not wasted on things that they are already competent to do. Thirdly that the ways they prefer to learn, and the range of preferences in any learner group, are acknowledged and allowed for.

> **! TIPS AND HINTS**
>
> Given the wide variation in learning styles and preferences it can be a useful practice to build a variety of methods into the design of the intervention.

Participation in learning is important for both sustaining motivation and enabling new learning to be integrated with existing knowledge and skills. The learning needs to be interesting and offer variety to sustain motivation and attention. There also needs to be some flexibility in a design to allow for differences in learners' preferred ways of learning. When adults are compelled to attend learning events against their will they tend to resist the experience and sometimes subvert them, with consequences for themselves, the trainers, and other learners. As well as participation, learners need opportunities to practise skills. Skills development requires practice and feedback and then further practice to use previous feedback and correct any errors. Feedback needs to be specific to the individual and immediately after the practice to be useful. Repeated practice is needed to embed a skill so that it can be applied with confidence.

Having clear outcomes for a training event has been shown to be helpful to learning. When these outcomes are clearly related to work applications then this provides additional benefits in using existing experience, focusing attention, and encouraging motivation to learn. Assessment during a learning event can have the benefit of identifying areas for improvement, confirming achievement, and offering a reward by means of formal recognition. The learners will return to work and be expected to use their learning. The design needs to try and minimize the gap between what they learn in the training situation and their work situation. This can be done through using the real work environment for the learning, using work based examples and materials, helping learners to relate what they have learned to their work situation through action plans, and building in line manager support.

Chapter 4 explained a range of learning theories. Taking experiential learning as one example, this can be applied to a wide variety of training methods. For instance, let us assume that you are designing a workshop on interviewing skills and want to incorporate role-play because this method allows learners to practise skills development. The initial role play represents the concrete experience. During this stage some learners can act as observers. Following the role play the role players, observers, and trainer(s) can discuss and reflect on what happened during the role play (e.g. what worked well? what didn't? etc). This represents the reflection stage. After an appropriate period of time the trainer can facilitate the third stage, drawing conclusions, by encouraging the learners to summarize on a flipchart key learning from the role play. This then provides the basis for the fourth stage as learners prepare to carry out a second role play, building upon the key learning points (with role-players and observers swapping roles). These stages can be enhanced considerably if the role play has been videoed; but the downside to this is that much more time is needed to incorporate the analysis of the video into the second and third stages.

(•) INSIGHTS INTO PRACTICE

A learning and development manager's perspective

Ian Yates, a Learning and Development Manager comments:

'The design of a training course is more complex and carries more weight than some people give it credit. I usually work on a ratio of 10:1. Ten hours preparation, research, script writing, exercise and scenario design, evaluation frameworks and testing for every one hour of training to be delivered. The work and effort that goes into the design will ultimately determine the success of the session. I learnt early on that the place to start when designing is the end—"the end defines the means". The obvious thing is the objectives, in other words what do you want people to be able to do as a consequence of the training. But that's just part of it. Equally important are:

1. What type of people will be attending and how many of them? Designing a session for 4 people is very different to designing a session for 20 people.

2. What venue will you be using and how convenient is it? If these people have to travel how fresh will they be when they get there? Will they be stressed because of the traffic and how will you overcome that if they are—bear in mind people learn best when they are relaxed?

3. Is the venue big enough for all your people and especially for the practical exercises that you have designed?

4. Is the venue too big—will people feel intimidated?

5. What are the likely learning styles of the attendees? Activists may get little from a slide show full of detail statistics.'

Summary

We have demonstrated that design is a very productive activity that is an iterative process. There are multiple decisions to be made that are all interdependent. There is no prescribed sequence for making design decisions and any decision made may need to be revised in the light of later decisions in developing the design. What can be asserted is that the best place to start design is with the need and the learning objectives that flow from that need. Then the gap between what the learners already know and can do compared to the desired learning objectives informs all subsequent issues. The casual observer of an experienced trainer designing training can overlook the expertise of the trainer in excluding from overt consideration many of the potential choices. This may reflect expertise in excluding unsuitable options in relation to specific learning objectives and also in personal preferences and comfort zone. Not all trainers can work in all areas and use the whole range of training methods with the full range of participants in terms of experience and seniority. Design is always a compromise, balancing the constraints against the needs and the standard of performance that needs to be achieved.

Review questions

1   What are the challenges and potential problems with translating an identified training need into a training objective?

2   What factors does the designer need to consider when deciding between the different methods available, as listed in the chapter?

3   Sequence is an issue in design: at the design process level when considering which decisions to make and in what order and at the within the design in sequencing learning activities. Consider what determines sequence at these two levels and what are the consequences of those decisions?

4   When, how, and with whom should a design be reviewed when it has been prepared?

5   How easy is blended learning to develop in a design and what factors need to be considered?

Suggestions for further reading

1   Simmonds, D. 2003. *Designing and Delivering Training.* London: CIPD.
    This is a good text for improving your understanding of the design process.

2   Macpherson, A., Elliot, M., Harris, I. and Homan, G. 2004. E-learning: reflections and evaluation of corporate programmes. *Human Resource Development International*, 7 (3): 295–313.
    This article provides some informative insights into e-learning.

3   Cowell, C., Hopkins, P. C., McWhorter, R. and Jorden, D. L. 2006. Alternative training methods. *Advances in Developing Human Resources*, 8 (4): 460–75.
    This article supplements the chapter's content on training methods.

4   Hansen, J. W. 2006. Training design: scenarios of the future. *Advances in Developing Human Resources*, 8 (4): 492–99.
    This article provides an interesting perspective on training design.

5   Dobbs, R. L. 2006. Development phase of systematic training: new technology lends assistance. *Advances in Developing Human Resources*, 8 (4): 500–13.
This article is useful for developing your understanding of the role of technology in the design process.

Case study

Acorn and a client centred approach to training

Established in 1992, Acorn is an award-winning business that is now Wales' leading recruitment and training organization, with an annual turnover of just under £100m. With offices across South Wales, the West Country, North Wales, Scotland, and the North West of England the company places 5,500 people into 750 different client companies each week and makes some 1,500 permanent placements each year. It is a previous winner of both best regional recruitment firm and best national firm at the Professional Recruiter Awards. Acorn's Learning & Development Division is highly regarded throughout the UK for its employer-led approach to training, learning, and development solutions. Its team of 30 training and development professionals deliver training to over 3,000 individuals per annum. The company has a particularly strong reputation in the area of Management Development and the following case study outlines how Acorn has worked very closely with a large leisure-resort employer to deliver a management development programme.

'The programme is typical of the innovative approach taken by Acorn to meet an employer's needs' explains Sarah John, Acorn's Commercial Director. 'In today's global economy businesses are under constant pressure to perform effectively to retain their competitive edge. As a consequence of ever-changing demands the quality of managers has become pivotal to the performance and long-term success of an organization. This client recognized that to achieve a strong market position they needed to invest in the development of their people. We responded by developing a bespoke approach to ensure the client received the exact level of support and guidance required. The challenge we faced was that the future business plans for the client required senior personnel not only to possess practical management skills but these skills had to evolve to meet changing business needs. Therefore in partnership with the client we were commissioned to design and deliver a development programme for senior managers geared around achieving the client's business objectives within a very dynamic market. It was agreed with the client that key performance indicators had to be built in to the development programme in order to measure achievement of objectives and to assess the impact of the programme on business performance'. This process took four meetings and involved four training and development consultants over a two month period. 'It was crucial to get the programme's objectives right', continues Sarah. 'After much discussion and consultation, which involved interviewing ten senior managers at the client organization, we arrived at four key objectives.'

Programme Objectives

1. To provide Senior Managers with the essential skills to develop operational teams in order to achieve individual, departmental, and corporate objectives.
2. Identification of on-going training needs to ensure effective use of management resources by developing the skills of middle management.
3. Development programme to support the corporate culture of attracting and retaining quality staff.
4. Programme to be tailored to accommodate the demanding work schedule of the Senior Managers involved.

'The client recognized that training and development is a key business driver directly affecting the company's performance', explained Sarah. 'We used our expertise in this area to design a management development programme that focuses on enhancing the practical and relevant skills that are needed to take the organization forward. We ensured that the programme was aligned with company objectives and that the client's investment in its management team would deliver a tangible return on investment. This was, and had to be, a very business-driven process—i.e., linked to the business plan, the corporate objectives, and the skills development plan. Following clarification of the client's requirements, in terms of identifiable business needs, it was possible to identify three key themes. These were managing change, managing self, and managing resources. To assist with the detailed design it was agreed with the client to analyse the learning styles of the managers who would be attending the programme. This was done by issuing 'Personal Styles' Questionnaires. This then enabled us to produce a modular programme that reflected managers' learning preferences. This has the advantage of ensuring that the trainers can tailor the delivery of the programme to have maximum impact on the delegates. As part of our service we always research possible sources of funding, such as the Welsh Assembly Workforce Development Plan, Sector Skills Council, and Business in Focus. Very often there is support available for up to 50 per cent of the cost of commercial delivery, although maximum funding is only usually available for accredited programmes, such as those involving national vocational qualifications. Once the programme was designed and agreed it was rolled out on-site. We developed a flexible approach to the delivery of the programme to accommodate the client's business needs. All modules were delivered on site and included role play, case studies, and practical assignments, which were all linked to business issues and objectives. In total there were 12 modules, each lasting one day. So, for a typical manager the whole programme took twelve months to complete. Evaluation and review was at the end of each module using 'End of Module' Evaluation form linked to key performance indicators or KPIs. These were then collated and reported in graphical format. At the same time future requirements were identified'.

In terms of the results of the programme, Sarah explains that 'Managers acquired a portfolio of skills enabling them to manage change, cope constructively with conflict, develop and motivate their teams, delegate effectively, and solve problems effectively. Skills were immediately converted into practical experience within the business and action plans were used to enable managers to achieve business objectives. What was particularly noticeable was that increased individual performance and satisfaction levels resulting in improved team work. More generally, the corporate culture and values were both developed and reinforced. The programme highlighted the client's commitment to long-term career pathways and enabled better succession planning. There was a review of internal systems identifying areas for improvement and sharing of best practice, for example, the development of an integrated customer service strategy. 'Overall' concludes Sarah, 'by investing in the development of senior personnel the client has been able to cascade the training internally through coaching and mentoring the next management tier. This has led to a culture of continued learning and development within the organization'.

Case questions

1. Why might an organization use a training consultancy to design, and also deliver and evaluate, a major training and development programme? What are the potential benefits?

2. To what extent has Acorn adhered to good design practice in this case? Draw upon relevant theory, concepts, and models to support your answer.

3. Convert the programme objectives shown in box 1 into specific learning objectives.

Online resource centre

Visit the supporting online resource centre for additional material that will help you with your research, essays, assignments, and revision.

 www.oxfordtextbooks.co.uk/orc/mankin/

8

Delivery of Learning and Development Interventions

Learning objectives

By the end of this chapter you should be able to:

* Explain the relationship between delivery and other stages in the systematic HRD cycle

* Describe the different ways in which interventions can be delivered

* Understand and explain the respective roles of the HRD practitioner and line manager in the delivery stage for different types of intervention

* Explain the skills needed to deliver different types of intervention

* Appreciate current trends in how interventions are delivered

Indicative content

■ The implications of organization development (OD) projects for HRD practitioners

■ Different roles of the trainer

■ The knowledge and skills required to be an effective trainer

■ How to design the layout of a training venue

■ Overcoming problems on training interventions

■ Emerging trends in training

■ How to be effective at career development

■ An overview of the role of secondments, development centres, and career counselling in career development

- The implications of online tutoring
- E-learning and blended learning interventions
- The requirements for effective facilitation
- How to be an effective coach and mentor
- Factors influencing the mentoring relationship
- Reasons for ineffective interventions
- A comparison between UK and US training methods

Key concepts

Trainer	Career counselling
Bite-sized training	Online tutoring
Project management	Facilitation
Problem-solving models	Action learning
Secondments	Coaching
Development centres	Mentoring

8.1 **Introduction**

When talking about delivery most people will conjure up the image of a trainer delivering a traditional classroom-based intervention. However, delivery can take different forms depending on the nature of the intervention. As D'Abate et al. (2003) observe:

> Interactions between a developer and learner can take many forms . . . It is increasingly important that human resource development professionals and other practitioners understand the developmental options available to them. (pp. 365–80)

Different 'development options' place different demands on the HRD practitioner, line manager, and learner. Coaching, mentoring, career counselling, action learning, online tutoring as part of an e-learning programme, and OD projects require the utilization of different skills and techniques by those delivering the intervention and also different approaches to learning by the learners. Even the delivery of training has changed over the years as HRD practitioners have been influenced by trends in management and organizational thinking. As was explained in chapter 2 TQM is an antecedent of HRD that acted as a catalyst for 'just-in-time' training interventions in the 1990s:

> The adoption of 'just-in-time' training means that training efforts are directed at those employees most in need of performance enhancement or improvement, focusing costs on staff most likely to bring future benefits to the business. While this kind of training is exacting of trainers' skills, adaptability and enthusiasm, it can unleash enormous benefits both from the trainers', trainees' and company perspective. Trainers are forced to reappraise their traditional modes of classroom delivery; trainees become more in control of their learning requirements; and companies ensure that training is faster, more customized, and individually driven. (Gilleard, 1996: 22)

This is how I delivered a great many formal interventions when I was both a TQM Manager and, subsequently, an HRD practitioner. This approach proved popular with line managers who felt the immediacy of many performance problems required a flexible approach from someone in my role.

What is critical is that the delivery phase of an HRD intervention is conducted in a professional manner as successful HRD practices have been shown to influence employee commitment to the organization (Bartlett and Kang, 2004). This also enhances the credibility of practitioners in the eyes of managers. For managers involved in the actual delivery phase it is an opportunity to develop and refine particular skills. Consequently, this chapter will focus on some of the principal modes of delivery starting with the role of project leader for organization development (OD) projects. This will be followed by a discussion of how formal classroom-based training is delivered. Subsequent sections will explore the implications of a range of HRD interventions that rely less on traditional training delivery methods. This reflects the breadth of the 'learning continuum' discussed in chapter 2 and is illustrated in figure 8.1.

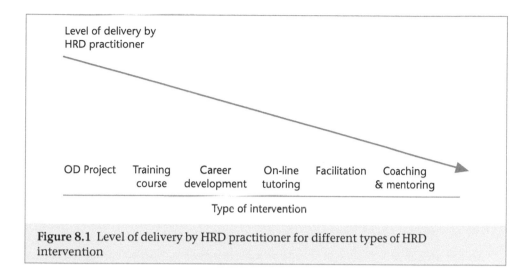

Figure 8.1 Level of delivery by HRD practitioner for different types of HRD intervention

8.2 The effective organization development (OD) project manager

> **TIPS AND HINTS**
>
> It is sometimes more useful to think about helping people to cope with change rather than viewing their concerns as being all about resistance to change.

Change, learning, and performance are inextricably linked as was explained in chapters 2 and 3. OD projects led by senior executives have been used in many organizations as a way to manage the implementation of changes which have strategic implications such as mergers and acquisitions, restructures, and new IT systems. However, the selection of the right project for 'a radical transformation can be a daunting task' (Morgan et al., 2007: 149). A project approach to the innovation and development of new products and services is becoming even more critical to competitive advantage in many industries (Kaplan and Norton, 2004). Whilst this approach has not been a characteristic of the developing economies in China and India it is believed to be only a matter of time before these two countries start to spearhead technological innovations (Engardio, 2007). This will see the emergence of a broader HRD approach in both countries, especially in China which is still very much at the training end of the 'learning continuum' (see chapters 1 and 2). In the US new products as a percentage of sales have actually fallen from 32.6 per cent in 1990 to 28 per cent in 2004 suggesting a shift from innovative products to improvements and modifications (Morgan et al., 2007).

The traditional focus of HRD-related OD projects has also involved incremental rather than transformational change (Swanson and Holton, 2001). This reflects the influence of TQM as an antecedent of HRD. Consequently, a requirement for the successful management of organization development projects is a combination of project management

skills and expertise in process improvement and problem solving techniques. HRD practitioners should already have some understanding of project management techniques
because of their experience in managing training programmes (Fabac, 2006):

> Upper management should ensure that those who are destined to manage training
> projects need skill development in project planning, project control, leadership,
> and communications. (ibid.: 544)

In terms of organization development projects the HRD practitioner should adopt the
role of catalyst or change agent (Gilley et al., 2002); while Swanson and Holton (2001:
245) refer to the role of the 'learning project manager'.

Key concept   Facilitation

Facilitation is about guiding and supporting a learner or group of learners with
the minimum of input.

Yorks (2005) stresses the importance of facilitation skills: what he terms 'facilitative
consultation' (p. 12). These are not unique to this particular role and are also required by
the 'effective trainer' (see section 8.3 below). However, the nature of OD projects makes
facilitation skills particularly critical to the successful implementation of the project. It is
not intended here to give a detailed explanation of project management and change processes as specialist texts can be used for this purpose. The problem solving approach to
TNA shown in figure 6.1 in chapter 6 can be used as a process-framework for managing
OD projects. The four stages in this model are similar to other models as illustrated in
table 8.1.

The identification of a relationship phase by Gilley et al. (2002) is an important point.
As Grieves (2003) observes the change agent needs to have the skills that enable him/her
to manage the client relationship effectively (e.g. sensitivity to client needs). In terms

	1st stage	2nd stage	3rd stage	4th stage
Mankin, 2009	Define nature of problem	Identify and prioritize causes	Identify and prioritize potential solutions	Implement and review changes
Swanson and Holton, 2001	1. Analyse and contract	2. Diagnose and feedback	3. Plan and develop	4. Implement 5. Evaluate and institutionalize
Gilley et al., 2002	1. Problem identification phase 2. The relationship phase (i.e. building relationships with client)	3. The diagnostic phase	4. The solution phase 5. The intervention phase	6. The evaluation phase

Table 8.1 Problem-solving models for OD

of implementing the change the principal challenge is often in finding ways to help employees cope with change (I prefer this term to that of 'resistance to change'). The input of line managers can be critical here as they are in the best position to provide feedback to the HRD practitioner about how employees are feeling. Change inevitably brings with it uncertainty and anxiety. These can be countered through a carefully managed strategy of consultation and involvement.

HRD practitioners who do not possess the skills needed to manage or facilitate change tend to demonstrate some of the following characteristics identified by Maycunich Gilley et al. (2003: 33):

- They are convinced that training is the solution to all performance problems (and, therefore, they have difficulty in embracing other approaches)
- They are unable to identify the root causes of poor performance
- They are convinced that performance will improve if learning takes place
- They are unable to make the transition from trainer to OD change agent

This highlights the importance of continuing professional development (see chapter 15). Unfortunately not all HRD practitioners are given the opportunity to develop expertise in OD projects because of perceptions about the role of the HRD function (i.e. seen as a function that provides training at an operational level). Given the trends highlighted in chapter 1 many HRD practitioners may need to find new ways in which they can expand their portfolio of skills in order to remain employable or provide a competitive outsourced service.

8.3 The effective trainer

> **Key concept**   Trainer
>
> A trainer is an expert at instructional techniques but is not necessarily a subject specialist.

As has been stated previously formal learning and development interventions, typically referred to as the 'training course' or 'training workshop' continue to play an important role in many organizations. Most HRD practitioners have had to develop the knowledge and skills required to be an effective trainer in order to be able to deliver such interventions successfully. Whilst all four stages in the HRD cycle are critical to the success of any training course or workshop, the demands made on the ability of the trainer are different at each of those four stages. Korte (2006) sums up the challenge of the delivery stage:

> There is a visceral 'moment of truth' when engaging an audience . . . All the efforts and best intentions of instructional analysts, designers, and developers surrender to the dynamics of the trainer and the learner during the implementation phase . . . it is through a relatively unpredictable process of question and answer and give and take that leads learners to the objectives that were established at an earlier time. (p. 514)

There is an old saying about trainers and teachers: 'those that can, do; those that can't, teach'. This underestimates the expertise needed to be an effective trainer. This is another reason why it can be useful for line managers to get involved in the delivery of training interventions. As Gibb (2002) observes:

> Being the best performer is not a sufficient condition for being an effective instructor. Some of the best performers are unable to engage with supporting the learning of others, and cannot perform well as instructors. The best instructors may rather be those who best grasp the 'business' of learning. (p. 86)

There is considerable variation in how formal learning and development interventions can be delivered. Gilley et al. (2002: 325) refer to five *primary instructional styles* of which the following three are most pertinent to this discussion:

- **Disseminator:** students will recognize this approach because the most commonly used method of presentation is the lecture. This approach is based on the assumption that learning is essentially about disseminating information and memorizing (often referred to as knowledge acquisition). Training content focuses on facts, concepts, models, and theories

- **Classroom instructor:** the emphasis is on information and the application of that information through classroom-based activities such as role play. This is the approach most people will be familiar with (e.g. the one day workshop on interviewing skills). It is reliant on the learner's ability to remember the information and the subsequent transfer of learning to the workplace; which, as the next chapter will discuss, is an inherently unreliable approach. When involved in such training I often say to participants: 'you will forget ninety percent of what I say by tomorrow morning'

- **Facilitator:** the aim of this style is to deepen the learner's level of existing knowledge through reflections on personal experiences. Gilley et al. (2002) refer to this as a process 'to crystallize the learners' experiences' (p. 325). In this way the learners' experiences become sources of learning and a benchmark for future comparisons. This approach does require learners to have some pre-existing level of understanding of facts, concepts, models, and theories.

The two other styles are 'philosophical instructor' (involving intellectual debate) and 'learning agent' (giving equal primacy to information and application). In many respects the latter style is aspirational, as can be seen from the authors' description of it:

> Learning agents must be masters of several teaching methods and experts in the discipline. By focusing simultaneously on information and its application, the integrator of learning [i.e. learning agent] can demonstrate concern for the learner and for the material, and promote a healthy relationship between them. (ibid: 325)

The knowledge and skills that are required by the effective trainer are summarized in table 8.2. These need to be developed and used in conjunction with how the trainer projects his/her personality. This should be done in a positive way that helps to build a trusting relationship with each learner.

The knowledge and skills need to be supplemented by personal attributes that encourage learning. Trainers need a high level of intuition to guide their utilization of the above knowledge and skills. This is something that is developed through experience. I have always made it a point to create what I term 'a safe learning environment' so that learners feel comfortable about making contributions and do not feel frightened to experiment and take risks. Humour and enthusiasm are also very important as these help to motivate learners although this should never be at the expense of learning. It is very easy to trivialize an issue in the eyes of the learner.

ACTIVITY 8.1

Think about a recent learning and development experience, such as a training workshop or a seminar. What knowledge and skills from table 8.2 did the tutor or HRD practitioner demonstrate? What aspects could he/she improve on? If you are a student then think about a recent session, such as a seminar, to answer these questions.

TIPS AND HINTS

Do not make assumptions about what the learners may or may not know about the subject.

Knowing the best methods for different types of training is important. As the CIPD point out (CIPD, 2007a), courses should involve learners:

- Working in small groups (ideally 4 to 6 members)
- Using real examples or up-to-date case studies
- Understanding how to transfer knowledge and skills to the workplace

As shall be seen in the next chapter it is the last point that is most contentious. Methods such as role play can be enhanced by not using participants for all the roles. For instance, using actors or outsiders can add realism to the activity. For recruitment and selection workshops I would advertise fictitious positions at a local college, and then invite short-listed candidates to the workshop to be interviewed by the participants. The feedback to learners from interviewees was much more powerful as a result. This reflects the importance of simulating realism wherever possible.

In many organizations more traditional instructional approaches have been embedded successfully into the day-to-day operations of the organization. A good example of this is the Toyota on-the-job development model (see chapter 3) which uses line supervisors as trainers who adhere to strict guidelines which include:

Always use a repetitive process of showing the student, letting the student try, and then letting the student practice with supervision . . . Never leave the student on her own until she is capable of reliably performing the work on her own. (Liker and Hoseus, 2008: 137)

(•) **INSIGHTS INTO PRACTICE**

Advice on delivery from an experienced training consultant

Jane Chilman, Director of People First Associates, comments:

'We change our delivery methods in line with the audience, their roles, seniority and particular needs. As trainers it is important to heed the following:

Do

- Be prepared
- Know your technology
- Know your subject matter
- Make it relevant
- Be enthusiastic about your topic
- Be supportive and encouraging
- Know your audience and what their expectations are and adapt your delivery and content to suit
- Make the subject matter interesting and real (through case studies, research, newspaper clippings)
- Keep PowerPoint slides simple and punchy and limit the number used
- Constantly assess learning, through tests, quizes, and questioning
- Use real life stories to support topics
- Let the delegates come up with the solutions
- Update information—when using research information try to make it recent

Don't

- Be late
- Do all the talking
- Assume all audiences are the same
- Discount answers if they are not what you were expecting—appreciate the contribution and see the value'

Toyota believes in using the workplace as the site for training. For many other organizations, and for different types of training, this is not practicable. Consequently, there are more organizations which are introducing imaginative and different settings for the delivery of interventions which reflect the organization's workplace-setting. For instance, the Malmaison and Hotel du Vin group provide hands-on training in the form of sending its managers to leading cookery schools for two days so that they will feel more confident working in a food-oriented organization (Clarke, 2007). AXA PPP Healthcare uses a blend of drama and online communications to raise awareness and understanding about issues such as discrimination (e.g. actors perform an improvised argument in the staff canteen and employees then comment online about the issues raised by the incident) (Clarke, 2006). Creative approaches have been a feature for some time of the training offered to communities by non-profit organizations (see *Media watch* box).

MEDIA WATCH BOX

Oxfam International

As part of a humanitarian project in Liberia which is focused on the prevention of disease training and education are being used to spread good practice in hygiene. As part of this initiative special songs containing hygiene messages have been written.

Source
http://www.oxfam.org/en/news/pressreleases2003/pr031003_liberia_update.htm (accessed 29 May 2008).

Room layout and equipment

The trainer should always check the room beforehand and make sure equipment is working as it should. In formal interventions careful consideration needs to be given to the layout of the training room and how this is located in relation to any syndicate/break-out rooms, social areas, support equipment (e.g. photocopier) and, where appropriate, to overnight accommodation. The trainer needs to consider how he/she will stand in relation to the learners and the 'U' shaped room layout remains the best tried and tested design for training interventions (see figure 8.2). This design enables:

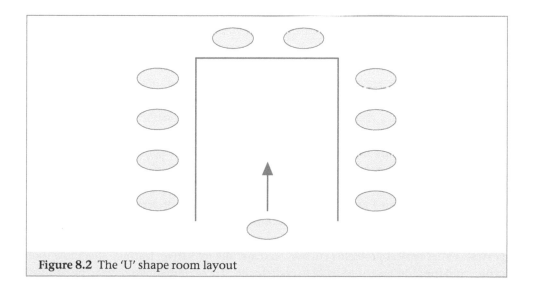

Figure 8.2 The 'U' shape room layout

- The trainer to maintain eye contact with all learners
- The trainer to be able to walk around in order to emphasize certain points
- The trainer to approach all learners without having to squeeze between rows of desks and chairs as in a conventional classroom
- The learners to maintain eye contact with all other learners
- The learners and the trainer to hear what is being said (there is nothing worse than learners talking to the backs of other learners as occurs in the conventional classroom)

Remember that running a training intervention is not the same as giving a presentation. It is not only acceptable, but also advantageous, to walk around the room, to make use of the U-shape layout, and to use expressive body language. Technology has introduced new aspects to the nature of the physical space used in the delivery of some interventions:

> Because of technology's impact on the delivery of training programmes, many training sites include instructor- and trainee-controlled equipment. For example, at Microsoft's customer briefing centre in Chicago, Illinois, 16 different computer platforms, ranging from laptops to mainframe systems, are available to use for training. Two seminar rooms include videoconferencing technology, which allows training sessions to be transmitted from Microsoft's corporate headquarters in Redmond, Washington, to Chicago. The Chicago site can link up to any of 25 Microsoft locations or a combination of 11 sites at once. (Noe, 2002: 132)

Overcoming problems

As both an educator and HRD practitioner I have encountered a range of problems in the training room, regardless of how well it is organized and equipped. There is nothing worse than encountering a wall of silence. Asking questions is an integral aspect of delivery and if the trainer is finding it difficult to get learners to contribute then the use of humour, incentives such as chocolates, and short icebreaker exercises can be applied. Icebreakers and energizers should be used at key times, such as at the start of the intervention and immediately following lunch. Popular examples of these include: telling other learners one truth and one lie about yourself and they have to guess which one is the lie. The challenge for the trainer is to keep learners engaged. Andrew Rae, director of Ten Minute Trainer, comments that trainers need to deliver sessions that address specific learning needs but are memorable (http://www.PersonnelToday.com 2007b). In many respects the trainer has to give a performance during classroom-based interventions. In this way he/she can stimulate learning through learners' participation in a range of methods and activities that engage learners. Often workshops and courses have been designed to cover all four of the learning styles/preferences discussed in chapter 4. This can be a problem though when a group of learners share a particular preference. This is why it is important to know about the learners (i.e. entry behaviour) in advance so that delivery can be varied accordingly. Lastly, patience and perseverance are essential qualities to possess. Other typical problems encountered are: the 'talkative' learner, 'the know-it-all cynic', and the 'don't-want-to-be-here participant'. These individuals have to be handled with a mix of firmness and tact so that their attitude does not disrupt the learning experience for other participants.

Good quality visuals, be they PowerPoint slides, acetates, pre-prepared flipcharts, and/or hand-outs are important. Using colour helps to improve learner retention (CIPD, 2007f). Peripheral vision can also be used to improve learner retention (e.g. posters pinned to the wall or displaying learner ideas on flipcharts pinned to the wall).

Props are a useful addition. I have used a wide range of props over the years, from piggy-banks to inflatable green aliens, to add interest to sessions, as well as asking learners to create their own props, such as three-dimensional models of key concepts. As Mary Brooks, director of Leadership and Management Training, comments: 'I always have a packet of balloons in my bag and use them to get learning points over, even with the most serious subjects' (http://www.PersonnelToday.com, 2007b).

Other problems, in particular environmental factors, can be overcome by ensuring the training venue is vetted in advance. Noe (2002: 133) provides a comprehensive list of such factors:

- Noise (e.g. from heating or ventilation systems, corridors, adjacent rooms, or outside)
- Colours (e.g. warm colours, such as pastel hues are better than dark hues which make the room feel smaller)
- Room structure (e.g. square-shaped rooms are much better than long, narrow ones)
- Lighting (e.g. adjustable, consistent lighting across the room is needed)
- Walls and floor covering (e.g. solid colours are preferable as patterns can be distracting to some people)
- Chairs (e.g. should have wheels and be able to swivel, and have backs that provide good support)
- Glare (e.g. eliminate any noticeable glare from metal surfaces, mirrors, or screens)
- Ceilings (e.g. ten foot high ceilings are preferable)
- Electrical outlets (e.g. outlets should be available at regular distances and around the room)
- Acoustics (e.g. do voice checks in advance to see if sound bounces off or is absorbed by walls)

ACTIVITY 8.2

Think about a recent learning and development experience, such as a training workshop or seminar. To what extent did the room used meet the requirements set out in the above list?

Emerging trends

The website of the Institution of Occupational Safety and Health declares that there need to be new and different approaches to training (http://www.iosh, 2007). This is a sentiment shared by many HRD practitioners who are using technology, 'bite-sized' modules, and on-the-job training to offer a broader range of learning and development 'solutions' to organizational managers. Bite-sized training delivery can be delivered face to face or via e-learning systems and usually refers to relatively short training sessions lasting between 30 minutes and two hours and which have a clearly defined set of outcomes. Bentley (2006) argues it can be an effective form of delivery for the following reasons:

- It can mirror the way we acquire skills generally
- Short sessions keep the topic fresh
- It is ideal for using accelerated training techniques that generate a tempo difficult to sustain over a longer intervention
- Transfer of learning is immediate
- Sessions can be repeated easily and quickly to a great many employees
- It is ideal for imparting practical advice such as changes to legislation

However, 'bite-size' training does not allow for effective group activities and discussions and the utilization of methods such as role play (Bentley, 2000). Consequently, it tends to be predicated on psychological theories of learning. The increased emphasis on delivery methods based on sociological theories is evident in various trends. For instance, the CIPD (2006a) note that induction programmes are involving less 'chalk and talk' and more 'active learning tasks' and 'sessions for cross-function team building'. The Pizza Express has 'how to' cards in each restaurant that explain how to do things the Pizza Express way (e.g. how to open a bottle of wine), and operate a 'buddy system' so that employees can spend several weeks working in one of the restaurants designated a centre of excellence (*People Management*, 10 August 2006: 16–17). The CIPD also note the increasing use of online and e-learning induction programmes and the implications of this trend for the HRD practitioner are discussed below.

MEDIA WATCH BOX

Induction at innocent, the fruit-drinks firm

Innocent, which is famous for its brand of fruit smoothies, believes in a 'happy people' strategy and this is reflected in their induction process. New employees receive a telephone call a week before they are due to start and are given a bouquet of flowers on their first day. They are given a different 'lunch buddy' every day to help them get to know people more quickly and eliminate any potential feelings of isolation. All employees can have a free breakfast if they turn up to work early, as well as a range of other employee-friendly benefits.[1]

This case illustrates how you can make induction both more memorable and much more fun. Obviously, how new employees are inducted and socialized into a new organization is a direct reflection of the culture.

Source
[1] *People Management*, 28 October 2004: 19.

8.4 **The effective career developer**

> **! TIPS AND HINTS**
>
> Career development interventions can be highly rewarding but also extremely time consuming.

Many performance problems are actually career related (Gilley et al., 2002). Consequently, many of the outputs from TNAs come under the heading of career development rather than learning and development; although the distinction in practice is often irrelevant to stakeholders. The distinction does matter though where there is a clear strategic intent by the organization to implement policies and processes that focus on the long-term development of the internal labour market so that future managers and leaders can be identified as well as specialist positions held by knowledge (or core) workers (see chapter 10). This type of approach results in the formulation of career plans which can then become the core focus of HRD expenditure:

> By focusing human capital investments and development programs on the relatively small number (often less than 10 per cent) of employees in strategic jobs, organizations can achieve breakthrough performance faster and less expensively than by diffuse HR spending. (Kaplan and Norton, 2004: 234)

Career development interventions need to be delivered in such a way that they do not raise unrealistic expectations about individuals' career aspirations. The challenge for the organization is to deliver interventions appropriate to the organizational context. Some popular methods include:

- Secondments
- Development centres
- Career counselling

A secondment involves an employee, usually a manager, spending a period of time working in a different department of the same organization or in a totally different organization (e.g. a supplier or customer). The CIPD (2007e) observe that organizations benefit from this approach but typically need to last for up to a year which may be too long for many managers or other categories of employee. This is because the secondment is intended to deepen and broaden an employee's experience and expertise which is difficult to achieve over shorter timescales. The role of the HRD practitioner is to ensure secondees are properly prepared for the secondment and debriefed at the end; that the secondment is monitored effectively and evaluated at the end. They can also act as a facilitator should any problems arise during the secondment.

Development centres (DC) are designed to replicate workplace processes through a mix of individual and group activities (e.g. individual presentation and/or in-tray exercise; problem-solving group activities etc.). Additionally psychometrics are used (e.g.

> **Key concept** Development centre
>
> A development centre is a structured HRD intervention comprising a blend of methods which are designed to measure participants' performance against a specified set of competencies. The outcomes are used to identify the career potential of participants and to produce customized career development plans.

personality questionnaires, interest inventories, and ability or aptitude tests). The delivery role of the HRD practitioner usually involves:

- Acting as an assessor during the DC
- Producing written feedback on how participants performed at the DC
- Facilitating the feedback process after the DC

However, development centres are labour intensive and expensive to run and therefore tend to be used by large organizations.

ACTIVITY 8.3

Carry out an Internet search and identify an example of a timetable for a development centre. What are the possible delivery implications of this design?

Career counselling is 'an important HRD task' (Gilley et al., 2002: 74) which provides an opportunity to develop or enhance inter-personal relationship skills. The counselling may be carried out by an HRD practitioner or a line manager with the HRD practitioner acting as a facilitator. It is a highly rewarding process but also can be very time consuming which is why many organizations do not view it as a priority.

MEDIA WATCH BOX

Career development in VectoGray Controls

VectoGray Controls, a subsidiary of GE's Oil and Gas business, has facilities in the UK, Singapore, and Australia and manufactures systems used as part of oil and gas drilling processes. Training is one of the company's main priorities and is heavily focused on employee retention through career development. The career development approach involves career planning reviews to identify employees ready for promotion and the provision of national vocational qualifications (in conjunction with local colleges).

Source
http://www.themanufacturer.com/uk/content/7780/All_under_control (accessed 26 March 2008).

INSIGHTS INTO PRACTICE

Career development in Brunei Shell Petroleum Company

This case illustrates one of the key trends identified in chapter 2: employees taking more responsibility for their own learning. It also highlights the emphasis on employee competence as the key determining factor for career progression. The development strategies referred to equate to the 'training' strategies specified in chapter 7.

Four key principles underpin the way in which the Brunei Shell Petroleum Company (BSP) approaches HRD. These include the principles that: responsibility for personal development and career management rest with the individual employee; and, development and career progression will be competence-based. To date the company has invested heavily in the education and development of 'home grown' talent (i.e. from the internal labour market). A career management framework for graduates specifies what they need to focus on in the first three to five years of their employment with the company (a similar framework for non-graduates also exists). This includes the formal induction programme which is organized by the company's Learning and Development department and is followed by a range of development strategies including: on-the-job learning and coaching; off-the-job training; and, mentoring. The company also sees experience gained in new environments as an important part of the development process. This approach has enabled BSP to drastically reduce its reliance on foreign professionals from 75 per cent in 1984 to 27 per cent by the end of 2004.

Source
Young, G. 2005. Finding, nurturing and developing the professional workforce—the BSP experience. In A. G. PG, HJ. Metusin and O. K. Beng (eds.) *HRD for Developing States and Companies: Proceedings of the 2005 Brunei Darussalem AEMC Convention*. Pasir Pang, Singapore: ISEAS Publications.

8.5 The effective online tutor

The growth in technology-based solutions which can be utilized by HRD practitioners has added a further dimension to the skills needed to deliver interventions effectively. Increasingly, many HRD practitioners are being asked to fulfil the role of online tutor with accredited training schemes in this form of tutoring now being offered by many specialist organizations. This approach to delivery is a feature of e-learning and blended learning interventions. Blended learning is about 'integrating face-to-face learning or training events with electronic tools, e.g. computer-based training' (Yorks, 2005: 293). The latter is generally referred to as e-learning which is, essentially 'any electronically assisted process that is used to acquire data, information, skills or knowledge' (ibid: 294). Blended learning packages can be based on the same principles as a traditional training intervention. For instance, a new blended learning package launched by Plateau Systems, based in Arlington, USA, uses interactive virtual learning technology to simulate an actual classroom experience (*Corporate Training and Development Advisor*, October 27 2007: 4). The concept of a classroom remains a comforting image for many employees.

Key concept   Online tutor

An online tutor is someone who understands how to support individual learners or groups of learners through a combination of instruction, facilitation, and coaching in a virtual environment.

The online tutor's role can be synchronous or asynchronous. Synchronous is when the tutor is online at the same time as a learner or group of learners so that any discussion can take place in real time. This usually takes place in a virtual discussion room at a pre-agreed date and time. Asynchronous is when the tutor simply responds to questions or discussion points at any time, in the same way most people check their email as and when is convenient depending on their particular job role. This can create delays but it would be very difficult, if not impossible, to justify the cost of an online tutor being available 24/7 to respond immediately to queries or to provide feedback. A survey by Rowan (2005: 52) identified the key drivers for asynchronous e-learning as:

1. Time schedule flexibility with self-paced format: 81%
2. Ability to reach a large audience with few resources: 66%
3. Cost savings over classroom: 62%
4. No live learner-to-learner and learner-to-instructor interaction is needed: 27%
5. Compliance issues that need quick action (e.g. health and safety): 27%
6. Other: 10%
7. Lack of available bandwidth to teach synchronous e-learning: 6%
8. Culture advocates synchronous e-learning: 6%
9. Lack of instructors to teach classroom or synchronous e-learning: 5%

Asked what skills are important to the delivery of blended learning, 75 per cent of respondents to a survey conducted by *Training* magazine, responded that the trainer must understand the needs of the learners and how they prefer to learn in order to blend the components of the intervention to achieve maximum delivery (Sparrow, 2003). In terms of e-learning (free-standing or as part of a blended-learning intervention), Hornik (2004) offers the following advice for the effective delivery of e-learning:

- Ensure there is a seamless interface between the online training package and other systems so that access is easy for the learner
- Have someone within reach who can answer questions about the e-learning package, such as an appropriately trained administrator or supervisor

- Provide a comfortable setting that minimizes unnecessary distractions and/or interruptions
- Allow sufficient time for each learner to complete the training

However, the CIPD's 2005 *Learning and Development Survey* highlighted that e-learning tends to be used for certain types of training (typically IT or technical training). There was less evidence that it was being used for soft skills. At this time content delivered via CD-ROMs was more prevalent than by intranets or the Internet. Tellingly, the equivalent survey for 2007 suggested there was a *gradual* growth in the use of e-learning (CIPD, 2007c). In terms of the 2008 survey (CIPD, 2008) there was limited evidence that the increased use of e-learning would continue. There is little doubt that technology will continue to impact on learning and development interventions and thus on the delivery aspect. It is possible to discern some emerging trends. For instance, the notion of 'bite-sized' training referred to above is ideally suited to technology-based delivery systems. For instance, a survey of 2000 HR executives, including training and development managers, carried out by the Boston-based consultancy Novations Group has revealed that 10 per cent of respondents are now utilizing the ipod as a delivery medium (Weinstein, 2007). It is likely that this figure will grow. Ipods and other brands of MP3 player are bringing audio learning back into vogue, particularly for topics such as leadership and management, and sales and product knowledge (http://www.PersonnelToday.com 2007a). This trend is also impacting on higher education where the lectures are being delivered via podcasts and the Internet at some universities in the US and UK (*The Times Higher Education*, 26 October 2007: 5).

The notion of 'bite-size' is being taken further by one company. Skill-Pill Mobile Learning (SPML), based in London, has launched 'skills pills', two-minute video and presentation clips that are sent to mobile devices as and when users need them (Charlton, 2007). Such delivery systems also facilitate a 24/7 approach to training. However, a 24/7 approach is not the preserve of technology-driven systems. Barnfield College, Luton is to run a new training facility at London Luton Airport that will remain open 24/7 to accommodate airport shift-working patterns (Vorster, 2007).

8.6 **The effective facilitator**

> **TIPS AND HINTS**
>
> When facilitating say as little as possible.

Being knowledgeable and skilful at facilitation is seen as one of the key attributes of the modern-day HRD practitioner, reflecting the shift from the training end of the 'learning continuum' to the learning end (see chapter 2). 'As learning becomes less formal, facilitation becomes more appropriate to the learning process' (Korte, 2006: 521). Stewart and Tansley (2002) argue that the facilitator role is essential in the era of the knowledge economy. The CIPD note that this can be a challenging role for those practitioners who have

	Knowledge of	Skills
Communicating	Verbal and non-verbal language	Speaking clearly, varying explanations to help learners understand, modulating voice, using eye contact and positive/encouraging non-verbal language; injecting humour, and telling anecdotes and stories; avoiding jargon and complicated language
	Giving (and receiving) constructive feedback	Active listening and providing feedback: the ability to listen to and respond effectively to learner inputs, such as questions, anecdotes, and presentations
	Different types of question	Asking open and closed and/or probing questions appropriately, for instance, to clarify learner understanding
Facilitating	Different learning theories; group dynamics	The ability to 'stand back': guiding and encouraging learners (rather than always telling them); allowing learners to discuss issues amongst themselves and to share stories with each other
Organizing	Time management	Managing time effectively; providing timely summaries of key points
Technical	Methods, media, and software	Using methods effectively; using technology and software (e.g. computer and data projector) effectively

Table 8.2 Knowledge and skills of the effective trainer

a controlling approach to their work as well as emphasizing that facilitation should be seen as a learning process in itself. Gilley et al. (2002) reinforce this emphasis on learning:

> The emphasis today is on questioning, listening, providing feedback, and learning transfer to bring about change in the learner. It is not enough to be a subject matter expert; [HRD practitioners] must understand how adults learn. (p. 165)

The skills listed in table 8.2 are transferable to other contexts, such as facilitating management teams as part of an internal consultancy role, giving presentations to senior management, and so on. In these contexts other skills, such as decision-making and problem solving are also important. The implications of these different skills sets are discussed also in chapters 13 and 15.

A commonly used HRD intervention that requires support from an appropriately experienced HRD practitioner adopting the role of facilitator is action learning. An action

---

Key concept   Action learning

Action learning involves a group of learners working together in an action learning set to solve real problems in the workplace. A series of meetings are held during which set members question and challenge the causes of the problem and potential solutions.

learning intervention shifts the focus from the classroom to the workplace. Action learning uses an actual work problem as a way to learn. Noe (2002) refers to it as a 'training method' while Gilley et al. (2002) describe it as both a 'process' and a 'program'. The facilitator guides the learning of those participating in the action learning set. As Waddill and Marquardt (2003) observe:

> It is one of the fundamental beliefs of action learning that we learn best when undertaking some action on which we reflect and from which we subsequently learn . . . The action learning facilitator establishes the pace to assure sufficient time for group members to reflect on the problem-solving . . . and to capture the learning. (pp. 411–23)

This is a very different role to that of an instructor or trainer delivering a traditional classroom-based intervention. Waddill and Marquardt (2003) expand on the approach adopted by a facilitator:

> She helps group members reflect on how they listen, how they may have reframed the problem, how they give each other feedback, how they are planning and working, and what assumptions may be shaping their beliefs and actions. The facilitator also helps participants focus on what they are achieving, what they are finding difficult, what processes they are employing, and the implications of these processes. (p. 423)

An important aspect of this role is the ability of the facilitator to empathize with set members and to understand where they are coming from and the reasons why (McGill and Beaty, 1992). This is a relational skill that an effective HRD practitioner needs for any delivery scenario.

Action learning involves both psychological (e.g. experiential) and sociological (e.g. situated) theories of learning. Users of action learning range from non-profit organizations such as the Broadway charity in the UK to the Tata Group in India (see *Insights into practice* box). However, there still needs to be more studies into the effectiveness of action learning:

INSIGHTS INTO PRACTICE

Tata Management Training Centre

The Tata Management Training Centre (TMTC) in Pune, India supports the Tata Group through the provision of training and education programmes. TMTC incorporates action learning as one of its key approaches to learning and development, encouraging managers to discuss issues and problems and share expertise to identify potential solutions.

Source
http://www.tata.com/0_our_commitment/employee_relations/learning/tmtc.htm (accessed 14 April 2008).

> Although action learning has not been formally evaluated, the process appears to maximise learning and transfer of training because it involves real-time problems employees are facing. Also, action learning can be useful for identifying dysfunctional team dynamics that can get in the way of effective problem solving. (Noe, 2002: 236)

8.7 **The effective coach**

Traditionally coaching has been seen as the preserve of line managers and selected direct reports although the use of internally designated coaches has been increasing in many organizations (Howe, 2008). The latter role involves creating a specialist role that can be filled by an HRD practitioner. The line manager's role in delivery will vary considerably from context to context. However, often individuals are promoted to a line manager role because of their technical competence rather than their ability to manage a group of people (Gilley et al., 2002):

> Thus, when confronted with difficult and complex problems, managers sometimes lack the competencies and abilities to correctly address them. (ibid: 74)

As was highlighted in chapter 5, coaching is an increasingly popular training method and provides an ideal opportunity for involving the line manager in the training and/or developing of his/her team members. Research by Knights and Poppleton (2007) shows that the type of involvement can vary:

• In formal coaching interventions the line manager plays a key role particularly in terms of setting business-related objectives and assessing the effectiveness of the coaching process

• Many organizations have invested resources to develop the coaching skills of line managers so that they use a coaching style of management with their own team members

• It appears that an increasing number of organizations are developing their line managers as coaches

• Some organizations have allowed coaching to emerge in an informal, organic manner

It is important that appropriate training is provided so that line managers can maximize the benefits of coaching. In this way, the HRD practitioner is helping to build a 'devolved learning' strategy (see HRD strategic choices in chapter 3). However, the CIPD (2007b) warn that the impact of coaching could be jeopardized because it is seen by some as a generic solution to training situations. Coaching can be a highly effective intervention where a one-to-one development relationship is the best approach to use. Alternative methods may be less labour intensive and less expensive but not necessarily more effective.

Smith and Sadler-Smith (2006) advise that for coaching to be effective the following conditions must apply:

> **⊙) INSIGHTS INTO PRACTICE**
>
> ## Coaching in the Royal College of Nursing (RCN)
>
> 'As part of its efforts to develop a coaching culture, the RCN recently launched an internal coaching programme . . . In May, the first 14 of a target group of 50 senior-level managers will have completed the programme. They will then act as coaches for the next tranche of managers starting the programme in June . . . as more and more employees receive coaching, there will be a knock-on effect, with a coaching style of management becoming more widespread . . . opportunities for executives to prac-tise what they learn needs to be built into any coaching skills development . . . One of the [main] difficulties in developing managers as coaches is that it requires a shift from telling to asking, which many managers resist'.
>
> **Source**
> Hall, L. 2007. Costume change. *People Management*, 5 April 2007: 42–3. (Originally published in *People Management*, 5 April 2007, and produced with permission)
> Liz Hall is currently editor of the magazine *Coaching at Work*.

- Tasks are carried out in the correct sequence
- Coaches have the relevant technical knowledge, good inter-personal skills and credibility
- Back-up material is provided for the learner to take away after the coaching session
- The learner is ready and self-motivated to learn from the coaching method

This advice illustrates the importance of effective TNA. For instance, task analysis is critical to the first point and an analysis of entry behaviour is critical to the fourth point.

8.8 The effective mentor

Mentoring has become an increasingly popular HRD intervention. Mentoring relation-ships can be both formal and informal (Hezlett and Gibson, 2005; Young et al., 2006). Informal mentoring relationships emerge and evolve and it is argued that mentoring works best when the relationship between mentor and mentee is characterized by chem-istry and mutuality (Bierema and Hill, 2005). Formal mentoring:

> involves an intense, one-to-one relationship in which an experienced, senior per-son (i.e. a mentor) provides assistance to a less experienced, more junior colleague (i.e. a protégé or mentee) in order to enhance the latter's professional and personal development. (Hezlett and Gibson, 2005: 446)

Mentors provide two types of support to protégés or mentees: career support and psycho-logical or social support (Young et al., 2006):

> Career support includes mentoring behaviours related to the career advancement of a protégé including giving advice, making the protégé visible to influential others, and protecting the protégé from political situations. Psychological or social support represents the more emotional side of mentoring and includes listening to a protégé's concerns and befriending and counselling a protégé. (p. 149)

Formal mentoring relationships require HRD practitioners to make matching decisions: which mentors and mentees should be paired together (Egan, 2005). These matching decisions can be critical to the success of the mentoring relationship. Research shows that mentors can also benefit from mentoring (Hezlett and Gibson, 2005) but this will not occur in a mis-matched relationship. Some organizations have introduced peer mentoring which enables mentors and mentees to be matched from a much wider and more diverse group of employees.

Factors which impact on the quality and duration of the relationship between mentor and mentee include:

• The scope of the discussions: how many topics or issues that are discussed (Hezlett and Gibson, 2005)

• The extent to which the relationship is characterized by goal setting and achievement (Egan, 2005)

• The frequency of meetings between mentor and mentee (Hezlett and Gibson, 2005); and the extent to which meetings are given priority in spite of any time constraints (Bierema and Hill, 2005)

• The level of influence the mentor has over the mentee (Hezlett and Gibson, 2005): this is linked to factors such as trust, respect, and integrity (i.e. the extent to which the mentor acts as a role model for the mentee)

• The extent to which the mentee believes that the mentor cares about him/her (Gibson, 2005)

There is a lack of research into how mentors and mentees learn from each other although the preliminary findings from a study by Hezlett (2005) suggest 'that protégé learning plays a pivotal role in mentoring relationships' (p. 506). She highlights an interesting finding from her research:

> Observation was one of the primary means of protégé learning. Most opportunities to observe arose when protégés watched their mentors work with others. This suggests that mentors should be encouraged to interact with their protégés in more than just one-to-one meetings. (ibid: 522)

There is considerable anecdotal evidence to support the view that mentors and mentees do learn from each other. For instance, Linda Pettit (2004) has written about the mutual learning that has taken place in several organizations as a result of mentoring programmes but her article also highlights the importance of good matching.

This reflects the importance of social learning theory discussed in chapter 4 and, in particular, Bandura's (1979) work. Egan (2005) has identified the degree of learning goal orientation (LGO) alignment or misalignment between mentor and mentee as an important factor:

> Protégés with high LGO benefit from mentors with high LGO, and high LGO mentors paired with low LGO protégés appear likely to attempt to positively influence protégé outcomes. HRD professionals may have to develop appropriate approaches toward mentors with low LGOs, providing them with relevant feedback or excluding them from the mentor role completely. (p. 502)

Mentoring does not always work. Some relationships can be dysfunctional due to a range of factors including: a lack of trust (Bierema and Hill, 2005), manipulative behaviour, and lack of mentor expertise (Hezlett and Gibson, 2005). Other barriers include: time constraints, the intrusion of work responsibilities, and geographic distance (Bierema and Hill, 2005).

Mentors require training (Gilley et al., 2002). For instance, to ensure that they understand that their role is to assist the mentee in making decisions which are in the mentee's best interest, rather than that of the mentor or organization (Gibson, 2005). Mentors may benefit also from training that gives them an opportunity to practise explaining information to someone else and an insight into how mentees may learn from them (Hezlett, 2005). However, in a study of mentoring programmes involving 17 companies from the US Fortune 500 list, Hegstad and Wentling (2004) noted:

> Apparently HRD specialists are not frequently enlisted to train mentors and protégés for their respective roles . . . In [orientation] sessions, potential participants were typically welcomed to the process and given information about guidelines and logistical details. Skill building was not a frequent priority in these sessions. (p. 443)

The above discussion is based on mentoring relationships characterized by meetings involving physical, face-to-face contact. Mentoring can also be virtual reflecting the globalized nature of many workplaces (Bierema and Hill, 2005):

MEDIA WATCH BOX

E-mentoring

The key to successful e-mentoring is having the right collaborative tools to create effective online discussions. Martyn Sloman of the CIPD points out that many organizations experimenting with e-mentoring tend to focus instead on online materials to support mentoring rather than creating a virtual environment within which mentoring can take place. Well known organizations that have set up e-mentoring programmes include IT firms such as IBM and Hewlett-Packard.

Source
People Management, 24 March 2005: 34–7.

> The mentor and protégé can literally be around the world from each other. Furthermore, virtual mentoring relationships can be struck up and nurtured using many technical mediums, including email, electronic mailing lists, chat groups, intranets, and computer conferencing . . . another potential affordance of virtual mentoring is time independence. Mentors and protégés can literally leave messages for each other at any time when asynchronous technologies are used. (p. 559)

As with other forms of e-learning this can be seen as a cheaper and more flexible approach than traditional programmes (Bierema and Hill, 2005).

Even if the manager is not acting as a mentor to anyone, he/she can still play an important facilitation role: acting as a facilitator of the mentoring relationship. For instance, keeping lines of communication open between the parties and being supportive of the mentee (Gilley et al., 2002).

ACTIVITY 8.4

Carry out a journal search in order to find a case study example of a mentoring programme. In what ways does this example help to further improve your understanding of mentoring?

8.9 Reasons for ineffective interventions

Many interventions fail because of poor design and/or training needs analysis. Often the delivery phase is excellent but transfer of training/learning fails to take place. However, some interventions fail because of problems with the delivery phase. This can be due to a range of factors; for instance, the incompetence, indifference, or inexperience of the HRD practitioner; as well as a lack of relevant knowledge or expertise on the part of the HRD practitioner. Woolnough (2006) describes the following as warning signs that there may be a problem with the person delivering the intervention:

- Negative feedback from learners (e.g. boring delivery; information overload; too much theory and not enough practice; too much 'chalk and talk' with learners being passive; poor presentation style, etc.)
- High drop-out rates from the intervention
- A drop in attendance or return on investment of an intervention that has been successful previously (with a different trainer)
- The trainer shows little interest in the organization's culture, values, or business interests (when he/she is an external training consultant)

To this list can be added:

- The trainer takes little interest in the learning outcomes (this can be a problem when someone else has carried out the design phase)

- The trainer fails to adhere to timings resulting in some aspects of the intervention being rushed or missed out completely

Bunch (2007) suggests that such failure can be linked to the organization's culture:

> Training failure can be the manifestation of the values, beliefs, and assumptions shared by members of various levels of organizational culture. The disregard for sound practices is an immediate cause of failure but also a reflection of cultural barriers that can circumvent the best-designed program. Beliefs that training is simple, unimportant, or pointless generate behaviours such as employing incompetent trainers [and] rejecting the recommendations of competent trainers. (p. 157)

In contrast, successful interventions are those that:

> Present new ideas and concepts (in-filling) and also apply and examine those ideas and concepts (drawing-out) provide the learner with maximum opportunity to develop new competencies and awareness. (Gilley et al., 2002: 327)

In order to present new ideas and concepts the trainer needs to act as a role model for learning. Unfortunately, trainers can be as opinionated as the next person and there are occasions when this can have a negative impact on an intervention. Keeping an open mind is difficult and challenging.

◉ INSIGHTS INTO PRACTICE:

Tips and hints from an HRD practitioner

Ian Yates, a Learning and Development Manager comments that: 'Delivery needs careful planning. The delivery style will depend very much on the way the script has been written in the first place so writing scripts for others to deliver can be very difficult. Before delivering the script for the first time do a couple of test runs and make sure that the material is linked so that one piece of information flows to another, especially if it is a script that you have not had any input into. This ensures continuity and makes it easier for the audience to understand and remain engaged. Trainers who are highly regarded will have practiced and practiced the scripts to ensure that the "links" work. One very important piece of advice that I was given early in my career was—never ad-lib, even the best actors or comedians script their ad-libs. The skill is to make it look like you have just pulled a gem from the depths of your memory. For new trainers who may be feeling nervous always remember: the attendees don't know what you don't know. So never be scared of the fact that you may not be able to answer a question. You can guarantee that some one in the room will know the answer. The skill is to be able to re-direct the question back to the audience and use it as a test as part of the course.'

8.10 **International trends**

The similarities and differences between US and UK perspectives were discussed in chapter 2. A survey published by Sparrow (2004) revealed some differences in how respondents on both sides of the Atlantic ranked specific 'training strategies' by effectiveness. Traditional 'training strategies' (e.g. trainer-led sessions, on-the-job training, and coaching) were ranked highest in the UK with blended learning in fourth place and e-learning in seventh. In contrast blended learning was ranked first in the US but e-learning was still relatively low in sixth place. The same survey also ranked training methods by efficiency (i.e. a focus on the cost involved in using a particular method). In the UK ranking trainer-led sessions fell from first to fourth with on-the-job training and coaching ranked first and second respectively. In the US blended learning was top again reflecting the extent to which this 'training strategy' is seen as both effective and efficient. E-learning was ranked second for efficiency (it was sixth in the UK). The survey also revealed that traditional trainer-led sessions are the most significant component of blended learning interventions rather than the e-learning element. Whilst an emphasis on efficiency is inevitable in many organizations where budget restrictions are in force, it is important to maintain a balance between efficiency and effectiveness. It is this balancing act that is the primary focus of the next chapter on evaluation of learning and development interventions.

These trends in the USA are supported by other surveys and anecdotal evidence. For instance, according to *Business Intelligence* magazine whilst classroom-based delivery remains the most popular form of intervention this is closely followed by asynchronous e-learning (blended learning was not included in the survey). Interestingly, on-the-job training, ranked highly in the UK, was one of the least popular approaches in the USA (Rowan, 2005). What was particularly interesting about this survey was the identification of drivers for classroom-based delivery (ibid: 51):

1. Need for instructor-learner interaction: 68%

2. Some subject matter requires supervision and hands-on experience: 65%

3. Learners need live interaction with other learners: 51%

4. The corporate culture advocates classroom-style training: 40%

5. Lack of technical infrastructure needed to support e-learning: 27%

6. Use of outside instructors who only offer classroom training: 13%

7. Tracks attendance and ensures completion: 13%

8. Other: 8%

In a study of adult learners in the US, Buch and Bartley (2002) discovered that regardless of their learning style or preference the respondents expressed a preference for classroom-based training:

> It seems that the learner audience will need time and knowledge to make the transition from the classroom—the primary learning mode they have known

since kindergarten—to fully accepting and benefiting from training in another format. This suggests a need for placing more emphasis on helping learners adjust to learning in a non-classroom environment. (p. 9)

Today e-learning has become much more accepted as a 'training strategy' in the UK although predictions about its future appear mixed when a survey of senior HR professionals is compared to the CIPD survey above. 'The Future of Learning' survey, sponsored by SkillSoft, revealed that online learning will form the single, largest part of their organizations' future training delivery (e-learning age, 2007).

In terms of management development, an increasing range of methods are being used by organizations as there is an apparent shift from traditional classroom-based interventions to learning interventions characterized by self-managed and workplace learning (CIPD, 2007d). The latter includes special projects; secondments; mentoring; executive coaching; and, action learning projects. An example of this shift is shown in the *Media watch* box. At the same time educational qualifications such as the MBA continue to be popular and universities find new ways to support the development of managers in what is still a highly lucrative but highly competitive market. The implications of these trends are discussed in chapter 15.

MEDIA WATCH BOX

Management development at Sony Europe

Sony Europe is based in Berlin, Germany and employs 9,000 people across Europe. Rather than focus on traditional topics such as strategy and structure Sony Europe have introduced a management development programme for senior executives that instead focuses on how to have better conversations and how to make better decisions. The programme is underpinned by the emotional-intelligence perspective on learning (see chapter 4) so learners are encouraged to understand their own feelings and how these can be used to improve performance.

Source
People Management, 23 August 2007: 34–7.

Summary

Delivery can take different forms depending on the nature of the intervention. What is critical is that the delivery phase of an HRD intervention is conducted in a professional manner by both HRD practitioners and line managers acting as coaches or mentors. There are a great many benefits to involving line managers in the delivery phase of certain types of intervention. The level of input by HRD practitioners at this stage will vary according to the nature of the intervention. To illustrate this point there was consideration of traditional training courses or workshops, career development activities, OD projects, online tutoring, and facilitation. Coaching and mentoring were used to illustrate how managers can play an important role in the delivery stage. The key knowledge and skills required by HRD practitioners were identified and discussed. It was shown that many of these skills are transferable across the different types of intervention but that certain skills were more important for specific interventions. International trends were also considered to highlight differences between the US and the UK. Blended learning is viewed as being the most effective and efficient 'training strategy' in the US whereas in the UK more traditional strategies were ranked higher.

Review questions

1   What are the principal knowledge and skills required by an HRD practitioner to be an effective trainer?

2   How has e-learning impacted on the delivery role of the HRD practitioner?

3   In what ways do the skills required to be an effective OD project manager differ from those needed to be an effective facilitator?

4   In what ways are the requirements of coaching different to mentoring?

5   What are the principal international trends?

Suggested further reading

1   Swanson, R. A. and Holton, E. F. 2001. *Foundations of Human Resource Development*. San Francisco, CA: Berrett-Koehler.

Chapters 12, 13, and 14 provide a detailed and informative discussion on Organization Development and related change processes.

2   Bierema, L. L. and Hill, J. R. 2005. Virtual mentoring and HRD. *Advances in Developing Human Resources*, 7 (4): 556–68.

This article offers an interesting insight into e-mentoring.

3   Fabac, J. N. 2006. Project management for systematic training. *Advances in Developing Human Resources*, 8 (4): 540–47.

This article provides a good overview of the importance of project management techniques and skills as part of a systematic approach to the design and implementation of OD interventions.

4   Bunch, K. J. 2007. Training failure as a consequence of organizational culture. *Human Resource Development Review*, 6 (2): 142–63.

This article provides an informative analysis of the relationship between culture and failed interventions.

5   e-learning age 2007. HR executives predict that the future of learning is online. *e-learning age*, February: 2.

This is well worth reading to gain some further insights into e-learning.

Case study

Training and development methods in Starbucks

Training in Starbucks is closely aligned with the development and promotion of the brand. Starbucks aims to please both its customers and its employees and its vision is to bring 'great coffee to everyone everywhere' and its mission statement makes a commitment to 'provide a great work environment and treat each other with respect and dignity'. The company want a diverse workforce that reflects local communities and is passionate about the company and its products; although its brand approach involves a standardized approach to the training of all frontline staff. Employees are called partners with the barista role being the most familiar to customers. Baristas receive a minimum of 24 hours training during the first four weeks of employment. Training courses for managers are provided by the Starbucks University. Managers attend classroom-based training for eight to twelve weeks and covers barista training (as above) as part of an in-depth familiarization with the company and its procedures and systems. The trainers are store and district managers who have the appropriate knowledge and experience to pass on to new managers.

Baristas are trained predominantly in the store under the supervision of the store manager or the assistant manager. The latter focus on practising the skills of coffee making, and also include tests. Baristas are given a training manual as part of the 'coffee passport' programme. It is a 94 page booklet which is divided into sections and the barista is given a written test to complete at the end of each section. It can take two days just to complete this process. Learning to differentiate between different aromas can take several weeks. Baristas have to taste every cup of coffee they make during training so they can learn how to describe the different flavours to customers. They are also given a free bag of coffee each week so that they can continue to refine their appreciation of the product outside the work environment.

Initial training covers a range of topics including the history of coffee and how to prepare drinks. They are also taught customer service and retail skills; and attend a four hour workshop specifically on how to brew the perfect cup of coffee. This training goes into a great deal of detail such as: **Handling coffee beans:** How to open a bag of coffee beans properly without spilling any of the contents; how to hold the bag to prevent air getting trapped; how to weigh the beans; and, how to put labels in the correct position on the bag (i.e. exactly half-an-inch above the company logo). **Preparing coffee and other beverages:** How to grind coffee beans; how to prepare the milk to the correct temperature; memorizing recipes for all the drinks on the menu; and, practising the making of drinks. They also learn how to customize drinks as this is an integral aspect of the company's commitment to its customers. **Additional topics include:** cleaning and cleanliness, learning about the Italian names, how to make eye contact with customers; and, weighing the exact quantity of coffee beans being purchased by a customer. An important part of the training is learning the three underpinning principles of working for Starbucks: maintaining and enhancing self-esteem; listening and acknowledging; and, asking for help. This reflects a strong emphasis on socializing new employees into the company culture. When training is completed baristas sign a promise to exceed customer expectations by always serving a perfect cup of coffee. As they develop baristas can investigate the possibility of becoming a 'Coffee Master' which demonstrates a high commitment and passion for coffee. A coffee master wears a black apron but to achieve this status must complete a specified number of hours training and pass a series of tests, as well as lead some coffee tastings. When a new store opens experienced baristas from other branches provide one-to-one training. The company believes its approach to training has immediate benefits in terms of the positive impact on customer service.

Sources

[1] Schultz, H. and Yang, D. J. 1997. *Pour Your Heart Into It: How Starbucks Built a Company One Cup at a Time*. New York: Hyperion.

[2] Crosby, L. A. and Johnson, S. L. 2003. Beyond brand awareness. *Marketing Management*, June: 10–11.

[3] Seiler, M. 2005. High performance. *Marketing Management*, Nov/Dec: 18–23.

[4] Michelli, J. A. 2007. *The Starbucks Experience: 5 Principles for Turning Ordinary into Extraordinary*. New York: McGraw-Hill.

[5] http://www.mhhe.com/business/management/thompson/11e/starbucks-2.html (accessed 14 April 2008).

[6] http://www.teaandcoffee.net/0104/coffee.htm (accessed 14 April 2008).

[7] http://www.workforce.com/section/11/25/39/42 (accessed 14 April 2008).

Case questions

1. What 'training strategies' and 'training' methods can you discern from the case?

2. Which learning theories can be discerned from the above strategies and methods?

3. What changes would you recommend to improve the delivery of training?

Online resource centre

Visit the supporting online resource centre for additional material that will help you with your research, essays, assignments, and revision.

 www.oxfordtextbooks.co.uk/orc/mankin/

The Evaluation of Learning and Development Interventions

David Simmonds

Learning objectives

By the end of this chapter you should be able to:

* Define the concept of evaluation and differentiate between internal validation, external validation, and evaluation

* Explain the salient differences between models of evaluation

* Apply an evaluation model to different organizational contexts

* Appreciate the business reasons for undertaking evaluation

Indicative content

■ The differences between internal validation, external validation, and evaluation

■ The purpose of evaluation

■ Different approaches to evaluation

■ Barriers to evaluation

■ Different models of evaluation (e.g. Kirkpatrick, Hamblin, Return on investment)

■ Criticisms of evaluation models

■ Adopting a business approach to evaluation and the role of financial measures

■ A detailed explanation of return on investment (ROI)

■ The implications of measuring performance

Key concepts

Internal validation

External validation

Evaluation

Transfer of learning/training

Return on Investment (ROI)

HR Effectiveness Index (HREI)

Human Capital Measurement

HR Profit Centre

Kirkpatrick model

9.1 **Introduction**

'At the most basic level the task of evaluation is counting . . . The most difficult tasks of evaluation are deciding *what* things to count and developing routine *methods* for counting them' (Cascio, 2003: 154). This chapter will focus on what can be termed type 1 evaluation. This focuses on the evaluation of discrete learning and development interventions (e.g. course, workshop, seminar, or a group of these within a specific intervention, such as basic IT skills' training). Type 1 evaluation comprises internal validation, external validation, and evaluation:

- **Internal validation** can be defined as the measurement of whether a training programme has achieved its behavioural objectives or programme outcomes. The most common form of internal validation is the end-of-course reaction questionnaire or *happy sheet*. This provides a 'snap-shot' of the learners' perception of the event. However, it has some flaws such as: learners are often in a hurry to leave and do not give it their full attention; some learners do not want to be totally honest for fear of upsetting the trainer; there is insufficient time for adequate self-reflection. Additional validation techniques that could be used during the training event itself are questions and answers; tests; exercises; etc.

- **External validation** is concerned with looking at the learning process and identifying whether the activity was based on a valid identification of training or learning needs that related to the organizational criterion of effectiveness.

- **Evaluation** is concerned with measuring the impact the training or learning has had on individual performance in the workplace and the contribution this makes to overall organizational performance.

Many HRD practitioners rarely go beyond the internal validation stage. Whilst innovative use of information technology has added much needed flexibility in training delivery practitioners have continued to struggle with the area of training evaluation. Stockbrokers and accountants have been evaluating organizational assets for centuries, but until Bloom (1956) highlighted a need for training practitioners to establish behavioural objectives for courses to facilitate the performance management of learners, little had been done in the training arena.

A great deal has been written about evaluation for many years. One of the fundamental tenets of the systematic approach to training is the need for evaluation of the learning objectives. Whilst being acknowledged for many years as having great importance, evaluation is rarely undertaken to any significant degree. It is somewhat curious that the development of evaluation processes has lagged behind the development of other aspects of the systematic approach, such as needs analysis, design, and delivery. Given that performance improvement has been a strong driver of training and development for many years you might have expected senior managers to have been putting constant pressure on practitioners to justify the training budget. Certainly, this situation has been changing more recently. The drive to prove that HRD adds value to an organization has become something of a mantra in recent years. Key initiatives have emphasized the importance of evaluation. For instance, in the UK the Investors in People (IIP) award has evaluation and review as one of its four major components; while a foundational element of the whole Total Quality Management approach is based on evaluation and review, assessment, and feedback. The emergence of e-learning (free-standing and as part of a blended-learning approach) has not altered this situation:

> With simplistic evaluation processes focusing on the number of hits on online systems, computer-based tests and reduced costs, the holistic evaluation required to measure real organisational impact is significantly lacking . . . without systematic and comprehensive evaluation, it is hard to see how e-learning as an HRD strategy can be developed to ensure the delivery of quality human resources so important to organisational strategy. (Macpherson et al., 2004: 307)

The difficulties faced in measuring the impact of e-learning on organizational performance remain the same as those for any learning and development programme (Reddy, 2002). This issue is discussed in more detail below in relation to return on investment (ROI).

Key concept   Return on investment (ROI)

Return on investment measures the rate of return, expressed as a percentage, on an investment in training. It is based on an assumption that the benefits resulting from training can be quantified. It can be applied to other types of HRD intervention such as organization development projects or career development programmes.

9.2 **The purpose of evaluation**

Preskill and Russ-Eft (2003) identified five critical issues for HRD professionals in the area of evaluation:

1. The need to show effectiveness in training
2. The need to describe the process and outcomes of training
3. The need to assess more than just the trainees' reactions
4. The need to be more strategically focused
5. The need to know how well money is being spent on training

It is evident from these five needs that a great deal of thought and effort needs to go into the evaluation process. Evaluation is a complex process that involves the design of a range of metrics that require the input of a range of stakeholders. Swart et al. (2005) assert that evaluation should address the needs of three distinct stakeholders:

• The participant: who wants to be able to gauge success
• The investor: who wants to be able to measure a return on investment

- The facilitator: who wants to be able to assess the effectiveness of the development design

To which Rae (2002) would add a fourth stakeholder:

- The training manager: who wants to be able to judge the outcomes of the training department

---

! TIPS AND HINTS

Evaluation can be a very time-consuming exercise and this can be a deterrent to many HRD practitioners.

Numerous types of evaluation are badly designed, and are often full of leading, loaded, or ambiguous questions. Many questionnaires have boxes to tick on a scale of one to five, and so people typically tick the middle box, in order not to upset the trainer, the manager, or the organization. As soon as the learners have fled from the training room, the trainer pounces upon these 'happy sheets', and receives a wonderful glow of warm affirmation. And such a collusive, shallow, superficial approach to evaluation does little to change the learners, the organization, or the trainers. In contrast, Shaw and Green (1999) posit that the key to effective evaluation lies in the demonstration of learning outcomes. Individual programmes of learning do not lend themselves to traditional assessment methods. It will be difficult to write an examination paper for a diverse group of work-based learners! Increasingly a portfolio approach, demonstrating involvement, is being adopted, where a variety of materials are presented. These may range from the more traditional project report to team meeting minutes and recordings of presentations. The key is the link between the learning undertaken and the appropriateness of the demonstration tool.

MEDIA WATCH BOX

Why evaluation matters

Too often the training and development budget is the first to be cut when a recession looms. This article from a supplement in the *Guardian* newspaper illustrates why it is important to be more cautious about this type of knee-jerk reaction to changes in the external environment.

The UK faces an economic slowdown as a result of the global credit crunch. Meanwhile the UK still faces long-term skills shortages. More astute firms will resist the temptation to reduce training budgets as to do so could result in the loss of key employees who are vital to future competitiveness.

Source
Guardian, 12 April 2008: 1 (HR Focus supplement).

A portfolio approach can be designed to capture many aspects of informal workplace learning. However, it can never capture the totality of an individual's learning. The evaluation of informal learning is highly problematic. However, developing an appreciation of reflective practice (both individually and within groups), can contribute to the evaluation process. But to be effective the support of the line manager is critical. To date there has been more focus on the line manager's role in the evaluation formal training activities. Chapter 11 will discuss ways in which line managers can support the evaluation of informal learning. At this stage it should be noted that little attention has been paid to this issue (Woodall, 2000).

O'Donnell and Garavan (1997) advocate the use of three categories of evaluation criteria, namely suitability, feasibility, and acceptability. Suitability will determine the fit with the organization's goals; feasibility can assess the practicality of HRD plans and policies; and acceptability requires an analysis of the overall organizational mind-set and cultural web. And Garavan et al. (1995) had earlier identified eight contextual factors, which impact on the form of the HRD function, and the type of activities in which it engages. These are the external environment and the organization's stakeholders, culture, technology, structure, change, size, and power.

Nevertheless, there are a number of reasons why training and development programmes are *not* evaluated.

ACTIVITY 9.1

What other ways of evaluating informal learning can you find? Search the internet, journals, and library for at least one approach to add to the above discussion.

There are many reasons why learning and development interventions are not always evaluated, including:

1. People are not convinced of the purpose or benefits of evaluation
2. They feel it will be too time-consuming
3. They believe that the costs of evaluating a training event will outweigh any benefits
4. No training objectives have been identified
5. Appropriate assessment criteria have not been agreed
6. People have difficulty in selecting key areas for assessment
7. They are unaware of the methods of evaluation and how they can be used
8. They do not have the time, expertise, or resources to analyse the learning results of any evaluation
9. People feel threatened
10. They may not actually want to hear any bad news
11. They may feel they are above such considerations
12. The organization or union has no agreed policy for evaluation to take place

Consequently, through a combination of experience and knowledge, it is possible to identify seven purposes for evaluation (see *Insights into practice* box).

INSIGHTS INTO PRACTICE

The seven purposes for evaluation

1. To validate tools and methods of training needs analysis
2. To confirm or revise the options available
3. To confirm or revise the training strategies chosen
4. To determine the trainee and trainer reactions
5. To assess the acquisition of knowledge, skills, and attitudes
6. To assess the trainee's performance in the workplace
7. To determine whether organizational goals are being met

Source
The author.

Mann and Robertson (1996) argue that the purpose of evaluation is often misunderstood. The primary purpose of evaluation is act as a diagnostic tool to identify how a particular programme can be improved; not to pass judgement on the designer. The results of an evaluation contribute to a decision-making process (Campbell, 1998). The evaluation results can demonstrate whether a programme has been useful by showing the benefits in terms of cost (this, in turn, contributes to type 2 evaluation discussed in chapter 13). Evaluations can help decide between alternative training programmes and between participants in future programmes. If an evaluation can show which trainees are likely to benefit most, then it will be more cost effective to offer future programmes to those types of learners. In addition, evaluations assess the clarity and validity of tests, questions, and exercises. They must measure the skills, knowledge, and attitudes that the programme is designed to develop.

MEDIA WATCH BOX

Measuring the benefits of mentoring

A mentoring initiative in the First Direct online bank has saved the firm £915,000 in recruitment and training costs as well as reducing increasing staff retention levels.

Source
People Management, 22 February 2007: 12.

Measuring the benefits of mentoring

A study reveals that formal mentoring programmes not only contribute to employee learning, which in turn contributes to organizational performance and competitiveness, but also make the organization more attractive to potential applicants.

Source
Allen, T. D. and O'Brien, K. E. 2006. Formal mentoring programs and organisational attraction. *Human Resource Development Quarterly*, 17 (1): 43–58.

Moreover, effective training evaluation can have beneficial legal implications. Legal issues have become important considerations in human resources. Employment tribunals often question the criteria for access to training and the value of training, especially when it is used as a requirement for promotion or recruitment. In those cases, evaluation data are required to show the relatedness of the training programme to the job.

There are a number of advocates of learning-through-assessment. Evaluation can reinforce for the participants major points developed in the learning event. A follow-up evaluation can reinforce the information covered in a programme by attempting to measure the results accomplished by participants. It reminds the participants of what they should have accomplished, or should be accomplishing.

There are many reasons why evaluation is not carried out effectively. For instance, Wang and Wilcox (2006) cite HRD practitioners who do not believe in evaluation, or who do not have the 'mind-set' needed to carry out evaluation or who lack confidence in their programmes as value-added interventions. Swanson (2005) reinforces the point about mindset, arguing that many HRD practitioners do not view evaluation as a core HRD activity. Bunch (2007) adds to this list: unskilled practitioners who provide flawed interventions; and, skilled practitioners who produced flawed interventions because they lack the necessary power to produce a valid programme. A study by Kim and Cervero (2007) reveals that although:

> HRD practitioners were recognised as powerful by controlling the evaluation process in a practical sense, they perceived themselves as powerless . . . perceived themselves as victims of the organisational culture because their evaluation practices were structured by the organisation's strategic needs, values and expectations.
> (p. 16)

Key concept   Transfer of learning

Traditionally referred to as transfer of training, the transfer of learning is the ability of the learner to transfer the knowledge and skills acquired from formal learning and development interventions successfully to the workplace.

Barriers to the effective transfer of learning from 'classroom' to workplace also impede evaluation processes. Such barriers include: participants who are afraid of change and are lacking in confidence, managers who do not provide support, and HRD practitioners who are suffering from work overload (Gilley et al., 2002). According to Lewis and Thornhill (1994), ineffective training evaluation is directly related to organizational cultures. In order to attempt to counteract this problem, and to change an organization's culture, those responsible for training evaluation should carefully consider the following action points:

- Attempt, first, to understand the organization's culture and organizational attitudes to evaluation

- Recognize all levels of the organization's culture in order to consider how positive attitudes can be fostered at all of these

- Determine measurable goals for changing attitudes to evaluation in the organization in relation to time

- Utilize Lewin's forcefield analysis to analyse the extent of the problem and the task to be undertaken and his approach of how to bring about change

- Adopt a proactive approach to the advancement of organizational level training evaluation by promoting this to senior management and by forging links with line managers and other key players in order to effect new organizational beliefs towards training evaluation

- Choose a suitable change strategy or strategies to promote new organizational beliefs towards training evaluation, through seeking answers to a number of critical questions

- Seek to involve a wide range of organizational participants in the implementation stage, in an attempt to change attitudes towards training evaluation

- Actively evaluate the results of this culture change attempt

Cultural factors have also been cited more recently by Desimone et al. (2002) and Bunch (2007). The latter comments that 'training failure can be a manifestation of the values, beliefs, and assumptions shared by members of various levels of organizational culture' (p. 157).

! TIPS AND HINTS

Do not assume that transfer of learning from the 'classroom' to the workplace happens automatically. Much thought and effort needs to be given to this phase of an intervention.

9.3 **Different models of evaluation**

Let us begin by looking at how training evaluation has been developed in the past. Out of much early work in the field of education there emerged several classical approaches to the evaluation of training and learning, the most well known of which is the Kirkpatrick model (1959) which has a hierarchical structure (see table 9.1).

Despite the fact that most trainers espouse this classic approach, almost unquestioningly, we must be aware that there are nevertheless important criticisms of the Kirkpatrick model (Swanson and Holton 2001):

- **Not supported by research:** Research has consistently shown that the levels within the taxonomy are not related, or only correlated at a low level.

- **Emphasis on reaction measures:** Research has shown that reaction measures have nearly a zero correlation with learning or performance outcome measures.

- **Not used:** The model is not widely used. Despite decades of urging people to use it, most do not find it a useful approach.

- **Can lead to incorrect decisions:** The model leaves out so many important variables that four-level data alone are insufficient to make correct and informed decisions about training program effectiveness.

Yorks (2005: 207) voiced the concerns of many HRD professionals when he stated that the relationship between Kirkpatrick's learning evaluation levels, while logically antecedent to one another, is 'neither linear nor causal'.

After the pioneering work by Bloom (1956) on the need for trainers to establish behavioural objectives for the purpose of performance management, over the next ten years there was a steady stream of research into training evaluation and there then emerged several models of evaluation that built upon Kirkpatrick's original four stages or offered an alternative perspective. Some of the key ones are shown in table 9.2.

The Industrial Society's (now Work Foundation) 'Carousel' model offered a surprisingly new approach, with six stages or phases:

Evaluation level	Questions
1. Reaction	What are participants' reactions at the end of the training? Were they *happy* with the training?
2. Learning	What did the participants *learn* from the training? Were the learning objectives achieved?
3. Behaviour	Has job performance changed? Did the participants change their *behaviour* based on what was learned?
4. Results	Did the behaviour change have a positive *effect* on the organization?

Table 9.1 The Kirkpatrick model of evaluation

Model	Levels	Comments
Warr et al. (1970)	4 (Context, Input, Reactions, Outputs)	Non-hierarchical. Usually referred to as the CIRO model.
Hamblin (1974)	5 (Reactions, Learning, Job behaviour, Organization, Ultimate value)	Hierarchical. Adds a fifth level to Kirkpatrick's model
Easterby-Smith (1986)	6 (Context, Administration, Process, Inputs, Outcomes, Organizational change)	Non-hierarchical. This model uses not only a different approach and more levels, but causes the evaluator to consider their perspective and purpose more thoughtfully
Worthen and Sanders (1987)	4 (Context, Input, Process, Product)	Sequential. Referred to as the CIPP model
Bushnell (1990)	4 (Input, Process, Output, Outcomes)	Sequential. Referred to as the IPO model
Fitz-enz (1994)	4 (Situation, Intervention, Impact, Value)	Sequential. Referred to as the TVS model

Table 9.2 Evaluation models

1. Recognize a business need
2. Define development objectives
3. Define learning processes
4. Experience learning processes
5. Use and reinforce learning
6. Judge the benefit to the organization

But even this approach has come in for criticism for its lack of definition about what constitutes a business need (Kearns, 2005). Other models are more a checklist, such as Rae (2002) who adopts a step-by-step approach from the TNA stage, the identification of training objectives, and the design of the evaluation process through to medium- and long-term evaluation analyses. Given the models and frameworks available, and their promotion by practitioners, it is surprising that over the years various studies and surveys have uncovered the low levels of their application in organizations. For instance, in 1991 Phillips found that in regard to American companies:

52% measure satisfaction with the training event/course (Level 1)

17% assess the application of the trained skills on the job (Level 3)

13% evaluate changes in organizational performance (Level 4)

5% look for skill acquisition immediately after the training (Level 2)

13% carry out no evaluation at all

The situation still hadn't changed by the eve of the millennium. Bassi and van Buren (1999) found that 45 per cent of the organizations they surveyed only gauged trainees' reactions. The fact that most practitioners and organizations were happy to conduct such low level evaluations is indicative of the traditional belief held by some that if training was taking place then employee and organizational performance would improve as a result. Through my own experience I have found that when performance measurement is based on 'happy sheet' ratings, there is little incentive for practitioners to spend hours undertaking the more effective evaluations when stakeholders don't request them.

The essential difficulty with much that underpins many of these approaches, however, is that they tend to be systems-based in their origin and linear in their application. Managers in general, and financial directors in particular, have demanded more robust measures of efficiency and effectiveness from trainers for many years. But those in training departments have often just shrugged their shoulders at the impossibility, the enormity, or the difficulty of such a task.

! TIPS AND HINTS

HRD practitioners in many organizations need to adopt a business-oriented approach to evaluation and learn how to talk the language of finance.

Attempts have been made to produce evaluation models that reflect the dynamics of organizational life rather than rely on the linearity and monopolistic prevalence of the Kirkpatrick model. For instance, Preskill and Russ-Eft (2003) offer senior managers an alternative model of five phases or processes, placed within a wider context. Hodges (2002) develops an increasingly complex model of measures in order to be able to assess the effectiveness of training. But this tends to compound, rather than to clarify, the meaning, purpose, relevance, and worth of the training—reducing it instead to abstruse financial data.

9.4 **Criticisms of evaluation models**

Holton and Naquin (2005) identified a fundamental flaw, common to all evaluation models and processes: they are not framed as decision-making models (see *Insights into practice* box). For evaluations to be effective, to be credible, and to overcome cultural resistance to their implementation, I believe that the needs of three key audiences must be met. Firstly, HRD practitioners need an approach, which is simple, timely, cost effective, and provides the tools for the job. Secondly, stakeholders want an approach which is easy to explain to others and metrics/outputs which can be used in comparison with others in the organization. Thirdly, academic researchers want to support an approach based on commonly accepted practices/theories, which produce consistent outcomes.

By considering the needs of our audiences it is possible to review the evaluation methods previously identified. As a method of improving training, neither Kirkpatrick's nor Hamblin's models help practitioners to select or implement the steps to be taken at each level, nor do they help to utilize the results. Whilst Level 1 and 2 data can support future programme design, the lack of emphasis on pre-training analysis makes it difficult to determine if a learner's performance gap has been overcome. Even though Burrow and Bernardinelli (2003) demonstrated that using open questions could quantify the amount of improvement, the complexity of collecting upper level data doesn't justify the effort if robust financial measures are not an outcome. In addition, if the effects of training cannot be isolated, the data loses credibility.

Researchers were also critical because too much emphasis was placed on reaction measures that have a zero correlation to performance outcome measures (Swanson and Holton, 2001; Laird, 2003). An implicit assumption of reaction measures is that participants are clear about their learning needs and that these needs are consistent with those identified at the preceding stages of the systematic approach (Wang and Wilcox, 2006). Whilst Holton (1996) had earlier suggested a model based on individual performance as opposed to behaviour, it still didn't give stakeholders a clear and comparable metric to use.

The work of Warr et al. was a step in the right direction but measuring output at the work unit and organizational level is complicated and doesn't provide practitioners or stakeholders with the simplicity they are looking for. Easterby-Smith and Fitz-enz do try to appeal to practitioners by encouraging evaluation teams to conduct more up-front work on both the context of the evaluation and the performance gap to be breached. In fact Zigarmi and Baynham (1997) were able to obtain positive results from a variety of pre- and post-training tests following a management development programme. However, the absence of a clear link between training design and evaluation, and the tools to realize the model are a drawback. The problem facing HRD practitioners is highlighted by Smith and Sadler-Smith (2006):

> Causal ambiguity has bedevilled much of the evaluation of training research at the results level . . . This may sometimes render investment in training decisions to be based more upon expert judgements than meticulously calculated bottom-line pay-offs. This is not to say that such analyses are impossible but they may be difficult to achieve in practice. (p. 195)

Rae's model (2002) does provide a more detailed process to follow and it may be worthy of further investigation.

In reality, the problem with all these models is the fact that in the workplace things don't separate into neat little steps that can be followed systematically and sequentially. A practitioner can devote hours to conducting a thorough needs analysis and design of an event only to see it fail for an unforeseen reason. If a line manager doesn't have the prerequisite skills to conduct a pre- and post-training analysis then any evaluation at higher levels will be flawed. The complexities of measuring application and implementation can be overcome with sufficient resources but if the needs of stakeholders aren't met, then there will be no support to facilitate the investment. Practitioners need to look for a broad based partnership within the workplace to share resources and time, establishing buy-in from stakeholders through the promise of hard financial data, as they are needed to encourage the application of learning in the workplace.

Lewis and Thornhill (1994) saw a link between ineffective evaluation and reluctance to change, which was rooted in an organization's culture. Key audiences need to be able

Level (Where?)	Index (Which?)	Question (What?)	Methods (How?)	Timing (When?)	Outcomes (How much?)
1. Reaction	Happiness	What were the *reactions* of the learners to the training activity?	Training records Learning styles Verbal questioning Observation Visual assessment Body language Interpersonal relationships Reaction questionnaire	Before During Immediately afterwards After a month	Are the trainees still motivated to learn? Has the credibility of the trainer / the programme been maintained or increased? What needs to be changed?
2. Learning	Learning	What *learning* was accomplished?	**Head**—assessing recall, understanding, application, analysis **Hands**—assessing manual, intellectual, and communication abilities **Heart**—assessing relevance, sincerity, and durability of attitudes **Holistic**—assessing integration of learning to the whole self	Before During Immediately afterwards After a month After 3 months After 9 months	*Internal* **validation** of changes to knowledge, skills and attitudes What has still to be learnt? What has been remembered? What needs to be changed?
3. Job performance	Application	What direct *changes* have there been to job performance?	Self-appraisal Peer appraisal Supervisory appraisal Subordinate appraisal Stakeholder analysis Activity sampling Interviews, discussions, and questionnaires Observation Performance indicators / targets	Before Immediately afterwards After a month After 3 months After 9 months	*External* **validation** of training and learning objectives What improvements to performance have been measured? What changes have been sustained? Any further changes?
4. Department/ Organization	Bottom-line value	What was the ultimate *value* of the training and learning?	Reporting processes / systems Performance indicators Cost / benefit analysis ROI Human capital investment analysis Strategic change	Before After 3 months After 9 months	**Evaluation** of training and learning objectives What has been the (financial / non-financial) benefit to the department / organization? What still needs to be changed?

Table 9.3 A composite model for the evaluation of training and learning

Source: Simmonds, 2003

> **◉ INSIGHTS INTO PRACTICE**
>
> ## Evaluation as a decision-making process
>
> A critical review of evaluation models reveals that most of these models are based on a rational-economic perspective. However, a critical review of literature on decision-making shows that the rational-economic approach does not work in practice; which may explain why evaluation is not as widely practised as theorists argue it should be.
>
> **Source**
> Holton, E. F. and Naquin, S. 2005. A critical analysis of HRD evaluation models from a decision-making perspective. *Human Resource Development Quarterly*, 16 (2): 257–80.

to see the benefits of the change and commit to it rather than have it forced upon them. The existence of 'internal permitting conditions', such as the amount of money and managerial time and energy devoted to an initiative, give an indication of the willingness to change (Lundberg, 1985). Lundberg also believes that change should be implemented in small palatable steps, which we need to consider when introducing a more strategic approach to training evaluation. It would be easy to introduce second order change if people could be programmed like machines to respond in particular ways without any resistance. But as this isn't the case, then strong leadership, a clear reason for change, and stakeholder involvement will be key to overcoming resistance.

From all these many and various approaches, we can now perhaps synthesize a composite model for the evaluation of training and learning. This is shown in table 9.3.

9.5 A business approach to evaluation

So, what is the current situation concerning training evaluation and how does the above model fit into this? Clearly new approaches to evaluation were required which addressed the failings of earlier approaches. The pioneering approaches below were closely tied to the growing realization for HRD practitioners that they needed to show the contribution their interventions were making to organizational success:

a) Return on Investment (ROI)

b) HR Effectiveness Index (HREI)

c) Human capital measurement

d) HR profit centre

a) The Return on Investment approach mirrors other financial evaluation tools by comparing the cost of HR programs to the benefits they deliver. In order to calculate ROI, evaluation experts such as Phillips are recommending the addition of a fifth level to Kirkpatrick's model. This requires collecting level 4 data, converting the results to monetary values, and then comparing those results with the cost of the training program. Even though collecting level 4 data is complicated, in its absence it is difficult to show that the organization has benefited from the learning and application of skills (see *Insights into practice* box). However, the economic and monetary focus within the process ignores the (sometimes intangible) value of training to the individual, and so could prove unpopular. However, as Wang and Wilcox (2006) observe:

> in training reality, the net program benefit is often entangled with other organisational variables and difficult to separate . . . In fact, if one can calculate the net benefit for a training program, it may become unnecessary to determine the ROI because the net benefit is the organisational impact of training, or the contribution that a training program makes for the organisation. (p. 535)

MEDIA WATCH BOX

Return on investment or return on expectations?

Ensuring the expectations of stakeholders are met is more important than producing financial measures. According to Martyn Sloman of the CIPD measuring the return on expectations is a more forward looking approach.[1]

This does assume that the two approaches are mutually exclusive which need not be the case.

Source
[1] *People Management*, 6 September 2007: 12.

---

b) The HR Effectiveness Index, first developed and used by General Electric in the 1950s, used a series of HR measures (e.g. revenue/employees, grievances, reward/operating expenses) which when combined form a single benchmark figure. By comparing training and development expenses with the total number of employees, for example, Phillips (1988) was able to establish a relationship between HR performance and organizational effectiveness. Nevertheless, being able to compare an organization's effectiveness against a competitor's doesn't necessarily provide the robust internal measure stakeholders and practitioners require.

c) The School of Human Capital Measurement categorizes employees as assets and attempts to place a value on them by using standard accounting principles to measure changes in their performance. Whilst Cascio (1993) believes the benefits of the measure can greatly outweigh the costs of implementation, the fundamental notion that people are assets and therefore owned by the organization is controversial given that companies are looking for greater flexibility.

d) The HR Profit Centre approach is based on the concept that the services HR functions provide should be cross-charged to the business unit consuming them (Mercer, 2002). Central to this is the notion that those same business units could purchase HRD services externally. In theory L&D practitioners are then encouraged to undertake effective evaluation of training to identify the processes they perform which add value and deliver cost reductions. If the services add value they will be in demand and revenue generated will be sufficient to show a profit. To realize such an approach would require a significant change in perception from seeing HR departments as expense centres, to them delivering profit (Pauly, 1993). A more client-focused attitude by practitioners must first be realized for this approach to be fully implemented (Phillips, 2001).

Now, at last, in the USA, Phillips (2002) and Swanson (2001) have led the profession in attempts to determine rigorous approaches to the analysis of return on investment (ROI) of training and learning. Over the years, there has been much debate about the difficulty of assessing the effectiveness of training and learning at these upper or wider levels. In this context, Phillips' ROI model (2002) for collecting level 5 evaluation data is a major contribution.

ACTIVITY 9.2

Write a short statement of not more than 250 words explaining why it is important to use financial measures to evaluate interventions. Seek feedback on this from colleagues and/or fellow students.

Like earlier models of evaluation, these approaches have shortfalls when meeting the needs of diverse stakeholders. Questions surround the objectivity of data, and the difficulty in isolating the financial benefits of a training program in order to demonstrate its contribution (Phillips, 2001). However, having considered these various evaluation approaches, I believe that the ROI process is worthy of further investigation, as it could provide stakeholders with a measure they can use to compare the ROI delivered.

(•) INSIGHTS INTO PRACTICE

ROI in practice

(i) A number of researchers have attempted to determine the ROI from training interventions. Gordon and Owens (1997) used the ROI process to measure payback from a basic skills training programme at **Otto Engineering.** Using a range of tools they were able to:

- assess skill levels pre- and post-training
- convert defect and productivity rates into monetary values
- isolate the improvement as a result of training through statistical analysis
- determine program costs including participants' wages, replacement overtime, and the time taken to undertake training

As a result they showed that the company received payback on their investment in training in 10.3 months. This supported earlier more subjective assertions from supervisors of how long it took to notice performance improvements on the factory floor. However, the low correlation between the cost of defects and the cost of quality training does cast some doubt on the statistical analysis method used to isolate the affects of training.

(ii) Stone et al. (1997) calculated a return on investment of 47.2% in the first year following the training programme contribution to a major change initiative for relationship bankers at the **First National Bank**. Complications arose when attempting to isolate the affects of training—scheduling difficulties made it difficult to use control groups, and the variables to be used for trend line analysis proved to be erratic. Therefore, participants' and managers' financial estimates were used to identify Level 3 and 4 outputs. Using such estimates can give rise to concerns of subjectivity but these were reduced by asking participants about the degree of confidence they had in their responses and getting managers to validate them. The research also identified positive intangible benefits as a result of the training that in the wider context of the change initiative at the bank may be of greater value in the long run.

(iii) Credibility is a key output of any training evaluation, a factor that seemed to have escaped Graff and Shriver (1997) when evaluating a negotiation skills course at **Texas Instrument Systems Group**. At first glance the reported ROI of 2,287% seems to be too good to be true, and by looking closely at their methodology it can be seen that the ROI calculation is weakened by neglecting the cost of training facilities and lost productivity, and the fact that only a third of participants responded or provided results. There was also a lack of pre event work to identify the performance gap, and no evidence of how the subjectivity of reported savings and profits by delegates was validated.

(iv) Nevertheless, looking at individual courses ROI forecasting can be a powerful aid when deciding where to deploy training resources (Graber et al., 1997). These researchers tested ROI forecasting at **Commonwealth Edison** to identify which met training needs delivered the greatest value. Considerable work was done up-front with a broad base of stakeholders to identify and weight the key accountabilities of each job. Competency levels were identified to determine the skills gap of each employee using a combination of questionnaires followed by meetings between managers and their employee to agree final ratings. Whilst assumptions were made as to the value of each employee, they were conservative in nature and by segregating employees into groups (professional, supervisory, middle management) deficiencies could be weighted to validate them. Programmes were evaluated based on the skills learnt and their cost, but no attempt was made to determine the extent of the application and implementation of those skills. Hypothetically, they were then in a position to determine the ROI for any person attending any course and prioritize which courses would deliver the greatest value. However, the workplace in general and training in particular rarely delivers uniform results. For example, assuming that benefits would be derived from simply attending a course doesn't take into account the difference in learning styles. (Shepherd, 1999)

9.6 **The return on investment (ROI) model of evaluation**

By taking note of the criticisms of the pioneering approaches, Phillips (2002) developed a model, which provides practitioners with a set of tools they can use to apply ROI. Stakeholders also have a metric that makes it possible to compare the bottom-line input of HR initiatives against other investments in the business. Even though academics comment that the application of ROI can still present difficulties, the model is seen as a move in the right direction (Simmonds, 2003). Phillips has produced a basic formula for calculating ROI within his model:

1. Collect level-4 evaluation data to determine if on-the-job application produces measurable results

2. Isolate the effects of the training program by using control groups, trend line analysis, or validated confidence levels in the monetary estimates provided

3. Convert the results to monetary benefits by dividing training results into hard data and soft data

4. Calculate the 'fully loaded' costs of training

5. Apply the ROI formula below to arrive at a comparable and credible metric:

$$\text{ROI} = \text{Net Program Benefits} \times 100$$

Program costs

It would be easy to dismiss the ROI approach as unsuitable in the not-for-profit sector, but the focus of the formula is on savings generated not profits produced. As we have seen from earlier examples, if we can demonstrate that savings are achieved from productivity and quality gains following a training intervention, an ROI calculation can be successfully completed even in the public sector or a voluntary organization. The ROI process can also be used as a diagnostic tool to assist the review of programme design and needs analysis.

How, then, can training evaluation progress in the future?

9.7 **The future of evaluation**

All the above approaches fall squarely within a rational economic paradigm. This limits their applicability and effectiveness.

There is a new development in the field of evaluation, which I have called the Ripple Model. Unlike other models of evaluating training, which are too often viewed as linear, static, or progressive, I believe evaluation should be perceived as a reflection of the people, systems, and processes in which it takes place. Consequently, it is constantly moving, dynamic, and organic.

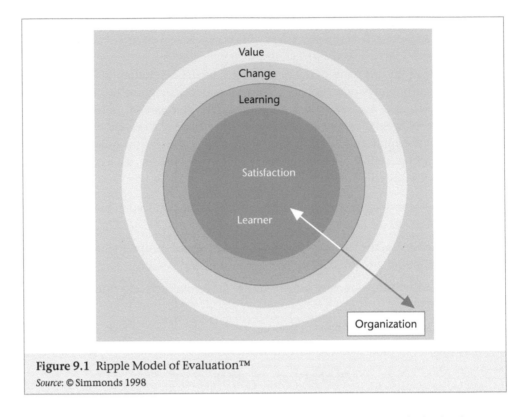

Figure 9.1 Ripple Model of Evaluation™
Source: © Simmonds 1998

At the centre is the requirement for the learner's needs to be satisfied. This becomes translated into learning, which in turn is transferred to the job and to the changed job performance. Finally, we determine its value to the wider organization.

As the ripples flow out, so different parts and aspects of work performance are impacted. Moreover, the greater the learning, so greater will be the ripples, creating wider and higher waves. These will impact an ever-widening group of others. For organizational change, therefore, there needs to a much larger impact from the learning.

However, evaluation occurs in more than one direction, for the ripples also flow back towards the centre. Since learning always takes place within a context, so the learning itself will be constrained and affected by, say, the organizational culture, financial imperatives, and stakeholder expectations. These will cause classic interference patterns to be set up between the ripples flowing from the centre and those coming from the boundary. Consequently, the organization will also affect the rate and scope of change and learning in the department and the individual.

Therefore evaluation measures must be undertaken, before, during, and after the learning, by the learner, by the trainer, and by the manager. Job performance must be measured **before** the learning takes place, against whatever criteria or measures are normally used for performance management in the working environment. For example it could be an assessment of the financial costs of placing a job advert; how quickly a student is enrolled by the postgraduate office at a university; how much time is spent in servicing a gas central heating boiler; or how late the trains arrive!

And then, **during** the training, people's reactions are assessed, and the learning can be measured. At the **end** of training, and through the transfer of learning, by means of a learning contract and by including action plans, projects, and assignments, the learning can be taken into the workplace and applied in a realistic environment, resulting in improved and changed job performance. This can then be measured using the same criteria and metrics as those used before the learning event. However, transfer of learning can take time to occur, as long as three to six months according to Wang and Wilcox (2006). Over the last 15 years there has been much progress in arriving at a better understanding of the transfer of learning. Despite this progress:

> The research done to date has provided only limited knowledge about *which* factors have the greatest impact on the transfer of [learning] and about *how* these factors affect transfer behaviour under different conditions and different kinds of training. (Maycunich Gilley et al., 2003: 196)

The extent to which this impacts upon the business unit, the shop, department, office, or factory will be the degree to which the ultimate **value** of the learning will be accomplished.

Internal validation of learning and training is a measurement of the extent to which the objectives have been accomplished. And this is tested in a number of different ways, but preferably during the learning event itself. *External validation* on the other hand is a measure of how far the learning has impacted upon job behaviour and job performance. *Evaluation* however is a measure of the worth or value of that learning to the wider organization, often in economic and financial terms, and this will include cost / benefit analysis and return-on-investment measures.

It is appropriate at this point to offer a health warning! It must be remembered that, in an organization which has little or no background or experience of effective evaluation systems, to introduce such an approach will necessitate a great deal of time, effort, and resource—probably at least 18 months. Moreover, some evaluation systems that I've encountered in the past have become so elaborate and intricate that their benefit is questionable in relation to their cost.

For evaluation to be effective it must be seen to be part of a continuous cycle of improvement which includes training as well as every other function and department in the organization. Where there is a history and a culture of change and quality improvement, this will be easier. Deming, Juran, Crosby, and Ishikawa are well known names in the development of quality management approaches. But fundamental and imperative to each of their systems is the need for evaluation, review, and feedback. Training is central and fundamental to any change management system and process, and evaluation is foundational to effective training and learning. Training itself must, therefore, include within it elements of review and assessment, change, and continuous improvement. These must be built into each learning event, each programme, each course, seminar, workshop, conference, mentoring, or coaching session (see *Media watch* box). There need to be milestones for review, appraisal, assessment, and evaluation. Feedback—honest, transparent, criterion-based feedback—is essential for improvement. Unless the trainer is open to receiving feedback on their performance, which is realistic, sincere, and truthful, then their own performance is unlikely to improve, becoming stuck in traditional methods and media. They will use hackneyed exercises, old jokes, and tired case studies that have long passed their sell-by-date, because it's easy and comfortable. Since the trainers haven't been told of the consequences of their delivery techniques, they are unaware of the outcomes and responses to such methods and media. Training professionals need, through continuous professional development, quality circles, and reflective practice, to lead in the development of professional practice. However, measuring the impact of some HRD interventions, such as mentoring programmes is difficult due to the lack of evaluation strategies for such programmes (Hezlett and Gibson, 2005).

MEDIA WATCH BOX

Evaluation and coaching

These two items illustrate how the evaluation of coaching is lagging behind the utilization of this popular intervention.

The CIPD's 2008 *Learning and Development Survey* shows that the number of organizations using coaching has increased from 63 to 71 per cent since the previous year's survey. Yet only 8 per cent evaluate coaching interventions.[1]

With only 27 per cent of organizations integrating coaching into HR and business strategies there is an increasing interest in finding ways to evaluate coaching. For instance, in the UK in order to develop an evaluation model the BBC has been interviewing employees who have received coaching to find out more about the impact of this intervention. The BBC also seeks feedback from its team of internal coaches through twice-yearly sessions. It is likely that more organizations will go down this route in order to better understand the efficacy of coaching.[2]

Sources
[1] *People Management*, 20 March 2008: 11.
[2] *People Management*, 10 August 2006: 34–6.

ACTIVITY 9.3

1. What are the potential implications for the credibility of HRD practitioners of the current gap between the usage and evaluation of coaching?
2. How could the Kirkpatrick model be used to evaluate coaching?

For our organizations to be able to change, and to make change happen, training is central and the core to the achievement of that purpose. But it is not sufficient to view the process as linear, straight line, or causal. Change and learning are not two-dimensional; they are multi-dimensional, dynamic, organic in approach, where there are webs, links, interfaces, relationships, and social connections. And it is difficult for us to even name all the parts, let alone understand the connections. Increasingly, training professionals must acknowledge the existence of work, learning, and change as interconnected parts of a complex adaptive system (Lewin and Regine, 1999). Instead, the role of the training practitioner is to facilitate and enable the generic transferability of skills, knowledge and attitudes so that employees can function more effectively. We must model such behaviour. Essential to that is the need for evaluation.

9.8 **Measuring performance**

We need to see evaluation in the context of normal performance measurement approaches. Here are just a few of the ways in which people's work is measured today in, say, an HR department:

- Labour turnover rates
- Number of customer complaints
- Cost, size, and effectiveness of recruitment adverts
- Speed of replacing staff
- Uptake of new initiatives, such as 360° feedback
- Implementation of appraisal
- Accuracy of payroll and pensions administration
- Results of employee relations negotiations

However, no matter which approach is adopted, performance measurement and management can only be effective when employed within a framework of quality management and continuous improvement.

Assessing the effectiveness of training and learning has a number of benefits:

1. Helps the learner to change performance
2. Confirms the extent to which the objectives have been achieved
3. Rewards the learner with knowledge of results
4. Assesses competence
5. Gives certification of competences for qualification purposes
6. Provides evidence of learning as a basis for further training
7. Identifies the need for remedial training
8. Identifies the learning gained
9. Provides evidence to revise the training design
10. Justifies use of resources (money, people, space, time, equipment)
11. Demonstrates the benefits of investment in training
12. Compares the costs / benefits of different training and learning methods

13. Provides evidence for marketing the training

14. Enables the credibility and profile of the training function to be raised.

Such benefits can be used to inform discussions between stakeholders and trainers. At this point, there is a useful distinction to be made between 'pay-back and pay-forward'.

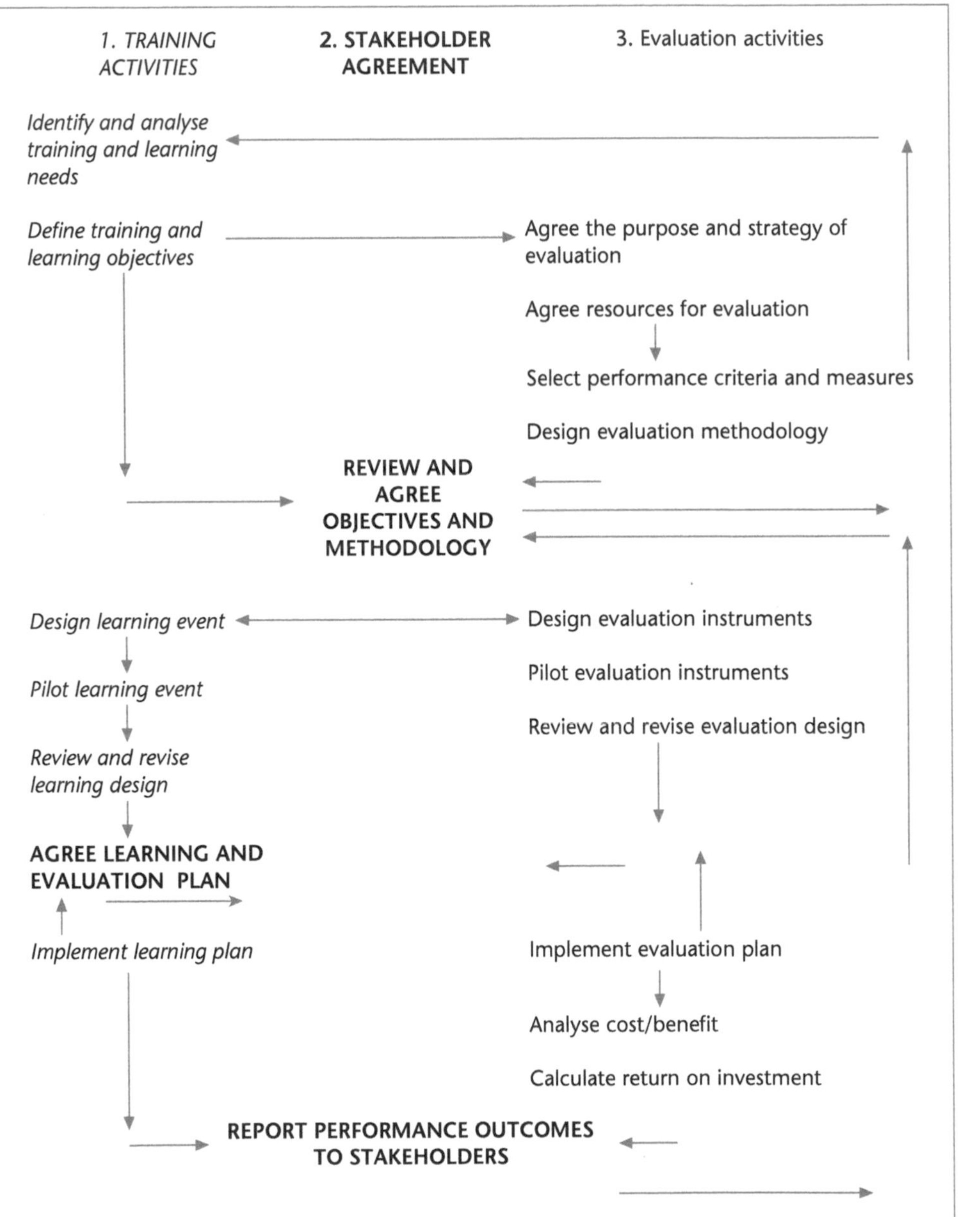

Figure 9.2 The Training Evaluation Process™

Source: © Simmonds 2005

Pay-back means a return on training investment measurable in financial turnover, such as profit or similar terms e.g. increases in sales, conversion of leads to sales etc. Pay-back evaluation suggests that the option to invest in training can be directly compared with other investment options using standard investment appraisal techniques. *Pay-forward*, on the other hand, means a benefit flowing from investment in training that cannot be expressed directly in financial terms. This may be in the form of cultural / behaviour change, increased identification on the part of staff with business objectives, or observed changes in individual or team behaviour. There are, therefore, a number of necessary steps in gaining agreement with stakeholders in the evaluation process. It is possible to see a number of flows within a dynamic whole:

As a result, training professionals must collaborate with stakeholders in agreeing:

1. That an identified problem represents a training need

2. The most appropriate training strategy

3. If the chosen strategy has been successfully implemented

4. If learning occurred, and to what extent

5. The use of learning outcomes (at an individual level)

6. The impact and worth of the learning (at an organizational level)

In the recent past, researchers have worked to construct balanced-scorecard-type metrics of HRD (Holton and Naquin, 2005). Fitz-enz (2000) has amalgamated a number of these approaches into a 'composite human capital scorecard', which highlights the following metrics for the evaluation of training and development activities:

• Training cost as percentage of payroll

• Total training hours provided

• Average number of hours of training per employee

• Training hours by function, job group

From these various models and approaches to evaluation it is possible to construct appropriate measures of training and learning that will be congruent with not only the organization's purpose, function, and culture, but also with its people and their many expectations. Helpfully for the training practitioner, Fitz-enz (2000) has tabulated a number of process and function metrics. Taken together, these can be used to apply different evaluative measures in various organizational settings (see table 9.4).

! TIPS AND HINTS

It is imperative that HRD professionals adopt a client-centred approach to evaluation, and employ measures of performance such as these that are known, transparent, and applicable to the appropriate function or department.

Marketing	Customer service
Marketing costs as percentage of sales	Service costs as percentage of sales
Advertising costs as percentage of sales	Mean time to respond and repair
Distribution costs as percentage of sales	Service unit cost
Sales administration costs as percentage of sales	Customer satisfaction level
Information services (IS)	**Finance**
IS costs as percentage of sales	Accounting costs as percentage of sales
Percentage of jobs completed on time and within budget	Aging of receivables
	Accuracy of cost accounting
Overtime costs	Percentage of filings on time
Backlog hours	Percentage of on-time closings
Value of regular reports (use paired comparison)	
Facilities	**Safety and security**
Work order response time	Safety and security costs as percentage of sales
Work order completion time	
Level of employee complaints	Accident rates
Maintenance costs as percentage of sales	Lost days level
Recycling percentages	Worker compensation costs
	Security incident rates
Purchasing	**Administrative services**
Purchasing costs as percentage of sales	General and administrative costs as percentage of sales
Average cost to process a requisition	
Average time to process a requisition	Outsourcing cost/benefit
Inventory costs	Average project response time
Percentage of purchases defective or rejected	Internal customer satisfaction level
	Percentage of projects completed on time and within budget

Table 9.4 The range of evaluative measures

Summary

Despite its acknowledged benefits, and in spite of the best intentions of trainers and their employers alike, training evaluation is still undertaken neither systematically nor with any degree of conviction.

The almost monopolistic influence of Kirkpatrick's model, together with his followers in the rational economic school, appears now at least to be waning. Researchers are willing to critique their approach, and to voice the concerns that many HRD practitioners have had for some time. The somewhat simplistic, and linear, methodology has enjoyed worldwide renown, but by no means universal success. Lacking validity, the model is perhaps starting to lose credibility.

Phillips and Swanson have led the way in offering a convincing alternative in their ROI frameworks. Case studies are emerging (Phillips, 2005) that appear to give credence to such an approach. Finance directors and line managers, in certain cultures and contexts, may be particularly pleased that at last training and development can be measured on an equal basis to other organizational functions. However, this reductionist paradigm, insisting as it does that training can only be assessed in tangible and financial terms, appears to overlook the very nature of human learning.

Fitz-enz, amongst others, seems to favour a more naturalistic, and holistic view that encourages a dynamic, connected, and organic approach. Reflection, feedback, and cycles of continuous improvement need to flow between the learner, the department, and the organization—and back again. The greater the learning, so greater will be the effects, creating wider and higher impact. These will impress an ever-widening group of stakeholders. For organizational change to be effective, therefore, there needs to a much larger impact from the learning. Integrated commitment to an organization-wide approach to appropriate and relevant training evaluation will have a significant part to play in achieving and sustaining organizational transformation and development.

Review questions

1 Define the following: internal validation, external validation, and evaluation.

2 What are some of the main barriers to the transfer of learning/training to the workplace?

3 Explain the four levels of the Kirkpatrick model.

4 What are some of the principal criticisms of evaluation models?

5 What are the potential advantages to using the return on investment (ROI) model?

Suggestions for further reading

1 Kirkpatrick, D. 1959. Techniques for evaluating training programmes Parts 1–4. *Journal of the American Society for Training and Development*, 13 (11), 13 (12), 14 (1), 14 (2).

   Collectively these represent the most influential discussion on evaluation to date.

2 Macpherson, A., Elliot, M., Harris, I. and Homan, G. 2004. E-learning: reflections and evaluation of corporate programmes. *Human Resource Development International*, 7 (3): 295–313.

   This article provides some useful insights into the evaluation of e-learning interventions.

3 Holton, E. and Naquin, S. 2005. A critical analysis of HRD evaluation models. *Human Resource Development Quarterly*, 16 (2): 257–80.

   This is a very good critique of evaluation models.

4 Kearns, P. 2005. *Evaluating the ROI from Learning*. London: CIPD.

   For those who want a more detailed explanation of this financial approach of evaluation.

5 Wang, G. G. and Wilcox, D. 2006. Training evaluation: knowing more than is practised. *Advances in Developing Human Resources*, 8 (4): 528–39.

   This article contains an interesting discussion on the evaluation process.

Case study

Costs of evaluating training through the UK Investors in People (IIP) award

The UK Department of Transport, Local Government and the Regions (DTLR) achieved Investors in People (IIP) recognition in mid-1999. IIP is a business improvement tool that is designed to improve organizational performance through the development of people. It comprises a framework which organizations can adapt to their own context. Once achieved the award is subject to periodic reviews based on a reassessment of the organization. In terms of the DTLR, they chose to be re-assessed in October 2001 so that should they fail in the re-assessment they still had six months to reach the required standard. The government had instructed each department to achieve IIP status by Dec 1999, and to retain accreditation. As the only political party at the time to hold accreditation, the Labour Party was satisfied of the benefits of IIP.

The costs involved therefore tend to be regarded as almost immaterial. In the grand scheme of government and departmental expenditure, they are also insignificant. The only *direct* measurable cost of reassessment was the fee paid to the assessor. This was £550 per day, and the assessment and report took 18 days (i.e. a total of £9,900). However, there were many hidden costs. A total of 180 staff from all grades were interviewed at an average cost of one hour each and an estimated salary cost of £30 per hour (i.e. a total of £5,400). These figures also exclude further additional costs such as accommodation. Preparing for the re-assessment included conducting an internal 'Health-check' carried out by staff from each Division (some 35 in DTLR). The training of a member of staff from each Division took 2 days. The average time spent on the 'Health-check' was 8 days, plus 3 person-days of interviews. The cost of 13 days × £30 × 7hrs × 35 divisions is £95,000. In addition, there is a three-person team in HR whose sole function is IIP matters, and a considerable part of their time was focused on these 'Health-checks', and then the re-assessment. An estimate of their time commitment would be two months at approximately £28,000.

The production of Action Plans in the department as a whole and then in each Division took yet further time. The identified Actions from these plans would require even more time to implement. An estimate might be 3 days in each Division at an approximate cost of £22,000. However, if an 'Action' involves 'all staff' this is a huge underestimate of the real costs. In addition there are supplementary costs that have not been calculated. Each Division was required to brief the staff and in particular the senior Team (any of whom might have been selected). Each Division produced its own briefing, since the IIP position and Actions within each are different. Distribution varied from an e-mail note to full Divisional meetings. Consequently, the total cost of re-assessment is realistically upwards of £160,000.

Case questions

1. In order to calculate the ROI of this initiative what further information do you need?

2. What are the potential benefits of an initiative like Investors in People and which benefits could you realistically quantify in financial terms?

3. What are the limitations of the ROI approach to evaluation?

Online resource centre

Visit the supporting online resource centre for additional material that will help you with your research, essays, assignments, and revision.

  www.oxfordtextbooks.co.uk/orc/mankin/

PART 3

The Key Themes in Human Resource Development

Part 3 explains key themes in human resource development. The topics covered reflect the evolving role of human resource development that was discussed in part 1. Topics such as the role of human resource development in small and medium sized enterprises and in corporate social responsibility have been neglected in many of the mainstream texts on the concept.

10

Managing or Nurturing Knowledge

Learning objectives

By the end of this chapter you should be able to:

* Define and explain the concepts of knowledge, knowledge management, and knowledge work

* Understand the principal perspectives on knowledge management

* Explain the differences between managing and nurturing knowledge

* Appreciate the relationship between formal and informal organizational structures and processes

* Explain the relationship between HRD and knowledge management

* Understand how HRD can support different knowledge management strategies

* Appreciate the importance of social spaces to knowledge creation and knowledge sharing

Indicative content

- The problematic nature of knowledge and the lack of any universal definition

- The relationship between tacit and explicit knowledge

- The principal perspectives on knowledge management: the objectivist and practice-based perspectives

- Intellectual capital as a source of competitive advantage

- The role of human and social capital theories

- The symbiotic relationship between formal and informal structures and processes (particularly in relation to communities of practice and social networks)

- The principal strategies for knowledge management: managing or controlling, nurturing or cultivating, and a balanced approach

- The implications of knowledge management, knowledge work, and knowledge workers for HRD strategy and processes

- Knowledge creation and knowledge sharing as the primary knowledge management processes

- The role of social spaces in maximizing knowledge creation and knowledge sharing

- The relationship between HRD and knowledge management and the need for the horizontal integration of HRD and HRM in order to maximize the benefits of an organization's knowledge management strategy

- The implications for learning of different knowledge management strategies

Key concepts

Knowledge

Knowledge work and workers

Knowledge intensive firm (KIF)

Professional service firm (PSF)

Knowledge management

Tacit and explicit knowledge

Codification

The objectivist perspective

The practice-based perspective

Communities of practice

Social networks

Intellectual capital

Knowledge creation and knowledge sharing

Social space

10.1 **Introduction**

In the UK the theory and practice of human resource development (HRD) has evolved in parallel to that of knowledge management (KM). The growth of interest in KM since the early 1990s reflects the extent to which we live in a society that has become increasingly dependent on knowledge (Delanty, 2001). We can see examples of this trend all around us, for instance: the expansion of the Internet, the continued development of mobile phone technology, and the advancements in treatment for a wide range of medical conditions. KM has become an important strategic consideration for organizations because increasingly knowledge is seen as the key to an organization's competitive advantage. This knowledge has been described as an organization's intellectual capital and comprises both human capital and social capital, thus reflecting a resource based view (RBV) of business strategy (explained in more detail in chapter 3):

> The metaphor of 'capital' draws our attention to the way human skills and relationships can theoretically represent assets for an organisation. (Newell et al., 2002: 77)

KM policies and processes are designed to manage these assets as effectively as possible, although as shall be discussed later in this chapter there is a difference in opinion about how this can best be achieved. In principle the experience that HRD practitioners have at designing, implementing, and evaluating HRD interventions is ideally suited to KM interventions. KM interventions require not only careful design and implementation but a rigorous approach to evaluation. KM processes, such as knowledge acquisition, knowledge creation, and knowledge sharing all involve learning processes (e.g. situated learning—see chapter 4). Indeed there is a tendency for HRD theorists to wax lyrically on this topic, for instance:

> It is clear that HRD skills and knowledge are critical to the success of knowledge management processes. (Gourlay, 2001: 40)

> Through the development of learning strategies . . . HRD can facilitate the unlocking of the organisation's potential and the means by which all the (dynamic) processes within an organisation can be better aligned with an organisation's business strategy. (Mankin, 2001: 75)

While in research reports for the CIPD Beaumont and Hunter (2002) argue that HRD practitioners are ideally placed to play a central role in knowledge management initiatives; and Stewart and Tansley (2002) believe they can play a fundamentally influential role. However, the reality is somewhat different with many organizations focusing on technology-based solutions to KM which privilege the expertise of computer specialists over that of HRD practitioners.

This chapter will attempt to define and explain a series of complex concepts in as straightforward a manner as possible. The first section discusses the concept of knowledge and is followed by a section dedicated to the concept of knowledge management.

The third section explains the emergence of knowledge work and knowledge workers. The fourth section analyses the relationship between human resource development and knowledge management and is followed by a discussion on how HRD can help with the development of human and social capital (i.e. intellectual capital as defined in chapter 2).

10.2 **Knowledge**

Key concept   Knowledge (part 1)

Knowledge is a complex, multi-faceted, and ambiguous concept (Blackler et al., 1998; Davenport and Prusak, 2000; Ahmed et al., 2002). Consequently, it is difficult to define (Alvesson, 2004).

It may seem odd that knowledge is so difficult to define given the way the term is referred to in everyday situations: be it references to our general knowledge (e.g. the popularity of quiz shows and pub quizzes), our specialist knowledge (e.g. the diversity of professional expertise), or our lack of knowledge about something (e.g. not knowing what came before the 'big bang' that 'kick-started' the universe some 14 billion years ago). However, the difficulty over definition becomes apparent when you refer to a typical dictionary definition:

> *n[oun]* that which is known; information, instruction; enlightenment, learning; practical skill; assured belief; acquaintance; cognizance (*law*). (*The Chambers Dictionary*, 2003: 823)

Any definition of knowledge will be dependent on the context within which the term is used. For instance, in organizational contexts knowledge is often defined in terms of its relationship to data and information. Given the significance of information and communications technology (ICT) to organizations this is not surprising. Knowledge is different to data and information. However, it is also argued that knowledge contains judgement (Davenport and Prusak, 2000), is about beliefs and commitment (Nonaka and Takeuchi, 1995), and has a far broader range of applicability than data and information (Delanty, 2001). These initial building blocks are illustrated in figure 10.1.

Although an interest in the concept of knowledge can be traced back to the 6th century BC (Lane Fox, 2005), a contemporary understanding of knowledge can be better understood by reference to the seminal work of Polanyi (1962, 1967) and Ryle (1949). Both argued that there is a practice or skills component in all knowledge which Polanyi described as 'tacit knowledge' and Ryle as 'knowing how'. Polanyi (1962, 1967) regarded tacit knowledge as *personal* knowledge residing with the individual which accrues or develops through experience. This is often referred to as an individual's skills or expertise. Such knowledge involves action (i.e. an individual *doing* something) and is usually context specific. Ryle (ibid.) uses the example of a boy playing chess to illustrate how *knowing how* is linked to action; Polanyi (ibid.) uses the example of learning how to ride a bicycle

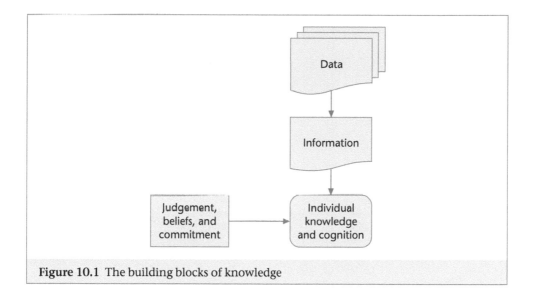

Figure 10.1 The building blocks of knowledge

to make the same point about *tacit knowledge* (as shall be discussed below this action orientation of knowledge was not fully appreciated in earlier KM strategies but has become an integral aspect of many recent KM strategies). Because tacit knowledge is acquired through experience Polanyi (1967) argued that it can be transferred from one person to another only through a long process of apprenticeship (this can be described as a process of osmosis). Spender (1996) describes tacit knowledge as *automatic* knowledge in acknowledgement of Polanyi's assertion that 'we can know more than we can tell' (1967: 4). It is difficult to articulate tacit knowledge because it is so deeply embedded within an individual's experience, judgement, and intuition (Ahmed et al., 2002). In a study of pizza parlours employees struggled to explain (verbally) how to hand-toss a pizza thus demonstrating the tacit nature of the process (Epple et al., 1996). These refinements in our understanding of knowledge are illustrated in figure 10.2.

ACTIVITY 10.1

Returning to Polanyi's example of learning how to ride a bicycle write down a set of instructions explaining how to ride a bicycle and share this with a relative, friend, or colleague. What is their reaction? Would it be better to do this exercise using an actual bicycle? How easy is it to explain how to balance, how to judge distances etc?

In contrast explicit knowledge is formal, abstract, or theoretical knowledge which relies on an individual's conceptual skills and cognitive abilities. It includes scientific knowledge which has enjoyed a privileged status within Western culture (Lam, 2000). University courses are heavily reliant on explicit knowledge: think about a typical lecture! Explicit knowledge can be stored in books, teaching/training hand-outs, diagrams, graphs, pictures, and computer drives. Many organizations have centralized repositories,

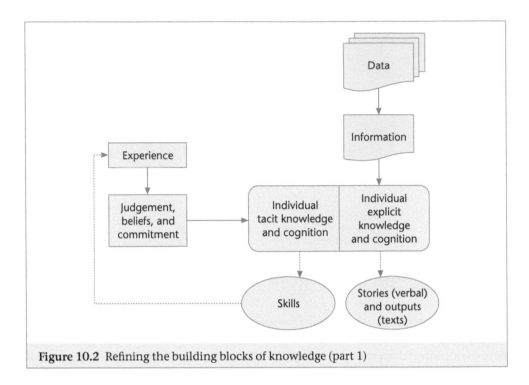

Figure 10.2 Refining the building blocks of knowledge (part 1)

often computerized, which can be accessed by individual organizational members who need to know more about a particular subject (e.g. products, processes, services etc). This is referred to as a *codification* strategy (i.e. knowledge is encoded in the different types of media listed above and can then be acquired by anyone accessing those media). It is also stored in the stories that individuals share with colleagues (Cook and Brown, 1999) and can take the form of knowing who knows what (Kogut and Zander, 1992) so that you know who to ask about a particular subject or problem even if you do not know about it yourself. Figure 10.3 shows these further refinements.

Key concept   Codification

Codification is based on the assumption that it is possible to encode knowledge as text, figures, or digital data. Many observers argue it is information rather than knowledge that is being encoded in this way.

The problem with codification is well summarized by Alvesson (2004):

The idea of making tacit knowledge explicit through codification is a popular one. Companies are expected to become less vulnerable to people leaving, taking their knowledge with them. Knowledge can also be reused, leading to increased efficiency or improved quality. The problem is, of course, that knowledge may not readily lend itself to capture and codification. (pp. 172–3)

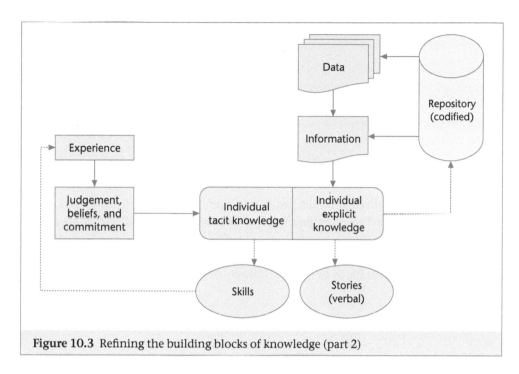

Figure 10.3 Refining the building blocks of knowledge (part 2)

These explanations of tacit and explicit knowledge may appear to be relatively straightforward. However, there is a great deal of contention about the relationship between tacit and explicit knowledge which has huge implications for the KM strategy adopted by any organization. While it is possible to distinguish conceptually between explicit and tacit knowledge, it is argued by many theorists that they are not separate and discrete in practice (Lam, 2000). Neither Polanyi nor Ryle subscribed to a reductionist view of knowledge. In both cases the distinction represents different interrelated *dimensions* of knowledge rather than different *types* of knowledge. It is argued that they are mutually constituted (Tsoukas, 1996) in what can be described as a symbiotic relationship (Alvesson, 2004). At the core of this debate is what appears to be a relatively straightforward question: is it possible to encode (and therefore articulate) tacit knowledge? If it is, then this suggests that tacit knowledge can be converted into explicit knowledge.

! TIPS AND HINTS

Training in the form of apprenticeships is well suited to the 'transfer' of tacit knowledge from an experienced to inexperienced employee.

So far the discussion has focused on tacit and explicit knowledge as an attribute of individuals. More recently, it has been argued that they have a collective or social dimension (i.e. both forms of knowledge can be held by groups as well as individuals). Spender (1996) refers to explicit group knowledge as *objectified* knowledge and to tacit group knowledge as *collective* knowledge. Examples of objectified knowledge include operating

---

Key concept   Knowledge (part 2)

There have been many attempts to capture the multifaceted nature of knowledge in a single definition, such as: 'Knowledge in organisations ranges from the complex, accumulated expertise that resides in individuals and is partly or largely inexpressible to much more structured and explicit content' (Davenport and Prusak, 2000: 70).

---

procedures and formalized routines; while examples of collective knowledge include 'informal organisational routines and ways of working, stories, and shared systems of understanding' (Hislop, 2005: 20). Spender (1996) argues that collective knowledge is what provides an organization with competitive advantage as this form of knowledge is difficult for rival organizations to imitate. Consequently, KM strategies need to achieve two outcomes:

1. Stimulate the creation of new collective knowledge (e.g. through a range of interventions; hence a role for the HRD practitioner).

2. Protect existing collective knowledge from degradation (e.g. as a result of high staff turnover; hence the importance of retention strategies).

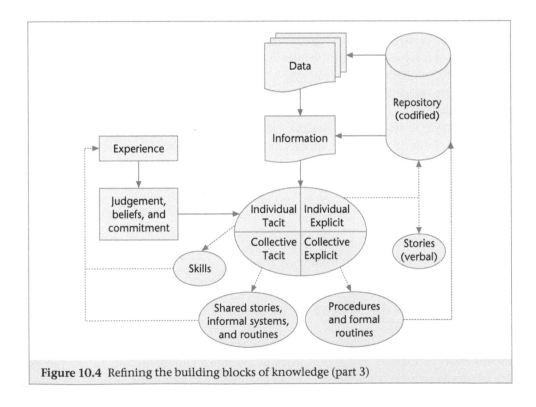

Figure 10.4 Refining the building blocks of knowledge (part 3)

However, there is a difference of opinion about how this can best be achieved: through the adoption of a traditional control approach (i.e. the *management* of knowledge) or through a facilitation approach (i.e. the *nurturing* of knowledge). For many theorists the use of the word 'management' in KM implies the control of processes that may be inherently uncontrollable (Von Krogh et al., 2000; Alvesson and Kärreman, 2001). Figure 10.4 shows the inclusion of collective forms of knowledge.

10.3 Knowledge management

There is a lack of any universal definition of KM. Noe (2002) defines knowledge management as:

> The process of enhancing company *performance* by designing and implementing tools, processes, systems, structures, and cultures to improve the creating, sharing, and use of knowledge. (p. 457; emphasis added)

This reflects a performance oriented approach to KM that is consistent with much of the literature on HRD, as discussed in chapter 2. In contrast, Scarborough et al. (1999) argue that KM processes enhance both learning and performance.

MEDIA WATCH BOX

Competitive advantage through knowledge

The management of knowledge is the key driver of organizational learning and organizations need to be generating new knowledge on a continuous basis if they are to remain competitive.

Source
People Management, 13 October 2005: 40–2.

To date the evolution of KM can be described in terms of waves (Huysman and de Wit, 2002) with each wave reflecting a different perspective on the nature of knowledge: the objectivist and practice-based perspectives (Hislop, 2005). In terms of the first wave objectivist perspective, knowledge has the following characteristics:

- **Knowledge is treated as an object or entity (Hislop, 2005).** Knowledge is seen as objective because it comprises facts and concepts. Spender (1996) refers to this as *conscious* knowledge because we have an awareness of its existence and are able to articulate it. Indeed, it is our ability to articulate such knowledge that makes it objective and places it in the 'public domain'.

- **Explicit knowledge is privileged over tacit knowledge (Hislop, 2005).** Tacit knowledge can be converted into explicit knowledge which can then be encoded and stored.

In principle, this makes knowledge relatively easy to transmit to others (Von Krogh et al., 2000).

- **Knowledge is derived from cognitive or intellectual processes (Hislop, 2005).** Cognition is understood as something that occurs within the individual mind (Patriotta, 2003). Consequently, knowledge acquisition and other related KM processes are dependent on cognitive learning theory (see chapter 4).

This first wave objectivist perspective is underpinned by human capital theory. An appreciation of the value of human capital within an organization is well established (Geroy and Venneberg, 2003). Becker (1964; 1975) popularized Schultz's (1961) human capital theory that asserts organizations derive economic value from employees' skills, competence, knowledge, and experience. From a strategic RBV knowledge is seen as a commodity in the same way as other resources, such as buildings, equipment, or stocks of raw materials.

! TIPS AND HINTS

It is difficult to place a value on intangible resources such as the human capital of employees. However, HRD practitioners who have developed expertise in evaluation are better placed to advise an organization on its approach to managing knowledge (and potentially enhance their professional credibility).

In contrast, from a second wave practice-based perspective knowledge has the following characteristics:

- **Knowledge is socially constructed (Hislop, 2005).** Knowledge is created when we converse with others. This may be face-to-face or via other media (e.g. phone, email, video-links, internet chat-rooms etc). From this perspective two things occur. First, social interaction stimulates individual cognition (Vygotsky, 1978). Second, cognition is no longer located solely within the individual mind but also needs to be understood as a complex social phenomenon (Nahapiet and Ghoshal, 1998). In effect cognition is situated within and distributed across a collective or group (Hutchins, 1994, 1996). In effect, the sum is greater than the individual parts.

- **Knowledge is embedded in practice (Hislop, 2005).** Given that cognition is situated within and distributed across a group then it is argued that much of the knowledge within an organization is socially embedded knowledge (Lin, 2002). From this perspective knowledge is inextricably linked with action (i.e. a work practice such as teaching, accountancy, law, engineering, or research and development). This knowledge tends to be tacit, highly personal, context specific, difficult to express in words, and therefore not easy to share with others (Von Krogh, 1998).

- **Knowledge is subjective (Baumard, 1999).** This means knowledge can be contested. Knowledge does not remain unchanged but is the subject of continuous, ongoing debates and exchanges (Seiler, 2004). From this perspective knowledge can be used as a term to represent the mundane aspects of everyday practices or the complexities of abstract thinking (Kalling and Styhre, 2003).

- **Tacit and explicit knowledge are inseparable (Hislop, 2005).** Explicit knowledge and tacit knowledge interact as individuals engage in their work practice. Consequently, it is 'impossible to totally disembody knowledge from people into a fully explicit form' (Hislop, 2005: 31).

The second wave is underpinned by social capital theory which highlights the role of informal groups and social networks.

Key concept   Social capital

A seminal definition of social capital is: 'the sum of actual and potential resources within, available through, and derived from the network of relationships possessed by an individual or social unit. Social capital thus comprises both the network and the assets that may be mobilized through that network' (Nahapiet and Ghoshal, 1998: 243).

Both forms of capital contribute to an organization's intellectual capital and are interlinked. Social capital provides the opportunities in which human capital can be applied (Burt, 1997). An individual needs access to informal groups and social networks if he/she is to perform well (Kessels and Poell, 2004). Informal groups often manifest in the form of communities of practice (Lave and Wenger, 1991; Brown and Duguid, 1991):

> Communities of practice are a *natural* part of organisational life. They will develop on their own and many will flourish, whether or not the organisation recognises them. Their health depends primarily on the *voluntary* engagement of their members and on the *emergence* of internal leadership. (Wenger et al., 2002: 12 —emphases added)

The key features of these two waves are summarized in table 10.1.

First wave	Second wave
Knowledge is objective (e.g. facts and figures)	Knowledge is socially constructed predominantly through face-to-face interaction and is therefore subjective
Tacit knowledge can be converted into explicit knowledge and stored (i.e. codified)	Tacit and explicit knowledge are two dimensions of knowledge rather than two different types of knowledge (i.e. they are inseparable)
Individual cognition is emphasized (i.e. knowledge is held by individual minds)	Situated and distributed cognition are emphasized (i.e. knowledge is embedded in work practices)
Psychological theories of learning are emphasized	Sociological theories of learning are emphasized

Table 10.1 Summary of the key features of the first and second waves of knowledge management

---

Key concepts Communities of practice and social networks

'Communities of practice are groups of people who share a concern, a set of problems, or a passion about a topic, and who deepen their knowledge and expertise in this area by interacting on an ongoing basis . . . Over time, they develop a unique perspective on their topic as well as a body of common knowledge, practices and approaches . . . They will tend to organize along friendship lines or within local geographical or organizational contexts rather than cover the whole organization (Wenger et al., 2002: 4–5 and 13).

'Communities of practice are different to social networks: all organizations have informal networks of people who communicate, share information, and build relationships and reputations. A community of practice is different from such a network in the sense that it is "about" something. It is not just a set of relationships' (Wenger et al., 2002: 43).

However, the focus on informal groups and networks means it has been difficult and challenging to find ways to operationalize tacit knowledge (Ambrosini and Bowman, 2001). Not only is much of this knowledge embedded in routines, which are ways of doing things that have consolidated over time (Nelson and Winter, 1982; Patriotta, 2003) but many of these routines are located within the informal relationships which are invisible to organizational managers. This has particular implications, as Hislop (2005) observes:

> The practice-based perspective on knowledge suggests that rather than being unitary and coherent, organisational knowledge bases are in fact fragmented and dispersed, being made up of specialised and specific knowledge communities which have some degree of overlapping 'common knowledge'. (p. 35)

Perhaps not surprisingly, despite the growth in second wave literature, there is still a tendency to view knowledge management systems as reliant on the information and communications technology that tend to characterize the first wave objectivist perspective. A study by Ruggles (1998) revealed that while senior managers do understand that knowledge is highly people-based they find it difficult to shed a technology-oriented mindset. There is also a view that much of what is termed knowledge management is in fact nothing more than information management (Beaumont and Hunter, 2002).

Key concept The informal or *shadow* organization

My own studies support the view that informal structures and processes (such as communities of practice) emerge, evolve, and co-exist with formal structures and processes in a symbiotic relationship. They can be described as a form of 'shadow' organization. They may not appear on an organizational chart but they impact daily on an individual's working life.

10.4 **Knowledge work and knowledge workers**

Increasingly, the terms 'knowledge work' and 'knowledge worker' have become popular. Noe (2002) defines knowledge workers as:

> Employees who own the means of producing a product or service. These employees have a specialised body of knowledge or expertise which they use to perform their jobs and contribute to company effectiveness. (p. 457)

This reflects the RBV of strategy discussed in chapter 3. From this perspective knowledge workers are presented as an occupational group that is very different from those associated with industrialized rather than knowledge economies (Scarborough et al., 1998).

MEDIA WATCH BOX

Too frightened to develop?

A key differentiator between high and low performing organizations is the willingness of employees to engage in knowledge sharing. Knowledge workers in particular need to be developed but some organizations are wary of doing so because they are frightened they will be poached by the competition.

Source
People Management, 15 July 2004: 25.

This has given risen to the identification of a particular type of organization that is most commonly associated with knowledge work: the knowledge intensive firms (KIF). The KIF:

> Can be loosely and preliminarily defined as organisations that offer to the market the use of fairly sophisticated knowledge or knowledge-based products. The products may be plans, prototypes, blueprints, or mass-produced products where the RandD cost outweighs manufacturing expenditure. The core of activities in these companies is based on the intellectual skills of a *very large proportion* of the labour force deployed in development, and often also in the sale of products and in service work. A *large section* of the employees typically have an academic education and relevant experience . . . there is a strong tendency for this type of organisation to employ a *large number* of graduates. (Alvesson, 2004: 17; emphases added)

Alevsesson (2004) proposes two types of KIF: the professional service firm (PSF) and research and development firms. Examples of PSFs are accountancy firms, management consultancy firms, advertising agencies, investment banks, and computer consultancy firms. Examples of RandD firms are science-based companies (e.g. biotech) and high tech companies that are based on engineering knowledge. Swart et al. (2003) argue that such organizations operate in highly unstable contexts and therefore have to develop new structures for coping with the demands placed on the firm.

However, the reality is that knowledge work is not restricted to these two types of organization. Garvey and Williamson (2002) refer to 'knowledge-productive' organizations which are capable of generating new ideas and ways of thinking that result in competitive advantage through improved products and services. Equally not all employees of such *knowledge* organization are necessarily knowledge workers. There is a further argument that all forms of work involve some form of knowledge. For instance, cleaning (agency sub-contractor staff), maintenance staff in a cleansing department, and healthcare assistants in care homes involve some degree of 'knowledgeable practice' involving tacit skills (Rainbird et al., 2004).

(•) INSIGHTS INTO PRACTICE

The rise of the knowledge worker

The phenomenal growth of professional services over the past 20 years means that one in four workers in the US and Western Europe now works for a professional services firm (PSF), be it in engineering, accountancy, the law, architecture, or consultancy.

Source
People Management, 11 August 2005: 25.

Knowledge workers are seen as stakeholders who possess specialist expertise and therefore take responsibility and control for their own learning and are far less likely to be forced into attending HRD interventions that they believe to be irrelevant to their needs (Stewart and Tansley, 2002). This has implications for the line management of knowledge workers. As Drucker (1998) observes, specialists (i.e. knowledge workers) cannot be told how to do their job. Consequently, as shall be argued below, a nurturing rather than controlling stance needs to be adopted.

ACTIVITY 10.2

What categories of employee could be termed knowledge workers in the following types of organization?

1. Advertising agency
2. University
3. Hospital
4. Estate agency
5. Police force
6. Supermarket

10.5 **Human resource development and knowledge management**

The relationship between HRD and KM needs to be placed within a broader HRM context. Swart et al. (2003) identify the following 'people management practices and processes' as critical to managing what they term 'knowledge-intensive situations' (p. 2):

- Attracting, developing, rewarding, and retaining human capital
- Recognizing the importance of social capital
- Building network management skills

This reflects the importance of both human and social capital and the need for a balanced approach (Swart et al., 2003). There are potential advantages to an organization if both the first wave objectivist and second wave practice-based perspectives are adopted as part of an integrated KM and HRD strategy. As Fuller et al. (2004) observe in relation to learning in the workplace:

> Stressing the situated character of knowledge fails to recognise that there are types of knowledge, such as theoretical ideas not connected to specific contexts, which are not always accessible on the job. (p. 3)

A more balanced approach can be achieved through the implementation of a range of HRD strategies or policy choices that should be viewed as complementary rather than either-or choices (Mankin, 2004). This approach was discussed in detail in chapter 3 (see figure 3.2). Table 10.2 shows the types of human resource management and development practices identified by Swart et al. (2003) that can be associated with each KM wave.

MEDIA WATCH BOX

Using training to transfer expertise

This case illustrates how formal training interventions can facilitate the transfer of knowledge from a specialist provider to an organizational context.

BMC Software has world-wide revenues of US$1.5 billion and specializes in providing software solutions that encompass a range of business systems. At the Dublin site, which produces a wide range of software products, the manufacturing and distribution manager wanted to use knowledge acquired from an external formal training programme in specific lean manufacturing techniques to achieve practical improvements. This has enabled him to reduce costs by a further 15 per cent and to work towards a more automated production process.

Source
http://www.themanufacturer.com/uk/content/7779/The_shape_of_knowledge (accessed 26 March 2008).

First wave (Individual development focus)	Second wave (Group-oriented focus)
Standardized performance appraisal based on human capital theory only. There is an emphasis on career management rather than career development	Performance appraisal acknowledges the contribution of both human and social capital. There is much more emphasis on career development with the individual taking responsibility for exploiting social networks and contacts to enhance his/her career progression
Formal training interventions that focus on socialisation and employability (i.e. developing transferable skills which will benefit the organization)	A blend of formal and informal learning opportunities that enable the individual to develop their employability for the benefit of themselves and the organization. Formal interventions often focus on workplace learning (e.g. mentoring and coaching). Informal learning is focused on shared work practice and situated in communities and social networks
Reward and recognition schemes based on individual performance	Team-based reward and recognition schemes
Time is devoted to individual development as a result of participation in external professional bodies	Frequent social activities involving organizational members (as well as external stakeholders). Social networks are exploited
Standardized work practices, routines, and procedures. An emphasis on employee consultation and limited involvement	A blend of standardized and informal work practices and routines. An emphasis on decision-making through employee participation or more extensive employee involvement

Table 10.2 HRD and HRM practices associates with the two KM waves
Source: Adapted and developed from information in Swart et al. (2003)

Consequently, both KM waves have implications for learning. For instance, the first wave stresses learning as a private process, as something that occurs inside individual minds; whereas the second wave stresses learning as a process anchored in social contexts. HRD practitioners should be able to respond to the demands created by each wave. For instance, they need to work collaboratively with IT specialists in order to maximize the human capital benefits of the first wave (Noe, 2002); although this can be problematic:

> Some organisations have experienced counterproductive turf battles between HRD and IT groups over the knowledge management domain, where collaboration, with both groups focused on learner needs, is the most useful approach. Organisational members need user-friendly information access and the capacity to conduct meaningful collaboration, either as needed or as part of ongoing collaborative groups. (Yorks, 2005: 247)

The reference to collaborative working is important. The creation of new knowledge is heavily reliant on knowledge sharing processes which involve social interaction:

> Knowledge assets increase with use: Ideas breed new ideas, and shared knowledge stays with the giver while it enriches the receiver. The potential for new ideas

arising from the stock of knowledge in any firm is practically limitless—particularly if the people in the firm are given opportunities to think, to learn, and to talk
with one another. (Davenport and Prusak, 2000: 17)

Although knowledge sharing through social interaction is seen as the primary process
for knowledge creation in the second wave practice-based perspective, the first wave
objectivist perspective undervalues the importance of social interaction (Von Krogh et al.,
2000). Swart et al. (2003) conclude from their study of six research and technology organizations that 'it is not just the knowledge and skills of the workforce that is critical but
also the knowledge-sharing processes within the firm which help maximize the benefit
of their expertise for the firm' (p. viii) (see *Insights into practice* box). It is as a result of
engaging with others that (a) personal knowledge is shared with others, through language, non-verbal expressions, and signs, and (b) that personal knowledge is (or rather
can be) modified and refined in the light of the knowledge and expertise of others. Even
personal knowledge that is refined through reading or listening still involves engagement
with social artefacts (e.g. books, audio-tapes). Articles and books are social artefacts which
act as triggers for individual learning. In this sense an individual is still actively engaging
within a social context albeit in a predominantly passive manner (i.e. *thinking* rather than
acting). However, the outcome of this passive learning is normally socially oriented and
requires active engagement (i.e. *acting*) in the work-world (e.g. research collaboration;
teaching; management discussion etc).

(•) INSIGHTS INTO PRACTICE

Sharing knowledge

'Often you have a problem with teaching and learning. You'll often find that other
people have had similar problems and help you with solutions . . . come and sound
off about teaching experiences and . . . things that have gone wrong. Share things
that have gone really well, but also things outside work as well: politics, the news,
what everyone's been doing. Basically, its very friendly' (Zoe, a lecturer in a northern
new university).[1]

   This quote illustrates the point made by Von Krogh et al. (2000: 45) that 'in order to
share personal knowledge, individuals must rely on others to listen and react to their
ideas. Constructive and helpful relations enable people to share their insights and
freely discuss their concerns'.

Source
[1] Research study carried out by the author.

Huysman and de Wit (2003) identify three types of knowledge sharing which encompass both first and second wave perspectives:

* **knowledge retrieval:** sharing from the organization to the individual. This emphasizes
  the first wave objectivist perspective which privileges explicit over tacit knowledge. For

instance, Arthur Anderson has an information system that can be accessed by 80,000 employees across the globe: 'This information system can be used to share training content, find information about potential clients, or post work problems on an electronic bulletin board' (Noe, 2002: 51).

- **Knowledge exchange:** sharing from individual to individual (often referred to as dyadic sharing). The sharing of explicit knowledge is relatively straightforward. In terms of tacit knowledge, the two individuals need to be in 'close physical proximity while the work is being done' (Von Krogh et al., 2000: 83).

- **Knowledge creation:** sharing among individuals. Such knowledge is often described as being *sticky* (Brown and Duguid, 1998) because it is context specific (see *Insights into practice* box). This reflects the second wave practice-based perspective as 'it seems reasonable to argue that if people share a practice, then they will share know *how*, or tacit knowledge' (Brown and Duguid, 2001: 204).

As table 10.3 illustrates there are barriers to and facilitators of knowledge sharing that HRD practitioners and line managers need to be cognizant of.

INSIGHTS INTO PRACTICE

The 'stickiness' of tacit knowledge

'Due to its social origins, knowledge moves differently *within* communities than it does *between* them. Within communities, knowledge is continuously embedded in practice and thus circulates easily. Members of a community implicitly share a sense of what practice is and what the standards for judgement are, and this supports the spread of knowledge. Without this sharing, the community disintegrates. Between communities, however, where by definition practice is no longer shared, the know-how and know-what embedded in practice must separate out for knowledge to circulate. These divisions become prominent and problematic. Different communities of practice have different standards, different ideas of what is significant, different priorities, and different evaluating criteria.'[1]

This is why members of communities of practices often demonstrate a silo mentality. It has been shown that individuals who identify with a sub-unit or sub-group than with the organization as a whole are less likely to share information outside of these sub-units/groups (Fisher et al., 1997). Consequently, whilst knowledge sharing may be a characteristic of relations within the community, knowledge transfer between communities may be problematic.

Source
[1] Brown, J. S. and Duguid, P. 2002. Organising knowledge. *California Management Review*, 40 (3): 90–111 and 100–1.

Barriers to knowledge sharing	Facilitators of knowledge sharing
Knowledge hoarding ('knowledge is power' syndrome)	Sympathetic organizational culture
Lack of social spaces (case study at end of chapter)	Shared physical location (face-to-face contact in shared offices or social spaces such as canteen, staff rooms, etc.) (See *Insights into practice* box)
Fear (fear of failure or loss of status)	Subordination of individual goals and associated actions to collectively defined and collectively enacted goals
Silo mentality.	Strong working relationships (regular contact; cooperation and collaboration; individuals motivated by communal norms; high levels of trust)
Perceived inequality in status	Status similarity

Table 10.3 Knowledge sharing: barriers and facilitators

Sources: Allen, 1977; Marwell and Oliver, 1988; Wellman and Wortly, 1990; Cohen and Zhou, 1991; Krackhardt, 1992; Orlikowski, 1993; Brown and Duguid, 1998; Leonard and Sensiper, 1998; Von Krogh, 1998; Leana and Van Buren, 1999; Davenport and Prusak, 2000; Pfeffer and Sutton, 2000; Käser and Miles, 2001; Michailova and Husted, 2003; Burgess, 2005; Hansen et al., 2005; Wasko and Faraj, 2005.

INSIGHTS INTO PRACTICE

Why the design of office buildings matters

A study of the pattern of movements by employees based in several office buildings reveals that some of their best work is the result of chance encounters with colleagues who work in different buildings and/or parts of the organization. This study was conducted by Space Syntax as part of the design process for the new BA Business Centre. The findings suggest 'that the work environment can impact directly on both the working atmosphere of an organization and the effectiveness with which its people interact. It is therefore important for organizations to capitalize on the "usefulness" of what people seem to do naturally at work—interact. The research suggests that in a well-managed organization management will bring together those individuals and groups that can see a "need" to interact to tackle a particular problem or project. Buildings could contribute by creating the physical environment that brings people together to interact in ways in which nobody could have predicted . . . [and] play a central role in innovation.'[1]

This illustrates the importance of well designed office buildings. Traditionally, the underpinning rationale for the design of new buildings or the redesign of existing buildings has tended to be for efficiency gains. The role of shared social spaces for knowledge sharing has been less appreciated.

Source
[1] Garvey, B. and Williamson, B. 2002. *Beyond Knowledge Management: Dialogue, Creativity and the Corporate Curriculum*. Harlow: Prentice Hall, pp. 22–3.

10.6 **Developing human and social capital**

An overarching results-driven rather than activity-based approach to HRD (Maycunich Gilley et al., 2003) is required if HRD practitioners are to support KM strategy effectively. As discussed in chapter 2 this is when HRD practitioners work collaboratively with management at all levels of the organization in order to improve organizational performance. This approach embraces both strategic and operational issues as well as both formal and informal learning activities. Garvey and Williamson (2002) note that high levels of HRD activity are associated with knowledge-productive organizations.

Traditionally:

> training departments have focused their resources on cognitive [know what] and advanced [know how] skills. But the real value of training may be in having employees understand the manufacturing or service process and the interrelationships between departments and divisions (system understanding). (Noe, 2002: 51)

This is very much a human capital perspective. Human capital is seen as something that can be developed through training and experience within the organization (Scarborough and Elias, 2002). Noe's (ibid) argument that intellectual capital requires HRD practitioners to adopt a systems perspective also reflects the importance of TQM to the evolution of HRD processes (see chapter 2). Systems understanding is in effect *know-why* which is about underlying cause-and-effect relationships (Quinn et al., 1998). With the emergence of knowledge management as an organizational priority *performance*-oriented HRD practitioners will expand both their questions and their solutions to a wider range of problems (Gilley et al., 2002).

However, as stated above, the technology-centred approach of the first wave tended to ignore any role for the HRD practitioner or treat it as subordinate (Gourlay, 2001). There was a lack of any 'meeting of minds' between the KM and HRD communities:

> Whereas knowledge management professionals may emphasise the provision of valuable information, but without the focus on learning, HRD professionals may focus on learning but lack the original sources of intellectual capital. (Brandenberg and Ellinger, 2003: 317)

In terms of knowledge creation (Nonaka and Takeuchi, 1995) that characterized the first wave objectivist perspective, a collective, shared view of knowledge is rejected on the basis that different individuals will interpret and store knowledge differently. This is consistent with the first wave emphasis on individual cognition: there is an external reality or physical world that exists independently of our individual cognitive systems and our individual cognitive systems are able to recreate and store representations of this external reality. The focus is on what happens inside an individual's head; on the processing structures of the brain and the symbolic representations of the mind (Patriotta, 2003). This is why from this perspective knowledge is treated as an object; as explicit, abstract, capable of being encoded and stored, and easy to transmit to others (Von Krogh, 1998). So whilst Nonaka (1994: 15) refers to 'communities of interaction' and acknowledges the role of social interaction, his model for knowledge creation falls short of a second wave perspective which gives primacy to the social and cultural context. He treats tacit and explicit as two types, rather than two dimensions of knowledge.

Key concept   Knowledge creation

The model for knowledge creation put forward by Nonaka and Takeuchi (1995) is based on four modes of knowledge sharing: socialization (i.e. sharing tacit knowledge through talking about personal experiences, often in the form of stories and anecdotes); externalization (i.e. converting tacit knowledge into explicit knowledge, although the mechanics of this remain contentious); combination (i.e. using information and explicit knowledge in new ways); and, internalization (i.e. the conversion of explicit knowledge into tacit knowledge).

Noe (2002) argues that training has a particularly important role in two of the four modes of knowledge sharing proposed by Nonaka and Takeuchi as part of their knowledge creation model (i.e. combination and internalization). Formal courses and seminars can be used for combination; training methods such as action learning, simulations, and on-the-job can be used for internalization. However, Poell and Van der Krogt (2003) argue that this knowledge creation model is not appropriate to professional organizations which are characterized by worker autonomy as:

> First, it assumes that workers will learn only within the boundaries set by management. They do not, however, take into account that workers organise a great deal of learning themselves, frequently irrespective of management expectations. Second, Nonaka and Takeuchi expect workers to learn according to rigid bureaucratic principles in a work context emphasising innovation. The theory of knowledge creation does not show how these contrary principles might be successfully integrated. (p. 400)

In this sense, the model falls squarely into learning as socialization (Mankin, 2004).

! TIPS AND HINTS

To help managers to better understand the role of social capital, ask them to list all the people (i.e. stakeholders) and groups (e.g. project teams, committees, networks etc) they work with or rely on to carry out their job effectively. Then ask them to categorize these as formal or informal and to make a subjective assessment about the effectiveness of each. Finally, ask them what is different about those people and groups which are the most effective.

The role of social capital has tended to be ignored by HRD theorists and practitioners (Mankin, 2004, 2005). In terms of developing social capital, HRD practitioners can support line managers in the building of knowledge networks and the creation of learning opportunities to secure the social capital benefits of the second wave (Stewart and Tansley, 2002):

> Work organisations are increasingly considered to be key sources of social capital, emphasising the importance of social networks, partnerships, collaboration and interaction, and knowledge sharing they provide. (Kessels and Poell, 2004: 151)

The challenge facing managers is captured aptly by Beaumont and Hunter (2002), who warn that if the knowledge of employees is to be exploited effectively then managers need to develop a much better understanding of how employees socially interact with each other and how new knowledge is created. This requires a nurturing approach by management. Beaumont and Hunter (2002) go on to suggest that management can achieve this through three strategies:

- **Compliance:** by establishing rules, procedures, and routines that are written into employees' contracts and enforced through managerial compliance. (This control-oriented approach can result in increased social capital as employees find ways to work around constraints imposed by management. However, this social capital remains invisible to management and may not be compatible with organizational goals and objectives).

- **Entrepreneurship:** management become more entrepreneurial (e.g. non-bureaucratic decision-making; shallow hierarchies; the development of an innovative and entrepreneurial culture). (My own research has highlighted the extent to which innovation is associated with informal structures and processes. Consequently, this strategy is heavily reliant on the emergence of social capital that is visible to management).

- **Employee participation:** management seek to increase employee commitment to the organization through a range of employee participation strategies (e.g. high levels of flexibility and autonomy among the workforce; an emphasis on performance-related pay; a performance appraisal system that monitors and rewards knowledge creation and sharing; profit-sharing or similar types of reward strategy) (This is compatible with the entrepreneurship strategy).

MEDIA WATCH BOX

HRD and innovation

A key challenge for HR practitioners generally is to find ways to leverage organizational knowledge. Making the case for global innovation in multinationals is one way the practitioner can take the lead and add value to the organization; although this is a difficult and challenging task that will require changes in mindsets, processes, and structures.

Source
People Management, 12 October 2006: 32–4.

ACTIVITY 10.3

What do you see as the potential barriers to each of the strategies suggested by Beaumont and Hunter (2002)?

However, as Gourlay (2001) observes:

> If managers are not clear about what they are trying to manage, it is difficult to see how knowledge management practices can be evaluated, or the effects of actions taken in the name of knowledge management understood, or the relationship of knowledge management to HRD and other management activities assessed. (p. 30)

Everything seems to come back to evaluation and as was highlighted in chapters 5 and 9 this is an aspect of HRD practice, as well as management practice generally, that is often ignored or undervalued.

Beaumont and Hunter (2002) claim that developing communities of practice provides an opportunity to leverage collective knowledge. Although this fails to appreciate fully the organic and emergent nature of communities of practice, it is argued that such groups can be *cultivated* (or *nurtured*) (Wenger et al., 2002). Nonaka has acknowledged that a more enabling role is required in which managers support rather than attempt to control knowledge creation processes. To achieve this Nonaka and his co-authors (Von Krogh et al., 2000) argue that organizations need to adopt five 'knowledge enablers', all of which have HRD implications:

1. **Instilling a knowledge vision:** this is 'firmly connected to an advancement strategy, one that emphasises a company's future performance and success' (ibid.: 102). Consequently, the KM strategy has to be fully integrated with the organization's business strategy in the same way as the HRD strategy. In this way the commitment needed from HRD practitioners to make the KM strategy work can be identified in the same way as the commitment needed from managers and employees generally. HRD practitioners can help achieve buy-in to the knowledge vision as part of their daily interactions, both formal and informal, with managers and employees.

2. **Managing conversations:** the importance of conversations to knowledge creation and sharing has been highlighted above. The authors suggest that managers need to create awareness of the importance of knowledge-creating conversations and encourage employee participation in such conversations. However, the notion that such conversations can be managed may not be conducive to an empowered informal learning HRD strategy that emphasizes nurturing rather than control.

3. **Mobilizing knowledge activists:** these are managers who understand knowledge processes and can mobilize employees to use knowledge more effectively. The HRD practitioner can support the identification and development of such managers, provide facilitation and formal HRD interventions when appropriate, and assist with the socialization process of new (and less 'aware') managers and employees.

INSIGHTS INTO PRACTICE

The role of training in knowledge enabling processes at Gemini Consulting

Consultants at Gemini Consulting 'rely on tacit, explicit, individual and social knowledge to serve their clients. The service they provide is knowledge about a particular area, and that knowledge is created and exchanged through various enabling processes—good conversations, recreation of local knowledge for better insights'. Consequently, these processes are embedded in the firm's culture and are pivotal to the successful achievement of the firm's strategy. The principal business objective is 'to excel in knowledge exchange and creation, benefiting its clients, employees and shareholders' and the core values of the firm are 'excellence, openness, trust, teamwork and mastery. Thus, knowledge sharing has always been important at this firm, and the implementation focus of its projects has made cooperative and mutually supportive behaviour a necessity. These values, in turn, have been reinforced by Gemini's leaders, performance evaluation systems, and corporate stories . . . It has become increasingly important to train consultants in the art of knowledge enabling, especially as this concerns how they personally can and must contribute. During training of new consultants, good practice is demonstrated and later reiterated by a knowledge "champion" on each project. Correspondingly, Gemini's incentive scheme has been realigned. While knowledge-creation activities are now completely and transparently recorded, their impact is assessed through performance evaluations similar to those for consultants' performance on project assignments.'[1]

This case is interesting for several reasons:

1. It illustrates the type of cultural context within which knowledge sharing processes are able to thrive.

2. It illustrates the role of a socialization HRD strategy which is supported by a number of 'champions' who, in effect, act as role models; as do Gemini's leaders. The importance of this in relation to learning processes was highlighted in chapter 4's discussion on social learning theory (specifically the work of Bandura). Role models can act as a catalyst for informal and incidental learning. Consequently, the impact of such role models on colleagues reflects a devolved informal learning HRD strategy.

3. The realignment of the reward strategy illustrates the importance of horizontal integration between HRD and HRM.

Source
[1] Von Krogh, G., Ichijo, K. and Nonaka, I. 2000. *Enabling Knowledge Creation: How to Unlock the Mystery of Tacit Knowledge and Release the Power of Innovation*. Oxford: Oxford University Press, pp. 240–53.

4. **Creating the right context:** this involves ensuring there are shared (social) spaces that foster emerging relationships (although the authors refer to 'micro-communities of knowledge' rather than the more widely used term communities of practice). Both the HRD practitioner and line manager can play an important role in the nurturing of a learning environment or climate that is conducive to the emergence and evolution of such communities.

5. **Globalizing local knowledge:** this enabler recognizes the fact that 'many midsize and large firms are no longer contained within national borders' (ibid.: 207). The HRD practitioner can assist managers in finding ways to facilitate the sharing of knowledge across and between subsidiaries that increasingly have cultural implications. Formal interventions in raising cultural awareness and preparing expatriate workers for international deployment do play a role, although these reflect a socialization HRD strategy. The authors concede that company training programmes do have an important role to play. More challenging is finding ways to overcome the silo mentality that pervades highly productive communities.

In terms of other KM processes, Liu et al. (2006) have focused on the implications for HRD of knowledge transfer processes between subsidiaries of multinational companies (MNCs). From a study of MNCs in the information technology industry in China they conclude that:

> The implications for HRD professionals are substantial. If knowledge transfer is key to successful MNCs, then personnel must be prepared to appreciate and participate in knowledge transfer. This will require a substantial amount of staff development and potentially a change in culture of the organisations to facilitate communication of the types of knowledge identified in the study. (ibid.: 550)

MEDIA WATCH BOX

Knowledge transfer can occur in the most unlikely of contexts

In Bombay hot meals are delivered to office workers each day by 5,000 *dabbawallas* who carry the meals in tins. This involves a complex logistical process that has been refined over the last hundred years. Multinationals, such as Microsoft, are now exploiting this system to promote their own products and services in India (e.g. giving the *dabbawallas* branded t-shirts to wear and getting them to distribute promotional leaflets). According to a spokesman for the *dabbawallas* the secrets of success are time management and customer service.

Source
The Times, 12 April 2007: 52.

(•) INSIGHTS INTO PRACTICE

Knowledge sharing at SCA Packaging

SCA Packaging is part of SCA (Svenska Cellulosa AB), a Swedish forestry company founded in 1929. SCA has been in the packaging business since the early 1960s. In the company knowledge is shared through a mix of processes (e.g. social interactions; staff collaboration; training; the distribution of texts). The focus is 'on methods and practices that have been successful elsewhere':

1. An example of social interaction is when employees visit successful plants for a specified period of time. 'Some plants have used this opportunity, and sent one of their own machine experts to visit peers at other plants for a couple of weeks spread out over a long period. In other cases, plants invite representatives or experts from other plants to come to visit and help work out problems or under-achievements. Another aspect of interaction refers to working together with cor-porate experts, for instance members of the Manufacturing department at the head office. This force spends part of its time leading or taking part in specific, tech-nical projects in local or regional units. Plants can also draw on resources at regional levels.'

2. 'Collaboration refers to situations whereby plants actually hire or exchange, with some permanency, key staff from other plants, or run joint development projects over a long period of time. This happens with some regularity.'

3. Training comprises courses for all types of employee. For instance, potential employees or employees who are perceived to have potential 'take part in a one-year (part-time) course on technical development training, including education in methods and technologies using a broad approach'. Also the company provides 'specific courses centred upon individual machine types . . . Here, SCAP may cooperate with machine suppliers or other external organizations [e.g. technical education institutes]. Any kind of machine worker can be invited to take part in this type of training.'

4. 'The key means by which SCAP tries to spread knowledge is through the distribu-tion of texts about production routines or about technical devices that could help improve certain production tasks.'[1]

This case illustrates how formal training, as discussed in chapters 5 to 9, is one of several strategies for the nurturing of knowledge sharing. The approach adopted by SCAP is not at all unusual in the manufacturing sector. Informal learning (see chap-ter 11) is implicit in the other strategies.

Source
[1] Kalling, T. and Styhre, A. 2003. *Knowledge Sharing in Organisations*. Copenhagen: Copenhagen Business School Press, pp. 81–91.

Liu et al. (2006) go on to describe how HRD practitioners will need to:

1. Understand how different types of knowledge require different practices for transfer, especially when this involves cross-cultural transfer.
2. Evaluate the effectiveness of each practice over time to ensure an organization maximizes its ability to transfer and integrate knowledge.

Herling (2001) refers to *knowledge engineering* and the role of the *knowledge engineer* who focuses on the replication of human expertise. This involves an understanding of expertise and the relationship between explicit and implicit (i.e. tacit) knowledge. This is seen as being important because the concept of human expertise is at the *core* of human resource development:

> It is the skills, knowledge, and experience of the organisation's human resources—in short, its expertise—that have become the new secret weapon in the competitive marketplace. (ibid.: 228)

This is, perhaps, little more than a re-labelling of the HRD practitioner's role in order to take advantage of the levels of interest in KM (although it could be argued that this approach is consistent with the American tendency to use a much wider range of job titles that reflects specific activities within the HRD function).

Summary

Knowledge is a problematic concept which lacks a universal definition. Consequently, more than one approach to the management of knowledge in organizations has emerged. These can be described in terms of waves with the first wave objectivist perspective followed by a second wave practice-based perspective. Both waves build on the work of Polanyi who differentiated between tacit and explicit knowledge. The first wave was underpinned by human capital theory and stressed the role of the individual and individual cognition. The second wave stressed the role of informal groups, such as communities of practice and social networks, and situated and distributed cognition. The second wave shifts the emphasis from the control of knowledge through compliance interventions to the nurturing of the context within which knowledge is created and shared. This corresponds to the shift from a HRD strategy based on socialization to one based much more on devolved and empowered informal learning (Mankin, 2004, 2007), as discussed in chapter 3.

The nurturing approach, in particular, requires HRD practitioners and line managers to work together in order to facilitate the emergence and development of informal knowledge sharing structures and processes. Knowledge sharing, and in particular face-to-face sharing, is a pivotal process underpinning the second wave. The development and facilitation of social capital (Stewart and Tansley, 2002; Swart et al., 2003) is thus central to HRD strategy-making. Figure 10.5 sets out the implications for KM and HRD of the two approaches available to an organization. Ideally, all four choices will be adopted in a particular blend that can be adapted over time as organizational circumstances change. Managing knowledge is very much a control-oriented approach whilst nurturing knowledge is much more about facilitation by HRD practitioners and line managers.

	Compliance	Facilitation
Group	1. The setting up of formal teams to enable the creation, sharing, and transfer of knowledge through formal collaboration 2. An emphasis on team-work, team goals, and incentives (including e-working) 3. Formal social activities	1. Creating a learning environment within which social capital flourishes: bringing individuals together, promoting diversity, and stimulating informal collaboration 2. Encouraging self-managed teams 3. Developing line managers as facilitators
Individual	1. Induction and staff development (e.g. managers as coaches and mentors) 2. Training in use of KM database and facilitating usage through formal projects 3. An emphasis on developing skills and employability 4. Formal L&D interventions on the implications of individual and group learning, and reflective practice	1. Raising awareness of social capital and the benefits it offers 2. Improving individual skills that impact on networking and relationship-building
	Managing knowledge	**Nurturing knowledge**

Figure 10.5 The implications of KM for HRD

Review questions

1 Why is it difficult to arrive at a universal definition of knowledge?

2 Explain the principal differences between the first wave objectivist and second wave practice-based perspectives.

3 Define and explain the concept of knowledge sharing.

4 How can HRD practitioners support the development of human capital?

5 How can line managers support the development of social capital?

Suggestions for further reading

1 Brown, J. S. and Duguid, P. 1991. Organisational learning and communities-of-practice: toward a unified view of working, learning, and innovation. *Organisation Science*, February, 2 (1): 40–57.

This remains a seminal article on the concept of communities of practice and the implications for organizations of informal structures and processes.

2 Gourlay, S. 2001. Knowledge management and HRD. *Human Resource Development International*, 4 (1): 27–46.

This is a theoretical discussion on the relationship between KM and HRD that is still valid today and includes an overview on different perspectives on knowledge.

3   Brown, J. S. and Duguid, P. 2002. Organising Knowledge. *California Management Review*, 40 (3): 90–111.

This article offers an alternative perspective to the management of knowledge.

4   Kalling, T. and Styhre, A. 2003. *Knowledge Sharing in Organisations*. Copenhagen: Copenhagen Business School Press.

This slim volume provides an excellent overview of KM and, in particular the role of knowledge sharing processes. Detailed case studies are provided.

5   Hislop, D. 2005. *Knowledge Management in Organisations*. Oxford: Oxford University Press.

This is an excellent text on all aspects of knowledge management.

Case study

KM in the new university sector and the need for space

My principal research interest has been the study of knowledge sharing processes in academic communities in post-1992 universities, mainly former polytechnics that are now referred to as 'new' universities. It is generally accepted that higher education is experiencing a period of profound change resulting from increased student numbers, reduced funding by central government, and tighter managerial controls. Increasingly, universities are expected to function like business organizations. The educational press in the UK has been highlighting the impact of these trends on academic practice; for instance, increased class sizes, less staff-student contact time, increased teaching. At the same time many universities have been closing down shared social spaces such as staff common rooms and staff canteens and rationalizing office space. At the business school of a UK northern new university participants commented as follows about this particular trend and the implications it has for how academics work:

> A big issue here is we don't have common rooms. We don't have staff common rooms . . . there was a premium on space, so the spaces were converted into either offices or teaching areas. Well, actually not teaching areas, conferences for letting out. So there was quite a rationalisation of space. So they just did away with them . . . Instead you go to the canteen now and you very seldom meet many staff. Staff just don't go. So the informal opportunities to meet and have a discussion without students being about are much less . . . Now we try to be electronic. I mean, the one thing you do get now is a lot of email. (George, an academic manager)

> When I first started here we had a staff common room. You would come in, you'd sit down and you'd start chatting to people. Now you've got your individual office. They got rid of the staff canteen about a year ago and over a year ago, the staff common room. If you went into the common room, the way the seating was arranged, it was long, sort of bench-like seats, curving round, that could take up to a dozen people, quite easily . . . and so you would inevitably be sitting down with someone you didn't know, whereas downstairs in the main canteen you go to a little table of four. I wouldn't dream of walking over to a table of people that I didn't know. You'd feel you were invading their space. And having a single office, although I really, really benefit from having a single office, I realise [that] in the past when you shared an office, you did have more connection with what was going on. (Kate, a senior lecturer)

As a department we had a room. A research room it was, where we had journals and books and also a meeting table and some easy chairs where we used to meet for coffee once a week. And all our other meetings were there. Now, we have got nothing to replace that. (Judy, a senior lecturer)

There will be two in one corner of the canteen and another two come down. Well they are with their pals so they are not going to go to that corner. So they will go to a corner around the corner so they can't even be seen. They won't make the effort to cross the room to join a different group. They have to be put in a small room to make that happen. (Nancy, an administrator)

People seem to speak to each other less here. Everyone shuts their door when they are in their room and the corridors are very quiet. There is hardly anyone who walks up and down them apart from the people that reside in the rooms there. So, why the rooms have to be shut every time, I don't know. Where I used to be was always quite friendly. People did keep their doors open there. I don't think any of them were ever kept shut. (Sophie, a senior lecturer)

A lot of staff are not particularly happy here because there are so many small aspects with design that just seem a shame. Given that we started with a blank sheet it should have been better. Everybody says the same thing, there are a number of things that are short-sighted . . . I mean, what they have done is combined a number of offices. Where you had perhaps one or two secretaries in one office where they would have had their own set of staff, now we have got four in one large office. I have never had a situation like I've got now where I know the staff but I can walk in and go to the pigeon holes and walk back out and nobody has said a word. I think that is partly just because of the size of the room but in the past there would have been communication. (John, a senior lecturer)

We are all in an open plan office, which we moved to in October, which, of course, has caused a little bit of friction because everybody was used to either sharing one office or having an individual office . . . I think one of the impacts has been that some people, including myself sometimes, despite my ability to concentrate on certain things, if I have something to do I will stay at home. I have purchased a lap-top which has enabled me to do that. So, sometimes, I think we are less there than we would be otherwise. However, the problem now is we can always see whenever somebody is here or not here, and what I may be in fact reflecting in my statement is that I know I am able to see that they are there. When before I was in my office I couldn't tell who was in their office or not in their office. So that may also be interesting, particularly in terms of the head of department's role, how she perceives whether people are around or not. (Tony, a senior lecturer)

Source
Research carried out by the author.

Case study questions

1. Assume you are a senior manager at the university. How might you justify the decision to close down the staff common room and staff canteen?

2. In what ways have the changes impacted on the business school's human and social capital?

3. What HRD interventions would you recommend to address the problems caused by the changes? Differentiate clearly between the role of the HRD practitioner and the line manager.

Online resource centre

Visit the supporting online resource centre for additional material that will help you with your research, essays, assignments, and revision.

 www.oxfordtextbooks.co.uk/orc/mankin/

11

Integrating Learning with Work

Learning objectives

By the end of this chapter you should be able to:

* Define and explain the concept of informal learning

* Understand the principal perspectives on informal learning

* Appreciate the relationship between formal and informal learning interventions

* Explain the factors influencing the growth of interest in informal learning

* Appreciate the importance of learning by doing in the workplace

* Demonstrate how to facilitate the integration of learning with work

* Understand and explain the role of the HRD practitioner and line manager in integrating learning in the workplace

Indicative content

■ The relationship between knowledge, knowledge management, and learning

■ Definitions of informal learning, incidental, and unintended learning

■ The importance of collaborative working

■ A learning model to explain the nature of informal learning

■ The tensions between controlling and nurturing informal learning

■ The role of development interactions

■ The concept of just-in-time (JIT) learning

■ The role of learning-by-doing in the workplace

■ The facilitators of and obstacles to integrating learning with work

- The role of the HRD practitioner and line manager in integrating learning in the workplace

- The relationship between the HRD cycle and the enhanced HRD cycle

- The role of technology and e-learning in facilitating informal learning

---

Key concepts

Informal learning	Just-in-time (JIT) learning
Incidental and unintended learning	Learning by doing
Development interactions	Enhanced HRD cycle

11.1 **Introduction**

The workplace has become conceptualized as an environment in which people learn (Andersen and Andersen, 2007) and various terms have emerged to describe this phenomenon, including *learning-in-context* (Matthews and Candy, 1999), *workplace learning* (Boud and Garrick, 1999) and *work-related learning* (Sambrook, 2005). In the past HRD practitioners and line managers have concentrated on specific on-the-job training interventions such as coaching, guided practice, and mentoring as well as competency-based programmes such as national vocational qualifications (NVQs). These interventions have been designed and implemented using the principles of the systematic training cycle or the HRD cycle (see chapter 5) and form part of an organization's overall HRD strategy. More recently, there has been growing interest in what is termed *informal* learning which is happening all the time in the workplace and falls outside an organization's formal learning system. Increasingly, organizations have been recognizing the potential of informal learning as a source of competitive advantage (Bell and Ford, 2007). This has arisen as a result of the growth of interest in knowledge and knowledge management, as discussed in the previous chapter, as well as the preceding interest in organizational learning and the learning organization (see chapters 2 and 3).

It is believed that informal learning in the workplace now accounts for the majority of learning in organizations (Ellinger, 2005). This type of learning can be planned; for instance, an individual identifies a scheduled project team meeting as an opportunity to learn about certain aspects of project management; an HR practitioner identifies a scheduled disciplinary meeting as an opportunity to learn more about how to handle such a meeting effectively. In these situations the informal learning can be described as *purposeful* (Jarvis, 2006) or *deliberate* (Doornbos et al., 2004) although there is no guarantee that the individual will necessarily learn anything. Informal learning can also be accidental or *incidental* (Matthews and Candy, 1999). This is when an individual has not anticipated learning something as a result of engaging in a work activity. Consequently, informal and incidental learning are embedded in the workplace; they are a natural phenomenon of organizational life and, as with the 'shadow' organization proposed in chapter 10, they are not the product of direct management control.

In effect, work and learning have come to be viewed as *intertwined* (Vera and Crossan, 2005) thus suggesting a performance-oriented perspective on workplace learning. However, it is still not clear how much workplace learning activity is actually occurring within organizations. Not only is it difficult to measure (Stern and Sommerlad, 1999) but it is also an under-researched topic (Eraut, 2004). Additionally, it is even less clear how much of this learning is supporting the achievement of organizational goals. It is likely that a significant proportion of informal and incidental learning is benefiting the career development of individuals more than it is necessarily benefiting the organization. This corresponds to the humanist perspective on learning that was discussed in chapter 2 (i.e. the purpose of learning is to enrich the individual). The different approaches to workplace learning are summarized in figure 11.1.

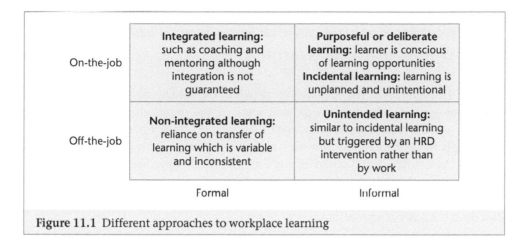

	Integrated learning: such as coaching and mentoring although integration is not guaranteed	**Purposeful or deliberate learning:** learner is conscious of learning opportunities **Incidental learning:** learning is unplanned and unintentional
On-the-job		
Off-the-job	**Non-integrated learning:** reliance on transfer of learning which is variable and inconsistent	**Unintended learning:** similar to incidental learning but triggered by an HRD intervention rather than by work
	Formal	Informal

Figure 11.1 Different approaches to workplace learning

Informal learning is posing new challenges for HRD practitioners who tend to know far more about structured, formal approaches to learning (Eddy et al., 2006). These are what most people tend to think of as being 'training' (Beattie, 2006). As with social capital in chapter 10 this chapter will argue that informal learning should be nurtured rather than managed. The content of this chapter is primarily devoted to purposeful or deliberate informal workplace learning. Incidental learning will be discussed where relevant; and, unintended learning will be used to illustrate the linkage between the HRD cycle which underpinned chapters 5 to 9 and an enhanced HRD cycle that incorporates informal learning (see below). The chapter starts with a brief clarification of the relationship between knowledge, knowledge management, and learning before moving onto a detailed explanation of the nature of informal learning, a consideration of the principal barriers and facilitators of informal learning, and a discussion of the role of HRD practitioners and line managers in integrating learning with work.

MEDIA WATCH BOX

The UK Government and informal learning

In January 2008 the UK Government published a consultative paper on informal learning in acknowledgement of the increasingly outdated nature of much of the adult learning provision in the UK.

Source
http://www.niace.org.uk/Conferences/older-informal.htm (accessed 1 June 2008).

11.2 **The relationship between knowledge, knowledge management, and learning**

Chapter 10 highlighted the relationship between knowledge management (KM) and human resource development (HRD) and some of the implications for learning (for instance see the definition of knowledge management by Scarborough et al., 1999). Learning is implicit in all KM processes, such as knowledge-acquisition, -creation, and -sharing. As Gourlay (2001) observes, any activities which have been designed to influence or manage learning have at some point also been concerned with influencing and managing knowledge. Learning involves both tacit and explicit knowledge and has been described variously as a process for:

• acquiring knowledge (Brown and Duguid, 2001)

• sharing knowledge (Quintas, 2002)

• creating new knowledge (Kogut and Zander, 1992).

Learning can be at the individual level, the group level, or the organizational level. Individual learning is dependent on individual cognition (see chapter 4) and from a KM perspective has been described as 'individual knowledge development' by Poell and Van der Krogt (2003a). Fenwick (2006) notes that individual learning is based on the assumption that an individual learns and then affects the group. This is consistent with the first wave objectivist perspective on KM where Nonaka (1994) described the process of *internalization* (i.e. the conversion of explicit knowledge into tacit knowledge) as bearing some similarity to the traditional notion of learning. In contrast from a second wave practice-based perspective on KM learning is seen as being intrinsically linked to the social processes within an organization (McAdam and Reid, 2001). Consequently, social interaction provides the primary experience for individuals (Jarvis, 2006) and therefore is pivotal to understanding how people learn (see *Insights into practice* box). Such social interaction tends to occur within groups (for instance, see chapter 10's discussion of communities-of-practice). This is why from this perspective cognition is described as being situated and distributed (again, see the discussion in chapter 10). In terms of learning at the organizational level KM has built on the body of literature on organizational learning (Prusak, 2001). For instance, a second wave practice-based perspective on KM views organizational learning as an institutionalizing process (Huysman, 2004) through which individual knowledge becomes organizational knowledge as a result of a practice becoming sufficiently regular and continuous to be described as institutional (Huysman and de Wit, 2003).

The most interesting discussions on the relationship between knowledge, knowledge management, and learning revolve around the second wave practice-based perspective. It is felt that the over-reliance on technology in the first wave objectivist perspective may have acted as an inhibitor to the learning and the development of expertise (Dreyfus and Dreyfus, 1997). Walton (1999) developed this theme further by speculating that the

Situated learning and knowledge sharing—linked processes

'We meet once a week and we talk through how we are going to run the tutorials and what activities we'll do and why we are doing them and that sort of thing . . . this is just something we do, we weren't directed to do it or following anyone else's model . . . I think it works very well because we all learn from each other. I mean, I am not telling them how to tackle this. People chip in and come up with good ideas and we use the email a lot and send ideas around and that sort of thing. And we share resources, so, if I produce a set of slides for use in the tutorial, we do copies and keep them in a drawer in the office so everybody can use them'. (Annie, a lecturer working in a UK southern new university).[1]

This example illustrates informal situated learning and how this involves knowledge sharing. This is a particular characteristic of communities of practice which provide an ideal learning environment (Brown and Duguid, 2000). Members of a community develop implicit ways of learning and working together (Leonard and Sensiper, 1998) and this reinforces the need to view learning and working as interrelated concepts.

Source
[1] Research study carried out by the author.

MEDIA WATCH BOX

Informal learning at Shell

This case illustrates the intimate relationship between organizational knowledge and learning processes.

At Shell knowledge management is regarded as being part of the company's informal learning processes. The concept of knowledge management is now being replaced by practices such as knowledge sharing, mentoring, job-shadowing, and coaching. These now form part of a workplace learning strategy which integrates traditional formal classroom-based learning interventions with work-based learning opportunities.

Source
http://findarticles.com/p/articles/mi_qa5362/ai_n21292770/pg_4 (accessed 5 June 2008).

knowledge organization 'with its concomitant value set of seeing the individual as only a source of net worth, has such an instrumental orientation that it fails to pick up how and why individuals learn' (p. 73). This is another illustration of the tension between performative and humanist perspectives on HRD discussed in chapters 2 and 3.

11.3 Informal learning in the workplace

> **Key concept**   Informal learning
>
> Informal learning is essentially learning that is 'predominantly unstructured, experiential, and noninstitutionalised' (Marsick and Volpe, 1999: 4) with the control of learning resting primarily in the hands of the learner (Marsick and Watkins, 1990).

Informal learning requires a new approach by management (Kessels and Poell, 2004): a nurturing rather than control approach (as advocated in chapter 10). Marsick and Watkins (1990) also differentiate between informal and incidental learning with the latter being a by product of some other activity. Often individuals are not necessarily conscious of learning having taken place (Eraut, 2000):

> People can learn without being aware of it and detect the changes in their thinking and behavioural repertoire only at a later point. Learning can happen either directly or indirectly via workplace experiences and with or without the mediation of verbal explanation. From an educational perspective, learning typically involves the setting of learning goals. In contrast, workplace learning need not have such goals and, if it does, they are usually work-related ones . . . The key purpose of activities at work and the prime objectives of workers are things other than learning. (Doornbos et al., 2004: 255–6)

Informal (and incidental) learning offer viable, if often unpredictable alternatives to formal learning opportunities. Informal learning takes place through processes such as story-telling and conversations as well as coaching and the mentoring of novices (Wenger et al., 2002). The latter is described by Lave and Wenger (1991) as a form of apprenticeship although this is not the same as formal apprenticeship schemes. Rather the term is used to explain how a novice practitioner develops into a skilled practitioner: 'the knowledge needed to do particular jobs is embedded within the associated tasks, processes and those who are already competent' (Fuller et al., 2004: 3). Individuals learn and develop from working in collaboration with their immediate colleagues and, consequently, learning is simultaneously individual and collective in nature (Fenwick, 2006). Hence the learning is *situated* in a particular work context giving rise to the concept of situated learning (Lave and Wenger, 1991) as a particular form of social learning. As was explained in chapter 10 this type of learning is associated with knowledge sharing where new knowledge is socially constructed. The dynamics of individual and social learning are captured in the learning model shown in figure 11.2.

In the model an individual's learning is anchored in his/her day-by-day work experiences. Learning occurs as a result of engaging with social artefacts, such as books, magazines, or the Internet, and taking part in social interactions. This means the boundaries between individual and social learning and between personal knowledge and socially

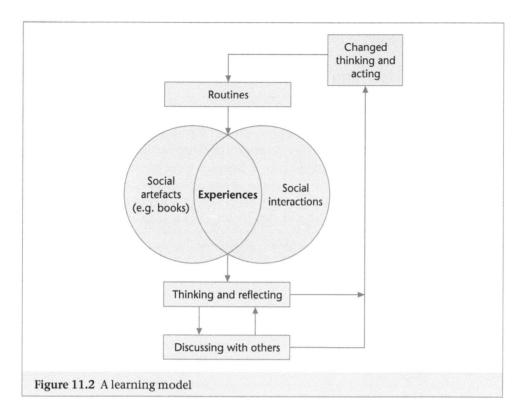

Figure 11.2 A learning model

constructed knowledge become blurred in a dynamically entwined relationship. Think-ing about and reflecting on the experience can be an individual activity and/or can involve discussions with others (e.g. immediate colleagues, mentor, line manager etc). For actual learning to take place there needs to be changes to how an individual thinks *and* acts in the workplace and for these to become embedded in new routines which, in turn, inform or influence new experiences. This is consistent with the explanations of experiential learning, situated learning, and reflective practice in chapter 4. Figure 11.3 shows an illustrative example.

In figure 11.3 the individual, who we shall call Kate, has received some feedback from colleagues on her approach to classroom-based teaching. Kate is trying to make sense of this feedback as it challenges some of her assumptions about how she should be teaching. Initially, she struggles to accept the feedback and is inclined to reject what she has been told. But to help her in thinking about and reflecting on the feedback she talks to colleagues about what she has been told, how she feels about it, and her ideas for changing her teaching approach. In between these discussions she continues to reflect by herself. This process takes several days before she reaches a decision about changing how she thinks and acts about teaching in the classroom. She experiments with some new approaches and reflects on these before making some permanent changes. This is when changes to how she thinks and acts become embedded as new routines which then inform subsequent performance (not only by her but her immediate colleagues who decide to reflect on their own teaching in the light of Kate's personal changes). This

MEDIA WATCH BOX

Is informal learning a threat to formal learning interventions?

Informal learning is seen as a threat to traditional formal learning because of the perceived ineffectiveness of the latter. Retention of classroom learning falls dramatically after a few days and to 10 per cent or less after three weeks. Evaluation data might be interpreted by some organizational managers as evidence of the HRD function's inability to direct resources to where they really matter—the workplace.

Source
http://www.trainingzone.co.uk/cgi-bin/item.cgi?id=173334 (accessed 2 June 2008).

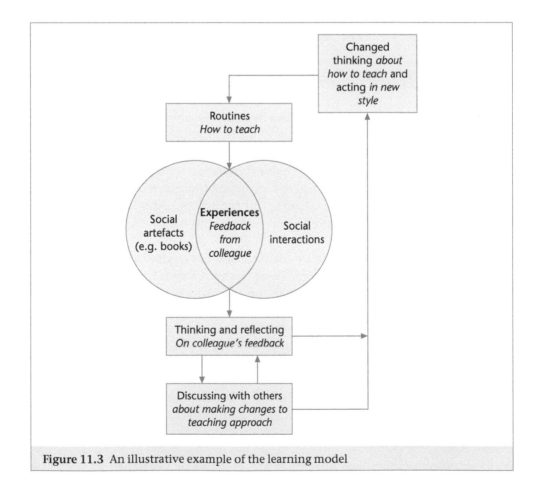

Figure 11.3 An illustrative example of the learning model

example illustrates how it is possible to externalize informal learning through a process of critical reflection. However, as chapter 4 explained, most people are not necessarily very good at reflecting critically on what has happened to them and usually need surprises to trigger reflection. For Kate the surprise was to receive feedback that she had not been expecting.

Another example is Thomas a customer services adviser in a national call centre. Thomas has been given a verbal warning for failing to adhere to company guidelines for handling customers who make a complaint. He has been told that his manner is often unhelpful and he is prone to sarcasm. He has been told that an experienced adviser will be listening to his calls and providing feedback and coaching where necessary. Thomas is initially resentful about the warning but after a few days chatting to some close colleagues he has calmed down and decided to give the coaching a try. Figure 11.4 sets out the sequence following the feedback from the coach who refers to taped conversations between Thomas and several customers and suggests Thomas discuss his feelings about

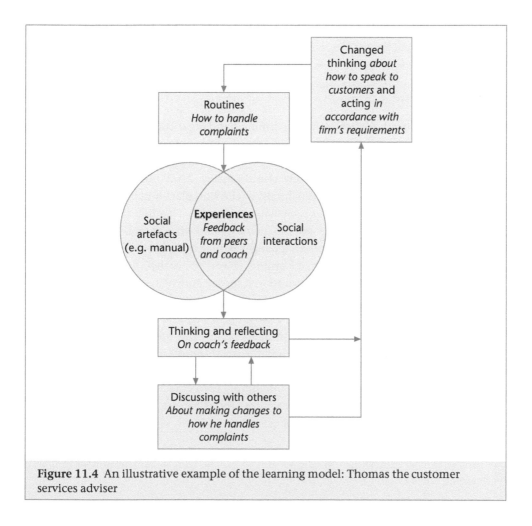

Figure 11.4 An illustrative example of the learning model: Thomas the customer services adviser

the feedback with colleagues as well. He also suggests that Thomas should re-familiarize himself with the firm's procedural manual for customer service advisers. As a result of deciding to engage with this process Thomas is acknowledging that he does need to change. The warning has acted as a trigger (see chapter 4) and it is through the combination of feedback from the coach and colleagues (i.e. peers) with a re-reading of the procedural manual that facilitates changes to how Thomas thinks and acts. This example also illustrates how learning is used as part of the socialization process (see, in particular, the discussion on behavioural learning theory in chapter 4).

ACTIVITY 11.1

Apply the learning model shown in figures 11.2, 11.3, and 11.4 to a recent learning experience that has happened to you. How easy was it for you to identify a relevant experience?

Historically, HRD practitioners and line managers have tended to ignore informal learning:

> Only recently did TandD professionals acknowledge the unstructured learning journey. Most TandD professionals had been only thinking about their structured training view of the world and not acknowledging the unstructured . . . [which] has not been viewed favourably. (Swanson and Holton, 2001: 207)

It has also been difficult for both HRD practitioners and organizational managers to get to grips with the concept of informal learning. It can be very difficult to distinguish between working and learning (Koopmans et al., 2006) and, as with social capital, informal learning is difficult to directly control. As Stewart and Tansley (2002) note informal learning is essentially invisible because it occurs naturally in the workplace and outside formal learning interventions and is therefore problematic to control. This highlights the principal dilemma facing HRD practitioners and line managers: to what extent should they try to make such learning explicit? A potential danger is that in the process of doing so they actually change the nature of informal learning. However, because informal learning can be deliberately encouraged by an organization (Marsick and Watkins, 1990) it is possible to nurture a context (i.e. create a learning climate) conducive to it through HRD strategy choices of 'devolved informal learning' and 'empowered informal learning', with the former focusing on the development of human capital and the latter the development of social capital (Mankin, 2004). In this way the organization is introducing what Yorks (2005) refers to as 'facilitated informal learning' (p. 156) although Swanson and Holton (2001) warn that 'there is also a danger in attempting to over-facilitate informal and incidental learning to the point that it really becomes formal learning' (p. 170).

! TIPS AND HINTS

'To develop the knowledge organization it is necessary to create an appropriate learning environment' (Mankin, 2001: 75).

Informal learning can also occur as a consequence of formal off-the-job interventions. For instance, as part of an initiative designed to develop individual management competencies, officers within Liverpool North Merseyside Police are offered places on a formal course but can opt to fill knowledge gaps through trying out new activities at work or asking colleagues for advice (Pickard, 2004). Indeed, HRD learning initiatives or programmes tend to involve a combination of different learning activities such as formal, informal and incidental, both on- and off-the-job (Poell and Van der Krogt, 2003b). In a study of HRD practitioners, Slotte et al. (2004) observed that 'our most notable results relate to the emphasis placed by participants on practical on-the-job training' and that 'HRD practitioners themselves attached great value to informal learning and its use as one component in more formal training activities' (p. 494).

A particular form of informal learning has been described as 'development interactions' by Eddy et al. (2006):

> Development interaction refers to interactions between two individuals with the intent of enhancing personal development or growth. They may address a variety of personal or professional topics, such as career advice, work-life support, and job or task guidance and involve individuals we refer to as 'advisers' and 'advisees' who respectively give and receive development advice. (p. 60)

My own research has shown this type of dyadic-learning is a particular characteristic of academic management teams in the new university sector. More generally, development interactions appear to reflect mentoring relationships although Eddy et al. (2006) state that the concept extends beyond traditional formal mentoring. Unlike the interactions that take place between two people in a formal mentoring relationship, development interactions are happening every day in virtually every organization (ibid.). A study of three occupation groups by Koopmans et al. (2006) suggests that for learning to be reciprocal in a dyadic relationship both individuals need to be aware of the supporting role they can offer to each other (i.e. they need to perceive the interaction between them as a potential learning opportunity). The extent to which this is achievable will depend on the extent to which the dyadic relationship is embedded in an appropriate learning environment.

Closely associated with informal learning is the notion of just-in-time (JIT) learning (Brandenberg and Ellinger, 2003) which, in terms of HRD strategic choices, requires a transition from *devolved* informal learning to *empowered* informal learning (Mankin, 2004). JIT learning is:

> Truly learner driven where the control shifts to learners, especially including groups of learners, who create their learning environment, select vehicles for learning, establish priorities and pace, and set expectations for outcomes. JIT learning is viewed as a dynamic and adaptive approach to learning where standards and outcomes are not controlled or contrived by designers, but are considered fundamentally user centred, user designed, and user managed. (Brandenberg and Ellinger, 2003: 309)

JIT learning can also impact on formal learning interventions if they are sufficiently 'dynamic, changeable and opportunistic' (Garvey and Williamson, 2002: 38). A further way of enhancing JIT learning and informal learning more generally is through raising people's awareness of learning styles (see *Media watch* box).

MEDIA WATCH BOX

Informal learning at Cisco

To what extent does an organization's sector influence its approach to informal learning? In this example Cisco, not surprisingly, relies on technology to facilitate informal learning by enabling employees to access Web-based material to suit their own needs.

In order to adopt a learning rather than training orientation at Cisco the Internet Learning Solutions Group decided to focus on helping employees become more effective in their jobs. This was achieved by using e-learning as a delivery system that could be accessed by employees whenever they felt motivated to learn. Underpinning this approach was a belief that learning also equates to communication and so email and voicemail systems can be used to support learning. These are relatively cheap systems to install and maintain. It is better to talk about learning and the impact this has on the business, and the relationship between learning and communication, than about training argues Mr Tom Kelly of Cisco. Employees are able to create their own learning content by accessing any of the millions of pages available to them on the Cisco Website. Mr Kelly argues that this gives control to the learner. The overall aim of this strategy is to integrate learning with work. Employees are able to access learning content for up to twenty minutes at a time.

Source
http://www.e-learningguru.com/articles/misc4_4a.htm (accessed 16 June 2008).

ACTIVITY 11.2

What are the potential advantages and disadvantages of using technology, such as e-learning systems, company intranets, and on-line discussion forums to support informal learning in the workplace?

11.4 Why the growth of interest in informal learning?

A range of factors have contributed to the heightened interest in informal learning, including:

- Employees are taking more responsibility for their own learning (Ellinger, 2005)
- Learning on-the-job offers potentially more opportunities for learners to choose their own learning activities (Berings et al., 2005)

- The ability of individuals to learn is increasingly being seen as an important competency (Matthews and Candy, 1999)

- The recognition of learning as a source of sustainable competitive advantage for organizations (Ellinger, 2005)

- Questions about the efficacy of formal workplace learning interventions (Brockman and Dirkx, 2006)

It has been known for some time that tacit knowledge in particular is acquired and developed through learning-by-doing (Zuboff, 1988). The emphasis on knowledge work and knowledge workers (see chapter 10) has raised awareness of the number of ways in which highly qualified individuals learn about their jobs outside structured or formal learning (Eraut et al., 1998).

Key concept   Learning-by-doing

Learning-by-doing places work practice at the centre of the learning process. It builds on both experiential and situated learning theories as discussed in chapter 4.

INSIGHTS INTO PRACTICE

Learning by doing on-the-job

'When anything comes in for the whole school I tend to get it because I can give the longest and most experience on it . . . I've had the chance to change some of the forms and the procedures we do for the timetabling. So it really is my way of doing it and the way I want it to be done. And so I get everyone else to work around it . . . I trained myself to change the procedures and the paperwork that goes behind the whole process and system . . . I told them how I was doing it and hoped that they would take up my way of doing it because I've been doing it for longer and I know that if you do it this way you don't get a response and if you do it that way, you do. In the other schools they have adopted some of my forms and procedures. I have been doing it for so long I pretty much know what [academic colleagues] are going to say as they answer'. (Marilyn, an administrator working in UK northern new university)[1]

This example illustrates the interconnectedness of learning and work as previously theorized and the extent to which tacit and explicit knowledge are learned on the job. The development of tacit knowledge includes an intuitive element captured nicely by her closing sentence.

Source
[1] Research study carried out by the author.

Informal learning has become attractive to organizational managers because it is also associated with action learning and problem solving (Swanson and Holton, 2001); as well as coaching and mentoring. These are popular HRD strategies that were highlighted in chapter 3. Action learning results in solutions to real work problems and is particularly attractive to knowledge workers who respond well to being exposed to complex problems (Quinn et al., 1998). Coaching can help specifically in the development of systems understanding or know-why (Noe, 2002) which are important aspects of problem solving; while mentoring can facilitate a wide range of work-based learning initiatives. However, the role of problem-solving as a form of informal learning is not restricted to knowledge workers. In a qualitative study of machine operators Brockman and Dirkx (2006) discovered that the machine operators viewed problem solving incidents as opportunities for learning. They also noted that even long serving employees still found such problem solving activities to be a positive learning experience.

However, learning-by-doing occurs within formal as well as informal contexts. In his study of new product projects, formal teams set up in three leading IT companies, Lynn (1998) identified three different forms of team learning: 'Within-Team Learning' or learning-by-doing at the intra-team level; 'Cross-Team Learning' or transplanting of experience at the inter-team level; 'Market-Learning' or knowledge gained external to the organization at the organization level. This also highlights that organizations still need to develop mechanisms for the transfer of learning between contexts as not all knowledge, such as theoretical ideas, is situated within a particular context (Fuller et al., 2004).

> **! TIPS AND HINTS**
>
> Not all jobs offer the same opportunities for learning (Nieuwenhuis and van Woerkom, 2007.

11.5 Facilitators of and obstacles to integrating learning with work

Swart et al. (2003) claim that data from their study of six organizations reveal that the majority of knowledge workers are apparently less interested in what they get paid and more interested in what they can learn. This suggests that in terms of knowledge work there is a need to reappraise the range of HRM and HRD incentives offered to this type of employee by the organization. The importance of this was discussed in chapter 10. However, this needs to be considered in relation to informal as well as formal learning opportunities, and how these can be maximized from the organization's point of view. Clarke (2005) notes from a study of hospices in the UK that in order to develop an effective learning environment an organization needs to implement a range of interventions that can support different types of learning. This supports the need for a range of HRD strategic choices, as proposed in chapter 3, and has implications for HRM policies, such as employee participation, employee involvement, performance management, and recruitment, selection and retention (thus illustrating the need for horizontal integration between HRD and HRM).

The development of an appropriate learning environment requires HRD practitioners and organizational managers to be familiar with those factors which can best facilitate the cultivation of such an environment and those that can act as an obstacle. These are summarized as positive and negative influences in table 11.1.

11.6 The role of the HRD practitioner and line manager in integrating learning in the workplace

Traditionally HRD practitioners and line managers have concentrated on interventions that are usually intended to have a direct impact on the development of an organization's human capital. In particular on 'learning as socialization' which involves the design and delivery of formal training and development interventions. Examples include: short courses, workshops, and seminars on a range of topics from employment legislation to presentation skills. Often such interventions are designed to help gain the trust of employees by signalling that the organization is investing in their future (Scarborough and Elias, 2002). These types of intervention reflect a systematic approach to HRD as discussed in chapter 5. In order to develop an organizational culture that supports the development of social as well as human capital HRD practitioners need to design and implement interventions that have an indirect impact on how people learn and develop informally (i.e. 'devolved informal learning' and 'empowered informal learning'). Examples include the development of awareness and skills in: reflective practice, facilitation and coaching of work-place learning, and learning how to learn (differently). In these situations the role of the HRD practitioner should be non-directive and reliant on the facilitation skills of the line manager.

In their study of effective and ineffective development interactions between two individuals, Eddy et al. (2006) discovered that the HRD practitioner's role needs to focus on helping employees engage in learning through self-discovery (rather than being highly directive). They argue that this facilitation approach can be devolved to line managers. Consequently, the HRD practitioner needs to design direct interventions for the development of line manager facilitation skills. This is exploiting the traditional knowledge and skills of HRD practitioners referred to earlier as well as providing opportunities for developing the expertise needed to nurture the development of informal learning. As well as helping to build collaborative networks and other forms of social capital and finding solutions to problems associated with learner motivation, Stewart and Tansley (2002) suggest that HRD practitioners need to broaden their role to encourage key stakeholders outside the organization, such as government, to support new approaches to learning. These approaches are essential for the future of the HRD profession as it is now clear that learning in the workplace is central to HRD (Sambrook, 2005). However, the lack of research studies does mean that empirical evidence of the role of the HRD practitioner in facilitating this type of learning remains inconclusive (Gubbins and Garavan, 2005).

Positive influence	Negative influence
Clear and supportive strategic vision and direction (e.g. having HRD policies that support the different forms of learning within the workplace; line managers acting as stewards of an organization's vision)	Lack of strategic vision and direction (e.g. HRD is not an integral element of the organization's vision and strategic goals; lack of support for informal learning from the HR function; lack of role clarity)
Management support for learning (e.g. creating and visibly supporting informal learning opportunities; acting as coaches or mentors; encouraging risk taking; instilling the importance of knowledge sharing and developing others; giving positive feedback and recognition; acting as a role model; line managers collectively lobbying senior managers for support; making learning a specific objective in line with other aspects of the business)	Lack of management support for learning (e.g. not valuing the role of learning; line managers who focus on control and telling people what to do; conflict between operational and developmental duties; lack of accountability)
Positive perceptions of learning (e.g. learning does add value; developing human capital brings competitive advantage)	Negative perceptions of learning (e.g. little of value will be gained from learning interventions)
Developing a culture committed to learning (e.g. general managers acting as role models; the level of expenditure on learning—'symbol of the training room'; having HRD skills in facilitation and coaching; willingness of individuals to learn; effective management development; encouraging individuals to ask questions and challenge)	Internal culture slow to change (e.g. people resisting change; people not willing to learn; trying to change too much too quickly; engrained management thinking; lack of adequate management development; regarding individuals who question and challenge as organizational deviants or as being dysfunctional; lack of role modelling by general managers; lack of HRD skills in facilitation and coaching)
Having the right work resources (e.g. such as a computer and telephone)	Work resources that distract employees and impede informal learning (e.g. lack of face-to-face contact due to ICT systems)
Promoting social capital (e.g. forming networks and participating in communities—this reflects the role of social capital; managers creating opportunities for people to learn in teams)	People who disrupt webs of relationships from forming (e.g. 'old guard cynicism'; hoarding knowledge)
Removing structural inhibitors (e.g. creating social spaces to encourage social interactions)	Structural inhibitors (e.g. physical barriers, such as the size and shape of the building and office layout; silo mentality)
Improved work design (e.g. redesigning work flows and activities; focusing on process improvement to free time; viewing problems as learning opportunities)	Lack of time (e.g. due to job pressures and responsibilities)

Table 11.1 Contextual factors that positively and negatively influence informal learning

Sources: Table based on Kolb, 1996; Marsick and Watkins, 1997; Garvey and Williamson, 2002; Stewart and Tansley, 2002; Billet, 2004; Clarke, 2005; Ellinger, 2005; Lohman, 2005; Sambrook, 2005; Beattie, 2006; and Brockman and Dirkx, 2006

That line managers are going to have a greater direct impact or influence on informal learning than HRD practitioners does raise potential tensions between them and HRD practitioners. For instance, in terms of encouraging social learning in the workplace Lohman (2005) suggests that HRD practitioners should be responsible for the strategic design of work areas to ensure that employees are located near to their colleagues, especially in the early stages of their career (see the above comments on apprenticeship). This approach builds on the discussion in chapter 5 of work design and redesign as an example of a formal OD approach that can be adopted by HRD practitioners. However, in terms of stimulating informal learning the design of work areas is arguably best left to managers and their team (see *Insights into practice* box). Those doing the job are in the best position to decide how a work area should be designed. The irony is that one of the biggest challenges facing HRD practitioners in the past has been getting managers to understand and engage with learning (Slotte et al., 2004).

The reality is that as section 11.5 illustrates line managers can be both a facilitator of and a barrier to the integration of learning in the workplace. However, the CIPD's 2007 *Learning and Development Survey* reveals that line managers are taking on greater responsibility for training, learning and development (Hutchinson et al., 2007). Referring to their own research studies Hutchinson et al. (2007) note that line managers are 'involved in

---

● ▶ INSIGHTS INTO PRACTICE

Redesigning work areas

'Dobbs (2000) described a number of organizations where managers had taken deliberate steps to promote informal learning. For example, in a manufacturing company the way work was designed militated against learning; employees rotated between jobs every few hours but never saw a job through from start to finish and hence were unable to see how the process as a whole functioned and how they contributed to this. In order to facilitate informal learning, the company moved its customer service department down to the shopfloor and introduced 10-minute overlaps between shifts so that employees had the chance to mingle with people from other shifts and other departments. When these conversations veer towards work, as they inevitably do, "simple moments of learning" take place (Dobbs, 2000). This contrasts with the perceptions of some managers that such congregations are unproductive and need to be guarded against as a waste of valuable work time.'[1]

As well as illustrating the importance of workplace design these cases highlight one of the main reasons why managers perceive informal learning, in the form of knowledge sharing, as a form of social loafing or laziness. It can be difficult to place value on something that is viewed as a distraction or waste of time.

Source
[1] Smith, P. J. and Sadler-Smith (2006) *Learning in Organisations: Complexities and Diversities*. Abingdon: Routledge, p. 135.

informal learning and development and in promoting knowledge-sharing and collaborative problem solving' (p. 39). This reflects the view from a decade earlier that managers have an important role to play in the facilitation of informal learning (Marsick and Watkins, 1997). Typical examples of informal learning that line managers can support directly or indirectly include mentoring, coaching, experimentation (which includes learning from mistakes), and networking. This means that increasingly managers need to be able to facilitate multiple developmental relationships (Rock and Garavan, 2006). This is a level of complexity not envisaged in the past when the role of the line manager was subordinate to that of the training expert. Now and in the future line managers, as well as appropriately skilled colleagues, will be much more intimately involved than HRD practitioners in the facilitation of these types of informal learning. Poell et al. (2006) refer to such people as 'informal workplace trainers' and suggest that HRD practitioners would benefit from collaborating with them as this would result in a much more integrated approach to workplace learning. The actual training of 'informal workplace trainers' can be carried out by the HRD practitioner. This, again, reflects the nurturing role of the HRD practitioner. As Brockman and Dirkx (2006) note:

> Helping supervisors and managers understand and recognise the power of the work context in shaping learning, development, and identity formation of frontline workers represents an important goal for HRD practice. Critical to this role is the fostering of an appropriate degree of worker autonomy within the learning process, together with appropriate support. (p. 217)

This is consistent with devolved informal and empowered informal learning strategies.

ACTIVITY 11.3

What specific skills or competencies do you feel are critical for line managers to demonstrate when facilitating informal learning?

11.7 The enhanced HRD cycle

Key concept   Enhanced HRD cycle

The enhanced HRD cycle explains the inter-relationships between formal and informal learning.

Taking all of the above points into consideration it is possible to arrive at an enhanced model of the HRD cycle which is illustrated in figure 11.5. Incidental learning is not made explicit in the model as this can be the product of any work process or activity whether formal or informal. Consequently the emphasis is on purposeful or deliberate informal learning with the placement of informal learning as the outer cycle reflecting the fact

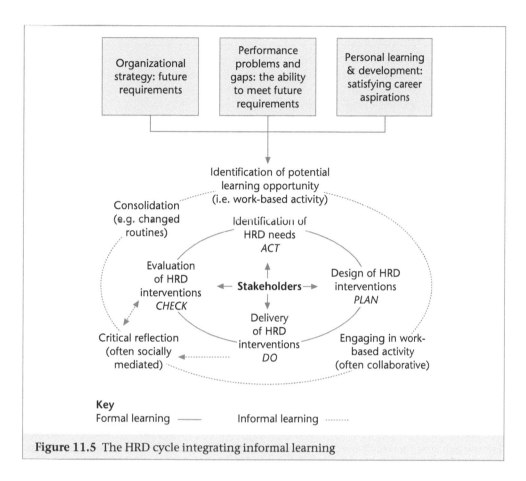

Figure 11.5 The HRD cycle integrating informal learning

that the majority of learning in an organization is informal and takes precedence over formal learning (Ellinger, 2005). However, *unintended learning* which was referred to in figure 11.1 above is made explicit. Unintended learning is similar to incidental learning but is triggered by an HRD intervention rather than by work. This may only happen in a minority of situations as argued by Doornbos et al. (2004) but should not be ignored. The outer cycle reflects the shadow organization referred to in chapter 10 where informal and formal processes and structures are interlinked in the form of a symbiotic relationship. Formal learning tends to focus on the individual and the acquisition of explicit knowledge. There are exceptions to this and many formal interventions are designed to allow participants to practise skills (e.g. role play; guided practice; coaching etc.) but often are reliant on the transfer of learning from the classroom to the workplace which chapters 5 and 9 highlighted as being an inconsistent process; indeed often being unreliable. Informal learning tends to focus on the social context and the acquisition and development of tacit knowledge, sometimes building on the explicit knowledge gained from formal interventions. However, there are also examples of informal learning which focus primarily on the individual and explicit knowledge, such as observation and imitation of others (as was discussed above this is a form of passive interaction with the social context).

> **! TIPS AND HINTS**
>
> Despite the growth of interest in the potential benefits of informal learning there is still a tendency for organizations to concentrate on the training of line managers as task-related coaches only (Hall, 2006). A broader and deeper level of coaching is needed to reflect a real shift in an organization's culture.

The first stage in the outer cycle is the identification of a potential learning opportunity (i.e. work-based activity) which may be in advance of the activity taking place or at the time it is actually happening. Examples of such activities include making mistakes, sharing knowledge, receiving feedback, and testing new ideas. Sometimes an individual may only be aware of learning having taken place after the activity when he/she reflects on what happened. This is indicative of incidental learning. On other occasions the learning (and reflection) may remain intuitive (an example of Polanyi's observation that we may know more than we can say which was discussed in chapter 10). Kessels and Poell (2004) argue that knowledge productive workplaces should encourage individuals to become self-directed learners. Self-directed learning was introduced in chapter 4 and involves learners taking primary responsibility for their own learning in terms of planning, implementation, and evaluation (Ellinger, 2004). In this way SDL can be viewed as one of the key learning processes for sustaining informal learning and maximizing the benefits for the learner and the organization. Although SDL tends to be individually driven it is interlinked with the other key processes which include situated (social) learning and knowledge sharing which involve social interaction. This is why the second stage in the outer cycle, engaging in work-based activity, is qualified as usually involving some form of collaboration. Most jobs tend to involve social interaction. Consequently, the stakeholders at the centre of the model need to be expanded from the learner, line manager, and HRD practitioner to include colleagues as learning collaborators. These relationships are critical to the nature and quality of informal learning in the workplace (Poell et al., 2006) and, in particular to the third stage in the outer cycle: critical reflection which is qualified as being often socially mediated.

In terms of the interaction between the formal and informal parts of the HRD cycle critical reflection can be triggered at the implementation and evaluation phases of the formal HRD cycle and, to a lesser extent at the identification of needs stage (depending on the level of involvement of the learner). Formal HRM interventions such as job enlargement and job enrichment can also act as a trigger. As was highlighted in chapter 4 there are different theories of critical reflection with the most well known being Kolb's experiential learning theory (van Woerkom, 2004); which is also the most often used learning theory by HRD practitioners. The fourth stage in the outer cycle is consolidation. This is when routines are changed as a result of the learning and corresponds to the changed routines stage in the learning model illustrated by figure 11.4 above. This outer cycle is driven by the learner but is, for the reasons given above:

- **Directly and indirectly influenced by the line manager in his/her role as a facilitator** of informal learning and co-collaborator in developmental relationships. This type of support is needed to address problems of low motivation to learn by employees (Stewart and Tansley, 2002). In a study of two voluntary organizations Beattie (2006) noted that the principal manager behaviours that fostered developmental relationships included caring (e.g. being approachable and supportive, reassuring and encouraging, empathizing), informing (e.g. sharing knowledge), being professional (e.g. setting standards and acting as a role model), advising (e.g. coaching, counselling, and guiding), assessing (e.g. providing feedback and identifying development needs), thinking (e.g. reflecting), and empowering (e.g. demonstrating trust and delegating).

- **Indirectly influenced by the HRD practitioner in his/her role as a designer of formal interventions** that train and develop the line manager as facilitator, coach, or mentor as well as the individual employee in transferable knowledge and skills (such as team-working and interpersonal skills; understanding learning and reflection etc.). An important aspect of a 'devolved informal learning' strategy, which in turn acts as a precursor to 'empowered informal learning', is making employees aware of their learning styles which was discussed in chapter 4. Both organizations and employees can benefit from an appreciation of learning styles (Berings et al., 2005). The concept of learning style was discussed in chapter 4 where the work of Honey and Mumford was cited. Helping individuals to better understand their preferences will help them to become more aware of how and when they are learning on-the-job and make it easier for them to reflect on how they may be changing the combination of learning activities to suit different aspects of the job.

- **Indirectly influenced by the HRD practitioner in his/her role in nurturing** an appropriate learning environment. This includes the provision of resources to support learning as Brown and Duguid (2000) argue that when people have a need they will learn effectively and quickly as long as the resources for learning are made available. In the future these resources are likely to be increasingly reliant on technology (see *Media watch* box).

Arguably, the enhanced HRD cycle reflects much more accurately the multifaceted nature of an organization's learning system and the shift from training to learning discussed in chapter 1 in relation to the learning continuum. Ideally, stakeholders in the enhanced HRD cycle should be working in tandem in order to address the obstacles to workplace learning referred to in section 11.5. The role of the HRD practitioner is control-oriented in the original HRD cycle because the cycle needs to be managed carefully if the HRD intervention is to be effective (see chapter 5). In terms of the enhanced cycle the HRD practitioner needs to facilitate the 'shadow' processes through the adoption of 'devolved informal learning' and 'empowered informal learning' strategies. The principal focus is on creating the right conditions for informal learning to take place. This includes knowledge productivity (Tillema, 2006) and associated knowledge management processes as discussed in chapter 10.

MEDIA WATCH BOX

The role of technology and virtual environments in facilitating informal learning

Although it has been argued that company intranets as well as web browsers, search engines, discussion forums, and more recently social networking sites and blogs can stimulate informal learning by individuals there is a lack of empirical evidence to support these claims. Company intranets focus on the provision of information. E-learning platforms tend to be highly structured and simulate formal interventions. The quality and reliability of much of the content on the Internet is highly questionable. The efficacy of knowledge databases was discussed in chapter 10 which also highlighted the preference for face-to-face contact by advocates of the second wave practice-based perspective. Will things change in the future? Probably. It is dangerous to try and predict technological advancements. For instance, no one foresaw the popularity of mobile phone texts or social network sites. Yet, it is highly likely that the younger generation will prove more inclined to take advantage of future technology-based informal learning solutions. Particularly if these new systems are better at replicating the informal learning that currently characterizes face-to-face contact in communities of practice and social networks.

An example of an organization that is trying to use technology for both formal and informal learning is Turner Construction in the US. The company introduced collaboration centres which, in conjunction with the company's computerized knowledge systems, allow employees to join formal or informal communities for the purpose of sharing knowledge through collaborative working and/or accessing learning information. The collaboration centres are specific to business functions or web-based formal learning interventions. Another example is the accounting firm Ernst and Young who expect their employees to have 24/7 access to the knowledge and expertise needed to satisfy individual professional development needs. The company's global leadership programme builds on this approach and makes use of formal and informal learning experiences through the use of feedback mechanisms, peer-to-peer interactions between partners, and internal and external coaches. Through this collaborative approach more experienced partners are able to pass on the expertise they have accumulated over the years.

Source
http://www.clomedia.com (accessed 29 April 2008).

INSIGHTS INTO PRACTICE

Global perspectives on workplace learning (from *Advances in Developing Human Resources* Volume 8 Edition 3)

Regular practice of karma yoga, including in *svadhyaya* (experiential learning), and adopting *antharavalokana* (introspection) help members of the organization to learn and adopt the appropriate methods that not only help them in satisfying individual needs but also organizational goals. (Ashock and Thimmappa, 2006: 333)

A Buddhist approach to HRD encourages experiential learning. We should encourage the learner to actively test the ideas we bring to practice. (Johansen and Gopalakrishna, 2006: 344)

Dialogic techniques, mentoring, and pair or foursome study groups . . . characterise the contemporary approaches to learning used by Jewish adults . . . The adult learner in Jewish tradition is strongly tied to the workplace. (Beck, 2006: 366–8)

Learning from a Maori worldview is seen as a gradual process with understanding emerging from experience and maturity. (Papuni and Bartlett, 2006: 405)

Ubuntuism discourages the notion that the individual should take precedence over community . . . it emphasises the need for cooperation, moral, emotional, and social support, and group work. (Nafukho, 2006: 410–12)

Sources

[1] Ashock, H. S. and Thimmappa, M. S. 2006. A Hindu worldview of adult learning in the workplace, pp. 329–36.

[2] Johansen, B-C. P. and Gopalakrishna, D. 2006. A Buddhist view of adult learning in the workplace, pp. 337–45.

[3] Beck, J. K. 2006. Jewish adult learning and the workplace, pp. 364–72.

[4] Papuni, H. T. and Bartlett, K. R. 2006. Maori and Pakeha perspectives of adult learning in *Aotearoa*/New Zealand workplaces, pp. 400–7.

[5] Nafukho, F. M. 2006. Ubuntu worldview: a traditional African view of adult learning in the workplace, pp. 408–15.

Summary

The extent to which workplace learning is encouraged or nurtured is arguably dependent more on the role of the manager than the HRD function/practitioner and/or formal HRD processes:

> Many organisations without formal HRD mechanisms nonetheless provide communities of learning and environments of practice that are extremely productive and developmental. The problem does not lie with structures. It lies with attitudes and expectations and commitments. It lies in the way in which particularly managers in organisations value the people with whom they work. (Garvey and Williamson, 2002: 134)

Self-reflection can be embedded through the interplay of devolved informal and empowered informal learning strategies. The challenge for organizations is to find ways to nurture an organization within which informal learning can flourish without having to resort to control-oriented strategies. The primary facilitator of informal learning is the line manager with support and guidance from the HRD practitioner.

As was highlighted in chapter 2 the prevailing perspectives on HRD may be predominantly Anglo-American at present but this situation is starting to change. The *Insights into practice* box offers a brief glimpse of different perspectives on workplace learning from around the world.

Review questions

1 Define and explain the concepts of informal, incidental, and unintended learning.

2 What is the relationship between knowledge, knowledge management, and learning?

3 What are the principal obstacles to informal learning developing in the workplace?

4 Explain the respective roles of the HRD practitioner and line manager in developing informal learning.

5 How can informal learning be triggered in the workplace?

Suggestions for further reading

1 Lave, J. and Wenger, E. 1991. *Situated Learning: Legitimate Peripheral Participation*. Cambridge: Cambridge University Press.

This remains a seminal text and is a relatively slim volume. It links together some of the central themes in chapters 10 and 11.

2 Billet, S. 2004. Learning through work: workplace participatory practices. In H. Rainbird, A. Fuller and A. Munro (eds.) *Workplace Learning in Context*. London: Routledge.

Anything by Billet is usually worth reading so even if you cannot get hold of this book you can still search for his articles on the subject.

3 Doornbos, A. J., Bolhus, S. and Simons, P. R-J. 2004. Modeling work-related learning on the basis of intentionality and developmental relatedness: a noneducational perspective. *Human Resource Development Review*, 3 (3): 250–74.

A good review of current theory and practice of workplace learning which explains and contrasts educational and non-educational perspectives.

4 Clarke, N. 2005. Workplace learning environment and its relationship with learning outcomes in healthcare organisations. *Human Resource Development International*, 8 (2): 185–205.

An interesting and informative discussion of workplace learning which is based on an empirical study of hospices in the UK.

5 Ellinger, A. D. 2005. Contextual factors influencing informal learning in a workplace setting: the case of reinventing itself company. *Human Resource Development Quarterly*, 16 (3): 389–415.

A highly informative analysis and discussion of the contextual factors that influence informal learning in the workplace based on a qualitative case study.

Case study

Informal learning in a hotel context

Swinton Park is an exclusive luxury hotel of 30 bedrooms located in North Yorkshire eight miles from Ripon. It is set in 200 acres of parklands and gardens, and offers a wide range of facilities to guests. It also has a Cookery School run by a celebrity chef. The hotel was opened in 2001 and employs about seventy full-time and part-time staff, although this number fluctuates due to seasonal demands. In April 2002 the Hotel was awarded Investors in People and since then has received several sector awards including 'Outstanding Customer Service Award' in 2006. The hotel's approach to training and development is a blend of formal and informal initiatives. Given the nature of most jobs at the hotel both induction and ongoing training are highly practical. New employees undertake a comprehensive induction followed by an informal staff review after three months. This socialization process is further supported by informal learning activities such as job shadowing which has been highly successful for the transfer of knowledge and skills from experienced individuals to new employees (although there have been some failures indicating that this approach does not suit everyone). Job shadowing is also used when employees are first promoted. The emphasis is on the relatively gradual accumulation of expertise rather than 'throwing people in at the deep end'. Experienced employees have also learnt from new employees who often have knowledge and skills gained from working in other organizations.

Ongoing training is predominantly on-the-job for managers and other employees and includes interventions such as job rotation which enables individuals to broaden their knowledge and skills as well as gain an insight into other aspects of the organization. Selection for this is based on a lottery system (taking names from a hat). Although the frequency of this intervention is affected by trading circumstances it is clearly a key aspect of the hotel's training and development strategy. A research study that involved a series of staff interviews reveals that employees learn informally through doing their work and resolving problems that they encounter on a daily basis. Employees are encouraged to try out new ideas for improving their jobs and if the idea is successful it will be adopted as a new work routine. The employees who were interviewed spoke positively about the opportunities available to them to learn and seemed to appreciate the interest taken in them by the owners and managers.

Employees are keen to acknowledge the help and support they receive from colleagues and it is apparent that this social aspect of work is seen as being very important. Managers stress the importance of teamwork as well as good communications and the sharing of information. Consequently, formal staff committees and meetings are held regularly and employees are able to submit feedback forms to management on any issue. Informal shift meetings tend to be held daily and employees are able to raise any issue they want at these. Support networks between individuals in different departments have also emerged and evolved over time.

Management believe in recognizing the efforts of their employees and also in providing them with customer feedback. Monthly work reviews are conducted to recognize any staff achievements and this approach is seen as being highly motivational by many employees. The hotel's owners would like to see a system that recognizes the organizational benefits of informal learning including some form of qualification for individual employee's informal learning. Full-time staff are also formally appraised on an annual basis.

Sources

[1] http://www.inflow.eu.com (Informal Learning Opportunities in the Workplace—Case Studies) (accessed 25 March 2008).

[2] http://www.swintonpark.com (accessed 27 March 2008).

[3] http://www.mrsconsultancy.com/Services/Pages/News/Swinton.htm (accessed 9 July 2008).

Case study questions

1. To what extent does the hotel's approach to training and development conform and/or differ to the theories and perspectives set out in the chapter?

2. To what extent does this case illustrate the importance of horizontal integration between HRD and HRM?

3. How feasible would it be to introduce a system that can measure the benefits of informal learning including the provision of a qualification for employees?

Online resource centre

Visit the supporting online resource centre for additional material that will help you with your research, essays, assignments, and revision.

 www.oxfordtextbooks.co.uk/orc/mankin/

12

HRD in Small and Medium Sized Enterprises (SMEs)

Rod Stone and David Mankin

Learning objectives

By the end of this chapter you should be able to:

* Appreciate variations in how small and medium sized enterprises (SMEs) are defined

* Explain the nature of HRD in SMEs

* Appreciate the principal differences between HRD practices in small and medium sized firms

* Understand the principal differences between HRD practices in SMEs and larger organizations

* Critically evaluate the potential contribution that HRD practices can make to SMEs

In order to achieve these objectives it is important that you not only read the chapter carefully but also complete the activities and review questions, and undertake some of the suggested further reading.

Indicative content

■ Definitions of small and medium sized enterprises (SMEs)

■ The nature and role of HRM practices and training in SMEs

■ The respective contributions of formal and informal learning to SME performance

■ The influence of the owner-manager/entrepreneur on business and HRD practices in SMEs

- Other factors influencing HRD practices in SMEs

- The quality of management expertise in SMEs

- The key strengths and weaknesses of SMEs

- The importance of individual competence to the intellectual capital of smaller firms

Key concepts

Small and medium sized enterprises (SMEs)

E-business

Competence (including core competence)

Entrepreneur

Formal and informal training and learning

12.1 **Introduction**

Small and medium sized enterprises (SMEs) play a key role in national economies particularly in countries such as Australia, Finland, Norway, South Korea, Spain, Taiwan, and the US. Across Europe there are approximately twenty million firms of which 99 per cent are SMEs that employ about 67 per cent of the total workforce (Gray, 2004); while in China there are 120 million 'township and enterprise ventures' that are predominantly small businesses employing five or less people (Fishman, 2006). In the US and Canada SMEs generate 85 per cent and 80 per cent of new jobs respectively (Montazemi, 2006). Many SMEs have been able to exploit technology and the Internet to compete in global markets for the first time (Ulrichch and Brockbank, 2005) although there are variations between nations. For instance, US manufacturing SMEs make better use of information technology than Canadian manufacturing SMEs (Montazemi, 2006). Governments are now recognizing the potential economic benefits of SMEs engaging in e-business (Brown et al., 2005). Additionally, the outsourcing of supply chains by larger organizations has provided many smaller firms with the opportunity to create niche markets supplying specialist products and/or services. This enables larger firms to exploit the levels of flexibility and innovation that characterize the activities of many SMEs (Tan et al., 2006).

It is only recently that SMEs have started to take an interest in HRM practices (Price, 2004) albeit that practices in smaller firms tend to be informal and ad hoc. Gray (2004) notes that due to resource constraints most SMEs 'take an instrumental approach to most HR matters and are likely to be aware of which activities offer value for money' (p. 466). Although there has been a lack of research into the role of HRD practices in SMEs there have been a variety of studies that focus on the impact of specific HRM practices such as performance management, recruitment, reward, and training. These have highlighted the extent to which many SMEs have very little or no training provision at all and those that do tend to adopt a pragmatic approach (Boxall and Purcell, 2008) that is based on 'small-firm, not large-firm, logic' (Hill, 2002: 141). This means that many of the concepts and models discussed in earlier chapters are not automatically applicable to SMEs. Medium sized firms may have some similarities with larger firms, such as an organizational structure based on functions, but the vast majority of SMEs tend to be small or very small businesses employing only a handful of people (see *Media watch* box). It is not surprising then that the primary influence on many SMEs is the owner-manager. For instance, a study of SMEs in India by Kasturi et al. (2006) reveals that it is the attitude of the owner-manager rather than the adoption of HRM practices that has the more significant impact on firm performance.

As with other practices, much of the learning and training that takes place in SMEs tends to be informal (Stewart and Tansley, 2002). In comparison to larger organizations SMEs are characterized by much lower levels of off-the-job training despite research showing that those firms which invest more in training tend to perform better. For instance, a study involving 168 fast-growth family-owned SMEs in the US reveals that there is a positive correlation between investment in training and firm performance (Carlson et al., 2006). The difficulty for many SMEs is that training can be expensive,

MEDIA WATCH BOX

International comparisons in the farming industry— UK and China

Across the globe farming knowledge and expertise accrues through experience which has been passed on from generation to generation by farming families. In the developed nations this approach has been supplemented with formal training and education (for instance, courses at agricultural colleges in the UK). The farming or agriculture sector tends to be ignored in much of the mainstream literature on business and management yet half of the world's population is still involved in farming. Agricultural practices may have been transformed by technology in developed nations, leading to fewer and bigger farms, but the small farm remains the dominant business model in this sector around the world. However, there are wide variations in what constitutes a small farm business as these two cases from the UK and China illustrate.

In the UK between 1995 and 2005 farming income fell by 60 per cent and 59,000 farm workers quit the industry. The majority of UK farmers make a net income of £20,000 or less. Upland hill farms and dairy farms have suffered the worst (7,000 dairy farms went out of business between 1994 and 2003). However, there are still opportunities for entrepreneurial farmers. Linda and Peter Williams run a farm and farm shop in Surrey. They started the business in 1999 when they spotted a gap in the market for local organic produce. At first they struggled financially and it was six years before they made a profit. Today they have six people working for them on a full-time basis and an annual turnover of £300,000. In contrast, in the far west of China Kasam Sayim is regarded as a relatively wealthy farmer. He owns one hectare of land and seven sheep and uses the land to grow grapes which he then sells, making US$5,300 in a good year (in other provinces annual income for farmers can be as low as US$12.50). He has six children who all have mobile phones and he communicates with one of his sons, who is studying at university, by email. Presently, 50 per cent of those employed in China at the end of 2003 were working in the agricultural sector. The small farming family is the primary and traditional agricultural model in China.

Sources

[1] Rifkin, J. 2000. *The End of Work: The Decline of the Globl Workforce and the Dawn of the Post-Market Era.* London: Penguin Books.

[2] Fishman, T. C. 2006. *China Inc: The relentless rise of the next great superpower.* London: Pocket Books.

[3] Ke, J., Chermack, T. J., Lee, Y-H. and Lin, J. 2006. National human resource development in transitioning societies in the developing world: the People's Republic of China. *Advances in Developing Human Resources,* 8 (1): 28–45.

[4] *New Scientist,* 10 November 2007: 60.

[5] Hutton, W. 2007. *The Writing on the Wall: China and the West in the 21st Century.* London: Little, Brown.

[6] *The Mail on Sunday,* 25 May 2008: 75.

[7] Kingsnorth, P. 2008. *Real England: The Battle Against the Bland.* London: Portobello Books.

it can create logistical problems such as finding staff cover, and there is no guarantee that any benefits will be realized. For many owner-managers training is regarded as a cost rather than an investment and many worry about an employee becoming too qualified and subsequently leaving or being poached. Not surprisingly, the take up of newer approaches to employee learning, such as e-learning, remain 'lacklustre' across Europe (Brown et al., 2006: 418).

12.2 Small and medium sized enterprises (SMEs)

SMEs defined

Presently there is no universal definition of a SME and this can make cross-border comparisons problematic. Most definitions tend to focus on numerical size which can infer the existence of a monolithic sector whereas the reality is a complex pattern of diversity within and between nations. Research studies have also not differentiated between factors such as ethnic and cultural background instead focusing on firm performance generally (Shoobridge, 2006). In Europe SMEs are defined as businesses with fewer than 250 employees (Hall, 2004). This is consistent with the European Commission's 1996 recommendations (cited in Stewart and Tansley, 2002):

- Very small or micro firms: 0 to 9 employees
- Small firms: 10 to 49 employees
- Medium firms: 50 to 249 employees

INSIGHTS INTO PRACTICE

The demise of small businesses

Wal-Mart, with 140 million consumers using its stores every week and an annual turnover of US$250 billion, is an illustration of how multinationals have been impacting on local communities and small businesses. The decision to locate stores out-of-town has been crucial to its success but this has resulted in fewer consumers using town centre stores. In addition the company has used its market power to minimize costs and maximize profits. Suppliers are squeezed (in the 1990s there was a campaign against the company's purchasing of clothing from suppliers who used child labour; this included the company being 'awarded' the title 'sweatshop retailer of the year'). Employees are squeezed (low wages; only half the 1.4 million workforce covered by health and medical benefits). Employee turnover remains high and, with expansion plans continuing, the company needs to find vast numbers of new employees every year. Recently, the company has had requests to build new stores rejected (e.g. Inglewood near Los Angeles in the US).

Sources
[1] Kay, J. 2004. *The Truth about Markets: Why Some Nations are Rich but Most Remain Poor.* London: Penguin Books.
[2] Saul, J. R. 2005. *The Collapse of Globalism: And the Reinvention of the World.* London: Atlantic Books.
[3] Woolf, M. 2005. *Why Globalisation Works.* London: Yale University Press.
[4] Fishman, T. C. 2006. *China Inc: The Rrelentless Rise of the Next Great Superpower.* London: Pocket Books.
[5] MacGillivray, A. 2006. *Globalisation.* London: Robinson.
[6] Stiglitz, J. 2007. *Making Globalisation Work.* London: Penguin Books.

Wal-Mart's approach to store expansion and the negative impact this has had on high street stores has also been replicated in the UK by leading supermarkets including Wal-Mart-owned Asda. This strategy has already enabled Tesco to capture over 30 per cent of the UK market. In some cases the supermarkets have been criticized for building stores bigger than that allowed under the planning process but then gaining retrospective permission for the change in size. The impact on town centres and small business has been huge: 30,000 independent retailers selling food, beverages, or tobacco have closed down over the last decade; 8,600 independent grocery stores closed down between 2000 and 2005; and, 13,000 independent newsagents closed down between 1995 and 2004. However, supermarkets have also been opening smaller stores, such as Tesco's Express stores and Sainsbury's Locals, that have impacted on the performance of independent retailers in towns and cities. Marks and Spencer is also opening smaller outlets; although the head of Asda argues that only 10 per cent of the anticipated £60 billion growth between 2008 and 2012 will come from these small stores. Meanwhile Waitrose is launching a new strategy of building up to 100 half sized stores in market towns which will specialize in selling local produce. The company's managing director is adamant that this will not have a negative impact on local independent food businesses arguing that Waitrose's approach creates a 'food culture' in the town which benefits everyone. The first store has already opened in the town of St. Neots which has a population of 30,000 and currently just one independent greengrocer which has survived to date by diversifying its product range to include flowers, plants, and pet food.

Sources
[1] Hutton, W. 2003. *The World We're In.* London: Abacus.
[2] Kingsnorth, P. 2008. *Real England: The Battle Against the Bland.* London: Portobello Books.
[3] *Guardian,* 3 May 2008: 41.
[4] *Guardian,* 17 May 2008: 16.

The vast majority of SMEs in Europe fall within the very small or micro firm category (Gray, 2004). In other countries there are different definitions. For instance, in their study of small to mid-size organizations in the US, Hite and McDonald (2006) refer to the Urban League's categorization whereby large organizations start at 5,000 or more employees (somewhat significantly higher than the 250 figure in Europe). In Australia they are defined as organizations with up to 199 employees (Kotey and Folker, 2007). In Indonesia

SMEs comprise micro enterprises (1 to 4 employees), small enterprises (5 to 19), and medium enterprises (20–99) with large organizations starting at 100 employees (Tambunan, 2007). While in China SMEs are defined as firms with less than 2,000 employees reflecting the labour-intensive nature of Chinese firms generally (Yu and Bell, 2007). Many of these smaller firms around the world are family-owned. They provide the 'backbone' of national economies although many are now being forced out of business by the market power of multinational corporations (Stiglitz, 2007), as illustrated in the *Insights into practice* box.

The role of the entrepreneur

> **Key concept**   Entrepreneur
>
> An entrepreneur is someone who sets up a business often at considerable personal risk and takes personal responsibility for the strategic and operational management of that business.

One of the characteristics of the global economy is the growth in entrepreneurial activities. The entrepreneur (owner-manager) is often the crucial factor in determining the international strategy for a SME (Ruzzier et al., 2007). It is for this reason that the government in Indonesia has included training in entrepreneurship in government-supported programmes (Tambunan, 2007). The number of adults starting their own business is one in eight in Brazil, one in ten in the US and one in twelve in Australia (Price, 2004). In the UK where it is one in 33 (ibid.) it is not only the younger generation who are adopting an entrepreneurial approach and setting up their own business; so too are the older generation (see *Media watch* box).

However, in a study of automotive and aerospace industry Brown et al. (2004) noted that UK-based SMEs suffer from:

- Poor management
- Inefficient work design
- Low productivity levels
- Failure to meet quality standards
- Failure to meet delivery schedules
- Inadequate employee skills
- Poor development of e-commerce
- Reliance on commodity products (rather than those that add value)

Lack of management expertise is believed to be crucial to explaining the high failure rate of small firms, for instance in Australia an estimated 30,000 fail annually (Doyle, 2007). Certain segments of the SME sector can experience particular difficulties. For instance, ethnic minority businesses, such as restaurants and retail outlets, tend to involve low cost

MEDIA WATCH BOX

The new generation of entrepreneurs

Rayment Kirby was in his sixties when he set up his own camera-making business. His cameras sell for up to £1,500 and are based on traditional designs. Mr Kirby is typical of a growing number of older people who are exploiting years of accumulated experience and becoming entrepreneurs rather than opting for retirement. Another example is Neilson Kite. Now 65 years old Mr Kite's business, called Tomorrow's Business, provides training and coaching interventions. Businesses that involve giving advice are particularly popular with older people.

Source
The Sunday Times (Business Section), 2 March 2008, p. 13.

labour-intensive processes and suffer from under-funding, poorly equipped and underinsured premises (Shoobridge, 2006). Under-funding is probably the most intractable problem facing ethnic minority small businesses in Europe and the US (Ram and Barrett, 2000). Dowling and Welch (2004) note that Asian family firms like to keep as much control as possible within the family (immediate or extended). This is likely to constrain the firm's ability to operate internationally.

12.3 Human resource development in SMEs

The principal strengths of SMEs

The two principal strengths of SMEs are the ability to be flexible about terms and conditions of employment and the ability to recognize the individuality of each employee (Goodwins, 2008). Theoretically, these should underpin HRD strategies for training and development as well as HRM strategies for recruitment, reward, and retention. Yet, in the UK 44 per cent of SMEs offer no formal training although this figure is 55 per cent for very small or micro firms and only 13 per cent for medium firms (Gray, 2004). In Korea and the electronics sector in India this lack of investment is one of the factors that differentiate SMEs from large firms (Singh et al., 2005; Jeon et al., 2006). Training and development is also less evident than other HRM practices in many SMEs in China which is consistent with findings from studies in the US and UK (Zheng et al., 2006). For instance, in a study in the US, Hite and McDonald (2006) note that SMEs tend to lack the time and resources to implement training programmes. While the findings from a study of differently sized Russian enterprises supports the generally held view that size is a crucial influencing factor on training and development practices with larger firms regarding it as an important long term investment rather than a cost (Ardichvili and Dirani, 2005).

> **! TIPS AND HINTS**
>
> It is more appropriate to refer to training than HRD when discussing small firms.

Factors influencing HRD practices in SMEs

Price (2004) identifies a range of factors influencing HRM practices in SMEs and from these can be selected the following which can have a particular an impact on HRD:

- Variability in the quality of communications (e.g. employees may not be aware of any of the firm's objectives)

- Variability in the levels of employee commitment (e.g. employees who relate to the owner-manager are likely to stay much longer)

- Change tends to be reactive (e.g. short term operational rather than long term strategic perspective)

- Competence is dependent on the personal knowledge held by employees and owner-manager (e.g. focus is on practical skills and learning from experience)

- Lack of creativity (e.g. a tendency to stick with known products and services)

- Cost consciousness (e.g. tight budgets means little cash for investment in training and development)

SMEs can be a major source of workforce skills, innovation and, increasingly for those in developed nations, of international trading, although operating internationally can stretch the limited resources available to the SME (Dowling and Welch, 2004). Innovation requires an investment in learning, training and development which can be achieved through a blend of formal and informal interventions: for instance, specialist courses for research and development personnel, project management skills for project leaders, the setting up of problem-solving teams, and the cultivation and facilitation of informal groups (see chapters 5, 10, and 11). These examples reflect the extent to which organizations need processes in place for managing organizational knowledge and learning. However, there has been relatively little research carried out by HRD academics on the nature of organizational knowledge and learning processes in SMEs. Whereas large organizations often have sophisticated knowledge management systems (technology- and people-based) the intellectual capital of SMEs tends to be held by individual employees (Camuffo and Comacchio, 2005). Consequently, competence development is critical to the growth of small firms (Salvato, 2007).

> **Key concept**   Competence
>
> Competence is the combination of an organization's technologies with the knowledge, skills, and abilities of its employees. It determines the viability and competitiveness of an organization.

INSIGHTS INTO PRACTICE

The role of personal knowledge in SMEs in Italy

This case comprises the results from two research studies that illustrate the importance of individual competence to smaller firms. Personal knowledge often constitutes a small firm's core competence.*

Small firms in Italy comprising 20 or less employees are characterized by high levels of production capacity but low levels of education. Employees with formal qualifications are in the minority. Data show that only 36 per cent of workers have successfully completed eight years of compulsory education; and only 8 per cent have a recognized vocational qualification. Yet many of these firms are competing in national and international markets and their employees are demonstrating high levels of competence in the jobs they do. This suggests that individual employees accrue, over time and through experience, tacit knowledge (also referred to as know-how or practical skills) that is invaluable to these firms. The findings from a study of small firms reveal that employees are able to carry out several jobs within a 'field of activity' shared with other employees. This conveys the nature of work in these small firms better than concepts such as tasks or jobs. The findings from another study of the individual competencies of 310 middle managers working in 46 SMEs in Italy revealed:

1. The personal knowledge of middle managers accrues through experience (i.e. learning by doing) and they are able to pass this knowledge (particularly tacit knowledge or know-how) onto others through a combination of goal oriented decision making, problem-solving, and the mentoring of new talent

2. Organizational knowledge is socially embedded. There is very limited evidence of technological know-how and in some cases the ability to use communications technology was nonexistent. This supports the generally held view that the acquisition of individual knowledge occurs predominantly within social contexts (see chapter 10)

3. Individual skills and competencies are the principal source of intellectual capital and competitive advantage

4. The core capabilities that were identified included: flexibility and cost reduction; incremental innovation (e.g. customization of products); and, commitment and social skills

Sources
[1] Meghnagi, S. 2004. Work organization, 'fields of activities' and workers' competence: the case of Italian small firms. In H. Rainbird, A. Fuller and A. Munro (eds.) *Workplace Learning in Context*. London: Routledge.
[2] Camuffo, A. and Comacchio, A. 2005. Linking intellectual capital and competitive advantage: a cross-firm competence model for north-east Italian SMEs in the manufacturing industry. *Human Resource Development International*, 8 (3): 361–77.
* A core competence is defined as 'a bundle of skills and technologies that enables a company to provide benefit to customers' (Hamel and Prahalad, 996: 219).

The increase in inter-firm networking (see below) is also highlighting the role of inter-firm competencies as a source of competitive advantage (Hann and Walsh, 2002). Such competencies will vary across nations and sectors. The three most critical competencies for SMEs in the electronics sector in India are: using information to optimize decision-making; introducing new technology; and, identifying market changes (Singh et al., 2005). Yet a study of SMEs in China suggests that SMEs should place greater emphasis on employee commitment as a way of improving firm performance (Zheng et al., 2006). This may simply reflect the current situation in China where the commercial focus has been on the mass-manufacture of low cost products.

ACTIVITY 12.1

What are the principal implications for the practice of HRD of the findings from the study of Italian SMEs discussed in the *Insights into practice* box?

Who takes responsibility for HRD in SMEs?

Most SMEs tend to value practical skills more than formal qualifications. Often the intellectual capital of a firm is represented by the actual entrepreneur (owner-manager) who determines the strategic direction of the SME (Ruzzier et al., 2007). The extent to which he/she is able to exploit his/her human and social capital can be the difference between a successful and unsuccessful business. Whilst knowledge is socially embedded in SMEs it is less likely that communities of practice (see chapter 10) will emerge in smaller firms as there are likely to be very few employees doing similar work (Smith and Sadler-Smith, 2006).

! TIPS AND HINTS

The social capital of most owner-managers is predominantly external to the firm in the form of contacts such as suppliers and customers. Maintaining these contacts as well as developing new ones is usually a major priority for such firms. The emphasis is less on the leveraging of new knowledge and more on ensuring the continued survival of the business.

SMEs, particularly smaller firms, are highly unlikely to have a dedicated HRD practitioner who can help the firm to develop its knowledge assets because of cost constraints. Smaller organizations tend to have a lean structure which makes it difficult to allocate specialist facilitation roles to assist with OD interventions, such as continuous improvement programmes (Thomas and Webb, 2003). This role is only found in medium sized firms which replicate the functional structure of large organizations. Even medium sized firms may have to employ such a person on a part-time basis and will lack the HRD infra-structure associated with larger firms (Walton, 1999). This equates to the one-person HRD model proposed by Gilley and Maycunich Gilley (2003) in which:

> HRD practitioners are jack-of-all-trades. In other words, a single person is respons-
> ible for identifying and analysing employees' needs; designing, developing, and
> implementing training programs; and evaluating their success . . . Therefore, the
> effectiveness of HRD often suffers. (pp. 19–20)

Normally the owner-manager in smaller firms takes responsibility for HRD although
he/she probably lacks any real understanding of training processes. Even an employee
designated with responsibility in a medium sized firm is unlikely to be professionally
qualified or passionate about the role (Gilley and Maycunich Gilley, 2003). This is in stark
contrast to the range of alternative models for the design and structure of the HRD function in large organizations which are discussed in the next chapter.

Organizational learning processes in SMEs

In terms of organizational learning processes, Salvato (2007) identifies the following
learning opportunities that can be exploited when a SME is adopting a strategy of growth
through acquisitions (a strategy normally associated with larger organizations): learning
from mistakes and learning from missed targets. These learning opportunities enable the
firm to develop employee competencies that can be leveraged by the firm in future situations. Learning from mistakes has also been shown as crucial to the effective implementation of lean manufacturing in an Indian SME (Kumar et al., 2006). A study involving 359
SMEs in Ireland reveals that entrepreneurially driven firms tend to adopt a more formal
approach to strategic planning as this helps them to learn about the external environment
and firm capabilities (Gibbons and O'Connor, 2005). This demonstrates an appreciation
of organizational knowledge and learning processes. The importance of strategic management has been demonstrated in other studies involving SMEs. For instance, Karami
(2005) shows that the adoption of formal or informal techniques for strategic management can have a positive impact on firm performance and, in particular, help to solve
organizational problems and reduce organizational conflict. He notes that informal
approaches in particular enable SMEs to respond quickly to changes in the market.

❗ TIPS AND HINTS

The structured, rational models of strategic management beloved by business schools
around the world have limited application to the SME context where much of a firm's
strategic planning, implementation, and review takes place in the head of one person
— the owner-manager.

12.4 **Formal HRD provision**

The principal types of formal HRD provision in SMEs

Formal HRD provision encompasses: organizational development projects; career development activities; training courses and workshops; business seminars and conferences;
education programmes; structured on-the-job training. These are typically characteristic

of larger organizations which have the advantage of: more resources, economies of scales, and a HRD infrastructure (e.g. HRD function whether centralized, decentralized, outsourced, or virtual—see chapter 13). For many SMES and particularly smaller firms the primary focus is on training. As a study of TQM practices in Malaysian SMEs by Rahman and Tannock (2005) shows the adoption of structured training programmes makes an important contribution to the successful implementation of organization-wide change programmes. This finding is supported by other studies, for instance: training plays a key role in the adoption of TQM practices in Australian SMEs particularly in the service sector (Prajogo and Brown, 2006); while in a case study investigation of lean manufacturing processes in a manufacturing SME in India training was one of several key factors affecting successful implementation (Kumar et al., 2006).

Although the cost of training is the biggest problem confronting SMEs (Hall, 2004) just over half the SMEs in the UK provide training for their employees at an annual cost of £5.8 billion (Bacon and Hoque, 2005). However, training is far less prevalent in small firms (Forde and MacKenzie, 2004) which have tended to concentrate on recruiting people who are already suitably qualified (Pattanayak, 2003). For those SMEs that do engage with training the most popular approach is formal on-the-job training (Webster et al., 2005). For instance, while 78 per cent of large firms in the UK construction sector support training leading to externally recognized qualifications, this figure is 44 per cent in medium sized and 38 per cent in small sized firms operating in the same sector (Forde and MacKenzie, 2004). Cost of training has also been identified as a problem in SMEs in China which to date have relied on readily available low-skilled labour producing low-cost products (Zheng et al., 2006). As China's economy continues to develop this situation is likely to change.

> **! TIPS AND HINTS**
>
> Sometimes it can be more effective to identify the costs of not training and the impact that this is likely to have on an organization's performance.

The vast majority of the world's firms are family-owned (Dowling and Welch, 2004). However, not only do family-owned SMEs invest far less in the training and development of employees than non-family firms (Carlson et al., 2006) there is also a consequent lack of management training. Owner-managers may have good technical skills but often lack effective managerial and associated business skills (Webster et al., 2005). Studies such as that of small family businesses in Finland confirm that there is a need for more management training and development (Malineu, 2001). The amount of management development taking place in any organization is directly linked to the size of the organization: the larger the organization the more there is and, conversely, the smaller the organization the less there is (Storey, 2004). Key management skills have been identified as: financial management; utilizing information; organizing and delegating; marketing; managing employees; handling technological change; scheduling production; and, purchase control (Doyle, 2007). Relying on existing knowledge and experience can lead to very mixed results depending on the competence of owner-managers who can have a very different mindset to managers working in larger organizations. For instance, many smaller firms focus on autonomy and independence rather than profits and growth (Gray, 1998). Owner-managers tend to possess tacit knowledge which has been accumulated through experience that is often narrowly focused and they often lack transferable skills. Much of their time is spent on reacting to operational demands and problems thus making it difficult to adopt a more strategic approach to the business (Brown et al., 2004).

Storey (2004) shows that there is a wide variation between countries over who are the major providers of management training for SMEs:

- Educational institutions and public organizations in Finland
- Private sector training consultants/firms and chambers of commerce/industry associations in Germany (all firms are required to be members of a local chamber of commerce)
- Chambers of commerce/industry associations and public organizations in Japan
- Private sector training consultants/firms and educational institutions in the US
- Educational institutions, private sector training consultants/firms, and chambers of commerce/industry associations in the UK

In the UK government initiatives that target SMEs have been emphasizing the importance of management training and development (Fuller-Love, 2006).

The advantages of smaller firms

However, smaller firms do have several advantages such as agility (i.e. the ability to respond very quickly to changes in skills requirements), informality, and shared values (Smith and Sadler-Smith, 2006). The size of the firm means that employees can acquire an overview and understanding of the firm's entire processes that is not always feasible in larger organizations (van den Berg et al., 2006). Size also means that they are often able to react faster to changing economic circumstances, such as a recession (van den Berg, 2006). These advantages explain why many larger organizations give so much autonomy to business units. The aim is to have business units that can respond quickly to changes 'on the ground' but which are able to exploit the benefits of corporate resources and its brand (Fung et al., 2008). Li and Fung, the world's largest sourcing company with annual sales of US$8 billion, has 170 business units with each comprising between 20 and 50 employees generating annual sales of US$20 to US$70 million (ibid.).

Government support for HRD in SMEs

Governments can implement a wide range of initiatives to support SMEs and facilitate higher levels of training and development. For instance, they can introduce tax reductions and/or rebates, and training subsidies (Nilsson et al., 2005). Government initiatives vary from country to country (see chapter 1) although there appears to be a consensus generally that an interventionist policy is needed to encourage SMEs to focus on training

MEDIA WATCH BOX

When size really does matter—the impact of the global economy on small haulage firms in the UK

There are approximately 150,000 small haulage firms in the UK that are now experiencing real difficulties as a result of the continuing global rise in the price of crude oil. In the last month alone the price of diesel has risen by 7 pence a litre. Many small haulage firms have gone into liquidation as these rises turn potential profits into losses. In comparison Eddie Stobart, a large haulage company, has been passing the additional fuel costs on to customers. Angry hauliers have decided to stage a protest in London to make their feelings known to the government. Since March this year the UK government has raised an extra £730 million through windfall taxes on North Sea oil companies.

Sources
[1] *Mail on Sunday*, 25 May 2008: 52.
[2] *Daily Express*, 26 May 2008: 1–2.

(Rigby, 2004). The UK is regarded as having the most developed approach to the financial support of small businesses in the whole of Europe (and also better than the US), for instance, tax incentives that encourage people to set up a business (Walburn, 2005). In contrast, in developing countries such as Indonesia there can be problems with the organization of training provision by local government (Tambunan, 2007). In Singapore government policies have failed to address the tradition of SMEs being characterized by little training and poorly skilled employees (Ashton et al., 2002). A study of SMEs in China reveals that the government has not provided SMEs with sufficient guidance and training on specific issues, such as managing in a socially responsible manner (Yu and Bell, 2007).

Some owners of SMEs are unaware of government initiatives while others are too busy to find out (Hall, 2004). Smaller businesses in the UK have proven difficult to persuade to support government training initiatives (Matlay, 2004). A key finding from a study in the tourism and hospitality sector in the UK identifies that whilst there is a wide range of training provision available in the sector it is often poorly understood and rarely accessed by firms (Dewhurst et al., 2007). In The Netherlands SMEs are not as successful as large organizations at securing training subsidies (van den Berg et al., 2006). There can also be problems of perception. Nilsson et al. (2005) report on a four year programme designed to upgrade business skills in eight SMEs in the tourism sector of Sweden. A range of approaches was adopted that included training courses, group activities, and group discussions but whilst these focused on content (i.e. to give participants tools and techniques) the entrepreneurs attending wanted consulting advice (ibid.). This mirrors the emphasis on customized training discussed above/below.

Direct impact (primary importance)	Indirect impact (secondary importance)
Market position (e.g. firms with low-cost products and services react to market changes and carry out little training)	Time constraints and logistics (e.g. lack of time; availability of cover; operational issues taking precedence; knowing how to get advice and support which can often be time consuming and involve highly bureaucratic processes)
Prevailing economy (i.e. favourable or unfavourable)	Cost of training provided by external consultants, training providers and education institutions (e.g. lack of funds/training budget)
Availability of relevant training (e.g. shortages in the training provision needed by the firm; lack of customized interventions)	Lack of in-house providers (i.e. reflection of firm's size)
Perceived value of training and development (e.g. concerns about the lack of any return on the investment)	Perceived lack of focus to business advice from external bodies; lack of training tailored to needs of the firm; learner motivation (e.g. can be inconsistent; lack of previous formal education)

Table 12.1 Factors impacting on training provision in SMEs in the UK
Sources: Based on Matlay, 2000; Sadler-Smith et al., 2000; Barclay, 2005; Doyle, 2007

Factors that impact on training provision in SMEs

A study by Matlay (2000) reveals a range of factors that have directly or indirectly impacted on training provision in small firms (see table 12.1 for an adapted and expanded version of these factors). Barriers identified in Australian small firms fall into three categories: features of the training (e.g. cost and relevance of external provision); features of the workforce (e.g. type of contract, levels of employee turnover); features of the firm (e.g. tendency for a short term focus, fear of qualified staff leaving or being poached; cost constraints) (Smith and Sadler-Smith, 2006). These barriers reflect constraints that can impact on the growth and development of SMEs generally: poor infrastructure (e.g. transport links, utilities, standard of premises; firms operating in isolated areas are unable to access the training); institution (e.g. lack of access to training; poor education standards; limited access to finance opportunities); and, economic issues (e.g. limited access to technology; lack of working capital) (Tambunan, 2007).

In tackling the challenges of the knowledge economy and providing effective training in organizations the government and employers in all types and size of organization need to address barriers to learning (Stewart and Tansley, 2002). These barriers are shown in figure 12.1 and can be seen to correspond with the factors of secondary importance in table 12.1 above.

> **! TIPS AND HINTS**
>
> Persuading some owner-managers to invest in HRD interventions that will address barriers to learning is rather like persuading someone with a serious drink problem to admit to being an alcoholic. But until this happens it is highly unlikely that the underlying causes of the problem(s) can ever be rectified.

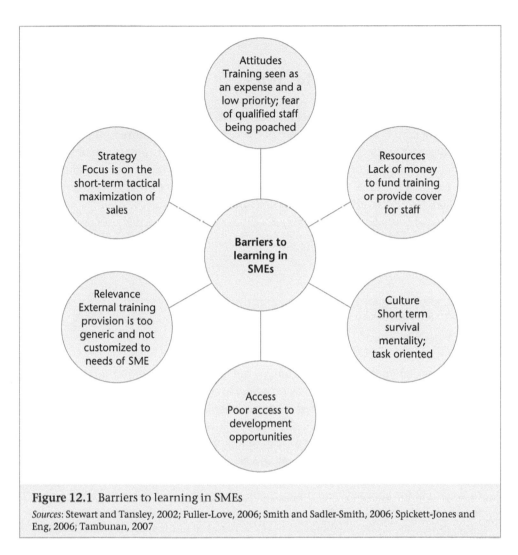

Figure 12.1 Barriers to learning in SMEs

Sources: Stewart and Tansley, 2002; Fuller-Love, 2006; Smith and Sadler-Smith, 2006; Spickett-Jones and Eng, 2006; Tambunan, 2007

Small business owners look to the government to maintain a stable economy and to provide financial incentives that encourage growth (see *Media watch* box). As Rigby (2004) notes government grants and funding schemes have been critical to the provision of training in small firms (see *Insights into practice* box).

ACTIVITY 12.2

Identify two government-led initiatives:

1. What are the main elements of the initiative?
2. What are the principal benefits of the initiatives for SMEs?
3. To what extent is it possible to evaluate the success of the initiative?

MEDIA WATCH BOX

Government support for SMEs

A report published by the Confederation of British Industry (CBI), the UK's employer association, contained harsh criticism of the Government's failure to support small businesses effectively. The report pointed out that the Government's Small Business Service, which is part of a government department, had failed to meet four of its seven targets over a five year period. The report highlighted that the Government had failed to build an effective enterprise culture.

Source
Independent on Sunday (Business Section), 14 August 2005: 4.

INSIGHTS INTO PRACTICE

SMEs and national policy in Spain

Small firms dominate the Spanish economy but less than half have historically offered any form of training (the figure may be as low as a quarter). In order to address this problem the Government shifted to an interventionist training policy based on 'Tripartite Agreements on Continuous Training' involving the Government, employers, and trade unions. Since 1992 a series of four year Agreements have been implemented. The Agreements require employers to consult employee representatives about the content of company training plans. Government funding schemes were set up as part of the approach and these schemes cover SMEs as well as larger organizations. These Agreements have impacted positively on the provision of training in small firms with significant increases in the number of employees receiving training (although there is still considerable scope for further improvement).

Source
Rigby, M. 2004. Training in Spain: an evaluation of the continuous training agreements (1993–2001) with particular reference to SMEs. *Human Resource Development International*, 7 (1): 23–37.

Non-government sources of support for HRD in SMEs

Aside from government initiatives there are a range of potential sources for the provision of HRD/TandD in the developed countries, such as: local schools; colleges and universities; training consultants; commercial course providers; professional institutes; trade unions; and, customers and suppliers. In China SMEs tend to rely on private providers of training as they lack any internal provision; this is in contrast to larger organizations that are state-owned or foreign-financed and which provide their employees with a wide range of training and development interventions (Venter, 2003). Providing support to SMEs needs to be at the local level as the majority of SMEs prefer personal contact (see *Media Watch Box*). They also tend to lack a qualified HR practitioner (see *Media Watch Box*).

MEDIA WATCH BOX

The state of HR in UK SMEs

These two extracts from the CIPD's *People Management* magazine illustrate two important characteristics of the majority of SMEs. First, the lack of specialist HRD roles in most SMES; second, the need for customized training interventions (although these are more expensive than many SMEs usually afford).

A study of 80 SMEs of 250 or less employees carried out in 2002 by Manchester Metropolitan University's business school revealed that only one in four employed a HR practitioner with CIPD qualifications.[1]

A pilot scheme was set up by the Department for Trade and Industry (DTI) in the UK to encourage smaller business to make use of shared HR services in order to improve their understanding of the HR implications of running a business. The initiative ran from August 2003 to March 2004 and involved 170 SMEs with 50 or fewer employees. One of the outcomes from the pilot was that the SMEs prefer services that are customized to meet their individual needs and include personal contact with a local provider.[2]

Sources
[1] *People Management*, 14 October 2004: 55.
[2] *People Management*, 28 October 2004: 29.

ACTIVITY 12.3

Imagine you are the managing director of a SME. What might be some of the potential advantages and disadvantages of each of the above mentioned sources for training provision:

1. Local schools, colleges, and universities

2. Training consultants

3. Commercial course providers

4. Professional institutes

5. Trade unions

6. Customers and suppliers

Differences between SMEs and large firms in the provision of training

The differences between SMEs and larger firms in terms of training and development provision are shown in table 12.2. There can also be specific differences between European nations. For instance, in terms of management development UK firms rely on educational provision more than other countries, whereas Norwegian and German firms rely more on internal provision, and Danish firms use a combination of methods (Mabey, 2004).

The role of technology in supporting HRD in SMEs

Many SMEs have assimilated technology and the Internet in order to compete at e-business (Raymond et al., 2005). As chapter 1 explained information and communications

	SMEs	Large firms
Learning needs	Often unique and idiosyncratic; many have no appraisal system	Often common to a particular role or unit; most have an appraisal system
Learning solutions	Predominantly on-the-job training that focuses on developing job-related skills; heavily reliant on informal learning but also oriented to formal qualifications (although often acquired through the recruitment of suitably qualified people); external provision often needs to be customized; limited reliance on traditional schemes such as apprenticeships	A blend of customized and off-the-shelf; much greater utilization of traditional schemes such as apprenticeships; informal learning not always leveraged by the organization
Training budget	58% of SMEs have a training budget but often small or non-existent in smaller firms	73% of large firms have a training budget
Logistics	Often difficult to provide cover for those being trained	Can be easier to provide cover (but not guaranteed as most large firms have operating constraints)
Training and development policies	67% of small firms have no management development policy; in the UK construction sector only 24% of small firms and 46% of medium sized firms have a formal training policy	59% of large firms have a management development policy; 69% of large firms in the construction sector have a formal training policy
Preferred learning methods	Predominantly internal provision (particularly on-the-job training)	Both internal and external provision is used (although little use made of job rotations and external placements)
Impact of management style	Values and attitude of the owner-manager have a very direct impact on whole organization	Values and attitudes of corporate leader can have a more diluted effect; also sub-cultures often exist in larger firms

Table 12.2 The differences between SMEs and larger firms in the provision of training and development

Sources: Hill, 2002; Forde and MacKenzie, 2004; Gray, 2004; Sadler-Smith and Smith, 2006; van den Berg, 2006

technologies have enabled business of different sizes to compete globally on a level playing field: the world has become flatter (Friedman, 2006). Raymond et al. (2005) cite a range of operational, managerial, and strategic advantages of e-business that include closer links with customers and other stakeholders (e.g. business partners), improved decision-making, improved competitor intelligence, and greater access to external expertise and other resources. SMEs face particular challenges when utilizing technology because they lack (Montazemi, 2006):

- IT specialists
- Finances to invest in an appropriate IT infrastructure
- Finances to invest in IT training
- The capacity to absorb failed IT projects

Raymond et al. (2005) studied data from 350 manufacturing SMEs in Canada and discovered that 30 per cent of the firms demonstrated this type of assimilation; and noted that to be successful there needs to be an investment in training and organizational development. Other countries are recognizing the potential of e-business. The Malaysian government has made it a requirement that all SMEs wishing to become or remain a government supplier must be able to access and use an online procurement system which involves attending a certified training programme (Salleh et al., 2006). In Korea the government is promoting the relevance and benefits of e-business for SMEs through both information and training initiatives (Jeon et al., 2006). Yet other research has shown that government policies have little impact on SME utilization of the Internet; rather it is pressure from customers that is more critical (Beckinsale et al., 2006).

! TIPS AND HINTS

Unlike many unsuccessful implementations in large organizations, e-learning programmes are ideally suited to SMEs where the lack of internal training provision and the cost of external interventions makes blended learning too difficult and costly to fund.

This reliance on technology should facilitate the introduction of e-learning programmes. However, the adoption of an e-learning strategy is problematic for many small and very small businesses as they tend to lack the necessary technology needed. This is in contrast to medium sized firms which are appropriately resourced and where employees tend to use technology a great deal as part of their day-to-day work (Stewart and Tansley, 2002). Based on an in-depth study in Ireland only 20 per cent of SMEs use e-learning due to the costs involved with other problems being learner motivation and the disruption to normal work duties (Brown et al., 2006). While in Australia existing levels of skill coupled with deeply engrained attitudes about all forms of training act as a barrier (see *Insights into practice* box).

(•) INSIGHTS INTO PRACTICE

Small firms in Australia

This case illustrates how attitudes about training need to change in many Australian small firms if technology is going to be exploited effectively as a medium for learning.

Small businesses with less than 20 employees dominate Australia's private sector. Information and communications technology has helped to boost productivity in the SME sector. Consequently, online training has the potential to overcome small business fears that training does not offer tangible benefits. Over 90 per cent of small business own a computer and nearly as many are connected to the Internet. However, a survey of 716 small businesses in Western Australia revealed that the majority of employees are not computer literate and therefore basic computer skills training is needed before a business can adopt online training. This can be a problem in a sector where training has been viewed traditionally as a cost not an investment: the need to do pre-training may simply fuel existing perceptions and frustrations about training. The study shows that an employee's willingness to engage with online training is linked to the level of education they have received. Owner-managers prefer flexible delivery of training (i.e. just-in-time delivery involving short, customized modules that are focused on specific business issues). This needs to be accompanied by appropriate support and advice. The study concluded that for online training to be successful there needs to be a commitment by owner-managers and employees to the concept of lifelong learning where training is viewed as an investment and not a cost.

Source
Webster, B., Walker, E. and Barrett, R. 2005. Small business and online training in Australia: who is willing to participate? *New Technology, Work and Employment*, 20 (3): 248–58.

The role of networks and local associations in the provision of training in SMEs

In order to take advantage of economies of scale SMEs can form local associations or networks in order to pool resources and share training provision (Hall, 2004). Such networks are a particular feature of the competitive response of SMEs in northern Italy's industrial sector (Hanna and Walsh, 2002). These networks are referred to as SME 'clusters' which form when there is an economic benefit to be gained by all the participating firms (Barclay, 2005). Market insights can be shared between firms in the network and so enhance the decision-making by individual SMEs (Spickett-Jones and Eng, 2006). A study of how SMEs use marketing networks in Northern Ireland and Australia reveals that owner-managers recognize that training can support the development of commercial skills in their employees although some would consider withdrawing from the network as the firm grows in order to carry out their own training (Gilmore et al., 2006).

Many small firms in the UK are members of a local Chamber of Commerce which holds meetings and events where members can share their experiences and learn from other business people. Lituchy and Rail (2000) note, in a UK study of bed and breakfast establishments and small inns, that tourist boards, chambers of commerce, or small business associations are ideally positioned to organize training at an affordable price. Collaborative learning approaches that involve several stakeholders (e.g. small firm, external learning advisers, university business school) and focus on firm-specific issues, in conjunction with generic interventions that develop team learning, can be very effective in this sector (Sadler-Smith, 2000). SMEs wanting to introduce firm-wide interventions, such as training in statistical quality control, need to pool resources through consortia involving local colleges and universities (Thomas and Webb, 2003). HRD interventions such as development centres (see chapter 8) can be countered by pooling resources in this way or by ensuring ongoing monitoring staff performance and development needs and addressing these as and when problems occur. Consultants can be very useful in providing expertise not available within the SME but they need to:

- Have experience of working in the SME sector
- Deliver on the promises they make
- Be cost effective
- See the project through and evaluate it at the end
- Have an ethical perspective
- Be a good communicator and listener

MEDIA WATCH BOX

The winning ways of some SMEs

The 2008 award for '*The Sunday Times* Best Small Company to Work For' competition has gone to the charity Christians Against Poverty (CAP). Based on data from over 32,000 employees some 513 SMEs were assessed against eight criteria including personal growth. CAP is a national debt counselling charity that employs 123 people. The charity has a head office in Bradford and 68 church-based centres throughout the UK. The charity's chief executive, Mr Matt Barlow, also took the leadership award. The previous year's winner was also a charity, P3, which came fourth this year but won the employee well-being award. The winner of the award for being best at training and development was Nicoll Curtain, a recruitment consultancy employing 52 people that was ranked second overall. The company's training budget is £15,000 and employees feel there are plenty of opportunities for personal growth. New starters are given a mentor to help with their socialization into the company.

Source
The Sunday Times 100 best small companies to work for 2008. *The Sunday Times*, 2 March 2008.

12.5 **Informal learning in SMEs**

Why informal learning is a feature of many SMEs

The employment relationship in small firms tends to be characterized by informal management approaches (Clark, 2007). This reflects cultural differences with larger firms where formal structures and processes tend to dominate. The principal learning process in small firms is learning-by-doing (Garengo et al., 2005) which tends to occur informally as part of everyday work practices. Therefore it is not surprising that the literature on SMEs has identified informal learning as one of the most commonly used approaches to training and development (Boxall and Purcell, 2008). The downside is that much of this type of learning can be unreliable: it includes accidental learning which may not always work in the favour of the firm (see chapter 11). A further problem is that there can be very limited opportunities for employees in SMEs to engage in activities commonly associated with structured informal learning such as project work or the swapping of job roles (Sambrook, 2005). In many SMEs it is the owner-manager who takes responsibility for informal workplace training. This is not particularly surprising given their role as the primary stakeholder (Garavan, 2007). In a study of Australian firms Poell et al. (2006) it was noted that owners who adopted the role of an informal workplace trainer (see chapter 11) focused much more on performance and provided higher levels of support than non-owners in the same role.

◉ INSIGHTS INTO PRACTICE

Informal learning in SMEs

The study involved in-depth interviews with owners and employees from a range of SMEs and revealed that informal learning is an important source of employee development:

1. Participants referred to learning from mistakes and experimentation (i.e. trial and error) as common ways of learning. They also prefer individual coaching and mentoring to formal training that leads to a qualification. Many of them emphasized the value of their previous experience

2. Participants use a combination of formal and informal on-the-job learning methods that build on their previous experience

3. SMEs want external training providers who fully understand the SME context and can provide learning interventions that are tailored to the needs of individual firms

Source
Doyle, L. and Hughes, M. 2004. *Learning Without Lessons: Supporting Learning in Small Businesses* (Research Report). London: Learning and Skills Development Agency (written in collaboration with N. Hudson and K. Stanford of the Small Firms Enterprise Development Initiative).

A potential problem with a reliance on informal learning-by-doing is highlighted by a study involving small business entrepreneurs. It was discovered that entrepreneurs prefer the identification of solutions that are relatively quick and easy to implement to those that necessarily optimize the learning process (Nieuwenhuis and van Woerkom, 2007). This can be seen as a form of short term pragmatism that reflects a 'gut feel' approach to business. This raises a difficulty for one of the contemporary arguments about HRD: that there should be a close convergence between HRD interventions and an organization's strategic objectives. This is very much a large organization model that does not fit the more fluid, demands-driven culture that characterizes many SMEs. As stated above the competence, behaviour, and attitude of owner-managers directly impact on small firm culture and firm performance. If the owner-manager views management of the firm through an operational- rather than strategic-lens it is highly unlikely that any training and development or informal learning that takes place is going to be directly linked to organizational objectives. Rather it is much more about a tacit acceptance of 'that's how we work here'.

Where training plans do exist they are likely to be both informal and disjointed often overshadowed by daily operational concerns. There is unlikely to be any real critical analysis of performance and the contribution of training and learning to this. There are many exceptions of course as illustrated by the findings of *The Sunday Times* '100 Best small companies to work for 2008' awards (see above). The criteria used for this award illustrate the range of factors that are critical to high levels of performance but are neglected by so many firms: employee perceptions of leadership and management style; personal growth through training and development; personal well being and the work-life balance; employee perceptions of team-working; reward and recognition; and, perceptions of the company (ibid.: 4–5).

(•) INSIGHTS INTO PRACTICE

SMEs and training in Vietnam

Vietnam's economy can be classified as being in transition from a centralized state control to a free market economy. Recently, Vietnamese firms have been introducing HRM practices including training. A study of 200 manufacturing SMEs located in Hanoi revealed that most firms had some form of training provision. The study differentiated between formal and informal learning opportunities and revealed that 84 per cent used some form of on-the-job informal training while 62 per cent offered formal training. However, the overall financial investment in training was small suggesting the firms do not see training as a key priority.

Source
King-Kaurani, S., Ngoc, S. D. and Askley-Cotler, C. 2006. Impact of human resource management: SME performance in Vietnam. *Journal of Developmental Entrepreneurship*, 11 (1): 79–95.

Summary

This chapter has discussed the critical role that SMEs play in national and global markets. Technology and the fragmentation of supply chains have enabled many SMEs to occupy niche markets that exploit the levels of flexibility and innovation commonly associated with this type of firm. However, definitions of a SME vary across the world although it is common practice to differentiate between medium- and small sized enterprises. Research investigating the nature and role of HRD in SMEs has been limited but several studies indicate that many smaller firms are unable to afford the cost of formal training and therefore rely on informal training and learning which can be ad hoc and inconsistent in its contribution to firm performance. Medium sized firms often replicate the functional structure of larger organizations and therefore employ someone in a HRD role although the level of expertise associated with such roles tends to be rather low.

A range of factors that impact on HRD in SMEs was identified and discussed along with several related barriers to learning. These need to be addressed by SMEs through firm initiatives often supported by government schemes that support training in smaller firms. Of critical importance is the development of employees' personal knowledge as this often represents the firm's core competence. In many cases it is the owner-manager's personal knowledge that is critical to firm performance. Competence can be developed through the adoption of processes for the management of organizational knowledge and learning although, again, this is likely to be a relatively informal set of processes in many SMEs which lack the formal infrastructures of larger organizations.

Review questions

1   How are SMEs defined in Europe?

2   How have SMEs been affected by changes in global markets?

3   What are the different approaches to training provision found in small firms and medium sized firms?

4   What are the principal barriers to learning in SMEs?

5   How important to the provision of training is the role of the entrepreneur or owner-manager?

Suggestions for further reading

1   Rigby, M. 2004. Training in Spain: an evaluation of the continuous training agreements (1993–2001) with particular reference to SMEs. *Human Resource Development International*, 7 (1): 23–37.

An interesting insight into how one country has attempted to address its poor track-record on skills training and the impact this has had on smaller firms.

2   Webster, B., Walker, E. and Barrett, R. 2005. Small business and online training in Australia: who is willing to participate? *New Technology, Work and Employment*, 20 (3): 248–58.

This article provides an insight into the attitudes of small businesses in Australia towards training generally.

3   Fuller-Love, N. 2006. Management development in small firms. *International Journal of Management Reviews*, 8 (3): 175–90.

This article contains a detailed and informative review of management training and development in UK SMEs.

4   Brown, L., Murphy, E. and Wade, V. 2006. Corporate eLearning: human resource development implications for large and small organizations. *Human Resource Development International*, 9 (3): 415–27.

This article focuses on the role of e-learning in different sized organizations.

5   Kotey, B. and Folker, C. 2007. Employee training in SMEs: effect of firm size and firm type—family and non-family. *Journal of Small Business Management*, 45 (2): 214–38.

This article contains a very useful review of the literature on training in SMEs.

Case study

1. Competence development in a Taiwan manufacturing SME

The case organization, a Taiwanese manufacturing SME, identified problems with the design and sales aspects of its business. These problems were linked to resource limitations and a lack of competence in these areas. Consequently, in order to be able to develop products and services the SME needed to expand its competence set (i.e. the set of competencies that are needed to support the daily operations of the firm). As part of an initiative aimed at achieving this, the firm implemented on-the-job training interventions covering: the management of factory operations, the various applications of computer-based information systems, and the utilization and maintenance of production facilities. The researchers concluded that these types of intervention are critical to expanding and developing the firm's competence set.[1]

2. Small family and non-family firms in Australia

This case involved the analysis of data from 448 family firms and 470 non-family firms. Respondents identified the category their firm belonged to although consideration was also given to additional factors. For family firms these included: who owned and controlled the firm, who were the primary decision-makers, how many family members were employed by the firm, and whether the business was inherited or acquired from parents. For the purposes of the study a small firm was defined as comprising 5 to 19 employees and a medium firm as 20 to 199 employees. On-the-job training was the preferred approach in both types of firm although differences in training methods were evident. For example, apprenticeships and trainee programmes were more popular in family firms. The utilization of formal training increases with firm size. The data suggest that smaller firms prefer an informal approach to training because this fits better with their approach to strategic management. These firms are more concerned with short term survival than with long term planning. Consequently, the preference is for job-specific, low cost interventions that address the immediate skills needs of the firm. For firms that survive the high-risk start-up phase and start growing in size there is a greater likelihood of a return on longer term training investments. Significant increases in formal training provision were observed for family firms comprising between 20 and 49 employees. However, in firms with 50 or more employees there were only relatively modest incremental increases. A significant gap was noted between the two types of firm with between 50 and 99 employees. It is at this size that the family firm preference for informal training and the non-family firm preference for formal training become particularly evident. As the non-family firm grows it has to focus much more on the training of existing employees and new recruits in order to achieve its strategic goals (this is because these firms are more reliant on external finance than family firms and therefore have to demonstrate the ability to sustain performance and growth).[2]

Sources

[1] Shee, D. Y. 2006. An analytic framework for competence set expansion: lessons learned from an SME. *Total Quality Management*, 17 (8): 981–97.

[2] Kotey, B. and Folker, C. 2007. Employee training in SMEs: effect of firm size and firm type—family and non-family. *Journal of Small Business Management*, 45 (2): 214–38.

Case questions

1. What are the advantages and disadvantages of the different approaches to training and development taken in the two case organizations?

2. What types of government initiatives could help these firms improve their training infrastructures?

Online resource centre

Visit the supporting online resource centre for additional material that will help you with your research, essays, assignments, and revision.

www.oxfordtextbooks.co.uk/orc/mankin/

Managing the HRD Function

Learning objectives

By the end of this chapter you should be able to:

* Explain the factors that influence the role, responsibilities, and structure of the HRD function

* Evaluate the different design options for a HRD function

* Discriminate between a strategically integrated and an operationally integrated HRD function

* Understand and explain the responsibilities of a HRD manager for managing processes, products, services, and people

* Distinguish between the strategic and operational responsibilities of the HRD manager

* Appreciate the importance of innovation, marketing, financial management, and evaluation to the role of the HRD function

In order to achieve these objectives it is important that you not only read the chapter carefully but also complete the activities and review questions, and undertake some of the suggested further reading.

Indicative content

■ The impact of an organization's strategy, size and design, internal and external stakeholders, culture and technology and communications infrastructure on the role, responsibilities, and structure of the HRD function

■ Design options for the HRD function including: centralized, outsourced, and virtual

■ The role of training centres and corporate universities

■ The different roles of a HRD consultant

■ The differences between a strategically integrated and an operationally integrated HRD function

■ The importance of standards and protocols to the reputation and credibility of the HRD function

■ The strategic and operational responsibilities of a HRD Manager for processes, products, services, and people

■ Managing stakeholders

■ The role of continuous improvement, knowledge management processes, and learning in developing an HRD function characterized by innovation

■ The importance of marketing and financial management to the HRD function

■ How the evaluation of the HRD function is different to the evaluation of discrete HRD interventions

Key concepts

The HRD function	Corporate universities
The HRD 'wheel'	Virtual functions
Added value	Outsourced function
Strategically integrated HRD	HRD consultants
Operationally integrated HRD	Marketing
Stakeholders	Type 2 evaluation
Training centres	

13.1 **Introduction**

The concept of a HRD function reflects a traditional approach to organizational design. Typically, responsibilities for HRD are split between a designated central department and operational functions (Price, 2004). The delineation in responsibilities may be defined in an organization's policies, regulations, and procedures but there can still be a blurring of the boundaries that can result in a variety of problems, from minor disagreements to major differences of opinion. Such conflict is not surprising given the different priorities and pressures that operational managers are usually coping with in most organizational contexts. Attitudes toward HRD vary tremendously and this presents the HRD function with many different challenges. From the perspective of the HRD manager issues such as the provision of training or the integration of learning into work are of paramount importance. This view may not be shared so wholeheartedly by many line managers who are immersed in the day-to-day running of the organization's operations, whether these are focused on sales, finance, production, or logistics.

The HRD function may appear on the organizational chart as a free-standing department or as part of the HRM department. Many organizations may not have any form of HR function at all (especially smaller enterprises as discussed in the previous chapter). Increasingly many organizations are using technology and telecommunications to link together disparately located individuals and teams as virtual functions; while other organizations are outsourcing the function. But what remains constant is the need for HRD practitioners to collaborate with a wide range of internal and external stakeholders in order to maximize the effectiveness of HRD practices (see table 13.1).

Maintaining effectiveness is about demonstrating how the HRD function adds value to an organization (Ulrich, 2007). In many organizations this is about being business-focused and linking learning to the wider organizational objectives and business needs (Slotte et al., 2004). The term 'business-focused' can be used generically and applied to organizations in other sectors (e.g. public and non-profit) because it communicates the financial and performance realities that all organizations face. However, the HRD manager has to contend with two potential dilemmas:

1. Success for the HRD function is dependent on the contribution of stakeholders who the HRD manager has no authority over. Consequently, how well these stakeholder relationships are managed will have a direct impact on the effectiveness of the HRD department.

2. Proving that HRD interventions do add value. It has been claimed that comprehensive training and development activities have produced beneficial organizational outcomes (Naquin and Holton, 2003; Bell and Ford, 2007) many of which can be measured in financial terms (Collins and Holton, 2004). Non-profit organizations will be concerned about maximizing the benefits of their work but in terms of deliverables are likely to focus on intangibles such as improvements in living conditions, education levels, and health standards.

The way in which these dilemmas are resolved varies from organization to organization. The factors influencing HRD strategy that were highlighted in chapter 3 impact directly

Internal stakeholders	External stakeholders
Senior managers (e.g. setting strategic objectives; making funding decisions; identifying OD projects)	Shareholders and investors; sponsors and trustees (e.g. impact of HRD on organizational performance)
Operational/Line managers (e.g. identifying training needs; assessing the impact of learning on performance; acting as coaches and mentors)	Communities (e.g. training delivered by non-profit organizations to address social and environmental issues)
Employees (e.g. participants on training interventions; learning informally in the workplace; identifying learning needs)	Trade associations and chambers of commerce (e.g. local HRD initiatives; sharing of HRD resources)
HRD practitioners who are embedded in operational functions (e.g. co-designing HRD interventions; co-delivering training courses; co-facilitating change processes)	HRD consultants and training providers (e.g. ensuring quality of provision; impact on HRD function's credibility)
	Education providers (e.g. accreditation of organizational training programmes)
	Professional institutes (e.g. influence on professional development and credibility of HRD personnel)

Table 13.1 Examples of internal and external stakeholders

on the role, responsibilities, and structure of the HRD function (i.e. organizational strategy and structure; organizational culture; and, human resource management—see figure 3.2 in chapter 3). Vertical strategic alignment, involving the integration of HRD strategy, policies, plans, and practices with business strategy, and the structure of the organization shape the way in which resources are deployed to support HRD (see also chapter 3 and figure 3.3). For instance, in larger organizations a HRD function usually works in collaboration with line managers. Responsibility for the implementation and review of HRD is shared between these two stakeholders and specific responsibilities can vary considerably. For instance, a centralized HRD function may be highly involved with strategic planning and implementation and has devolved operational responsibilities for HRD to line managers. Conversely, the HRD function may have limited involvement in strategic planning and implementation and be much more involved in operational issues, thus reducing the role and responsibilities of line managers. Organizational culture is important because the values and beliefs of an organization have a direct impact on organizational knowledge and learning processes and thus influence the role, responsibilities, and structure of the HRD function. For instance, organizational cultures that are learning-oriented are less likely to require a large HRD function. Such cultures are characterized by the HRD strategic choices of devolved and empowered informal learning (see section 3.3 and figure 3.7 in chapter 3). Here primary responsibility for the practice of HRD rests with the line manager and employee. The HRD practitioner is still an important stakeholder but his/her role is more strategic and focused on the ongoing nurturing of the organization's culture. In this situation specialist HRD expertise can be accessed through outsourced provision.

HRM is important because HRD functions tend to be integrated within HRM functions, which also reflects their conceptual relationship (see chapters 2 and 3). Often this can make horizontal alignment between HRD and HRM strategies, policies, plans, and practices easier (see chapter 3 and figure 3.3). In this situation the function can be centralized, decentralized, outsourced, or even virtual depending on the strategic and operational roles and responsibilities of both HRM and HRD practitioners. There is no universal structural model for a HR function. These issues are developed in much more detail below.

Throughout this chapter the generic term HRD manager will be used to signify the head of the HRD function, although in reality job titles, roles, and responsibilities vary considerably. For instance, Gilley et al. (2002) propose five categories of roles: HRD manager, learning agents (i.e. instructors), instructional designers, performance engineers, and HRD consultants (these are in addition to the other role typologies discussed in chapter 3).

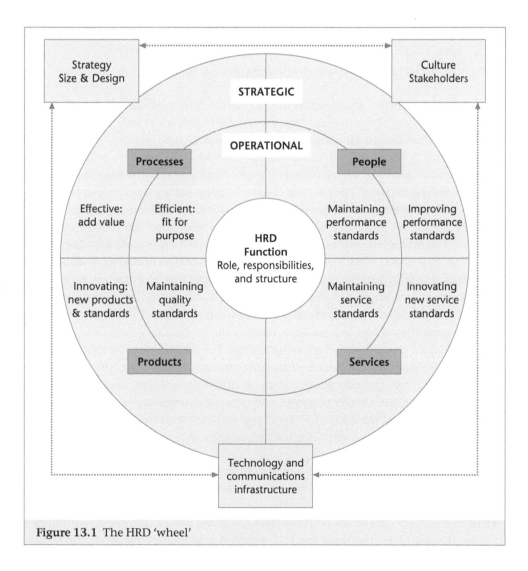

Figure 13.1 The HRD 'wheel'

The content of the chapter will be linked to the concept of the HRD 'wheel' shown in figure 13.1 which can be used as an analytical model. The HRD 'wheel' illustrates how the principal factors that influence the role, responsibilities, and structure (and therefore the purpose) of the HRD function are an organization's strategy, size and design, culture, stakeholders, and technology and communications infrastructure. These are interlinked in ways which are unique to each organization. Theoretically the HRD function has strategic and operational responsibilities although the former may be minimal or even non-existent in some organizations. These responsibilities revolve around four categories: People, Processes, Products, and Services. The 'wheel' provides generic differentiators between the strategic and operational characteristics of each of these categories. For instance, operational HRD processes are characterized by efficiency (i.e. that they are fit for purpose) while strategic HRD processes are characterized by effectiveness (i.e. adding value).

13.2 The HRD wheel: factors influencing the role, responsibilities, and structure of the HRD function

The role, responsibilities, and structure of the HRD function are influenced by a range of factors, the first of which is the organization's strategy. This is not only in terms of what the strategy is but also how it is formulated, implemented, and reviewed. The nature and extent of the HRD function's involvement in these processes tends to reflect how the function and its activities are perceived by senior management. The second is size and design of the organization. The previous chapter highlighted the simplicity of HRD functions in smaller enterprises. In larger organizations which have more complex designs there are a range of options available for the structure of the HRD function such as: centralized, decentralized, outsourced, and virtual. In turn there is more than one variant of each of these (see section 13.5 below). The third factor is stakeholders, both internal and external. Shrewd judgements need to me made about who to influence, how best to influence them, and when to influence. The fourth is organizational culture; although the reality is that many organizations are a mix of sub-cultures. Culture can be driven by a particular stakeholder (e.g. as Anita Roddick did in the Body Shop) and is heavily influenced by the prevailing management ideology. The fifth and final factor is the organization's technology and communications infrastructure. Many organizations are using 'global connectivity' to underpin the work of virtual departments and teams, virtual knowledge sharing and transfer processes, and virtual learning (i.e. e-learning).

Chapter 3 discussed these topics in detail and you may wish to re-familiarize yourself with the contents of that chapter. Illustrative examples of how the five factors influence HRD are shown in table 13.2.

There are several different design options for the structure of the HRD function and these are discussed in detail in section 13.5 below. These are, in effect, overarching options as design specifics will vary considerably between organizations. This reflects the extent to which the role of the HRD manager can entail a wide range of responsibilities as listed in table 13.3. The aim of any HRD function is to manage processes and people,

Factor	Illustrative examples
Strategy	*The strategic goals of the organization require the identification of HRD implications so that an overall HRD plan can be formulated*: This is often a reactive process by the HRD function reflecting relatively low levels of status, influence, and credibility. It tends to be associated with an activity-based approach to HRD that is characterized by a pre-occupation with formal training activities (Gilley et al., 2003). This is typical of many centralized training departments which have adopted a training centre approach, operate as a cost centre, and focus on short term planning (e.g. conforming to the organization's annual financial planning cycle). The espoused aim of the HRD function is typically to improve organizational effectiveness through training (Blanchard and Thacker, 2004)
	The formulation and implementation of the organization's strategy requires input by the HRD function on an ongoing basis: In these situations the HRD manager has relatively high levels of status, influence, and credibility that can actually exceed those associated with his/her formal position in the organizational structure. It tends to be associated with a results-driven approach in which the HRD function works in partnership with key stakeholders (Gilley et al., 2003). Strategic goals require the adoption of a long term perspective and can involve HRD strategies such as the building of an organizational infrastructure that leverages both formal and informal learning (Ellinger, 2004). This is best achieved through a decentralized HRD function which is embedded across an organization's operations (often drawing upon outsourced resources and supported by a small, specialized group of HRD practitioners working at head office)
Size and design	*As larger organizations in particular have adapted to global trends by introducing more flexible organizational designs the HRD function has had to move away from the traditional centralized model*: Organizations comprising business units often maintain a small team of trainers with responsibility for the delivery of basic skills programmes (Yorks, 2005). Global organizations can address economies of scale through e-learning interventions as the support of e-learning does not require large centralized training centres which incur high overhead costs (see also technology and communications infrastructure below). E-learning can still be supported by a centralized function but one which is much smaller and comprising a team of instructional designers; equally it can be supported by specialist outsourced providers. Supplementary classroom-based provision as part of a blended learning intervention can be supported by decentralized teams of trainers and/or locally sourced training consultants
Stakeholders	*Different strategies are required for managing relationships with different stakeholders*: For instance, a HRD manager or practitioner requires a high level of political acumen to work in partnership successfully with senior managers coupled with a good understanding of the external context (e.g. market trends; trading conditions; changes in government funding of the public sector; etc). They need to develop an intuitive feel for when it is best to: challenge or compromise; persuade through rational argument or rely on emotional pleas; use resources to influence decision-making in one area of operations or divert the resources elsewhere

Table 13.2 Factors that influence the role, responsibilities, and structure of the HRD function

Factor	Illustrative examples
Organizational culture	*The role of the HRD function is to support the socialization process*: A basic activity of the HRD function is the induction and socialization of new employees. This involves adherence to organizational values and beliefs and can entail the utilization of personality questionnaires and associated psychometric instruments (e.g. as found in development centres). The use of competency frameworks for both recruitment and development purposes has been criticized as a 'cloning' mechanism.
	The role of the HRD function is to develop a culture characterized by learning: This requires the cultivation of organizational learning processes which can be problematic in organizations with a strong unitary ideology. For instance, a common strategy is to encourage double-loop learning (see chapter 4) but this can be viewed by managers as a source of conflict and dysfunctional behaviour. Often there is a gap between the rhetoric of organizational leaders and the realities that confront employees. For instance, managers who look for 'quick fix' training solutions rather than addressing the underlying causes of problems
Technology and communications infrastructure	*The technology and communications infrastructure can facilitate virtual working*: Knowledge creation, sharing, and transfer have become processes of strategic importance in many organizations. Much of this activity is increasingly cross-functional collaboration which has been described as a form of 'entwinement' (Marques, 2006). The HRD function can be entwined by embedding aspects of the HRD function in operational functions without the necessity for any physical decentralization (i.e. a form of virtual decentralization). Virtual work can also involve a combination of teleworking (i.e. working away from an organization's offices) as well as working in virtual teams involving external stakeholders (Noe, 2002)
	The technology and communications infrastructure can facilitate virtual learning: For instance, Nestlé, with over 200,000 employees spread across hundreds of locations, has adopted a distance learning approach based on e-learning with courses structured around short modules of between five and seven minutes duration (Marquardt, 2004). As stated above there are several structural options for this type of provision

Table 13.2 *(cont'd)*

products and services in such a way that they add value to the organization (Ulrich and Brockbank, 2005). This can best be achieved through a strategic role where the focus is on value-added processes, improved performance standards, and the innovation of new products and service standards. This is in contrast to an operational role where the focus is on efficiency and maintenance of standards (see figure 13.1).

> **! TIPS AND HINTS**
>
> A key priority for a newly appointed HRD manager is the identification of products, services, and processes that add value.

	Operational (efficiency)	Strategic (adding value)
Processes	• Control and coordination of HRD activities (e.g. the four stages in the HRD cycle) • Managing the function's budget • Managing the organization's HRD budget • Evaluating the effectiveness of individual HRD interventions (i.e. type 1 evaluation) • Maintaining management Information systems	• Providing strategic leadership for the function (e.g. creating a vision for the HRD function; publishing a mission statement and set of values) • Monitoring the internal and external environments for changes that have HRD implications • Long term planning of organization's HRD needs • Production of the HRD strategy and HRD policy • Integrating learning into the organization's strategic and operational structures and processes • Nurturing the development of social capital • Monitoring and reviewing knowledge sharing and knowledge transfer processes • Marketing the HRD function • Evaluating the effectiveness of the HRD function (i.e. type 2 evaluation)
People	• Maintaining regular contact with stakeholders (internal and external) • Managing and developing HRD personnel (including HRD consultants) • Supporting workplace trainers	• Managing key stakeholders (internal and external): delivering what matters to stakeholders • Building strategic partnerships within the organization • Building and maintaining collaborative networks (e.g. trade associations) • Supporting line managers (e.g. developing their ability to develop human capital and to nurture social capital; developing their ability to think strategically)
Products	• Maintaining the quality and currency of HRD interventions and resources (e.g. libraries; learning resource centres; intranets; e-learning content; training materials such as slides, hand-outs, and workbooks) • Monitoring technological developments (e.g. implications for e-learning and blended learning)	• Auditing HRD interventions and resources to identify those that add most value to the organization • Innovating new products
Services	• Maintaining high service standards • Monitoring technological developments (e.g. computerized administration systems)	• Creating a customer service strategy • Auditing HRD services to identify those that add most value to the organization • Innovating new services (anticipating customer needs)

Table 13.3 Responsibilities of the HRD manager

Sources: Mankin, 2000, 2001, 2005; Gilley et al., 2002; Ulrich and Brockbank, 2005; Yorks, 2005

ACTIVITY 13.1

What are likely to be the principal features of a HRD function's customer services strategy?

Chapter	Processes	Products	Services
3	Strategic planning, implementation, and evaluation	HRD strategy, policy, and plans.	Conducting an organizational analysis; evaluating HRD strategy, policy and plans and identifying improvements
4	Learning theories	Customized HRD interventions (e.g. training workshop; e-learning programme; coaching session)	Helping managers and employees to understand: how they learn, how they can learn differently; how they can become reflective practitioners; how they can take responsibility for their own learning
5, 6	HRD cycle	Specific TNA/Problem identification techniques	Carrying out a TNA/Problem identification investigation
5, 7	HRD cycle	Design models and techniques for different types of intervention	Interpreting TNA data including entry behaviour; analysing causes of problems; designing HRD interventions
5, 8	HRD cycle	Different types of HRD intervention including 'training-the-trainer' options	Delivery of a HRD intervention (e.g. instructing, coaching, project leading, facilitating); facilitating or supporting the delivery of an HRD intervention by another stakeholder (e.g. line manager)
5, 9	HRD cycle	Specific evaluation models and techniques	Carrying out an evaluation
10	Knowledge Management systems for the creation, sharing and transfer of knowledge	Training interventions on related topics (e.g. teambuilding, inter-personal skills, building collaborative networks); management development programmes (e.g. understanding how to nurture intellectual capital)	TNA, design, delivery, and evaluation of HRD interventions; supporting line managers (e.g. coaching and facilitating)
11	Enhanced HRD cycle	HRD interventions for developing employee learning competencies; management development programmes (e.g. understanding how to support informal learning)	TNA, design, delivery, and evaluation of HRD interventions; supporting line managers (e.g. coaching and facilitating)

Table 13.4 Processes, products, and services

Previous chapters have explained many of the processes, products, and services provided by HRD functions and these have been summarized in table 13.4. Subsequent sections will focus on those aspects not previously discussed before moving on to a section covering the management of people (e.g. stakeholders, HRD personnel).

13.3 The HRD wheel: managing processes, products, and services

The key requirements

In order to manage processes, products, and services effectively the HRD manager needs to understand about innovation, marketing, financial management, and evaluation. In order to be innovative the HRD function needs to be characterized by an ethos that is committed to:

- **Continuous improvement:** chapter 2 explained how the total quality management philosophy has informed the evolution of HRD. The adoption of *kaizen* techniques, such as brainstorming, cause and effect analysis, and incremental problem solving (see PDCA in chapter 11), in conjunction with an open style of management, that encourages team-work and empowerment, is critical.

- **Knowledge creation, sharing and transfer:** chapter 10 explained the different perspectives on knowledge management. An approach that blends the utilization of technology and face-to-face contact is likely to create the necessary synergies. Such an approach complements the commitment to continuous improvement.

- **Learning:** chapter 4 explained a range of learning theories which were subsequently developed in term of formal learning (chapters 5 to 9) and informal learning (chapter 11). Reflective practice in particular should be encouraged within the function along with experimentation and learning from mistakes. Social learning theory is critical to both continuous improvement and knowledge management. Ideally, the HRD function should evolve into a community of practice (see chapter 10).

Through these approaches it will be possible for the HRD function to rise to the challenges of operating at a strategic level: developing processes that are not just efficient and fit for purpose but are also effective and add value; innovating new products and standards rather than simply maintaining existing products and quality standards; and, innovating new service standards rather than simply maintaining existing standards. The skills implications of this are discussed in chapter 15.

! TIPS AND HINTS

In order to promote the role of learning and reflective practice HRD practitioners need to act as role models. This requires them to be willing to critically reflect on their own actions and behaviour (Mankin, 2001).

Marketing the HRD function

Marketing is important because it focuses on issues such as: customer/market segmentation, the price of products and services, and the need for added value. The HRD function needs to operate as if it is a free-standing business which is customer-oriented, regardless of sector and whether it is technically a cost-centre or a profit-centre. To be customer-oriented means understanding the needs of target market segments and the starting point for this is understanding an organization's strategy and then building a relationship with customers (i.e. key stakeholders) so that their needs can be anticipated (Fung et al., 2008). Linked to this is the creation of a customer service strategy and philosophy which establishes the standards and protocols for maintaining and improving the function's products and services. According to Gilley et al. (2002) this is an important initiative for establishing credibility. The key steps in adopting a marketing strategy are shown as a marketing cycle in figure 13.2.

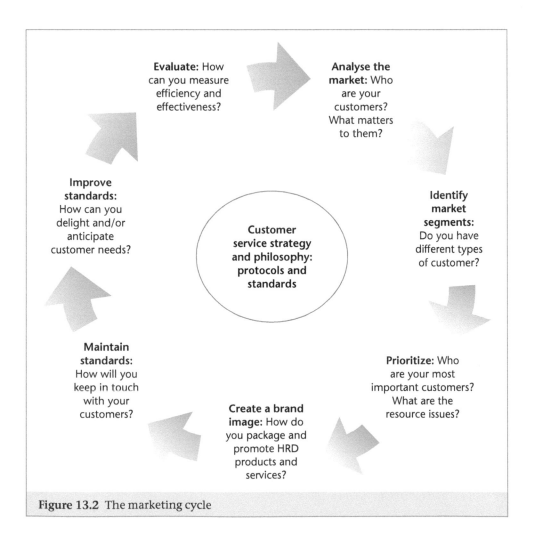

Figure 13.2 The marketing cycle

> **Key concept** Marketing
>
> The acquisition and retention of customers through the identification of customer needs and the communication to those customers of the benefits an organization's products and services will offer them.

> **! TIPS AND HINTS**
>
> It may seem odd to ask a HRD manager who has worked in an organization for several years and who may feel confident in his/her knowledge and understanding of that organization, to undertake a market analysis. However, one of the key ingredients for an effective HRD function is an *effective* planning process that is not based purely upon a narrow range of assumptions and perceptions.

Analysing the market and identifying market segments enables the HRD manager to make decisions about the allocation of resources to support different customer needs. This should encompass both supply-led and customer-driven needs. Indeed, adopting this marketing approach actually means that all needs become customer-driven as the supply-led needs discussed in chapter 5 are generated by the organization's senior management who are themselves a stakeholder group (i.e. a market segment). The importance of brand image should not be trivialized or underestimated. Do not dismiss it as some superficial cosmetic exercise that has nothing to do with the HRD function. You simply need to look at how corporate universities market themselves to appreciate the importance of brand image (for instance see the *Insights into practice* box on Motorola later in this chapter). This part of the marketing cycle is about how you package and promote the products and service of the HRD function and has implications for the next stages which cover the maintenance and improvement of the standards that reflect the brand image created. HRD practitioners and support staff, external consultants, and guest trainers can have a dramatic positive or negative impact on how the HRD function is perceived by stakeholders. The different approaches to evaluation are discussed in more detail below. An important point to note at this stage is that customers buy benefits not features and these benefits should be identified at an early stage (as discussed in chapter 5 in relation to the HRD cycle). Outputs from the evaluation process feed into a new and/or ongoing analysis of the market. The marketing analysis can be part of an integrated approach to the analysis of organizational needs as part of the formulation of a HRD strategy (see chapter 5) and an organizational TNA (see chapters 5 and 6).

The financial management of the HRD function

Financial management is critical in an era when vast sums are expended on HRD interventions. A significant proportion of training budgets is spent on salaries for HRD personnel. For instance, of the US$54.2 billon budgeted on training by US organizations with a hundred or more employees, US$39.1 billion was spent on salaries with the remaining US$15.1 billion used to cover the costs of external services such as seminars and conferences (Blanchard and Thacker, 2004). Managing the costs of HRD activities is about efficiency *and* effectiveness: the maximization of added value through the HRD budget. By shifting to an added value orientation HRD functions can become value centres rather than cost centres although this is very difficult in practice (Carliner, 2004). Yet an increasing number of training departments in the US are now charging other departments for their services as they come under pressure from senior management to justify their role (Blanchard and Thacker, 2004). It is important that the HRD function starts thinking about the cost implications of any HRD intervention before the TNA/problem identification stage so that internal stakeholders can be provided with an estimate of the costs for different types of intervention based on factors such as the number of days preparation needed for each day of delivery (Blanchard and Thacker, 2004). This approach is in fact shifting the focus from purely financial management to a form of commercial management or to put it more prosaically it's about managing the HRD function like a business. The skills implications of this are discussed in chapter 15.

ACTIVITY 13.2

Can you find any examples of internal HRD functions that are managed as a business or seem to be moving in this direction? What appear to be the practical implications of this approach? For instance, does it influence how HRD practitioners engage with key stakeholders? Search resources such as the Internet, library search engines, and HRD-related publications (e.g. *People Management*) or websites (e.g. http://www.cipd.co.uk).

A critical aspect of financial management is the HRD budget, or as it is more commonly referred to, the training budget. The allocation of expenditure needs to reflect the strategic priorities of the organization (see the discussion on vertical strategic alignment in chapter 3). At the same time there are legal requirements that have to be met (e.g. health and safety; employment legislation; environment) as well as ethical and social responsibilities (see chapter 14).

Evaluating the effectiveness of the HRD function

The final element in this section is evaluation which is also the final stage in the marketing cycle. The HRD function needs to identify a comprehensive process (Yorks, 2005) that incorporates a range of HRD metrics that are meaningful to stakeholders in the organization (Yorks, 2004). Increasingly, the effectiveness of HRD is also being evaluated by looking at its impact on external stakeholders such as suppliers and customers (Garavan, 2007). This requires type 2 evaluation which is a broader, more holistic approach than type 1 evaluation which focuses on discrete HRD interventions and was discussed in chapters 5 and 9. The results from type 1 evaluations should be incorporated into type 2 as there is an important complementary relationship between the two levels. Some of the key requirements for type 2 evaluation include:

- Clearly defined performance objectives that are linked to the HRD strategy (which in turn is linked to the organizational strategy)
- A focus on added value (i.e. measuring efficiency and effectiveness)
- The utilization of qualitative and quantitative metrics (e.g. data from attitude surveys is combined with data from an analysis of the returns on investment)

! TIPS AND HINTS

The feedback given to stakeholders must be honest and transparent even if the news is not always good. Some initiatives are bound to fail or succeed only partially. This is an inescapable feature of organizational life.

One of the problems with evaluation feedback is that there is a need for more research into how managers respond to and utilize evaluation data. Several studies indicate that managers in business corporations are more interested in evaluation reports that emphasize business results rather than participant reactions, learning and behaviour changes (Mattson, 2003). It is up to the HRD manager to explain why it is important to consider both types of data output.

Key concept   Added-value

Added value is about identifying what really matters to key stakeholders and delivering the services and products that achieve this. In many respects it builds on the total quality management ethos of delivering products and services that create 'customer delight'.

The balanced scorecard, benchmarking, and return on investment (ROI) can be used for type 2 evaluation. The balanced-scorecard mentioned briefly in chapter 3 was developed by Kaplan and Norton (1993, 1996) and is particularly relevant because of the incorporation of non-financial data as a key measurement of organizational performance. These non-financial measures cover customer satisfaction, internal processes, and the organization's innovation and improvement activities; and, are seen as the drivers of an organization's future financial performance. This captures organizational learning processes and also links the assessment of HRD activities with the wider accountability of the HR function generally (Yorks, 2005). Learning and growth are seen as important strategic drivers and this can help the HRD manager to position the activities of the HRD function at a more strategic level. Put simply, the balanced scorecard is an attempt to put strategy and vision rather than control at the centre of measurement processes (Kaplan and Norton, 1993, 1996). Indeed they argue that the objectives in the learning and growth perspective are the drivers for achieving outstanding results. They recommend three core

---

INSIGHTS INTO PRACTICE

Using the balanced scorecard

Tata Steel is part of the Tata Group of companies and has been using the balanced scorecard as a way of bringing about change in the company by focusing on key results areas that are broader in scope than those covered by traditional financial measures. Strategy is broken down into its constituent elements and performance tracked across the company using the key result areas. This is designed to be a transparent process that starts with the managing director and senior managers who are expected to act as role models. The company values its employees and invests heavily in learning and development as well as reward and recognition schemes. This reflects the company's commitment to a culture characterized by an empowered workforce, customer-driven excellence, and ethical and socially responsible management practices. The latter is focused on improving the lives of the company's employees and the communities it serves*. The balanced scorecard is ideally suited to this combination of 'hard' and 'soft' measures.

Sources
[1] Anand, M. and Singh, K. 2006. Case Analysis III. *Vikalpa*, 31 (3): 138–42.
[2] Shesadri, D. V. R. and Tripathy, A. 2006. Reinventing a giant corporation: the case of Tata Steel. *Vikalpa*, 31 (1): 133–46.
* See also chapter 14.

---

measurements for learning and growth: employee satisfaction (e.g. attitude surveys); employee retention; and employee productivity.

Benchmarking involves scanning the external environment, identifying practices that lead to superior performance, and replicating these in your own organization. It is akin to the idea of best practice. During the era of business process re-engineering in the 1990s it was argued that if you are going to benchmark then it should be against the best in the world rather than simply the best in a given sector (Hammer and Champy, 1993). Return on investment (ROI) was discussed in detail in chapter 9 in relation to type 1 evaluation. However, it can also be used in the overall assessment of the HRD function's performance because it can provide a quantification of benefits that should satisfy those stakeholders who appreciate a commercial approach to managing the HRD function.

13.4 The HRD wheel: managing people

There are two aspects to this: managing stakeholders, both internal and external, and managing those who work in the HRD function, such as HRD practitioners and administrators. From an operational perspective the aim is to maintain performance standards; from a strategic perspective it is to improve those standards.

Managing stakeholders

In chapters 2 and 3 it was suggested that managing stakeholder relationships is a challenging and complex task that is influenced by the structure of the HRD function. For instance, a centralized function may operate at too much of a distance from line managers; an outsourced function can be denied regular contact with key stakeholders; a decentralized function can lack access to senior managers based at head office. The evolution in technology and communications and the emergence of virtual collaboration has gone some way to addressing these shortcomings; although many would argue technology can never better face-to-face contact. Building strategic partnerships with key stakeholders is seen as a critical activity for the HRD function (Gilley et al., 2002) and the importance of this approach was explained in chapter 3. As stated earlier the HRD function needs to demonstrate the ability to deliver what really matters to stakeholders (Ulrich and Brockbank, 2005). The ability to select from a range of influencing tactics is necessary for developing and strengthening its role within the organization; and Gilley and Maycunich Gilley (2002) suggest the HRD function needs to acquire 'important sponsors and advocates who [can] help its image within the organization' (p. 21).

Part of the HRD function's role is also to 'safeguard the voice of the stakeholders' (Swanson, 2002: 138). Bierema and D'Abundo (2003) propose that, in line with a 'socially conscious' approach to HRD (see chapters 1 and 14), the HRD function should act as an advocate for a wide range of stakeholders including customers, suppliers, and citizens as well as employees. This advocate role involves the HRD manager making senior management aware of these stakeholder groups when strategic planning and implementation are undertaken (ibid). HRD practitioners should be concerned with the well-being of employees and should monitor the workplace, investigate causes of ill health, and initiate changes to the work environment accordingly (Gilbreath and Montesino, 2006). This requires an expansion of the role of the HRD practitioner. In the UK this particular responsibility would be shared between the line manager and the health and safety specialist.

An important aspect of managing both internal and external stakeholders is the management of networks that span functional and organizational boundaries. These comprise: networks that HRD practitioners are members of and networks that the HRD practitioner can use to leverage to support learning. Hawley and Taylor (2006) suggest that HRD practitioners in the US should be working more actively with local business associations, such as chambers of commerce and trade associations, for the provision of training. Similar associations exist in other countries but function in different ways. For instance, in Germany they are larger and more unified than in France which is characterized by a rather fragmented approach (Hawley and Taylor, 2006).

Managing HRD practitioners and support staff

The HRD manager needs to be skilled in leadership skills as well as management practices. He/she has an implicit obligation to act as a role model in how he/she manages HRD practitioners and support staff (e.g. training administrator). This involves helping them to engage in reflective practice in order to develop their professional competence. Lombardozzi (2007) suggests this includes:

> Help[ing] them to be more conscious of the ideas that underlie their approaches . . . Ask[ing] them to articulate their assumptions and explain how they are applying theories and models . . . Ask[ing] whether research continues to support the theories, or if newer research findings are shifting in some way. (p. 210)

An effective function invests in the training and development of its own people (Ulrich and Brockbank, 2005). Often the HRD function has an indirect responsibility for part-time workplace trainers such as health and safety staff who spend some of their time designing and delivering a range of specialist courses. However, there is another breed of workplace trainer: individuals who help colleagues learn informally in the workplace but whose role has not been formalized (Poell et al., 2006). This was discussed in chapter 11 because these trainers play a more important role in the facilitation of informal learning than

---

INSIGHTS INTO PRACTICE

The thoughts of HRD practitioners

The following list of actions was devised by a group of HRD practitioners attending a part-time course leading to a professional qualification:

Involve stakeholders

Prove there is a business case for interventions

Link with organizational objectives

Be proactive not defensive

Put evaluation not validation to the top

Market yourself

Develop your competencies (e.g. influencing, negotiating, communication, planning, team-working)

Create a policy

Talk value not costs

Decentralize decision-making

Use role models and good practice already established

Balance organizational learning and individual learning

Use customer and supplier skills

Refute the perception that training is a punishment for poor performance

Don't come over as an expert

Source
Rod Stone (co-author of chapter 12).

MEDIA WATCH BOX

Training centres in the US

These examples illustrate how training centres are a popular option for the provision of training to external stakeholders by non-profit organizations. They are examples of very different specialist training centres that cater for particular market segments and therefore have adjusted their products and services accordingly. They are funded in very different ways.

The Manchester Community Resource Centre in the US is a non-profit agency that was opened in 1998 to provide a range of services to low-income residents living in the local community. The aim of the centre is to help individuals attain self-sufficiency in terms of their work and social lives (for instance, there is a life skills programme which assists learners with parenting skills, nutritional skills, and personal finances). Today services include: employment services to help people become employed; education services to improve people's skills; and, a number of other more specific services (e.g. health, volunteer opportunities). The centre has attracted media coverage because of its job readiness training for people who are finding it difficult to gain employment because of language or cultural difficulties. Many of the learners are immigrants or refugees. A key feature of the centre's approach to training is the restriction of class sizes to a maximum of six. This is because many of the learners do not feel comfortable in a traditional classroom setting.

Sources

[1] *NH Business Review*, 9–22 November 2007: 31–2.
[2] http://www.mcrcnh.com.html (accessed 22 May 2008).
[3] http://www.volunteermatch.org/orgs/org42907.html (accessed 22 May 2008).

The new Johnson and Johnson Diabetes Institute in the Silicon Valley of California is the first training centre of its kind in the US. The institute was set up to help tackle a growing epidemic of diabetes cases in the US which are estimated to be costing the country some US$174 billion annually. The institute is focusing on local communities because this is where there has been a historic shortage of skills in diabetes management. It will provide free training to healthcare practitioners involved with caring for patients with diabetes such as community-based nurses. Specialists in diabetes have designed the course which lasts two days and is offered twice weekly. The institute is part of a global initiative and also has a training facility in Japan and is planning to open new centres in China and France in 2008. As part of its expansion plans the institute is considering the introduction of distance learning courses.

Sources

[1] *Drug Store News*, 17 March 2008: 24.
[2] http://www.jjdi.us/about/news.aspx (accessed 22 May 2008).

professional HRD practitioners (ibid). The HRD function can support them by providing access to training to develop coaching and facilitation skills. There are also a variety of reasons why organizations make use of outsourced HRD consultants, including: providing fresh ideas, flexibility (using additional resources), and taking advantage of specialist expertise (Czerniawska, 2002). To these can be added: objectivity, acting as a catalyst for change, and the possession of analytical skills refined in a wide range of organizational settings (Gilley et al., 2002).

13.5 Design options for the HRD function

In the light of the above discussion we now need to consider design options for the HRD function and the implications of these for the various elements of the HRD wheel. Although larger organizations often have a centralized HRD function of some kind, be it part of the HRM department or free-standing (Blanchard and Thacker, 2004), there are different ways in which a centralized function can be structured. Additionally, more organizations have been streamlining their centralized functions and/or moving to decentralized or outsourced options. Carliner (2004) has identified six types of business model that can be adopted by an HRD function:

- **Consulting firm:** consulting firms tend to bid for individual projects which focus on specific performance issues. Typically the consulting firm will adopt an approach that Wykes (2003) refers to as 'performance-focused HRD'. This is where the HRD consultant works through a series of stages in a systematic and methodical manner: assessment of the performance gap, analysis of the causes of the problem, selection of the solution and design, implementation and evaluation. This is consistent with the principles that underpin the systematic training and HRD cycles featured in chapter 5. Consulting firms tend to offer a wide and diverse range of training solutions that are intended to address an equally wide and diverse range of performance issues. This is how the outsourced HRD functions tend to operate.

- **Internal profit centre:** HRD functions that operate as an internal profit centre charge other functions in the organization for the products and services they provide. This approach can be used by both centralized and decentralized HRD functions. Centralized functions often incorporate a training centre or have access to an external residential centre. Not surprisingly, their performance is measured in terms of their ability to make a profit.

- **Internal cost centre:** internal cost centres tend to focus on a narrower range of HRD activities than profit centres because of budget constraints. They also can operate on a centralized or decentralized basis. In many respects the centralized cost centre approach is the traditional model for a HRD function in larger organizations.

- **Leveraged expertise:** leveraged expertise tends to involve a small team of HRD practitioners who focus on the identification of training needs and then train subject experts in how to deliver and manage the training. This approach is often used by centralized

HRD functions such as training or learning centres, or corporate universities (see below), which first decide the courses to be offered and then identify who will teach these courses.

- **Development shop:** development shops tend to focus on the development of courses or programmes for a particular industry or sector. The client provides details of the needs analysis and outline course or programme plans and the development shop is responsible for the refining these and producing the courses. HRD providers operating as development shops tend to be external to the client organization and are another example of an outsourced function.

- **Course marketers:** course marketers are training providers who build a reputation for delivering specialist courses which are sold off-the-shelf or customized for clients. This is typically another example of an outsourced function.

MEDIA WATCH BOX

Decentralized training at the European Commission

The European Commission (EC), which employs 30,000 civil servants across 37 directorate-generals based mainly in Brussels and Luxembourg, is now characterized by coaching, mentoring, and on-the-job learning rather than formal training courses as in the past. This change is the result of a new strategic training framework that was introduced to help the EC achieve its stated strategic aim of becoming a learning organization. As part of this new approach small learning and development teams were set up within each directorate-general, a new appraisal scheme linked to learning and development was created, and every employee was given an individual training plan. It is anticipated that the number of centrally organized interventions will gradually decrease each year as decentralized events increase. Recently, further changes have been introduced such as using managers as trainers, offering more flexible training interventions, and making some interventions shorter. More changes are in the pipeline as a result of consultations with stakeholders such as the implementation of knowledge management and better utilization of internal resources.[1]

This illustrates a move away from a traditional centralized training model to a decentralized learning and development model although many more changes are still needed as indicated. It also illustrates an attempt to link individual learning needs to the strategic direction of the EC through the appraisal system. The implementation of knowledge management supports the argument that HRD can play a key role in maintenance of knowledge management systems (it also adds a further strategic dimension to the role of HRD).

Source
[1] Cottell, C. 2007. Commission accomplished. *People Management*, 12 July: 34–7.

As Carliner (2004) rightly points out, in many larger organizations there may be a mix or blend of models although one tends to be dominant. These models along with other perspectives on the role and structure of the HRD function have been amalgamated and adapted as shown in table 13.5 (some of these were also discussed in chapter 3). The table highlights the role, responsibilities (i.e. financial, focus and expertise headings); and structure; along with some of the advantages and disadvantages of each option.

ACTIVITY 13.3

How easy is it to find organizational examples of each of the options for the design of a HRD function as listed in table 13.5? As before use search engines for the Internet and library, as well as relevant websites and trade publications.

In terms of the strategic integration of HRD the most crucial role is that of business partner (Ulrich and Brockbank, 2005) or enabler (Yorks, 2005). This role was initially discussed in chapter 3, and is associated with the results-driven approach to HRD which focuses on added value and is consistent with the HRD model in chapter 3 which illustrated how HRD interventions are intended to support change through learning *and* improved performance.

INSIGHTS INTO PRACTICE

Training departments around the world

62.3% of companies in the Catalan region of Spain have a training department, with a higher presence in service industries and larger companies (in terms of size and turnover).[1]

In China local and central government personnel departments have responsibility for the training of China's public servants and the awarding of certificates to those who complete a course successfully.[2]

Sources
[1] Huerta, M. E., Audet, X. L. A. and Peregort, O. P. 2006. In-company training in Catalonia: organisational structure, funding, evaluation and economic impact. *International Journal of Training and Development*, 10 (2): 140–63.
[2] Shan, A. 2004. Present situation, problems, and prospect of China's public servant training. *International Journal of Public Administration*, 27 (3 and 4): 219–38.

Centralized HRD functions

The corporate head office is often seen as the logical place to locate personnel who have responsibility for establishing company-wide standards and protocols which set out how the company expects people to behave when working together (Bryan and Joyce, 2007). HRD standards and protocols can cover: level of customer service, standard of training

Options	Characteristics and implications for HRD wheel
Centralized as part of the HRM function • Activity-based approach to HRD • Vendor-driven (i.e. HRD source formal training from a wide range of external providers)	**Role** • Broker (sources suppliers) • Administrator **Structure** • Very small team: as few as one person in smaller organizations **Financial** • Part of the HRM cost centre **Operational focus** • Efficient processes (i.e. fit for purpose): the systematic training cycle, validation rather than evaluation • Maintaining performance standards of trainers and support staff (e.g. performance reviews) • Maintaining the quality standards of products such as training courses and workshops (e.g. based on validation data) • Maintaining service standards (e.g. efficient coordination and administration of services such as training needs analysis) **Expertise** • Predominantly administrative • Basic coordination of training • Limited understanding of HRD (primarily training) **Advantages** • Consistency of approach • Relatively straightforward to control **Disadvantages** • Lack of HRD expertise • 'Hit and miss' approach to addressing needs of the organization
Centralized and separate from the HRM function • Activity-based approach to HRD • Vendor-customized (i.e. internal HRD practitioners focus on instructional design with in-house delivery delegated to trainers and/or consultants)	**Role** • Instructional designer • Administrative expert **Structure** • Training centre • Corporate university **Financial** • Internal cost centre or • Internal profit centre **Operational focus** • Efficient processes (i.e. fit for purpose): the systematic training cycle, validation rather than evaluation

Table 13.5 Design options for the HRD function

Sources: Gilley and Maycunich Gilley, 2002; Gilley et al., 2002; Noe, 2002; Carliner, 2004; Ulrich and Brockbank, 2005; Yorks, 2005

Options	Characteristics and implications for HRD wheel
	• Maintaining performance standards of trainers and support staff (e.g. performance reviews) • Maintaining the quality standards of products such as training courses and workshops (e.g. based on validation data) • Maintaining service standards (e.g. efficient coordination and administration of services such as training needs analysis) **Expertise** • Instructional design • Leveraged expertise • More complex coordination role • Building relationships to better understand client needs • Knowledge of the organization's operations **Advantages** • Creates a brand identity for the HRD function • Consistency of approach • Can disseminate training to relatively large numbers of employees **Disadvantages** • Expensive to maintain • Expertise narrowly focused on design and delivery • Lack of flexibility
Outsourced—Operationally integrated • Activity-based approach to HRD • Vendor-driven (i.e. course marketers are sourced to deliver courses) • Vendor-customized (i.e. external HRD practitioners focus on instructional design and courses are delivered by trainers who deliver the training in-house)	**Role** • HRD consultant • Functional expert (specialization) **Structure** • Development shops • Course marketers **Financial** • Internal cost centre or • Internal profit centre **Operational focus** • Efficient processes (i.e. fit for purpose): the systematic training cycle, validation rather than evaluation • Maintaining performance standards of trainers and support staff (e.g. performance reviews) • Maintaining the quality standards of products such as training courses and workshops (e.g. based on validation data) • Maintaining service standards (e.g. efficient coordination and administration of services such as training needs analysis) **Expertise** • Instructional design • Leveraged expertise (internal and external)

Table 13.5 *(cont'd)*

Options	Characteristics and implications for HRD wheel
	Advantages • Exploiting the benefits of internal and external specialist expertise • More suited to flexible budgeting **Disadvantages** • Initial relationship building and familiarization with the organization can be time consuming • Restricted availability of HRD expertise
Decentralized • Results-driven approach to HRD • HRD is integrated into several operational departments	**Role** • Performance engineer • Strategic partner/Enabler **Structure** • Devolved • Small teams **Financial** • Integrated into department budgets **Strategic focus** • Effective processes (i.e. added value through improved organizational performance): the enhanced HRD cycle, evaluation as well as validation • Improving the performance standards of HRD practitioners and support staff (e.g. emphasizing continuing professional development, development reviews, career development strategies) • Innovating new HRD products and standards (e.g. integration of learning with work) • Innovating new HRD service standards (e.g. applying TQM principles, delighting customers) **Expertise** • Formal and informal learning • Leveraging expertise • Building collaborative relationships with managers (understanding how managers think) • Commercial acumen (understanding the organization's operations combined with a basic understanding of strategic issues) **Advantages** • Focuses on added value • Strategic integration of HRD **Disadvantages** • Potential for silo mentality in operational functions (i.e. lack of inter-functional knowledge sharing and transfer) • Duplication of some costs

Table 13.5 *(cont'd)*

Options	Characteristics and implications for HRD wheel
Outsourced—Strategically integrated • Results-driven approach to HRD • HRD is fully integrated into all aspects of the organization's operations. • HRD interventions are project-led by external consultants who develop long term collaborations with the client organization (trust-building)	**Role** • Strategic partner/enabler • HRD consultant **Structure** • Consulting firms **Financial** • Devolved cost or profit centres **Strategic focus** • Effective processes (i.e. added value through strategic integration of HRD and improved organizational performance): the enhanced HRD cycle, evaluation as well as validation, managing change, organization development projects • Improving the performance standards of HRD practitioners and support staff (e.g. emphasizing continuing professional development, development reviews, career development strategies) • Innovating new HRD products and standards (e.g. e-learning and blended learning, integration of learning with work) • Innovating new HRD service standards (e.g. applying TQM principles, delighting customers) **Expertise** • Strategic acumen • Project management • Change management • Performance management • Leadership **Advantages** • Access to specialist expertise • Responsive to flexible budgeting **Disadvantages** • Too reliant on external expertise • Potential for lack of in-house competency building in HRD practices
Virtual • Activity-based and/or Results-driven approach to HRD • Vendor-customized (i.e. HRD practitioners fulfil two functions: instructional design and delivery of e-learning; providing internal consultancy)	**Role** • Instructional (e-learning) designer • HRD consultant (internal) • Strategic partner/enabler (results-driven HRD only) **Structure** • Structural versatility **Financial** • Internal cost centre or • Internal profit centre

Table 13.5 (*cont'd*)

Options	Characteristics and implications for HRD wheel
	Operational or strategic focus • Efficient processes (i.e. fit for purpose): the systematic training cycle, validation rather than evaluation (activity-based HRD) • Effective processes (i.e. added value through strategic integration of HRD and improved organizational performance): the enhanced HRD cycle, evaluation as well as validation, managing change, organization development projects (results-driven HRD) • Maintaining performance standards of trainers and support staff (e.g. performance reviews) (activity-based HRD) • Improving the performance standards of HRD practitioners and support staff (e.g. emphasizing continuing professional development, development reviews, career development strategies) (results-driven HRD) • Maintaining the quality standards of products such as training courses and workshops (e.g. based on validation data) (activity-based HRD) • Innovating new HRD products and standards (e.g. e-learning and blended learning, integration of learning with work) (results-driven HRD) • Maintaining service standards (e.g. efficient coordination and administration of services such as training needs analysis) (activity-based HRD) • Innovating new HRD service standards (e.g. applying TQM principles, delighting customers) (results-driven HRD) **Expertise** • E-learning systems • Project management • Performance management **Advantages** • Ideally suited to multisite organizations (e.g. national, regional, and global) • Offers flexible access to learning resources • Economies of scale **Disadvantages** • Start-up costs can be very high • Lack of face-to-face contact (unless implemented as part of a blended learning strategy)

Table 13.5 *(cont'd)*

delivery, evaluation criteria, expectations of how learners will behave on training courses, criteria for the level of collaboration between HRD practitioners and line managers. These standards and protocols are usually articulated through a mix of: the HRD policy, the HRD mission statement, and HRD procedures and practices. They are also communicated in different ways through the behaviour of HRD practitioners and support staff that come into contact with stakeholders.

> **! TIPS AND HINTS**
>
> A professionally managed HRD function can make an important contribution to an organization's reputation and image. Organizations with good reputations are able to attract and retain more talented employees which in turn can increase the likelihood of sustained competitive advantage (Joo and McLean, 2006).

Centralized functions in large organizations, such as multinationals, usually focus on corporate-level development such as leadership skills for senior managers, core-competency programmes and organization-wide initiatives (Yorks, 2005). However, as table 13.5 illustrates centralized functions are usually associated with an activity-based approach to HRD. It is too easy to make the assumption that because a function is associated with a corporate headquarters it must therefore be strategic. Many corporate HRD functions take the form of training centres and corporate universities which tend to operate from a supply-led perspective that is associated with formal training and development interventions (see chapter 5). This fails to address issues such as the integration of learning into the workplace (see chapter 11). In many global organizations, such as McGraw-Hill and Johnson Wax trainers are sent from corporate headquarters to train at sites around the world (Marquardt et al., 2004). This is a form of operationally integrated training rather than strategically integrated learning.

Training centres

Training centres remain a popular approach whether the organization is national or global, private, non-profit, or public sector. Multinationals often set up training centres in countries where they have operations to ensure standards of training remain consistent with the company's culture and values, policies, and practices that emanate from the global head office (usually in the 'home' country). Often companies enter into co-operative agreements with local institutions, such as vocational schools and colleges, to make use of pre-existing facilities. The agreement can also include access to staff expertise at these institutions. These agreements are similar in principle to many of the partnerships that exist between organizations and higher education colleges and universities. It is not uncommon for internal training and development programmes to be accredited against a college or university award as this increases the credibility of the HRD function's provision (while providing an additional income stream for the educational institution). In the past learning resource centres have been particularly popular as a way of encouraging employees to take more responsibility for their own learning. These allow employees access to a wide range of materials and media (e.g. books, audio tapes, DVDs etc).

MEDIA WATCH BOX

Corporate training centres in India

These examples illustrate the huge investments being made in employee learning by the new breed of global companies emerging from one of the world's leading developing economies. The size and scale of these centres is more akin to a university campus.

Tata Consultancy Services (TCS) is part of the Tata Group of companies based in India (see also chapters 3 and 14). In 1998 the company set up the Learning and Development Centre in Technopark, Thiruvananthapuram. Covering 58,000 square feet the centre has: 18 classrooms, an auditorium, a conference hall, discussion rooms, and a library. There are also some 300 personal computers connected by servers. The centre can accommodate over 600 people at any one time and is supported by 30 full-time staff, comprising ten with a technical background, 17 who specialize in soft skills and three who handle the administration. The centre provides a wide range of programmes including a six week initial learning programme (ILP) for new recruits. This programme is also offered at four other centres in the US, China, Hungary, and Uruguay.[1]

Infosys Technologies, an outsourcing software service firm employing 75,000 people and with annual sales of US$3.1 billion, has a US$280 million training centre in Mysore, India, that has 58 high-tech classrooms for lectures and practical work. The campus also includes cinemas, sports facilities including one of the largest gyms in India, a hair salon, and halls of residence that cater for thousands of learners. Some courses last several months; for instance new recruits attend a 14 week course which encompasses technical and soft skills (e.g. team building and communication). The company likes to recruit people who are well qualified but also who demonstrate a willingness to learn. The campus has some very strict rules such as no alcohol. Not surprisingly as it is a software service firm much of its general training is heavily reliant on technology and e-learning. There is also a knowledge database that contains company case studies to help inform new projects.[2,3,4]

Sources

[1] http://www.tata.com/0_our_commitment/employee_relations/articles/20060907_grooming.htm (accessed 4 April 2008).

[2] Anon. (2006) Outsourcing twist, *Communications of the ACM*, 49 (10), p. 9.

[3] http://money.cnn.com/2006/03/15/magazines/fortune/infosys_fortune_032006/ (accessed 22 May 2008).

[4] http://www.iht.com/articles/2007/09/24/business/outsource.php (accessed 22 May 2008).

MEDIA WATCH BOX

A health and safety training centre in the US

This example of a training centre offers an interesting contrast to those shown in the *'Insights into practice'* box. It operates on a much smaller scale and focuses on practical training rather than the type of classroom-based activity associated with corporate universities.

Two local companies renovated a warehouse in East Syracuse, USA, in order to set up a safety training centre. The centre covers 10,000 square feet but only 1,200 square feet is used for classrooms. The majority of the centre comprises areas for simulating particular environments so that students can practise safety techniques (e.g. the centre contains two roofs built inches off the ground). Originally intended for use by the two companies it has since been decided to make the facilities available to all members of the local business community.

Source
Tampone, K. 2006. New safety-training center opens in East Syracuse, *The Central New York Business Journal* (Education and Training), 11 August: 16.

Corporate universities

The corporate university model is usually associated with multinationals. In many cases it is simply a re-branding of an existing centralized training and development centre or equivalent (e.g. learning centre) that offers a range of formal interventions delivered on 'campus' or over an intranet or the Internet. In others the focus has shifted beyond the original centre's preoccupation with training to incorporate a wider range of strategies that can stimulate employee learning and expand the company's knowledge base (Blass, 2001). Corporate universities can be found in the US, Europe, and Asia: for instance, in 1998 the automotive company Daimler-Benz became the first company to set up a corporate university in Germany (Jarvis, 2001). The catalyst for this model was the Walt Disney Company in the US (Walton, 1999; Blass, 2001). Since the end of the 1990s there has been a steady growth in this type of provision particularly in Europe (Marquardt, 2004). Examples of corporate universities include: Motorola University, Disney Institute, Harley-Davidson University, and Intel University (Yorks, 2005) as well as McDonald's Hamburger University and in the UK, Unipart University (Walton, 1999). Noe (2002) cites Motorola University as an excellent example (see *Insights into practice* box). The decision to set up a corporate university can sometimes transform an organization's approach to training and development. First National Bank in Colorado focused on limited training provision before it set up a corporate university in 2001 which expanded the provision to training *and* education, including e-learning, classroom-based instruction, and educational resources (Cocbeo, 2004).

Key concept   The corporate university

The corporate university is an extension of an old style training school model found predominantly in the US. In many respects it is a branding exercise that copies the traditional university model and is designed to signal to stakeholders a strategic-level response to learning and development.

Although corporate universities may symbolize the role of learning in the 'strategic thrust of the company' (Yorks, 2005: 74), this does not mean the approach adopted is always results-driven HRD. Corporate universities are a centralized function and these are often focused on activity-based HRD. Although it is often argued that corporate universities have a strategic dimension in that they link employee learning to the organization's strategy, unless learning processes become fully integrated across the organization this strategic dimension remains something of an illusion. The centrality of the corporate university acts against this process of integration. A study by Morin and Renaud (2004) of a major Canadian financial institution, which had set up a corporate university in 1995, discovered that participation in the university's programmes had only a very small positive effect on individual job performance. Although this might suggest a low return on investment they do stress that many of the benefits associated with a corporate university remain intangible. This reflects the general debate on evaluation covered in chapter 9. Corporate universities can operate as a cost-centre or a profit-centre (e.g. Motorola University is an example of the latter).

Decentralized HRD functions

Companies such as IBM and 3M operate on a decentralized basis: IBM divides its global provision of training into five geographical units; while 3M has devolved responsibility to each of its subsidiaries (Marquardt et al., 2004). As table 13.5 indicates decentralized HRD functions tend to be results-driven and used as a way of integrating training and/or learning into operational functions. However, decentralization can take other forms. For instance, Yorks (2005) suggests that the decentralized model involves the devolving of basic entry-level training; although this can sometimes include more advanced technical skills and management development that is specific to the decentralized unit. This suggests an activity-based approach to HRD and provides a useful reminder of the generic nature of the models discussed in this chapter. An example of a decentralized design using Toyota is shown in the *Insights into practice* box.

Outsourced HRD functions

Based on a review of literature on the subject of outsourcing and an analysis of data from over 300 organizations, Gainey and Klaas (2005) have identified that:

> **◉) INSIGHTS INTO PRACTICE**
>
> ## Motorola University
>
> The motto of Motorola University is 'right knowledge, right now'. The university was founded in 1989 and employs full-time and part-time staff in a variety of roles including writing, developing, delivering, and translating. All members of the teaching staff have to undergo a 160 hour certification course. Many in the teaching staff are recently retired employees and people who have retired from other companies. The curriculum provides a wide range of courses covering engineering, manufacturing, sales, and marketing. While relational skills (e.g. customer care, negotiating etc.) are the responsibility solely of Motorola personnel other technical and business skills, such as numeracy and accountancy, are developed in partnership with local colleges and schools. Employees are expected to undergo 40 hours of job-related education every year. The company also expects its supply and distribution chains to participate in the university's programmes. With an annual investment of US$225 million the university provides over 3,500 learning interventions. Regional centres provide 85% of training across the US arm of the company with online e-learning being increasingly pivotal to the university's education strategy. Learners studying at the regional centres are able to combine online study with face-to-face group activities. The university promotes itself as a global leader in corporate education to potential clients who can enter into a business partnership with Motorola University to implement the company's Six Sigma© system for process improvement into their own organizations. Consequently the university is providing clients with both customized consulting services and education services that are underpinned by the university's vast store of knowledge and expertise. As part of this service it is constantly updating its materials to reflect the latest lessons learned from implementation projects. The concept has been expanded to include Motorola Universities for Europe, Africa, and the Middle East. The university operates as a profit-centre. Return on investment (ROI) and 'tribal stories' are used to measure the effectiveness of the university's interventions.
>
> **Sources**
> [1] Walton, J. 1999. *Strategic Human Resource Development*. Harlow: Prentice Hall.
> [2] Blass, E. 2001. What's in a name? A comparative study of the traditional public university and the corporate university. *Human Resource Development International*, 4 (2): 153–72.
> [3] Jarvis, P. 2001. *Universities and Corporate Universities*. London: Kogan Page.
> [4] Noe, R. A. 2002. *Employee Training and Development* (2nd edition). New York: McGraw-Hill.
> [5] http://meetingsnet.com/corporatesmeetingsincentives/meetings_motorola_university_changing/ (accessed 22 May 2008).
> [6] http://www.motorola.com/content.jsp?globalObjectId=3082 (accessed 22 May 2008).

- The outsourcing of the HRD function is becoming increasingly common (however there are risks associated with this approach which can be minimized by having a detailed contractual agreement in place).

- Trust between the organization and the training provider is the single most important factor in determining the success of the outsourcing relationship.

INSIGHTS INTO PRACTICE

Toyota's decentralized approach in the United States

This case illustrates how training and learning can be embedded in work practices to achieve strategic goals. In Toyota training is inextricably linked with continuous improvement projects and problem solving activities which are integral to the company's strategy often referred to as the 'Toyota Way' (see also the case in chapter 3).

Globally line managers and supervisors are used as trainers and are responsible for the majority of training in Toyota. This includes running classroom sessions provided at the sites as well as on-the-job training which is carried out while employees are working on the assembly line. This reflects the company's commitment to focusing activities at the level of *gemba* (the work site) so that employees learn-by-doing. The concept of *gemba* is a key aspect of Toyota's commitment to *kaizen* (continuous improvement) as part of the Toyota Production System (TPS). If additional trainers are needed to deliver classroom sessions the company ensures they have production experience. All trainers have to be formally certified. In the US a central human resources department retains responsibility for company level training and development and adopts a partnering role with manufacturing operations. In addition, in 1998 one of Toyota's subsidiaries, Toyota Motor Services, set up the University of Toyota in the Silicon Valley of California. The university provides induction training for new employees and offers a range of courses on leadership, strategic thinking, lean thinking, how to do on-the-job development, and other Toyota business practices. Employees are also sent to the Toyota Institute in Japan for training as facilitators (again reflecting the company's commitment to *kaizen*). Meanwhile as part of Toyota's global strategy the company has committed to the opening of three regional training centres (known as Global Production Centres) in Thailand, the UK, and Kentucky in the US.

Sources
[1] Liker, J. K. and Meier, D. P. 2007. *Toyota Talent: Developing Your People the Toyota Way.* New York: McGraw-Hill.
[2] Liker, J. K. and Hoseus, M. 2008. *Toyota Culture: The Heart and Soul of the Toyota Way.* New York: McGraw-Hill (written in conjunction with the Centre for Quality People and Organisations).

- Organizations rely on training providers for two reasons: cost savings and specialist expertise.
- Regular and ongoing communications between the two parties is crucial.

The outsourced HRD consultant faces a variety of challenges when undertaking a project with a new client. Not only do they need to learn about the organization very quickly (e.g. about its culture, strategy, structure etc) but they also need to identify what type of relationship the client is seeking. This will determine the role adopted by the consultant. Marquardt et al. (2004) identifies eight roles that can be adopted which range from very directive to non-directive:

1. **Advocate:** the consultant tries to persuade the client to accept a particular recommendation. For instance, that an OD project needs to be set up to tackle problems with work design in a government department.

2. **Informational specialist:** the consultant has a particular expertise that the client wants to utilize. For instance, the consultant specializes in presentation skills training.

3. **Trainer/Educator:** the consultant advises the client on an appropriate training strategy and assists with the design process. For instance, that the best approach to a management development programme is not a conventional classroom-based series of workshops but a blend of interventions including mentoring, action learning projects, and e-learning.

4. **Joint Problem Solver:** the consultant and client collaborate to solve a particular problem. For instance how to improve hygiene on hospital wards.

5. **Identifier of Alternatives and Linker to Resources:** rather than suggesting one particular approach or recommendation, as in the Advocate role, the consultant proposes: a range of alternatives, the criteria for evaluating each of them, and the resources needed to solve the problem. For instance, identifying the advantages and disadvantages of different change management strategies and highlighting the resource implications of each.

6. **Fact Finder:** the consultant specializes in data collection and analysis. For instance, the conducting the TNA stage of the systematic HRD cycle and presenting the findings to the client (see the Tom Holden Vortex© case study in chapter 6).

7. **Process Counsellor:** the role of the consultant is to help the client understand how to analyse processes and tackle problems. For instance, educating managers in action learning but not being involved in the actual action learning projects.

8. **Objective Observer:** this is a facilitation role in which the consultant stands back, asking questions or giving feedback only when necessary. For instance facilitating strategic planning meetings in which ownership of the process, content, and outputs must remain with the client.

There is no guarantee that an outsourced HRD provider will demonstrate the same level of commitment to the client organization as an internal HRD practitioner would do. Consequently, the client needs to establish clearly defined selection criteria. In addition, time should be devoted to building a relationship based on mutual trust and respect.

Key concept Outsourcing

Contracting with external organizations or individuals, who possess specialist expertise and can fulfil specific projects for an organization, instead of employing an in-house function or individual specialist.

Virtual HRD functions

Information and communications technologies provide senior managers with opportunities to redesign the structure of organizations so that collaboration between individuals and groups is enhanced (Bryan and Joyce, 2007). This can involve significant levels of online working (e.g. virtual teams that span the globe) and it is important that HRD practitioners are able to contribute to this process (e.g. online facilitation of discussion groups, the development of e-learning). This trend also raises questions about the design of the HRD function. Noe (2002) predicted that 'training' departments would become virtual 'training' organizations which operate according to three guiding principles: employees have primary responsibility for learning; workplace learning is the most effective approach to learning; and, the most important relationship for converting training into improved performance is that between the manager and the employee. This is consistent with trends discussed in other chapters (e.g. chapter 2 on the evolution of HRD; chapter 11 on the integration of learning with work). Many virtual HRD functions take the form of a corporate university (Yorks, 2005). For instance, in Canada in 2000 the company Sierra Systems launched an online corporate university for its 900 employees; while at the opposite end of the scale in France the France Telecom University was set up to provide intranet-based training for over 100,000 employees (Jarvis, 2001).

Key concept   The virtual function

A virtual function comprises a team or a number of teams that are dispersed physically and geographically but who utilize information and communications technology to work collaboratively in order to achieve shared goals that add value to an organization.

MEDIA WATCH BOX

Virtual learning centres

This example illustrates how one organization is using a virtual training centre to integrate learning and development into the working lives of its employees.

The US company Kelly Services launched the virtual Kelly Learning Centre in Puerto Rico to provide on-line training for its employees. At an annual cost of US$250,000 the new virtual learning centre has the capacity to deliver some 200 web-based training courses. This training is provided free to permanent and temporary employees who can study at their own pace. Courses range from software training to skills development in areas such as time management.

Source
Caribbean Business, 13 September 2007: 9.

Summary

There are a range of alternatives for the design and structure of the HRD function including centralized, decentralized, outsourced, and virtual models. These models tend to be associated with larger organizations although medium-sized enterprises may have someone filling a full-time or part-time role as a HRD practitioner (although they are likely to have limited experience and expertise). The role and structure of the HRD function is influenced by an organization's strategy, size and design, stakeholders (internal and external), organizational culture, and an organization's technology and communications infrastructure. Popular approaches to the design of the HRD function have been centralized training centres and corporate universities which focus on formal HRD interventions.

Whatever structure exists it remains important for the HRD manager to manage four key areas: processes, people, products, and services as illustrated in the HRD 'wheel' shown in figure 13.1. The 'wheel' also differentiates between strategic and operational activities and the list of design options in table 13.5 highlighted which designs are commonly associated with these different levels. A key aspect of a strategic level role is working in collaboration with key stakeholders, such as senior and line managers. This links back to the discussion on HRD strategy in chapter 3. The principal focus of the HRD function should be finding ways to add value to an organization and this is reflected in the strategic level requirements of processes, products, and services. To achieve this aim the HRD manager needs to create a functional ethos that embraces continuous improvement, knowledge creation, sharing and transfer processes, and learning processes. At the same time he/she also needs to market the HRD function, manage the function's finances, and evaluate the overall effectiveness of the HRD function using type 2 evaluation methods. These are demanding and challenging tasks that require high levels of expertise in a range of competencies that are discussed in the next chapter.

Review questions

1   What are the principal factors that influence the role, responsibilities, and structure of the HRD function?

2   What is the difference between a strategically integrated and an operationally integrated HRD function?

3   Define and explain the concept of a corporate university.

4   What are the seven stages in the marketing cycle?

5   Explain the difference between type 1 and type 2 evaluation.

Suggestions for further reading

1   Czerniawska, F. 2002. *Management Consultancy: What Next?* Basingstoke: Palgrave Macmillan.

    This book provides some interesting and informative insights into the role of consultants generally.

2   Carliner, S. 2004. Business models for training and performance improvement departments. *Human Resource Development Review*, 3 (3): 275–93.

This supplements the chapter's discussion on different design options for the HRD function.

3   Gainey, T. W. and Klaas, B. S. 2005. **Outsourcing relationships between firms and their training providers: the role of trust.** *Human Resource Development Quarterly*, 16 (1): 7–25.

This article highlights the crucial role of trust in outsourced relationships between the client and the training provider.

4   Poell, R. F., Van der Krogt, F. J., Vermulst, A. A., Harris, R. and Simons, M. 2006. **Roles of informal workplace trainers in different organisational contexts: empirical evidence from Australian companies.** *Human Resource Development Quarterley*, 17 (2): 175–98.

This article includes an interesting discussion on the role of informal workplace trainers and their relationship to the formal HRD function.

5   Garavan, T. N. 2007. **A strategic perspective on human resource development.** *Advances in Developing Human Resources*, 9 (1): 11–30.

This article should be treated as required reading for both this chapter and chapter 3.

Case study

Managing the HRD budget

Concrete Co is a leading manufacturer of concrete building materials for the construction sector. The company has just under 2,500 employees distributed across the country in six production sites, eleven regional distribution centres, and a head office which includes a small HRD department headed by a training and development manager supported by two full-time trainers (one a specialist in IT training) and an administrator. The research and development centre is located at the site of the company's largest factory. Recently trading conditions have become very difficult as the global credit crunch impacts on house-building in particular. Plans to expand into plasterboard and associated products have been post-poned although the acquisition of two regional businesses specializing in leading-edge roof-ing materials is still proceeding. The aim is to merge these into a new division and rationalize costs further by relocating certain functions, including research and development, to the company's existing head office location. The long term goal of the company remains establishing itself as the market leader although the timescale for achieving this has had to be extended. It currently trails its main rival by 11 per cent in terms of market share. As part of this strategy it has invested heavily in new technologies (not only in production and related functions, but also in terms of: distribution and customer service, sales and marketing, and research and development). HRM policies are focused on recruiting and retaining the best talent; HRD policies have been focused on developing competence in innovation, customer care, and process improvement. However, as a consequence of trading conditions the board of directors has decided to reduce the company training budget by 50% from 600,000 to 300,000 euros. The HRD manager has been asked to review the proposed training plan which currently comprises:

1. MBA sponsorship for one director and three senior managers as part of the company's ongoing commitment to supporting the career development of high-fliers: $1 \times 41,000$ euros, $3 \times 27,000$ euros

2. Ongoing sponsorship of five staff taking professional qualifications: $1 \times 4,000$ euros; $1 \times 3,800$ euros; $1 \times 3,500$ euros; and, $2 \times 3,400$ euros

3. Ongoing health and safety training: 20 days training at 600 euros per day

4. Ongoing technical skills training for process operatives: 35 days training at 500 euros per day

5. The initial design costs for a new e-learning programme for customer service staff which is going to be implemented in 18 months time: 95,000 euros

6. Ongoing open-learning programme for customer service staff (to be replaced in 18 months time by the new e-learning programme): 27 days of workshops at 1,100 euros per day plus materials costs of 5,800 euros

7. New product training for sales and customer services staff to support a new product launch in six months time: 21 days at 300 euros per day

8. Induction training for new staff: 12 days at 300 euros per day

9. Ongoing development centres for sales representatives and sales managers: 6 events lasting 2 days each at 3,000 euros per day

10. Ongoing IT training using an external provider: 40 days of workshops and 10 surgery days at 800 euros per day

11. Internal IT training: 100 days at 100 euros per day

12. Management development workshops for middle managers: 12 days at 1,000 euros per day (external trainers) plus 6 days at 100 euros per day (TandD Manager and trainer)

13. Ongoing sponsorship of research and development specialists at 48,000 euros per annum (this includes conferences, seminars, and technical programmes)

14. Contingency to cover unforeseen requests (based on previous two years' experience): 40,000 euros

Case questions

Imagine that you are the training and development manager and you have to decide which initiatives to support:

1. What programmes will be cut from the training plan?

2. What criteria will you use to prioritize your decisions?

3. Are there any ways in which you could reduce costs so that some of the programmes can be implemented in a different way?

4. What changes, if any, could you make to the design and structure of the HRD department?

5. What are the potential implications for the company of the decision to reduce the training budget?

Online resource centre

Visit the supporting online resource centre for additional material that will help you with your research, essays, assignments, and revision.

 www.oxfordtextbooks.co.uk/orc/mankin/

The Ethical Practitioner

Learning objectives

By the end of this chapter you should be able to:

* Define and explain the concepts of business ethics and corporate social responsibility

* Explain the implications of key global trends for the ethical and socially responsible management of organizations

* Analyse organizational approaches to business ethics and corporate social responsibility using shareholder and stakeholder theories

* Appreciate the role of organizational and professional codes of conduct

* Explain the different types of HRD intervention that organizations can use to support strategies for business ethics and corporate social responsibility

* Apply the four principal responsibilities of corporate social responsibility to different organizational contexts

* Understand and explain why it is important for HRD practitioners to behave in an ethical manner

Indicative content

■ The impact of key global trends, such as demographic changes, poverty, and environmental degradation, on organizations

■ An explanation of business ethics and the implications this has for managers and professionals, such as HRD practitioners

■ The ethical and socially responsible ways in which organizations can be managed

■ The role of codes of conduct and what constitutes unethical practice

■ The four principal responsibilities of corporate social responsibility

■ How HRD interventions can support strategies for business ethics and corporate social responsibility

■ The benefits of managing an organization in an ethical and socially responsible manner

■ The drawbacks of managing an organization in an unethical and socially irresponsible manner

■ Differences in approach between established and developing economies

---

Key concepts

Business ethics

Corporate social responsibility

Demographic transition

Global poverty

Environmental degradation and climate change

The 'dark' and 'grey' sides of organizations

Codes of conduct

Shareholder theory

Stakeholder theory

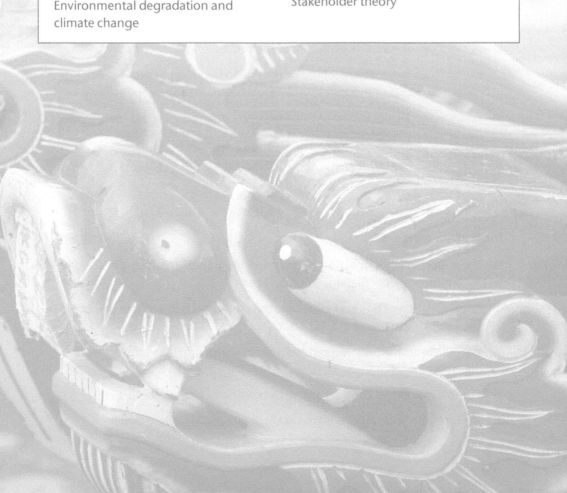

14.1 **Introduction**

Chapter 1 highlighted the impact of globalization on organizations generally. The 'credit crunch' of 2007–8 illustrates how markets around the world have become integrated and how problems in the United States can trigger financial and economic instability in other countries. The 'credit crunch' was caused by a housing crisis in the US, where warnings went unheeded about reckless lending in the form of subprime-mortgages to low-income families, and this plunged the world's financial markets into crisis (Samuelson, 2008). Within months the United Kingdom was facing an economic slowdown after 15 years of continued economic growth (Kaletsky, 2008). In contrast, the continued economic development of China, India, and Russia illustrates how the balance of power in the global economy is shifting from the US to these emerging markets (Bew, 2008). However, this economic perspective on globalization remains contentious: opponents argue that an economic focus is too narrow and that globalization should be seen primarily as a social process (MacGillivray, 2006). Only then can the social, health, and ethical dimensions of globalization be fully realized. Across the world population distribution is increasingly characterized by the process of urbanization: more and more people are migrating to urban areas (Friedman, 2000). This can be seen on a large scale in China as rural, predominantly female, workers are attracted to factories specializing in toys, shoes, and clothes (Cooke, 2004). This process of urbanization brings with it a wide range of social, healths and environmental implications, such as: the disintegration of traditional, rural communities; the need for more housing, medical care, and education; the provision of food and basic supplies needed for daily living; and, the degradation of the environment.

Green groups, in particular, see globalization as a threat to the world environment (Turner, 2001). They argue that a global market is characterized by a competitive exploitation of natural resources and a lack of adequate conservation strategies (Gray, 1998). Green concerns are now gaining more coverage in British and international media thus raising public awareness of issues such as global warming and climate change, greenhouse gases, and the dangers of deforestation. Organizations have responded to these concerns by developing policies on how to manage their operations in an ethically and socially responsible manner. The concept of corporate social responsibility (CSR) has emerged to explain this 'new' approach, building on the existing and more narrowly focused concept of business ethics. This shift can be seen in a range of changing organizational priorities, for instance: sourcing more products ethically (e.g. the growing commitment to Fairtrade products), the implementation of diversity policies that go beyond the minimum requirements of equal opportunities legislation, the increased use of environmentally-friendly machinery in manufacturing operations, and the increased re-use of recycled materials. Increasingly organizations have been developing strategies and policies for CSR and publicizing these to customers, suppliers, shareholders, and employees; as well as to other relevant stakeholders, such as national and regional governments. Consumers and the media are much more aware of the social and environmental responsibilities of organizations. However, some business executives still indulge in socially irresponsible and unacceptable behaviour (Idowu and Papasolomou, 2007) as illustrated in the *Media watch* boxes in this chapter.

There has been good coverage of the relationship between HRD and business ethics in HRD literature. However, there needs to be much more discussion on the relationship between CSR and HRD. HRD scholars rarely cover the topic in any depth while those in other disciplines rarely mention a role for HRD apart from limited references to training interventions (often restricted to a single sentence!). Consequently, the aim of this chapter is to attempt to address this deficiency. The first part of the chapter will consider in more detail the global trends impacting on business ethics and CSR before moving onto separate discussions of business ethics and CSR. These discussions will consider how HRD practitioners in particular can support an ethical and socially responsible approach to managing an organization. Although all types of organization operating in all sectors are affected by business ethics and CSR the chapter will pay particular attention to business organizations, referred to as business corporations. This is because many of the media examples of unethical and anti-social behaviour have tended to be associated with the private sector.

MEDIA WATCH BOX

Ethical and socially responsible behaviour?

These three examples illustrate different aspects of this chapter's topic.

In early 2008 the International Monetary Fund (IMF) estimated that global losses due to the 'credit crunch' could eventually total £500 billion, almost US$1 trillion. (*Daily Mail*, 9 April 2008: 72; *The Times*, 9 April 2008: 40)

In April 2008 water company Severn Trent was fined £35.8 million for deliberately falsifying key performance data which distorted the level of service being offered to customers. This misled Ofwat, the industry regulator, into allowing the water company to charge higher prices until 2010. This followed a fine of £20.3m for Southern Water in December 2007, also for providing Ofwat with misleading information. (*Daily Mail*, 9 April 2008: 17; *The Times*, 9 April 2008: 43)

In April 2008 it was reported that the HSBC Bank had admitted to losing the confidential personal data of 370,000 customers when a computer disk with password-protection only went missing in the post. According to the bank's own security guidelines the data should have been encrypted and sent electronically—not put in the post. (*Daily Mail*, 8 April 2008: 17)

14.2 **Global trends**

Demographic trends

The world's population has doubled from three billion to over six billion since 1960 and is predicted to reach somewhere between ten and twelve billion this century before subsiding. Whilst AIDS, famine, and wars devastate central African countries the birth-rate continues to rise elsewhere, particularly in India. This may prove to be a long term advantage for India over its main economic rival China. In China the policy of one-child families is predicted to reduce China's working population within the next decade (Engardio, 2007). Meanwhile the birth-rate in the developed world is starting to slow down and decline. For instance, in the US the population will continue to grow although the rate of growth will be below any previous period apart from the Great Depression (Noe, 2002). In the UK universities face the prospect of declining numbers of 18 to 20 year olds after 2011 when the number of people in that age group is predicted to fall sharply from 2.61 million to 1.79 million (*The Times Higher Education Supplement*, 24 March 2006: 5). These statistics reflect the extent to which the world is in state of demographic transition (Sachs, 2008).

Key concept   Demographic transition

'According to the theory of demographic transition . . . the total fertility rate declines with a lag, leading to a massive onetime bulge of population as the society transitions from high fertility and high mortality to low fertility and low mortality. At both the start and end of the transition, the overall population growth is low, but during the transition, the population soars. The world has been in that transition, claims the theory, for the past two hundred years. In fifty years' time, or earlier with good policies, the world will complete the transition and enter an era of population stability' (Sachs, 2008: 172).

The main implication for developed nations is the prospect of an older and more diverse workforce. With a decline in the number of new entrants into the job market because of the falling birth-rate there may need to be further reviews of the retirement age. This trend is compounded by the fact that in developed nations people are living longer and the impact this is having on pensions is well documented in the British media. For instance, it is predicted that by the mid 2020s the number of people aged 55 or older in the US will increase by 73 per cent (Ulrich and Brockbank, 2005). Increasingly all types of organization will become more reliant on the older worker. At the same the populations of developed countries are becoming more culturally diverse. This trend has been accelerated in the UK through the expansion of the European Union and the subsequent influx of people from East European countries, especially Poland. At the same time recruitment of employees from abroad is also increasing. In 2005 20 per cent of British companies reported that they had recruited employees from abroad to fill a wide range of positions, skilled and unskilled, managerial and professional (*The Times*, 12 September 2005: 44). Over the last two decades the number of women in managerial and professional roles has been increasing and today the number of male and female workers is roughly equal although it is still rare to find women in the top ranks of leading organizations in the US (Bierema, 2005). Although the number of female directors in the UK's top 100 companies has been rising they still remain in a minority (*Independent on Sunday*, 17 April 2005: 8). Interestingly, however, it is predicted that within the next 20 years women will own

60 per cent of the wealth in the UK, rising from 48 per cent in 2005 (*Independent*, 22 April 2005: 15).

Global poverty

An issue closely related to that of demographics is the problem of global poverty. We live in an age when rock/pop stars bring national leaders to task with high-profile media coverage (e.g. Live Aid in 1985, and Live8 in 2005). Even if the outcomes fall short of a great many people's expectations it is apparent that this form of pressure does deliver some, albeit limited results. It has been claimed that under globalization the total number of people living in basic poverty has actually grown from 2.5 to 2.7 billion (Saul, 2005). The supporters of globalization refute these claims pointing out that more global markets are needed to raise the living standards of the poor (Wolf, 2005). The World Trade Organization (WTO), itself a product of globalization, has been attacked by the critics of globalization as being: secretive and under the influence of corporations to force countries to repeal laws intended to protect the consumer and the environment (Bakan, 2004). Africa is the poorest continent on the planet and the only one that has actually grown poorer over the last thirty years (Guest, 2004). Aid agencies have been lobbying for an end to European Union subsidies that penalize African exports and create food-mountains (that could be used to alleviate the suffering of millions struggling to survive in Third World countries). The European Union's Common Agricultural Policy (CAP) has become the battleground for fierce debates in recent years.

Key concept   Global poverty

'The world is in a race between economic growth and population growth, and so far population growth is winning. Even as the percentages of people living in poverty are falling, the absolute number is rising' (Stiglitz, 2007: 10).

In the year to April 2008 world food prices rose by an average of 57 per cent (*Daily Mail*, 12 April 2008, p. 101). There are several reasons for this trend: poor harvests in Europe for three consecutive years, recent crop failures in countries such as India, droughts in countries such as Australia, increasing demand for bio-fuels because of rising oil costs, and the soaring demand for food products in the developing economies of China and India (Wehrfritz and Overdorf, 2008). As more and more people in India and China get richer so the demand for food rises. By April 2008 world food stocks stood at an all time low of just 40 days' worth (*Daily Mail*, 15 April, 2008: 12). At the same time the gulf between the world's poorest and richest communities is widening. Although on a different scale and of a different nature the UK also has a poverty problem with around 3.5 million poor people living in working households but on desperately low incomes (Toynbee, 2003). The gap between rich and poor in the UK is widening and the difference in life expectancy between the poorest and most affluent areas in the country is now 11 years.

The environment

We now live in a disposable society. In the USA you can buy a DVD player which has been manufactured in China for as little as US$30 (Fishman, 2005). This has become possible because of cheap labour costs in Asian factories, with China now being the world's leading manufacturer and exporter of clothing, shoes, toys, watches, and tools (Engardio, 2007). It is often cheaper to buy a new product than to get the existing one repaired. In the UK we dispose of 180 million tons of waste each year and spend nearly £3 billion annually for its collection and disposal. In 2008 the supermarket plastic carrier-bag became the media symbol of this profligacy. Across the globe natural resources, such as oil, gas, iron ore, water, and timber, are being consumed at a faster rate than at any previous period. The USA and China are the world's biggest polluters; and, the problems in China are going to get much worse as its economic growth continues (Hertsgaard, 2000). Industrial smog and untreated sewage are two of the principal by-products of the developing economy in China (Kynge, 2006). We are living in an era in which many people fear that 'ecocide' is the primary threat to civilization. This is the term used by Jared Diamond for unintentional ecological suicide. He argues that many business corporations are among the 'most environmentally destructive forces' that exist today (Diamond, 2005: 23).

Key concept   Climate change

[T]he economic costs of letting climate change happen greatly outweigh the economic costs of tackling it (Monbiot, 2006: 49).

We have reached a situation where organizations and individuals within organizations can no longer claim to be working in isolation from the environment. As various reports have illustrated in recent years the vast majority of human activity is contributing in some way to climate change. The Stern report, commissioned by the British government, warns that the global economic cost of climate change could reach 20 per cent of world GDP if nothing is done to halt or minimize the current trends. Examples of environmental damage appear in the news media on an almost daily basis: the collapse of the huge Larsen B ice shelf in Antarctica; the threat of rising sea levels caused by the melting of the Greenland ice cap; the destruction of up to 2.5 million acres of rainforest in Ecuador as a result of oil exploration; and, the collapse of natural fish stocks in the North Sea. In the UK it is somewhat ironic that the cheapest form of internal, and short-haul travel is the most damaging to the environment (i.e. by aeroplane) whilst the most expensive and least damaging to the environment is the most criticized (i.e. train travel). It is situations like this that have prompted environmentalists to argue for 'true cost economics' which incorporates the environmental prices for any service or commodity. Yet, following high-profile political meetings, such as the G8 summit at Gleneagles, Scotland in July 2005, the subsequent newspaper headlines remained consistently downbeat and moribund. Of course, global warming is a highly contentious issue. Political and economic concerns act as constraints on the implementation of changes that might reverse current trends (although some scientists already fear that we are at the 'tipping point' and any changes, even dramatic ones such as a significant decrease in carbon dioxide emissions, will prove ineffectual). It can be argued that this situation, along with other ethical concerns (such as child labour, low wages, and poor working conditions) represent the *dark-side* of globalization. Any global regulation of environmental standards is going to be highly problematic when goods produced by environmentally accountable firms cost more than similar goods produced by enterprises that are at liberty to pollute (Gray, 1998). Indeed many industries that have declined in Europe because of pressure to improve environmental as well as health and safety standards, have been supplanted to the Asian sub continent. For instance, 90 per cent of the world's ship-breaking industry is now found in India, Bangladesh, China, and Pakistan, countries which have less rigorous environmental and safety standards (*The Times*, 11 February 2006: 51).

MEDIA WATCH BOX

Natura and CSR

Natura is Brazil's leading cosmetics company and has placed CSR initiatives at the heart of its business strategy. The company's commitment to the sustainability of product ingredients, in conjunction with its approach to innovation and distribution, has contributed to significant increases in sales turnover and net income.

Source
World Business, 4, July–August 2006: 32–5.

At the heart of these issues is an energy crisis. Oil supplies are declining (although they are still a long way from being exhausted), demand for natural gas is rising, and there are shortages of electric power in developing countries such as India and China. Political tensions compound this problem, not only in the Middle East (oil) but also in West Africa (oil and natural gas), and Eastern Europe (natural gas). The Artic is the latest political battleground as the melting of the ice pack opens up previously inaccessible reserves of oil and gas. Nuclear power is a thorny issue. James Lovelock, the originator of the Gaia Theory (i.e. the planet is a self-regulating system) suggests that utilizing nuclear power is the only way to counteract the environmental damage caused by burning fossil fuels (Lovelock, 2006). The demand for energy continues to rise and with this increased demand comes increased damage to the environment. Consequently, organizations are increasingly developing strategies based on sustainable development. The concept of sustainability was first developed in the forestry industry and has since become widely used (Zink, 2005). It is now seen as a source of competitive advantage (Harford, 2006).

ACTIVITY 14.1

Carry out a search of recent media articles about each of the above mentioned global trends: demographic changes, global poverty, and environmental degradation. To what extent do these articles support or refute the explanations given above?

14.3 **Business ethics**

In the introduction reference was made to the 'dark' side of organizations. Those activities described as being 'dark', such as fraud, bribery, discrimination, or bullying and harassment, are covered by legislation. Unfortunately, there will always be some organizations who attempt to avoid even their legal responsibilities (Boxall and Purcell, 2008). However, there is also a 'grey' side to organizations and those activities described as being 'grey' fall within the realm of business ethics. An example of a 'grey' activity is the mark up on organic food in supermarkets (Harford, 2007). Another example is to choose not to release certain information about a product that may have an impact on the well-being of some people within the wider community. It is not the organization that makes such decisions but individuals working on behalf of the organization. Consequently, society expects managers and professionals to behave in a particular way (Lantos, 2001). That way is in an ethical manner.

MEDIA WATCH BOX

A typical day's coverage?

In one edition of the *Independent* newspaper the following business news items were reported:

1. Mr Robert Cearsolo, finance director of Spain's Guggeheim Museum, is being sued by the museum for the alleged embezzlement of £400,000

2. The Office of Fair Trading has charged 112 construction companies for allegedly colluding over prices when tendering for public sector building contracts

3. Following a four-month long investigation Mr Lee Kun-hee, chairman of Samsung, has been charged with tax evasion

Source
Independent, 18 April 2008: 24, 42, 44.

TIPS AND HINTS

To behave ethically involves building relationships between stakeholders based on trust (Kanter, 1996).

Building relationships with stakeholders based on trust can be in a micro-context, such as a middle manager interacting with his/her direct reports on a daily basis, or a macro-context, such as senior managers negotiating with external stakeholders over a multi-million pound acquisition or merger that can have implications for thousands of people (e.g. employees will be concerned about job security; shareholders will be concerned about their financial investment). To abuse or misuse these relationships would be to engage in unethical behaviour (Kanter, 1996). To ensure unethical behaviour does not occur organizations need to develop self-regulatory practices that are based on clearly defined ethical guidelines (Dowling and Welch, 2004). These are typically referred to as codes of conduct which in the globalized economy can be used to ensure that all members in a long and dispersed supply chain understand how they are expected to behave

---

(•) ▶ INSIGHTS INTO PRACTICE

The Enron scandal

Enron was created in the mid-1980s from the merger of two companies involved in operating natural gas pipelines. Over a ten year period from 1989 the company's sales increased from US$4.6 billion to US$40.1 billion. The Enron scandal was characterized by greed and arrogance. Senior executives were involved in breaking the law through a series of complicated financial deceptions. The company's accounts were manufactured to conceal substantial financial losses. Over a period of several years senior managers took large bonuses from poorly performing subsidiaries and exploited flaws in the financial reporting systems. Enron exploited the political influence it had built up over a number of years, gained from making political donations, to remove government restrictions on how it operated its business. This then enabled the company to engage in further illegal and unethical but lucrative practices (e.g. creating an artificial energy shortage to drive up electricity prices and therefore boost profits). Amnesty International even set up an investigation into the company for allegedly allowing its private police to attack villagers in India who objected to the building of a power station because of its impact on the local environment and community. Enron is a classic example of the difference between rhetoric and reality. The company published an annual CSR report which set out various targets such as reducing greenhouse-gas emissions and making pledges about a putting range of CSR issues at the core of its operations. Diversity was promoted. It was named the 'most innovative' company by the US *Fortune* magazine for five consecutive years from the mid 1990s and won several prestigious awards. Although Enron was able to fool a wide range of stakeholders (e.g. investors, employees, customers, suppliers etc) it was unable to continue fooling the market. The company ran out of cash to keep unprofitable subsidiaries afloat and filed for bankruptcy protection in December 2001 provoking allegations of fraud and corruption. In the previous year the CEO of Enron, Jeffrey Skilling, had sold his stock-options in the company for US$270 million.

Sources
[1] Bakan, J. 2004. *The Corporation: The Pathological Pursuit of Profit and Power*. London: Constable.
[2] Kay, J. 2004. *The Truth About Markets: Why Some Nations Are Rich But Most Remain Poor*. London: Penguin Books.
[3] Wheen, F. 2004. *How Mumbo-Jumbo Conquered the World*. London: Harper Perennial.
[4] Ulrich, D. and Brockbank, W. 2005. *The HR Value Proposition*. Boston, MA: Harvard Business School Press.
[5] Wolf, M. 2005. *Why Globalisation Works*. New Haven: Yale Nota Bene/Yale University Press.

and act (Fung et al., 2007). Such codes are self-regularity because ethical behaviour is not necessarily regulated by legislation. Business ethics is about 'the study of business situations, activities, and decisions where issues of right and wrong are addressed' (Crane and Matten, 2007: 5). The authors are referring to what is *morally* right or wrong. However, this does not automatically equate to what is *legally* right or wrong (hence the differentiation between the 'grey' side and the 'dark' side).

The notion that something is morally right or wrong suggests that ethical standards are universal. However, it can be argued firstly, that economic values are simply different to those personal values which guide us in our private lives and, consequently, any behaviour which is aimed at maximizing profit is acceptable within a business context (Kay, 2004). Secondly, that business ethics are relative to the cultural context (Dowling and Welch, 2004). Multi-national companies, in particular, face the complexity of operating in culturally diverse environments and having to decide whether or not to adjust corporate values to suit local ethical standards (Dowling and Welch, 2004). The values of an organization are often set out in published mission statements. It is these values that reflect the standards by which an organization operates (Ulrich and Brockbank, 2005). The dilemma is that the rhetoric can be very different to the reality of organizational practices (see *Insights into practice* box).

MEDIA WATCH BOX

Ethical and socially responsible behaviour?

Until the practice was banned by legislation in 1999, many German corporations kept a slush fund to bribe foreign officials in order to secure orders (*Independent* 6 August 2005: 25).

In January 2004 the news broke that the oil giant Shell had misreported its oil reserves by nearly 4 billion barrels. Subsequently, the US Justice Department decided not to take any criminal action against Shell over the affair. However, Shell agreed to pay US$90m (£50m) in damages to a group of US employee shareholders who had taken legal action against the company (*Independent*, 13 July 2005: 55).

In March 2008 Brendan Barber, TUC general secretary, called for an end to the exploitation of migrant workers by unscrupulous employers, citing a *Labour Force Survey* that revealed that at least 170,000 workers do not receive the UK's minimum wage (*People Management*, 6 March 2008).

Business ethics is important because it is being increasingly seen by consumers, pressure groups, the media, and corporate managers as being good for business (Crane and Matten, 2007). A good example of this is the promotion and stocking of an ever wider range of Fairtrade products in supermarkets with Stuart Rose, CEO of Marks and Spencer recently admitting that increasingly consumers want to see clear evidence of ethical behaviour by large corporations (Lamb, 2008).

ACTIVITY 14.2

Use the Internet to find an example of a code of conduct. What strikes you most about the language that is used in the code?

14.4 **HRD and business ethics**

The HRD profession has a responsibility to create a profession that behaves in a morally responsible manner (Hatcher, 2003; Ulrich and Brockbank, 2005). This is because all aspects of HRD practice have ethical implications (Hatcher, 2006) and involve making moral choices (Fisher, 2005). These choices will reflect directly on the personal integrity and credibility of practitioners (Garavan, 2007). In the US the Academy of Human Resource Development (AHRD), which was founded in 1993, has published 'Standards on Ethics and Integrity', while in the UK the CIPD has published a code of conduct for HR practitioners that requires all members, regardless of membership grade, to behave within the law and in accordance with particular standards set out by the institute (CIPD, 2008a). Members' actions must be underpinned by diligence, integrity, and honesty; and must be seen to enhance the CIPD's standing and good name. The code also sets out the disciplinary procedures for complaints made against members. Codes of conduct not only require professionals to behave in an appropriate manner but also tend to require professionals to give something back to society (Lantos, 2001). For instance, the CIPD code requires members to act in the *public* interest. Ultimately such codes are a sign of a strong profession (Bunch, 2007).

Key concept   Code of conduct

A code of conduct sets out the way in which employees or members of a occupational group are expected to behave when carrying out their work responsibilities.

Russ-Eft and Hatcher (2003) argue that given the ethical issues raised by globalization there is now a need for a global code of ethics for HRD which can guide practitioners in how to counter unethical values and behaviours that have emerged across global markets. However an ethical code:

> is sometimes better seen as a symbolic vehicle supporting the political interests of the profession by promoting its image as highly respectable and credible than as a set of norms that in practice ensure morally superior behaviour on the part of professionals. (Alvesson, 2004: 35)

The reality is that for a great many different reasons, such as pressure from senior managers or the need to ensure the survival of a business, it is not feasible for a HRD practitioner to always act as a role model. The way in which an organization's human resources are *developed* tends to mirror how they are *managed*: 'from an ethical perspective, they should not be treated as a "means *only*", and it is this restriction that makes all the difference in terms of business ethics' (Crane and Matten, 2007: 267). Unfortunately, a great many organizations do regard employees as a 'means only'.

So what else can a HRD practitioner do? An important role is to help educate organizational leaders so that they better understand the importance of ethics and how this can be integrated into the business (Maycunich Gilley et al., 2003). In this way, as suggested in chapter 1, HRD can act as the *conscience* of the organization (Marquardt and Berger, 2003; Maycunich Gilley et al., 2003). This has also been termed providing the organization with *ethical stewardship* (Dowling and Welch, 2004). However, there are two problems with this perspective. First, how can HRD practitioners extend their influence into the boardroom? To continue in a subordinate role in an organization that operates unethically is to be complicit in that behaviour (Russ-Eft and Hatcher, 2003). Yet, as has been highlighted in previous chapters, in many organizations HRD practitioners find themselves in such a subordinate role. Consequently, practitioners need to develop the ability to influence key stakeholders without having the prerequisite formal power (May et al., 2003).

Second, how can they ensure ethical decisions are made? There is a potential danger that performance-oriented perspective on HRD may obscure the ethical implications of some situations. Swanson and Holton (2001) suggest that HRD practitioners have both an ethical and moral obligation to ensure that such obfuscation does not occur. Hatcher (2002) believes though that for far too long HRD practitioners have emphasized economic gain over responsibility to society and that this has contributed to unethical behaviour in business corporations. This suggests that the humanist perspective on HRD is more likely to adhere to an ethical approach to the development of people than the performance perspective (see chapter 2 for an explanation of these two perspectives).

MEDIA WATCH BOX

CSR and career development

An online survey of over 1,500 private sector employees has revealed that younger employees are moving to the public and non-profit sectors. The Institute for Employment Studies has suggested that private sector employers could improve employee retention if they helped similarly motivated employees to get involved in worthwhile activities.[1]

The private sector, and in particular multinational corporations, has the resources to help millions of people out of the poverty trap.[2]

Sources
[1] *People Management*, 15 May 2008: 49.
[2] http://www.oxfam.org.uk/oxfam_in_action/issues/private_sector.html (accessed 29 May 2008).

A particular dilemma facing the HRD practitioner is that whilst research indicates most large business corporations have a code of conduct many of these organizations do not provide any training in the code (Dowling and Welch, 2004). From a practitioner perspective this is disappointing as there are many different ways in which training can support an organization's code. They can help employees to understand the difference between bribes and legitimate gifts (Dowling and Welch, 2004). For instance, LRN is an online business that provides legal and ethics education to a range of global companies that includes helping employees to understand when they are allowed to accept a gift (Friedman, 2006). Li and Fung, which sources over two billion garments and consumer goods each year and has an annual turnover of US$8 billion, provides training for its suppliers on social responsibility and workers' rights (Fung et al., 2007). They can help employees to develop negotiation skills to handle problems that can arise when operating in different cultures (Dowling and Welch, 2004). They can also provide pre-departure training for expatriates that should include ethics and the implications of working in a different culture (Dowling and Welch, 2004).

There are other more indirect ways in which the HRD practitioner can support both an organization's code of conduct as well as their professional code (be it the CIPD or AHRD). For instance, the maintenance of security and confidentiality are critical to the credibility of practitioners. The 'trainer' is often viewed as a 'safe pair of hands' to confide in and can act as an informal conduit between different departments and levels of management within an organization. Further, formal HRD interventions such as training courses, workshops, and seminars do not function outside existing employment legislation. The HRD practitioner needs to be conversant with relevant legislation, such as discrimination, when carrying out any aspect of his/her role. For instance, at the TNA and design stages of the STC (see chapter 5), it may be necessary to take into account any cases of special needs among the potential participants (such as access for anyone who is physically disabled); ensuring any tests to assess training needs are non-discriminatory (and do not exclude anyone for the wrong reasons). In terms of delivery, cultural sensitivity is important. I recall a guest speaker who was due to give a talk to a group of managers I was working with on a teambuilding intervention. On entering the room and asking participants to explain who they were he commented to the only ethnic member of the group, 'Oh, you're the one with the funny name, aren't you'.

> **! TIPS AND HINTS**
>
> In order to maintain credibility the HRD practitioner must act with integrity and discretion when passing on feedback from participants.

As globalization has changed the way in which many organizations now operate it has also brought the need for effective diversity policies within organizations. Diversity makes good business sense in a globalized environment (McKenna and Beech, 2002) and a commitment to it involves rebuilding the culture of an organization (Higginbotham, 2004). Hite (2004) argues that HRD practitioners can play a key role in this process by:

- Revising policies and practices to ensure equal access to management development opportunities (this can be extended to embrace all levels and category of employee)
- Implementing diversity training processes that address inequities and prepare for organizational change
- Influencing recruitment and selection processes by ensuring criteria used to identify potential candidates are inclusive

All of these are consistent with the standards set out in the CIPD's code of conduct. Indeed, there has been a proliferation of diversity training programmes across the US and research shows that training is a key factor in managing diversity (Hite and McDonald, 2006). Diversity training can help all employees to better understand how differences are useful to an organization (Blanchard and Thacker, 2004). Noe (2002) argues that diversity training programmes are important to the management of diversity. He defines this type of intervention as 'training designed to change employee attitudes about diversity and/or developing skills needed to work with a diverse work force' (p. 337). Examples of this are workshops at 3M in which managers explore their attitudes towards a range of stereo-typical statements about race, gender, and age (Noe, 2002); and, a training programme for senior executives at Centrica, which has been cascaded down to other levels, where role play is used to make individuals think about how their careers may have been different if they had been born into a different ethnic group, with a disability or as a different gender (Arkin, 2005). The Tata Group provide new employees with training that includes the appreciation of other cultures, tips on personal grooming, and business etiquette (Tata Group, 2008). Wentling's (2004) study of diversity initiatives in multinational corporations identified diversity training and education as playing an important role in avoiding the potential failure of diversity initiatives:

> Training and education were considered effective tools to assist in removing barriers such as people not understanding the value of diversity, slow involvement, resistance to change and unwillingness to participate. Diversity training was a way to communicate the importance of diversity and its impact on the organization. (p. 177)

She argues that HRD practitioners need to develop short and long term strategies to address diversity issues.

ACTIVITY 14.3

Can you find any other examples of how training interventions are being used to support diversity training? To make your search as wide as possible include academic journal articles and textbooks as well Internet search engines.

However, these approaches need to be placed within the context of creating an appropriate learning environment, as discussed in previous chapters. This strategy can help employees at all levels to challenge their own prejudices and assumptions about diversity (Awbrey, 2007). As previously discussed this involves line managers adopting a facilitation role. The development of social capital (empowered informal learning) includes the cultivation of networks. Many organizations have been attempting to use networks to increase opportunities for women and other groups without realizing the hidden complexities of this approach (Bierema, 2005). As was explained in chapters 10 and 11, social capital emerges and evolves and attempts to control and manage it directly usually fail.

> **! TIPS AND HINTS**
>
> Cultivating the context (learning environment) for career development purposes requires an approach that is more subtle than the implementation of traditional training interventions, such as diversity training programmes.

14.5 Corporate social responsibility (CSR)

Corporate social responsibility (CSR) is an ambiguous and problematic concept that is difficult to operationalize (Pedersen, 2006). Consequently, there are no easy solutions to how an organization can best implement a CSR strategy. This suggests the need for experimentation based on learning-by-doing: testing out different strategies and gauging reactions to these. It also makes it difficult to determine the true, underlying reasons why organizations adopt a CSR policy/strategy. As Crane and Matten (2007) observe it is sometimes impossible to determine corporate motives. Is a business corporation being altruistic or simply trying to maximize profit? Or is it simply about making good business decisions? What has become apparent is that in the developed world there is a significant market for 'green' or 'eco' products and services. For instance, in the US some 63 million 'green' consumers purchase US$226.8 billion worth of goods and services that come under the heading of LOHAS—Lifestyle and Health and Sustainability (Crawford and Scaletta, 2005). In the UK the growth in Fairtrade-branded and organic products in supermarkets illustrates that many consumers are willing to pay a premium for ethically sourced products that, in turn, can help to increase profits. This does raise the question as to whether the underlying reasons for CSR is economic, ethical, or altruistic.

CSR has an internal as well as external focus although it is the latter that tends to receive more media coverage. The external focus is about the impact of an organization's activities on communities, the environment, and external stakeholders such as customers and suppliers. The internal focus is about how an organization is managed and the impact this has on employees. This internal focus includes practices such as human resource management, and health and safety, as well as the management of any impact on the environment and natural resources (Zink, 2005). This internal focus includes diversity management, as discussed in the previous section, as well as strategies for lifelong learning (Packer and Sharrar, 2003). From this it can be seen that the boundaries between the concepts of business ethics and CSR become blurred. Increasingly, because of the external focus, countries around the world, such as the UK, France, and South Africa, are requiring leading businesses to report in some way on their CSR activities (Idowu and Papasolomou, 2007). In the UK 80 per cent of companies in the FTSE 100 voluntarily issue annual CSR reports (Idowu and Papasolomou, 2007). The leading supermarkets in the UK now report on a range of environmental issues, such as energy consumption, use of raw materials, waste, volume of packaging, and recycling (Comfort et al., 2005). Drinks company innocent donates 10 per cent of its annual profits to support non-governmental organizations in the countries it sources its ingredients from (Warren, 2008).

In terms of understanding the impact on organizations of CSR it is important to appreciate two particular theories: shareholder theory and stakeholder theory. These two theories reflect the tensions that exist between the two competing perspectives on globalization referred to above. Shareholder theory gives priority to profit maximization based on a corporation's legal obligations to generate shareholder wealth (Key, 1999). This is consistent with the economic perspective on globalization referred to above. Stakeholder theory looks beyond profit maximization and focuses on social and environmental values, based on a corporation's moral obligations to all those who have a stake in the business (Freeman, 2001). This reflects the social perspective on globalization referred to above. However, this delineation between economic and social is an artificial one as economic decisions tend to have social consequences (Pedersen, 2006). A CSR strategy underpinned by shareholder theory encourages a short term perspective. Zink (2005) cites several financial scandals, involving US corporations, that have been caused through the adoption of a short term perspective: Enron (where losses and debts were hidden in various subsidiaries); World Com (US$3.9 billion was wrongly accounted); and, Adelphia Communication (who invented 500,000 subscribers). Shareholder theory is more controversial in the UK than the US because commercial practices in the UK are underpinned by the values of European capitalism which emphasize the need for clear codes of conduct at the highest levels in organizations (Hutton, 2003). This may be a contentious perspective but it does correspond to other differences between the US and the UK/Europe. For instance, in terms of the UK/Europe's renewed emphasis on the rights of employees following a tradition of employee participation and involvement which has been markedly stronger than in the US (Boxall and Purcell, 2008). This illustrates that cultural differences over how business should be conducted exist even when a common language is shared.

However, shareholder theory has been criticized as an overly simplistic view given that business organizations have to satisfy the needs of stakeholders other than shareholders (Freeman et al., 2004). Stakeholder theory enables an organization to adopt a longer term perspective. Stakeholder theory looks beyond shareholder value to embrace a wide range of stakeholders. It is being increasingly recognized that long term sustainability relies not just on the shareholder but on all other stakeholders relevant to the organization (Zink, 2005). This perspective increasingly underpins organizational approaches to CSR (Burchell and Cook, 2006) as a successful CSR strategy involves a two-way relationship between business corporations, as well as other types of large organization, and the societies within which they interact (Werther and Chandler, 2006). MNCs, in particular, interact with a wide range of societies across the globe both directly (e.g. subsidiaries are located in different countries) and indirectly (e.g. sourcing of raw materials).

Consequently, organizations need to wrestle with a balancing act between economic, ethical, and social objectives (Lantos, 2001).

(•)) INSIGHTS INTO PRACTICE

CSR in an SME

Boss Design is a SME that manufactures high quality office seating and furniture. The company is based in Dudley in the UK and employs just over 170 people. CSR is an integral part of the company's business strategy. Recently accredited to the Furniture Industry Sustainability Programme the company has become carbon neutral through various initiatives including: reducing the amount of air travel by introducing video-conferencing; and, recycling 130 tonnes of customer waste (that in the past would have been thrown away in landfill sites).

Source
http://www.themanufacturer.com/uk/content/7984/Greener_and_leaner (accessed 26 March 2008).

As Crane and Matten (2007) observe, CSR encompasses the following responsibilities:

- **Economic:** business corporations exist to make a profit for shareholders while providing other stakeholders with economic benefits such as fair-paying jobs for employees and good quality products for customers (Lantos, 2002). Equally, other types of organization, such as local government, health, charities etc need to adhere to economic and financial principles to ensure their continued existence.

- **Legal:** all organizations operate within the context of a legal framework which can reflect national, regional, and international legislation. The emphasis is on compliance (Maycunich Gilley et al., 2003).

- **Ethical:** This is the 'grey' area as discussed above. Organizations may not be legally required to operate in a particular way but may choose to do so because of some over-riding moral obligation. This is about doing something because it is *right* to do so (Lantos, 2002).

- **Philanthropic:** this is where an organization exercises 'discretion to improve the quality of life of employees, local communities, and ultimately society in general' (ibid.: 50). This has been termed *altruistic* by Lantos (2002) and often manifests as organizations making significant charitable donations. There is a link here to the fifth layer of HRD evaluation labelled 'ultimate value' that was discussed in chapter 9.

The need to achieve a balance reflects the fact that the overlap between economic and social benefit is at the heart of a successful CSR policy (Werther and Chandler, 2006). However, from an international perspective different CSR responsibilities are emphasized in different parts of the world (Crane and Matten, 2007). These are shown in table 14.1.

There is some concern about the CSR stance that is emerging in the three principal developing economies: China, India, and Russia (see *Insights into practice* box).

Country/region	Prominent CSR responsibility	Examples
United States	Economic	Provide customers with products and services of real value; earn a good return on any investments; create wealth
Mainland Europe	Legal	Compliance-based approaches: employee rights in the workplace; EU information and consultation directives; health and safety legislation; Equal Opportunities policy
Europe (including UK)	Ethical	Diversity implies a more holistic approach with diversity policy going beyond the minimum legal requirements of Equal Opportunities policy
United States	Philanthropic	Days Inn recruit homeless people as reservation sales agents and allow them to stay in a hotel room until they can afford their own accommodation; in 1997 Johnson and Johnson gave away US$132 million in cash and products mainly to hospital-related causes

Table 14.1 International perspectives

Sources: Lantos, 2001, 2002; Douglas, 2004; Crane and Matten, 2007

◉ INSIGHTS INTO PRACTICE

The CSR implications in the three principal developing economies: China, India, and Russia

China

An indigenous form of capitalism has emerged in China which is built upon a bed-rock of tight state control of the economy. Initially, state-owned and small family-run firms provided the basis of economic expansion. More recently larger home-grown companies and multinationals have emerged which are developing an understanding of foreign markets. Investment in research and design is increasing as companies vie to develop their own brands. The growth in China's economy can be explained by several factors that would have CSR implications in other, established economies such as the US, UK, and Europe: the low wages paid to factory workers reflecting workers' lack of bargaining power and their compliant nature (although they are by no means the cheapest workforce in the world); poor enforcement of environmental laws, thus discouraging investment in clean technologies and conservation of natural resources (for instance, China is one of the world's most wasteful users of oil). The rapid economic growth is sustained because other countries buy the products China's factories manufacture while China's home market is expanding rapidly (e.g. it is the fastest growing market in the world for motor cars). Manufacturing companies are both energy- and pollution-intensive. There is a huge demand for raw materials such as steel, timber, and cement that is having a knock-on effect on other economies.

Hundreds of coal-fired power stations are being built each year. The result of this growth and demand for raw materials has been environmental degradation due to rising greenhouse-gas emissions, industrial pollution (including acid rain falling on 30% of the country's land), increasingly scarce water supplies, and large-scale construction projects; as well as increased poverty in many rural areas. This reflects China's poor track record on environmental issues. In terms of social costs, people are dying younger because of industrial smog in the cities and medical care for an increasingly aging population is poor. In order to increase food production China has embraced the use of technology, for instance genetically modified (GM) rice, and is investing heavily in biotech research (e.g. research into human embryonic stem cells). Corruption is widespread although not as bad as in countries such as India and Russia according to an international index published in 2001. In order to have a slice of China's home market many Western businesses have been prepared to bargain away patent rights (e.g. drug companies) and share intellectual property with Chinese businesses (e.g. automotive companies). There is extensive counterfeiting of Western products, from designer fashion labels to cars. It is these problems that are preventing Western power companies who specialize in more environmentally-friendly solutions from entering China's energy market.

India

The opening up of India's economy to foreign trade, investment, and competition can be traced back to 1991. Capitalism in the country is built on a caste system that has been criticized by many people from other cultures as oppressive but which has proven to be highly stable as a social system. In the past major development projects have been hindered by endemic corruption within India's bureaucratic and political structures. It is a country that seems to be characterized by disorder and social networks based on nepotism. Despite the economic growth many in India remain desperately poor. Often unemployed parents have to send their children to work in sweatshops as it is easier for children to find this type of work than it is for adults. Estimates of the number of people in India living in poverty vary from 260 million to 470 million. In the impoverished rural areas standards of education are very poor. However, despite the inefficiencies of the state education system, there is still a large pool of well-educated, financially literate, and highly motivated workers (mainly the result of an expanding private education sector). In terms of the environment, air quality in large cities is poor, enforcement of environmental laws is weak, and water is becoming increasingly scarce. Dirty water is causing the deaths of hundreds of thousands of children each year. Deforestation is contributing to problems of soil erosion, which in turn impacts on farming. People still remember the Union Carbide scandal at Bhopal in 1984 when there was a major leak from the plant causing death and illness to many thousands. The abandoned plant remains today along with 25 tonnes of toxic waste. Eventually the company paid out US$470 million in compensation although this was relatively little given the scale of the disaster.

Russia

Following the collapse of the Soviet Union in 1991 Boris Yeltsin's post-communist government tried and failed to introduce an American-style economy in Russia. The 1990s were characterized by what has been termed *anarchic* capitalism as Russia became a *bandit* economy (there was extensive corruption and organized criminal activity taking place throughout the 1990s). The privatization of state-controlled enterprises resulted in the creation of a new wealthy minority, the so-called 'oligarchs'. Although ordinary workers received shares many were forced to sell these in order to purchase basic provisions as the economy floundered and living standards declined (many Russians ended up living in poverty or found themselves destitute). State institutions were unable to pay workers and pensions were paid late. Pollution has been another major problem although this was largely inherited from the old Soviet system which viewed nature simply as a resource to be exploited. As a result foreign investors became increasingly reluctant to invest in the Russian economy. Since the election of President Putin there has been a turnaround in the economy. This period has witnessed the evolution of an indigenous form of capitalism which is built on a form of state control not dissimilar to that found in the old-style Soviet Union. Approximately 75% of property and land is still owned by the state. However, in recent years inward investment has been booming. Eager to exploit Russia's vast reserves of natural resources Western companies have had to establish political as well as business connections in order to do business in the country thus raising some ethical questions.

Sources

[1] Gray, J. 1999. *False Dawn: The Delusions of Global Capitalism*. London: Granta Books.
[2] Tully, M. and Wright, G. 2003. *India in Slow Motion*. London: Penguin Books.
[3] Guest, R. 2004. *The Shackled Continent: Africa's Past, Present and Future*. London: Pan Books.
[4] Engardio, P. 2007. *Chindia: How China and India Are Revolutionising Global Business*. New York: McGraw-Hill.
[5] Fishman, T. C. 2006. *ChinaInc: The Relentless Rise of the Next Great Superpower*. London: Pocket Books.
[6] Friedman, T. L. 2006. *The World is Flat: The Globalised World in the Twenty-first Century*. London: Penguin Books.
[7] Kay, J. 2004. *The Truth About Markets: Why Some Nations are Rich but Most Remain Poor*. London: Penguin Books.
[8] Lucas, E. 2008. *The New Cold War: How the Kremlin Menaces Both Russia and the West*. London: Bloomsbury.
[9] Luce, E. 2006. *In Spite of the Gods*. London: Little, Brown.
[10] Mishra, P. 2006. *Temptations of the West*. London: Picador.
[11] Ohmae, K. 2005. *The Next Global Stage: Challenges and Opportunities in our Borderless World*. Upper Saddle River, NJ: Wharton School Publishing.
[12] Saul, J. R. 2005. *The Collapse of Globalism*. London: Atlantic Books.
[13] Wolf, M. 2005. *Why Globalisation Works*. New Haven: Yale Nota Bene/Yale University Press.

A study by Idowu and Papasolomou (2007) led them to conclude that managers *genuinely* believe that CSR is good for business. Some of the most successful companies are also those who are the most socially responsible (Lantos, 2001). For instance, HSBC have set up environmental partnership programmes with various non-profit organizations including WWF and Earthwatch (*People Management*, 11th January 2007, pp. 32–5). While

The organization	The employee	The consumer	Society
Improves and enhances company image and reputation	Increases employee trust in management	The consumer feels good about buying products from companies they trust	NGOs want to work with companies they trust
Attracts new customers	Attracts new employees	The consumer will talk positively to family, friends, and colleagues about the company	Alleviation of social ills
Increases customer satisfaction and builds longer term customer relationships	Increases employee satisfaction, motivation and morale		Development of the arts and sport through company sponsorship initiatives
Accumulation of customer goodwill	Improves employee retention		
Employee benefits result in higher productivity			
Limits government interference			
Sources of finance are more readily available			
Minimizes the likelihood and cost of fines and legal actions			

Table 14.2 The benefits of CSR

Sources: Based on and developed from the following: Lantos, 2001, 2002; Rees and McBain, 2004; Crawford and Scarletta, 2005; Werther and Chandler, 2006; Crane and Matten, 2007

Starbucks is committed to the promotion of sustainability (http://www.starbucks.co.uk 2008) although the company has been criticized by fair-trade campaigners for how Ethiopian farmers are rewarded for their coffee crops (http://www.news.bbc.co.uk 2008). The benefits of CSR to different stakeholders are shown in table 14.2. The benefits are many because CSR influences all aspects of an organization's operations (Werther and Chandler, 2006).

! TIPS AND HINTS

It has been shown that consumers tend to view organizations that actively support CSR as honest and more reliable (Lantos, 2001).

The organization	The employee	The consumer	Society
Poor publicity—impacting on company image and reputation	Less commitment to the company	Views the CSR cause as a publicity stunt	Environmental degradation
Loss of customer goodwill	Lower levels of productivity	Takes custom elsewhere	Breakdown in community cohesion
Consumer boycotts products and/or services thereby reducing turnover		Makes derogatory remarks about the company to family, friends, and colleagues	
Increases the likelihood of fines and litigation thereby adding to the costs of the business			

Table 14.3 The potential problems of a poor approach to CSR

Sources: Based on and developed from the following: Lantos, 2001, 2002; Werther and Chandler, 2006; Crane and Matten, 2007

The consequences of having a poor, ill conceived, or indifferent approach to CSR is shown in table 14.3. This also includes the implications of adopting a controversial cause which can divide public opinion. It is wiser to avoid these (Lantos, 2001).

Even companies that are perceived as actively supporting CSR can be liable to accusations of hypocrisy; for instance, the Body Shop maintains it is against animal testing but does not always make clear on their labelling that ingredients in products may have involved tests on animals by other companies (Werther and Chandler, 2006).

14.6 Human resource development (HRD) and corporate social responsibility (CSR)

A key aspect of organizations acting in a socially responsible manner is an investment in human capital (Zink, 2005). This is easier for organizations that have a surplus of resources to invest in this way (Pedersen, 2006). Consequently, HRD practice should be at the heart of any CSR strategy. But what exactly is the role of HRD in this process? In the non-HRD literature the role is usually restricted to the provision of training. Training employees to do their jobs more effectively is seen as having a positive effect on performance resulting in satisfied customers and better financial gains for the organization (Crawford and Scalleta, 2005). Training can be focused specifically on CSR or on helping employees in ways that reflect an organization's commitment to CSR. For instance, in the provision of training and education interventions to help employees manage personal financial debt. The 2008 'Credit Crunch' has plunged many families in the UK into financial hardship. GlaxoSmithKline has a financial education programme in place which is designed to help employees manage their finances (Syedin, 2008). Training is one way in which the leading supermarkets in the UK demonstrate their commitment to CSR

(Comfort et al., 2005). Training is also being used by other organizations. For instance, E.ON UK, the power company, has been training staff, who have volunteered to be 'green champions', how to conduct environmental audits and how to educate other employees about CSR (Johnson, 2008). Training can assist managers to engage with CSR particularly those who need help in adjusting their behaviour toward the concept (as with many preceding concepts many managers may simply dismiss CSR as the latest 'fad' and only pay lip-service/offer limited support to CSR policies, systems of reporting, and operational practices). Rees and McBain (2004) observe that many managers are left untrained or poorly briefed on the implications of CSR. Yet a European Commission action plan on CSR published in 2002 recommended that management schools should include training on CSR (Zink, 2005).

In terms of the HRD literature, the HRD role is seen as being more influential at a strategic level. For instance, Hatcher (2004) argues HRD practitioners should be developing democratic values in the workplace and focusing more on social justice than performance improvement. While Packer and Sharrar (2003) argue that HRD departments can be turned into what they term HHBD departments: Helping Human Beings Develop departments. This is emphasizing a holistic approach to development that is consistent with a socially responsible approach to work (Bates and Chen, 2005). Given that socially conscious organizations are likely to conduct social audits in order to reflect on and evaluate CSR initiatives and identify improvements (Maycunich Gilley et al., 2003) there is a potential role for the HRD practitioner in:

• The design, implementation, and review of the social audit

• The design, implementation, and evaluation of improvement projects

• The communication of CSR benefits through daily HRD practice

There is also an initial and then ongoing educational role that spans the design of induction and CSR awareness sessions for existing employees. This can be achieved through a combination of technology-based and face-to-face interventions. Maycunich Gilley et al. (2003) refer to this approach as *socially conscious* HRD which has both an educative and supportive role:

> HRD has a responsibility to create a socially conscious work environment that benefits the whole social system, not just the organisation . . . HRD has a unique opportunity to educate organisations about social responsibility and use HRD strategies to integrate social consciousness into organisational activities that have the potential to effect significant social change. (pp. 216–17)

This is a challenging agenda and links back to the emergence of national HRD discussed in chapters 1 and 2. Maycunich Gilley et al. (2003) suggest that HRD practitioners should:

• Act as an advocate for employees when an organization breaches the psychological contract

• Ensure that decisions are arrived at democratically by involving all stakeholders

• Teach and promote ethical management and leadership

• Challenge and improve traditional performance measures to include socially responsible metrics

- Analyse and negotiate power relations in 'a manner that facilitates socially conscious thought and action in organizations' (p. 229)

This is very much an American perspective on the role of HRD. In the UK much of the above would be said to fall within the remit of the HRM practitioner.

Summary

The modern consumer of products and services is becoming increasingly sophisticated in their understanding of global trends, such as population growth, global poverty, and environmental degradation. This means that organizations, and particularly business corporations, need to manage their operations in ethically and socially responsible ways. Increasingly, CSR is being seen as a source of competitive advantage. CSR builds on the concept of business ethics and an organization's approach can be informed by one of two competing theories: shareholder or stakeholder theory. The latter perspective is gaining primacy.

As part of this trend HRD practitioners are required to behave in a professional and ethical manner. In the UK and US the practice of HRD (and HR generally) is subject to professional codes of conduct published by the CIPD and AHRD respectively. In this way, HRD practitioners can play a leading role in managing a range of CSR strategies, such as diversity or environmental protection, through the cultivation of an appropriate culture. This is consistent with the development of an appropriate learning environment as explained in chapters 10 and 11. For instance, in terms of diversity the learning environment should be one that encourages individuals to question their own prejudices and assumptions. Traditional training interventions, in line with the systematic approach explained in chapters 5 to 9, are commonly used to help managers and employees understand the importance of ethical and socially responsible management practices.

Review questions

1 Why is it important for HRD practitioners to behave in an ethical manner?

2 What is a code of conduct and how is it used by organizations and professional institutes?

3 Define and explain the concept of corporate social responsibility (CSR).

4 What are the benefits for an organization of adopting a CSR policy?

5 What are the principal ways in which the HRD practitioner can support an organization's CSR policy?

Suggestions for further reading

1 Fisher, C. 2005. HRD attitudes: or the roles and ethical stances of human resource developers. *Human Resource Development International*, 8 (2): 239–55.

This article challenges the notion that HRD is inherently good and discusses the implications of having to make moral choices.

2   Pedersen, E. R. 2006. Making corporate social responsibility (CSR) operable: how companies translate stakeholder dialogue into practice. *Business and Society Review*, 111 (2): 137–63.

An interesting article that focuses on the practical implications of CSR.

3   Crane, A. and Matten, D. 2007. *Business Ethics*. Oxford: Oxford University Press.

This is an excellent textbook on the topic of business ethics and the implications for a range of stakeholders.

4   Idowu, S. O. and Papasolomou, I. 2007. Are the corporate social responsibility matters based on good intentions or false pretences? An empirical study of the motivations behind the issuing of CSR reports by UK companies. *Corporate Governance*, 7 (2): 136–47.

This is worth reading to find out more about the underlying reasons why organizations support CSR.

5   Russ-Eft, D. and Hatcher, T. 2008. The issue of international values and beliefs: the debate for a global HRD code of ethics. *Advances in Developing Human Resources*, 5 (3): 296–307.

An up-to-date discussion on the topic of global codes of ethics (also referred to as codes of conduct).

Case study

Tata Group and CSR

The Tata Group, based in India, has an annual turnover of US$28.8 billion (2006–7) and comprises 98 operating companies covering seven business sectors including ICT, chemicals, engineering, and energy. The group employs just under 300,000 people in over 80 countries. Leading subsidiaries include Tata Steel, Tata Motors, Tata Tea, and Tata Consultancy Services. The Tata Group is committed to CSR and has published five core values: integrity, understanding, excellence, unity, and responsibility. Integrity stresses conducting business fairly and honestly; understanding is about showing respect and compassion and working for the benefit of communities; excellence is about standards; unity focuses on building relationships based on tolerance and understanding as well as mutual co-operation; and, responsibility is about being responsible to the communities and environments within which the group operates. There is a company code of conduct containing 25 clauses that provide the standards for how the Tata group conducts its business operations. These clauses include, for instance: national interest (e.g. respecting other countries' cultures); financial reporting and records (e.g. accurate financial records); equal opportunities employer (e.g. compliance with legislation); gifts and donations (e.g. not receiving or offering illegal payments); health, safety and environment (e.g. compliance with regulations); corporate citizenship (e.g. actively improving the quality of life of those people in the communities the business operates in); ethical conduct (e.g. all employees to behave in a professional and honest manner); and, reporting concerns (e.g. employees should report any violation of the code of conduct). In addition the company has a process referred to as 'Management of Business Ethics' which includes a commitment to train employees on ethical issues. New employees are expected to sign an allegiance to the company's code of conduct during induction training. These mechanisms illustrate how the company believes in fulfilling its duties to all those affected by its business operations. To help achieve this each Tata has a group ethics council and each of its subsidiary companies has its own ethics counsellor. However, there have been some blemishes. For instance, ActionAid has accused some companies, including Tata Tea, of low wages and inhuman working conditions on some tea plantations in India.

For much of its history the Tata Group has adhered to a strict set of legal and ethical values. These values can be traced back to the company's founder Jamsetji Tata. Tata Steel Ltd, established in 1907, was responsible for implementing what were regarded as pioneering employee welfare initiatives nearly 100 years ago: the eight-hour working day (1912), the provision of free medical care (1915), and maternity benefits (1928). More recently, in 1989 the company introduced a pension scheme. Additionally the company ran hospitals and schools. Tata Steel is regarded as a pioneer in CSR and has a vision statement that makes explicit its commitment to the communities it serves. It has won several awards for its commitment to CSR and is one of only a small number of Indian companies invited to join a major UN-sponsored programme called 'Global Compact'. However, over time some of its interventions started to impact negatively on the company's core business resulting in job cuts forcing the company to change its business strategy and redesign its welfare programmes. Today Tata Steel is supporting a range of initiatives that focus on rural development. These include the provision of health and education services in remote areas. Schemes such as water resource management and training in modern farming practices are designed to help communities generate incomes and sustainable livelihoods. Recently, the company adopted the Social Accountability (SA) 8000 standard. This promotes responsible behaviour towards workers supplied by Tata's contractors. Some 11,000 or so employees do unpaid voluntary community work during the weekend. This is an indication of the extent to which Tata's values are embedded in the company's culture. Part of a year-long development programme for graduates, recruited from leading business schools, is a seven week assignment spent in a rural community aimed at instilling in them an understanding of what rural life is really like in India. For example, some graduate trainees have had to live in a community of craftsmen and artisans learning about craft skills and the community itself so that they could identify ways in which the Tata Group could help the community. In this way graduate trainees are exposed to the group's CSR philosophy. Through the assignment the graduate trainees are able to better understand the ethics of the company. During the year-long programme graduate trainees are also provided with a mentor.

Sources

[1] Ulrich, D. and Brockbank, W. 2005. *The HR Value Proposition*. Boston, MA: Harvard Business School Press.

[2] Engardio, P. 2007. *Chindia: How China and India Are Revolutionising Global Business*. New York: McGraw-Hill.

[3] Ethical Corporation 2008. Asia-Pacific: corporate responsibility in India. Flying the flag the Tata way, http://www.ethicalcorp.com/content.asp?ContentID=4299 (accessed 14 April 2008).

[4] Tata Group 2008. web-pages:
  a) Tata Steel: a benchmark in corporate social responsibility. http://www.tata.com/tata_steel/releases/20040316 (accessed 14 April 2008).
  b) Tata Steel. http://www.tata.com/tata_steel/index.htm (accessed 14 April 2008).
  c) Tata Group profile. http://www.tata.com/0_about_us/group_profile.htm (accessed 14 April 2008).
  d) Leadership with trust. http://www.tata.com/0_about_us/values_purpose.htm (accessed 14 April 2008).
  e) About us. http://www.tsrds.org/keyfocus.asp (accessed 14 April 2008).
  f) TAS. http://www.tata.com/0_our_commitment/employee_relations/learning/tas.htm (accessed 14 April 2008).
  g) The lamp of rustic learning. http://www.tata.com/0_our_commitment/employee_relations/articles/20050121_rural.htm (accessed 14 April 2008).
  h) Fan-TAS-tic fifty. http://www.tata.com/0_our_commitment/employee_relations/20070713_overview.htm (accessed 14 April 2008).

i) A rich rubric of ethics. http://www.tata.com/0_our_commitment/corporate_governance/overview.htm (accessed 14 April 2008).

j) Tata code of conduct 2008. http://www.tata.com/0_our_commitment/corporate_governance/code_of_conduct.htm (accessed 14 April 2008).

k) Fair practices. http://www.tata.com/0_our_commitment/corporate_governance/fair_practices.htm (accessed 14 April 2008).

l) The covenant and the code. http://www.tata.com/0_our_commitment/corporate_governance/articles/20050122 (accessed 14 April 2008).

Case questions

1. Using Crane and Matten's (2007) set of four CSR responsibilities, identify the approach to CSR that Tata has adopted.

2. What other aspects of business ethics and CSR theory can you discern in the case?

3. What explicit approaches to training and development have been adopted by Tata? Drawing upon your knowledge of chapters 5 to 11 what approaches appear to be implicit?

Online resource centre

Visit the supporting online resource centre for additional material that will help you with your research, essays, assignments, and revision.

 www.oxfordtextbooks.co.uk/orc/mankin/

Continuing Professional Development and Reflective Practice

Learning objectives

By the end of this chapter you should be able to:

* Define and explain the concept of continuing professional development

* Discriminate between continuing professional development and continuing professional education

* Understand and explain the principal HRD competencies for HRD practitioners, line managers, and employees

* Understand some of the key trends that are likely to affect the theory and practice of HRD in the future

* Understand the principal future challenges facing HRD practitioners

In order to achieve these objectives it is important that you not only read the chapter carefully but also complete the activities and review questions, and undertake some of the suggested further reading.

Indicative content

■ Definitions of continuing professional development and continuous professional education

■ Key competencies for HRD practitioners, line managers, and employees

■ Future trends affecting organizations

■ The HRD implications of these future trends

- The potential benefits for organizations of these future trends
- The principal internal factors influencing HRD
- The principal challenges facing HRD practitioners in the future

Key concepts

Continuing professional
development (CPD)

Continuing professional education
(CPE)

15.1 **Introduction**

The importance of continuing professional development has been highlighted in many of the preceding chapters. Chapter 2 made the point that for many professional HRD practitioners, such as members of the Chartered Institute of Personnel and Development (CIPD), development activities, including education programmes, are an integral aspect of an individual's continuing professional development (CPD). However, managers and employees, as the other two primary stakeholders in the enhanced HRD cycle (see chapter 11), also need to demonstrate a commitment to CPD in terms of lifelong learning in order to sustain their employability. The career development paths of these three stakeholders may be very different but their development needs overlap in several aspects of HRD practice. These overlaps are shown in table 15.1 below which summarizes the principal competencies needed for the effective practice of HRD. It can be seen from this table that the HRD practitioner and the line manager require competencies that allow them to assume a shared responsibility for the management of many aspects of HRD practice. The employee tends to be involved in a learning role and has limited input in management decisions.

Approaches to CPD tend to be relatively mechanistic and involve the imposition of a methodology for reflective practice that does not suit all learners. In many respects this is inevitable as organizations and professional associations need to monitor tangible outputs from CPD that can be articulated in a relatively straightforward manner. The danger is that this becomes a 'ticking-the-box' exercise which fails to instil a genuine understanding of reflective practice. Critically reflecting on your own actions and behaviour is probably one of the most difficult things to do and organizations and professional associations often lack the resources to support this effectively. Certainly, mentoring and coaching (both formal and informal) can help but these methods need time and money. Ultimately the concept of reflective practice needs to be deeply embedded in the organizational and/or occupational culture so that it is seen as a normal everyday activity. This is important also because existing approaches to CPD do not necessarily capture the benefits of informal learning as many individuals are unaware that such learning has occurred (see chapter 11). Arguably the current situation illustrates the continuing influence on strategies and methodologies for CPD of traditional rational models for HRD (e.g. the systematic training cycle discussed in chapter 5).

The emphasis placed on CPD by professional associations, such as the CIPD, reflects the ongoing professionalization of HRM and HRD occupational roles. This is a global trend as illustrated by a Tanzanian example in the *Insights into practice* box later in this chapter. Several implications of this trend have been highlighted in earlier chapters, for instance: strategic credibility (chapter 3), and ethical and socially responsible practice (chapter 14). However, there are four dilemmas confronting the HRD profession. First, many organizations employ HRD practitioners who do not possess formal qualifications or membership of a professional association (and therefore are not subject to any code of ethics or conduct). Second, as chapter 12 explained, in the vast majority of SMEs responsibility for HRD practice rests with owner-managers, who tend to lack formal management qualifications. Third, the reality facing many HRD practitioners is that 'the practice of HRD and the professional expertise in HRD is in constant danger of remaining an unused resource in organizations' (Hytönen, 2003: 134). Fourth, as Fenwick (2005) observes HRD practitioners can find themselves marginalized if they challenge prevailing organizational ideologies and practices.

The first two sections in this chapter (15.2 and 15.3) focus respectively on a discussion of the concept of CPD and the key competencies needed by stakeholders for the effective practice of HRD. The ongoing challenge facing HRD practitioners and line managers in particular is finding ways to keep their competencies updated in the face of a turbulent external environment. Chapter 1 set out the principal characteristics of globalization and the implications of this for organizations generally and the practice of HRD specifically (see tables 1.2 and 1.3). Section 15.4 below builds on these trends by highlighting some of the current predictions about how global markets, organizational structures and technologies may change in the future and the potential implications for the practice of HRD (see table 15.2). This is followed in section 15.5 by a summary of the principal challenges facing HRD practitioners, line managers, and employees. The final section focuses on international trends, building on the original discussion in chapter 1. The chapter closes with a case study based on the career profile of a training and development consultant employed by Acorn, a training and recruitment firm based in South Wales.

15.2 Key competencies for the practice of HRD

A wide range of knowledge and skills has been identified in the preceding chapters and these have been categorized as stakeholder HRD competencies in table 15.1. The categories are: strategic acumen; commercial acumen; leadership; technical (strategic); technical (operational); and, critical reflection. This is linked to figures 15.1, 15.2, and 15.3 which summarize the key HRD competencies for each of the three stakeholders: HRD practitioner; line manager; and, employee. The terms used to describe categories have been amended where appropriate to reflect the different roles of the three stakeholders. For instance, employee involvement in strategy is normally very limited or non-existent.

There are other ways to categorize such competencies and there are omissions. For instance, conflict resolution was not made explicit in the book but this is needed in a highly fluid and ambiguous context. What I have tried to do is avoid producing a list of generic competencies which could fit any organizational role. Collectively the table does reflect the primary competencies needed for the business partner role which is regarded as 'one of the most important activities in which HRD professionals may engage' (Gilley et al., 2002: 408). Although many responsibilities have been devolved to line managers and/or outsourced to external providers there is still an expectation in many organizational contexts that the HRD practitioner will possess all-round expertise in the practice of HRD. Clearly, preceding chapters have illustrated that the role of the HRD practitioner does vary considerably from organization to organization and in many other contexts he/she would not be expected to possess all the above competencies; or possess them to the same level of competence. Rather line managers or owner-managers assume

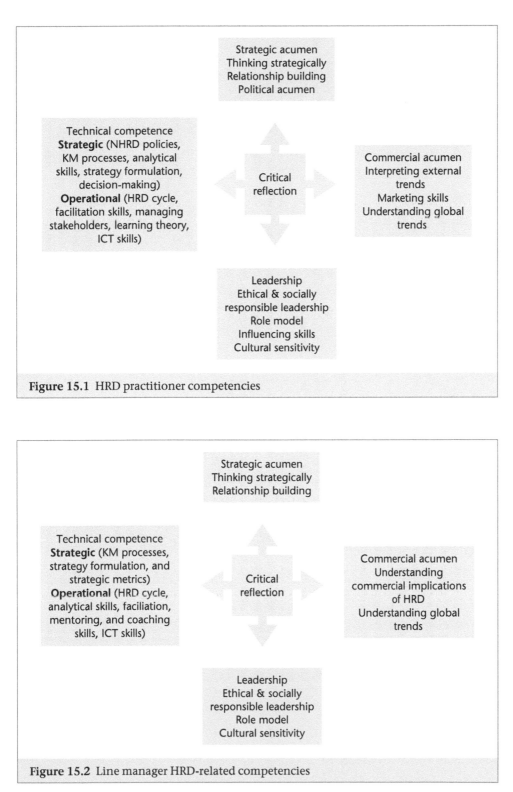

Figure 15.1 HRD practitioner competencies

Figure 15.2 Line manager HRD-related competencies

Competencies	HRD practitioner	Line Manager	Employee
Strategic acumen	Able to think strategically (1, 3, 13); able to operate as strategic partner (2, 3, 13); understands how HRD interventions can add value (3, 5, 9); able to differentiate between 'activity-based' and 'results-driven' approaches to HRD (2, 3, 5, 13); knows how to 'think globally but act locally' (1); able to build relationships with external HRD stakeholders at regional and national levels (1, 13); skilled at negotiating organizational politics (2, 13)	Able to think strategically (3, 12); able to operate as business partner (2, 3); knows how to 'think globally but act locally' (1)	Understands how his/her role is linked to strategic goals and objectives (3)
Commercial acumen	Able to make a business case to justify an organization's investment in HRD (2, 3, 13); knowledgeable about global trends and the global economy (1); able to scan and analyse external environment (3); knows how to market the HRD function (13); knows how to run the HRD function as a business (13)	Understands the commercial implications of HRD interventions (3, 5, 6, 12); understands global trends (1)	Understands the implications of training for work role (5, 6); understands the need for improved performance (5, 6)
Leadership	Demonstrates ethical and socially responsible leadership (1, 14); able to lead as well as manage the HRD function (13); demonstrates leadership to organizational members: understands and enacts his/her responsibilities for learning and development (2, 3, 5, 6, 7, 8, 9, 11, 12, 13, 14); able to lead projects (7, 8, 9); able to influence others, to negotiate effectively, and to communicate ideas with fluency (3); demonstrates political acumen (2, 13); able to demonstrate cultural sensitivity (1, 2, 3, 13, 14)	Demonstrates ethical and socially responsible leadership (14); demonstrates leadership to peers and subordinates: understands and enacts his/her responsibilities for learning and development (2, 3, 5, 6, 9, 11, 12); demonstrates cultural sensitivity (1, 2, 3, 12)	Able to respond to specific ethical and socially responsible training interventions (14); builds relationships with peers: understands and enacts his/her responsibilities for learning and development (2, 5, 6, 9, 11, 12)
Technical (strategic)	Knowledgeable about different national HRD policies and practices (1); understands knowledge management processes (e.g. knowledge creation, sharing and transfer) (1, 10); knowledgeable about intellectual capital (human and social capital) theory; able to balance the implications of humanist and performance perspectives on learning and HRD (2); able to analyse external and internal environments (strategic 'scanning') (3); able to identify an appropriate blend of strategic HRD choices (3); knows how to formulate a HRD strategy, policy, and plans; knowledgeable about strategic metrics (e.g. 'balanced scorecard') (3); able to analyse	Able to support specific HRD strategic choices (3); knowledgeable about strategic metrics (e.g. 'balanced scorecard') (3); understands the organization's vision and mission (3); understands the relationship between individual goals and objectives and organizational goals and objectives (3);	Able to respond to specific HRD strategic choices (3); understands the organization's vision and mission (3); understands the relationship between individual goals and objectives and organizational goals and objectives (3); skilled in

	'training' needs at the organizational level (2); understands cultural differences and the implications of these for formal and informal learning (1); able to facilitate the creation of a learning-oriented culture (2); skilled at decision-making (minimizing the effects of 'bounded rationality') (3); knowledgeable and skilled in change management (1); skilled in information and communications technologies (10)	understands knowledge management processes (10); skilled in information and communications technologies (10)	information and communications technologies (10)
Technical (operational)	Knowledgeable about and skilled in the design, delivery, and evaluation of global training in a multinational environment (1); able to analyse 'training' needs at department and individual levels (2, 5, 6); knows how to develop operational HRD plans (e.g. training plans for departments and individuals) (3); skilled at coaching, mentoring, and facilitation (1); understands learning theories and the implications for practice (1, 2, 4, 7); able to design a wide range of HRD interventions (5, 7, 10, 11); able to deliver a wide range of HRD interventions that directly impact on individual organizational members (5, 8); able to deliver a wide range of HRD interventions that indirectly impact on individual organizational members (10, 11); understands how to learn and how to learn differently (4); knowledgeable about project management processes and techniques (7); able to manage multiple external stakeholders involved in projects (7, 8, 9, 13); able to facilitate change management interventions (3, 5, 8, 10, 11, 13); understands the importance of customer service (13)	Knowledgeable about the design, delivery, and evaluation of global training in a multinational environment (2); able to analyse 'training' needs at department and individual levels (2); understands about operational HRD plans (e.g. training plans for departments and individuals) (3); skilled at coaching, mentoring, and facilitation (1); understands aspects of learning theory (1, 2); understands how to learn and how to learn differently (4)	Understands aspects of learning theory (1, 2, 4); understands how to learn and how to learn differently (4); able to assess own training needs (5, 6); able to evaluate training interventions (5, 9); able to coach peers (8)
Critical reflection	Able to act as a role model for reflective practice (2, 4); demonstrates career consciousness (2); understands the application of learning theory (4)	Able to critically reflect on own actions and behaviours (essential for cultural 'rewiring' of managers) (3, 4); able to act as a role model for reflective practice (2); demonstrates career consciousness (2)	Demonstrates career consciousness (2); understands how to critically reflect on own performance (4)

Table 15.1 Stakeholder HRD competencies highlighted in chapters 1 to 14

Note: The numbers in brackets indicate the relevant chapters

INSIGHTS INTO PRACTICE

Developing trainers in Toyota

Toyota's approach to the development of trainers is based on the following belief: 'Almost anyone can learn the fundamentals of training. Intuitive skills, however, tend to be inherent in the personal makeup of the individual. It is possible to bring out latent abilities in individuals, but it is easier if the basic raw material is present to begin with' (p. 65). The key competencies for trainers identified by Toyota include:

Intuitive

A willingness and ability to learn

Adaptability and flexibility

Concern for others

Patience

Persistence

Taking responsibility

Confidence and leadership

A questioning nature

Learnable

Observation and job analysis

Communication skills

Attention to detail

Knowledge of the job

Respect for colleagues

Source
Liker, J. K. and Meier, D. P. 2007. *Toyota Talent: Developing your People the Toyota Way*. New York: McGraw-Hill.

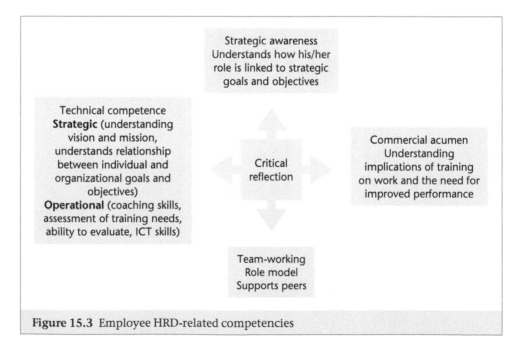

Figure 15.3 Employee HRD-related competencies

additional responsibilities for HRD practice. The question is whether or not they are able to acquire and exercise this expertise effectively or as effectively as HRD practitioners. Consequently, the competencies listed in the table and illustrated in the figures must be treated as generalizations. I have chosen to highlight specific aspects of each of the competencies and you may wish to discuss with other students whether you agree with my selection. Critical reflection has been placed in the centre because this impacts on all the other competencies.

Having identified the key HRD competencies for the three principal stakeholders it is now necessary to discuss the concept of continuing professional development in more detail.

15.3 **Continuing professional development**

> **Key concept** Continuing professional development
>
> Continuing professional development (CPD) is an ongoing learning process that focuses on developing professional expertise and the ability to learn more effectively. Pivotal to CPD is the concept of reflective practice (i.e. the ability to reflect critically).

Continuing professional development (CPD) is closely associated with career development. For instance, members of the CIPD must demonstrate evidence of CPD in order to progress through the different levels of membership and, in turn, make themselves eligible for promotion to more senior HR roles. Consequently, it is important that CPD is not viewed as a 'stand-alone' activity but as an integral part of an organization's HRD strategy. Any individual engaging in CPD needs as much support as possible from his/her organization. This may be in terms of financial support, time to study, opportunities to maximise learning in the workplace or access to relevant equipment, such as a computer for e-learning. Obviously, the degree of support will vary considerably from one organization to another. Research shows that employees who have higher levels of job satisfaction are more likely to be willing to learn new skills (Chen et al., 2004).

A great deal of the literature on personal development assumes that learners are free to be themselves, encouraged to be critical thinkers and free to participate in learning activities (Garavan et al., 2004). The emphasis is on the individual learner and the assumption often made by organizations is that critical reflection is an isolated activity (see *Insights into practice* box). This is probably because CPD is about self-development. It is a process in which individuals are expected to take time-out to focus on their own, *personal* development rather than the development of others. However, given the importance of formal and informal groups and collaborative working (discussed in chapters 10 and 11), there is much merit in using colleagues to facilitate personal development. As chapter 10 explained much of an individual's work is carried out as part of a shared practice with colleagues. In many respects CPD is a journey of discovery and as with any journey you need to plan the route, identify stopping points for refreshments, and/or sleep and also make contingency arrangements to minimize the unexpected (e.g. a good quality map, maybe even a compass). It is also about being a role model and being seen to 'practise what you preach'. There is little point in promoting any aspect of learning and development within an organization if you are not seen to apply the same processes to yourself. Arguably, a large amount of an HRD practitioner's credibility rests on his/her ability to actively demonstrate that learning and development is not simply something they talk about (Mankin, 2003a).

INSIGHTS INTO PRACTICE

A personal reflection

At a CIPD conference I attended the guest speaker talked about CPD as an exercise in personal reflection that was based on cognitive theories of learning (see chapter 4). He went on to explain that recently he had visited one of his clients (a leading blue chip company) and had to criticize their managers for allowing staff to use the new 'thinking rooms' for group meetings and discussions. The rationale for this position: he tried to argue that employees must reflect in silence and that is the purpose of these rooms. There was no acknowledgement of sociological perspectives on learning (see chapter 4). Indeed, he appeared oblivious to the existence of these alternative perspectives.

Source
The author.

TIPS AND HINTS

Rather than simply focusing on what you have done and listing all the courses, workshops, and seminars you have attended you need to think about *how* you have developed and how you want to develop in the future. This will involve you in answering some questions and identifying what is different about you compared with, for instance 12 months earlier. Have your colleagues commented on your work or your competence over the past year? What did you do as a result of any comments made? Have you offered feedback to colleagues and how have they reacted to it? What does their reaction tell you about yourself? This process also requires you to reflect upon your own competence. This can be a simple self-assessment exercise based on the knowledge and skills needed to carry out your present role effectively. You may also wish to compare this assessment to the levels of knowledge and skills required for other roles that interest you. Any gaps can then be used as the starting point for your CPD plan. You can carry out a similar exercise if you are a full-time student (see Activity 15.1).

Source
Adapted from Mankin 2003a.

> **ACTIVITY 15.1**
>
> Design a simple self-assessment checklist based on the knowledge and skills needed for you present role if you are a part-time student. If you are a full-time student base the checklist on the knowledge and skills required by employers (this should be available to you in a course programme or similar document as a paper copy or online). What gaps have you identified? How might these be addressed? Are there any resource implications?

> **Key concept**   Continuing professional education
>
> Sleezer et al. (2004) refer to the importance of continuing professional education (CPE) for HRD practitioners with CPE being defined as 'the ongoing learning needs of professionals' (p. 21). It differs from CPD because it focuses specifically on educational programmes/qualifications.

Unlike HRD which focuses on both learning and performance, CPE focuses on learning only (ibid.). This demonstrates the linkage between career development and lifelong learning (see chapters 2 and 3). The reason why CPE is regarded as important is because the 'fast pace' of research and scholarly activity carried out by academics can quickly render a practitioner's knowledge out of date (ibid.). There are probably many practitioners who would argue that it is the 'fast pace' of change in the global economy rather than in research and scholarship that is driving the need for CPE (see references to the gap between theory and practice in chapters 1 and 2). Although academics draw distinctions between the theory and practice of CPE and HRD the reality is that practitioners are less concerned by such distinctions.

There is also a problem with anchoring the lifelong learning needs of practitioners in CPE because of its focus on education. As chapter 10 illustrated the bulk of learning by professionals occurs informally in the workplace rather than in the classroom. Hence Kuchinke's (2007) pragmatic suggestion that education programmes 'should encourage work-based learning' and would benefit from 'increased emphasis on melding classroom learning with work projects or employment' (p. 121). This is likely to be a more successful route for embedding reflective practice in the workplace. Reflective practice is arguably the most critical aspect of CPD. As Lombardozzi (2007) comments: 'Reflective practitioners add the critical reflection component to their work, constantly looking for ways to improve their practice' (p. 210). This approach requires real commitment which is why it is so important for HRD practitioners to act as role models (as well as line managers and employees doing the same in turn).

> **! TIPS AND HINTS**
>
> Always keep a notebook or audio-recorder of some sort handy so that you can capture your thoughts and feelings as things happen. You can then write this up later as part of a formal CPD record.

INSIGHTS INTO PRACTICE

CPD in the construction sector of Tanzania

This example illustrates a HRD profession that is anchored at the training-end of the 'learning continuum' (see chapter 2) where any concept of professional status is at best a nascent one.

At present there is no formal postgraduate qualification that trainers, who work in the construction sector of Tanzania, can take to demonstrate their professional competence. Existing programmes are 'fragmented and lack overall strategy and continuity' (p. 440). Yet, there is a need for a continuous development programme in this area. A particular problem is that construction firms 'need to be educated on the economic merits of training and to develop internal capabilities of training' (p. 459). The authors propose the introduction of a training accreditation and certification scheme funded through an industry-specific training levy as a starting point. This would overcome the present obstacle of a lack of funding for such a scheme.

Source
Debrah, Y. A. and Ofori, G. 2006. Human resource development of professionals in an emerging economy: the case of the Tanzanian construction industry. *International Journal of Human Resource Management*, 17 (3): 440–63.

ACTIVITY 15.2

Brainstorm a list of learning opportunities that you have encountered over the last 12 months and then rank these in terms of which have been the most beneficial for your CPD. Study the ranking carefully and identify what it is about certain opportunities that make them better learning opportunities for you. Are there some opportunities which you have missed or, perhaps, undervalued? If so, why is this and what can you do to improve the situation in the future?

MEDIA WATCH BOX

Strategies for supporting learning

The CIPD's 2007 *Learning and Development Survey* has highlighted strategies for developing a learning climate. These reflect many of these issues covered in preceding chapters, including: helping line managers to support learning; developing line managers as coaches; encouraging workplace learning; aligning the learning strategy with the business strategy; and, empowering employees.

Source
People Management, 20 March 2008: 38–9.

15.4 **Looking to the future**

Marsick (2007) argues that we need to rethink both the practice and theory of HRD 'in the changing, global economy' (p. 89). HRD practitioners are being increasingly challenged by the dynamics of a changing workplace (Garavan et al., 2007) and the 'ability of corporations to maintain flexibility and change rapidly is not a luxury but a necessity in today's business environment' (Monaghan and Cervero, 2006: 381). Consequently a major concern for the HRD profession is 'its receptiveness and ability to adjust to changing conditions in organizations' (Ruona et al., 2003: 275). This is why it is important that HRD practitioners are able to embrace change and ambiguity (Mankin, 2001).

Chapter 1 explained some of the key trends associated with globalization but will these continue unabated in the future or will new trends, with new implications for HRD, emerge? Some of the predictions are summarized in table 15.2 which uses the same categories as table 1.2 in chapter 1 with the addition of business models to the 'organizational structures' category. Not surprisingly, the table features new jargon to describe future trends including 'prosumers' and the 'wiki workplace' (Tapscott and Williams, 2008), 'globality' (Sirkin et al., 2008), and 'learnability' (Sirkin et al., 2008). The HRD implications remain consistent with those identified in table 1.3 in chapter 1. What has changed is the terminology and some of the specifics of the trends.

What benefits are these predicted trends likely to offer organizations? First, Tapscott and Williams (2008) argue that the 'wiki workplace' offers 'powerful new levers to cut costs, innovate faster, [and] cocreate with customers and partners' (page 2). Second, Merrifield et al. (2008) argue that the value of service-oriented architecture or SOA has not yet been realized:

> When software is designed this way and placed on an intranet or the internet, anyone using SOA—any business unit in a firm and any customer or supplier—can plug in or remotely access the same software . . . Unfortunately, few companies are using SOA to create more productive and focused organisations or to slash costs by purging duplicative operations and technologies. They are not revisiting the fundamental design of their operations. (pp. 75–6)

Consequently, this approach has the potential to impact hugely on the organizational structures and business models category in table 15.2. Third, Elkington and Hartigan (2008) note that globally there are some four billion low-income consumers (including 2.86 billion in Asia with a combined income of US$3.47 trillion) and that the business models being developed by social and environmental entrepreneurs are demonstrating how this market of the future, referred to as the 'base of the pyramid' or BOP, can be tapped into (see *Insights into practice* box).

It can be seen from the HRD implications identified in table 15.2 that a common theme of the predicted trends is collaboration and the role of technology and organizational structures in leveraging the outputs from this collaboration (i.e. value creation in the form of new markets and/or new products and services). Consequently, organizational knowledge and learning processes are becoming ever more critical to effective organizational

	Predicted trends	HRD implications
Global competition	• Customers are replaced by 'prosumers' who co-create rather than simply consume goods and services (Tapscott and Williams, 2008) • 'Globality' will characterize global markets (Sirkin et al, 2008): 'Globality is not a new and different term for globalisation, it's the name for a new and different global reality in which we'll all be competing with everyone, from everywhere, for everything . . . a whole new mindset that embraces profit and competition as well as sustainability and collaboration' (ibid.: 1–2) • Global competition will be replaced by global co-operation in order to meet the challenges of sustainable development (Sachs, 2008)	• Integrating the learning needs of 'prosumers' into the organization's HRD strategy • Developing and improving learning and development processes to develop and retain talented employees (Sirkin et al., 2008: 93, refer to an employee's 'learnability' which is 'the person's inherent ability to learn, rather than just the applicant's academic credentials or knowledge of technical or other business content') • Facilitating collaborative activities (e.g. innovation projects) • Facilitating inter-organization and inter-government collaboration (the latter is a national HRD role)
Information and communications technology	• A growth in connectivity in the form of 'Web-enabled communities' which focus on innovation and wealth creation as well as social development (Tapscott and Williams, 2008) • The next generation will use technology to its full potential (Penn and Zalesne, 2008) • Using 'service-oriented architecture' to design and deploy software that supports business activities (Merrifield et al., 2008): 'It is becoming possible to design many business activities as Lego-like software components that can be easily put together and taken apart' (ibid.: 74)	• Understanding how technology can be used to sustain competitive advantage • Developing an organization's collaborative capabilities • Facilitating online collaboration • Embracing technology as a vehicle for learning
Organizational structures and business models	• The 'wiki workplace': based on community, mass collaboration across boundaries and self-organization in contrast to traditional corporate structures based on hierarchy and control (Tapscott and Williams, 2008)	• Supporting knowledge transfer processes • Developing employee competence in entrepreneurial skills (e.g. risk-taking) • Developing employee competence in creativity and innovation

Table 15.2 Predicted trends
Additional sources: Ulrich and Brockbank, 2005; Brown et al., 2006

Predicted trends	HRD implications
• The emergence of the business-web (or b-web) which are 'clusters of businesses that come together over the Internet' to create wealth and 'are predicated on a new kind of interenterprise collaboration' (Tapscott and Williams, 2008: 57) • The continued growth in multiunit enterprises: 'a geographically dispersed organization built from standard units such as branches, service centres, hotels, restaurants, and stores, which are aggregated into larger geographic groupings such as districts, regions, and divisions' (Garvin and Levesque, 2008: 108) (not to be confused with the traditional multidivisional organizational structure) • A growth in social and environmental entrepreneurs who bring a new perspective on value creation by tackling what are seen by mainstream institutions and organizations as intractable problems with high risk solutions (Elkington and Hartigan, 2008): 'All pursue social or environmental ends that the markets have largely or totally failed to address' (ibid.: 31)	• The design, implementation, and review of HRD interventions aimed at value creation through improvements in social, health, education, and the environment • Supporting organization design processes

Table 15.2 (cont'd)

! TIPS AND HINTS

One of the best ways for thinking about future trends is to read material which has nothing at all to do with your profession. For instance, if you are a HRD practitioner or aspire to be, then read non-fiction subjects such as popular science or travel. This can help to develop your conceptual skills by looking at situations in new and different ways and thereby gaining insights into potential trends that hadn't previously occurred to you.

---

performance. The role of HRD practitioners in encouraging collaboration is not new, for instance see Gilley et al., 2002. However, what is now more pertinent is the need for HRD practitioners to become much more involved in knowledge management and informal learning processes (see chapters 10 and 11 respectively). The HRD profession has been relatively slow to embrace the concept of knowledge management and associated concepts

◉ INSIGHTS INTO PRACTICE

SKS Microfinance

SKS Microfinance was set up by Vikram Akula in 1998 and now has a sales turnover of US$250 million. The company provides unsecured business micro-loans to over two million low-income customers in India. The entrepreneurial principles underpinning the company's strategy are: the application of a profit-oriented approach to attract investors; the standardisation of products, processes and training; and, using local knowledge to build the customer base. The company is now exploiting its vast network of customers by making deals with other companies, such as Nokia and ICICI Lombard, to promote their products and services to its customers.

Source
Akula, V. 2008. Business basics at the base of the pyramid. *Harvard Business Review*, June: 53–7.

Key concept   Social and environmental entrepreneurs

Social and environmental entrepreneurs operate across a spectrum of enterprises, from the purely charitable to the purely commercial. But because many of the markets they address are immature, they tend to skew toward the nonprofit end. (Elkington and Hartigan, 2008: 3)

MEDIA WATCH BOX

The continuing rise of technology

Using mobile phones to distribute novels has been highly successful in China and this has prompted Penguin to introduce the same system in India.[1]

Tesco intends using its loyalty card technology to monitor the spending habits of over 60 million customers globally.[2]

Sources
[1] *Guardian*, 29 March 2008: 28.
[2] *The Times*, 12 April 2008: 51.

---

such as social capital (see chapter 10). Facilitating knowledge formation processes such as knowledge sharing and knowledge transfer provide an opportunity for the HRD function to enhance its influence and reputation at a strategic level. This is particularly pertinent given the view that successful strategy implementation is closely associated with information flows and the ability to convert decisions into action (Neilson et al., 2008). This suggests that the factors influencing HRD strategy in figure 3.2 in chapter 3 should

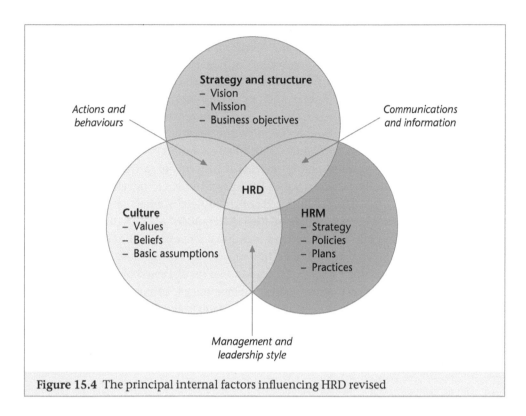

Figure 15.4 The principal internal factors influencing HRD revised

be modified as shown in figure 15.4. Communications and information were included in the original version of this model (Mankin, 2001):

> If an organisation's communications, and information systems, are ineffective, it is likely that the achievement of strategic goals will be inhibited. (p. 70)

Mankin (2001) argued that this problem was a consequence of ineffective decision-making. The original model also included actions and behaviours, which are influenced by both the organization's culture and arrangements for information processing, and management and leadership style, which influences both the organization's culture and the role and purpose of HRM/HRD. These elements have also been added to the figure.

To what extent do these predictions support a humanist and/or performance perspective on learning? Many HRD practitioners are attracted to the profession because of their desire to help others; in other words, 'because of people-oriented humanistic values' (Marsick, 2007: 89). Humanism was discussed in chapters 2, 3, and 4 and can be summarized as:

> *humanism* treats individual freedom, autonomy, and personal experience as key to learning and development. It sees humans as essentially good, intrinsically motivated to higher levels of learning and development, and able to examine and draw meaning from experience. (Johansen and McLean, 2006: 325; emphasis in original)

In one sense the new forms of mass online collaboration predicted by Tapscott and Williams (2008) would suggest an organic environment within which humanism can thrive. However, given the focus on innovation and wealth creation there will inevitably be tensions with the performance perspective. This suggests that the present tensions will continue to be a feature of HRD theory and practice. However, as chapter 1 argued new indigenous forms of HRD are likely to emerge in the future which will challenge prevailing Western perspectives that currently dominate the literature. This supports the notion that HRD is an evolving concept (Mankin, 2001); and evolution involves change. Marsick (2007) feels the most important change needed is in terms of 'a fresh and closer link with our customers' (p. 89) which requires HRD practitioners to develop their role as a broker: someone who can handle the needs of multiple customers and help different stakeholders understand the perspective of other stakeholders. Marsick (ibid.) is, in effect, suggesting a facilitation role but not one in a traditional sense where the HRD practitioner is facilitating learning activities. Rather her suggestion corresponds with the move towards a much more strategic role for the practitioner (as discussed in chapter 3). This is also when learning is viewed as a core strategic competency for an organization (Garavan et al., 2007). It appears that 'a sense of duty to be strategic governs the mindset of' HRD practitioners (Kim and Cervero, 2007: 16) but to what extent can the HRD function, where it exists, truly establish itself at the strategic level? Only time can tell.

MEDIA WATCH BOX

Changing career patterns for HRD practitioners?

Future changes to career patterns are predicted for senior HR practitioners as a result of the shift from managing large HR departments to the facilitation of change and management of stakeholder relationships. Increasingly, front-line staff in HR service centres are customer service specialists rather than HR practitioners. The latter are tending to fill specialist HR roles.

Source
People Management, 5 May 2005: 15.

15.5 **The principal challenges**

Based on the above discussions it is likely that HRD practitioners will continue to be confronted by a range of challenges (see figure 15.5):

- **Adopting a leadership role:** May (2007) argues that the biggest problem facing the HRD profession is 'the inability of most HRD professionals to bring leadership to the mission-critical functions of their organization' (p. 127). To succeed practitioners need

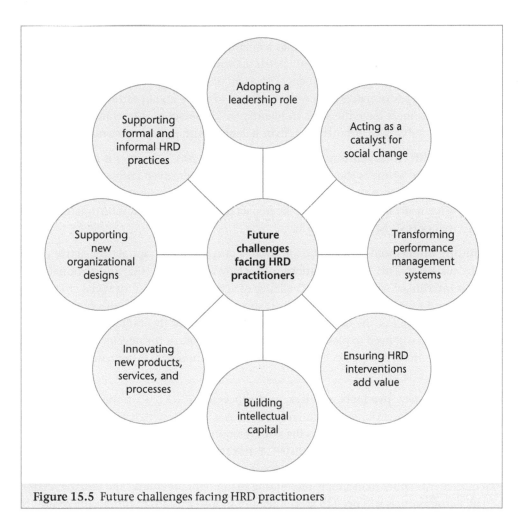

Figure 15.5 Future challenges facing HRD practitioners

to gain respect and credibility in the eyes of managers, which can be achieved partly through gaining line management experience (ibid.), a point that has been stressed earlier in the book, and above, in relation to the development of both strategic and commercial acumen. The importance of integrity and credibility is highlighted by influential academics such as Garavan (2007).

- **Acting as a catalyst for social change:** this is a somewhat contentious perspective that has been the focus of debate amongst academics rather than practitioners. Chapter 1 referred to socially responsible HRD and this theme was developed further in chapter 14. This involves striving for the creation of human workplaces and serving 'as the conscience of the organization' (Dewey and Carter, 2003: 253). The influence of human capital theory has resulted in a rather narrow economic perspective on HRD although the emergence of intellectual capital (including social capital) and national HRD will go some way to offsetting this (see chapter 1).

- **Transforming performance management systems:** in many organizations perform-ance management systems function as something that is done *to* rather than *for* the employee (Buchner, 2007). There still needs to be more emphasis on the developmental aspects of performance management. This is an opportunity for a better blend of the humanist and performance perspectives referred to above and in earlier chapters. 'HRD professionals must have the skills to identify valid measures of learning and growth' (Bing et al., 2003: 346) but this needs to be balanced with performance metrics.

- **Ensuring HRD interventions add value:** as Bunch (2007) observes it is not just real failure that undermines the HRD profession but also perceived failure. Having lots of positive comments at the validation stage does not bring credibility to the practice of HRD. What really matters is proving the impact of HRD interventions on organizational performance (see chapters 9 and 13).

- **Building intellectual capital:** the shift from a purely human capital perspective needs to be sustained. This has implications for socially responsible HRD and national HRD and is interlinked with the above challenge of acting as a catalyst for social change. As Dewey and Carter (2003) observe, albeit somewhat emotively: 'Intellectual capital is the true lifeblood of the organization' (p. 253). As part of this building process 'HRD professionals will need to play an increasingly strong role in the development of global and multicultural competencies throughout the organization' (Marquardt and Berger, 2003: 293).

- **Innovating new products, services, and processes:** HRD practitioners need to find 'new ways to address emerging skill requirements, and to design developmental experi-ences so that the organization has the skills it requires at the right time' (Garavan et al., 2007: 6). Innovation is closely associated with knowledge creation, sharing, and transfer processes. Consequently, HRD practitioners will need to start anticipating knowledge requirements rather than simply responding to them (Brandenburg and Ellinger, 2003). 'HRD professionals will need to keep abreast of industry trends in promoting creativity and inventiveness' (Marquardt et al., 2004: 340).

- **Supporting new organizational designs:** Table 15.2 above highlighted the import-ance of organizational structures (and business models). Chapter 12 looked at some of the differences between SMEs and larger firms. Over recent years organizational designs have attempted to replicate the benefits of smaller organizations through the creation of smaller subsidiaries or business units. The outsourcing of supply chains has also resulted in SMEs becoming a more integral component within many larger organiza-tions. Many of the businesses that have benefited from the Internet and e-commerce are SMEs. Is this trend likely to continue? Almost certainly; particularly in the light of surveys that highlight how employees within smaller firms are more engaged (Brown et al., 2007). HRD practitioners can use their skills in organization development and pro-ject management to help organizations maximize the benefits of size and changing technologies when redesigning organizational structures.

- **Supporting formal and informal HRD practices:** Formal learning and development interventions such as training courses and workshops will continue to play an important role. Indeed the HRD profession is characterized by a greater understanding of formal, structured learning than it is of informal learning (Eddy et al., 2006). The importance of informal structures and processes was highlighted in part 3 of the book. In the future the focus will continue to be on blending the formal and informal.

MEDIA WATCH BOX

Formal training interventions are still important

In order to improve employees' understanding of basic customer service skills in branches of Curry's and PC World the ailing parent company, DSG, has set up academies in stores to improve the capability of its 20,000 employees to perform basic skills including how to greet customers and explain the benefits and features of products.

Source
Daily Mail, 27 June 2008: 9.

15.6 International trends

As explained in chapter 1 the dominant economies of the twenty-first century are likely to be China and India, although Haass (2008) argues that there will be multiple concentrations of power with the European Union, Russia, and Japan also playing a prominent role. It is likely that the US will continue to be at the forefront of innovations in science and technology given its strong higher education system (Zakaria, 2008). The impact of China and India though should not be underestimated:

> Combine China's rise with that of India and the globe has seen nothing like it since America's emergence in the nineteenth century . . . A stylised view of patterns of economic development would characterise the nineteenth century as European, the twentieth as American and, though we are only a few years into it, the twenty-first century as belonging to China and India. (Smith, 2008: 171–2)

Smith (2008) goes on to warn though that we should be cautious about the scale of China and India's economic potential for several reasons, including: it is misleading to focus on the size of their populations given the levels of poverty in both countries and the burden this will impose on their economies; the impact on prices of natural resources, such as oil, gas, and timber, due to the rate of consumption of these resources in both countries; and, the prospect of increased protectionism by Western economies (i.e. a reversal of economic globalization). Also China and India are in demographic decline and some argue that this problem can best be averted through an increase in immigrants (Zakaria, 2008). Ironically, it is these types of problem that social and environmental entrepreneurs, referred to above, see 'as opportunities in disguise' (Elkington and Hartigan, 2008: 88).

MEDIA WATCH BOX

Can the future be predicted?

China will need economic policies that shift the emphasis from foreign to domestic consumption if its current growth is to be sustained. While the US will no longer be the major economic power it has been historically. However, just over a decade ago everyone was predicting that Japan would overtake the US which never happened.[1] Presently, China's industrial sectors, and in particular its steel industry, benefit from significant energy subsidies from the government which help to keep costs and prices down. However, in the future this could change suddenly and force costs and prices up.[2] It is predicted that e-commerce will have a much bigger impact in China than elsewhere and it will be China that generates new business models for this type of business rather than the West.[3]

China and India will soon stop being reliant on Western universities and research centres for science-based innovation as spending on indigenous research centres continues to increase.[4]

Goldman Sachs has predicted that by 2050 the US economy will have fallen to third place behind China and India.[5]

Sources
[1] *Newsweek*, 9 June 2008: 61.
[2] *Harvard Business Review*, June 2008: 25–6.
[3] The world in 2008, *Economist*, 2008: 84.
[4] *The Times*, 17 January 2007: 51.
[5] *Guardian* (Money Supplement), 11 August 2007: 5.

One of the criticisms of economic globalization is the extent to which organizations are displacing nation states and the consequent implications this is having for decision-making processes which are becoming increasingly undemocratic (Hatcher, 2004). This is consistent with the anti-globalization views highlighted in chapter 1. As Stiglitz (2006) argues:

> What is needed, if we are to make globalisation work, is an international economic regime in which the well-being of the developed and developing countries are better balanced: a new *global social contract* between developed and less developed countries. (p. 285; emphasis in original).

This is consistent with the aspirations associated with national HRD and ethical and socially responsible HRD practice in organizations (particularly in multinationals because of their global influence). The dilemma confronting many HRD practitioners is increased 'shareholder pressure for short-term profits' (May et al., 2003: 321) reflecting the financial imperatives driving many organizations and, in turn, the role and purpose of HRD. While

Sachs (2008) points out 'our limited capacity to cooperate' (p. 7), Porritt (2007) argues that the primary problem is the incompatibility between capitalism and sustainability:

> Sustainability is about the long term, about working within limits, about making more from less, about accommodation with others to secure equilibrium—and it demands a deep and often disconcerting re-engagement with the natural world. Contemporary capitalism responds to the shortest of short terms, abominates the very notion of limits, celebrates excess, accepts that its 'invisible hand' will fashion as many losers as winners—and has no connectedness with the natural world other than as a dumping ground and a store of raw materials. (p. 327)

This is an emotive subject. Concerns over environmental degradation will continue given the extent to which the world is presently trapped in a political impasse:

> The governments of the rich nations complain that there is no point in cutting their own [carbon] emissions if emissions are to continue to grow in China and India. The governments of China and India complain that limiting their pollution is a waste of time if the richer countries—whose output per head is still far greater than theirs—are not prepared to make the necessary reductions. (Monbiot, 2006: 213)

Western governments should be taking the lead in tackling this issue by making economic sacrifices (Mahbubani, 2008). Until this happens it is unlikely that the balance sought by Stiglitz (2006) can be achieved.

Summary

Continuing professional development (CPD) is underpinned by reflective practice. This is a critical competence not only for HRD practitioners but also for other key stakeholders (i.e. line managers and employees). Approaches to CPD tend to be rather mechanistic and this creates problems for embedding critical reflection in organizational cultures. CPD needs to cover a range of competencies for all three stakeholders and is closely associated with the concepts of lifelong learning and career development. Global trends indicate that stakeholders involved in the practice of HRD need to be conscious of the importance of CPD. Many of these trends were identified and discussed in chapter 1. It is extremely difficult trying to predict how these trends might develop in the future and what new trends might emerge. Taleb (2008) refers to the unexpected and unpredictable as 'black swan' events:

> Black swan logic makes *what you don't know* far more relevant than what you do know . . . we act as though we are able to predict historical events . . . What is surprising is not the magnitude of our forecast errors, but our absence of awareness of it. (pp. xix–xx)

This statement highlights the importance of learning and reflective practice in making us aware of what is happening around us, why it is happening, and how it might happen differently. Ultimately, that is what continuing professional development is all about.

Review questions

1 Define and explain the concept of continuing professional development (CPD).

2 How is continuing professional education (CPE) different to CPD?

3 What are the principal competencies needed by HRD practitioners?

4 What are the principal challenges facing the HRD practitioner in the future?

5 In what ways are these challenges different to the implications of globalization for HRD practice identified in chapter 1?

Suggestions for further reading

1 Marquardt, M., Berger, N. and Loan, P. 2004. *HRD in the Age of Globalisation*. New York: Basic Books.

   Although published in 2004 this text is still relatively current with a final chapter on future trends that is still topical.

2 Elkington, J. and Hartigan, P. 2008. *The Power of Unreasonable People: How Social Entrepreneurs Create Markets that Change the World*. Boston, MA: Harvard Business Press.

   An interesting and stimulating text on the role of social and environmental entrepreneurs in the development of new business models for tapping into low income markets.

3 Smith, D. 2008. *The Dragon and the Elephant: China, India and the New World Order*. London: Profile Books.

   This is worth reading for its analysis of the economic rise of China and India and the implications of this for other countries.

4 Zakaria, F. 2008. The future of American power: how America can survive the rise of the rest. *Foreign Affairs*, May/June: 18–43.

   This is an informative discussion on the future prospects of the world's leading economy and includes comparisons with historical competitors (e.g. the UK) and current and future competitors (e.g. China and India).

5 Merrifield, R., Calhoun, J. and Stevens, D. 2008. The next revolution in productivity. *Harvard Business Review*, June: 72–80.

   This article provides an interesting insight into the potential impact of technology on organizational design.

Case Study

The Biography of a Professional Trainer

Fiona Argent is a training and development consultant with Acorn, the recruitment and training organization featured in chapter 6. She is a chartered fellow of the CIPD and has worked for Acorn for the last five years on a part-time basis researching, designing, and delivering customized and bespoke development programmes across the UK. These are a mixture of accredited and non-accredited programmes. But how did she come to this point in her career? Fiona originally studied for an HND in Hotel Catering and Institutional Management at Brighton Polytechnic. While on this course she gained experience working in a variety of roles in hospitality environments that required not only a good working knowledge of relevant legislation but also fast-moving, 'on the feet' decision making skills coupled with a high degree of people management skills. The combination of the HND course and on-the-job work experience enabled Fiona to develop both the skills and theory needed to run a business in this sector. In particular, she learnt first-hand about the challenges of business planning, budgeting, and recruitment. However, she wanted to develop further her HR knowledge which she felt would be critical to any future employment ambitions. Consequently, upon completion of the HND she was unsure what route her future career should take, and in 1990 embarked on a post-graduate Institute of Personnel Management (IPM) course at Thames Valley College (the IPM eventually merged with the Institute of Training and Development to form the CIPD). During this course she spent a placement at Town and Country catering within terminal 4 at Heathrow airport, where her role was to write a new induction programme for new staff within the land-side and air-side operations. This is where she first discovered an interest in training and development.

Following the successful completion of the IPM course Fiona's first role was a six month contract working as part of the Ebbw Vale Garden Festival training team. As assistant training officer her key task involved the design and delivery of a a NVQ-based training programme for the 800 staff who would provide the customer-facing and behind-the-scenes roles required to make the Garden Festival a success. As part of this role she completed the D32 qualification needed to become a NVQ assessor. The Ebbw Vale Garden Festival was a successful project bringing in over 2 million visitors to Wales and generating a huge boost to the local economy. Following this project it was evident that a career in vocationally based training could be both challenging and rewarding. Consequently, Fiona's next employment was with LINK Training. LINK was known across South Wales as a private vocational training provider, contracting with the Training and Enterprise Councils (latterly ELWa and now part of the Welsh Assembly), to meet their objectives for the training and development of employed and unemployed individuals across a wide range of industry sectors. Fiona's role was focused on the development and implementation of National Vocational Qualifications. This entailed the completion of a Training and Development Diploma with the Institute of Training and Development (ITD), which then allowed her to upgrade from graduate membership of the newly formed IPD to full member status. She also completed the D33, D34, and D36 assessor awards to enhance her portfolio of knowledge and skills in NVQ programmes. This helped her to progress her career as a regional training adviser which involved her in the launch of the first Customer Service qualifications with Peacock Group. Very quickly Fiona's role had become much wider. LINK was renamed Spring Skills and formed part of a National Training Provider with over 22,000 learners following NVQ programmes at any one time—the remit was now to provide an 'added value' service through bespoke NVQ programmes that met clients' business objectives.

As the 1990s progressed Fiona became even more involved with the Sector Skills Councils (SSCs) and the development of new programmes, qualifications, and government initiatives. This included advising one SSC on the need to adapt the criteria of their new qualification to meet industry requirements and piloting a national project with them. The next corporate challenge Fiona faced was the introduction of Modern Apprenticeships. This was a key role for Fiona as she needed to understand the delivery models, relate them to Spring's client base and 'real' situations, manage the pilot programmes within Spring, train and develop staff, produce guidance for the business, and keep the Executive Board updated regularly on progress. Having gained this experience, Fiona then left Spring and spent the next 10 years working as a self-employed Professional Management Trainer. Because of the skills and knowledge Fiona had built up over the years she was still in demand to support her former colleagues at Spring, employers, and the wider educational network, in the design, development, and delivery of a wide range of programmes to support client needs (accredited and non-accredited). During this time Fiona's membership of the CIPD was upgraded to that of chartered fellow.

This has proved to further develop Fiona as she has been exposed to the challenges of self-employment as well as the rewards of being able to decide on projects to support. For instance, she has recently led the delivery of a programme for 14–19 year olds as part of the Welsh Assembly's programme to widen options for students in full time education and her comment following the first day was 'I couldn't use the lesson plan, if I'd taken my eyes off them, (the pupils), for 10 seconds they'd have disappeared!!' Then at the other end of the scale she has recently been approved as a HRD Adviser for the Welsh Assembly's Workforce Development, Programme where she will meet HR Directors and Business owners to support them in the design of their Learning strategies to meet their business plans, access funding for them, and mentor them to work towards IiP (Investors in People).

Case questions

1. What has been more critical to Fiona's career development: formal qualifications or on-the-job practical experience?

2. What appear to be Fiona's principal strengths, in terms of knowledge and skills, as a training and development consultant?

Online resource centre

Visit the supporting online resource centre for additional material that will help you with your research, essays, assignments, and revision.

 www.oxfordtextbooks.co.uk/orc/mankin/

GLOSSARY

Action learning Action learning involves a group of learners working together in an action learning set to solve real problems in the workplace. A series of meetings are held during which set members question and challenge the causes of the problem and potential solutions.

Added value Added value is about identifying what really matters to key stakeholders and delivering the services and products that achieve this. In many respects it builds on the total quality management ethos of delivering products and services that create 'customer delight'.

Attitude survey Attitude surveys are organization-wide questionnaires that attempt to identify how employees feel about the organization on a range of issues such as leadership and management style, values, and culture, reward and recognition, and so on. They are regarded as a useful qualitative measure that can inform decisions about HRD interventions.

Blended learning Blended learning is where a range of learning methods, underpinned by a range of learning theories, are combined or blended together. This usually involves some form of e-learning as part of the combination.

Business ethics Business ethics 'is the study of business situations, activities, and decisions where issues of right and wrong are addressed' (Crane and Matten, 2007: 5).

Capabilities Capabilities are 'the capacity of an organisation to use resources, get things done, and behave in ways that accomplish goals. They characterise how people think and behave in the context of the organization . . . Capabilities define what the organisation does well' (Ulrich and Brockbank, 2005: 49). See also core competence.

Career development Career development is a planned and structured response to the career aspirations of key employees.

Coaching Coaching is where a peer or manager works with an employee to motivate him or her, help him or her develop skills, and provide reinforcement and feedback (Noe, 2002: 452).

Code of conduct A code of conduct sets out the way in which employees or members of an occupational group are expected to behave when carrying out their work responsibilities. Also referred to as a code of ethics.

Codification Codification is based on the assumption that it is possible to encode knowledge as text, figures, or digital data. Many observers argue it is information rather than knowledge that is being encoded in this way. See also knowledge management.

Cognition Cognition involves the development of representations or mental models of the world around us within an individual's mind (Bowden and Marton, 2004). See also situated cognition.

Communities of practice 'Communities of practice are groups of people who share a concern, a set of problems, or a passion about a topic, and who deepen their knowledge and expertise in this area by interacting on an ongoing basis . . . Over time, they develop a unique perspective on their topic as well as a body of common knowledge, practices and approaches . . . They will tend to organize along friendship lines or within local geographical or organizational contexts rather than cover the whole organization' (Wenger et al., 2002: 4–5 and 13)

Competence Competence is the ability of an individual to do a particular job to a high standard.

Competencies Competencies are 'a broad grouping of knowledge, skills, and attitudes that enable a person to be successful at a number of similar tasks' (Blanchard and Thacker, 2004: 9).

Continuing professional development Continuing professional development (CPD) is an ongoing learning process that focuses on developing professional expertise and the ability to learn more effectively. Pivotal to CPD is the concept of reflective practice (i.e. the ability to reflect critically).

Core competence Core competence is the combination of an organization's technologies with the knowledge, skills, and abilities of its employees. It determines the viability and competitiveness of an organization. See also capabilities.

Corporate social responsibility (CSR) Corporate social responsibility 'encompasses the economic, legal, ethical, and philanthropic expectations placed on organisations by society at a given point in time' (Crane and Matten, 2007: 49).

Corporate university The corporate university is an extension of an old style training school model found predominantly in the US. In many respects it is a branding exercise that copies the traditional university model and is designed to signal to stakeholders a strategic-level response to learning and development.

Development Development is much broader than training and usually has a longer term focus. It is concerned with the enhancement of an individual's personal portfolio of knowledge, skills, and abilities (i.e. competencies). See also education.

Development centre A development centre is a structured HRD intervention comprising a blend of methods that are designed to measure participants' performance against a specified set of competencies. The outcomes are used to identify the career potential of participants and to produce customized career development plans.

Education Education can range from courses in basic literacy and numeracy through to post-graduate qualifications such as an MBA. National HRD policies have a very strong focus on education.

E-learning E-learning is a learning and development delivery system that relies on technology and normally requires the learner to engage in self-directed study. It is not a learning theory.

Emotional intelligence Emotional intelligence is about dealing with emotions effectively and can be viewed as an ability or competency (McEnrue and Groves, 2006).

Enhanced HRD cycle The enhanced HRD cycle explains the inter-relationships between formal and informal learning. See also the HRD cycle.

Evaluation Evaluation is concerned with measuring the impact training or learning has had on individual performance in the workplace and the contribution this makes to overall organizational performance.

Explicit knowledge Explicit knowledge is formal, abstract, or theoretical knowledge which relies on an individual's conceptual skills and cognitive abilities.

External validation External validation involves looking at the learning process and identifying whether the activity was based on a valid identification of training or learning needs that related to the organizational criterion of effectiveness.

Facilitation Facilitation is about guiding and supporting a learner or group of learners with the minimum of input.

Globalization Globalization is about the creation of a borderless global economy that allows unhindered movement of finance, products, services, information, and people.

Horizontal strategic alignment (also referred to as horizontal alignment) Horizontal strategic alignment is the process by which HRD strategy, policies, plans, and practices are aligned with an organization's HRM strategy, policies, plans, and practices.

Human capital Becker (1964, 1975) popularized Schultz's (1961) human capital theory that organization's derive economic value from employees' skills, competence, knowledge, and experience. Shultz (ibid.) argued that human capital can be developed through education and training.

Humanism Humanism 'treats individual freedom, autonomy, and personal experience as key to learning and development. It sees humans as essentially good, intrinsically motivated to higher levels of learning and development, and able to examine and draw meaning from experience' (Johansen and McLean, 2006: 325).

Human resource development (HRD) Human resource development encompasses a range of organizational practices that focus on learning: training, learning, and development; workplace learning; career development and lifelong learning; organization development; organizational knowledge and learning.

Human resource development (HRD) cycle The HRD cycle builds on the systematic training cycle (STC) by providing a methodical step-by-step approach to the key stages in developing HRD interventions that span learning and development, career development and lifelong learning, and organization development and organizational knowledge and learning. Like the STC it comprises four stages: identifying HRD needs, design, delivery, and evaluation of HRD interventions.

Human resource development policy The HRD policy should communicate an organization's HRD philosophy to all employees so that informed decisions can be made about HRD activities.

Informal learning Informal learning is essentially learning that is 'predominantly unstructured, experiential, and noninstitutionalised' (Marsick and Volpe, 1999: 4) with the control of learning resting primarily in the hands of the learner (Marsick and Watkins, 1990).

Intellectual capital Intellectual capital comprises the intangible assets of an organization including both human capital and social capital.

Internal validation Internal validation involves the measurement of whether a training programme has achieved its behavioural objectives or programme outcomes.

Job or task analysis A job or task analysis involves 'a structured questionnaire that consists of a listing of tasks comprising a particular job' that has been put together by the employees who perform that job (Wexley and Latham, 2002: 58).

Knowledge Knowledge is a complex, multifaceted concept which lacks a universal definition. Often discussed as comprising explicit and tacit dimensions. See also explicit knowledge and tacit knowledge.

Learning There is no universal definition of learning. Learning at the individual level is about the acquisition of new knowledge and how this changes the individual in some way (e.g. in terms of how they think about something, or how they carry out a task, or how they behave). See also: lifelong learning, social and situated learning, learning organization, organizational learning, and reflective practice.

Learning objective A learning objective is an explicit statement of what a learner is expected to be able to understand and/or do as a result of participating in a HRD intervention. Often referred to as a 'training' objective.

Learning organization A learning organization is 'an organisation which learns powerfully and collectively and is continually transforming itself to better collect, manage, and use knowledge for corporate success. It empowers people within and outside the company to learn as they work' (Marquardt, 1996: 19). See also organizational learning.

Learning styles or learning preferences Learning styles or learning preferences explain how information is organized and processed by individuals (i.e. how we prefer to *think* about something). Honey and Mumford (1992) have identified four learning styles: activist; reflector; theorist; and pragmatist. Each one is associated with one of the four stages in the experiential learning cycle.

Lifelong learning Lifelong learning is the ongoing acquisition of knowledge and skills by study and experience throughout the duration of an individual's career.

Mentoring Mentoring involves a more experienced and usually more senior person helping a less experienced employee through discussion and guidance. It is a developmental relationship which is focused on supporting the employee's ability to achieve his or her career ambitions.

National human resource development (NHRD) National human resource development is intended to provide a coherent set of policies for the social and economic development of a country. It encompasses a wide range of concerns including: public health, environmental protection, diversity, education, and vocational training. The way in which national HRD is handled varies from country to country.

National vocational education and training (NVET) National vocational education and training is focused on developing a country's human capital and represents a strategic response to the long term skills needs of its indigenous private, public, and non-profit sectors.

Organization development (OD) Organization development is a systematic and methodical approach to the management of change that is aimed at improving organizational performance and competitiveness.

Organizational learning Organizational learning focuses on the actual learning processes which explain how individuals and groups learn (e.g. the individual acting as an agent of the organization; group members learning from each other) and how that learning can become institutionalized. See also the learning organization.

Outsourcing Outsourcing involves contracting with external organizations or individuals, who possess specialist expertise and can fulfil specific projects for an organization, instead of employing an in-house function or individual specialist.

Psychological contract The psychological contract is the set of unwritten reciprocal expectations between an organization and an individual employee (Schein, 1978). It reflects the existence of an emotional as well as economic attachment to the organization which is highly subjective and subject to change (Boxall and Purcell, 2008).

Reflective practice Reflective practice involves thinking critically about specific incidents and examining what happened, how it happened, and why it happened. The outcome of this process is often some form of learning that involves an adjustment to how we think and act in the world.

Resource based view (RBV) The resource based view is based on the assumption that organizations can develop human and technical resources that help the organization secure competitive advantage but are difficult for competitors to imitate.

Return on investment (ROI) Return on investment measures the rate of return, expressed as a percentage, on an investment in training. It is based on an assumption that the benefits resulting from training can be quantified. It can be applied to other types of HRD intervention such as organization development projects or career development programmes.

Self-directed learning (SDL) Self-directed learning is where individuals take responsibility for identifying their own learning needs and for managing the learning process.

Situated cognition Cognition is situated in the workplace, distributed across group members, and learning occurs as a result of social interaction between group members.

Situated learning Situated learning is where learning is *situated* in a real-life or work setting, usually within the same community or social network, and is about developing individual competence through discussions with colleagues, mentors, and specialist experts.

Social capital Social capital is: 'the sum of actual and potential resources within, available through, and derived from the network of relationships possessed by an individual or social unit. Social capital thus comprises both the network and the assets that may be mobilised through that network' (Nahapiet and Ghoshal, 1998: 243). See also intellectual capital.

Social learning Social learning, or as it is often termed social cognitive theory, is where learning takes place as a result of engaging in social activities. This includes passive engagement, such as observation and listening, and active engagement, actually contributing to discussions.

Strategic human resource development (SHRD) Strategic human resource development is when HRD strategy, policies, plans, and practices are vertically and horizontally aligned and learning is embedded in the organization's strategic processes.

Supply chain The supply chain is the network of organizations that are involved in the processes that create value for customers in the form of products and/or services.

Systematic training cycle (STC) The systematic training cycle is one of several different terms used to describe a methodical step-by-step approach to the key stages in developing a training intervention: identification of needs, design, delivery, and evaluation.

Tacit knowledge Tacit knowledge is the practice or skills dimension of knowledge which accrues over time. It is often referred to as an individual's skills or expertise. Spender (1996) describes tacit knowledge as *automatic* knowledge in acknowledgement of Polanyi's assertion that 'we can know more than we can tell' (1967: 4). It is difficult to articulate tacit knowledge because it is so deeply embedded within an individual's experience, judgement, and intuition (Ahmed et al., 2002).

Task analysis See job analysis.

Trainer A trainer is an expert at instructional techniques but is not necessarily a subject specialist.

Training Training involves planned instruction in a particular skill or practice and is intended to result in changed behaviour in the workplace leading to improved performance.

Training needs analysis (TNA) A training needs analysis is a formal and systematic process for analysing the learning and development needs of employees and is usually compiled at three levels: the individual, the department, and the organization. Sometimes referred to as the identification of training needs (ITN).

Training method Training methods are the different ways in which specific elements within an intervention can be delivered to learners.

Training objective See learning objective.

Training strategy A 'training' or learning strategy is a specific approach to the delivery of the HRD intervention that guides the design process.

Transfer of training Traditionally referred to as transfer of training, the transfer of learning is the ability of the learner to transfer the knowledge and skills acquired from a formal learning and development interventions successfully to the workplace. Also referred to as the transfer of learning.

Validation See internal validation and external validation

Vertical strategic alignment (also referred to as vertical alignment) The process by which HRD strategy, policies, and plans are aligned with an organization's strategic goals and objectives.

BIBLIOGRAPHY

Ahmed, P. K., Kok, L. K. and Loh, A. Y. E. 2002. *Learning Through Knowledge Management.* Oxford: Butterworth-Heinemann.

Al-Dosary, A. S. and Rahman, S. M. 2005. Saudization (localisation)—a critical review. *Human Resource Development International*, 8 (4): 495–502.

Allen, T. J. 1977. *Managing the Flow of Technology.* Cambridge, MA: MIT Press.

Allen, W. C. 2006. Overview and evolution of the ADDIE training system. *Advances in Developing Human Resources*, 8 (4): 430–41.

Allen, T. D. and O'Brien, K. E. 2006. Formal mentoring programs and organisational attraction. *Human Resource Development Quarterly*, 17 (1): 43–58.

Alvesson, M. 2004. *Knowledge Work and Knowledge-Intensive Firms.* Oxford: Oxford University Press.

Alvesson, M. and Kärreman, D. 2001. Odd couple: making sense of the curious concept of knowledge management. *Journal of Management Studies*, 38 (7): 995–1018.

Ambrosini, V. and Bowman, C. 2001. Tacit knowledge: some suggestions for operationalisation. *Journal of Management Studies*, 38 (6): 811–29.

Amighini, A. and Rabellotti, R. 2006. How do Italian footwear industrial districts face globalisation? 14 (4): 485–502.

Andersen, V. and Andersen, A. S. 2007. Learning environment at work: dilemmas facing professional employees. *Human Resource Development Review*, 6 (2): 185–207.

Aragón-Sánchez, A. and Sánchez-Márin, G. 2005. Strategic orientation, management characteristics, and performance: a study of Spanish SMEs. *Journal of Small Business Management*, 43 (3): 287–308.

Ardichvili, A. and Dirani, K. 2005. Human capital practices of Russian enterprises. *Human Resource Development International*, 8 (4): 403–18.

Argyris, C. 1995. Action science and organisational learning. *Journal of Managerial Psychology*, 10 (6): 20–6.

Argyris, C. and Schön, D. 1974. *Theory in Practice: Increasing Professional Effectiveness.* San Francisco, CA: Jossey-Bass.

Argyris, C. and Schön, D. A. 1996. *Organisational Learning II: Theory, Method, and Practice.* Reading, MA: Addison-Wesley Publishing.

Arkin, A. 2005. Hidden talents. *People Management*, 14 July: 26–30.

Ashworth, L. 2005. It's time HR professionals got their teeth into bite-sized training programmes. *People Management*, 5 May: 42.

Awbrey, S. M. 2007. The dynamics of vertical and horizontal diversity in organisation and society. *Human Resource Development Review*, 6 (1): 7–32.

Bacon, N. and Hoque, K. 2005. HRM in the SME sector: valuable employees and coercive networks. *International Journal of Human Resource Management*, 16 (110): 1976–999.

Baddeley, M. 2006. Convergence or divergence? The impacts of globalisation on growth and inequality in less developed countries. *International Review of Applied Economics*, 20 (3): 391–410.

Bakan, J. 2004. *The Corporation: The Pathological Pursuit of Profit and Power.* London: Constable.

Bandura, A. 1977. *Social Learning Theory.* Englewood Cliffs, NJ: Prentice Hall.

Barclay, I. 2005. Supply chain management in SMEs—benchmarking best practice core competencies. *Journal of General Management*, 30 (3): 35–50.

Bartlett, K. R. and Kang, D. 2004. Training and organisational commitment among nurses following industry and organisational change in New Zealand and the United States. *Human Resource Development International*, 7 (4): 423–40.

Bartlett, K. R. and Rodgers, J. 2004. HRD as national policy in the Pacific Islands. *Advances in Developing Human Resources*, 6 (3): 307–14.

Bassi, L. J. and van Buren, M. E. 1999. *The 1999 ASTD State of the Industry Report.* Alexandria, VA: ASTD.

Bates, R. and Holton, E. F. 2004. Linking workplace literacy skills and transfer system perceptions. *Human Resource Development Quarterly*, 15 (2): 153–70.

Bates, R. and Chen, H-C. 2005. Value priorities of human resource development professionals. *Human Resource Development Quarterly*, 16 (3): 345–68.

Beattie, R. S. 2006. Line managers and workplace learning: learning from the voluntary sector. *Human Resource Development International*, 9 (1): 99–119.

Beaumont, P. B. and Hunter, L. C. 2002. *Managing Knowledge Workers.* London: CIPD.

Becker, G. 1964. *Human Capital: A Theoretical and Empirical Analysis with Special Reference to Education*. New York: Columbia University Press.

Becker, G. 1975. *Human Capital: A Theoretical and Empirical Analysis with Special Reference to Education* (2nd edition). New York: Columbia University Press.

Beckinsale, M., Levy, M. and Powell, P. 2006. Exploring Internet adoption drivers in SMEs. *Electronic Markets*, 16 (4): 361–70.

Bell, B. S. and Ford, J. K. 2007. Reactions to skill assessment: the forgotten factor in explaining motivation to learn. *Human Resource Development Quarterly*, 18 (1): 33–62.

Bentley, R. 2006. Can a little really beat a lot? *Training and Coaching Today*, April: 6.

Berings, M. G. M. C., Poell, R. F. and Simons, P. R-J. 2005. Conceptualising on-the-job learning styles. *Human Resource Development Review*, 4 (4): 373–400.

Bertels, T. and Savage, C. M. 1998. Tough questions on knowledge management. In G. von Krogh, J. Roos and D. Kleine (eds.) *Knowing in Firms: Understanding, Managing and Measuring Knowledge*. London: Sage Publications.

Bew, R. 2008. Twin track. *Economist: The World in 2008,*: 21.

Bhatnagar, J. 2005. The power of psychological empowerment as an antecedent to organisational commitment in Indian managers. *Human Resource Development International*, 8 (4): 419–33.

Bierema, L. L. 2005. Women's networks: a career development intervention or impediment? *Human Resource Development International*, 8 (2): 207–24.

Bierema, L., Bing, J. and Carter, T. 2002. The global pendulum. *Training and Development*, 56: 72.

Bierema, L. L. and D'Abundo, M. 2003. Socially conscious HRD. In A. Maycunich Gilley, J. L. Callahan and L. L. Bierema (eds.) *Critical Issues in HRD: A New Agenda for the Twenty-first Century*. Cambridge, MA: Perseus Publishing.

Billet, S. 2004. Learning through work: workplace participatory practices. In H. Rainbird, A. Fuller and A. Munro (eds.) *Workplace Learning in Context*. London: Routledge.

Bing, J. W., Kehrhahn, M. and Short, D. C. 2003. Challenges to the field of human resources development. *Advances in Developing Human Resources*, 5 (3): 342–51.

Blackler, F., Crump, N. and McDonald, S. 1998. Knowledge, organisations and competition. In G. von Krogh, J. Roos and D. Kleine (eds.) *Knowing in Firms: Understanding, Managing and Measuring Knowledge*. London: Sage Publications.

Blanchard, P. N. and Thacker, J. W. 2004. *Effective Training: Systems, Strategies, and Practices.* Upper Saddle River, NJ: Prentice Hall.

Blass, E. 2001. What's in a name? A comparative study of the traditional public university and the corporate university. *Human Resource Development International*, 4 (2): 153–72.

Bloom, B. S. (ed.) 1956. *Taxonomy of Educational Objectives, the Classification of Educational Goals —Handbook I: Cognitive Domain.* New York: McKay.

Boon, J., Rusman, E., van der Link, M. and Tattersall, C. 2005. Developing a critical review om e-learning trend reports: trend watching or trend setting? *International Journal of Training and Development* 9 (3): 205–11.

Boud, D. and Garrick, J. 1999. Understandings of workplace learning. In D. Boud and J. Garrick (eds.) *Understanding Learning at Work*. London: Routledge.

Boud, D., Keogh, R. and Walker, D. 1985. What is reflection in learning? In D. Boud, R. Keogh and D. Walker (eds.) *Reflection: Turning Experience into Learning*. London: Routledge.

Bowden, J. and Marton, F. 2004. *The University of Learning: Beyond Quality and Competence.* London: Routledge-Falmer.

Boxall, P. and Purcell, J. 2008. *Strategy and Human Resource Management* (2nd edition). Basingstoke: Palgrave Macmillan.

Boydell, T. and Leary, M. 1996. *Identifying Training Needs.* CIPD: London.

Brandenberg, D. C. and Ellinger, A. D. 2003. The future: just-in-time learning expectations and potential implications for human resource development. *Advances in Developing Human Resources*, 5 (3): 308–20.

Brassington, F. and Pettitt, S. 2003. *Principles of Marketing.* Harlow: Prentice Hall.

Bratton J. and Gold, J. 2007. *Human Resource Management: Theory and Practice* (4th edition). Basingstoke: Palgrave Macmillan.

Brewster, C. 2004. Developing managers in Europe. *Advances in Developing Human Resources*, 6 (4): 399–403.

Brockman, J. L. and Dirkx, J. M. 2006. Learning to become a machine operator: the dialogical relationship between context, self, and content. *Human Resource Development Quarterly*, 17 (2): 199–221.

Brown, J. S. and Duguid, P. 1991. Organisational learning and communities-of-practice: toward a unified view of working, learning, and innovation in *Organisation Science*, February, 2 (1): 40–57.

Brown, J. S. and Duguid, P. 1998. Organising knowledge. *California Management Review*, 40 (3): 90–111.

Brown, J. S. and Duguid, P. 2000. *The Social Life of Information.* Boston, MA: Harvard Business School Press.

Brown, J. S. and Duguid, P. 2001. Knowledge and organisation: a social-practice perspective. *Organisation Science*, 12 (2): 198–213.

Brown, A., Rhodes, E. and Carter, R. 2004. Supporting learning in advanced supply systems in the automotive and aerospace industries. In H. Rainbird, A. Fuller and A. Munro (eds.) *Workplace Learning in Context.* London: Routledge.

Brown, D. H., Lockett, N. and Schubert, P. 2005. Preface to the focus theme section 'SMEs and e-business'. *Electronic Markets*, 15 (2): 76–9.

Brown, L., Murphy, E. and Wade, V. 2006. Corporate elearning: human resource development implications for large and small organisations. *Human Resource Development International*, 9 (3): 415–27.

Brown, A., Roddan, M. and Nilsson, L. 2007. The time of your life. *People Management*, 26 July: 40–3.

Buch, K. and Bartley, S. 2002. Learning style and training delivery mode preference. *Journal of Workplace Learning*, 14 (1): 5–10.

Buchner, T. W. 2007. Performance management theory: a look from the performer's perspective with implications for HRD. *Human Resource Development International*, 10 (1): 59–74.

Burchell, J. and Cook, J. 2006. It's good to talk? Examining attitudes towards corporate social responsibility dialogue and engagement processes. *Business Ethics: A European Review*, 15 (2): 154–70.

Burgess, D. 2005. What motivates employees to transfer knowledge outside their work unit? *Journal of Business Communication*, 42 (4): 324–48.

Burns, P. 2001. *Entrepreneurship and Small Businesses.* Basingstoke: Palgrave.

Bunch, K. J. 2007. Training failure as a consequence of organisational culture. *Human Resource Development Review*, 6 (2): 142–63.

Burt, R. S. 1997. The contingent value of social capital. *Administrative Science Quarterly*, 42 (2): 339–65.

Bushnell, D. 1990. Input, process, output: a model for evaluating training. *Training and Development Journal*, 44 (3): 41–3.

Bryan, L. L. and Joyce, C. I. 2007. *Mobilising Minds: Creating Wealth from Talent in the 21st-Century Organisation.* New York: McGraw-Hill.

CIPD 2006a. Induction (Factsheet) http://www.cipd.co.uk/subjects/recruitmen/induction (accessed 25 October 2007).

CIPD 2007a. Learner-centred courses (Factsheet) http://www.cipd.co.uk/subjects/training/trnprogram (accessed 25 October 2007).

CIPD 2007b. Coaching (Factsheet) http://www.cipd.co.uk/subjects/lrnanddev/coachmentor (accessed 25 October 2007).

CIPD 2007c. E-learning: progress and prospects (Factsheet) http://www.cipd.co.uk/subjects/lrnanddev/elearning (accessed 25 October 2007).

CIPD 2007d. International management development: an overview (Factsheet) http://www.cipd.co.uk/subjects/intlhr (accessed 25 October 2007).

CIPD 2007e. Secondment (Factsheet) http://www.cipd.co.uk/subjects/lrnanddev/secondment (accessed 25 October 2007).

CIPD 2007f. Creative learning methods (Factsheet) http://www.cipd.co.uk/subjects/training/trnmethods (accessed 25 October 2007).

CIPD 2008. *The 2008 Learning and Development Survey.* London: CIPD.

CIPD 2008a. Code of professional conduct and disciplinary procedures. http://www.cipd.co.uk (accessed 17 April 2008).

Callahan, J. L. 2003. Organisational learning: a reflective and representative critical issue for HRD. In A. Maycunich Gilley, J. L. Callahan and L. L. Bierema (eds.) *Critical Issues in HRD: A New Agenda for the Twenty-first Century.* Cambridge, MA: Perseus Publishing.

Campbell, C. P. 1998. Training course/program evaluation: principles and practices. *Journal of European Industrial Training*, 22 (8): 323–44.

Camuffo, A. and Comacchio, A. 2005. Linking intellectual capital and competitive advantage: a cross-firm competence model for north-east Italian SMEs in the manufacturing industry. *Human Resource Development International*, 8 (3): 361–77.

Carey, S. 2000. The organisation of the training function in large firms. In H. Rainbird (ed.) *Training in the Workplace.* Basingstoke: Macmillan.

Carliner, S. 2004. Business models for training and performance improvement departments. *Human Resource Development Review*, 3 (3): 275–93.

Carlson, D. S., Upton, N. and Seaman, S. 2006. The impact on human resource practices and compensation design on performance: an analysis of family-owned SMEs. *Journal of Small Business Management*, 44 (4): 531–43.

Carmeli, A. and Weisberg, J. 2006. Exploring turnover intentions among three professional groups of employees. *Human Resource Development International*, 9 (2): 191–206.

Carnevale, A. P., and Schulz, E. R. 1990. *Return on Investment: Accounting for Training.* Alexandra, VA: ASTD.

Carnevale, A. P., Gainer, L. J. and Meltzer, A. S. 1990. *Workplace Basics: The Essential Skills Employers Want.* Alexandria, VA: ASTD.

Carter, S. D. 2005. The growth of supply of occupational-based training and certification in the United States, 1990–2003. *Human Resource Development Quartely*, 16 (1): 33–54.

Cascio, W. F. 2003. Invited reaction: the effects of alternative reports of human resource development results on managerial support. *Human Resource Development Quarterly*, 14 (2): 153–8.

Chandler, A. D. 1962. *Strategy and Structure.* Cambridge, MA: MIT Press.

Chen, T-Y., Chang, P-L. and Yeh, C-W. 2004. An investigation of career development programs, job satisfaction, professional development and productivity: the case of Taiwan. *Human Resource Development International*, 7 (4): 441–63.

Cho, E. and McLean, G. N. 2004. What we discovered about NHRD and what it means for HRD. *Advances in Developing Human Resources*, 6 (3): 382–93.

Clardy, A. 2005. Reputation, goodwill, and loss: entering the employee training audit equation. *Human Resource Development Review*, 4 (3): 279–304.

Clarke, N. 2004. HRD and the challenges of assessing learning in the workplace. *International Journal of Training and Development*, 8 (2): 140–56.

Clarke, E. 2006. Act of faith. *People Management*, 9 November: 36–7.

Clarke, E. 2006. Power brokers. *People Management*, 18 May: 40–2.

Clarke, E. 2007. Enjoy your stay. *People Management*, 5 April: 34–7.

Clarke, N. 2005. Workplace learning environment and its relationship with learning outcomes in healthcare organisations. *Human Resource Development International*, 8 (2): 185–205.

Clarke, L. and Winch, C. 2007. Introduction. In L. Clarke and C. Winch (eds.) *Vocational Education: International Approaches, Developments and Systems.* London: Routledge.

Cocbeo, S. 2004. If you build it, they will learn. *ABA Banking Journal*, February: 22–6.

Cohen, B. P. and Zhou, X. 1991. Status processes in enduring work groups. *American Sociology Review*, 56: 170–88.

Collins, D. B. and Holton, E. F. 2004. The effectiveness of managerial leadership development programs: a meta-analysis of studies from 1982 to 2001. *Human Resource Development Quarterly*, 15 (2): 217–48.

Comfort, P. J., Comfort, D., Hillier, D. and Eastwood, I. 2005. Corporate social responsibility: a case study of the UK's leading food retailers. *British Food Journal*, 107 (6): 423–35.

Cooke, F. L. 2004. Foreign firms in China: modelling HRM in a toy manufacturing corporation. *Human Resource Management Journal*, 14 (3): 31–52.

Cooke, F. L. 2005. Vocational and enterprise training in China: policy, practice and prospect. *Journal of the Asia Pacific Economy*, 10 (1): 26–55.

Cowell, C., Hopkins, P. C., McWhorter, R. and Jorden, D. L. 2006. Alternative training methods. *Advances in Developing Human Resources*, 8 (4): 460–75.

Cox, J. B., Estrada, S. D., Lynham, S. A. and Motii, N. 2005. Defining human resource development in Morocco: an exploratory inquiry. *Human Resource Development International*, 8 (4): 435–47.

Craig, M. 1994. *Analysing Learning Needs.* Aldershot: Gower.

Crane, A. and Matten, D. 2007. *Business Ethics* (2nd edition). Oxford: Oxford University Press.

Crawford, D. and Scaletta, T. 2005. The balanced scorecard and corporate social responsibility: aligning values for profit. *CMA Management*, October: 20–7.

Cromwell, S. E. and Kolb, J. A. 2004. An examination of work-environment support factors affecting transfer of supervisory skills training to the workplace. *Human Resource Development Quarterly*, 15 (4): 449–71.

Cross, R., Borgatti, S. P. and Parker, A., 2002. Making invisible work visible: using social network analysis to support strategic collaboration. *California Management Review*, 44 (2): 25–46.

Cunningham, I. and Dawes, G. 1997. Problematic premises, presumptions, presuppositions and practices in management education and training. In J. Burgoyne and M. Reynolds (eds.) *Management Learning: Integrating Perspectives in Theory and Practice.* London: Sage.

Cunningham, P. M. 2004. Critical pedagogy and implications for human resource development. *Advances in Developing Human Resources*, 6 (2): 226–40.

Czerniawska, F. 2002. *Management Consultancy: What Next?* Basingstoke: Palgrave Macmillan.

D'Abate, C. P., Eddy, E. and Tannenbaum, S. I. 2003. What's in a name? A literature-based approach to understanding mentoring, coaching, and other constructs that describe developmental interactions. *Human Resource Development Review*, 2 (4): 360–84.

Danielson, M. M. 2004. A theory of continuous socialisation for organisational renewal. *Human Resource Development Review*, 3 (4): 354–84.

Das, G. 2006. The India model. *Foreign Affairs*, 85 (4): 2–16.

Davenport, T. H. and Prusak, L. 2000. *Working Knowledge: How Organisations Manage What They Know.* Boston, MA: Harvard Business School Press.

Delanty, G. 2001. *Challenging Knowledge: The University in the Knowledge Society*. Buckingham: SRHE and Open University Press.

Desimone, R. L., Werner, J. M. and Harris, D. M. 2002. *Human Resource Development*. Cincinnati, OH: South-Western.

Dewhurst, H., Dewhurst, P. and Livesey, R. 2007. Tourism and hospitality SME training needs and provision: a sub-regional analysis. *Tourism and Hospitality Research*, 7 (2): 131–43.

Dewey, J. 1916. *Democracy and Education*. London: Macmillan.

Dewey, J. D. and Carter, T. J. 2003. Exploring the future of HRD: the first future search conference for a profession. *Advances in Developing Human Resources*, 5 (93): 245–56.

Diamond, J. 2005. *Collapse: How Societies Choose to Fail or Survive*. London: Penguin Books.

Dilworth, L. 2003. Searching for the future of HRD. *Advances in Developing Human Resources*, 5 (3): 241–4.

Dirani, K. 2006. Exploring socio-cultural factors that influence HRD practices in Lebanon. *Human Resource Development International*, 9 (1): 85–98.

Dirkx, J. M., Gilley, J. W. and Gilley, A. M. 2004. Change theory in CPE and HRD: toward a holistic view of learning and change in work. *Advances in Developing Human Resources*, 6 (1): 35–51.

Dobbs, R. L. 2006. Development phase of systematic training: new technology lends assistance. *Advances in Developing Human Resources*, 8 (4): 500–13.

Dooley, K. E., Lindner, J. R., Dooley, L. M. and Alagaraja, M. 2004. Behaviourally anchored competencies: evaluation tool for training via distance. *Human Resource Development International*, 7 (3): 315–32.

Doornbos, A. J., Bolhus, S. and Simons, P. R-J. 2004. Modeling work-related learning on the basis of intentionality and developmental relatedness: a noneducational perspective. *Human Resource Development Review*, 3 (3): 250–74.

Douglas, D. 2004. Ethical challenges of an increasingly diverse workforce: the paradox of change. *Human Resource Development International*, 7 (2): 197–210.

Dowling, P. J. and Welch, D. E. 2004. *International Human Resource Management: Managing People in a Multinational Context* (4th edition). London: Thomson.

Doyle, M. 2007. Management development. In J. Beardwell and T. Claydon (eds.) *Human Resource Management: A Contemporary Approach* (5th edition). Harlow: Prentice-Hall.

Dreyfus, H. and Dreyfus, S. 1997. Why computers may never think like people. In R. L. Ruggles (ed.) *Knowledge Management Tools*. Boston: Butterworth-Heinemann.

Drucker, P. F. 1998. The coming of the new organisation. In *Harvard Business Review on Knowledge Management*. Boston, MA: Harvard Business School Press.

Dymski, G. A. 2005. Financial globalisation, social exclusion and financial crisis. *International Review of Applied Economics*, 19 (4): 439–57.

Easterby-smith, M. 1986. *Evaluation of Management Education, Training and Development*. Aldershot: Gower.

Easterby Smith, M. and Araujo, L. 1999. Organisational learning: current debates and opportunities. In M. Easterby-Smith, J. Burgoyne and L. Araujo (eds.) *Organisational Learning and the Learning Organisation*. London: Sage.

Eddy, E. R., D'Abate, C. P., Tannenbaum, S. I., Givens-Skeaton, S. and Robinson, G. 2006. Key characteristics of effective and ineffective developmental interactions. *Human Resource Development Quarterly*, 17 (1): 59–84.

Egan, T. M., Yang, B. and Bartlett, K. R. 2004. The effects of organisational learning culture and job satisfaction on motivation to transfer of learning and turnover intention. *Human Resource Development Quarterly*, 15 (3): 279–301.

Egan, T. M., Upton, M. G. and Lynham, S. A. 2006. Career development: load-bearing wall or window dressing? Exploring definitions, theories, and prospects for HRD-related theory building. *Human Resource Development Review*, 5 (4): 442–77.

e-learning age 2007. HR executives predict that the future of learning is online. *e-learning age*, February: 2.

Elkjaer, B. 2000. Learning and getting to know: the case of knowledge workers. *Human Resource Development International*, 3 (3): 343–59.

Elkington, J. and Hartigan, P. 2008. *The Power of Unreasonable People: How Social Entrepreneurs Create Markets that Change the World*. Boston, MA: Harvard Business Press.

Ellinger, A. D. 2004. The concept of self-directed learning and its implications for human resource development. *Advances in Developing Human Resources*, 6 (2): 158–77.

Ellinger, A. D. 2005. Contextual factors influencing informal learning in a workplace setting: the case of 'reinventing itself company'. *Human Resource Development Quarterly*, 16 (3): 389–415.

Engardio, P. 2007. *Chindia: How China and India Are Revolutionising Global Business*. New York: McGraw-Hill.

Epple, D., Argote, L. and Murphy, K. 1996. An empirical investigation of the micro structure of knowledge acquisition and transfer through learning by doing. *Operations Research*, 44: 77–86.

Eraut, M. 1994. *Developing Professional Knowledge and Competence*. London: Falmer Press.

Eraut, M. 2000. Non-formal learning, implicit learning and tacit knowledge in professional work. In F. Coffield (ed.) *The Necessity of Informal Learning*. Bristol: The Policy Press.

Eraut, M. 2004. Transfer of knowledge between education and workplace. In H. Rainbird, A. Fuller and A. Munro (eds.) *Workplace Learning in Context*. London: Routledge.

Eraut, M., Alderton, J., Cole, G. and Senker, P. 1998. Learning from other people at work. In F. Coffield (ed.) *Learning at Work*. Bristol: Policy Press.

Espedal, B. 2004. Management and leadership development in Norway: discrepancies between talk and action. *Advances in Developing Human Resources*, 6 (4).

Fabac, J. N. 2006. Project management for systematic training. *Advances in Developing Human Resources*, 8 (4): 540–7.

Fenwick, T. 2005. Conceptions of critical HRD: dilemmas for theory and practice., *Human Resource Development International*, 8 (2): 225–38.

Fenwick, T. 2006. Toward enriched conceptions of work learning: participation, expansion, and translation among individuals with/in activity, *Human Resource Development Review*, 5 (3): 285–302.

Ferguson, N. 2004. *Empire: How Britain Made the Modern World*. London: Penguin.

Finland's Ministry of Education 2008. Adult education in Finland. http://www.minedu.fi (accessed 29 May 2008).

Fishman, T. C. 2006. *China Inc*. New York: Simon and Schuster.

Fitz-enz, J. 2000. *ROI of Human Capital: Measuring Economic Value of Employee Performance*. New York: AMACOM.

Forde, C. and MacKenzie, R. 2004. Cementing skills: training and labour use in UK construction. *Human Resource Management Journal*, 14 (3): 74–88.

Freeman, R. E., Wicks, A. C. and Parmar, B. 2004. Stakeholder theory and 'the corporate objective revisited'. *Organisation Science*, 15 (3): 364–9.

Friedman, T. L. 2000. *The Lexus and the Olive Tree: Understanding Globalisation*, New York: Anchor Books.

Friedman, T. L. 2006. *The World is Flat: The Globalised World in the Twenty-first Century*. London: Penguin Books.

Fuller, D. B. and Thun, E. 2006. China's global path. *World Business*, 4 July–August: 36–41.

Fuller, A., Munro, A. and Rainbird, H. 2004. Introduction and overview. In H. Rainbird, A. Fuller and A. Munro (eds.) *Workplace Learning in Context*. London: Routledge.

Fuller-Love, N. 2006. Management development in small firms. *International Journal of Management Reviews*, 8 (3): 175–90.

Fung, V. K., Fung, W. K. and Wind, Y. 2008. *Competing in a Flat World: Building Enterprises for a Borderless World*. Upper Saddle River, NJ: Wharton School Publishing.

Gainey, T. W. and Klaas, B. S. 2005. Outsourcing relationships between firms and their training providers: the role of trust. *Human Resource Development Quarterly*, 16 (1): 7–25.

Garavan, T. N. 1991. Strategic human resource development. *Journal of European Industrial Training*, 15: 17–30.

Garavan, T. N. 2007. A strategic perspective on human resource development. *Advances in Developing Human Resources*, 9 (1): 11–30.

Garavan, T. N., Costine, P. and Ileraty, N. 1995. The emergence of strategic human resource development. *Journal of European Industrial Training*, 19 (10): 4–10.

Garavan, T. N., McGuire, D. and O'Donnell, D. 2004. Exploring human resource development: a levels of analysis approach. *Human Resource Development Review*, 3 (4): 417–41.

Garavan, T. N., O'Donnell, D., McGuire, D. and Watson, S. 2007. Exploring perspectives on human resource development. *Advances in Developing Human Resources*, 9 (1): 3–10.

Garengo, P., Biazzo, S. and Bititci, U. S. 2005. Performance measurement systems in SMEs: A review for a research agenda. *International Journal of Management Reviews*, 7 (1): 25–47.

Garvey, B. and Williamson, B. 2002. *Beyond Knowledge Management: Dialogue, Creativity and the Corporate Curriculum*. Harlow: Prentice Hall.

Garvin, D. A. and Levesque, L. C. 2008. The multi-unit enterprise. *Harvard Business Review*, June: 106–17.

Géhin, J-P. 2007. Vocational education in France: a turbulent history and peripheral role. In L. Clarke and C. Winch (eds.) *Vocational Education: International Approaches, Developments and Systems*. London: Routledge.

Gergen, K. J. 1995. Social construction and the educational process. In L. Steffe (ed). *Alternative Epistemologies in Education*. Hillsdale, NJ: Erlbaum.

Geroy, G. D. and Venneberg, D. L. 2003. A view to human capital metrics. In A. Maycunich, J. L. Callahan and L. L. Bierema (eds.) *Critical Issues in HRD*. Cambridge, MA: Perseus.

Ghosal, S. and Bartlett, C. A. 2005. Rebuilding behavioural context: a blueprint for corporate renewal. In J. Birkinshaw and G. Piramal (eds.) *Sumantra Ghosal on Management: A Force for Good*. Harlow: Prentice Hall.

Ghosal, S. and Gratton, L. 2005. Integrating the enterprise. In J. Birkinshaw and G. Piramal (eds.) *Sumantra Ghosal on Management: A Force for Good*. Harlow: Prentice Hall.

Ghosal, S. and Moran, P. 2005. Towards a good theory of management. In J. Birkinshaw and G. Piramal (eds.) *Sumantra Ghosal on Management: A Force for Good*. Harlow: Prentice Hall.

Gibb, S. 2002. *Learning and Development: Processes, Practices and Perspectives at Work*. Basingstoke: Palgrave Macmillan.

Gibbons, P. T. and O'Connor, T. 2005. Influences on strategic planning processes among Irish SMEs. *Journal of Small Business Management*, 43 (2): 170–86.

Gilbreath, B. and Montesino, M. U. 2006. 'Expanding the HRD role: improving employee well-being and organisational performance. *Human Resource Development International*, 9 (4): 563–71.

Gilleard, J. 1996. Delivering training down the line. *Industrial and Commercial Training*, 28 (7): 22–7.

Gilley, J. W., Eggland, S. A. and Maycunich Gilley, A. 2002. *Principles of Human Resource Development* (2nd edition). Cambridge, MA: Perseus Publishing.

Gilley, J. W. and Maycunich Gilley, A. 2003. *Strategically Integrated HRD: Six Transformational Roles in Creating Results-driven Programs* (2nd edition). Cambridge, MA: Perseus Publishing.

Gilmore, A., Carson, D., Grant, K., O'Donnell, A., Laney, R. and Pickett, B. 2006. Networking in SMEs: findings from Australia and Ireland. *Irish Marketing Review*, 18 (1–2): 21–8.

Gold, J., Rodgers, H. and Smith, V. 2003. What is the future for the human resource development professional? A UK perspective. *Human Resource Development International*, 6 (1): 437–58.

Goodwins, S. 2008. Perfectly formed. *People Management*, 24 January: 22–3.

Gough, R., Holland, P. and Teicher, J. 2006. Conclusion: globalisation, labour standards and flexibility in the Asia-Pacific region. *Asia Pacific Business Review*, 12 (2): 257–60.

Gourlay, S. 2001. Knowledge management and HRD *Human Resource Development International*, 4 (1): 27–46.

Gray, C. 1998. *Enterprise and Culture*. London: Routledge.

Gray, J. 2000. *False Dawn: The Delusions of Global Capitalism*. London: Granta Books.

Gray, C. 2004. Management development in small and medium enterprises. *Advances in Developing Human Resources*, 6 (4): 451–69.

Greer, B. M., Maltbia, T. E. and Scott, C. L. 2006. Supplier diversity: a missing link in human resource development. *Human Resource Development Quarerly*, 17 (3): 325–41.

Greinert, W-D. 2007. The German philosophy of vocational education. In L. Clarke and C. Winch (eds.) *Vocational Education: International Approaches, Developments and Systems* (trans. J. Fraser). London: Routledge .

Grieves, J. 2003. *Strategic Human Resource Development*. London: Sage.

Griffin, C. 2001. From education policy to lifelong learning strategies. In P. Jarvis (ed.) *The Age of Learning: Education and the Knowledge Society*. London: Kogan Page.

Griffin, C. and Brownhill, B. 2001. The learning society. In P. Jarvis (ed.) *The Age of Learning: Education and the Knowledge Society*. London: Kogan Page.

Griffiths, J. 2004. Partnership drives worldwide change. *People Management*, 2 September: 12.

Guarlerzi, D. 2007. Globalisation reconsidered. *International Journal of Political Economy*, 36 (1): 3–29.

Gubbins, M. C. and Garavan, T. N. 2005. Studying HRD practitioners: a social capital model. *Human Resource Development Review*, 4 (2): 189–218.

Guest, R. 2004. *The Shackled Continent: Africa's Past, Present and Future*. London: Pan Books.

Haass, R. N. 2008. The age of nonpolarity: what will follow U.S. dominance. *Foreign Affairs*, May/June: 44–56.

Hackett, P. 2002. *Introduction to Training* (updated edition with minor revisions).

Hackett, P. 2003. *Training Practice*. London: CIPD.

Hager, P. 2007. Towards a new paradigm of vocational learning. In L. Clarke and C. Winch (eds.) *Vocational Education: International Approaches, Developments and Systems*. London: Routledge.

Hall, K. 2005. Global division. *People Management*, 24 March: 44–5.

Hall, L. 2006. Inside job. *People Management*, 10 August: 34–6.

Halliday, J. 2007. Social justice and vocational education> In L. Clarke and C. Winch (eds.) *Vocational Education: International Approaches, Developments and Systems*. London: Routledge.

Hamblin, A. C. 1974. *Evaluation and Control of Training*. Maidenhead: McGraw-Hill.

Hamel, G. and Prahalad, C. K. 1996. *Competing for the Future*. Boston, MA: Harvard Business School Press.

Hammer, M. and Champy, J. 1993. *Reengineering the Corporation: A Manifesto for Business Revolution*. New York,: HarperCollins.

Hanna, V. and Walsh, K. 2002. Small firm networks: a successful approach to innovation? *Research and Development Management*, 32 (3): 201–7.

Hansen, J. W. 2006. Training design: scenarios of the future. *Advances in Developing Human Resources*, 8 (4): 492–9.

Hansen, M. T., Mors, M. L. and Løvås, B. 2005. Knowledge sharing in organisations: multiple networks, multiple phases. *Academy of Management Journal*, 48 (5): 776–93.

Harford, T. 2007. *The Undercover Economist*. London: Abacus.

Harrison, R. and Kessels, J. 2004. *Human Resource Development in a Knowledge Economy: An Organisational View*. Palgrave Macmillan: Basingstoke.

Hatcher, T. 2002. *Ethics and HRD: A New Approach to Leading Responsible Organisations*. Oxford: Perseus.

Hatcher, T. 2003. World views that inhibit HRD's social responsibility. In M. Lee (ed.) *HRD in a Complex World*. London: Routledge.

Hatcher, T. 2004. On democracy and the workplace: HRD's battle with DDD (democracy deficit disorder). *Human Resource Development Quarterly*, 15 (2): 125–9.

Hatcher, T. 2006. An editor's challenge to human resource development. *Human Resource Development Quarterly*, 17 (1): 1–4.

Hawley, J. D. and Taylor, J. C. 2006. How business associations use interorganisational networks to achieve workforce development goals: implications for human resource development. *Human Resource Development Review Human Resource Development International*, 9 (4): 485–508.

Hegstad, C. D. and Wentling, R. M. 2005. Organisational antecedents and moderators that impact on the effectiveness of exemplary programs in fortune 500 companies in the United States. *Human Resource Development International*, 8 (4): 467–87.

Herling, R. W. 2001. Operational definitions of expertise and competence. In Swanson, R. A. and Holton, E. F. (eds.) *Foundations of Human Resource Development*. San Francisco, CA: Berrett-Koehler.

Herling, R. W. 2003. Bounded rationality and the implications for HRD. *Advances in Developing Human Resources*, 5 (4): 393–407.

Hezlett, S. A. and Gibson, S. K. 2005. Mentoring and human resource development: where we are and where we need to go. *Advances in Developing Human Resources*, 7 (4): 446–69.

Higginbotham, E. 2004. Invited reaction: black and white women managers: access to opportunity. *Human Resource Development Quarterly*, 15 (2): 147–52.

Hill, R. 2002. Researching HRD in small organisations. In J. McGoldrick, J. Stewart and S. Watson (eds.) *Understanding Human Resource Development*. London: Routledge.

Hite, L. M. 2004. Black and white women managers: access to opportunity. *Human Resource Development Quarterly*, 15 (2): 131–46.

Hite, L. M. and McDonald, K. S. 2006. Diversity training pitfalls and possibilities: an exploration of small and mid-size US organisations. *Human Resource Development International*, 9 (3): 365–77.

Hislop, D. 2005. *Knowledge Management in Organisations*. Oxford: Oxford University Press.

Hodges, T. 2002. *Linking Learning and Performance*. Boston, MA: Butterworth-Heinemann.

Holton, E. F. 1996. The flawed 4-level evaluation model. *Human Resource Development Quarterly*, 7 (1): 5–21.

Holton, E. and Naquin, S. 2005. A critical analysis of HRD evaluation models. *Human Resource Development Quarterly*, 16 (2): 257–80

Holton, E. F., Swanson, R. A. and Naquin, S. S. 2001. Andragogy in practice: clarifying the andragogical model of adult learning. *Performance Improvement Quarterly*, 14 (1): 118–43.

Honey, P. and Mumford, A. 1992. *The Manual of Learning Styles*. Maidenhead: Peter Honey.

Houldsworth, E. 2004. Managing performance. In D. Rees and R. McBain (eds.) *People Management: Challenges and Opportunities*. Basingstoke: Palgrave Macmillan.

Hutchins, E. 1994. *Cognition in the Wild*. Cambridge, MA: MIT Press.

Hutchins, E. 1996. Learning to navigate. In S. Chaiklin and J. Lave (eds.) *Understanding Practice*. New York: Cambridge University Press.

Hutchinson, S., Purcel, J. and Winkler, V. 2007. Golden gate. *People Management*, 19 April: 38–40.

Hutton, T. 2003. *The World We're In*. London: Abacus.

Huysman, M. 2004. Communities of practice: facilitating social learning while frustrating organisational learning. In H. Tsoukas and N. Mylonopoulos (eds.) *Organisations as Knolwedge Systems*. Basingstoke: Palgrave Macmillan.

Huysman, M. and de Wit, D. 2002. *Knowledge Sharing in Practice*. Dordrecht, Netherlands: Kluwer Academic Publishers.

Huysman, M. and de Wit, D. 2003. A critical evaluation of knowledge management practices. In M. Ackerman, V. Pipek and V. Wulf (eds.)

Sharing Knowledge: Beyond Knowledge Management. Cambridge, MA: MIT Press.

Hytönen, T. 2003. International briefing 14: training and development in Finland. *International Journal of Training and Development,* 7 (2): 124–37.

Idowu, S. O. and Papasolomou, I. 2007. Are the corporate social responsibility matters based on good intentions or false pretences? An empirical study of the motivations behind the issuing of CSR reports by UK companies. *Corporate Governance,* 7 (2): 136–47.

Iles, P. and Yolles, M. 2003. International HRD alliances in viable knowledge migration and development: the Czech Academic Link Project. *Human Resource Development International,* 6 (3): 301–24.

James, P. 2007. Reframing the nation-state: re-thinking the Australian dream from the local to the global. *Futures,* 39 (2–3): 169–84.

Jarvis, P. 2001. The public recognition of learning. In P. Jarvis (ed.) *The Age of Learning: Education and the Knowledge Society.* London: Kogan Page.

Jarvis, P. 2001. *Universities and Corporate Universities.* London: Kogan Page.

Jarvis, P. 2006. *Towards a Comprehensive Theory of Human Learning.* Abingdon: Routledge.

Jarvis, J. 2006. Training budgets squeezed. *CIPD Impact,* 15.

Jenkins, R. 2005. Globalisation of Production, Employment and Poverty: Three Macro-Meso-Micro Studies. *The European Journal of Development Research,* 17 (4): 601–25.

Jenkins, R. 2006. Contrasting perspectives on globalisation and labour in South Africa. *Progress in Development Studies,* 6 (3): 185–200.

Jeon, B. N., Han, K. S. and Lee, M. J. 2006. Determining factors for the adoption of e-business: the case of SMEs in Korea. *Applied Economics,* 38: 1905–19.

Jeris, L. S., Johnson, J. R. and Anthony, C. C. 2002. HRD involvement in merger and acquisition decisions and strategy development: four organisational portraits. *International Journal of Training and Development,* 6 (6): 2–12.

Jeris, L., Johnson, K., Isopahkala, U., Winterton, J. and Anthony, K. 2005. The politics of competence: views from around the globe. *Human Resource Development International,* 8 (3): 379–84.

Johansen, B-C. and McLean, G. N. 2006. Worldviews of adult learning: a core concept in human resource development. *Advances in Developing Human Resources,* 8 (3): 321–28.

Johnson, M. E. 2006. Supply chain management: technology, globalisation, and policy at a cross-roads. *Interfaces,* 36 (3): 191–3.

Johnson, R. 2008. E. ON's ahead. *People Management,* 7 February: 24–7.

Joo, B-K. 2005. Executive coaching: a conceptual framework from an integrative review of practice and research. *Human Resource Development Review,* 4 (4): 462–88.

Kaletsky, A. 2008. The storm to come. *Economist: The World in 2008*: 35.

Kanter, R. M. 1996. Beyond the cowboy and the corpocrat. In K. Starkey (ed.) *How Organisations Learn.* London: International Thomson Press.

Kaplan, R. S. and Norton, D. P. 1993. Putting the Balanced Scorecard to work. In *Harvard Business Review on Measuring Corporate Performance.* Boston, MA: Harvard Business School Press.

Kaplan, R. S. and Norton, D. P., 1996. *Translating Strategy into Action—The Balanced Scorecard.* Boston, MA: Harvard Business School Press.

Kaplan, R. S. and Norton, D. P. 2004. *Strategy Maps: Converting Intangible Assets into Tangible Outcomes.* Boston, MA: Harvard Business School Press.

Karami, A. 2005. An exploration of the chief executive officers (CEOs) perception of strategic management process: the case of British high tech SMES. *Corporate Ownership & Control,* 2 (4): 62–9.

Käser, P. A. W. and Miles, R. E. 2001. Knowledge activists: the cultivation of motivation and trust properties of knowledge sharing relationships. *Academy of Management Proceedings,* ODC: D1–D6.

Kasturi, P., Orlov, A. G. and Roufagalas, J. 2006. HRM systems architecture and firm performance: evidence from SMEs in a developing country. *International Journal of Commerce and Management,* 16 (3–4): 178–96.

Kay, J. 2004. *The Truth About Markets: Why Some Nations are Rich but Most Remain Poor.* London: Penguin Books.

Kearns, P. 2005. *Evaluating the ROI from Learning.* London: CIPD.

Keep, E. 2007. The multiple paradoxes of state power in the English education and training system. In L. Clarke and C. Winch (eds.) *Vocational Education: International approaches, developments and systems.* London: Routledge.

Kessels, J. W. M. and Poell, R. F. 2004. Andragogy and social capital theory: the implications for human resource development. *Advances in Developing Human Resources,* 6 (2): 146–57.

Kessels, J. W. M. and Poell, R. F. 2004. Andragogy and social capital theory: the implications for human resource development. *Advances in Developing Human Resources,* 6 (2): 146–57.

Key, S. 1999. Toward a new theory of the firm: a critique of stakeholder 'theory'. *Management Decisions,* 37 (4): 317–28.

Kim, P. S. 1999. Globalisation of human resource management: a cross-cultural perspective for the public sector. *Public Personnel Management*, 28 (2): 227–43.

Kim, H. 2004. Transfer of Training as a Socio-political process. *Human Resource Development Quarterly*, 15 (4): 497–501.

Kim, H. and Cervero, R. M. 2007. How power relations structure the evaluation process for HRD programmes. *Human Resource Development International*, 10 (1): 5–20.

Kingsnorth, P. 2008. *Real England: The Battle Against the Bland*. London: Portobello Books.

Kirkpatrick, D. 1959. Techniques for evaluating training programmes Parts 1–4. *Journal of the American Society for Training and Development*, 13 (11), 13 (12), 14 (1), 14 (2).

Klein, N. 2008. *The Shock Doctrine*. London: Penguin Books.

Knasel, E., Meed, J. and Rossetti, A. 2000. *Learn for your life—A Blueprint for Continuous Learning*. London: Pearson.

Knights, A. and Poppleton, A. 2007. *Coaching in Organisations (Research Insight)*. London: CIPD.

Kogut, B. and Zander, U. 1992. Knowledge of the firm, combinative capabilities and the replication of technology. *Organisation Science*, 3 (3): 383–97.

Köhler, W. 1925. *The Mentality of Apes*. London: Routledge and Kegan Paul.

Kolb, D. A. 1984. *Experiential Learning: Experience as the Source of Learning and Development*. Englewood Cliffs, NJ: Prentice-Hall.

Kolb, D. A. 1996. Management and the learning process. In K. Starky (ed.) *How Organisations Learn*. London: International Thomson.

Koopmans, H., Doornbos, A. J. and van Eekelen, I, M. 2006. Learning in interactive work situations: it takes two to tango; why not invite both partners to dance? *Human Resource Development Quarterly*, 17 (2): 135–58.

Korte, R. F. 2006. Training implementation: variations affecting delivery, *Advances in Developing Human Resources*, 8 (4): 514–27.

Kotey, B. and Folker, C. 2007. Employee training in SMEs: effect of firm size and firm type—family and non-family, *Journal of Small Business Management*, 45 (2): 214–38.

Krackhardt, D. 1992. The strength of strong ties: the importance of philos in organisations. In N. Nohria and R. Eccles (eds.) *Organisations and Networks: Structure, Form, and Action*. Boston, MA: Harvard Business School Press.

Kuchinke, K. P. 2003. Contingent HRD: toward a theory of variation and differentiation in formal human resource development. *Human Resource Development Review*, 2 (3): 294–309.

Kuchinke, K. P. 2004. Theorising and practicing HRD: extending the dialogue over the roles of scholarship and practice in the field. *Human Resource Development International*, 7 (4): 535–9.

Kuchinke, K. P. 2007. Birds of a feather? The critique of the North American business school and its implications for educating HRD practitioners. *Human Resource Development Review*, 6 (2): 111–26.

Kumar, M., Antony, J., Singh, R. K., Tiwari, M. K. and Perry, D. 2006. Implementing the lean sigma framework in an Indian SME: a case study, *Production Planning and Control*, 17 (4): 407–23.

Kynge, J. 2006. *China Shakes the World: The Rise of a Hungry* Nation. London: Weidenfeld and Nicolson.

Laird, D. 2003. *Approaches to Training and Development*. Cambridge, MA: Perseus.

Lam, A. 2000. Tacit knowledge, organisational learning and societal institutions: an integrated framework. *Organisation Studies*, 21 (3): 487–513.

Lamb, H. 2008. *Fighting the Banana Wars and Other Fairtrade Battles*. London: Rider.

Lane Fox, R. 2005. *The Classical World: An Epic History from Homer to Hadrian*. London: Allen Lane.

Lansbury, R. D., Kwon, S-H. and Suh, C-S. 2006. Globalisation and employment relations in the Korean auto industry: the case of the Hyundai Motor Company in Korea, Canada and India. *Asia Pacific Business Review*, 12 (2): 131–47.

Lantos, G. P. 2001. The boundaries of strategic corporate social responsibility. *Journal of Consumer Marketing*, 18 (7): 595–630.

Lantos, G. P. 2002. The ethicality of altruistic corporate social responsibility. *Journal of Consumer Marketing*, 19 (3): 205–30.

Lave and Wenger 1991. *Situated Learning: Legitimate Peripheral Participation*. Cambridge: Cambridge University Press.

Leana, C. R. and Van Buren III, H. J. 1999. Organisational social capital and employment practices. *Academy of Management Review*, 24 (3): 538–55.

Le Deist, F. D. and Winterton, J. 2005. What is competence?, *Human Resource Development International*, 8 (1): 27–46.

Lee, G. and Beard, D. 1994. *Development Centres*. Maidenhead: McGraw-Hill.

Lee, M. 2004. National human resource development in the United Kingdom. *Advances in Developing Human Resources*, 6 (3): 334–45.

Lee, M. 2007. Human resource development from a holistic perspective. *Advances in Developing Human Resources*, 9 (1): 97–110.

Leonard, D. and Sensiper, S. 1998. The role of tacit knowledge in group innovation. *California Management Review*, 40 (3): 112–32.

Lewis, P. and Thornhill, A. 1994. The evaluation of training: an organisation culture approach. *Journal of European Industrial Training*, 18 (8): 25–32.

Lewis, T. 2007. School reform in America: can Dewey's ideas save high school vocational education?. In L. Clarke and C. Winch (eds.) *Vocational Education: International Approaches, Developments and Systems*. London: Routledge.

Liker, J. K. and Meier, D. P. 2007. *Toyota Talent: Developing Your People the Toyota Way*. New York: McGraw-Hill.

Liker, J. K. and Hoseus, M. 2008. *Toyota Culture: The Heart and Soul of the Toyota Way*. New York: McGraw-Hill (written in collaboration with the Center for Quality People and Organisations).

Lim, D. H. and Morris, M. L. 2006. Influence of trainee characteristics, instructional satisfaction, and oganisational climate on perceived learning and training transfer. *Human Resource Development Quarterly*, 17 (1): 85–115.

Lin, N. 2002. *Social Capital: A Theory of Social Structure and Action*. Cambridge: Cambridge University Press.

Littlepage, G. E. and Brower, G. 2004. Team assessment when members have low reading proficiency. *Human Resource Development Quarterly*, 15 (3): 323–38.

Littrell, L. N. and Salas, E. 2005. A review of cross-cultural training: best practices, guidelines, and research needs. *Human Resource Development Review*, 4 (3): 305–34.

Littrell, L. N., Salas, E., Hess, K. P., Paley, M. and Riedel, S. 2006. Expatriate preparation: a critical analysis of 25 years of cross-cultural training research, *Human Resource Development Review*, 5 (3): 355–88.

Lituchy, T. R. and Rail, A. 2000. Bed and breakfasts, small inns, and the Internet: the impact of technology on the globalisation of small businesses. *Journal of International Marketing*, 8 (2): 86–97.

Liu, Y., Pucel, D. J. and Bartlett, K. R. 2006. Knowledge Transfer practices in multinational corporations in China's information technology industry. *Human Resource Development International*, 9 (4): 529–52.

Lohman, M. C. 2004. The development of a multirater instrument for assessing employee problem-solving skill. *Human Resource Development Quarterly*, 15 (3): 303–21.

Lohman, M. C. 2005. A survey of factors influencing the engagement of two professional groups in informal workplace learning activities.

Human Resource Development Quarterly, 16 (4): 501–27.

Lombardozzi, C. 2007. Avoiding malpractice in HRD . . . Five imperatives for HRD professionals in organisations. *Human Resource Development Review*, 6 (2): 208–16.

London, M. 2003. Antecedents and consequences of self-verification: implications for individual and group development. *Human Resource Development Review*, 2 (3): 273–93.

London, M. 2003a. *Job Feedback: Giving, Seeking, and Using Feedback for Performance Improvement* (2nd edition). Mahwah, NJ: Lawrence Erlbaum.

Lopez, S. P., Peon, J. M. M. and Ordas, C. J. V. 2005. Human resource practices, organisational learning and business performance. *Human Resource Development International*, 8 (2): 147–64.

Lovelock, J. 2006. *The Revenge of Gaia*. London: Allen Lane.

Lowy, A., Kelleher, D. and Finestone, P. 1986. Management learning: beyond programme design. *Training and Development Journal*, 40 (6): 34–7.

Lucas, B. 2003. Method to the madness. *People Management*, 23 October: 61.

Lundberg, C. C. 1985. On the feasibility of cultural intervention. In P. J. Frost, L. F. Moore, M. R. Louis, C. C. Lundberg and J. Martin (eds.) *Organisational Culture*. Newbury Park, CA: Sage.

Luthans, F., Vogelgeasang, G. R. and Lester, P. B. 2006. Developing the psychological capital of resiliency. *Human Resource Development Review*, 5 (1): 25–44.

Lynham, S. A. and Cunningham, P. W. 2006. National human resource development in transitioning societies in the developing world: concept and challenges. *Advances in Developing Human Resources*, 8 (1): 116–35.

Lynn, G. S. 1998. New product team learning: developing and profiting from your knowledge capital. *California Management Review*, 40 (4): 74–93.

MacGillivray, A. 2006. *Globalisation*. London: Robinson.

Macpherson, A., Elliot, M., Harris, I. and Homan, G. 2004. E-learning: reflections and evaluation of corporate programmes. *Human Resource Development International*, 7 (3): 295–313.

McAdam, R. and Reid, R. 2001. SME and large organisation perceptions of knowledge management: comparisons and contrasts. *Journal of Knowledge Management*, 5 (3): 231–41.

McClelland, D. C. 1973. Testing for competence rather than for intelligence. *American Psychologist*, January: 1–14.

McClernon, T. 2006. Rivals to systematic training. *Advances in Developing Human Resources*, 8 (4): 442–59.

McCracken, M. 2004. Understanding managerial propensity to participate in learning activities: the case of the Scottish life assurance company. *Human Resource Development International*, 7 (4): 501–17.

McDonald, K. S. and Hite, L. M. 2005. Reviving the relevance of career development in human resource development. *Human Resource Development Review*, 4 (4): 418–39.

McDowall-Long, K. 2004. Mentoring relationships: implications for practitioners and suggestions for future research. *Human Resource Development International*, 7 (4): 519–34.

McEnrue, M. P. and Groves, K. 2006. Choosing among tests of emotional intelligence: what is the evidence? *Human Resource Development Quarterly*, 17 (1): 9–42.

McGuire, D., Cross, C. and O'Donnell, D. 2005. Why humanistic approaches in HRD won't work. *Human Resource Development Quarterly*, 16 (1): 131–7.

McGuire, D., Garavan, T. N., O'Donnell, D. and Watson, S. 2007. Metaperspectives and HRD: lessons for research and practice. *Advances in Developing Human Resources*, 9 (1): 120–39.

McKenna, E. and Beech, N. 2002. *Human Resource Management: A Concise Analysis*. Harlow: Prentice Hall.

McLagan, P. 1989. *Models of HRD Practice*. Alexandria, VA: ASTD Press.

McLean, G. N. 2004. National human resource development: what in the world is it?, *Advances in Developing Human Resources*, 6 (3): 269–75.

McLean, G. N. 2006. Rethinking adult learning in the workplace. *Advances in Developing Human Resources*, 8 (3): 416–23.

McLean, G. N., Yang, B., Kuo, M-H. C., Tolbert, A. S. and Larkin, C. 2005. Development and initial validation of an instrument measuring managerial coaching skill. *Human Resource Development Quarterly*, 16 (2): 157–78.

Mabey, C. 2004. Developing managers in Europe: policies, practices, and impact. *Advances in Developing Human Resources*, 6 (4): 404–27.

Mabey, C. and Thomson, A. 2000. *Achieving Management Excellence*. London: Institute of Management.

Mahbubani, K. 2008. The case against the West: America and Europe in the Asian century. *Foreign Affairs*, May/June: 111–24.

Mankin, D. P. 2001. A model for human resource development. *Human Resource Development International*, 4 (1): 65–85.

Mankin, D. P. 2000. *Managing the Training Function*. Slough: Thames Valley University.

Mankin, D. P. 2003. Ambiguity and elusiveness: the principal characteristics of the relationship between HRM and HRD. The innovating HRM conference. University of Twente, The Netherlands (Dutch HRM Network), November.

Mankin, D. P. 2003a. *An Introduction to CTP*. Slough: Thames Valley University.

Mankin, D. P. 2004. Nurturing social capital: the principal lever in developing HRD's contribution to organisational success? Presented at the *Fifth Conference on HRD Research and Practice across Europe*. Limerick, Ireland, May.

Mankin, D. P. 2005. Nurturing social capital: the principal lever in developing HRD's contribution to organisational success? In N. Rohmetra (ed.) *Human Resource Development: Challenges and Opportunities*. Anmol Publications PVT Ltd.

Mankin, D. P. 2007. The implications of knowledge sharing in academic communities for academic development. The Eighth Conference on HRD Research and Practice across Europe, Oxford, June.

Mann, S. and Robertson, I. T. 1996. What should training evaluation evaluate? *Journal of European Industrial Training*, 20 (9): 14–20.

Marchington, M. and Wilkinson, A. 1996. *Core Personnel and Development*, London: IPD.

Margaryan, A., Collis, B. and Cooke, A. 2004. Activity-based blended learning. *Human Resource Development International*, 7 (2): 265–74.

Marquardt, M. J. 2002. Globalisation and HRD. In A. M. Gilley, J. L. Callahan and L. L. Bierema (eds.) *Critical Issues in HRD*. Cambridge, MA: Perseus Publishing.

Marquardt, M. J. 2005. Globalisation: the pathway to prosperity, freedom and peace. *Human Resource Development International*, 8 (1): 127–9.

Marquardt, M. J. and Berger, N. O. 2003. The future: globalisation and new roles for HRD. *Advances in Developing Human Resources*, 5 (3): 283–95.

Marquardt, M., Berger, N. and Loan, P. 2004. *HRD in the Age of Globalisation: A Practical Guide to Workplace Learning in the Third Millennium*. New York: Basic Books.

Marques, J. F. 2006. The new human resource department: a cross-functional unit. *Human Resource Development Quarterly*, 17 (1): 117–23.

Marsick, V. J. 2007. HRD research and practice: strengths, weaknesses, opportunities and threats. *Human Resource Development International*, 10 (1): 89–91.

Marsick, V. J. and Volpe, M. 1999. The nature and need for informal learning. *Advances in Developing Human Resources*, 3: 1–9.

Marsick, V. J. and Watkins, K. 1990. *Informal and Incidental Learning in the Workplace*. London: Routledge.

Marsick, V. J. and Watkins, K. 1997. Lessons from informal and incidental learning. In J. Burgoyne and M. Reynolds (eds.) *Management Learning: Integrating Perspectives in Theory and Practice*. London: Sage.

Marton, F. and Ramsden, P. 1988. What does it take to improve learning? In P. Ramsden (ed.) *Improving Learning: New Perspectives*. London: Kogan Page.

Marwell, G. and Oliver, P. 1988. Social networks and collective action: a theory of the critical mass III. *American Journal of Sociology*, 94 (3): 502–34.

Matlay, H. 2000. Training and the small firm. In S. Carter and D. Jones-Evans (eds.) *Enterprise and Small Business: Principles, Practice and Policy*. Harlow: Prentice-Hall.

Matlay, H. 2004. Contemporary training initiatives in Britain: a small business perspective. *Journal of Small Business and Enterprise Development*, 11 (4): 504–13.

Mathews, S. 1997. *Designing and Managing a Training and Development Strategy*. London: Pitman.

Matthews, J. H. and Candy, P. C. 1999. New dimensions in the dynamics of learning and knowledge. In D. Boud and J. Garrick (eds.) *Understanding Learning at Work*. London: Routledge.

Mattson, B. W. 2003. The effects of alternative reports of human resource development results on managerial support. *Human Resource Development Quarterly*, 14 (2): 127–51.

May, G. L. 2007. Invited reaction: birds of a feather? HRD and business schools should flock together. *Human Resource Development Review*, 6 (2): 127–31.

May, G. L., Sherlock, J. J. and Mabry, C. K. 2003. The future: the drive for shareholder value and implications for HRD. *Advances in Developing Human Resources*, 5 (3): 321–31.

Maycunich Gilley, A., Callahan, J. L. and Bierema, L. L. 2003. *Critical Issues in HRD: A New Agenda for the Twenty-first Century*. Cambridge, MA: Perseus Publishing.

Mayo, A. 1998. *Creating a Training and Development Strategy*. London: IPD.

Merrifield, R., Calhoun, J. and Stevens, D. 2008. The next revolution in productivity. *Harvard Business Review*, June: 72–80.

Megginson, D. 1996. Planned and emergent learning. *Management Learning*, 27 (4): 411–28.

Metcalfe, B. D. and Rees, C. J. 2005. Theorising advances in international human resource development. *Human Resource Development International*, 8 (4): 449–65.

Michailova, S. and Husted, K. 2003. Knowledge-sharing hostility in Russian firms. *California Management Review*, 45 (3): 59–77.

Mintzberg, H. 1994. *The Rise and Fall of Strategic Planning*. New York: Prentice Hall.

Mishkin, F. S. 2007. Is financial globalisation beneficial? *Journal of Money, Credit and Banking*, 39 (2–3): 259–94.

Monaghan, C. H. and Cervero, R. M. 2006. Impact of critical management studies courses on learners' attitudes and beliefs. *Human Resource Development International*, 9 (3): 379–96.

Monbiot, G. 2006. *Heat*. London: Allen Lane.

Montazemi, A. R. 2006. How they manage IT: SMEs in Canada and the US. *Communications of the ACM*, 49 (12): 109–12.

Morgan, M., Levitt, R. E. and Malck, W. 2007. *Executing Your Strategy: How to Break it Down and Get it Done*. Boston, MA: Harvard Business School Publishing.

Morin, L. and Renaud, S. 2004. Participation in corporate university training: its effect on individual job performance. *Canadian Journal of Administrative Sciences*, 21 (4): 295–306.

Mumford, A. 1988. Learning to learn and management self-development. In M. Pedlar, J. Burgoyne and T. Boydell (eds.) *Applying Self-development in Oganisations*. Hemel Hempstead: Prentice Hall.

Mumford, A. and Gold, J. 2004. *Management Development* (4th edition). London: CIPD.

Nahapiet, J. and Ghoshal, S. 1998. Social capital, intellectual capital, and the organisational advantage. *Academy of Management Review*, 23 (2): 242–66.

Naquin, S. S. and Holton, E. 2003. Motivation to improve work through learning in human resource development. *Human Resource Development International*, 6 (3): 355–70.

Neilson, G. L., Martin, K. L. and Powers, E. 2008. The secrets to successful strategy execution. *Harvard Business Review*, June: 60–70.

Nieuwenhuis, L. F. M. and van Woerkom, M. 2007. Goal rationalities as a framework for evaluating the learning potential of the workplace. *Human Resource Development Review*, 6 (1): 64–83.

Nelson, R. R. and Winter, S. G. 1982. *An Evolutionary Theory of Economic Change*. Cambridge, MA: Harvard University Press.

Newell, S., Robertson, M., Scarborough, H. and Swan, J. 2002. *Managing Knowledge Work*. Basingstoke: Palgrave.

Nijhof, W. J. 2004. Is the HRD profession in the Netherlands changing? *Human Resource Development International*, 7 (1): 57–71.

Nijhof, W. J. 2005. Lifelong learning as a European skill formation policy. *Human Resource Development Review*, 4 (4): 401–17.

Nilsson, P. A., Petersen, T. and Wanhill, S. 2005. Public support for tourism SMEs in peripheral areas: the Arjeplog project, Northern Sweden. *The Services Industries Journal*, 25 (4): 579–99.

Noe, R. A. 1986. Trainee attributes and attitudes: neglected influences on training effectiveness. *Academy of Management Review*, 11: 736–49.

Noe, R. A. 2002. *Employee Training and Development* (2nd edition), New York: McGraw-Hill.

Nonaka, I. 1994. A dynamic theory of organisational knowledge creation. *Organisation Science*, 5 (1): 14–37.

Nonaka, I. and Takeuchi, H. 1995. *The Knowledge-Creating Company*. New York: Oxford University Press.

O'Donnell, D. and Garavan, T. N. 1997. Viewpoint: linking training policy and practice to organisational goals. *Journal of European Industrial Training*, 21 (8–9): 301–9.

O'Donnell, D., McGuire, D. and Cross, C. 2006. Critically challenging some assumptions in HRD. *International Journal of Training and Development*, 10 (1): 4–16.

Ohmae, K. 2005. *The Next Global Stage: Challenges and Opportunities in Our Borderless World*. Upper Saddle River, NJ: Wharton School Publishing.

Orlikowski, W. 1993. Learning from notes: organisational issues in groupware implementation. *Information Society*, 9: 237–50.

Osman-Gani, A. M. 2004. Human capital development in Singapore: an analysis of national policy perspectives. *Advances in Developing Human Resources*, 6 (3): 269–75.

Özçelik, G. and Ferman, M. 2006. Competency approach to human resource management: outcomes and contributions in a Turkish cultural context. *Human Resource Development Review*, 5 (1): 72–91.

Packer, A. H. and Sharrar, G. K. 2003. Linking lifelong learning, corporate social responsibility, and the changing nature of work. *Advances in Developing Human Resources*, 5 (3): 332–41.

Palmer, R. 1999. The identification of organisational and individual training and development needs. In J. Wilson (ed.) *Human Resource Development*. London: Kogan Page.

Paprock, K. E. 2006. National human resource development in transitioning societies in the developing world: introductory overview. *Advances in Developing Human Resources*, 8 (1): 12–27.

Parry, K. W. and Sinha, P. N. 2005. Researching the trainability of transformational organisational leadership. *Human Resource Development International*, 8 (2): 165–83.

Patriotta, G. 2003. *Organisational Knowledge in the Making: How Firms Create, Use and Institutionalise Knowledge*. Oxford: Oxford University Press.

Pattanayak, B. 2003. Gaining competitive advantage and business success through strategic HRD: an Indian experience. *Human Resource Development International*, 6 (3): 405–11.

Pavlov, I. 1927. *Conditioned Reflexes*. Oxford: Oxford University Press.

Pedersen, E. R. 2006. Making corporate social responsibility (CSR) operable: how companies translate stakeholder dialogue into practice. *Business and Society Review*, 111 (2): 137–63.

Pedlar, M. (ed.) 1991. *Action Learning in Practice*. Brookfield, VT: Gower.

Penn, M. J. and Zalesne, E. K. 2008. *Micro Trends: Surprising Tales of the Way We Live Today*. London: Penguin Books.

Petranek, G. F. 2004. Global human resource development: the four C approach. *Human Resource Development Quarterly*, 15 (2): 249–52.

Petridou, E. and Glaveli, N. 2003. Human resource development in a challenging financial environment: the case of a Greek bank. *Human Resource Development International*, 6 (4): 547–58.

Pfeffer, J. and Sutton, R. 2000. *The Knowing–Doing Gap: How Smart Companies Turn Knowledge Into Action*. Boston, MA: Harvard Business School Press.

Phillips, J. 1991. *Handbook of Training Evaluation and Measurement Methods* (2nd edition). Houston, TX: Gulf Publishing.

Phillips, J. 2001. How to measure returns on HR investment. *People Management*, 22 November: 48–50.

Piaget, J. 1929. *The Child's Conception of the World*. London: Routledge and Kegan Paul.

Pickard, J. 2004. Mersey beat. *People Management*, 11 November: 28–30.

Pickersgill, R. 2001. Skills formation in Australia beyond 2000: 'flexibility' and vocational education and training policy. *International Journal of Employment Studies*, 9 (1): 121–39.

Poell, R. F. and Van der Krogt, F. J. 2003a. Learning strategies of workers in the knowledge-creating company. *Human Resource Development International*, 6 (3): 387–403.

Poell, R. F. and Van der Krogt, F. J. 2003b. Learning-program creation in work organisations. *Human Resource Development Review*, 2 (3): 252–72.

Poell, R. F., Van der Krogt, F. J., Vermulst, A. A., Harris, R. and Simons, M. 2006. Roles of informal workplace trainers in different organisational contexts: empirical evidence from Australian companies. *Human Resource Development Quarterly*, 17 (2): 175–98.

Polanyi, M. 1962. *Personal Knowledge: Towards a Post-Critical Philosophy*. London: Routledge.

Polanyi, M. 1967. *The Tacit Dimension*. London: Routledge.

Porritt, J. 2007. *Capitalism: As if the World Matters*. London: Earthscan.

Porter, M. E. 1980. *Competitive Strategy*. New York: Free Press.

Porter, M. E. 1985. *Competitive Advantage*. New York: Free Press.

Porter, M. E. 1991. Towards a Dynamic Theory of Strategy. *Strategic Management Journal*, 12 (S): 95–117.

Prajogo, D. I. and Brown, A. 2006. Approaches to adopting quality in SMEs and the impact on quality management practices and performance. *Total Quality Management*, 17 (5): 555–66.

Preskill, H. and Russ-Eft, D. 2003. A framework for reframing HRD evaluation, practice and research. In A. Maycunich Gilley, J. L. Callahan and L. L. Bierema (eds.) *Critical Issues in HRD: A New Agenda for the Twenty-first Century*. Cambridge, MA: Perseus.

Price, A. 2004. *Human Resource Management in a Business Context*. London: Thomson.

Pring, R. 2007. 14–19 and lifelong learning: distinguishing between academic and vocational learning. In L. Clarke and C. Winch (eds.) *Vocational Education: International Approaches, Developments and Systems*. London: Routledge.

Prusak, L. 2001. Where did knowledge management come from? *IBM Systems Journal*, 40 (4): 1002–7.

Purcell, J., Kinnie, N., Hutchinson, S., Rayton, B. and Swart, J. 2003. *Understanding the People and Performance Link: Unlocking the Black Box*. London: CIPD.

Quinn, J. B., Anderson, P. and Finkelstein, S. 1998. *Managing Professional Intellect: Making the Most of the Best*, in *Harvard Business Review on Knowledge Management*. Boston, MA: Harvard Business School Press.

Quintas, P. 2002. Managing knowledge in a new century. In S. Little, P. Quintas and T. Ray (eds.) *Managing Knowledge: An Essential Reader*. London: Sage.

Rae, L. 2002. *Trainer Assessment*. Gower: Aldershot.

Rahman, M. N. AB and Tannock, J. D. T. 2005. TQM best practices: experiences of Malaysian SMEs. *Total Quality Management*, 16 (4): 491–503.

Rainbird, H., Munro, A. and Holly, L. 2004. The employment relationship and workplace learning. In H. Rainbird, A. Fuller and A. Munro (eds.) *Workplace Learning in Context*. London: Routledge.

Ram, M. and Barrett, G. 2000. Ethnicity and enterprise. In S. Carter and D. Jones-Evans (eds.) *Enterprise and Small Business: Principles, Practice and Policy*. Harlow: Prentice-Hall.

Ramirez, M. 2004. Comparing European approaches to management education, training, and development. *Advances in Developing Human Resources*, 6 (4): 428–50.

Ramsden, P. 1992. *Learning to Teach in Higher Education*. London: Routledge.

Rao, T. V. 2004. Human resource development as national policy in India. *Advances in Developing Human Resources*, 6 (3): 288–96.

Raymond, L., Bergeron, and Blili, S. 2005. The assimilation of e-business in manufacturing SMEs: determinants and effects on growth and internationalisation. *Electronic Markets*, 15 (2): 106–18.

Reddy, A. 2002. E-learning ROI calculations: is a cost/benefit analysis a better approach? *e-learning*, 3 (1): 30–2.

Rees, D. 2004. The culturally fluent manager. In D. Rees and R. McBain (eds.) *People Management: Challenges and Opportunities*. Basingstoke: Palgrave Macmillan.

Rees, D. and McBain, R. 2004. *People Management: Challenges and Opportunities*. Basingstoke: Palgrave Macmillan.

Reid, M. A., Barrington, H. and Brown, M. 2004. *Human Resource Development: Beyond Training Interventions* (7th edition). London: CIPD.

Revans, R. 1983. *The ABC of Action Learning*. London: Chartwell-Bratt.

Revans, R. 1991. Action learning: its origins and nature. In M. Pedlar (ed.) *Action Learning in Practice*. Brookfield, VT: Gower.

Reynolds, J., Caley, L. and Mason, R. 2002. *How do People Learn?* (CIPD Research Report). London: CIPD.

Rigby, M. 2004. Training in Spain: an evaluation of the continuous training agreements 1993–2001 with particular reference to SMEs. *Human Resource Development International*, 7 (1): 23–37.

Roberts, P. B. 2006. Analysis: the defining phase of systematic training. *Advances in Developing Human Resources*, 8 (4): 476–91.

Rocco, T. S., Stein, D. and Chan, L. 2003. An exploratory examination on age and HRD policy development. *Human Resource Development Review*, 2 (2): 155–80.

Roth, G. L. 2004. CPE and HRD: research and practice within systems and across boundaries. *Advances in Developing Human Resources*, 6 (1): 9–19.

Rowan, L. 2005. Change and stasis in learning delivery. *Business Intelligence*, July: 50–2.

Rowold, J. 2007. The impact of personality on training-related aspects of motivation: test of a longitudinal model. *Human Resource Development Quarterly*, 18 (1): 9–31.

Rock, A. D. and Garavan, T. N. 2006. Reconceptualising developmental relationships. *Human Resource Development Review*, 5 (3): 330–54.

Rothkopf, D. 2008. *Superclass: The Global Power Elite and the World they are Making*. London: Little Brown.

Ruggles, R. 1998. The state of the notion: knowledge management in practice. *California Management Review*, 40 (3): 80–9.

Ruona, E. A., Lynham, S. A. and Chermack, T. J. 2003. Insights on emerging trends and the future of human resource development. *Advances in Developing Human Resources*, 5 (3): 272–82.

Russ-Eft, D. 2004. Customer service competencies: a global look. *Human Resource Development International*, 7 (2): 211–31.

Russ-Eft, D. and Hatcher, T. 2003. The issue of international values and beliefs: the debate for a global HRD code of ethics. *Advances in Developing Human Resources*, 5 (3): 296–307.

Ruzzier, M., Antoncic, B., Hisrich, R. D. and Konecnik, M. 2007. Human capital and SME internationalisation: a structural equation modeling study. *Canadian Journal of Administrative Sciences*, 24: 15–29.

Ryle, G. 1990 [1949]. *The Concept of Mind*. London: Penguin Books.

Sachs, J. D. 2008. *Common Wealth: Economics for a Crowded Planet*. London: Allen Lane.

Sadler-Smith, E. and Smith, P. J. 2006. Technical rationality and professional artistry in HRD practice. *Human Resource Development International*, 9 (2): 271–81.

Sadler-Smith, E., Gardiner, P., Badger, B., Chaston, I. and Stubberfield, J. 2000. Using collaborative learning to develop small firms. *Human Resource Development International*, 3 (3): 285–306.

Salas, E. and Cannon-Bowers, J. A. 2001. The science of training: a decade of progress. *Annual Review of Psychology*, 52: 471–99.

Salleh, N. A. M., Rohde, F. and Green, P. 2006. The effect of enacted capabilities on adoption of a government electronic procurements system by Malaysian SMEs. *Electronic Markets*, 16 (4): 292–310.

Sallis, E. and Jones, G. 2002. *Knowledge Management in Education: Enhancing Learning and Education*. London: Kogan Page.

Salvato, C., Lassino, U. and Wikland, J. 2007. Dynamics of external growth in SMEs: a process model of acquisition capabilities emergence. *Schmalenbach Business Review*, July, 59: 282–305.

Sambrook, S. 2005. Factors influencing the context and process of work-related learning: synthesised findings from two research projects. *Human Resource Development International*, 8 (1): 101–20.

Sambrook, S. and Stewart, J. 1999. Influencing factors on lifelong learning and HRD practices: comparison of seven European countries. Paper presented at the European Conference on Educational Research, Lahti, Finland, 22–5 September.

Sambrook, S. and Stewart, J. 2000. Factors influencing learning in European learning-oriented organisations: issues for management. *Journal of European Industrial Training*, 24 (2/3/4): 209–19.

Samuelson, R. J. 2008. High finance laid low. *Newsweek*, 14 April: 48.

Saul, J. R. 2005. *The Collapse of Globalism*. London: Atlantic Books.

Scarborough, H. and Carter, C. 2000. *Investigating Knowledge Management*. London: CIPD.

Scarborough, H. and Elias, J. 2002. *Evaluating Human Capital* (Research report). London: CIPD.

Scarborough, H., Swan, J. and Preston, J. 1999. *Investigating Knowledge Management*. London: CIPD.

Scarborough, H., Swan, J. A. and Preston, J. 1998. *Knowledge Management and the Learning Organisation*. London: IPD.

Shaw, M. and Green, J. 1999. Continuous professional development: emerging trends in the UK. *Quality Assurance in Education*, 7 (3): 169–77.

Schein, E. H. 1992. *Organisational Culture and Leadership* (2nd edition). San Francisco, CA: Jossey-Bass.

Schön, D. 1983. *The Reflective Practitioner: How Professionals Think in Action*. New York: Basic Books.

Schön, D. A. 1991. *The Reflective Practitioner: How Professionals Think in Action*. Aldershot: Ashgate.

Scully-Russ, E. 2005. Agency versus structure: path dependency and choice in low-wage labour markets. *Human Resource Development Review*, 4 (3): 254–78.

Seiler, T. B. 2004. The human foundation of knowledge management. in H. Tsoukas and N. Mylonopoulos (eds.) *Organisations as Knowledge Systems*. Basingstoke: Palgrave Macmillan.

Selmer, J. 2006. Munificence of parent corporate contexts and expatriate cross-cultural training in China. *Asia Pacific Business Review*, 12 (1): 39–51.

Senker, P. 2000. What and how do engineers learn? In H. Rainbird (ed.) *Training in the Workplace*. Basingstoke: Macmillan.

Seshadri, D. V. R. and Tripathy, A. 2006. Reinventing a giant corporation: the case of Tata Steel. *Vikalpa*, 31 (3): 131–4.

Shoobridge, G. E. 2006. Multi-ethnic workforce and business performance: review and synthesis of the empirical literature. *Human Resource Development Review*, 5 (1): 92–137.

Short, D. C. and Callahan, J. L. 2005. 'Would I work for a global corporation?' And other ethical questions for HRD. *Human Resource Development International*, 8 (1): 121–5.

Shoobridge, G. E. 2006. Multi-ethnic workforce and business performance: review and synthesis of the empirical literature. *Human Resource Development Review*, 5 (1): 92–137.

Short, D. C. 2006. Closing the gap between research and practice in HRD. *Human Resource Development Quarterly*, 17 (3): 343–50.

Shultz, T. W. 1961. Education and economic growth. In N. B. Henry (ed.) *Social Forces Influencing American Education*. Chicago, IL: University of Chicago Press.

Schultz, T. W. 1961. Investment in human capital. *American Economic Review*, 51 (1): 1–17.

Simon, H. A. 1985. Human nature in politics: the dialogue of psychology with political science. *American political Science Review*, 79 (2): 293–304.

Simmonds, D. 2003. *Designing and Delivering Training*. London: CIPD.

Simms, J. 2005. Seasoned greetings. *People Management*, 19 May: 36–8.

Singh, R. K., Garg, S. K. and Deshmukh, S. G. 2005. Development of flexible strategies by Indian SMEs in electronics sector in emerging economy. *Global Journal of Flexible Systems Management*, 6 (2): 15–26.

Sirkin, H. L., Hemerling, J. W. and Bhattacharya, A. K. 2008. *Globality: Competing with Everyone from Everywhere for Everything*. London: Headline Publishing Group.

Skinner, B. F. 1974. *About Behaviourism*. London: Jonathan Cape.

Skule, S. 2004. Learning conditions at work: a framework to understand and assess informal learning in the workplace. *International Journal of Training and Development*, 8 (1): 8–20.

Sleezer, C. M., Conti, G. J. and Nolan, R. E. 2004. Comparing CPE and HRD programs: definitions, theoretical foundations, outcomes, and measures of quality. *Advances in Developing Human Resources*, 6 (1): 20–34.

Sloman, M. 1994. *A Handbook for Training Strategy*. Aldershot: Gower.

Sloman, M. 2005. Branching out. *People Management*, 24 November: 38–40.

Sloman, M. 2007. *The Changing World of the Trainer: Emerging Good Practice*. Oxford: Butterworth-Heinemann.

Sloman, M. and Reynolds, J. 2003. Developing the e-learning community. *Human Resource Development International*, 6 (2): 259–72.

Slotte, V., Tynjälä, P. and Hytönen, T. 2004. How do HRD practitioners describe learning at work? *Human Resource Development International*, 7 (4): 481–99.

Smedley, T. 2007. Catch the express train. *People Management*, 4 October: 26–9.

Smethurst, S. 2005. Course of treatment. *People Management*, 9 March: 34–6.

Smith, A. 1999. International briefing 4: training and development in Australia. *International Journal of Training and Development*, 3 (4): 301–13.

Smith, A. 2006. Engagement or irrelevance? HRD and the world of policy and practice. *Human Resource Development Review*, 5 (4): 395–9.

Smith, P. J. 2002. Modern learning methods: rhetoric and reality—further to Sadler-Smith et al. *Personnel Review*, 31 (1): 103–13.

Smith, D. 2008. *The Dragon and the Elephant: China, India and the New World Order*. London: Profile Books.

Smith, P. J. and Sadler-Smith, E. 2006. *Learning in Organisations: Complexities and Diversities*. London: Routledge.

Sparrow, S. 2003. Blended learning spices up the training mix. *Training Magazine*, November.

Sparrow, S. 2004. Transatlantic trends. http://www.PersonnelToday.com/Articles (accessed 25 October 2007).

Spender, J. C. 1996. Organisational knowledge, learning and memory: three concepts in search of a theory. *Journal of Organisational Change*, 9 (1): 63–78.

Spickett-Jones, J. G. and Eng, T-Y. 2006. SMEs and the strategic context for communication. *Journal of Marketing Communications*, 12 (3): 225–43.

Starbuck, W. H. and Hedberg, B. 2001. How organisations learn from success and failure. In M. Dierkes, A. B. Antal, J. Child and I. Nonaka (eds.) *Handbook of Organisational Learning and Knowledge*. Oxford: Oxford University Press.

Stark, J. 2005. The state of globalisation. *The International Economy*, Spring: 52–70.

Stern, E. and Sommerlad, E. 1999. *Workplace Learning, Culture and Performance*. London: IPD.

Stewart, J. and McGoldrick, J. 1996. Editors' introduction. In J. Stewart and J. McGoldrick (eds.) *Human Resource Development: Perspectives, Strategies and Practice*. London: Pitman Publishing.

Stewart, J. and Tansley, C. 2002. *Training in the Knowledge Economy* (Research report). London: CIPD.

Stiglitz, J. E. 2002. *Globalisation and Its Discontents*. New York: W. W. Norton.

Stiglitz, J. 2007. *Making Globalisation Work*. London: Penguin Books.

Storey, D. J. 2004. Exploring the link, among small firms, between management training and firm performance: a comparison between the UK and other OECD countries. *International Journal of Human Resource Management*, 15 (1): 112–30.

Swanson, R. A. 2001. *Assessing the Financial Benefits of Human Resource Development*. Cambridge, MA: Persesus.

Swanson, R. A. 2002. Postmodern garage sale. *Human Resource Development Review*, 2 (1): 269–72.

Swanson, R. A. 2005. Evaluation, a state of mind. *Advances in Developing Human Resources*, 7 (1): 16–21.

Swanson, R. A. and Holton, E. F. 2001a. *Foundations of Human Resource Development*. San Francisco, CA: Berrett-Koehler.

Swart, J., Kinnie, N. and Purcell, J. 2003. *People Performance in Knowledge-Intensive Firms* (Research report). London: CIPD.

Syedain, H. 2008. The money trap. *People Management*, 10 January: 24–9.

Taleb, N. N. 2008. *The Black Swan: The Impact of the Highly Probable*. London: Penguin Books.

Tambunan, T. 2007. Entrepreneurship development: SMEs in Indonesia. *Journal of Developmental Entrepreneurship*, 12 (1): 95–118.

Tan, E. N., Smith, G. and Saads, M. 2006. Managing the global supply chain: a SME perspective. *Production Planning & Control*, 17 (3): 238–46.

Tapscott, D. and Williams, A. D. 2008. *Wikinomics: How Mass Collaboration Changes Everything*. London: Atlantic Books.

Tata Group 2008. Grooming global managers. http://www.tata.com/0_our_commitment/ employee_relations/artciles/20060907_groom (accessed 14 April 2008).

Thomas, A. J. and Webb, D. 2003. Quality systems implementation in Welsh small- to medium-sized enterprises: a global comparison and a model for change. *Proceedings of the Institution of Mechanical Engineers*, 217 (Part B): 573–9.

Tillema, H. H. 2006. Authenticity in knowledge-productive learning: what drives knowledge construction in collaborative enquiry? *Human Resource Development International*, 9 (2): 173–90.

Torraco, R. J. 2004. Challenges and choices for theoretical research in human resource development. *Human Resource Development Quarterly*, 15 (2): 171–88.

Torraco, R. J. and Swanson, R. A. 2001. The strategic roles of human resource development. In Swanson, R. A. and Holton, E. F. (eds.) *Foundations of Human Resource Development*. San Francisco, CA: Berrett-Koehler, pp. 339–57.

Torraco, R. J. and Yorks, L. 2007. Do practitioners compromise scholarly standards? Do scholars comprehend the rigors of practice? Can a theory journal be a viable bridge across the chasm? *Human Resource Development Review*, 6 (1): 3–6.

Toynbee, P. 2003. *Hard Work: Life in Low-Pay Britain*. London: Bloomsbury.

Tsoukas, H. 1996. The firm as a distributed knowledge system: a social constructionist approach. *Strategic Management Journal*, 17 (Winter Special Edition): 11–25.

Turner, A. 2001. *Just Capital: The Liberal Economy*. London: Macmillan.

Ulrich, D. 2007. Dreams: where human resource development is headed to deliver value. *Human Resource Development Quarterly*, 18 (1): 1–8.

Ulrich, D. and Brockbank, W. 2005. *The HR Value Proposition*. Boston, MA: Harvard Business School Press.

Van den Berg, N., Meijers, F. and Sprengers, M. 2006. More vocational education and supplementary training through equalisation of costs? An analysis of a training and development fund in the Netherlands. *Human Resource Development International*, 9 (1): 5–24.

Van der Sluis, L. E. C. and Poell, R. F. 2003. The impact on career development of learning opportunities and learning behaviour at work. *Human Resource Development Quarterly*, 14 (2): 159–80.

Van Horn, C. E. 2006. Mega-trends in the American workforce. *Human Resource Development Quarterly*, 17 (4): 475–9.

Van Woerkom, M. 2004. The concept of critical reflection and its implications for human resource development. *Advances in Developing Human Resources*, 6 (2): 178–92.

Vaughn, R. H. 2005. *The Professional Trainer*. San Francisco, CA: Berrett-Koehler.

Venter, K. 2003. Building on formal education: employers' approaches to the training and development of new recruits in the People's Republic of China. *International Journal of Training and Development*, 7 (3): 186–202.

Vera, D. and Crossan, M. 2005. Organisational learning and knowledge management: toward an integrative framework. In M. Easterby-Smith and M. A. Lyles (eds.), *Handbook of Organisational Learning and Knowledge Management*. Oxford: Blackwell.

Von Krogh, G. 1998. Care in knowledge creation. *California Management Review*, 40 (3): 133–53.

Von Krogh, G., Ichijo, K. and Nonaka, I. 2000. *Enabling Knowledge Creation: How to Unlock the Mystery of Tacit Knowledge and Release the Power of Innovation*. Oxford: Oxford University Press.

Vygotsky, L. S. 1978. *Mind in Society: The Development of Higher Psychological Processes*. Cambridge, MA: Harvard University Press.

Waddill, D. D. and Marquardt, M. 2003. Adult learning orientations and action learning. *Human Resource Development Review*, 2 (4): 406–29.

Waddill, D. D. 2006. Action e-learning: an exploratory case study of action learning applied online. *Human Resource Development International*, 9 (2): 157–71.

Wain, D. 2007. Learning's centre. *People Management*, 19 April: 34–6.

Walburn, D. 2005. The Lisbon Agenda: regional performance in a two speed Europe. The important contribution of local programmes of SME support. *Local Economy*, 20 (3): 305–8.

Wallerstein, I. 2004. *The Uncertainties of Knowledge*. Philadelphia: Temple University Press.

Walton, J. 1999. *Strategic Human Resource Development*. Harlow: Prentice Hall.

Wang, G. G. and Holton, E. F. 2005. Neoclassical and institutional economics as foundations for human resource development theory. *Human Resource Development Review*, 4 (1): 86–108.

Wang, G. G. and Wilcox, D. 2006. Training evaluation: knowing more than is practised. *Advances in Developing Human Resources*, 8 (4): 528–39.

Wang, X. and McLean, G. N. 2007. The dilemma of defining international human resource development. *Human Resource Development Review*, 6 (1): 96–108.

Wang, J., Wang, G. G., Ruona, W. E. A. and Rojewski, J. W. 2005. Confucian values and the implications for international HRD. *Human Resource Development International*, 8 (3): 311–26.

Wang, J. and Wang, G. G. 2006. Exploring national human resource development: a case of China management development in a transitioning context. *Human Resource Development Review*, 5 (2): 176–201.

Warr, P. B., Bird, M. and Rackham, M. 1970. *Evaluation of Management Training*. Aldershot: Gower Press.

Warren, C. 2008. A crushing victory. *People Management*, 21 February: 38–40.

Wasko, M. M. and Faraj, S. 2005. Why should I share? Examining social capital and knowledge contribution in electronic networks of practice. *MIS Quarterly*, 29 (1): 35–57.

Water, M. 1995. *Globalisation*. London: Routledge.

Webster, B. Walker, E. and Barrett, R. 2005. Small business and online training in Australia: who is willing to participate? *New Technology, Work and Employment*, 20 (3): 248–58.

Wellman, B. and Wortley, S. 1990. Different strokes for different folks: community ties and social support. *American Journal of Sociology*, 96: 558–88.

Wells, D. L., Moorman, R. H. and Werner, J. M. 2007. The impact of the perceived purpose of electronic performance monitoring on an array of attitudinal variables. *Human Resource Development Quarterly*, 18 (1): 121–38.

Wenger, E. 1998. *Communities of Practice: Learning, Meaning, and Identity*. Cambridge: Cambridge University Press.

Wenger, E., McDermott, R. and Snyder, W. M. 2002. *Cultivating Communities of Practice*. Boston, MA: Harvard Business School Press.

Wentling, R. M. 2004. Factors that assist and barriers that hinder the success of diversity initiatives in multinational companies. *Human Resource Development International*, 7 (2): 165–80.

Wernerfelt, B. 1984. A resource-based view of the firm. *Strategic Management Journal*, 5 (2): 171–80.

Wexley, K. N. and Latham, G. P. 2002. *Developing and Training Human Resources in Organisations* (3rd edition). Upper Saddle River, NJ: Prentice Hall.

Winch, C. 2007. Vocational education, work and the aims of economic activity. In L. Clarke and C. Winch (eds.) *Vocational Education: International Approaches, Developments and Systems*. London: Routledge.

Winkler, V. 2007. Line managers fail to support staff development. *Impact*, March, 19: 16–17.

Wolf, M. 2005. *Why Globalisation Works*. New Haven and London: Yale University Press.

Woodall, J. 2000. Corporate support for work-based management development. *Human Resource Management Journal*, 10 (1): 18–32.

Woodall, J. 2005. Theoretical frameworks for comparing HRD in an international context. *Human Resource Development International*, 8 (4): 399–402.

Worthen, B. R. and Sanders, J. R. 1987. *Educational Evaluation*. New York: Longman.

Wykes, L. M. 2003. Performance-focused HRD. In A. Maycunich Gilley, J. L. Callahan and L. L. Bierema (eds.) *Critical Issues in HRD: A New Agenda for the Twenty-first Century*. Cambridge, MA: Perseus Publishing.

Wynne, A. 2006. Small world. *People Management*, 18 May: 16–17.

Xiao, J. 2006. Survey ranking of job competencies by perceived employee importance: comparing China's three regions. *Human Resource Development Quarterly*, 17 (4): 371–402.

Xiao, J. and Lo, L. N. K. 2005. The education and training of employees in 12 countries in

China. *Journal of Education and Work*, 18 (3): 283–303.

Xie, J. and Wu, G. 2001. International briefing 10: training and development in the People's Republic of China. *International Journal of Training and Development*, 5 (3): 223–32.

Yang, B. 2004. Can adult learning theory provide a foundation for human resource development? *Advances in Developing Human Resources*, 6 (2): 129–45.

Yang, B. and Zhang, D. 2003. A theoretical comparison of American and Chinese culture and impacts on human resource theory and practice. *International Journal of Human Resource Development and Management*, 3 (4): 338–58.

Yang, B., Zhang, D. and Zhang, M. 2004. National human resource development in the People's Republic of China. *Advances in Developing Human Resources*, 6 (3): 297–306.

Yorks, L. 2004. Toward a political economy model for comparative analysis of the role of strategic human resource development leadership. *Human Resource Development Review*, 3 (3): 189–208.

Yorks, L. 2005. *Strategic Human Resource Development*. Mason, OH: Thomson South-Western.

Yorks, L. and Nikolaides, A. 2006. Complexity and emergent communicative learning: an opportunity for HRD scholarship. *Human Resource Development Review*, 5 (2): 143–7.

Yu, J. and Bell, J. N. B. 2007. Building a sustainable business in China's small and medium-sized enterprises (SMEs). *Journal of Environmental Assessment Policy and Management*, 9 (1): 19–53.

Zakaria, F. 2008. The future of American power: how America can survive the rise of the rest. *Foreign Affairs*, May/June: 18–43.

Zhao, C. L. 2005. Management of corporate culture through local managers' training in foreign companies in China: a qualitative analysis. *International Journal of Training and Development*, 9 (4): 232–55.

Zheng, C., Morrison, M. and O'Neill, G. 2006. An empirical study of high performance HRM practices in Chinese SMEs, *International Journal of Human Resource Management*, 17 (10): 1772–803.

Zink, K. J. 2005. Stakeholder orientation and corporate social responsibility as a precondition for sustainability. *Total Quality Management*, 16 (8–9): 1041–52.

Zuboff, S. 1988. *In the Age of the Smart Machine*. New York: Basic Books.

Websites

http://www.news.bbc.co.uk/2/hi/business/625514.htm (accessed 14 April 2008).

http://www.PersonnelToday.com 2007b. http://www.PersonnelToday.com/Articles/ArticleID=42326 (accessed 25 October 2007).

http://www.starbucks.co.uk/en-GB/_Social+Responsibility/Commitment+to+Origins.htm (accessed 14 April 2008).

INDEX